ISBN 978-1-332-84725-9
PIBN 10199658

1 MONTH OF
FREE
READING

at
www.ForgottenBooks.com

By purchasing this book you are eligible for one month membership to ForgottenBooks.com, giving you unlimited access to our entire collection of over 700,000 titles via our web site and mobile apps.

To claim your free month visit:

www.forgottenbooks.com/free199658

THE STORY OF OLD FORT PLAIN AND THE MIDDLE MOHAWK VALLEY

(WITH FIVE MAPS)

A Review of Mohawk Valley history from 1609 to the time of the writing of this book (1912-1914,) treating particularly of the central region comprised in the present Counties of Herkimer, Montgomery and Fulton. Especial attention is given to western Montgomery County and the region within a twenty mile radius of the Revolutionary fortification of old Fort Plain, including the Canajoharie and Palatine districts of then Tryon County

Written, Compiled, and Edited by

NELSON GREENE

O'CONNOR BROTHERS :: :: :: PUBLISHERS

FORT PLAIN, NEW YORK

1915

THIS BOOK IS DEDICATED, IN AFFECTIONATE
REMEMBRANCE, TO MY GRANDMOTHER, EMILY
HERKIMER GREENE. BORN IN THE EARLY
YEARS OF THE NINETEENTH CENTURY, HER
LONG LIFE COVERED MUCH OF THE GROWTH
AND DEVELOPMENT OF THE MOHAWK VALLEY
FROM WILDERNESS TO CIVILIZATION, AND,
HER STORIES OF THE EARLY DAYS PROMPTED
THE INTEREST WHICH EVENTUALLY LED THE
WRITER TO THE PREPARATION
OF THIS VOLUME.

Mohawk, ever-flowing.

Mohawk, ever-flowing—curving broadly, hill-born, mountain-bound, meadow-edged; its valley the nation's roadway, the nation's boatway—linking east to west, oceans to lakes; scurried by trains, by motor cars, thousands daily speeding along its banks, hill encompassed.

Mohawk, ever-flowing—river of the first days.

In the evening shadows, in the night shadows, the spirit lurk of the savage days; the lean red man pushing his live canoe o'er the rippling dark waters—on the nearby pine hill his bark cabin, on the flats his waving cornfield; vaguely gray seen through the river bank trees, the settler's stone house; from the flatland's edge the forest rising, all encompassing; the fisherman's skiff silently drifting past silhouetted giant elms; whisper of night wind in the great treetops; weird glow light of rising full, yellow moon.

Mohawk, ever-flowing—river of days of darkness, of battle, of death, of suffering; in the evening darkness, in the night darkness the spirit lurk of red days of blood; shot, zip of tomahawk, wail of crushed infant, death gasp of hero mother; the sturdy old farmer in bloody death clinch with the lithe, wriggling red man; scarlet midnight gleam of burning homestead.

Mohawk, ever-flowing—great river of old. In the hilltop twilight, dim spirit figure mighty, towering—the nation-maker, mounted, from a high pathway wisely viewing future vistas.

Mohawk, ever-flowing—river of the nation. Here the building of the nation—wisely, foolishly, strongly, recklessly, blusteringly, bravely—bridges, turnpikes, prairie schooners wending westward, canals, boats, railways, rattling engines, endless car-trains, flying trollies, speeding motor cars; hamlets, towns, cities, bare brick factories belching black smoke.

Mohawk, ever-flowing—river of the present. Comes a birdman flying the twilight heavens eastward; to him the earthdusk over-shadowing dull silver endless snake shapes of river, of canal; man-piloted great air bird flying, curving, settling on green hill meadow.

Mohawk, ever-flowing—river of our day. The steam car, electric car, flying past wide, dusty cities—standing brick bare in the summer sun—teeming with life—aimless, well-directed—streets, buildings, men, children, women, beauty, various clothes, strange hats, cars, carts, trucks, vehicles, hurrying, hither, thither, hustle, bustle—aimless, well-directed.

Mohawk, ever-flowing—river of now—from rushing railroad car, from flying motor car the speeding traveler, seeing village houses twinkling white amid green leaves, church spires rising amid the trees; school bells ringing, children running; on the village park the ball players, running, batting, catching; the great red barn standing upon a knoll amid wide, yellow grain fields; horses galloping the pasture from rushing train; cattle—black and white spots upon the distant meadow.

Mohawk, ever-flowing eastward—river no more; wide, full, waterway winding past great locks, great bridges, floating great boats—but still the same mysterious lines of flowing high hills, the same bordering green meadows.

Mohawk, ever-flowing—spirit of old, symbol of today, mysterious with suggestions of days to come.

Mohawk, ever-flowing.

TABLE OF CONTENTS

NOTE.—It is suggested that the reader of this book follow this order in reading this work

First: Read the Fifteen School Dates (p. 322) in the Mohawk Valley Chronologies in the appendix.

Second: Read the Mohawk Valley Chronology (p. 307), which starts the appendix.

Third: Read the main body of the book.

Fourth: At the conclusion of each chapter turn to the appendix and read therein the matter relative to the chapter in the main body of the book, which the reader has just completed. The appendix additions carry the main body chapter heads, to which the appendix matter properly belongs and to which they will be added in any future editions of this work.

This book can be read in connection with Lossing's "Empire State" or (for a shorter work) Hendrick's "Brief (School) History of the Empire State."

TABLE OF CONTENTS

TABLE OF CONTENTS

TABLE OF CONTENTS

ADDITIONAL CORRECTIONS.

In the Introduction, on page xiv, thirty-fifth line read "white winter slumber" for "while winter slumber."

In the Appendix, p. 351, fifth line from the bottom, first column, read "history of countries" for "history of counties."

In the Appendix on p. 354, the statement is made that "At Poughkeepsie in 1786, the New York State Assembly ratified the United States Constitution, making the ninth state to take such action and thus putting it into effect." This is an error. It was in 1788 that the State Assembly met at Poughkeepsie to consider the adoption of the National Constitution framed at Annapolis in 1786. While in session news was received that New Hampshire had ratified the Constitution. It was the ninth state so to do and its action put the national government into effect. It was then up to New York to ratify or secede from the United States. A majority of the state legislators were against ratifying and it was only the great efforts of Alexander Hamilton that secured New York's approval by the close vote of 30 to 27. See Lossing's "Empire State," Chapter 23.

In the Appendix, page 377, first column, seventh line from the top, read "New York State Revolutionary troops" for "New York State Revolutionary militia."

In the Appendix, page 382, second column, fifth line from the top, read "250 loaded coal cars" instead of "250 loaded freight cars."

In the Appendix, page 396, second column, fifth line from the bottom, read "Statue of Baron Steuben" instead of "Statute of Baron Steuben."

In the acknowledgment of assistance rendered the editor of this work by living (1914) writers on the Mohawk valley and others, the name of Mrs. A. T. Smith of Fultonville, N. Y., is omitted. On page 230 appears an extract from one of Mrs. Smith's writings, "A Ramble, Visit to a Colonial House."

An earnest effort has been made to correct the errors which have crept into this work during its preparation. These mistakes will be eliminated in any future editions of this book.

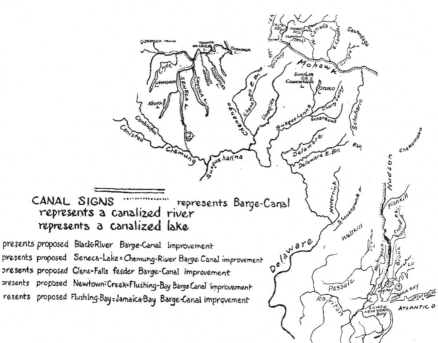

CANAL SIGNS ············· represents Barge-Canal
represents a canalized river
represents a canalized lake

presents proposed Black-River Barge-Canal improvement
presents proposed Seneca-Lake=Chemung-River Barge Canal improvement
oresents proposed Glens-Falls feeder Barge-Canal improvement
oresents proposed Newtown-Creek=Flushing-Bay Barge-Canal improvement
resents proposed Flushing-Bay=Jamaica-Bay Barge-Canal improvement

NEW YORK STATE RIVERS.

Here are seen the principal rivers and river systems of New York State, including also those of northeastern New Jersey, which empty into the mouth of the Hudson. The greatest river systems in the order of their importance to New York State are the Hudson, the Oswego, the St. Lawrence (including Lake Champlain), the Genesee, the Susquehanna, the Delaware, the Black, and the Allegheny. The borders of New York State are not here shown and it will interest the student (of any age) to supply them. New York contains two of the three principal drainage systems of the United States—these three are the Atlantic, the Gulf of Mexico and the Pacific systems. The Allegheny river, traversing a portion of southwestern New York State, represents the Gulf drainage system, while all the other streams lie within the Atlantic system. New York State, generally speaking, is bordered by Lake Erie and the Niagara river on the west, Lake Ontario and the St. Lawrence on the north, Lake Champlain and the watershed of the Hudson on the east and portions of the watersheds of the Allegheny, Susquehanna and Delaware rivers on the south. Attention is called to the remarkable Hudson (including the Mohawk) and Oswego river systems, which form such a large part of the New York State Barge Canal. The canalized portions of these rivers are represented by dots alongside their channels. Note the canal signs which indicate proposed future unions of streams and their canalization. See Chapter V., Series II., P. 171, "The Mohawk River and Watershed;" also Chapter VI., Third Series, "Geological Review of the Middle Mohawk Valley."

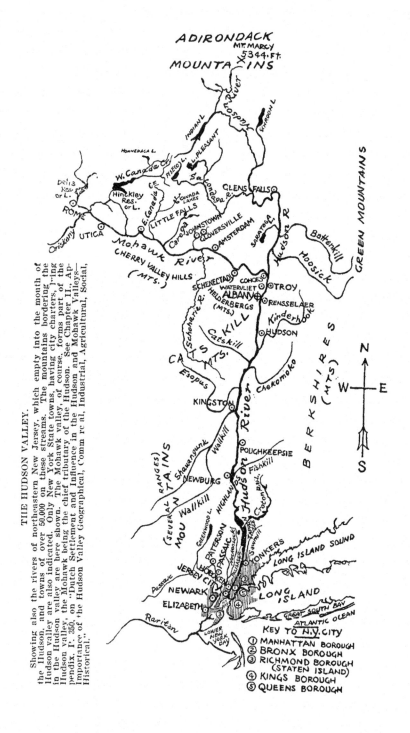

THE HUDSON VALLEY.

Showing also the rivers of northeastern New Jersey, which empty into the mouth of the Hudson, and towns of over 50,000 on these streams. The mountains bordering the Hudson valley are also indicated. Only New York State towns, having city charters, l-ing in the Hudson valley are here shown. The Mohawk valley, of course, forms part of the Hudson valley, the Mohawk being the chief tributary of the Hudson. See Chapter II., Appendix, P. 350, on "Dutch Settlement and Influence in the Hudson and Mohawk Valleys—Importance of the Hudson Valley Geographical, Commercial, Industrial, Agricultural, Social, Historical."

KEY TO N.Y. CITY
① MANHATTAN BOROUGH
② BRONX BOROUGH
③ RICHMOND BOROUGH (STATEN ISLAND)
④ KINGS BOROUGH
⑤ QUEENS BOROUGH

OSWEGO CO.

MADISON CO.

OTSEGO CO.

SARATOGA CO.

ALBANY CO.

DELAWARE Co.

N W S

THE MOHAWK VALLEY AND THE SIX MOHAWK VALLEY COUNTIES.

The above map co___ ____ ____ ___ the entire Mohawk valley and shows the six ___ valley ____ of Oneida, ___ (except the northern part), Montgomery, Fulton, Schoharie and Schenectady. Portions of the ___ ____ ___ (with the exception of Montgomery county) comprise parts of other watersheds but three-quarters of the territory of ___ counties here ___ lie within the Mohawk valley. Small parts of the M___ hawk watershed lying in Madison, Hamilton, ___ and ___ counties are not ___ the ___. The northern half of Herkimer ____ unty is omitted, as its ___ ___ of this ___ ___ to the ___ prevents it's ___ ____ within the limits ___ ___ is ___ to the key in the upper right and, furthermore, it belongs geographically to the Black river approximately ___ 200 population (in 1910) are here shown as ___ as some ___ smaller centers of ___ ____ historic ___. This map will be ____ useful in ca___ ___ with the use of a state ___ (the Rand & M___) ___ly pocket ___ is ___ ___) and separate ____ part. It should ___ be studied with reference to ___ the maps of the New ___ state river ____ and of the Hudson valley (of ___ with ___ map of the Mohawk ___ ___ watershed (on p. 172). So ___ as the ___ of this ___ ___ this is the first ___ of a ___ of the six ___wk valley ___ appearing separately. See Chapter II, Appendix, P. 350, "The Six Mohawk Valley Counties and the ___k Valley Considered as a ___torical and ___al Unit."

: xMcKeever

: . Key:—

INTRODUCTION

In 1776 an American fort was erected, in the district of Canajoharie of Tryon county, at the then mouth of the Otsquago creek, on a bluff in the Sand Hill section of the present village of Fort Plain. Legend has it that there was some sort of fortification before that date and this is not improbable as here was the beginning of the Otsego trail through the Otsquago valley and the site in question is one naturally suited for defense. The fort built in the year of the Independence declaration was a regular army post and continued as such until Washington's visit in 1783, and for some years after. It is with this fortification that the story deals and with lands adjoining, of which it was a natural center.

Artificial boundaries of territory are often confusing and somewhat ridiculous. The Mohawk forms a natural division between the north and south side sections about Fort Plain and it is fitting that these two neighborhoods should be treated as separate localities. Aside from supposed convenience to the citizens at election times and to facilitate town government, there is no reason whatever why we should try in our minds to conceive the township of Canajoharie as set off in any way from the town of Minden. Walk back on the hills toward Seebers Lane; look off to the east and you will see the stream of the Mohawk separating you from the fertile hills of beautiful Palatine. But where you stand (if it is on the high hill about a mile southeast of Fort Plain village) you will see no line or natural boundary cutting off the farms of Minden from those of Canajoharie. So, in treating of the land, people or events of the valley, it is more vitally important to consider the sections naturally set apart than those which consist solely of imaginary lines drawn upon maps.

In the following chapters, the story of old Fort Plain will be found to be interwoven with that of the old Canajoharie and Palatine districts of Tryon county. The acute mind of Sir William Johnson, in his division of the districts of Tryon, merely drew on his map the natural boundaries which ran through the county. This middle region of the Mohawk valley is set off from the upper part to the west of Little Falls by the range which cuts squarely across the Mohawk, known by the name of Fall Hill. To the east a similar barrier exists in the picturesque hill formations which rise from the Mohawk flats on each side, known as The Noses. The Mohawk here breaks through a high ridge which separates this mid section from the eastern part of the valley. Johnson fittingly named this region north of the river, Palatine, and that to the south Canajoharie, and these formed the Palatine and Canajoharie districts of Troyn county. The name Canajoharie had probably been applied to its section from early Indian times. Five districts were set off and the other three were Mohawk, on both sides of the river from the line of Schenectady county west to the Noses, and from Fall Hill west, Kingsland to the north of the Mohawk and German Flats to the south. The districts north of the river were supposed to run to the Canadian line, while those to the south embraced territory to the northern boundary of Pennsylvania. However, most of the population was gathered along the Mohawk river and its tributary, the Schoharie, and the history of Tryon county is in reality that of the Mohawk valley; which is another instance where actual natural territory and boundaries must be considered rather than the dot and dash divisions of the maps.

These two districts mentioned extend along the Mohawk for a distance of about twenty miles. The townships of Montgomery county that form part of old Canajoharie and Palatine are Minden, Canajoharie, part of Root (to the west of the Big Nose), Palatine and St. Johnsville. This publication deals with these five towns, as well as the older districts, and, as Fort Plain is approximately at their geographical center, it is fitting that the title of this narrative should be "The Story of Old Fort Plain." So the object of this work is to tell the tale of the Mohawk country between the Noses and Fall Hill and to relate as well all that can be gathered of importance with reference to the chief and central Revolutionary fortification of the territory in question, which was known as Fort Plain.

It is interesting to realize that we have a prior authority, for the consideration of local history from this point, in that eminent New York state historian, Benson J. Lossing, particularly adapted to his task by being a descendant of the first Holland settlers. In his wonderfully interesting "Pictorial Field Book of the Revolution," he says: "At Fort Plain I was joined by my traveling companions * * * and made it my headquarters for three days, while visiting places of interest in the vicinity. It being a central point in the hostile move ments in Tryon county, from the time of the flight of St. Leger from before Fort Stanwix until the close of the war, we will plant our telescope of observation here for a time, and view the most important occurrences within this particular sweep of its speculum." To do exactly this and, in addition, to continue our view of life and events from the Revolutionary time to the present, is the mission of "The Story of Old Fort Plain."

The need has been felt of a continuous narrative of the fort and the conditions existing in its surrounding territory. The former chronicles of events and life about here were largely obscure and what could be obtained was imbedded in a mass of other material in local history. Fort Plain was next to Forts Dayton and Herkimer, the most advanced New York frontier post, during the last years of the war and seems to have been the most important. From here Willett issued on his heroic marches to victorious battles; here was the headquarters of the chief officers concerned in the Klock's field battle; here and within cannon shot occurred some of the most tragic and thrilling incidents of the Revolution in Tryon county. From here was heard Brown's brave stand at Stone Arabia, and from here was seen the glare from Currytown's burning farm-houses. Here was heard the rattle of the rifles of the victorious Americans on Klock's Field. This fort housed the settlers fleeing from the tomahawk and torch of the Indian and Tory. It was once, by Fort Plain's women, successfully defended by a feminine ruse. It remained a tower of patriot strength during the whole contest and finally at its close housed the great commander—Washington himself. Here

came Gansevoort, Gov. Clinton, Col. Dayton, Gen. Clinton, the despised Van
Rensselaer, probably Gen. Arnold, as well as many members of the committee of
safety and of the county militia. Here commanded the mighty Willett and the
sterling warrior Clyde. Through the dreadful, bloody struggle, which decimated
the population and almost destroyed a thriving farming section, Fort Plain
stood a tower of strength to keep alive in a great territory the soul of American
liberty and the spirit of American civilization and culture. This it did and,
when the horrors of the conflict were past and its dead buried, some back of the
church near by, the batteaux again floated on the river at its feet, within
its sight blackened ruins were replaced by houses and barns and the plowman
was once more seen tilling the neglected fields on the distant slopes. Civilization
resumed its work in the valley and the task of old Fort Plain was done. But
its story still remains for those who wish to learn it.

The placing of the fortification was evidently largely a matter of geography.
Its hill was capable of defense on all sides and was commanded by no higher
ground which could be used as a base of attack at that time. It could be provided with its necessary water from a good spring directly under its walls. It
had a view of the country for miles in all directions. The road from Fort
Stanwix to Schenectady ran along the foot of the hill. It, of course, was of easy
access from the river at its base and commanded this highway of freight
traffic, and a ferry was here then as at a later date. Its location at the beginning of the Otsego trail or carry, as mentioned, probably influenced its site
and here then the Otsquago flowed into the Mohawk. Boys who swam in the
river before the beginning of the Barge canal remember "the low," as they called
it and this shallow in the river, then about opposite the knitting mills, was undoubtedly the remains of the rift which always existed in the Mohawk below the
outlets of contributory streams. The mouth of the Garoga valley, penetrating a
great extent of the country to the north, lay about two miles away and at that
point the old Indian trail from Canada, by way of Lake George, joined the Mohawk river trails. Furthermore Fort Plain was located in the midst of the
Palatine settlements of which Fort Herkimer and Fort Dayton defended the
western and Fort Hunter the eastern end. Everything made this the natural
site of what was later an important frontier post and the base of several military operations vitally affecting the settlers of the Mohawk valley. Here at
Sand Hill, was a Reformed church, a river ferry, one or two traders and probably a tiny hamlet at the time of the erection of this defense. Of course the
fear of invasion of the state by British forces and Indian allies, from Canada
through the Mohawk valley, was the prime reason for the renovation of Forts
Stanwix and Herkimer and the building of Fort Dayton diagonally opposite, at
the present site of Herkimer, and of Fort Plain in the center of the Canajoharie
district in the year of the Declaration of Independence.

The time dealt with lends added interest to a sketch of its people, places and
events on account of its remoteness. Although we are separated from it by only
about a century and a half of time (since the date of the erection of Fort Plain),
the vital changes of that period have given American life an absolutely different
phase. Up to the building of the Erie canal the details of human existence had
been the same, practically, for centuries. Today we live in a different world
from our American forebears of 1776.

The main part of these sketches is founded upon "Beer's Illustrated History of Montgomery and Fulton Counties, 1878," Lossing's "Field Book of the Revolution" and Simms's "Frontiersmen of New York." Large parts of these works have been used bodily. Other authorities whose material has been made use of are Lossing's "Empire State," Benton's "History of Herkimer County" and the "Documentary History of New York." While no claim is made for especial originality in its preparation, a great mass of material has been arranged in proper chronological sequence, which, the writer believes, is the first instance of its having been done in relation to the Revolutionary history of Fort Plain and the region about it. In order to make a continuous narrative, dealing with the men of this territory, the Oriskany campaign is included. It is presumed about half of the provincials concerned in this movement came from these two districts and the history of the men themselves of old Canajoharie and old Palatine is fully as vital as the study of events and places. An endeavor has been made to give a picture of different periods and, to this end, much detail has been necessary.

The history of the middle Mohawk valley can, for convenience, be divided into four sections.

The first is from its discovery about 1616, to the formation of Tryon county in 1772. This is the time of Indian life and of white settlement.

The second period is from 1772 to 1783, embracing the Revolutionary war.

The third is from 1783 to the division of Montgomery county into Fulton and Montgomery counties in 1838, covering the years of highway improvement, bridge building, canal digging, railroad construction and early town development.

The fourth is from 1838 to the present day, and it is hoped that teachers and parents will, in future years, carry on this story for the young reader up to the time in which he or she reads this book.

Many people have the idea that local history means, almost entirely, the events transpiring about here during the Revolution. That such an impression is erroneous is shown by the fact that, in this work, the recital of events hereabouts, during the War of Independence, occupies only about one-third of the space. Conditions have been so varied and so many elements have entered into the story of this valley of the northland that there is much to scan beside the tragedies, conflicts and life of the first war with England. Our chronicle is not alone local but touches at every point the development of our national life, and this is particularly true because the valley has always been, from the earliest times, one of the great highways of traffic, trade and travel between east and west.

No section of our country affords more glowing historical pictures than the Mohawk country. Here are found all the elements that go to the making of the story of man from the stone age to the present era of a complicated civilization. The French priests and the Dutch traders discovered here red savages, who were living under conditions similar to those of prehistoric man in Europe. Of the latter we have only the most fragmentary knowledge, but, of their equivalent brethren in America, we know as much as we do of our own frontier ancestors. In the earliest days in the valley, of which we have historical knowledge, we find much of the Mohawk Indian life centered in the old Canajoharie district. This lends to the study of the most warlike tribe of the powerful Iroquois republic an added and poignant local interest.

The story of this great and beautiful valley of the Mohawk is soon told in brief. While it has been ages in the making, the reader can close his eyes and, in less time than it takes in the telling, its varied and colorful pictures sweep before his mental vision.

Centuries, probably, after the great glacial ice sheet started ebbing toward the north, it turned the waters of some of the Great Lakes down through the valley to the Hudson sea inlet, making our river a great rushing torrent, large in volume and magnificent to the view. Before the mighty stream dwindled to its present course, back, through the great forest covering the old glacial bed and along the river, came slinking red human beings close, in brain and body, to the beasts they slew for food and clothing. Here, in the ages before the dread ice came slowly and irresistibly from the dead and frozen north, perhaps had been men not unlike them, living wild lives in the wilderness among the stranger wild animals of that distant day.

Gradually these savages, of the period after the great ice sheet, grew in the ruder arts of civilization; while, outside of their immediate bands, their lust for human blood and love of cruel spectacles probably increased. Then came red warriors from the north down upon the homes of these valley barbarians and began a bloody war of extermination. Suddenly from the forests, these vermilion-faced, befeathered, naked savages rush out and with club and arrow, with stone axe and knife, they murder the startled people of the Mohawk villages. A hideous spectacle ensues—men, women and children are stabbed, struck down, brained and scalped, only a few escaping to later burn and agonize for the bestial enjoyment of the red raiders. To save themselves, the Mohawks, with their brethren of the other four tribes, join in the great league of the Iroquois family. They drive back their foes, inflicting equally murderous and inhuman punishment, and become the virtual rulers of the red men of the entire eastern country.

Years after this, but upon a long ago day, a Mohawk stood in front of his village on a slope overlooking the bright and winding stream. Bronzed and naked to his breech cloth and deerskin leggins, with knife in belt and bow in hand, his sharp eyes scanned the summer scene. At his feet lay the flatlands of the valley, green with the promising crop of Indian corn. Gently back from these open spaces sloped the giant hills clad in a glorious forest unbroken to the summits of the fartherest ridges. In the distance a herd of deer stepped lightly to the river edge and drank, and far on high an eagle soared in the milky blue sky. A pleasing sight—a view of primeval nature undisturbed. Entered, upon this quiet scene, a man in a canoe. Around a willow-bordered bend in the placid river he came paddling down stream and the red man saw that he was clad in strange garments and that he was white—a sight which filled him with superstitious amazement—which meant the end of his race in the valley. This was the first of the French priests whose mission of religion brought them among the valley Iroquois.

As the river and its banks move quickly by, to this silent, serious white man, so the scene changes rapidly after his advent. The Dutch traders, in still stranger clothes, bring guns and rum to exchange with the Indians for their splendid wilderness furs. After them follow red-coated soldiers and traders of another race—the English. Then come, toiling painfully, up the banks of the

river, sturdy, patient men of a brother blood—the Germans. The Mohawks begin to lose their land and we soon find them, few in numbers, confined to two villages, one at the Schoharie creek and the other in the western Canajoharie district. To them the white men seem to come in swarms. They fell the trees and clear and till the land while the smoke from the burning prostrate forest giants clouds the sky. White women, little children, and strange new animals follow these woodsmen, who build yet larger houses of stone, who make wagon paths through the woods and who bring their flatboats, up and down the river, laden with grain, furs and many kinds of goods. These valley Europeans eat, drink, play, dance, love, sing, breed, work and die, like people the world over.

Then, as now, spring comes to the Mohawk, flooding the white and grey valley with sudden warmth, making every tiny rivulet a rushing torrent and filling the river with its yearly flood of brown turbid water and rushing ice. The rough clearings are plowed and planted and heavy crops soon cover the fertile soil. Forest, field, hillside—all are green, green in every shade; green everywhere is the valley, except the winding river reflecting the whitish blue sky. Then the harvest time dots the verdant landscape with fields of brown and yellow and through flatland and meadow resounds the swish of scythe and cradle. Autumn colors the woods with a riot of scarlet, yellows and browns and the open spaces and the river margin sparkle with the azure and sheen of aster, golden rod, wild sunflower. Corn shocks rustle and nod and yellow pumpkins glow like giant oranges amidst the stubble. Now is the beauty of the vale of the Mohawk at its best, while the air is filled with subtle haze and the glorious autumn landscape drowses in the noontide of a perfect Indian summer. Mohawk and white hunter bring home deer and wild turkey; the small boy scours the woods for hickory and butter nut. In the branches chatters the thrifty squirrel as the quiet air is startled by the crack and boom of rifle and gun. In the cabins and stone houses, wives and daughters bake and brew for autumn feasts and merrymakings. At night the great harvest moon, full-orbed, hangs in the sky flooding, with its greenish yellow light, a landscape of mystery, through which gleams the winding ribbon river—a scene inspiring that pensive seriousness which seems to possess the valley, even in its gayest autumn or tenderest springtime phases.

And now down again comes the soft mantle of snow and the great hills and vales are once more wrapped in their while winter slumber.

And so, for years, runs along the life of the pioneer beside the Mohawk. But after a time these white men of different nations begin to differ among themselves and fall to quarreling violently. The velvet and red-coated turn upon the men of homespun and buckskin; war to the death breaks out, while the valley reeks with horrid slaughter.

The embittered Indians join the red coats, glad of a foe on whom to wreak vengeance for their stolen hunting grounds. As is usual the payment for this dread struggle of the Revolution is made in the lives of tender children and loving women as well as in those of enraged men. What had once been strong men of Tryon county lie rotting, to the number of two hundred on the field of Oriskany.

Here particularly are shown all those revolting horrors of war which, when generally and constantly realized, will eliminate such bloody struggles from the of civilized peoples—war which is no more essential to the development of nations than Indian barbarities are requisite to the cultivation of intrepid manhood.

But the naked Indian, the velvet and the red coat are driven back. Sadly, the men of homespun and buckskin drop their guns, bury their dead, rebuild their burned and plundered homes and turn again to the task of tilling their neglected fields.

Such is nature that, in ten year's time, the Mohawk skirts a country again smiling with plentiful harvests, and through the trees along its banks show solid houses and barns filled with corn and wheat and all the bountiful products of a fertile soil. Then men tire of the hardships of boating on the river and dig themselves a canal in which to float still larger freight craft, and great is the rejoicing when it is done. Bridges are built across the Mohawk and soon, close along its edge, the engine of steam on iron tracks goes rushing by, before the gaze of the astonished farmer and his affrighted family. Villages with smoking factories dot the twin courses of the Mohawk and the Erie, broad cultivated fields have replaced the giant forest which live only in a few scattered woods. And here is the valley of our day, from whence, at the trumpet's blare which proclaimed a nation's peril, thousands of our men fare forth to fight and die on southern fields.

Here is the valley of four hundred thousand people, where were but ten thousand when St. Leger came down upon Fort Schuyler; our valley which has always been a great highway, by land and water, since the day of the Indian trails and the river flatboat—great and growing greater with its railroads over which hundreds of trains speed daily; its highways traversed by countless automobiles; its barge canal, soon to carry a large share of the country's east and west commerce: our valley, with its schools, societies, clubs, churches, theaters, fairs, factories, stores, bustling villages, great cities, tiny hamlets, fertile farms —with its restless, discontented human population, sharing in the trouble and perplexity of the nation's industrial and political problems—but yet withal our northland valley of old, shorn of its noble forest but with the same everlasting hills rising in slope on slope, from the winding river to noble heights along the horizon.

This in brief, is the story of the Mohawk. And what of the future—who knows what it may be, before the great green forest of yore again comes back over these rolling hills, yes and before that day when the dread cold encompasses it all once more—perhaps forever.

NELSON GREENE.

Fort Plain, New York, September 15, 1912.

THE STORY OF OLD FORT PLAIN

(FIRST SERIES 1616-1783)

CHAPTER I.

The Mohawks and Iroquois—A Dutch Journey Through the Canajoharie District in 1634—Local Indian Villages and Trails.

It is no part of this narrative to deal at length with the Indian inhabitants of the valley, who ceased to be people of this territory at the building of the Fort Plain fortification. The reader is referred to works dealing with the Mohawks and the Iroquois. That the aboriginal inhabitants of the Mohawk valley were a peculiar combination of shrewdness, semi-civilization, childishness and the blackest savagery, goes without saying. They cultivated the native vegetables on the river flats and some of the native fruits on nearby· slopes. They made maple sugar, raised tobacco and trapped and fished, and handed on to the first white settlers their knowledge of the native soil and its products. The Mohawks wore skins for clothing and made cabins of saplings and bark, which were of ·considerable size at times. A stockade surrounded their villages. With them is concerned a legend of Hiawatha. The members of the original five nations, in the order of their distribution from east to west, were Mohawks, Oneidas, Onondagas, Cayugas and Senecas. These were joined by the Tuscaroras in 1714, and the Iroquois, after that year, were known as the Six Nations. As the Mohawks were the most warlike tribe the war chief of the Iroquois was selected from the ranks of these valley savages. At the time of the Dutch occupation, the total Iroquois population is estimated at 13,000, and must then have

been considerably greater than a century later. Seventeenth century accounts would indicate at least double the number of Mohawks living along the river, compared with eighteenth century figures obtainable. Sir William Johnson, at one time, gives the available fighting strength of the Mohawks as 150 warriors, which seems a very low figure. However the tribe could not . have much exceeded six hundred people, as their castle at Fort Hunter (in the eighteenth century) is described as their largest village, and only contained 30 huts. The Great Hendrick and Joseph Brant are the leading figures of the Mohawks in the century preceding the Revolution. Both were residents of the old Canajoharie district which we are considering. The famous Seneca chief Cornplanter comes into our story and he had local interest as being the son of John Abeel, a Fort Plain trader. All of these are considered at greater length later.

Mr. John Fea of Amsterdam is the author of a very interesting article on "Indian Trails of the Mohawk Valley," which was published in the Fort Plain Standard in December, 1908. From this publication are taken the extracts which follow. The trip of the Dutch explorers, which Mr. Fea narrated, is of great local interest because it covers so much of the old Canajobarie district along the Mohawk and describes in detail the Indian villages of that tribe, of which a great part seems to have been located in the district mentioned.

Mr. Fea's paper says that this was "an expedition to the Mohawk and

Seneca Indians' country undertaken by three Dutchmen with five Mohawk Indians as guides in 1634-5. To us their journey through our own part of the Mohawk valley ought to be especially interesting, as they proceed from one Indian village to another. This journal is the earliest written description of the Mohawk valley. * * * * The motive of the expedition from Fort Orange, as stated in the journal, was to investigate the movements of the French traders, who were holding out greater inducements than the Dutch were giving, thereby persuading the Mohawks to go and trade their rich furs in Canada. They left Fort Orange on Dec. 11, 1634. During a journey of two days' time they covered 49½ English miles. This brought them up the Mohawk valley on the north side of the river to Yosts, near the 'Nose,' at a little house in which they lodged over night. This Indian house, according to this journal, was one-half mile from the first castle, which was built on a high hill, where they found 36 houses in rows like a street. The name of the castle was Onekagonka. The evidence of this village can be found on the bank of Wasontah creek on the Vrooman farm near the 'Nose.' After three days sojourn at Onekagonka they continued westward over the ice on the river a Dutch half mile [a Dutch mile equalling two and one-fourth English miles] past a village of nine houses, named Canowarode. This is the present county house site [on the north side of the Mohawk] and the buildings are all on the Indian village site. They went another Dutch half mile and passed a village of 12 houses, named Senatsycrosy. They had then arrived at Sprakers. They continued past Sprakers one Dutch mile and came to the second castle with 12 houses built on a hill. This castle was named Canagere. The expedition remained at Canagere three days. They received a supply of stores from Fort Orange. Among the stuff was ham, beer, salt, tobacco for the savages and a bottle of brandy. Three Indian women came from the Senecas peddling fish. They

had salmon, dried and fresh, also a good quantity of green tobacco to sell.

"Here the party employed an Indian to act as guide to the Senecas. As a retainer for his services they gave him half a yard of cloth, two axes, two knives, two pairs of awls and a pair of shoes. On this day, Dec. 19, [1634] there was a great rainfall. This castle Canagere was on the Horatio Nellis farm. Dec. 20 they departed from the second castle and marched a Dutch mile to a stream they had to cross. The water ran swiftly. Big cakes of ice came drifting along; the rainfall of the previous day loosened the ice and they were in great danger if they lost their footing. Here then we behold Canajoharie creek.

"After going another Dutch half mile they arrived at the third castle, named Sochanidisse. It had 32 houses and was on a very high hill. It was on the projecting point of land in the Happy Hollow district west of Canajoharie on the Brown farm. They remained over night at this castle. The journal makes mention of plenty of flat land in the vicinity. They exchanged here one awl for a beaver skin.

"Dec. 21 they started very early in the morning for the fourth castle. After marching one-half Dutch mile they came to a village with only nine houses, named Osquage. The chief's name was Ognoho, 'the wolf.' This was at Prospect hill, near Fort Plain. They saw a big stream that their guide did not dare cross as the water had risen from the heavy rainfall, so they postponed their journey until the next day. The stream we recognize is the raging Otsquago. The next day they waded through the stream and, after going one-half Dutch mile, came to a village of 14 houses, named Cawoge. This was on the Lipe farm west of Fort Plain [at the site of the Revolutionary post]. After going another Dutch mile they arrived at the fourth and last castle of the Mohawks, named Tenotoge. This was the largest village in the valley at that period. There were 55 houses, some 100 paces long. Here is mentioned a very definite landmark on the trail. 'The Kill (river), we spoke about before, runs past here, and the course is mostly north by west and south by east.' So reads the journal.

"Tenotoge was on the Sponable and Moyer farms, two miles northwest of Fort Plain. Accompanied by Andrew H. Moyer, I counted 69 deep and well defined corn pits on adjoining land, then owned by Adam Failing. The whole site covered about ten acres of ground. Abundant evidence of palisades was found by the Moyer family when they broke up the ground. This large and important Indian castle has never been mentioned in New York state aboriginal records.

"At St. Johnsville the river course is due east. It then commences to curve southerly and from Palatine Church its course is almost due south to Fort Plain, a distance of three miles. On the elevated ground west of the river, nearly opposite Palatine Church, was located the great Mohawk castle, Tenotoge. From this elevation they saw the Mohawk river course north and south as we may see it today. At this point the old Canadian trail was intersected at the river. From here they [the Dutch explorers] departed over the wilderness trail westward, passing the south edge of the Timmerman farm at Dutchtown, and what was known by the pioneers of Dutchdorf as the old Indian trail to the Senecas."

This important castle of the Mohawks must have been the largest village, inhabited by human beings, in this section of the present state of New York; and it was located centrally within the limits of the present town of Minden. Its site was doubtless influenced by the junction of the Canadian trail with the river trail at the Caroga ford.

"The whole Mohawk valley at an early period was interlaced with Indian trails. The main ones from the Hudson river passed along both sides of the Mohawk. From the head of Lake George two trails led to the Mohawk river. The first led southwestward through a valley between Potash

and Bucktail mountains in Warren county to the ford at Luzerne on the Hudson river below the mouth of the Sacandaga, thence along the Sacandaga to the Vlaie at Northampton. On leaving the Vlaie the trail took a westward direction along the south side of Mayfield creek to Kingsborough, thence down the Cayadutta to Johnstown, continuing its course on the west side of the Cayadutta to the present village of Sammonsville. From this place the trail took a circuitous course over Klipse hill, thence through Stone Arabia to the ford at the mouth of Caroga creek. This was the principal route from the west into Canada via Lake George and was a favorite route traversed by the Oneidas, and as such possibly gives reason why, in 1751, William Johnson secured from the Indians, for 'himself and others,' the Kingsborough tract of land, and later taking up his residence on the great Indian trail that passed through it."

CHAPTER II.

1616-1772—Indians—Mohawk Valley Discovery—Settlement—Sir William Johnson.

The Mohawks were the most eastern of the Five Nations. They claimed a region extending from Albany, on the Hudson, westerly to the headwaters of the Susquehanna and Delaware, and thence northerly to the St. Lawrence river and embracing all the land between this river and Lake Champlain. Their actual northern limits were not definitely fixed, but they appear to have claimed as hunting grounds, all the lands between the St. Lawrence and St. Johns river. This was a subject of continual dispute between them and other tribes. Canada was settled by the French in 1608. In 1609 Champlain and his party of Canadian Indians defeated a band of Iroquois (probably Mohawks), in battle, in the present town of Ticonderoga between Lake George and Crown Point. In 1615 Champlain and ten other Frenchmen joined the Hurons and Adirondacks in an expedition against the Five Nations. The Iroquois signally defeated this force, in the Onondaga country. Champlain was wounded twice and the invaders fled back to Canada. The first white man to explore this region was probably a Canadian Franciscian priest, LaCarnon, who entered this field as missionary in 1616 and was undoubtedly the first white man to behold the upper reaches of this famous river and its beautiful valley. In 1609 Dutch sailors from the Half Moon passed the mouth of the Mohawk and the Dutch may have then penetrated its lower valley a short distance. Jesuits, who in the interests of trade, as well as religion, went alone and unarmed, succeeded the Francisians in 1633. Three of these Jesuits suffered martyrdom at the hands of the Mohawks. The captivity and fate of Jogues exemplify the persistence of the Jesuits and the heroism with which they met death. In 1642 he and and a number of others were captured by Iroquois on the St. Lawrence. They came into the hands of the Mohawks near Lake George and were compelled to run the gauntlet. On reaching the villages of the Mohawks, Jogues was made to run the gauntlet twice more for their amusement, agonizing a white man being then a novelty to the savages. During his captivity he was frequently tortured with the most heartless cruelty. His fingers and toes were removed joint by joint and his body and limbs mutilated with burning sticks and hot irons. He suffered in this way for 15 months, when, through the influence of the Dutch, he was released and returned to France. He came back to the Mohawk in 1646 to prosecute his missionary work. The savages did not take kindly to him or his teachings and he was put to death by the most excruciating tortures, the Indians of course, being masters of the knowledge of every conceivable pain and agony which could be inflicted on the human body. The site of this martyrdom was at the Mohawk village of Caughnawaga, where Fonda now stands. The Jesuits kept up their missionary work on these same savages and finally, in 1670, converted them and induced them to move to Canada.

In 1659, the Mohawks, suffering from their conflicts with the French and from the crippling of their warriors by the sale of liquor to them by the Dutch, sent a delegation to Albany asking that the sale of spirits be suppressed among them and for aid against their enemies. A council concerning these matters was held between the Dutch and Mohawks at Caughnawaga in 1659, which was the first ever held in the Mohawk country. The governor of Canada, in 1666, tried to destroy the Mohawks, but only succeeded in burning their villages, as the warriors took to the woods. Troubles between the Mohicans and Mohawks followed, without much advantage to either. The Iroquois, including the Mohawks, were thoroughly won over to the English side by Gov. Dongan in 1684. In 1690 the French and Indians descended on Schenectady and burned that town; 60 people were killed and 27 captured, a few of the survivors escaping through the deep snow to Albany. In 1693 Count Frontenac captured the lower and middle Mohawk castles without much trouble, but had a hard fight at the upper castle; 300 Mohawks were taken prisoners. The people of Schenectady failed to warn their Indian neighbors, which greatly incensed them. Schuyler, with the Albany militia, pursued this French party and retook 50 Mohawk captives. For the last half century of the tribal existence of the Mohawks in the valley, they had but two castles, one called Canajoharie, situated at the present Indian Castle, in the town of Danube, Herkimer county, and the other, called Dyiondarogon, on the lower or east bank of the Schoharie creek at its junction with the Mohawk.

The first white valley settlement was by the Dutch in 1663 at Schenectady, under the Dutch rule of the colony. The next west of Schenectady was that of Heinrich Frey at Palatine Bridge in 1688. Their country, devastated by war, in 1708, a large body of German immigrants, from the Palatinate on the Rhine, landed in New York and were settled on the Hudson, where their treatment by the province is open to great criticism. In 1711 their number was said to be 1,761, but they had no idea of remaining in their deplorable condition. In the expedition of Col. Nicholson for the reduction of Canada in 1711, 300 Palatines enlisted to escape their condition of almost servitude. In 1711 some of them moved to the Schoharie valley and some are supposed to have settled in Palatine about that date. They are said to have threaded on foot an intricate Indian trail, bearing upon their backs their worldly possessions, consisting of "a few rude tools, a scanty supply of provisions, a meagre wardrobe, and a small number of rusty firearms." In 1723 numbers of the Palatines emigrated to Pennsylvania, others moved up and settled in the districts of Canajoharie and Palatine and along the Mohawk, and by 1725 there were settlements of these Germans extending up the river from the "Noses" to German Flats, the eastern part of the valley being settled by Dutch farmers.

October 19, 1723, the Stone Arabia patent was granted to 27 Palatines, who, with their families, numbered 127 persons. The tract conveyed by this deed contained 12,700 acres. The names of these pioneer settlers of the district which was later to become Palatine were: Digert, Schell, Cremse, Garlack, Dillinbeck, Emiger, Vocks, Lawyer, Feink, Frey, Diegert, Coppernoll, Peiper, Seibert, Casselman, Fink, Ingolt, Erchart, Nelse.

The story of the Mohawk valley from 1738 to 1772, the date of the formation of Tryon county, is largely the biography of that picturesque figure, Sir William Johnson. In order that the reader may better understand the subsequent history of the Canajoharie and Palatine districts, the following account is given of Sir William's life, taken from Beers' history:

"Sir William Johnson was born at Warrentown in the county of Down, Ireland, in 1715. In 1738, at the age of 23, he was sent into the Mohawk valley to superintend a large estate, the title to which had been acquired by his uncle, Sir Peter Warren, a British admiral. This tract containing some 15,000 acres, lay along the south bank of the Mohawk near the mouth of Schoharie creek, and mostly within the present town of Florida. It was called, from its proprietor, Warrensbush. Here Johnson came to promote his uncle's interests by the sale of small farms and his own interests by acquiring and cultivating land for himself, and their joint interests by keeping a store in which they were partners. In 1743 he became connected with the fur trade at Oswego and derived a great revenue from this and other dealings with the Indians. Having early resolved to remain in the Mohawk valley, he applied himself earnestly to the study of the character and language of the natives. By freely mingling with them and adopting their habits when it suited his interests, he soon gained their good will and confidence, and gradually acquired an ascendancy over them never possessed by any other European. A few years after Johnson's arrival on the Mohawk he purchased a tract of land on the north side of the river. In 1744 he built a gristmill on a small stream flowing into the Mohawk from the north, about three miles west of the present city of Amsterdam. He also erected a stone mansion at this place for his own residence, calling it Fort Johnson. [This fine old building still stands and bears its own name, which it has also given to the town about it and the railroad station there.] Johnson also bought, from time to time, great tracts of land north of the Mohawk, and at some distance from it, mostly within the present limit of Fulton county. He subsequently became possessed, by gift from the Indians which was confirmed by the Crown, of the great tract of land in what is now Herkimer county, known as the Royal Grant.

"The Mohawk river early became the great thoroughfare toward Lake Ontario for the Colonists in prosecuting their trade with the Indians. Gov. Burnet realized the importance of controlling the lake for the purpose of commerce and resistance to the encroachments of the French and accordingly established in 1722 a trading post and in 1727 a fort at Oswego. The French met this measure by the construction of defenses at Niagara, to intercept the trade from the upper lakes. This movement was ineffectually opposed by the Iroquois, who, to obtain assistance from the English, gave a deed of their territory to the King of England, who was to protect them in the possession of it. To defend the frontier, which was exposed to invasions by the French, especially after their erection of the fortification of Crown Point, settlements were proposed and Capt. Campbell, a Highland chief, came over in 1737 to view the lands offered, which were 30,000 acres. Four hundred Scotch adults came over and many of them settled in and about Saratoga, becoming the pioneers of that section, as the Palatines were of the upper half of the Mohawk. This settlement was surprised by French and Indians in 1745 who burned all the buildings and killed or captured almost the whole population, 30 families being massacred. The village of Hoosic was similarly destroyed, and consternation prevailed in the outlying settlements, many of the people fleeing to Albany. The Six Nations wavered in their attachment to the English. At this juncture, Sir William Johnson was entrusted with the sole management of the Iroquois. [He succeeded Col. Schuyler of Albany, the former Indian commissioner.] It is his services in this most important and delicate position, wherein he stood for a large part of his life as the mediator between two races, whose position and aims made them almost inevitably hostile, that constitutes his strongest claim to lasting and favorable remembrance. His knowledge of the language, customs and manners of the Indians, and the complete confidence which they always reposed in him, qualified him for this position. A high officer of his government, he was also

in 1746 formally invested by the Mohawks with the rank of a chief in that nation, to whom he was afterward known as Warraghegagey. In Indian costume he shortly after led the tribe to a council at Albany. He was appointed a colonel in the British ser vice about this time, and by his direction of the Colonial troops and the Iroquois warriors, the frontier settle ments were to a great extent saved from devastation by the French and their Indian allies, the settlements to the north of Albany, being an unhappy exception, while occasional murders and scalpings occurred even along the Mohawk. Johnson's influence with the Indians was increased by his having a Mohawk woman, Molly Brant, a sister of the famous Chief Joseph Brant, living with him as his wife the latter part of his life.

"Peace nominally existed between France and England from 1748 to 1756, but hostilities between their American colonies broke out as early as 1754. In the following year, 1755, Col. Johnson was appointed a major general and led the expedition against Crown Point which resulted in the distastrous defeat of the French near Lake George. At the same time with his military promotion he was reappointed superintendent of Indian affairs, having resigned that office in 1750, on account of the neglect of the government to pay some of his claims. On resuming the superintendency, General Johnson held a council with the Iroquois at his house, Fort Johnson, which resulted in about 250 of their warriors following him to Lake George. The victory there gained was the only one in a generally disastrous year, and General Johnson's services were rewarded by a baronetcy and the sum of £5,000 voted by Parliament. He was also thereafter paid £600 annually as the salary of his office over the Indians.

"In the spring of 1756 measures were taken for fortifying the portages between Schenectady and Oswego, by way of the Mohawk, Wood creek, Oneida lake and the Oswego river, with a view to keeping open communication between Albany and the fort at Oswego. The latter was in danger of being taken by the French. Tardily moved the provincial authorities and it was but a few days before Oswego was invested that Gen. Webb was sent with a regiment to reinforce the garrison and Sir William Johnson, with two battalions of militia and a body of Indians, shortly followed. Before Webb reached Oneida lake, he was informed that the besieged post had surrendered, and he promptly turned about and fled down the Mohawk to German Flats, where he met Johnson's force. The fort at Oswego was demolished by the French, greatly to the satisfaction of most of the Iroquois, who had always regarded it with alarm, and who now made treaties with the victors; and the Mohawk valley, exposed to the enemy was ranged by scalping parties of Canadian savages.

"The Mohawks, through the influence of Sir William Johnson, remained faithful to the English. The Baronet, with a view to counteract the impression made upon the Six Nations by the French successes, summoned them to meet him in council at Fort Johnson, in June, 1756. Previous to their assembling a circumstance occurred which rendered negotiations at once necessary and less hopeful. A party of Mohawks, while loitering around Fort Hunter, became involved in a quarrel with some soldiers of the garrison, resulting in some of the Indians being severely wounded. The Mohawk tribe felt extremely revengeful, but Johnson succeeded in pacifying them and winning over the Oneidas and Tuscaroras to the English interest. In the beginning of August, 1756, Sir William Johnson led a party of Indian warriors and militia to the relief of Fort William Henry at the head of Lake George, which was besieged by Montcalm; but on reaching Fort Edward his progress was arrested by the cowardice of Gen. Webb, who was there in command, and who used his superior authority to leave the besieged fortress to its fate, which was a speedy surrender. The provincials, thoroughly disgusted by the disasters incurred through incompetency and

cowardice of their English officers, now deserted in great numbers, and the Indians followed suit.

"Soon after the capture of Fort William Henry, rumors gained circulation that a large force of French and Indians was preparing to invade the settlements along the Mohawk. The Palatines who had settled on the Burnets field Patent, were evidently most exposed, and feeling but poorly protected by what fortifications there were among them, they were several times during the autumn on the point of deserting their dwellings and removing to the settlements further down the river which were better defended. The rumors seeming to prove groundless, they became careless and finally neglected all precautions against an attack. Meanwhile an expedition of about 300 Canadian, French and Indians, under command of one Belletre, came down from Canada by way of the Black river, and at 3 o'clock in the morning of Nov. 12, 1756, the Palatine village, at the present site of Herkimer, was surrounded. This settlement contained 60 dwellings and 4 blockhouses and the inhabitants were aroused by the horrid warwhoop, which was the signal of attack. The invaders rushed upon the blockhouses and were met with an active fire of musketry. The little garrison soon seemed to become panic stricken, both by the overwhelming numbers and the bloodcurdling yells of the savages and the active fighting of the French. The mayor of the village, who was in command, opened the door of one blockhouse and called for quarter. The garrisons of the other blockhouses followed his example. These feeble defences, with all the other buildings in the settlement, were fired and the inhabitants, in attempting to escape were tomahawked and scalped. About 40 of the Germans were thus massacred, and more than 100 persons, men, women and children, were carried into captivity by the marauders as they retired laden with booty. This they did not do, until they had destroyed a great amount of grain and provisions, and as Belletre reported, slaughtered 3,000 cattle, as many sheep, and 1,500 horses [figures now generally supposed to be exaggerated beyond any semblance of truth.]

"Although the marauders hastily withdrew the entire valley was thrown into panic. Many of the inhabitants of the other Mohawk settlements hastened to send their goods to Albany and Schenectady with the intention of following them, and for a time the upper towns were threatened with entire desertion. The Palatine settlement at Fort Herkimer, near the one whose destruction has been related, was similarly visited in April, 1758. Lieut. Herkimer was here in command. The militia, under Sir William Johnson, rendezvoused at Canajoharie, but the enemy withdrew and did not after appear in force in this quarter. About this time Johnson, with 300 Indian warriors, chiefly Mohawks, joined Abercrombie's expedition against Crown Point, where the English were disastrously repulsed. Fear again reigned in the Mohawk valley but the French did not follow up their advantage in this quarter.

"In spite of this disaster, the successes of the English, elsewhere in 1758, made so favorable an impression on the Six Nations, that Sir William Johnson was enabled to bring nearly 1,000 warriors to join Gen. Prideaux's expedition against Niagara in the following summer, which the Baronet conducted to a successful issue after Prideaux's death by the accidental explosion of a shell. Sir William in 1760, led 1,300 Iroquois warriors in Gen. Amherst's expedition against Montreal which extinguished the French power in America."

Sir William removed in 1763 to Johnstown where he built himself a residence and buildings on his great estate. Here grew up the county seat of the new and great county of Tryon, formed in 1772, and here he died, as elsewhere described, in 1774. Sir William Johnson was perhaps the most remarkable man of the many who figure in the record of Tryon county. Nothing in the state's history is more interesting than this spot of civiliza-

tion in a vast, savage wilderness, presided over by an Irish gentleman who was at once a benevolent dictator and a virtual regent over a territory larger than some famous kingdoms of history, and over a white people struggling toward civilization and the red men who were trying to keep their wild domains for their hunting grounds.

The well known story of how Johnson became possessed of the Royal Grant deserves a place here. Sir William Johnson obtained over 60,000 acres of choice land, now lying chiefly in Herkimer county, north of the Mohawk, in the following manner: The Mohawk sachem, Hendrick, being at the baronet's house, saw a richly embroidered coat and coveted it. The next morning he said to Sir William:

"Brother, me dream last night."

"Indeed, what did my red brother dream" asked Johnson.

"Me dream that coat be mine."

"It is yours," said the shrewd Irish baronet.

Not long afterward Sir William visited the chief, and he too, had a dream.

"Brother, I dreamed last night," said Johnson,

"What did my pale-faced brother dream?" asked Hendrick.

"I dreamed that this tract of land was mine," describing a square bounded on the south by the Mohawk, on the east by Canada creek, and north and west by objects equally well known.

Hendrick was astounded. He saw the enormity of the request, but was not to be outdone in generosity. He sat thoughtfully for a moment and then said, "Brother, the land is yours, but you must not dream again."

The title was confirmed by the British government and the tract was called the Royal Grant.

———

King Hendrick (also called the Great Hendrick) occupied, in the early eighteenth century, a position in the Mohawk tribe, similar to that held by Brant at the time of the Revolution. Hendrick was born about 1680 and generally lived at the upper Mohawk castle (in Danube), being thus a resident of the old Canajoharie district. He stood high in the estimation of Sir William Johnson and was one of the most active and sagacious sachems of his time. Hendrick, with a large body of Iroquois, accompanied Johnson on his Lake George expedition and was killed in the action (Sept. 8, 1755) which resulted in a victory against the French and Indians under Baron Dieskau. Prior to this battle, Johnson determined to send out a small party to meet Dieskau's advance and the opinion of Hendrick was asked. He shrewdly said: "If they are to fight they are too few; if they are to be killed they are too many." His objection to the proposition to separate them into three divisions was quite as sensibly and laconically expressed. Taking three sticks and putting them together, he remarked, "Put them together and you can't break them. Take them one by one and you can break them easily." Johnson was guided by the opinion of Hendrick and a force of 1,200 men in one body under Col. Williams was sent out to meet the French and Indians. Before commencing their march, Hendrick mounted a gun-carriage and harangued his warriors in a strain of eloquence which had a powerful effect upon them. He was then over 70 years old. His head was covered with long white locks and every warrior loved him with the deepest veneration. Lieut.-Col. Pomeroy, who was present and heard this Indian oration, said that, although he did not understand a word of the language, such was the animation of Hendrick, the fire of his eye, the force of his gestures, the strength of his emphasis, the apparent propriety of the inflections of his voice, and the natural appearance of his whole manner, that he himself was more deeply affected by this speech than with any other he had ever heard. In the battle which followed, resulting in the rout of the Canadian force, Hendrick was killed,

Baron Dieskau was mortally wounded and Johnson was wounded in the thigh. Lossing speaks of Gen Johnson's conduct in this campaign as "careless and apathetic." Hendrick visited England and had his portrait painted in a full court dress which was presented to him by the king. This Mohawk sachem is one of the greatest characters in the history of the remarkable tribe of savage residents of this valley. In 1754, commissioners from the different colonies met at Albany to consider plans for a general colonial alliance, and to this conference the Six Nations were invited. This Albany council was the initial step in the formation of the United States of America. Hendrick attended and delivered a telling speech in reference to the inefficient military policy of the British governors. This address shows the frankness and common sense of the old warrior and is reported as follows:

"Brethren, we have not as yet confirmed the peace with them. (Meaning the French-Indian allies.) 'Tis your fault, brethren, we are not strengthened by conquest, for we should have gone and taken Crown Point, but you hindered us. We had concluded to go and take it, but were told it was too late, that the ice would not bear us. Instead of this you burned your own fort at Sarraghtogee [near old Fort Hardy] and ran away from it, which was a shame and scandal to you. Look about your country and see; you have no fortifications about you—no, not even to this city. 'Tis but one step from Canada hither, and the French may easily come and turn you out of doors. Brethren, you were desirous we should open our minds and our hearts to you; look at the French, they are men—they are fortifying everywhere; but, we are ashamed to say it, you are like women, bare and open, without any fortifications."

CHAPTER III.

1774—Johnson Hall—Sir William, Sir John, Joseph and Molly Brant.

While Johnstown was not in the districts of either Canajoharie or Palatine, but was located in the Mohawk district, still it was the county seat and thus of importance to all of Tryon. The influence of the Johnson party was so strong before the Revolution and they formed such a large element of the Tory invaders of the valley that a glance at the Johnson Hall of pre-Revolutionary times is in order. This was the real seat of government in Tryon county. From the following standard accounts may readily be gained the secret of Sir William Johnson's tremendous popularity with the Indians and with all classes of the settlers. Prior to the Revolution Johnson Hall was the center of the political and social life of the county and for the people of its five districts of Mohawk, Canajoharie, Palatine, German Flats and Kingsland.

Beer's History of Montgomery and Fulton Counties (1878) gives the following account of Johnson Hall and the life about it prior to the death of Sir William Johnson in 1774: "After a residence of 24 years in the eastern part of the present county of Montgomery [at Fort Johnson], during which he had gained an immense estate by the profits of trade and the generosity of his Indian neighbors and had won a baronetcy by his successful campaign against the French and their Indian allies in 1755, Sir William removed to a stately mansion finished by him in the spring of 1763. The motive assigned for the baronet's removal to this neighborhood is the promotion of settlements on his large domains hereabouts, on which he had already settled over one hundred families, generally leasing but sometimes selling the land. Among those to whom he leased, with the supposed purpose of establishing a baronial estate for his descendants, were Dr. William Adams; Gilbert Tice, innkeeper; Peter Young, miller; William Phillips, wagon-maker; James Davis, hatter; Peter Yost, tanner; Adrian Van Sickler, Maj. John Little and Zephaniah Bachelor.

"Johnson Hall, as Sir William Johnson named his new residence, at Johnstown, was at that time one of the finest mansions in the state outside of New York city. During its eleven years occupancy, like his former home on the Mohawk, it was a place of frequent resort for his Indian friends for grave councils and for less serious affairs. Here at the Hall, Johnson had the Indians hold annually a tournament of their national games. Concerning this, Gov. Seymour wrote: 'It was from this spot that the agents went forth to treat with the Indians of the west, and keep the chain of friendship bright. Here came the scouts from the forests and lakes of the north to tell of any dangerous movements of the enemy. Here were written the reports to the Crown, which were to shape the policy of nations; and to this place were sent orders that called upon the settlers and savages to go out upon the war path.' Among the more illustrious guests of Colonial times, who divided with the Iroquois braves, the hospitalities of Johnson Hall were: Lady O'Brian, daughter of the Earl of Ilchester; Lord Gordon, whom Sir John Johnson accompanied to England, where he was knighted; Sir Henry Moore, governor of New York; Gov. Franklin of New Jersey, and other Colonial dignitaries. [Johnson Hall is still (1912) standing at Johnstown and is a most interesting place of resort for those who care for matters concerning Colonial New York and its life.] It is a wooden building sixty feet in length by forty in width, and two stories high, facing southeastwardly across lands sloping to the adjoining creek, on the higher ground beyond which the city stands. A spacious hall, fifteen feet wide crossed it in the center, into which on each floor opened large and lofty rooms wainscoted with pine panels and heavy carved work. At either end of the northwestern wall, a little apart from the house stood a square stone structure, loopholed, to serve as a blockhouse for the defense of the Hall. They were part of the fortifications, including a stockade, thrown up around the Hall in 1763, in apprehension of an attack by the western tribes under Pontiac.

"Whatever time Sir William's official duties left him, was actively employed in the improvement of his estate and the condition of agriculture in the settlement. We find him obtaining superior seed oats from Saybrook, Conn., scions for grafting from Philadelphia, fruit trees from New London and choice seed from England. He delighted in horticulture and had a famous garden and nursery to the south of the Hall. He was the first to introduce sheep and blooded horses in the Mohawk valley. Fairs were held under his supervision at Johnstown, the baronet paying the premiums. His own farming was done by ten or fifteen slaves under an overseer named Flood. They and their families lived in cabins built for them across Cayadutta creek from the Hall. They dressed very much like the Indians, but wore coats made from blankets on the place. Sir William's legal af fairs were conducted by a lawyer secretary named Lefferty, who was the county surrogate at the time of John son's death. A family physician nam ed Daly was retained by the baronet, serving also as his social companion in numerous pleasure excursions. A butler, a gardener, a tailor and a black smith were among the employes at the Hall, across the road from which the last two had shops.

"Sir William took a constant and lively interest in the welfare of his tenants, not only extending his bounty to their material needs, but providing for their spiritual and intellectual wants. One of his devices for their entertainment was the institution of 'sport days' at the Hall, at which the yeomanry of the neighborhood competed in the field sports of England, especially boxing and footracing. In the latter the contestants sometimes ran with their feet in bags [the modern sack race] and more amusement was furnished by horse races in which the riders faced backward; by the chase of the greased pig and the climbing of the greased pole; and by the efforts, of another class of competitors, to make the wryest face and sing the worst song, the winner being rewarded with a bearskin jacket and a few pounds of tobacco. A bladder of Scotch snuff was awarded to the greatest scold in a contest between two old women.

"Johnson died July 11, 1774, aged 59 years. He had long been liable to at tacks of dysentery. In combating his disease he had, in 1767, visited and drunk of the spring, now famous as the High Rock of Saratoga. He is believed to have been the first white man to visit this spring, whose medical virtues had been reported to him by the Mohawks, a band of whom accompanied him to the spot, bearing him part of the way through the wilderness on a litter. His cure was only partial but even that becoming known, was the foundation of the popularity of the Saratoga springs. At the time of Sir William's death, the Indians were exasperated over the outrages committed upon them by the Ohio frontiersmen, including the butchery of the famous Logan's kindred. The Iroquois had come with an indignant complaint to Johnson Hall. On the day the baronet died, he addressed them for over two hours under a burning sun. Immediately after he was taken with an acute attack of his malady and shortly died. Johnson had prophesied that he would never live to take part in the struggle which all saw was then impending.

"The baronet's funeral took place on the Wednesday following his death and the pall bearers included Gov. Franklin of New Jersey and the judges of the New York supreme court. Among the cortege of 2,000 people who followed the remains to their burial, under the chancel of the stone church which Sir William had erected in the village, were the 600 Indians who had gathered at the Hall. These, on the next day, performed their ceremony of condolence before the friends of the deceased, presenting symbolic belts of wampum with an appropriate address."

Lossing in his "Pictorial Field Book of the Revolution," says of Johnson and Johnson's Hall: "Here Sir William lived in all the elegance and comparative power of a English baron of the Middle Ages. * * * * * * * * * * * His Hall was his castle and. around it, beyond the wings a heavy stone breastwork, about twelve feet high, was thrown up. Invested with the power and influence of an Indian agent of his government in its transactions with the Confederated Six Nations, possessed of a fine person and dignity of manners, and a certain style of oratory that pleased the Indians, he acquired an ascendancy over the tribes never before held by a white man. When in 1760, General Amherst embarked at Oswego on his expedition to Canada, Sir William Johnson brought to him at that place, 1,000 Indian warriors of the Six Nations, which was the largest number that had ever been seen in arms at one time in the cause of England. He made confidants of many of the chiefs, and to them was in the habit of giving a diploma testifying to their good conduct. His house was the resort of the sachems of the Six Nations for counsel and for trade, and there the presents, sent out by his government, were annually distributed to the Indians. On these occasions he amused himself and gratified his guests by fetes and games, many of which were highly ludicrous. Young Indians and squaws were often seen running foot races or wrestling for trinkets, and feats of astonishing agility were frequently performed by the Indians of both sexes. * * * * * Sir William had two wives, although they were not made so until they had lived long with the baronet. Simms says that his first wife was a young German girl, who

according to the custom of the times, had been sold to a man named Phillips living in the Mohawk valley, to pay her passage money to the captain of the emigrant ship in which she came to this country. She was a handsome girl and attracted considerable attention. A neighbor of Sir William, who had heard him express a determination never to marry, asked him why he did not get the pretty German girl for a housekeeper. He replied "I will." Not long afterward the neighbor called at Phillips's and inquired where the 'High Dutch' girl was. Phillips replied, 'Johnson, that tammed Irishman came tother day and offered me five pounds for her, threatening to horsewhip me and steal her if I would not sell her. I thought five pounds petter than a flogging and took it, and he's got the gal.' She was the mother of Sir John Johnson and two daughters, who became the wives respectively of Guy Johnson and Daniel Claus. These two girls, who were left by their dying mother to the care of a friend, were educated almost in solitude. That friend was the widow of an officer who was killed in battle, and, retiring from the world, devoted her whole time to the care of these children. They were carefully instructed in religious duties, and in various kinds of needlework, but were themselves kept entirely from society. At the age of sixteen, they had never seen a lady, except their mother and her friend, or a gentleman, except Sir William, who visited their room daily. Their dress was not conformed to the fashions, but always consisted of wrappers of finest chintz over green silk petticoats. Their hair, which was long and beautiful, was tied behind with a simple band of ribbon. After their marriage they soon acquired the habits of society, and made excellent wives. When she [the German wife] was on her deathbed Sir William was married to her in order to legitimate her children. After her death, her place was supplied by Molly Brant, sister of the Mohawk sachem, by whom he had several children. Toward the close of his life, Sir William married her in order to legitimate her children also, and her descendants are now some of the most respected people in upper Canada. Sir William's first interview and acquaintance with her * * * have considerable romance. She was a very sprightly and beautiful girl, about sixteen, when he first saw her at a militia muster. One of the field officers, riding upon a fine horse came near her and, by way of banter, she asked permission to mount behind. Not supposing she could perform the exploit, he said she might. At the word, she leaped upon the crupper with the agility of a gazelle. The horse sprang off at full speed, and clinging to the officer, her blanket flying and her dark hair streaming in the wind, she flew about the parade ground as swift as an arrow. The baronet, who was a witness of the spectacle, admiring the spirit of the young squaw and becoming enamored of her person, took her home as his wife. According to Indian customs, this act made her really his wife, and in all her relations of wife and mother she was very exemplary."

Joseph Brant was the strongest supporter of the Tory cause among the Iroquois. He was a full-hooded Mohawk. His father was a chief of the Onondaga nation and had three sons in the army with Sir William Johnson, under King Hendrick, in the battle at Lake George in 1755. Joseph Brant, his youngest son, whose Indian name was Thayendanegea, which signified a bundle of sticks or, in other words, strength, was born on the banks of the Ohio in 1742, whither his parents immigrated from the Mohawk valley. His mother returned to Canajoharie [district] with Mary or Molly and Thayendanegea or Joseph. His father Tehowaghwengaraghkwin, a chief of the Wolf tribe of the Mohawks, seems to have died in the Ohio country. Joseph's mother, after her return, married an Indian named Carrabigo (news-carrier), whom the whites named Barnet; but by way of contrae-

tion, he was called Barut and finally, Brant. Thayendanegea became known as Brant's Joseph or Joseph Brant. Sir William Johnson sent the young Mohawk to the school of Dr. Wheelock of Lebanon Crank (now Columbia), Connecticut, and, after he was well educated, employed him as secretary and as agent in public affairs. He was employed as missionary interpreter from 1762 to 1765 and exerted himself for the religious instruction of the tribe. When the Revolution broke out, he attached himself to the British cause, and in 1775 left the Mohawk valley, went to Canada and finally to England, where his education, and his business and social connection with Sir William Johnson, gave him free access to the nobility. The Earl of Warwick commissioned Romney, the eminent painter, to make a portrait of him for his collection, and from this celebrated painting most of the pictures of Brant have been reproduced. Throughout the Revolution, at the head of the Indian forces, he was engaged in warfare chiefly upon the border settlements of New York and Pennsylvania, in connection with the Johnsons and Butlers. He held a colonel's commission from the King but he is generally called Captain Brant. After the peace in 1783, Brant again visited England, and on returning to America, devoted himself to the social and religious improvement of the Mohawks who were settled upon the Grand River in upper Canada upon lands procured for them by Brant from Haldimand, governor of the province. This territory embraced six miles on both sides of the river from its mouth to its source. He translated the Gospel of St. Mark into the Mohawk language, and in many ways his efforts, for the uplifting of his people, were successful. He died at his residence at the head of Lake Ontario, Nov. 24, 1807, aged 65.

Sir John Johnson was the son of Sir William Johnson by his German wife. He was born in 1742 and succeeded to his father's title and estate in 1774.

He was unsocial and without any of his father's brilliant cleverness. Soon after the close of the war, Sir John went to England and on returning in 1785, settled in Canada. He was appointed superintendent and inspector general of Indian affairs in North America and for several years he was a member of the Canadian legislative council. To compensate him for the loss of his Tryon county property through confiscation, the British government made him several grants of land. He died at the house of his daughter, Mrs. Bowes, in Montreal, in 1830, aged 88 years. His son, Adam Gordon Johnson, succeeded him in his title.

John Butler was one of the leading Tories of Tryon county during the war of the Revolution. Before the war he was in close official connection with Sir William Johnson and, after his death, with his son and nephew, Sir John and Guy Johnson. When he fled with the Johnsons to Canada, his family were left behind and were subsequently exchanged for the wife and children of Colonel Samuel Campbell of Cherry Valley. He was active in the predatory warfare that so long distressed Tryon county, and commanded the 1,100 Tories and Indians who perpetrated the infamous Wyoming massacre in 1778. He was of the Tory and Indian force that fought Sullivan and Clinton in the Indian country in 1779. He accompanied Sir John Johnson in his Schoharie and Mohawk valley raid of 1780 which ended so disastrously for them at Klock's Field. After the war he went to Canada. His property upon the Mohawk was confiscated, but he was made an Indian agent, succeeding Guy Johnson at a salary of $2,000 per year and was granted a pension, as a military officer, of $1,000 more. Like his son, Walter, he was detested for his cruelties by the more honorable English officers and, after the massacre at Wyoming, Sir Frederic Haldimand, then Governor of Canada, sent word that he did not wish to see him. It is but justice to Col. Butler to say that he was far more humane than his son Walter. He died in Canada about 1800.

CHAPTER IV.

Minden from 1720-1738—Sir George Clarke, Governor of the Province of New York, Establishes a Forest Home at Fort Plain—1750, the Reformed Church and First Store Established—1755, a Minden Tragedy of the French War.

The years immediately succeeding 1720, when German settlers first located along the Mohawk in the Canajoharie district, was a time of land clearing, building, and rude agriculture—a period similar to that experienced in the first few decades after settlement in all parts of the valley. The land was cleared, rude farming was carried on and log and stone houses and barns were built.

The first event of importance transpiring, in the Canajoharie district, was the advent of the Colonial governor of the state, Sir George Clarke, who, about 1738, built a summer lodge, on the first rise of ground from the flats almost in the center of the present village of Fort Plain.

At this time the Mohawk country was still practically an unknown forest wilderness, with the exception of the district immediately along the river, which was already cleared in spots and which was then being rapidly opened up and settled.

This Clarke place was a house of two stories, with a hall passing through the center and large square rooms on either side. The second floor was reached by a broad stairway, with white oak bannisters and easy steps of the same material. The house had a frontage of nearly forty feet and its walls were built of a slaty stone taken from the bed of the neighboring Otsquago. The steps to the front door were of slate also, but a limestone step used at one of its doors still serves its purpose. The Gov. Clarke house was, for its time, a structure of considerable pretension. It is said to have been erected by Clarke so as to remove two sons of "fast proclivities" from their New York city associations. For a few years the Clarke family resided here in a commanding position, employing a force of slaves about the house and its plantation. At the river's bank, the governor had a good landing for his bateaux and pleasure boats. Clarke brought to his forest home several goats, then a novelty in the region, and, at one time, several of them strayed away and were lost. They were finally found on the high ground several miles southwest of Fort Plain, and this spot was afterward called Geissenberg—goat hill. The Clarke family evidently did not stay at their Mohawk valley home any great length of time and about 1742 they abandoned the place, which was probably never anything more than a summer hunting and fishing lodge. The house then acquired the reputation of being haunted and was allowed to stand empty and decay. In 1807, Dr. Joshua Webster and Jonathan Stickney, who had come into the country shortly before from New England, built a tannery across the creek from the material in this old Colonial mansion.

About 1750 George Crouse settled next north to the Clarke property and built a log house which was burned by Brant in 1780. Isaac Paris later became possessed of the Gov. Clarke place, and he sold it to George Crouse jr. The residence, occupied for many years by the late A. J. Wagner, was built on the cellar of the Clarke mansion by Col. Robert Crouse.

Sir George Clarke was acting governor of New York state from 1736 to 1743. He was at that time reckoned an adventurer by many and was in constant conflict with the Colonial state assembly. It was during his weak administration (in 1741), and at the time he was a resident of the Canajoharie district, that the famous "negro plot" excited New York city. The baronet had an underground interest in the Corry patent granted in 1737. This consisted of 25,400 acres

in the present towns of Root, Glen and Charleston in Montgomery county and in Schoharie county. It is not improbable that Sir George built his Fort Plain hunting lodge to enable him to secretly look after his "property," as it was being surveyed and laid out in plots and farms for rental at this very time.

He could not have an open interest in the patent as the English law forbade a Colonial governor being interested in grants of land made by the government. Governor Clarke returned to England in 1745 with a big fortune "mysteriously gathered," as one of his historians puts it. On his way over he was captured by a French cruiser, but was soon released. He died in Cheshire, England, in 1763, aged 84 years. His Montgomery and Schoharie property was left to his two sons, George and Edward, for whom it is said the Fort Plain house was built and who had remained in New York after their father left the country. George died childless in England and Edward died in 1744, leaving one son, George Hyde Clarke, who succeeded to the property. Corry sold his share of the patent, but it was confiscated by the state during the Revolution, on account of the Toryism of the owners. George Hyde Clarke remained in New York during the war, and, siding with the patriots, was confirmed in the large landed possessions of his father. The property descended from father to son, each succeeding owner bearing the name of George Clarke. The dissensions, incendiarism and legal warfare, incident to the breaking up of this great estate, occurred within comparatively recent years.

———

In 1750 the Reformed church of Canajoharie was established at Sand Hill (later Fort Plain) and about the same time William Seeber opened his store and became Minden's first trader. The settlement and development of the Minden section of the Canajoharie district, into a fertile agricultural section, was going forward rapidly at this period and that mentioned in the foregoing part of this chapter.

During the French and Indian war the districts of Palatine and Canajoharie had suffered but little, although here and there scalping parties of Indians had cut down unfortunate settlers. One of these incidents, of particularly tragic character, occurred near Fort Plain in the westerly part of the town of Minden. About 1755, the year of the beginning of hostilities, John Markell, who married Anna Timmerman, daughter of a pioneer settler of St. Johnsville, settled in the western part of the town. Markell and his wife left home one day, she carrying an infant in her arms. They had not gone far when they saw a party of a dozen hostile Indian warriors approaching in the very path they were traveling and only a few rods distant. Markell, knowing escape was impossible, exclaimed: "Anna, unser zeit ist aus!" (Anna, our time is up.) The next instant he fell, a bullet passing through his body into that of his wife. They both fell to the ground, the child dropping from the woman's arms, and she lay upon her face, feigning death. Markell was at once tomahawked and scalped. One Indian said about the woman, "Better knock her on the head." Another replied, "No, squaw's dead now!" and reaching down he drew his knife around her crown, placed his knees against her shoulders, seized her scalp with his teeth and, in an instant, it was torn from her head. One of the party snatched the crying infant from the ground by one of its legs and dashed its brains out against a tree. The savages did not stop to strip the victims and Mrs. Markell was left on the ground supposedly dead. She revived and managed to get to a neighbor's house, where she was cared for and recovered. She later married Christian Getman of Ephratah, where she died in 1821 at the age of 85 years, making her about 21 at the time of her frightful experience. Such were the perils that, at times, surrounded the settlers of the New York border, and

which, twenty years later, threatened the people even under the walls of Fort Plain.

CHAPTER V.

1772—Tryon County and the Canajoharie and Palatine Districts.

German or Dutch settlers had come into the present town of Minden about the year 1720 and shortly after that date the influx of settlers, principally Palatinate Germans, was probably quite rapid. The Indian settlements in 1776 were mainly confined to the lower Mohawk castle at Fort Hunter and to the upper one at what is now Indian Castle in the western end of the then Canajoharie district.

Much of the confusion, attending the names of localities in reading local history, can be avoided by a knowledge of the boundaries of the five districts of Tryon county, which was formed in 1772, from the county of Albany. Most of its inhabitants then were settled along the Mohawk river and in the Schoharie valley but these five districts had a tremendous extent.

The eastern border of Tryon county, named after the governor of that day, ran from the Pennsylvania border due north from the Delaware river through what is now Schoharie county and along the eastern limits of the present counties of Montgomery, Fulton and Hamilton to the Canadian border and embraced the entire state west of this line. Instead of townships it was divided into five large districts. The most eastern of these was called Mohawk and consisted of a strip of the state between the east line of the county already mentioned and a parallel line crossing the Mohawk river at the "Noses." The Palatine district extended indefinitely northward from the river between the "Noses" on the east and on the west a north and south line crossing the river at Little Falls. With the same breadth on the opposite side of the river the Canajoharie district extended south to the Pennsylvania line. North of the Mohawk and west of the Palatine dis trict as far as settlements extended was the Kingsland district, while south of the river extending westward, from Little Falls to Fort Stanwix and southerly to the Pennsylvania line, was the German Flats district. These divisions were made March 24, 1772, and were suggested by Sir William Johnson. The name of the Palatine district was at first Stone Arabia, but was changed to Palatine a year after this division. All these names except Kingsland, are retained in townships in the counties of Herkimer and Montgomery, comprising minute areas compared with their original size.

The district of Palatine took its name from the German settlers from the Palatinate while that of Canajoharie was derived from the name of the famous creek. This stream's name comes from the huge pothole located almost at the beginning of the picturesque gorge leading to the falls. The title, Canajoharie, according to Brant, means, in Mohawk dialect, "the pot which washes itself." From the foregoing it will be seen that the affairs of Fort Plain are more immediately concerned with the districts of Canajoharie and Palatine, of the county of Tryon. Also that the Revolutionary name Canajoharie, applies to a large district, extending over 20 miles along the river, and not to the present comparatively small township of that name. A reference to Canajoharie of that time might mean any point in the present towns of Root, Canajoharie, Minden or Danube, or the districts back of these from the river. So when Washington speaks of going to Canajoharie he means the military post in that district located at Fort Plain. Fort Canajoharie in 1757 was located in Danube and the upper Mohawk village near the same place was called the Canajoharie Castle. Herkimer's residence was in the Canajoharie district near its western end and he represented that district in the Tryon county committee of safety and was also the colonel of the district's militia as well as brigadier general of that of the entire county. A realization of the extent and boundaries of the district of Canajoharie of the Revolution will aid in acquiring accurate knowledge of the history of that time.

The first January Tuesday the voters in each district were to elect a supervisor, two assessors and one collector of taxes. Four judges, six assistant judges, a number of justices of the peace, a clerk and a coroner were appointed by Governor Tryon, all but the clerk being Sir William Johnson's nominees. The first court of general quarter sessions was held at Johnstown, the county seat, on September 8, 1772. The bench consisted of Guy Johnson, John Butler and Peter Conyne, judges; John Johnson, Daniel Claus, John Wells and Jelles Fonda, assistant judges; John Collins, Joseph Chew, Adam Loucks, John Frey, Peter Ten Broeck and —— Young, justices. It will be seen that Sir William Johnson was practically dictator of the new county as the majority of the above officers were his Tory henchmen. Sir William Johnson was also major general commanding all the militia north of the highlands of the Hudson. He took great pride in his militia and their soldierly appearance. Governor Tryon in his tour of the Mohawk valley in 1772 reviewed three regiments of Tryon county militia at Johnstown, Burnetsfield and German Flats, respectively, numbering in all 1400 men. This military training of the Mohawk valley men was undoubtedly of great value to them in the following conflict.

It was almost entirely the influence of Sir William Johnson which made Tryon county a region unfavorable to the cause of independence. He had created a county seat at Johnstown and a powerful following about him. As Indian commissioner and general of all the militia he was supreme as a director of affairs. Johnson had practically absolute power over the Iroquois and an almost equally strong influence over a large portion of the white population. His domains in the Mohawk valley included the 66,000 acres, mostly in what is now Herkimer county and which in 1760 were given him by the Mohawks, in the pos session of which he was confirmed by the crown and which led to its being called the Royal Grant. Aside from this his landed estate was large and his henchmen and numerous tenantry added to his political strength, which was increased still further by his great personal popularity with all classes. By the Indians, not only of the Six Nations, but also of the western tribes, which had fallen within the circle of his influence, the baronet was regarded with the greatest veneration in spite of his unassuming sociability and his familiar manners incident to a border life. This tremendous influence over these Indian warriors was on his death in July, 1774, transferred to his son, Sir John Johnson, who succeeded to his position as major general of the militia, to his title and most of his estate, and also to his son-in-law, Col. Guy Johnson, who became superintendent of Indian affairs. The Johnsons had the added support of Molly Brant, a Mohawk, who had been Sir William Johnson's housekeeper and who, with her brother, Joseph Brant, had great influence with their tribe. Joseph Brant had been in the service of the elder Johnson and upon his death became secretary to Guy Johnson. Thus a great, though diminished, Tory influence still emanated from Johnson Hall. Its proprietor was in close official and political relations with Col. John Butler, a wealthy and influential resident of the county, and his son Walter, whose names are infamous on account of their brutal and bloody deeds during the Revolution. The Johnson family, together with other gentlemen of Tory inclinations, owned large estates in the neighborhood and so far controlled a belt of the Mohawk valley as to largely prevent the circulation of intelligence unfavorable to England.

Unlike Sir William Johnson, his successors at Johnson Hall were very unpopular with the farming population, which was composed in the main of the Dutch and Palatines.

The first election in the county occurred pursuant to writs issued Nov. 25, 1772. Colonel Guy Johnson and

Hendrick Frey were chosen to represent the county in the state assembly, where they took their seats Jan. 11, 1773.

The men of the Johnson party and others aforementioned will be found deeply concerned in later military operations around Fort Plain.

William Tryon was a native of Ireland and an officer in the British service. He married Miss Wake, a relative of the Earl of Hillsborough, secretary for the colonies. Thus connected, he was a favorite of government, and was appointed lieutenant governor of North Carolina in 1765, later becoming governor. In 1771 he was called to fill the same office in New York. The history of his administration in North Caroline is a record of extortion, folly and crime. During his administration in New York the Revolution broke out and he was the last royal governor of the state, though nominally succeeded in office by Gen. Robertson, when he returned to England. His property in North Carolina and New York was confiscated.

CHAPTER VI.

Population of Tryon in 1757 and 1776 Ft. Johnson—The Highways.

The white settlers of the five districts of Tryon county were generally the Dutch, who had gradually extended their settlements westward from Schenectady and occupied the eastern part of the county, and the Germans from the Palatinate on the Rhine, who had located farther west. These were the general limits of the settlers but the two nationalities had considerably intermingled and intermarried prior to the Revolution, forming an element largely known as "Mohawk Dutch." In the whole valley at the Revolutionary period the writer ventures the opinion that, of this Teutonic population, two-thirds were Palatine Germans and one-third were of Holland Dutch blood. These people were not disposed to submit to new-fledged aristocrats who assumed a high and mighty style in dealing with the Tryon yeomanry. This element, while it included many Tories, was the backbone of the Whig party in the valley. Before the building of Fort Plain in 1776 they had largely sided with the American cause and had taken decided steps for its furtherance.

There was a considerable number of Irish and Scotch in the county, some, as at Johnstown, being Tories while others, as at the Cherry Valley settlement, were ardent patriots for the most part. On the eve of the Revolution and at the time of the inauguration of Fort Plain as an American outpost, the white population of the entire county was estimated at 10,000 and the militia available for the patriot cause at about 2,500 men. The Indian population along the Mohawk may have approximated 1,000 or even less.

At this period the only settlement in the valley which could be dignified by the name of town was Schenectady, where the first river settlement had been made by the Dutch in 1663. There was a considerable village at Johnstown and a Dutch hamlet at Caughnawaga. At Cherry Valley there was a settlement mostly of Scotch, and at Fort Herkimer and the Palatine village, at West Canada creek, hamlets of Palatine Germans. At Fort Hunter and at Sand Hill were probably the beginnings of settlements. Johnstown was assuming importance, as it was made the county seat of Tryon when it was set off from Albany county in 1772, and it was also the seat of the powerful Johnson party.

Everything tended against concentration of settlers in towns. Almost the entire population, with the exception of a few traders and mechanics, was engaged in farming and clearing the land. The Mohawk, in the early days being the highway of commerce, tended to keep the population near it and the farms as a rule extended back from the flats on to the slopes. This brought the dwellings along the river into fairly close proximity and, if we trust a French account of 1757, we will find at that early day a surprising number of houses

noted along the Mohawk from East Creek to Schenectady, a distance of about 50 miles.

This old record gives a good idea of the Canajoharie and Palatine districts in the mid-eighteenth century. It mentions that the road was "good for all sorts of carriages" from Fort Kouari, later Fort Herkimer, about opposite the mouth of West Canada creek, in the town of German Flats, to Fort Cannatchocari, which was at the upper Mohawk castle, in the present town of Danube. This was a stockade 15 feet high and 100 paces square. The account continues as follows: "From Fort Cannatchocari to Fort Hunter is about 12 leagues; the road is pretty good, carriages pass over it; it continues along the banks of the Mohawk river. About a hundred houses, at greater or less distance from one another we found within this length of road. There are some situated also about half a league in the interior. The inhabitants of this section are Germans who compose a company of about 100 men.

"Fort Hunter is situated on the borders of the Mohawk river and is of the same form as that of Cannatchocari, with the exception that it is twice as large. There is likewise a house at each curtain. The cannon at each bastion are from 7 to 9 pounders. The pickets of this fort are higher than those of Cannatchocari. There is a church or temple in the middle of the fort; in the interior of the fort are also some thirty cabins of Mohawk Indians, which is the most considerable village. This fort like that of Cannatchocari has no ditch; there's only a large swing door at the entrance.

"Leaving Fort Hunter, a creek [Schoharie] is passed at the mouth of which that fort is located. It can be forded and crossed in batteaux in summer, and on the ice in winter. There are some houses outside under the protection of the fort, in which the country people seek shelter when they fear or learn that an Indian or French war party is in the field.

"From Fort Hunter to Chenectadi

or Corlar is seven leagues. The public carriage way continues along the right [south] bank of the Mohawk river. About 20 to 30 houses are found within this distance separated the one from the other from about a quarter to half a league. The inhabitants of this section are Dutch. They form a company, with some other inhabitants on the left bank of the Mohawk river, about 600 [?] men strong."

This account puts Fort Hunter on the wrong side of the Schoharie, an error of the French narrator.

Possibly the "600 men" referred to the militia of the town of Schenectady and its surrounding farming territory.

The above gives an idea of the population then on the south side of the river. Beginning again at the west at East Canada creek, the writer gives a similar account of the north side of the Mohawk from East Canada creek to Schenectady.

"After fording Canada creek, we continue along the left [north] bank of the Mohawk river and high road, which is passable for carts, for twelve leagues, to Col. Johnson's mansion [at Fort Johnson]. In the whole of the distance the soil is very good. About five hundred houses are erected at a distance one from the other. The greatest number of those on the bank of the river are built of stone, and those at a greater distance in the interior are about half a league off; they are new settlements, built of wood.

"There is not a fort in the whole of this distance of 12 leagues. There is but one farmer's house, built of stone, that is somewhat fortified and surrounded with pickets. It is situate on the banks of the river, three leagues from where [East] Canada creek empties into the Mohawk river. The inhabitants of this country are Germans. They form four companies of 100 men each.

"Col. Johnson's mansion is situated on the borders of the left [north] bank of the Mohawk. It is three stories high, built of stone, with portholes and a parapet and flanked with four bastions, on which are some small guns. In the same yard, on both sides of the mansion, there are two small houses. That on the right of the entrance is a store and that on the left is designed for workmen, negroes and other domestics. The yard gate is a heavy swing gate, well ironed; it is on the Mohawk river side; from this gate to the river there is about 200 paces of level ground. The high road passes there. A small rivulet, coming from the north, empties into the Mohawk river, about 200 paces below the enclosure of the yard. On this stream there is a mill about 50 paces distant from the house; below the mill is the miller's house where grain and flour are stored, and on the other side of the creek, 100 paces from the mill, is a barn in which cattle and fodder are kept. One hundred and fifty paces from Col. Johnson's mansion, at the north side, on the left bank of the little creek, is a little hill on which is a small house with portholes, where ordinarily is kept a guard of honour of some twenty men which serves also as an advanced post.

"From Col. Johnson's house to Chenectadi is counted seven leagues; the road is good, all sorts of vehicles pass over it. About twenty houses are found from point to point on this road * * * In the whole country of the Mohawk river there are nine companies of militia under Col. Johnson; eight only remain, that of the village of Palatines [at Herkimer] being no longer in existence, the greater part having been defeated by M. de Belletre's detachment. Col. Johnson assembles these companies when he has news of any expedition which may concern the Mohawk river."

Here we have a good description of the location of the settlers in a considerable portion of the Mohawk valley in 1757. With the exception of more houses and buildings and a largely increased population, conditions were probably similar in 1776. In addition it must be realized that from East Creek, on both sides of the river westward to German Flats and beyond there was a large number of dwellings and a considerable settlement of Palatine Germans. The account gives us a fair idea of what had been accomplished in the way of erecting large farmhouses, their necessary buildings, mills, and the opening up of plantations on a considerable scale in the instance of Johnson's place at ,Fort Johnson. Similar establishments were present, on a somewhat smaller plan, along the river and some of the dwellings were undoubtedly as large and in a way as comfortable as those of today. As a well known instance that of Gen. Herkimer can be cited, which was built in 1764. From this account, the population was practically composed of German and Dutch farmers. In the Canajoharie district there were probably, at this early date, more than 75 houses and in the Palatine district more than 400 dwellings. Together the two districts contained probably over 500 men liable to militia service and possibly a population of 2,500, if the French account is correct in its figures. The number of the dwellings and of the population had very largely increased by 1776, to what extent it is difficult to estimate, but it is not improbable that it had almost doubled. The highways will be seen to be fair in their condition, at least in some parts, and much better than would be casually supposed, and in general civilized society in the valley was at no low stage.

CHAPTER VII.

1772—Tryon County People—Farming, Religious and Social Life—Sports and Pastimes of the Days Before the Revolution.

There is a large element of population in the valley today which is descended from what we call the "Mohawk Dutch," for want of a better name. It has strong virtues and like all other strains of humanity certain deficiencies. Both were noted by early writers. However it is difficult to imagine a population better suited to stand the brunt of those early hardships and struggles. They made ideal frontiersmen, as a rule good soldiers and founders of American institutions and liberty in government, strong in

their political and religious ideals. If they are, at that early date, criticised in their farming methods or for the number of the "tippling houses" they supported, the hardships of turning a great forest country into a civilized farming section must be borne in mind. They produced public leaders of integrity with high, unselfish ideals and the quality of their minds, as shown in their acts and writings, proved them men in every sense of the word. Necessarily of bodily strength and vigor, the average of their masculinity and equipment for true men's work was of a standard to be envied by the male population of today. They showed some inclination toward learning which writers say, at the Revolution, had resulted in the establishment of schools in many of their valley settlements.

Both Palatines and Dutch had suffered untold hardships for their religion. In defense of their Reformed faith in their European homes they had been murdered, robbed and persecuted to the utmost limit. The presence of the Palatines in their Mohawk valley homes was largely due to these facts. Under such circumstances they took their religion seriously. Mostly of the Calvinistic belief they established Reformed churches and some of the Lutheran faith in the valley shortly after their settlement. At the birth of Fort Plain, in the Canajoharie and Palatine districts, there were Reformed churches at Fort Plain (1750), at St. Johnsville (1756) and at Stone Arabia (1711). Lutheran churches were at Stone Arabia (established between 1711 and 1732) and at Caroga Creek, now Palatine Church (in 1770). Near the Canajoharie castle (now Indian Castle) a church, largely for the use of the Indians, had been erected under the auspices of Sir William Johnson. The dominies of that day were frequently men of strong character and fit leaders of the spiritual and intellectual life of their parishioners. The labors of those of the Reformed faith have resulted in making the Mohawk valley one of the strongest districts of that church. The life of the Reformed church of Sand Hill (now of Fort Plain) is closely bound up with that of the fort built close to it and it was just out of gunshot of the post that it was burned during . the Tory and Indian raid in 1780. Preaching in these churches was in either the German or Dutch language or in both at intervals. After the Revolution English was introduced and, in some churches, preaching was in all three languages until English supplanted the others in the early nineteenth century.

That early farming methods in the Mohawk valley were open to criticism is shown by the following letter to the English Society for the Promotion of the Arts by Sir William Johnson, dated Johnson Hall, Feb. 27, 1765. The letter in part follows:

"The state of Agriculture in this country is very low, and in short likely to remain so to the great Detriment of the Province, which might otherwise draw many resources from so extensive and valuable a Country, but the turn of the old settlers here is not much calculated for improvement, content with the meer necessaries of Life, they dont chuse to purchase its superfluities at the expence of Labour, neither will they hazard the smallest matter for the most reasonable prospect of gain, and this principle will probably subsist as long as that of their equality, which is at present at such a pitch that the conduct of one neighbor can but little influence that of another.

"Wheat which in my opinion must shortly prove a drug, is in fact what they principally concern themselves about and they are not easily to be convinced that the Culture of other articles will tend more to their advantage. If a few of the Machines made use of for the breaking of hemp was distributed amongst those who have Land proper for the purpose it might give rise to the culture of it— or if one only properly constructed was sent as a model, it might Stir up a spirit of Industry amongst them, but Seed is greatly wanted, & Cannot be procured in these parts, and the Ger-

mains (who are most Industrious people here) are in general in too low circumstances to concern themselves in anything attended with the smallest Expence, their Plantations being as yet in their infancy, & with regard to the old Settlers amongst the Germans who live farther to the Westward, they have generally adopted the Sentiments of the rest of the inhabitants. The country Likewise labours under the disadvantage of narrow, and (in many places) bad roads, which would be still worse did I not take care that the inhabitants laboured to repair them according to law. The ill Condition of Public roads is a Great obstruction to husbandry; the high wages of labouring men, and the great number of tepling houses are likewise articles which very much want Regulation. These disagreeable circumstances must for some time retard the Progress of husbandry. I could heartily wish I had more leisure to attend to these necessary articles of improvements to promote which my Influence and Example should not be wanting. I have formerly had pease very well split at my mills, and I shall set the same forward amongst the people as far as I can. I have Likewise sent for Collections of many Seeds, and useful grasses which I shall Encourage them to raise, and from the great wants of stock, even for home use, & Consumption, I am doing all I can to turn the inhabitants to raising these necessary articles, for the purchase of which, a good deal of Cash has hither to been annually carried into the N. England Collonies.

"Before I set the Examples, no farmer on the Mohock River ever raised so much as a single Load of Hay, at present some raise above one Hundred, the like was the case in regard to sheep, to which they were intire strangers until I introduced them, & I have the Satisfaction to see them at present possess many other articles, the result of my former Labors for promoting their welfare and interests. My own tenants amounting to about 100 Families are not as yet in circumstances to do much, they were settled at great Expence and hazard during the heat of [French] War, and it was principally (I may venture to affirm, solely) owing to their residence & mine, that the rest of the inhabitant did not all abandon their settlements at that Distressful Period; But tho' my Tennants are considerably in my Debt, I shall yet give them all the assistance I can for encouraging any useful Branches of Husbandry, which I shall contribute to promote thro'out the rest of the Country to the utmost of my power, and Communicate to you any material article which may occur upon that 'Subject.' "

At the period of this letter and in the following decade a few grist and saw mills and similar industries were springing up in the valley where there was convenient water power. This letter gives us a vivid portrayal of one of New York's most interesting and sterling provincial characters, as well as the farming conditions in the Tryon county of that time and in its Canajobarie and Palatine districts.

Pioneer life was as hard as human life could well be. It required the strongest types of manhood, womanhood and even childhood to clear and cultivate this great wooded wilderness. First went up the log house cabins and barns to be followed later by those of stone and sawn lumber. After the sturdy woodman felled the trees they were burned of their limbs and leaves and the ground was left strewn with their blackened trunks. To pile these together, when dry enough, so that another firing would consume them was the dirty job of "logging up." It was largely done by "bees," to which the frontiersmen rallied in numbers adequate to the heavy work to be done. Severe as that was, an afternoon at it left the young men with vim enough for a wrestling match, after they had rested long enough to devour the generous supper with which the housewife feasted them.

The grain grown on the fields thus laboriously cleared was threshed with the flail or by driving horses over it and winnowed by dropping it through a natural draft of air instead of the artificial draft of the fanning mill. When ready for market it was mostly drawn to Albany, some three days being required for the journey. Rude lumber wagons or ox carts, or wood shod sleighs were the common vehicles for all occasions. Much of the grain also went down the river by bateaux to Schenectady.

A variety of work then went on indoors as well as out, which long ago ceased generally to be done in private houses. Every good mother taught her daughters a broad range of domestic duties, from washing dishes and log cabin floors to weaving and making up fine linen. The home was the factory as well and in it took place the making from flax and wool of the fabrics which the household needed. The houses resounded with the hum of the spinning wheel and loom and other machinery which the housewives used to make the family garments. The entire family were proud to appear in this goodly homespun even at church. Itinerant shoemakers made tours of the farmhouses, working at each place as long as the family footgear demanded, this being known as "whipping the cat." Common brogans were worn for the most part by the settlers. Many of the vegetables cultivated by their Mohawk Indian predecessors were adopted by their German and Dutch successors. Without tea or coffee, they made a drink of dried peas and sweetened it with maple sugar, the procuring of which they learned from the red man.

In regard to Christmas time in the valley the missionary Kirkland wrote as follows in his diary in 1789:

"The manner in wch. ye ppl. in yse parts keep Xmas day in commemor'g of the Birth of ye Saviour, as ya pretend is very affect'g and strik'g. They generally assemble for read'g prayers, or Divine service—but after, they eat drink and make merry. They allow of no work or servile labour on ye day and ye following—their servants are free—but drinking, swearing, fighting and frolic'g are not only allowed, but seem to be essential to ye joy of ye day."

The most common beverages drunk by the men of Revolutionary times were "flip" and "kill devil." "Flip" was made of beer brewed from malt and hops, to which was added sugar and liquor—the whole heated with a hot iron. "Kill devil" was made like flip, except that cider was substituted for beer. The price of each was one York shilling for a quart mug. Half a mug usually served two persons.

Freemasonry had a foothold in the valley prior to the Revolution and Sir William Johnson and Col. Nicholas Herkimer were both members of the Johnstown lodge. Also as showing the wilderness state of the country, it is said that wolves were so common in Dutchtown in the town of Minden that sheep had to be folded nights as late as 1773. All the wild animals of the present Adirondack wilderness were numerous about the Mohawk settlements in their earliest days.

Schools were located in many of the Tryon county settlements at the beginning of the Revolution. The first pedagogue in Dutchtown was John Pickard. As showing the early settlers' superstitions regarding sanitation and medical practise it may here be related that after Fort Willett was built he kept school in a hut within the palisade. Toward the close of the war he sickened and died of some disease prevalent in the fort at that time. A lad named Owen, living in the Henry Sanders family, caught a live skunk, which was set at liberty in the fort and "the disease was stayed." After the war, a Hessian named Glazier, who came into the state under Burgoyne, kept the Dutchtown school instructing in both German and English. Such instruction was probably mostly confined to the three Rs. School punishments were extremely severe and whipping a scholars' hands with a ruler until they bled was no unusual means of correction. One Palatine boy is said to have been so whipped in school on eighteen different occasions.

That a Tryon county woman could handle a gun is shown by an anecdote of the wife of the brave Captain Gardiner, of Oriskany fame, who lived near Fultonville: "His wife, like many of her sex on the frontier, on an emergency, could use firearms. On some occasion, when her husband was away from home in the service of his country, she saw from her house a flock of pigeons alighting upon the fence and ground not far off. She resolved to give them a salute and, hastily loaded an old musket, forgetting to draw out the ramrod. She left the house cautiously, gained a position within close gunshot, aimed at the pigeons on the fence, and blazed away. To her own surprise, and that of several of her family, who, from the window saw her fire, seven of the birds sitting upon a rail, were spitted on the ramrod in which condition they were taken to the house."

As befitted frontiersmen, their sports were rough and violent. They included rifle contests, wrestling, foot racing and horse racing. Horse races, on tracks and on the river ice, were greatly in vogue in the latter half of the eighteenth century, excepting the war period. The Low Dutch of the eastern end of the valley were famed for horse racing and even for running their horses from the foot of every hill two-thirds of the way up. Often between Schenectady and Albany were several farm wagons or sleighs trying titles for leadership at the hazard of a serious collision. Of this class of citizens at Schenectady was the well-to-do burgher Charick Van de Bogert, an old gentleman of worthy but eccentric character. He had a fine sleigh on the back of which was painted in Dutch the words, "Not to lend today but tomorrow." He had a span of horses named Cowper and Crown, which he raced successfully and which responded intelligently to his whip signals for the start and finish of a brush on the road. In his last illness, his affection for his team, induced the family to have the horses brought to his window where he patted them and bade them good-bye. He then turned to a close friend who was with him and asked him to drive the bier to the burial plot behind his beloved team, instead of having male bearers for the distance as was the valley custom. Van de Bogert requested his friend to touch the horses with his gad after a certain manner at a set point in the road and to again touch them in a different fashion at a farther point. Shortly after this the old gentleman expired and his funeral arrangements were ordered according to his wish. The friend who drove the hearse obeyed the deceased's wishes as to the whip signals. The well-trained team responded and the worthy Dutchman made his final earthly ride behind his well-loved span at the racing clip in which he delighted.

There were favorite race-courses in the valley, near Rotterdam, at Fort Hunter, at Conyne's tavern on the north river side a few miles further up. At Sand Flats, at Caughnawaga or Fonda was one of the most frequented. In the Canajoharie-Palatine districts there were race courses at Seebers Lane, on the flats at Canajoharie and at George Wagner's flats in Palatine. Every fall at Herkimer, horse racing was held on the flats at that place and it is not improbable that annual meetings such as these were the nuclei of the later county fairs. Such events were also common in the Schoharie valley. There was much drinking and gambling at all these races and the crowds assembled like those seen at county fairs.

There is every evidence that the men of those days had mighty athletes among them who were developed by the hard life of the day, instead of by modern training methods. Besides the foregoing sports and the usual crude field sports such as jumping, hurling the stone, etc., fighting bouts for purses were not uncommon.

A few years before the death of Sir William Johnson, he had in his employ a fellow countryman named Mc-Carthy, who was reputed the best pugilist in the Mohawk valley. The baronet offered to pit him against anyone. Major Jelles Fonda, tired of hearing this challenge, unearthed a mighty Dutchman named John Van Loan, in the Schoharie valley and made a journey of some fifty miles to secure him. Van Loan agreed to enter the ring for a ten-pound note. A big crowd assembled at Caughnawaga to see the contest. There was much betting, particularly on McCarthy. Van Loan appeared in a shirt and tight-fitting breeches of dressed deerskin. McCarthy tried hard but the Schoharie fighter was too strong and agile and eventually soundly whipped Sir William's pet, who had to be carried from the ring. This was probably one of many pugilistic and wrestling contests witnessed by crowds of settlers. Brutal they were but they were the physical expression of sport among men of iron and should not be judged by the tender standards of a delicate and soft age.

It will, of course, be understood that fishing, trapping and hunting, formed a large part of the vocations of the earliest settlers, who also availed themselves largely of the skins of game for clothing and other purposes, deerskin or buckskin forming a large part of this attire, particularly for sport or work in the woods.

Autumn husking bees and country dances were recreations of the river side folks and it is easy to see that here was no Puritan community but one which enjoyed the good things of life, after periods of strenuous toil. Barns and dwellings were raised by "bees" in which the neighborhood participated. Sports, dancing and solid and liquid refreshments followed in profusion. The final feast seemed an indispensable part of all social and most religious observances.

As the Dutch were such a considerable portion of the valley population, particularly in the eastern end and were scattered largely through the remainder some idea of their characteristics may be gained from Mrs. Grant's word pictures of life, in Albany in the middle of the eighteenth century, included in her "Memoirs of an American Lady." These things would apply to the Low Dutch of the town of Schenectady or, with a rural setting, to those in other parts of the valley and we must remember that the Dutch influence and customs were very strong in every part of the state in those days, including Tryon county.

Mrs. Grant says that the houses were very neat within and without and were of stone or brick. The streets were broad and lined with shade trees. Each house had its garden and before each door a tree was planted and shaded the stoops or porches, which were furnished with spacious seats on which domestic groups were seated on summer evenings. Each family had a cow, fed in a common pasture at the end of the town. At evening the herd returned altogether of their own accord, with their tinkling bells hung at their necks, along the wide and grassy street, to their wonted sheltering trees, to be milked at their master's doors. On pleasant evenings the stoops were filled with groups of old and young of both sexes discussing grave questions or gayly chatting and singing together. The mischievous gossip was unknown for intercourse was so free and friendship so real that there was no place for such a creature, and politicians seldom disturbed these social gatherings. A peculiar social custom arranged the young people in congenial companies, composed of equal numbers, of both sexes, quite small children being admitted, and the association continued until maturity. The result was a perfect knowledge of each other and happy and suitable marriages resulted. The summer amusements of the young were simple, the principal one being picnics, often held upon the pretty islands near Albany or in "the bush." These were days of pure enjoyment for everybody was unrestrained by conventionalities. In winter the frozen Hudson would be alive with merry skaters of both sexes. Small evening parties were frequent and were generally the sequel of quilting parties. The young men sometimes enjoyed convivial parties at taverns but habitual drunkenness was extremely rare.

Slavery was common in the valley and some plantations had a score or more slaves. The price of labor was so enormously high, because of the sparse population, that the importation of negroes had become a prime industrial necessity and they were then very numerous in the province of New York. Mrs. Grant speaks of slavery in Albany and her remarks are pertinent to the valley as well. She says:

"African slavery was seen at Albany and vicinity in its mildest form. It was softened by gentleness and mutual attachments. It appeared patriarchial and a real blessing to the negroes. Master and slave stood in the relation of friends. Immoralities were rare. There was no hatred engendered by neglect, cruelty and injustice; and such excitements as the 'Negro Plots' of 1712 and 1741 in New York city were impossible. Industry and frugality ranked among the cardinal virtues of the people."

These seem to have been negro slave conditions in this section up to 1827, when slavery was finally abolished in New York. The slaves were allowed much liberty and had their full share of celebrations and jollifications such as Christmas and New Year. Many were freed by their owners, for good service or other reasons and in all the local records we find few incidents of cruelty or abuse on the part of the white man to the black. There is an instance of a slave woman born in the Herkimer family at Danube who lived for years in Little Falls and was looked after and finally buried by the Herkimer grandchildren of her early master.

A number of conditions tended to mold public thought into a Revolutionary form. There were discouragements to settlement and some of the English governors had been avaricious, bigoted and tyrannical. The lavish grants of much of the best land to their favorites and tools were special hindrances to the rapid increase of population. The holders of large estates rated their lands so high that poorer persons could neither buy or lease farms.

It is not the province of this account to treat in detail of the grants of land in Tryon county. Suffice to say that these transactions frequently seemed to be honey-combed with every form of corruption known to Colonial adventurers and crooks. Such methods were well exemplified in the Corry patent which, tradition has it, was secured in part by Gov. Clarke for himself, although it was against the Colonial law for a governor to acquire land by free grant. This is the well known property which was the scene of so much miserable trouble, arson and crime during the years of its last proprietorship under a George Clarke. These grants angered both Indians and settlers and tended, among many other things, to make the true American of the day distrust and hate his state government and mother country. For the most part the Dutch and Palatine grantees seem to have settled upon and improved for their own use the lands given them.

Benson J. Lossing's "Empire State," says:

"In the state of New York the Dutch language was so generally used in some of the counties that sheriffs found it difficult to procure persons sufficiently acquainted with the English tongue to serve as jurors in the courts. Among the wealthiest people considerable luxury in table, dress and furniture was exhibited, yet there was an aspect of homely comfort through society. Both sexes, of all except the highest classes, were neglectful of intellectual cultivation. The schools were of a low order. 'The instructors want instruction,' wrote a contemporary. The English language where it was spoken was much corrupted. The placid good humor of the Dutch seemed to largely pervade the province, including men and women, and there seemed to have prevailed an uncommon degree of virtue and domestic felicity. The population is reported as industrious, hospitable, as a rule sober, and intent upon money-making.

"The people generally were religious. The principal church organizations were the Dutch Reformed, the Lutheran, English Episcopal and the Presbyterian. This was due to the racial elements of the state's settlers which were Dutch, German, English, Scotch, Irish and Huguenot French, and these elements penetrated to some extent into practically all the counties of the province, including Tryon. There was much freedom of thought and action among the people that fostered a spirit of independence. They were not bound hand and foot by rigid religious and political creeds, as were the people of New England, but were thoroughly imbued with the toleration inherited from the first Dutch settlers, and theological disputes were seldom indulged in."

Here and there were men of acute intelligence and fine minds who possessed initiative and the power of expressing themselves simply, clearly and forcibly. These were the leaders who were to be in the van in the impending struggle.

All the foregoing pictures to us the Mohawk valley people, their lands, customs, manners and play at the period just antedating the war for independence and the building of Fort Plain. This account is considered worthy of its length in portraying the men and women who were to be actors in and around this frontier out post, for after all the human element is more important than the dead walls of the old fort and both played their part on this stage of war and peace.

CHAPTER VIII.

1774 to 1777—Growth of the American Liberty Movement—Tryon County Committee of Safety and Militia.

At the opening of the Revolution the Mohawk valley had enjoyed 20 years of peace and consequent development and prosperity. Its people had almost forgotten the horrors of the French and Indian depredations during the last contest between England and France which resulted in the latter's loss of Canada.

In 1774, the strong American sentiment for independence took form in Tryon county at a meeting held in the Palatine district which warmly approved the calling of a Continental

congress for mutual consultation of
the colonies upon their grievances
against England. A set of resolutions
was drawn up setting forth the Am-
erieau cause and correspondence was
opened with the patriots of New York
city. The Johnson party early in
1775 published a set of resolutions ap-
proving English acts and went about
securing signatures, which excited the
indignation of the majority of the
Tryon county population who were
Whigs. Most of the Tryon county officials signed the Johnson petition.
The Whigs held meetings and the first
one, of three hundred patriots, assembled at Caughnawaga to raise a liberty pole. This was broken up by an
armed party of Tories headed by Sir
John Johnson. Young Jacob Sammons
interrupted a fiery speech of Col. Guy
Johnson and was severely beaten by
the Tories. Further patriotic meetings were held and at the second held
at the house of Adam Loucks in Palatine, a committee to correspond with
those of other districts was formed,
this being the beginning of the Tryon
County Committee of Safety. Johnson now armed further his fortifications at the Hall and organized and
equipped his Tory Scotch highlanders.
In view of these affairs the Palatine
committee addressed a letter to the
Albany committee setting forth the
situation in the county and asking
that the shipment of ammunition into
it from Albany be supervised so that
the Tories could not further arm
themselves. Evidences soon appeared
that Johnson was endeavoring to secure the support of the Six Nations.
His personal army now amounted to
500 men and he had cut off free communication between Albany and the
upper valley settlements. The Palatine committee, May 21, protested
against Johnson's course and the German Flats and Kingsland districts
were invited to cooperate with them.

May 24, 1775, the committees of all
the districts but Mohawk met at the
house of William Seeber in Canajoharie (at Fort Plain) and adopted resolutions of united action between the
districts. Delegates were sent to Al-

bany and Schenectady to confer with
those committees. This was the first
meeting of the Tryon County Committee of Safety and was held close to
the site of the later fortification. May
25, the Tryon county and Albany
committees held a council with the
Mohawks at Guy Park without apparent results. On May 29, again at the
house of William Seeber, near Fort
Plain, a resolution was passed prohibiting all trade with persons who had
not signed the article of association
and slaves were not to be allowed off
their master's premises without a permit. Any person disobeying these instructions was to be considered an
enemy of the patriot cause. The first
full meeting of the county committee
was held in the western part of the
Canajoharie district, June 2, 1775, at
the house of Warner Tygert a neighbor
and relative of General Herkimer. The
names of the committee at that
meeting follow:

Canajoharie District—Nicholas Her-
kimer, Ebenezer Cox, William Seeber,
John Moore, Samuel Campbell, Samuel
Clyde, Thomas Henry, John Pickard.

Kingsland and German Flats Dis-
tricts—Edward Wall, William Petry,
John Petry, Marcus Petry, Augustinus
Hess, Frederick Ahrendorf, George
Wents, Michael E. Ittig, Frederick
Fox, George Herkimer, Duncan Mc-
Dougall, Frederick Hilmer, John
Franck.

Mohawk District—John Marlett,
John Bliven, Abraham Van Horn,
Adam Fonda Frederick Fisher, Samp-
son Sammons, William Schuyler, Vol-
kert Veeder, James McMaster, Daniel
Lane.

Palatine District—Isaac Paris, John
Frey, Christopher P. Yates, Andrew
Fink jr., Andrew Reeber, Peter Wag-
goner, Daniel McDougall, Jacob Klock,
George Ecker jr., Harmanus Van
Slyck, Christopher W. Fox and An-
thony Van Vechten.

Of the members from the Canajoharie district, Herkimer and Cox lived
in the present town of Danube, Seeber
and Pickard in Minden, Henry in Harpersfield and Campbell and Clyde in
Cherry Valley.

Christopher P. Yates was chosen chairman of the county committee and Edward Wall and Nicholas Herkimer were selected to deliver a letter of protest to Col. Guy Johnson against his Tory stand. Col. Johnson returned a politic but non-committal letter to this deputation. He appointed a council at German Flats but did not hold it but went on to Fort Stanwix, taking with him his family, a number of dependents and a great body of Mohawk Indians, who left their valley homes never to return except in war parties and against their old neighbors.

On June 11, 1775, the committee chose Christopher P. Yates and John Marlett as delegates to the provincial congress. This meeting was held at the house of Gose Van Alstine (now known as Fort Rensselaer in the village of Canajoharie). Rev. Mr. Kirkland arranged a council of the Oneidas and Tuscaroras with the committee and Albany delegates at German Flats, June 28, 1775, which largely resulted in the friendly attitude of the Oneidas and Tuscaroras during the war.

July 3 the committee granted the petition of certain settlers for permission to form themselves into militia companies. The Tory mayor of Albany, who was fleeing west, was stopped by Capt. George Herkimer and the rangers and his batteau was searched but nothing contraband was found. By this time Guy Johnson and his party had pushed on to Ontario, far beyond the reach of angry patriots, and wrote back a hostile letter in reply to a pacific one sent him by the provincial congress. From Oswego Johnson went to Montreal accompanied by many warriors of the Six Nations. The Tryon county settlers feared that he would soon collect an army, and cooperating with John Johnson, sweep the valley of the patriots. The committee now assumed the civic and military functions of the county and began to have trouble with John Johnson over its assumption of the sheriff's duties and use of the jail and also over the formation of patriot companies in the vicinity

of the hall. Congress ordered Gen. Schuyler to capture the military stores at Johnson Hall and disarm and disperse the Johnson Tory party. Jan. 18, 1776, Schuyler and his force met Col. Herkimer and the Tryon county militia at Caughnawaga. On the 19th at Johnstown, Sir John Johnson delivered up his war supplies and his 300 Scotch highlanders were disarmed. Col. Herkimer remained and brought in 100 Tories, who were disarmed. Johnson continuing his work for the Tory cause, in May, 1776, Col. Dayton was sent to capture him. Johnson escaped to Canada with many of his followers, striking into the northern wilderness as the Continentals were entering Johnstown, and leaving in such haste that he buried his plate and valuables. Lady Johnson was removed to Albany where she was held as hostage for her husband's actions. Johnson took a commission as colonel under the British and organized two battalions, from the Tories who followed him, which were called the Royal Greens. These Tryon county Tories surpassed the Indians in their barbaric acts on subsequent raids into the Mohawk valley and in their depredations around Fort Plain. A large part of the Tory population soon left Tryon county for Canada. Sir John's estate and that of some sixty other Tories, were confiscated by the patriot government. The Whigs were now formed into companies by the different district committees. Aug. 22, 1776, the following were named, by a majority of votes, as field officers for the different districts:

Canajoharie, 1st Battalion—1st Col., Nicholas Herkimer; Lieut.-Col., Ebenezer Cox; major, Robert Wells; adjutant, Samuel Clyde.

Palatine, 2nd Battalion—Col., Jacob Klock; Lieut.-Col., Peter Waggoner; major, Harmanus Van Slyck; adjutant, Anthony Van Vechten.

Mohawk, 3rd Battalion—Col., Frederick Fisher; Lieut.-Col., Adam Fonda; major, John Bliven; adjutant, Robt. Yates.

Kingsland and German Flats, 4th Battalion—Col., Han Yost Herkimer;

Lieut.-Col., Peter Bellinger; major, Han Yost Shoemaker; adjutant, Jno. Demooth.

At the same time Nicholas Herkimer was appointed "Chief Colonel Commander of the County of Tryon." Following his unsuccessful attempt to arrest Johnson, Col. Dayton was commissioned by Gen. Schuyler, in command of the northern army at Albany, to strengthen the valley defenses. Forts Dayton and Plain were erected, all of which work was under Col. Dayton's supervision. He also repaired and strengthened Fort Stanwix (later Schuyler) and Fort Herkimer.

Four weeks after the Tryon county militia organization was effected, a battalion of "Minute men" (scouts or rangers) was formed with George Herkimer, brother of Nicholas, as its colonel and Samuel Campbell as its lieutenant-colonel.

In the spring of 1777 Brant, with a large party of Indians, came down from Canada to Unadilla. Gen. Schuyler ordered Col. Herkimer to confer with Brant, as the two latter had been on friendly terms prior to the Revolution. Herkimer and 450 Tryon county militia and regular troops accordingly proceeded to Unadilla and met Brant, who had 500 well armed warriors under him. Two conferences between the two commanders were ineffectual, a conflict was narrowly avoided and the American militia returned to the Mohawk.

––––––

In 1777 occurred the establishment and organization of an independent state government (succeeding the Provincial Congress) and the framing of a constitution for the government of the commonwealth. The new "Convention of Representatives of the State of New York" met in White Plains in July and representatives were present from the then fourteen counties of the state—namely, New York, Richmond, Kings, Queens, Suffolk, Westchester, Dutchess, Orange, Ulster, Albany, Tryon, Charlotte, Cumberland and Gloucester. The last two counties formed a part of the present state of Vermont. The members representing Tryon were: William Harper, Isaac Paris, Mr. Vedder, John Morse, Benjamin Newkirk.

––––––

Gen. Philip Schuyler, who disarmed Johnson and his followers at Johnstown in 1776, was connected with many of the military movements in this locality through being the commander of the American army of the north during the early part of the war with headquarters at Albany. He was born in Albany, 1733, and came of a Dutch family which had been prominently connected with the affairs of the city and the colony from its earliest days. Schuyler joined the British Colonial forces during the French war and became a major. Two days after the battle of Bunker Hill, congress made him a major-general and placed him in command of the northern department. In the expedition against Canada, Schuyler commanded that by way of Lake Champlain. He was compelled, owing to ill health, to relinquish his command to Montgomery after taking Isle au Noix, on Sorel river. The failure of the Canadian expedition excited much hostility to Schuyler and insinuations were made against his loyalty. This became so offensive that he sent congress his resignation which that body declined to accept in the autumn of 1776. In April, 1777, Schuyler demanded a court of inquiry, which approved his management. During this time he had continued in command at Albany and his influence with the Indians is said to have been of great value to the American cause. Gen. Schuyler sent aid, in August, 1777, to Fort Schuyler, under Arnold, in response to the plea of Col. Willett. This was opposed by his generals in council, but his wise and prompt action saved the fort, the valley and perhaps the nation. Schuyler resisted Burgoyne's advance but was superseded by Gates at the mouth of the Mohawk, where he had taken up a fortified position in September, 1777. Thus he was robbed of the fruits of the victory at Saratoga. 1778-81 he was a member of congress and in 1789 and 1797 went to the United States senate from New York. In the New York senate he contributed largely to the code of laws adopted by the state and was an active promoter of the canal system. The Inland Lock Navigation Co. was incorporated in 1792, for the improvement of Mohawk river traffic, and Gen. Philip Schuyler was elected its president. One of his daughters married Alexander Hamilton. Schuyler died in Albany in 1804, aged 70. He is considered one of the leading figures of New York's Revolutionary period.

Lossing gives the following origin of the terms, Whig and Tory: "They were copied by us from the political vocabulary of Great Britain and were first used here to distinguish the opposing parties in the Revolution about 1770. The term originated during the reign of Charles II., or about that time. Bishop Burnet, in his History gives the following explanation: 'The southwest counties of Scotland have seldom corn [grain] enough to serve them round the year; and the northern parts, producing more than they need, those in the west come in the summer to buy at Leith the stores that come from the north; and from a word 'whiggam,' used in driving their horses, all that drove were called 'whiggamores' and shorter, 'whigs.' Now in that year after the news came down of Duke Hamilton's defeat, the ministers animated their people to rise and march to Edinburg, and then came up marching at the head of other parishes, with unheard of fury, praying and preaching all the way as they came. The Marquis of Argyle and his party came and headed them, they being about six thousand. This was called the Whiggamores' inroad, and ever after that all that opposed the courts came, in contempt, to be called Whigg; and from Scotland the word was brought into England, where it is now one of our unhappy terms of distinction. Subsequently, all whose party bias was democratic were called Whigs. The origin of the word Tory is not so well attested. The Irish mal-

contents, half robbers and half insurgents, who harassed the English in Ireland at the time of the massacre in 1640, were the first to whom the epithet was applied. It was also applied to the court party as a term of reproach."

The following is a brief resume of events and their dates preceding and contributory to the Revolution and also of the principal events of the war from 1775 to the summer of 1777, when hostilities began in the Mohawk valley. It is prepared with especial reference to the history of New York state.

Albany convention (of delegates from eight colonies), 1754. New York congress of 1765, called to protest against the Stamp Act of 1765; formation of the Sons of Liberty in New York city and conflict between them and British troops, Jan. 18, 1770, resulting in bloodshed (Appleton's Encyclopedia says "this irregular fighting was the real beginning of the Revolutionary war."); Boston massacre, 1770; Boston tea party, Dec. 16, 1773; organization of "Mohawks" in New York in 1773 and repetition of "Boston tea party" in New York harbor, April, 1774; Continental congress in Philadelphia, Sept. 5, 1773 (in reality an assemblage of the patriot committees from the different colonies), sitting also during 1774; battle of Lexington, April 19, 1775; American capture of Ticonderoga, May 10, 1775; second Continental congress, May 10, 1775; battle of Bunker Hill, June 17, 1775; Washington made commander-in-chief of the American army, June 15, 1775; American defeat under Montgomery at Quebec, Dec. 31, 1775; declaration of independence, July 4, 1776; evacuation of Boston by British, Mar. 17, 1776; American defeat on Long Island, Aug. 27, 1776; American defeats of Fort Washington, Manhattan, and Fort Lee, New Jersey, in fall of 1776, and retreat across New Jersey; American victory at Trenton, Dec. 26, 1776; American victory of Princeton, Jan. 3, 1777; Adoption of state constitution at Kingston (Esopus) April 21,

1777, the legislators having removed there from White Plains on account of the nearness of the British force, occupying New York city; Burgoyne's British army assembled at Cumberland Point, Lake Champlain, June, 1777, and captured Crown Point, June 30, 1777; St. Leger's British army assembles at Oswego for invasion of Mohawk valley and junction with Burgoyne at Albany, July, 1777; George Clinton sworn in as governor of New York, July 31, 1777.

CHAPTER IX.

1776—The Building of Fort Plain— Other Forts Near Here.

At the close of the French war there were, in the valley, army fortifications at Fort Stanwix (now Rome, erected 1758), at Fort Herkimer (1756) and at Fort Hunter (1711), besides other fortified places such as Fort Johnson. Early in 1776 Col. Elias Dayton was sent to repair Fort Stanwix and he probably had supervision over the repairs to Fort Herkimer and the erection of Fort Plain and Fort Dayton at Herkimer, which bears his name.

The site of Fort Plain, on the rise just west of the present cemetery, at the extreme western end of the village limits, has already been noted. Simms says it was constructed mainly by farmers. Its form was an irregular quadrangle with earth and log bastions or block houses and embrasures at opposite corners a strong block house within in the center and also barracks. Cannon in the block-houses could command the fort on all sides. It enclosed from a third to a half acre of ground but when settlers began to be killed and burned out, the survivors came here in such numbers that the space was found too small for the public needs. Three or four comfortable huts were accordingly made along the verge of the hill. The adjacent spring furnished water and supplies were probably stored in the center block-house. There were two large apple trees within the fort inclosure. Its entrance was on the south-easterly side toward a road leading up to the ravine on that side

to it. Lossing says it had block-houses in each corner; Simms says they were in opposite corners of the quadrangle.

The plateau on which it stood is of penninsular form and, across the neck or isthmus, a breastwork was thrown up. The fort extended along the south-eastern brow of this hill and the block-house was about one hundred yards northwest on the edge of the northern slope of the hill. There is a tradition that nearby settlers aided in the erection of this defense. The boss carpenter, John Dederick, was allowed to name the fort. It is stated that he named it Fort Plain on account of its plain or fine view of open country and because from here operations of an enemy could be so plainly detected. It is said to have been not so named because the fortification was situated on a diminutive plain, as it was.

There is a possibility that it might have been named thus because, from this height looking over the trees which lined the near-by Otsquago, an unbroken view of the treeless flats, stretching four miles away to Canajoharie, was obtained. This was in strong contrast to the densely wooded slopes and heights stretching away to entire circle of the horizon around the fort. The outlook at that day must have been superb with the big woods cleared in spots only near the river and the heights covered by the great trees of the virgin forest. The Metropolitan Museum in New York houses a painting by Wyant called "The Mohawk Valley." It is a considerable canvas, showing the river before the coming of the white man and is impressive in its wooded hills and its treeless flat lands with the Mohawk winding through them. It suggests strongly what might have been the view at one time from Fort Plain. However we will accept the Simms statement that the fort received its name on account of the fine, open, plain or unobstructed view.

An acquaintance with the other regular military posts of the time seems to show that of them all it was the best located for defense. Fort Plain was the first Revolutionary fortification and the most important within the Canajoharie-Palatine districts. Fort Canajoharie at Danube was a stockade erected during the French war to protect the Mohawks but did not figure in the conflict for independence.

Who commanded first at Fort Plain is not known and it probably was not regularly garrisoned until 1777. It formed a key for communication with and protection of the Schoharie, Cherry Valley and Unadilla settlements and was the chief protection of the Canajoharie and Palatine districts. About 1780-1 it became the headquarters of the officer commanding this and the several military posts in this vicinity. Col. Marinus Willett was its commander for several seasons and he is believed to have been here constantly about 1781-2. He occupied the eastern one of the huts situated on the side hill below the pickets a rod or two from the spring. Col. Clyde was in command here in 1783. The blockhouse, which will be noted later, was built to still further strengthen the defenses here in the fall of 1780 and the spring of 1781, and was merely a part of the fortifications here and not a separate post. Fort Plain must have been considered of formidable strength for it never was attacked directly by the considerable forces of the enemy who operated in this section at different times. The land on which the post stood was part of the Lipe farm.

Five smaller fortifications were in the vicinity of Fort Plain. Commencing westerly Fort Windecker, Fort Willett, Fort Plank and Fort Clyde were only two or three miles apart, the first three being nearly on a north and south line, curving easterly to embrace the last fort named, and being in something like a half circle around Fort Plain on its western side. During the latter part of the war this line of forts, with the regular army post toward the center, made this section one of the best defended on the Tryon county frontier, and one historian says enabled the surviving to furnish most of the bread for the district. Fort Paris, at Stone Arabia, was the fifth fortification immediately about the central defense of Fort Plain.

Fort Windecker, built in 1777, was a palisaded small enclosure surrounding the dwelling of Johannes Windecker. It was nearly eight miles west of north from the latter upon the river road. It had the usual signal gun and probably contained a small block-house. This place, like similar posts, had at least one sentinel on duty at night, who was posted usually outside the pickets at this place.

Fort Willett was a palisaded inclosure on the highest ground in the Dutchtown section and was situated over four miles from Fort Plain on land now owned by William Zimmerman. This stockade was completed in the spring of 1781 and had ample room for huts for all the adjacent families. It had the block-house cor ners and an alarm gun. As it was iso lated from any dwelling, it had a good sized oven, the ruins of which re mained for many years. The timber for its pickets was cut on adjoining farms and was drawn together by the owners of them. Like other palisades, the pickets were the trunks of straight trees of different kinds, of about a foot thickness through the butt, and cut long enough to be sunk three or four feet in the ground and to rise above it about a dozen or more. On the completion of this defense, Col. Willett rode out with a squad of his men from Fort Plain to see it. He was much pleased with the condition of things and said "You have a nice little fort here; what do you call it?" "It has no name yet; wont you give it one?" was the answer. Col. Willett replied, "Well, this is one of the nicest little forts on the frontier, and you may call it after me, if you please." A cheer went up at this, so the name of Willett became connected with the town in which he lived and fought for several years. The old south shore turnpike running through the Greenbush section of Fort Plain village is named Willett street after this very capable Revolutionary commander. At the end of the war each family who had contributed pickets for the building of Fort Willett drew home their share and the fortification was demolished in the same manner as the many others when their use for purposes of defense had ceased.

Fort Plank was established in 1776 and was situated two and a half miles west of Fort Plain and one and a quarter miles in a direct line southerly from the Mohawk. Here then lived Frederick Plank, a whig, whose house was palisaded in a square enclosure with block-house corners. From its nearness to the settlements at Dutchtown and Geissenberg it served as a safe retreat for a score or two of families. Capt. Joseph House, a militia officer living with Plank, usually commanded in the absence of field officers. More or less troops were kept at this station through the war.

Fort Clyde was established in 1777 to protect the Freysbush settlers. It bore the name of Col. Samuel Clyde of Cherry Valley, who doubtless superintended its construction. This was not a palisaded dwelling but a fort by itself, like that at Fort Plain and Fort Willett. It was an enclosure large enough to hold huts for the accommodation of refugees and a strong blockhouse in the center. A signal gun was mounted as at all such posts. It was about three miles south of Fort Plain and topped a sightly knoll on what was the old Gen. George H. Nellis farm. It is believed Col. Clyde exercised a sort of paternal supervision over this fort, where part of a company of rangers or drafted militia was stationed.

In the Palatine district similarly adjacent to Fort Plain stood Fort Paris. It was three or four miles to the northeast of Fort Plain and stood upon the summit of ground half a mile to the north of the Stone Arabia churches. It was a palisade enclosing strong block-houses and was of a size to accommodate a garrison of 200 or 300 men. The fort was commenced in December, 1776, and completed in the spring of 1777.

This was an important post and was usually manned by a company or two of rangers. Col. Klock and Lieut.-Col. Wagner had much to do with its immediate command. In the fall and winter of 1779 it became the headquarters of Col. Frederick Visscher, who commanded this and its adjacent military posts, including Fort Plain. This headquarters was changed to Fort Plain in 1780-1, probably with the advent of Col. Willett to command the American forces in the valley. Fort Paris was named after Col. Isaac Paris. The post was ordered built by the Tryon County Committee of Safety, Dec. 19, 1776, and was largely erected by Capt. Christian Getman's company of rangers "under the sole direction and command of Isaac Paris, Esq.," to quote the language of the committee. It was located on what is now the Shull farm and was built of solid hewn timber and was two stories high with the upper story projecting over the lower on all sides. After it was taken down, early in the nineteenth century, its timbers were used in building structures now in existence in that section.

Besides these more important posts around Fort Plain there were numerous stockaded dwellings called forts generally named from the families who owned them. A small stockaded stone dwelling named Fort Keyser was located about a mile south of Stone Arabia.

In the present village of Canajoharie on the east side of the creek stood the stockaded stone dwelling of Philip Van Alstine. A mile or two southwest of this on the Mapletown road and a mile from the creek stood Fort Ehle. Lieut. Cornelius Van Evera and Ensign John Van Evera were on duty in and around this fort.

In the eastern part of the town of St. Johnsville stood "Fort House," named after its builder, although it was the home of Christian Klock. The house of Jacob Zimmerman was also stockaded. Both of these stockades repulsed repeated attacks of the enemy. Fort Hill, which was situated on an eminence in the western part of the town of St. Johnsville, was erected during the French war. It was repaired and used during the Revolution.

Thus before a blow had been struck, the settlers of Tryon county had realized the gravity of the situation and were prepared for defense.

After his unsuccessful attempt to arrest Sir John Johnson in May, in the summer of 1776, Col. Dayton was sent by Gen. Schuyler to look after the defenses in the Mohawk valley. He started the reconstruction of Fort Stanwix (Schuyler), which work was not entirely completed when invested by the enemy in the following year. Col. Dayton is supposed to have had official supervision of the renovation of Fort Herkimer and of the construction of Fort Dayton, which bears his name, at the site of Herkimer. It is reasonable to suppose that he supervised the erection of Fort Plain at the same time. Elias Dayton was born in Elizabethtown, New Jersey, in 1735. He joined the Colonial army during the French and Indian war. He was a member of the corps called "Jersey Blues," raised in 1759 by Edward Hart, the father of John Hart, one of the signers of the Declaration of Independence. With that corps Dayton fought under Wolfe at Quebec. He was one of the Committee of Safety at Elizabethtown at the beginning of the Revolution. In February, 1778, congress appointed him colonel of a New Jersey regiment, and in 1782 he was promoted to the rank of brigadier-general. He was in several of the principal battles of the Revolution and had three horses shot under him—one at Germantown, one at Springfield and one at Crosswick Bridge. He was the first president of the Society of the Cincinnati of New Jersey and, during the life of Washington, enjoyed the warm personal friendship of the national leader. He died at Elizabethtown in 1807, aged 72 years.

Three forts were erected in the Schoharie valley in the fall of 1777, the central being the first one built. It was known during the Revolution as the Middle Fort and, Simms says,

"stood on the farm long owned by Ralph Manning, about half a mile east of north from the present Middleburgh railroad station." It was built by soldiers and citizens, the farmers drawing the material together and the soldiers doing a great part of the building. The Upper Fort was situated five miles west of south from the Middle Fort. It was begun in the fall of 1777 and completed the following summer. The Lower Fort, situated six miles north of the Middle Fort. The stone church, still standing one mile north of the court house, was enclosed within the palisades of this fortification.

CHAPTER X.

1776—Adjacent Settlers and Buildings —Some Thrilling Incidents.

The following deals with some of the buildings and families immediately around Fort Plain and in the Canajoharie-Palatine districts during the Revolutionary period, 1775-1783.

Across the river from the fort was the dwelling and farm of Peter W. Wormuth, whose son Matthew was shot down in 1778 while carrying despatches between Fort Plain and Cherry Valley. Here Washington stopped and remained over night on his visit to Fort Plain in 1783. Directly across the river was the Wagner farm where a ferry ran later and probably then.

Beside the Lipe family an immediate neighbor of Fort Plain, on the Minden side of the river, was William H. Seeber, who had a store and dwelling on the late Adam Lipe place. His store was opened about 1750 and he traded here during the French war. He was a member of the Tryon County Committee of Safety of the Canajoharie district and a major of militia in the battalion from the same district. He was wounded at Oriskany and died 126 days after at his home. Two of his sons were with him in this battle. One, Audolph, was killed on the field and the other, Capt. Jacob W. Seeber, fell with a wounded leg and died shortly after it was amputated at Fort Herkimer. The land on which Fort Plain was built was owned by Johannes Lipe, who had a dwelling and barns next to it.

A neighbor of considerable size and importance at the time was the first Reformed Dutch church of Canajoharie, situated at Sand Hill, about a third of a mile north of the fort, and a little distance above the Abeel place on the Dutchtown road. This was a wooden building and stood on a sightly place on the westerly side of the road at what is now the old Sand Hill cemetery. At the time of its burning by Brant, Dominie Gros was its pastor, and from that time to the close of the war he preached in a barn on the Lipe farm in the ravine through which the road ran from the river up to Fort Plain. This barn was removed to make way for another in 1859. Another old dwelling a few yards below it gave way in 1875 to a brick dwelling. One of the ancient wooden structures standing on the left side almost at the beginning of the Dutchtown road is said to be the old parsonage. These buildings, with several others were so near the fort that they were never molested. One of these was the Young house which was superseded by the former Williams residence on Canal street. Several of these old Sand Hill wooden structures have been destroyed by fire in comparatively recent years. •

Other adjoining property was that of John Abeel, a Dutch trader of Albany, who came into this part of the Canajoharie district in 1757. He was the father of the Seneca chief, Cornplanter, as mentioned elsewhere, and was engaged in the fur trade among the Six Nations when he became enamored of a Seneca girl. Abeel was captured near his home in the raid of 1780 by Brant and Cornplanter and was released by the latter. The half-breed son later visited his relatives at Fort Plain. George Crouse built a log house to the south of the fort and between it and the Governor Clarke place. This cabin was burned by Brant in 1780. The Clarke wilderness home is mentioned at length in an early chapter.

The Clarke property came into the possession of Isaac Paris jr., who built a large store upon it in 1786 (now the Bleecker house). Paris built this store after the Revolution but he must have owned the Clarke property as early as 1782 as he sold part of it to George Crouse jr. and Col. Willett, who boarded with Crouse, advised the latter to buy it. Willett did not command here after 1782. The land was to be paid for in wheat at 18 cents per skipple (three pecks). Later Col. Robert Crouse built a house on the cellar of the Clarke mansion and this was later the residence now standing of the late A. J. Wagner. The Crouse farm, on which so much of Fort Plain was built, was probably the original Clarke property.

Among the soldiers and people of the country surrounding Fort Plain in the districts of Palatine and Canajobarie, who had experiences in the war we summarize the following· from Beer's ·History: "John Brookman was carried captive to Canada by the Indians and màde to run the gauntlet; Castine Bellinger, who was taken by the Indians to Canada when only three years old, where she afterward married and refused to return when found by her father, Frederick Bellinger; Christian, Jacob and Peter Bellinger, who were captured by the Indians, the last two tomahawked and scalped and Christian held for three years as a slave; Nicholas Casler, John Casler, a baker for the army who is said to have kneaded dough with his feet; Jacob Conkling, mate of the brig Middleton; John Chisley; George Clock; Abram Copeman, a Revolutionary major; George Dievendorff, a captain; John Dievendorff, who escaped from captivity two years after he had been taken by the Indians; Henry Dievendorff, who was shot at Oriskany by an Indian who was immediately killed by William Cox; Jacob Dievendorff, a captain, who passed safely through the war; George Davis, who was in the battles with Burgoyne and at one time with two other patriots, captured three Tories, whom Davis took to Albany; John Peter Dunckel; John Dillenbeck, a captain; George Dillenbeck, brother of the former, who in the war lost an eye from an Indian bullet and after drew a pension; Cornelius Flint; Mrs. Dr. Frame, murdered by Indians while trying to escape to Fort Nellis; Peter Flagg, a soldier at Fort Plain under Col. Willett; Henry J. Failing; John Gremps, a fifteen-year-old patriot soldier who was killed at Oriskany; Peter Gremps, who put out a fire kindled by Indians in his house, with a barrel of swill, during the Stone Arabia raid; Christian Hufnail; Peter H. House; Samuel Howe; Rudolph Keller, who was taken to Canada by the Indians and died of consumption when he returned within six months; Peter Lambert, a spy; John Lambert, who was captured by the Indians when twelve years old and on his return two years after was known only to his mother by a scar on his arm, and could not eat regular food but would go into the woods and cook for himself, Indian fashion; Adam Lipe, wounded during the war; John Lipe; George Lambert, a butcher in the army; Moses Lowell, soldier; Francis Lighthall; Isaac Miller, who was taken by the Indians, scalped and left for dead but revived, reached friends and recovered; John Miller, a soldier and one of the pursuers of Brant; Jacob Matthews; Solomon, John Henry, Jacob and Henry Moyer, soldiers, the last wounded in the shoulder; Nicholas Pace; John Roof, a soldier at Oriskany; John Roof, another of the same name, a soldier at the Johnstown battle; Henry and Peter Sitts, the latter of whom, while riding with Wormuth from Cherry Valley to Fort Plain, had his horse shot down and, falling under it, was captured and kept in Canada during the war; Barbara Schenck, captured by the Indians while pulling flax and taken thinly dressed and barefoot to Canada with her baby and a girl of eleven, were cared for by a Tory who recognized them, later returned to their home, except the daughter, who mar-

ried and went to New England; Henry Sanders, whose head was scratched by a bullet at Oriskany; Peter and John Snyder; Henry Seeber, a paymaster in the army; Henry Timmerman, who was sixteen when he was in the block-house at St. Johnsville when it was attacked by Brant; Giles Van Vost; Nicholas Van Slyke, a boatman on the Mohawk, who boasted of having killed 47 Indians, but who was finally killed by them and his body mutilated; Jacob Wagner; Jos. H. Wiles;——Wilkes, grandfather of Matthew Wilkes, a scout; M. Wormuth, who was shot dead when Sitts was taken; Henry Waffle; G. Walrath, who was captured by the Indians but killed his guard and escaped into a swamp, where he covered himself with mud and eluded search; Jacob Walrath, George Yoneker, Adam, John and Nancy Yordon, the latter of whom was taken a prisoner to Canada and there married; Christian Young and Henry Galler, who was killed in the war."

It is impossible to give the names of all who participated in the Revolution. More of these soldiers' names will be found in the Canajoharie and Palatine names on the Oriskany roster. Other Minden families are considered at greater length in the chapter on Brant's Minden raid of 1780.

In the Palatine district, among other neighbors of Fort Plain, was the patriot Major John Frey and his Tory brother, Hendrick Frey, both sons of Heinrich Frey jr., who was possibly the first white child born in the wilderness west of Schenectady. Henrich Frey sr., in 1689, had settled on 300 acres of land, at the now town of Palatine Bridge, where he built a log cabin. This was succeeded in 1739 by a stone dwelling which is often called Fort Frey, and is still standing. It had a row of portholes on all sides and was stockaded during the French war and occupied by several companies of soldiers. Col. Hendrick Frey, being the oldest son, inherited his father's landed estate which had grown to be of large size. He was educated at the school of Rev. Mr.

Dunlap in Cherry Valley, and married a sister of Gen. Herkimer. He had been a colonel of Colonial troops under the Johnsons and with Guy Johnson had been the first to represent Tryon county in the assembly. After some delay Col. Hendrick Frey went over to the cause of England.

Major John Frey was born in 1740 and later educated also at Cherry Valley. He married a niece of Gen. Herkimer. At the age of sixteen he joined Bradstreet's expedition, to take Fort Niagara from the French, with the rank of lieutenant. He was a justice of Tryon county, a member of the Committee of Safety and in 1776 its chairman. He was the first sheriff of Tryon county elected by the people. At Oriskany, Maj. Frey was wounded in the arm and taken a prisoner to Canada. It is said that he was in danger of being killed by his own brother, a Tory, after the battle. He held important offices and died at the age of 93.

Peter Wagner lived on what is now the Smith farm in the town of Palatine and in sight of the Fort Plain location. His stone house was fortified and called Fort Wagner during the war. He was a member of the Committee of Safety and lieutenant-colonel in the Palatine battalion at Oriskany.

Captains William Fox jr., Christopher P. Fox and Christopher W. Fox, commanded companies the first, second and third companies of the Palatine battalion. Their home was near Palatine Church. They fought at Oriskany and Christopher P. Fox was killed there.

Peter Fox of near Palatine Church, was at Oriskany where he shot an Indian. He also fought at Klock's Field, near his home.

In the Palatine district, other settlers and soldiers adjacent to Fort Plain were John Cook of Stone Arabia, who was wounded in the jaw, but escaped, at Oriskany; Johannes Schnell of Palatine, who lost all his sons at Oriskany; Philip Nellis of Palatine, who was wounded in the shoulder at Oriskany; Conrad Kilts of

Palatine, who fought at Oriskany, Johnstown and Stone Arabia, and was at Col. Brown's side when he fell; George Spraker of Sprakers, who with his four sons fought in the Revolution, and the tavern built on his place was famous as the Spraker tavern; John Wohlgemuth of Palatine, a soldier stationed for a time at Fort Plain; John Marcellus of Palatine, a minute man, who was stationed for a time at Fort Paris; Peter Loucks, first lieutenant of the third company of the Palatine battalion; Adam Loucks of Stone Arabia, at whose house was held meetings of the Committee of Safety; Isaac Paris, a member of the county committee, of Stone Arabia, who fought as a colonel under Herkimer at Oriskany and who was stripped, kicked and clubbed by the Tories and finally barbarously murdered by the Indians; County Committeemen Andrew Reber, who then occupied the Nellis property near the Fort Plain railroad station; Major John Eisenlord, who was an excellent penman and secretary of the county committee, and a man of good education and considerable wealth and who was killed at Oriskany.

Andrew Fink of Palatine was a member of the Committee of Safety. He joined the Second New York regiment under Col. Goove Van Schaick, in 1775, and was a first lieutenant in the company commanded by Capt. Christopher P. Yates. He was later promoted to a captaincy and in 1781 became a major and served under Col. Willett at Fort Plain and in the surrounding territory. In the campaign of 1778 he was with the army under the immediate command of Washington and was in the battle of Monmouth. He fought at Johnstown under Willett in 1781. George Ecker jr., a member of the Committee of Safety, lived about a mile north of Palatine Bridge.

Captain Andrew Dillenbeck of Stone Arabia was the hero of a fight at Oriskany which resulted in his death.

Jacob I. Snell of Palatine fought under Col. Brown at Stone Arabia. After that officer fell, Snell attempted to escape when he was chased by Indians, wounded in the shoulder, scalped and left to die. He revived, reached Fort Paris and eventually recovered. His oldest brother was killed in the battle.

Malachi Bauder was a soldier at Fort Paris and there kept his family for safety. One August Sunday morning he went to his home to examine the premises, taking along two of his sons, Malachi and Leonard, aged ten and twelve years. After going about the place for some time Malachi senior became drowsy and lay down in his orchard under the trees and went to sleep, the two boys meantime playing about the house. A small party of Indians stole up at the time, and seeing the boys, captured them and took them to Canada. After a time they were exchanged and shipped for home, with other prisoners, by way of Lake Champlain. At a landing Malachi strayed away and the boat left him. After a year or more his father getting trace of him left for New England, found his son and brought him back.

Dr. George Vache was without doubt, the first physician in Palatine. During the Revolution he was in the army. On one occasion he was pursued by Indians and, with his horse, swam the Mohawk three times in one night, each time being warned by a little dog which closely followed him. Dr. Younglove was a surgeon and was with Herkimer's army at Oriskany and was captured. His thrilling story is related elsewhere.

In the present Canajoharie township, in 1770, were grist mills on the Canajoharie creek, owned by Gose Van Alstine and Col. Hendrick Frey.

The present town of St. Johnsville was settled about 1725. Most of the early settlers were Germans. Among them were families named Hellebrandt, Waters, Getman, Van Riepen, Walrath and Klock. The first settlement in the present village of St. Johnsville was made in 1776 by Jacob Zimmerman, who built the first grist mill in the town soon after. As early as 1756 a Reformed church was erect-

ed in the eastern part of the town by Christian Klock. The Rev. Mr. Rosenkrantz was the first preacher and Rev. John Henry Disland, the second. Christopher Nellis kept a tavern in 1783 and a store in 1801. Capt. Jacob Klock, at whose house the Committee of Safety met, June 16, 1775, lived about a mile below the village of St. Johnsville. He was a member of the Tryon County Committee of Safety, and in September, 1775, was appointed colonel of the Second (Palatine) Battalion of the Tryon county committee, which position he held till the close of the war. Capt. Christian House was an earnest patriot of the Revolution. He lived at that time near the west line of St. Johnsville township. He converted his house into a fort and stockaded it at his own expense. He served the American cause faithfully during the war and died soon after. Capt. House was buried in an old burial plot, still in existence near the former site of Fort House, where lie the ashes of many a gallant soldier of the Revolution. Near where the East Creek depot now stands, Andrew Helmbold was surprised by Indians while plowing. He was slain, but succeeded in killing two of the savages with a paddle which he carried on his plow.

The town of Root was formerly in part a portion of the old Canajoharie district. Some of its pre-Revolutionary settlers were families by the names of Keller, Meyers, Bellinger, Tanner, Lewis and Dievendorff.

The town of Danube, now in Herkimer county, formed the extreme western part of the Revolutionary Canajoharie district and was probably settled at about the same period as the rest of the district (some time between 1720 and 1730). It is of considerable interest as it contains the residence of Gen. Herkimer and the monument to him in the adjoining family plot. Danube also was the seat of the upper Canajoharie Mohawk castle. Here a fort was built by Sir William Johnson to protect the friendly Mohawks, from French incursion, in 1755. Here a church was also built by Sir William Johnson, under the supervision it is said, of Samuel Clyde of Cherry Valley, about 1760. Joseph Brant, in his younger years, was a resident of the Mohawk Castle and an intimate acquaintance sprang up between him and Herkimer when they were young men. Old King Hendrick, the celebrated Mohawk chief, who fell fighting under Johnson at Lake George, is said to have passed his last years here. During the Revolution hostile Indians tried to steal the bell of the old Castle church, but forgot to secure the clapper and its clanging in the night aroused the German settlers, who sallied forth and recaptured it.

The town of Manheim, of Herkimer county, formed the extreme western end of the old Palatine district. Benton places its settlement at about 1755. Among the names of the pre-Revolutionary settlers are Timmerman, Schnell, Reimensnyder, Boyer, Keyser, Van Slyke, Newman, Shaver, Klacks, Adle, Garter. There were nine men of the Schnell or Snell family who went into the Oriskany battle under Herkimer. Two returned and seven were killed.

CHAPTER XI.
1777—Oriskany—Willett's Trip—Arnold's March—Enemy Flees.

In the summer of 1777 the intended invasion of the Mohawk valley by St. Leger was seasonably announced to the Tryon county authorities by Thomas Spencer, an Oneida half-breed sachem, who had learned of it in Canada on a spying expedition. He reported that there were 700 Indians and 400 British regulars at Oswego, who were to be later joined by 600 Tories, for the invasion of the valley to effect a junction with Burgoyne at Albany. For a time this startling news seemed to throw the Tryon county Whigs into a panic and many wavered in their Continental allegiance. The valley Tories remaining took on new heart and activity. The militia rangers constantly scouted the frontier and the farmers went armed

at their work. Letters of John Jay and General Schuyler at this time sternly criticise the Tryon county Whigs for their panic-stricken condition and lack of self-reliance. Schuyler wrote that he had sent Col. Van Schaick's and Col. Wesson's regiments into Tryon county and says further: "But if I may be allowed to judge of the temper of Gen. Herkimer and the committee of Tryon county, from their letters to me, nothing would satisfy them unless I march the whole army into that quarter. With deference to the better judgment of the Council of Safety, I cannot by any means think it prudent to bring on an open rupture with the savages at the present time. The inhabitants of Tryon county are already too much inclined to lay down their arms and take whatever terms the enemy may be pleased to afford them. Half the militia from this (Tryon) county and the neighboring state of Massachusetts we have been under the necessity of dismissing; but the whole should go."

In the light of the truly heroic part the Mohawk valley men played in the conflicts which followed, the opinion must prevail that Gen. Schuyler did not read aright the temper of these militia men. A few days prior to the date of this letter written from Fort Edward, July 18, 1777, the county committee had been called upon to reinforce Fort Stanwix, or Fort Schuyler, as later called. Of the 200 militia ordered to muster and garrison this post, only a part responded. They had also ordered two companies of regular troops, stationed at different points in the county under their direction, to go to Fort Schuyler. These regulars made various excuses, among them that their duties as scouts unfitted them for garrison work, but they reluctantly complied. Realizing that Tryon county must depend practically on its own men to resist this invasion, Gen. Herkimer, on July 17, 1777, issued a proclamation announcing that 2,000 "Christians and savages" had assembled at Oswego for a descent upon the Mohawk valley, and warning the entire population to be ready at a moment's notice to take the field in fighting order, the men from 16 to 60 for active service and the aged and infirm to defend the women and children at points where they might gather for safety. Those who did not voluntarily muster for service when called upon were to be brought along by force. At this time many valley men were fighting in other American armies.

The Oneida chief, Thomas Spencer, warned the committee, on July 30, that the enemy would be upon Fort Schuyler in a few days. On Aug. 2, Lieut.-Col. Mellon, of Col. Wesson's regiment, arrived at the fort with two batteaux of provisions and ammunition and a reinforcement of 200 men, both sorely needed. As the last load of supplies was hurried into the stockade, the vanguard of St. Leger's army broke from the surrounding forest.

St. Leger came down on Fort Schuyler from Oswego by way of Oneida lake and Wood creek, boating his supplies in flat boats through those waterways. His progress was considerably delayed in Wood creek by the tactics of the Americans, who had felled trees across that stream. This delay in the British advance was of vital value to Gansevoort's force at Fort Schuyler.

This advance party of the enemy was commanded by Lieut. Bird and Joseph Brant. Col. Gansevoort commanding the fort had 750 men with six weeks provisions and plenty of small arm ammunition, but not many cartridges for the cannon, there being only about nine per day for six weeks. The garrison had no flag when the enemy appeared, but a curious patchwork, conforming to the recent congressional regulations, soon waved over the fort. Shirts were cut up to form the white stripes, the red was supplied by pieces of scarlet cloth and the ground for the stars was made from a blue cloak. This is said to have been the earliest use of the stars and stripes in regular siege and battle. On Aug. 3, St. Leger arrived in front of the fort with his entire force and demanded its surrender, sending

in a pompous manifesto at the same time, both matters being treated with derision by Gansevoort and his men. Active hostilities at once began, several soldiers in the fort being killed by the enemy's gun fire on the first and second days.

At the news of St. Leger's investment of Fort Schuyler, Gen. Herkimer summoned the militia to action. Not only the militia, but most of the members of the county committee took the field. The patriots concentrated at Fort Dayton to the number of over 800. This Tryon militia was composed almost entirely of farmers, some in uniform and others in homespun and buckskin.

Molly Brant, then at the Canajoharie Castle, warned St. Leger of Herkimer's intended advance. The non-combatants, women, children, aged and infirm, were gathered in the valley forts during this movement. Forts Dayton, Herkimer, Plain, Paris, Johnstown, Hunter and the smaller posts held their quota of these defenseless ones. A few able-bodied men were probably assigned to each fort, in addition to the boys, old men and infirm, who were expected to aid in the defense. These posts were also the rendezvous of the militia of the neighborhood for the march to German Flats.

At Fort Dayton was a garrison consisting of part of Col. Wesson's Massachusetts regiment, but Herkimer left them there and set out on his march, starting on August 4. The patriot Tryon county regiment followed the road on the north side of the river, passing through the clearings, which became more and more infrequent, and plunging into the dense forests. On account of the great number of wagons which were being convoyed, the little army was strung out for a distance of two miles or more. Most of these oxcarts were loaded with supplies and provisions for Fort Schuyler. The progress of these wagons along the narrow trail was difficult and the advance of the American militia was necessarily slow. The first night's camp was made west of Staring creek, about twelve miles from Fort Dayton.

On the morning of August 5, Herkimer and his men pushed on westward until they came to the ford opposite old Fort Schuyler, where they crossed to the south bank. The American force might have continued on the north side, but this would have necessitated the transportation of all the ox-carts across the river at Fort Schuyler, in the face of the enemy, and the Tryon county general judged this too hazardous a proceeding. This ford was at the present site of Utica. Herkimer's camp on that night (August 5) extended between the Oriskany creek and Sauquoit creek, upward of two miles through the forest. It was guarded on the west by Oriskany bluff and on the east by the Mohawk river. Three scouts were sent forward to inform Col. Gansevoort of the approach of Herkimer's force. The discharge of three cannon at the fort was to be the signal of their arrival there and for Herkimer to advance upon the enemy while Gansevoort made a sortie against their camp. The scouts sent to Gansevoort by Herkimer were Helmer, Demuth and an unknown.

With the wisdom of an old frontier fighter, it was Herkimer's intention to stop at this point on the morning of August 6 and do some reconnoitering, while awaiting the expected signals.

St. Leger, aware of the patriot advance, had sent a detachment of Indians under Brant and Tories under Col. Butler and Major Watts to meet them. Herkimer's subordinates were anxious to advance before the expected signal from the fort and on the morning of August 6, became practically mutinous. His officers attacked him violently for the delay and Cols. Cox and Paris denounced him as a coward and a Tory. Calmly the general told them that he considered himself charged with the care as well as the leadership of his men and did not wish to place them in a perilous position from which it would be impossible to extricate them; he added that those who were boasting loudest

of their courage, would be first to run in the face of the enemy, and satisfied the clamor of his officious subordinates by giving the order "Vorwaert." With great shouting the undisciplined militia grasped their arms and rushed forward. Doubtless Gen. Herkimer realized that his officers and men, or a considerable part of them, would have gone on without him, and hence he gave the order to advance.

The line of march soon led into a curving ravine with a marshy bottom, traversed by a causeway of logs and earth. Along this road the patriots were rushing hastily forward when the advance guard was shot down and the forest rang with Indian yells. The enemy cut off the baggage train and the rear battalion of Col. Visscher, which was pushed back in a disorderly retreat, although Capt. Gardinier's company and some others of Visscher's men succeeded in pushing forward and joining the American main body. They were pursued and badly punished by the Indians. The 600 men left in the ravine were thrown into confusion and for a time seemed likely to be annihilated, as the slaughter was terrific. Although undisciplined and insubordinate, they were not panicstricken and soon were fighting back effectively against an enemy of more than double their number.

Early in the action Gen. Herkimer was severely wounded by a bullet which shattered one of his legs just below the knee and killed his horse. Directing his saddle to be placed against a tree, and having his wounds bound as well as possible, he lit his pipe, supported himself by his saddle and calmly directed the battle.

After an hour of fighting with the foe closing gradually in upon them, Captain Seeber, without orders, threw the remnant of his men into a circle, the better to repel the attacks of the enemy. This example was followed by other sections of Herkimer's little army, whose defense from then became so effective that it was thought necessary for a part of the Royal Greens and Butler's Rangers to make a bayonet charge. Thus old valley neighbors fought each other in this deadly hand-to-hand combat, when a heavy thunderstorm broke upon the fighters in the little ravine. The Tories drew off and there was a lull in the conflict. Herkimer's men took advantage of this to concentrate upon an advantageous piece of ground. Another piece of tactics now adopted was to place two men behind a single tree to fire alternately, thus protecting each other from the savages, who, when a marksman was alone, rushed upon him and tomahawked him as soon as he had fired and before he could reload. Meanwhile the Indians, good for nothing at the point of the bayonet and being severely punished were wavering.

The signal gun from the fort now sounded gratefully upon the ears of the grimly-fighting farmers. Col. Willett was assaulting St. Leger's camp. Here Brant tried an Indian trick of sending a company of Johnson's Greens disguised with American hats toward the patriots. Capt. Jacob Gardinier of Visscher's regiment, was the first to detect the stratagem. To Lieut. Jacob Sammons, who thought them friends, said Gardinier: "Not so; don't you see them green coats?" They were hailed by Captain Gardinier, just at which moment one of his own men, seeing a friend, as he supposed, approaching, sprang forward and offered his hand, which was grasped and he was drawn into the advancing corps a prisoner. The American struggled to free himself and Gardinier, jumping into the melee, killed the Tory captor with the blow of a spontoon. Instantly the captain was set upon by several of the enemy, one of whom he slew, and wounded another. Three of the foe now grappled with Gardinier and hurled him to

the ground and held him there while one of the "Greens" pinioned his thigh to the ground with a bayonet. Another attempted to thrust a bayonet into his chest, but he caught it and jerked its owner down upon his body where he held him as a protection, until Adam Miller, one of his own men, came to his rescue and, with his clubbed musket, brained one of the assailants who was holding down the fighting captain. The other two now turned upon Miller, when Gardinier, partly rising, snatched up his spear and killed one of them, who proved to be Captain McDonald of Johnson's Greens, who is believed to have been the invader of the Schoharie settlements a short time before. In one of these terrible hand-to-hand fights, Captain Watts was fearfully wounded and taken prisoner, and Captains Hare and Wilson of Johnson's Greens were killed.

The enemy being thus unmasked, a bloody fight at close quarters ensued. Bayonets, clubbed guns, swords, pistols, tomahawks, war clubs, spears and knives were used with murderous effeet. In this fierce melee the valley farmers had the advantage and killed and beat back their enemies. until the Indians sounded their call of retreat, "Oonah, oonah," and slunk back into the forest. Thus deserted, the Tories fled, leaving the field in the possession of the Tryon county militia, whom a miracle had saved from extermination. During the six hours of conflict nearly 200 Americans had been killed. The wooded glen was littered with hundreds of wounded, dead and dying of both forces. The loss of the enemy was about 200, including 100 Indians.

The enemy precipitately retired from the field and left the provincials master of it at about 3 o'clock in the afternoon. The decimated battalions were, by their surviving commanders as far as practicable, hastily reorganized. The wounded, having been placed upon rude litters, the troops took up their mournful retrograde march, and encamped that night on the site of old Fort Schuyler (now Utica), eight miles from the battlefield. From this point, Gen. Herkimer and Capt. Jacob Seeber and possibly one or two others of the wounded, were taken down the river in a boat to Fort Herkimer. At this place, Capt. Seeber was left with a broken leg, which was amputated and he bled to death. Gen. Herkimer was taken to his home below Little Falls—probably in a boat to the head of the rapid— and died there ten days later. It is stated that Lieut.-Col. Campbell and Major Clyde brought off the shattered troops.

———

Colonel Willett, on the way down the valley to obtain relief from Gen. Schuyler for the fort bearing his name, wrote a letter concerning the siege by St. Leger and Willett's sortie. It was published in the Connecticut Courant, August 27, 1777, and is in part as follows:

"On Saturday evening, Aug. 2d, five battoes arrived with stores for the garrison. About the same time, we discovered a number of fires, a little better than a mile from the northwest of the fort. The stores were all got safe in, and the troops which were a guard to the batteaux marched up. [This was part of a Massachusetts regiment under Lieut. Col. Mellon from Fort Dayton.] The Captain of the bateaux and a few of his men, delaying their time about the boats, were fired on by a party of Indians, which killed one man and wounded two, the Captain himself was taken prisoner.

"Next morning the enemy appeared in the edge of the woods about a mile below the fort, where they took post, in order to invest it upon that quarter and to cut off the communication with the country from whence they sent in a flag, who told us of their great power, strength and determination, in such a manner as gave us reason to suppose they were not possessed of strength to take the fort. Our answer was, our determination to support it.

"All day on Monday, we were much annoyed by a sharp fire of musketry from the Indians and German riflemen as our men were obliged to be exposed on the works, killed one man and wounded seven. The day after, the firing was not so heavy, and our men were under better cover; all the damage was one man killed by a rifle ball. This evening [Tuesday, Aug. 5], indicated something in contemplation by the enemy. The Indians were uncommouly noisy, they made most horrid yellings great part of the evening in the woods, hardly a mile from the fort. A few cannon shot were fired among them.

[The batteaux guard, which brought into Fort Schuyler, the five boatloads of supplies were part of Col. Wesson's Massachusetts regiment from Fort Dayton, under command of Lieut. Col. Mellon. The German riflemen, referred to, composed a company of St. Leger's very mixed force of British valley Tories, Indians and these Germans.]

"Wednesday morning there was an unusual silence. We discovered some of the enemy marching along the edge of the woods downwards. About 11 o'clock three men got into the fort, who brought a letter from Gen. Herkimer of the Tryon County militia, advising us that he was at Eriska [Oriskany], eight miles off, with a part of his militia and purposed to force his way to the fort for our relief. In order to render him what service we could, it was agreed that I should make a sally from the fort with 250 men, consisting of one-half Gansevoort's and one-half Massachusetts ditto, and one field piece—an iron three pounder.

"The men were instantly paraded and I ordered the following disposition to be made. [Here follows the arrangement of his troops and plan of march.] Nothing could be more fortunate than this enterprise. We totally routed two of the enemy's encampments, destroyed all the provisions that were in them, brought off upwards of 50 brass kettles and more than 100 blankets. [two articles which were much needed.] With a quantity of muskets, tomahawks, spears, ammunition, clothing, deerskins, a variety of Indian affairs and five colors—the whole of which, on our return to the fort, were displayed on our flag-staff under the Continental flag. The Indians took chiefly to the woods, the rest of the troops then at the posts, to the river. The number of men lost by the enemy is uncertain, six lay dead in their encampment, two of which were Indians; several scattered about in the woods; but their greatest loss appeared to be in crossing the river, and no inconsiderable number upon the opposite shore. I was happy in preventing the men from scalping even the Indians, being desirous, if possible, to teach Indians humanity; but the men were much better employed, and kept in excellent order. We were out so long that a number of British regulars, accompanied by what Indians, etc., could be rallied, had marched down to a thicket on the other side of the river, about 50 yards from the road we were to cross on our return. Near this place I had ordered the field piece. The ambush was not quite formed when we discovered them, and gave them a well-directed fire. Here, especially, Maj. Bedlow with his field piece, did considerable execution. Here, also, the enemy were annoyed by a fire of several cannon from the fort, as they marched round to form the ambuscade. The enemy's fire was very wild, and although we were much exposed, did no execution at all. We brought in four prisoners, three of whom were wounded. * * * From these prisoners we received the first accounts of Gen. Herkimer's militia being ambuscaded on their march, and of the severe battle they had with them about two hours before, which gave us reason to think they had, for the present, given up their design of marching to the fort. I should not do justice to the officers and soldiers who were with me on this enterprise, if I was not, in most positive terms, to assure their countrymen that they, in general, behaved with the greatest gallantry on this occasion; and, next to the very kind and signal interposition of Divine Providence, which was powerfully manifested in their favor, it was undoubtedly owing to that noble intrepidity which discovered itself in this attack, and struck the enemy with such a panic as disenabled them from taking pains to direct their fire, that we had not one man killed or wounded. The officers, in general, behaved so well that it is hardly right to mention the names of any particular ones for their singular valor. But, so remarkably intrepid was Capt. Van Benscoten [he commanded the advance guard of 30 men] and so rapid was his attack, that it demands from me this testimony of his extraordinary spirit."

Among the effects taken from the enemy's camp were several bundles of papers and letters, which had been taken from Gen. Herkimer's baggage wagons a few hours before, not yet opened, one of which was for Col. Willett. There were also papers of Sir John Johnson, St. Leger and other officers of the enemy's camp, some of which were of service. Willett writes further: "That evening (August 8) it was agreed by the field officers that I should undertake with Lieut. Stockwell—who is a good woodsman—to endeavor to get down into the country and procure such force as would extirpate the miscreant band. After a severe march, of about 50 miles, through the wilderness, we in safety arrived at this place" (supposed to mean Fort Dayton, but as Fort Plain is 50 miles from Fort Schuyler, it may be that this letter was written from the local fort). This was a heroic and hazardous enterprise and resulted in bringing up Arnold's force.

From the day of Oriskany until the enemy reached Oswego on their retreat a number of American prisoners were barbarously beaten and murdered by Tories and Indians. Col. Paris of Palatine and Robert Crouse of Minden were among these. Some of these victims were eaten by the Indians.

A letter of Col. Claus shows the desire of the Tryon county Tories to murder and pilfer the homes of their old neighbors after the battle: "Sir

John Johnson proposed (while siege of Fort Schuyler was still being prosecuted) to march down the country with about 200 men, and I intended joining him with a sufficient body of Indians, but the Brigadier (St. Leger) said he could not spare the men, and disapproved of it. The inhabitants in general were ready (as we afterward learned) to submit and come in. A flag was sent to invite the inhabitants to submit and be forgiven, and assurance given to prevent the Indians from being outrageous; but the commanding officers of the German Flats (Fort Dayton) hearing of it seized the flag, consisting of Ensign Butler of the Eighth Regiment, ten soldiers and three Indians, and took them up as spies. A few days after, Gen. Arnold, coming with some cannon and a reinforcement, made the inhabitants return to their obedience." Simms says Claus's opinion that the Tryon county settlers were ready to submit was a delusion.

St. Leger now made new demands for surrender on Gansevoort, who was ignorant of the result of the effort of Herkimer's men, but who replied that he would defend the fort to the last extremity. Siege operations were renewed with increasing vigor but the British artillery was too light to be effective. It was feared the garrison might be starved into a surrender if not relieved, and accordingly on the night of the 10th of August, Col. Willett and Maj. Stockwell set out to pass the enemy's lines and rally the support of the county militia with whom Willett was deservedly popular. Reaching Stillwater after a most perilous journey, Col. Willett induced Gen. Schuyler to send Gen. Arnold with a Massachusetts regiment of 800 men for the relief of Fort Schuyler. The force set out the next day, accompanied by Col. Willett, and reached Fort Dayton where it waited for the militia to assemble, which they did in considerable numbers, considering their recent losses at Oriskany.

St. Leger issued manifestos to the people of Tryon county signed by Sir John Johnson and Cols. Butler and Claus, in which he hoped by threats of Indian barbarities to induce Col. Gansevoort to surrender. In trying to circulate this document down the valley, Walter Butler was arrested by Wesson near Fort Dayton, tried as a spy before Gen. Arnold, and convicted but was saved from death by the intercession of American officers who knew him. Butler was sent to Albany and imprisoned. Gen. Arnold issued a stirring proclamation calculated to neutralize the effect of the Tory manifesto in the valley.

The address issued by Arnold at Fort Dayton, to counteract the Tory proclamation, was well calculated to awe the timid and give courage to the wavering Whigs. The prestige of his name gave great weight to it. He prefaced it with a flourish of his title and position as follows: "By the Honorable Benedict Arnold, Esq., general and commander-in-chief of the army of the United States of America on the Mohawk River."

He denounced a certain Barry St. Leger "a leader of a banditti of robbers, murderers and traitors, composed of savages of America and more savage Britons," and denounced him as a seducer of the ignorant and unthinking from the cause of freedom, and as threatening ruin and destruction to the people. He then offered a free pardon to all who had joined him or upheld him, "whether savages, Germans, Americans or Britons" provided they laid down their arms and made oath of allegiance to the United States within three days. But if they persisted in their "wicked courses" and "were determined to draw on themselves the just vengeance of Heaven and their exasperated country, they must expect no mercy from either."

St. Leger ran forward his trenches to within 150 yards of the fort, but the accurate firing of the garrison prevented a nearer approach. His weak artillery had little effect. The defenders, utterly ignorant of any relief approaching, began to be apprehensive and some suggested surrender. Gansevoort stoutly maintained he would defend the fort to the last extremity and would then try to cut his way out at night. This proved unnecessary as, on the 22d of August, to the surprise and mystification of the fort's defenders, the enemy suddenly broke camp and vanished.

This was the result of the celebrated ruse adopted by Arnold who had captured an eccentric Tory supposed to be half-witted, in company with Butler. His name was Han Yost Schuyler and his sentence of death was remitted if he should carry out Arnold's instructions. Schuyler's brother was retained as hostage for his behavior. Bullets were fired through Schuyler's coat and he was sent on his mission, while arrangements were made with an Oneida Indian to reach St. Leger at the same time. Both arrived at short intervals and told an extravagant story of the force on the way to raise the siege. When questioned closely as to the numbers of the provincials marching up the valley the tale-bearers merely pointed to the leaves on the trees. The effect of this story upon the Tory force and particularly upon the Indians can be imagined after the losses they had suffered. The retreat, to Oneida lake and Oswego, was begun at once and, disgusted by the conduct of the campaign, the Indians stripped, robbed and even murdered their late allies. Schuyler next day deserted from the retreating enemy, and returned to Fort Schuyler where he told his story and was received with lively demonstrations of joy. Gansevoort sent a party after the flying enemy, which returned with a number of prisoners, a large quantity of spoil, and St. Leger's desk and private papers.

General Arnold sent out from Fort Dayton to Fort Schuyler, after Schuyler's departure, a force of 900 soldiers. At the Oriskany battleground they were compelled to make a wide detour on account of the terrible stench from the battlefield. Many gruesome sights came to the soldiers' notice, mention of which is added later. Burials of the bodies had been contemplated but could not be carried out, as the officers feared for the health of the soldiers. At Fort Schuyler, Arnold's arrival was greeted with a military salute and great cheering and demonstrations on the part of the garrison. In all probability, had the enemy not run, they would have been soundly beaten by Arnold's and Gansevoort's men, cut up and disheartened as the British force was by their encounter with Herkimer and his Mohawk valley men at Oriskany. Arnold's force undoubtedly contained several hundred of the Tryon county militia who had fought on that famous field two weeks before. Gen. Arnold and his regiment shortly thereafter turned back and marched down the valley to Cohoes where he joined the American army gathered to oppose Burgoyne at the mouth of the Mohawk. His intrepid valor and immense aid, in the subsequent battles of Stillwater, which wiped out the British army, are well known.

Whether the action of Herkimer and his men at Oriskany is regarded as an actual defeat, a drawn battle or a practical victory, nevertheless the successful defense of Fort Schuyler was one of the causes which contributed to Burgoyne's defeat at Saratoga. It is to be doubted whether the St. Leger force would have been intimidated so easily had not they suffered severely at the hands of the Tryon county militia. In all the word story of armed conflict there is no more desperate or heroic fight recorded than that in the wooded glen of Oriskany.

In the valley homes was great mourning For such a small population, the losses were almost overwhelming. In some families the male members were almost or even entirely wiped out in some instances. It was many a long weary year before the sorrow and suffering caused by the sacrifices at Oriskany had been forgotten in the valley of the Mohawk.

In closing the Oriskany campaign the following letter from the chairman of the committee to the Albany committee, written three days after the battle, will be found of interest:

German Flats Committee Chamber.
August 9, 1777.

Gentlemen: Just arrived Capt. Demuth and John Adam Helmer, the bearer hereof, with an account that they arrived with some difficulty at Fort Schuyler, the 6th of the month, being sent there by Gen. Herkimer. Before he set out for the field of battle, he requested some assistance from the fort in order to make an effort to facilitate our march on the fort. Two hundred and six men were granted. They made a sally, encountered the enemy, killed many, destroyed the tents of the enemy and came off victorious to the fort. The commander (of the fort) desired them to acquaint us, and his superiors, that he is wanting assistance, and thinks to stand out so long that timely ass'stance could come to his relief.

Concerning the battle: On our side, all accounts agreed, that a number of the enemy is killed; the flower of our militia either killed or wounded, except 150, who stood the field and forced the enemy to retreat; the wounded were brought off by those brave men; the dead they left on the field for want of proper support. We will not take upon us to tell of the behavior of the rear. So far as we know, they took to flight the first firing. Gen. Herkimer is wounded; Col. Cox seemingly killed, and a great many officers are among the slain. We are surrounded by Tories, a party of 100 of whom are now on their march through the woods. We refer you for further information to the bearer. Major Watts of the enemy is killed. Joseph Brant, William Johnson, several Tories and a number of Indians.

Gentlemen, we pray you will send us succor. By the death of most part of our committee officers, the field officers and General being wounded, everything is out of order; the people entirely dispirited; our county as Esopus unrepresented, so that we can not hope to stand it any longer without your aid; we will not mention the shocking aspect our fields do show. Faithful to our country, we remain

Your sorrowful brethren,
The few members of this committee.
Peter J. Dygert, Chairman.

To the Chairman of the Committee of Albany.

Dygert was in error as to the death of Brant and also as to the march of the 100 Tories. Probably many rumors were rife in the valley immediately after Oriskany.

William Johnson was a half-breed Mohawk and a reputed son of Sir William Johnson.

CHAPTER XII.

1777—A Contemporary Account of the Battle at Oriskany—Lossing on Willett's Journey to Schuyler for Aid—The Oriskany Roster.

A contemporary account of the Oriskany battle is appended. This was published in the Pennsylvania Even ing Post, Aug. 19 and 21, 1777, and is reprinted from that very interesting volume, "Diary of the American Revolution:"

"Aug. 7:—Yesterday, about nine o'clock, an engagement ensued between a part of the militia of Tryon county, under the command of General Herkimer, and a party of savages, Tories and regulars, a short distance from Fort Stanwix [Fort Schuyler]. It lasted till three o'clock in the afternoon, when the British thought proper to retire, leaving General Herkimer master of the field. Unluckily, however, the General and some valuable officers got wounded or killed in the beginning.. But this did in nowise intimidate the ardor of the men, and the general, although he had two wounds, did not leave the field till the action was over. He seated himself on a log, with his sword drawn, animating his men.

"About one o'clock, Colonel Gansevoort having received information of General Herkimer's march, sent out Lieutenant-Colonel Willett, with two hundred men, to attack an encampment of the British, and thereby facilitate General Herkimer's march. In this the colonel succeeded, for after an engagement of an hour he had completely routed the enemy and taken one captain and four privates. The baggage taken was very considerable, such as money, bear skins, officers' baggage and camp equipage; one of the soldiers had for his share a scarlet coat, trimmed with gold lace to the full, and three laced hats. When Colonel Willett returned to the fort, he discovered two hundred regulars in full march to attack him. He immediately ordered his men to prepare for battle, and, having a field piece with him, Captain Savage so directed its fire as to play in concert with one out of the fort; these, with a brisk fire from his small arms, soon made these heroes scamper off with great loss. Colonel Willett then marched with his booty into the fort, having not a single man killed or wounded.

"General St. Leger, who commands the enemy's force in that quarter, soon after sent in a flag to demand the delivery of the fort, offering that the garrison should march out with their baggage, and not be molested by the savages; that, if this was not complied with, he would not answer for the conduct of the Indians, if the garrison fell into their hands; that General Burgoyne was in possession of Albany. Colonel Gansevoort, after animadverting on the barbarity and disgraceful conduct of the British officers, in suffering women and children to be butchered as they had done, informed the flag that he was resolved to defend the fort to the last, and that he would never give it up so long as there was a man left to defend it."

———

Lossing's "Field Book of the Revolution" says of the heroic expedition of Willett and Stockwell to get aid for Fort Schuyler:

"Meanwhile the people in the Mohawk valley were in the greatest consternation. St. Leger had arrived from Oswego and was besieging Fort Schuyler, while the Tories and Indians were spreading death and desolation on every hand. Colonel Gansevoort, with a handful of men, was closely shut up in the fort. General Herkimer, with the brave militia of Tryon county, had been defeated at Oriskany, and the people below hourly expected the flood of destroyers to pour down upon them. It was a fearful emergency. Without aid all would be lost. Brave hearts were ready for bold deeds. * * * * * Colonel Willett volunteered to be the messenger, and on a very stormy night, when shower after shower came down furiously, he and Lieutenant Stockwell left the fort, by the sally port, at ten o'clock, each armed with a spear, and

crept upon their hands and knees along a morass to the river. They crossed it upon a log and were soon beyond the line of drowsy sentinels. It was very dark, their pathway was in a thick and tangled wood, and they soon lost their way. The barking of a dog apprised them of their proximity to an Indian camp, and for hours they stood still, fearing to advance or retreat. The clouds broke away toward dawn and the morning star in the east. like the light of hope, revealed to them their desired course. They then pushed on in a zig zag way, and, like the Indians, sometimes traversed the bed of a stream to foil pursuers that might be upon their trail. They reached German Flatts in safety and, mounting fleet horses, hurried down the valley to the headquarters of General Schuyler who had already heard of the defeat of Herkimer and was devising means for the succor of the garrison at Fort Schuyler.

"The American army of the north, then at Stillwater, was in wretched condition and in no shape to offer battle to the advancing forces under Burgoyne. Its commander, Schuyler, ordered a retreat to the Mohawk, and it was during this movement, while the Americans were retiring slowly down the Hudson, that Willett and Stockwell came, asking aid, to the headquarters at Stillwater.

"Not a moment was to be lost. The subjugation of the whole valley would inevitably follow the surrender of Fort Schuyler and, the victors gaining strength, would fall like an avalanche upon Albany, or, by junction, swell the approaching army of Burgoyne. The prudent foresight and far-reaching humanity of General Schuyler at once dictated his course. He called a council and proposed sending a detachment immediately to the relief of Fort Schuyler. His officers opposed him with the plea that his whole force was not then sufficient to stay the oncoming of Burgoyne. The clearer judgment of Schuyler made him persist in his opinion, and he earnestly sought them to agree with him. While pacing the floor in anxious solicitude,

he overheard the half-whispered remark, 'He means to weaken the
army.' Wheeling suddenly toward the
slanderer and those around him, and
unconsciously biting into several
pieces a pipe he was smoking, he in-
dignantly exclaimed, 'Gentlemen, I
shall take the responsibility upon myself; where is the brigadier that will
take command of the relief? I shall
beat up for volunteers tomorrow.' The
brave and impulsive Arnold, ever
ready for deeds of daring, at once
stepped forward and offered his services. The next morning the drum
beat and eight hundred stalwart men
were enrolled for the service before
meridian. Fort Schuyler was saved
and the forces of St. Leger were scattered to the winds."

Subsequently Schuyler retreated to
the Mohawk and fortified Van
Schaick's and Haver's island at the
mouth of that stream where it empties
into the Hudson. Schuyler ordered
the grain in his own fields at Saratoga
to be burned, in his retreat, to prevent
the enemy reaping it. The following
is taken from Lossing:

"That seemed to be the most eligible point [the islands at the Mohawk's
mouth] at which to make a stand in
defense of Albany against the approaches of the enemy from the north
and from the west. At that time there
were no bridges across the Hudson
or the Mohawk, and both streams
were too deep to be fordable except
in seasons of extreme drought. There
was a ferry across the Mohawk, five
miles above the falls (defended by the
left wing under Gen. Arnold), and
another across the Hudson at Half
Moon Point or Waterford. The
'sprouts' of the Mohawk, between the
islands, were usually fordable; and as
Burgoyne would not, of course, cross
the Hudson or attempt the ferry upon
the Mohawk, where a few resolute
men could successfully oppose him,
his path was of necessity directly
across the mouth of the river. Fortifications were accordingly thrown up
on the islands and upon the mainland,
faint traces of which are still visible."

Aug. 6, 1777, occurred the battle of
Oriskany. On Aug. 22, St. Leger and
his force fled from before Fort Schuyler. Aug. 16, the New Hampshire
militia, under Stark, beat the enemy
at Bennington. Gen. Schuyler's army
of the north began to be greatly reinforced about this time when Gen.
Gates superseded him. On Sep. 19 occurred the first battle of Stillwater,
which was a virtual defeat for the
British. On Oct. 7, 1777, Burgoyne was
decisively beaten and started to fall
back. Oct. 17, the British army surrendered to the American force. Over
2,000 of the 6,000 captives were German mercenaries.

Burgoyne's surrender is said to have
been somewhat hastened by an American cannon ball which crossed his
breakfast table during a council of the
British officers.

―――――

Benedict Arnold was born in Nor
wich, Conn., in 1740, a descendant of
Benedict Arnold, one of Rhode Island's
early governors. From 1763 to 1767
he kept a drug and book store in New
Haven. At the outbreak of the Revolution he was in command of a volunteer company of that city and marched
to Cambridge with it. He was in many
of the stirring events of the war, up
to his treason in 1780. Among his
greatest services were his gallant
leadership at Saratoga and his clever
conduct of the relief of Fort Schuyler. He held commands in the
British army during the latter part of
the war and at its end went to England. From 1786 to 1793 he was in
business at St. Johns, N. B., where he
was so dishonest in his dealings that
he was hung in effigy by a mob. He
died in London in 1804, aged 63 years.

―――――

Col. Peter Gansevoort, the intrepid
commander of Fort Schuyler, was a
Revolutionary patriot and soldier
of the highest type and he deserves a niche in the hall of fame
dedicated to the heroes of the Revolution. Gansevoort was born in Albany,
July 17, 1749. He accompanied Montgomery into Canada in 1775, with the
rank of major, and the next year he
was appointed a colonel in the New

York line, which commission he held when he defended Fort Schuyler against St. Leger. For his gallant defense of that post he received the thanks of congress, and in 1781 was promoted to the rank of brigadier-general by the state of New York. After the war he was for many years a military agent. He held several offices of trust and "was always esteemed for his bravery and judgment as a soldier and for his fidelity, intelligence, and probity as a citizen." He died July 2, 1812, aged 62 years.

Of the 800 or more who constituted the patriot army at Oriskany only the following soldiers are recorded. Some of these are known also to have come from certain Tryon county sections, and wherever this is verified, it is given. The word, Mohawk, refers to the present town of Montgomery county. The letter K appended stands for killed; W for wounded; P for prisoner. Following is the "Oriskany roster:"

Abram, Arndt, Minden
Alter, Jacob, Minden
K. Ayer, Frederick, Schuyler
Bellinger, Col. Peter, German Flats
P. Bellinger, Lieut. Col. Frederick, German Flats
Bell, Capt. Geo. Henry, Fall Hill
K. Bell, Joseph, Fall Hill
K. Bell, Nicholas, Fall Hill
W. Bigbread, Capt. John, Palatine
Bauder, Melchert, Palatine
Boyer, John, Remesnyderbush
K. Bowman, Capt. Jacob, Canajoharie
P. Blauvelt, Maj. (supposed murdered), Mohawk
Bellinger, Adam
K. Bliven, Maj. John, Florida, Mohawk committee
Bellinger, John
K. Billington, Samuel, Palatine Committee of Safety
Billington, ——, Palatine
Bargy, Peter, Frankfort
K. Cox, Col. Ebenezer, Danube, Canajoharie committee
Campbell, Lieut. Col. Samuel, Cherry Valley, Canajoharie committee
Clyde, Maj. Samuel, Cherry Valley, Canajoharie committee
Copeman, Capt. Abram, Canajoharie
Covenhoven (now Conover), Isaac, Glen
Casler, Jacob, Minden
Casler, John, Minden
Casler, Adam, Minden

Clock, John I., St. Johnsville
W. Cook, John, Palatine
Coppernoll, Richard, Minden
Cox, William, Minden
K. Crouse, Robert, Minden
Crouse, George, Minden
Clemens, Jacob, Schuyler
W. Conover, Peter
K. Cunningham, Andrew, Amsterdam
Collier, Jacob, Florida
K. Campbell, Lieut. Robert, Cherry Valley
K. Dievendorf, Capt. Henry. Minden
K. Dillenbeck, Capt. Andrew, Palatine
K. Davis, Capt. John James, Mohawk
K. Davis, Martinus, Mohawk
Dievendorf, John, Minden
Dunckel, Francis, Freysbush
Dygert, Peter, Palatine
Dunckel, Hon. (John) Peter, Minden
Dunckel, Hon. Garret, Minden
Dunckel, Hon. Nicholas, Minden
K. Davis, Benjamin, Mohawk
Dockstader, John, German Flats
K. Davy, Capt. Thomas, Springfield
K. Dygert, John, Palatine Committee of Safety
Dygert, Capt. William, German Flats
Demuth, Capt. Marx, Deerfield
DeGraff, Nicholas, Amsterdam
Degraff, Capt. Immanuel, Amsterdam
Dygert, Peter S., German Flats
Dygert, George, German Flats
Dorn, Peter, Johnstown
K. Eisenlord, Maj. John, Palatine (secretary county committee)
Empie, Jacob, Palatine
Ehle, William, Palatine
P. Ehle, Peter
Eysler, John, Remesnyderbush
W. & P. Frey, Maj. John, Palatine Palatine committee
K. Fox, Capt. Christopher P., Palatine
W. Fox, Capt. Christopher W., Palatine, Palatine committee
Fox, Peter, Palatine
Fox, William, Palatine
Fox, Charles, Palatine
Fox, Christopher, Palatine
W. Folts, Conrad, Herkimer
K. Failing, Jacob, Canajoharie
W. Failing, Henry, Canajoharie
Failing, Henry N., Canajoharie
Fralick. Valentine, Palatine
Fonda, Jelles, Mohawk
Fonda, Adam, Mohawk, Mohawk committee
Frank, Adam
Gardinier, Capt. Jacob, Glen
W. Gardinier, Lieut. Samuel, Glen
W. & K. Grant, Lieut. Petrus, Amsterdam
Geortner, Peter, Minden
Geortner, George, Canajoharie
K. Gray, Nicholas, Palatine
Gray, Lieut. Samuel, Herkimer
K. Graves, Capt. ——,
Gremps, John (15 years old), Palatine
Gros, Capt. Lawrence, Minden.

Gray, Silas, Florida
W. Groot, Lieut. Petrus, Amsterdam
Harter, Henry, German Flats
K. Herkimer, Gen. Nicholas, Danube, member Canajoharie committee
Herkimer, Capt. George, Fort Herkimer, member German Flats committee
K. Helmer, Capt. Frederick, German Flats, German Flats committee
Helmer, John Adam, German Flats [Sent to fort by Gen. Herkimer]
House, Lieut. John Joseph, Minden
K. Hunt, Lieut. Abel (supposed), Florida
Huffnail, Christian
K. Hawn, Conrad, Herkimer
K. Hiller, ——, Fairfield [shot from a tree-top]
Huyck, John, Palatine
Hand, Marcus, Florida
Hall, William, Glen
Hill, Nicholas
Klock, Jacob I., Palatine
K. Klepsaddle, Maj. Enos, German Flats
Kilts, Conrad, Palatine
Kilts, Peter, Palatine
Keller, Andrew, Palatine
Keller, Jacob, Palatine
Keller, Solomon, Palatine
Klock, John, St. Johnsville
Klock, Col. Jacob G., St. Johnsville, member Palatine committee
Klepsaddle, Jacob, German Flats
Loucks, Lieut. Peter, Palatine
Lintner, George, Minden
Lighthall, ——, Palatine
Longshore, Solomon, Canajoharie
Louns, Henry, Canajoharie
P. Lighthall, Francis, Ephratah
Louis, Col., a St. Regis Indian with Oneidas. [He held a Lieutenant's commission, and was usually called Colonel.]
K. Moyer, Jacob, Fairfield [found with his throat cut.]
Miller, Adam, Glen
Miller, Jelles, Minden
Miller, John P., Minden
Miller, Henry, Minden
Murray, David, Florida
McMaster, Lieut. David, Florida
K. Markell, Jacob, Springfield
K. Merckley, William, Palatine
Myers, Jacob, German Flats
Myers, Joseph, Herkimer
Mowers, Conrad, supposed Danube
Mowers, ——
Mowers, ——, brothers
W. Nellis, Philip, Palatine
Nellis, Christian, Palatine
Nellis, John D., Palatine
Nestell, Peter, Palatine
Newkirk, John, Florida
Newkirk, Garret, son of John, Florida
K. Paris, Hon. Isaac (murdered), Palatine Committee of Safety
K. Paris, Peter, son of Isaac, Palatine
Petry, Dr. William, Fort Herkimer Committee of Safety

K. Pettingill, ——, Mohawk
K. Petry, Lieut. Dederick Marcus, German Flats, German Flats committee
Petry, John Marks, German Flats
K. Pettingall, ——, town of Mohawk
Putman, Ensign Richard, Johnstown
K. Putman, Martinus, Johnstown
K. Phillips, Cornelius, Florida
W. Price, Adam, Canajoharie
Pickard, Nicholas, Canajoharie
K. Petry, John, Herkimer, German Flats committee
W. Petry, Joseph, Herkimer
K. Petry, Lieut. Han Yost, Herkimer
Pritchard, Nicholas, Minden
Quackenbush, Lieut. Abm. D., Glen
W. Rechtor, Capt. Nicholas, Ephratah
W. Radnour, Jacob, Minden
Rother, John, Minden
K. Raysnor, George, Minden
Roof, Johannes, Fort Stanwix; afterwards captain of exempts at Canajoharie
Roof, John, a son (Col. of militia after the war)
Rasbach, Marx, Kingsland
Ritter, ——, Fairfield. Suffrenus Casselman, a tory, boasted of having cut Ritter's throat.
Sammons, Sampson, Mohawk Committee of Safety
Sammons, Jacob, Mohawk
Shoemaker, Rudolph, Canajoharie
Scholl, Ensign John Yost, Ephratah
Sitts, Peter, Palatine
K. Sharrar, Christian, Herkimer
K. Sharrar, ——, a school teacher, Remesnyderbush
Staring, Hendrick, Schuyler
Shoemaker, Thomas, Herkimer
Siebert, Rudolph
Shults, George, Stone Arabia
Shaull, Henry, Herkimer
Shimmel, ——, Herkimer
Sanders, Henry, Minden
W. Shafer, William
K. Seeber, Major William H., Minden, Canajoharie district committee
K. Seeber, Capt. Jacob, Minden
K. Seeber, Suffrenus, Canajoharie
K. Seeber, Audolph, sons of William S., Minden
K. Seeber, James, Canajoharie
W. Seeber, Henry, Canajoharie
Seeber, Lieut. John, Canajoharie
K. Spencer, Henry (interpreter), an Oneida
Schell, Christian, Schellsbush
Smith, George, Palatine
Smith, Henry,
Swarts, Lieut. Jeremiah, Mohawk
Sillenbeck, John G.
Shults, John, Palatine
Shults, George, Stone Arabia
Sommer, Peter
Stowitts, Philip G. P., Root
K. Snell, Joseph, Snellsbush (now Manheim)
K. Snell, Jacob, Snellsbush
K. Snell, Frederick, Snellsbush

K. Snell, Suffrenus, Snellsbush
Snell, Peter, Snellsbush
Snell, George, Snellsbush
K. Snell, John, Stone Arabia
K. Snell, John, Jun., a fifer, Stone
Arabia
K. Snell, Jacob, a committee man,
Stone Arabia
P. Sponable, John, Palatine
Thum, Adam, St. Johnsville
Thompson, Henry, Glen
Timmerman, Jacob, St. Johnsville
W. Timmerman, Lieut. Henry, St.
Johnsville
Timmerman, Conrad, St. Johns-
ville
Visscher, Capt. John, Mohawk
W. Visscher, Col. Frederick, Mohawk,
Mohawk committee
Van Alstyne, Martin C., Canajo-
harie
Van Deusen, George, Canajoharie
Vedder, Henry
W. Vols, Conrad, German Flats
Vols, Lieut. Jacob, German Flats
K. Van Slyke, Maj. Harmanus,
Palatine, Palatine committee
K. Van Slyke, Nicholas, a fifer,
Palatine
Van Horne, Cornelius, Florida
Van Horne, Henry, Florida
Van Slyke, ——, Canajoharie
K. Van Antwerp, John, Glen
Wagner, Lieut. Col. Peter, Palatine,
Palatine committee
Wormuth, ——, Palatine
Wagner, Lieut. Peter, Palatine
W. Wagner, George, Palatine
Wagner, John, Palatine (sons of
Lieut. Col. Peter Wagner)
Wagner, Jacob, Minden
Wagner, John, Canajoharie
P. Walrath, Garret, Minden
W. Walter, George, Palatine
K. Westerman, Peter, Minden
K. Wohlever, John, Fort Herkimer
Wohlever, Richard, Fort Herkimer
Wohlever, Peter Fort Herkimer
Wohlever, Abram, Fort Herkimer
P. Walrath, Lieut. Henry, Herkimer
Weaver, Jacob, German Flats
Weaver, Peter James, German Flats
Widrick, Michael, Schuyler
K. Wrenkle, Lawrence, Fort Herkimer
Walrath, Jacob, Palatine
P. Walrath, Henry, Herkimer
Yates, Capt. Robert, supposed
Root
W. Yerdon, Nicholas, supposed Minden
P. Younglove, Moses, surgeon, Stone
Arabia
P. Youker, Jacob, Oppenheim
W. Zimmerman, Henry, St. Johnsville

This list of names indicates that Herkimer's regiment was composed three-quarters of German farmers, with some Dutch from the eastern part of the county, while the balance of one-quarter consisted of men with Scotch, Irish, English, Welsh, Swiss and names of indeterminate nationality. The foregoing roster contains 256 names, the largest list yet published and gives the identity of a little less than one-third of the Tryon militia of Oriskany. Further research would probably add more men to this record. The homes of 225 of the 256 are given. Of these 225, the Palatine district furnished 71 and the Canajoharie 66—137 combined. This great proportion of the regiment from this midsection of the valley may be due largely to the fact that more effort has been made to identify the men of Oriskany hereabouts, particularly by Simms. Of the five western Montgomery towns, Palatine furnishes to this list 55, Minden 35, Canajoharie 21, St. Johnsville 8, Root 2, a total of 119. At least 20 of the patriots were members of the Tryon County Committee of Safety.

The loss of the American force at Oriskany is variously stated by writers of the period. One account gives it as 160 killed and another as 160 killed and wounded. Whatever it was it was large for the force engaged, and the loss of the enemy at Oriskany and during Willett's sortie was fully as great as that of the provincials.

Assuming the patriot force, which set out from Fort Dayton for Oriskany, to have numbered 850 men, the roster here published comprises about two-sevenths of this valley regiment. This list, out of 256 names, has 63 killed, 24 wounded and 11 prisoners. The same proportion carried out would make the Oriskany losses 224 killed, 84 wounded and 37 prisoners. This probably is not accurate as to deaths, as more names of killed soldiers were probably remembered and recorded and put on the roster than of the wounded, prisoners or unharmed. The proportion of wounded and prisoners may be assumed to be correct so that the opinion may be risked that the American losses were about 160 killed, 80 wounded and 40 prisoners, a total patriot loss of 280. As 40 Senecas were killed, on the British side, it may be assumed that, aside from the prisoners, the enemy's loss was as great and possibly greater, and this would indicate a total casualty list of 2,800 engaged at Oriskany and Willett's sortie of 500 killed and wounded. This is merely ventured as an opinion, and the true or full extent of the terrible losses at Oriskany (said to have been the bloodiest battle of the Revolution) on both sides will probably never be known. Certainly scores of dead were left by the provincials on the field and similarly, on the enemy's side, scores were buried by the Indians and Tories or were left lying in the forest where the battle was fought. Scores of wounded were carried down the valley by the patriots and back to the British and savage camps by the enemy. The patriot wounded were frequently slaughtered where they lay, many of the Americans being found, with their throats cut where they fell, by their comrades after the savage foe retreated. Here, as in many other Revolutionary conflicts, the Indians acted like bloodthirsty, cowardly wild beasts and, in many instances, their Tory comrades outdid them in deeds of bloody bestiality. The brave men, who went to this wood of death with Herkimer, came from the confines of the present counties of Montgomery, Fulton, Herkimer, Oneida and Otsego, all from the Mohawk valley with the exception of the men from the Cherry Valley and Springfield settlements.

After the battle of Oriskany a song, commemorative of the event was composed, and for a long time sung in the Mohawk valley, of which the following is a stanza:

"Brave Herkimer, our General's dead,
    And Colonel Cox is slain;
And many more and valiant men,
    We ne'er shall see again."

CHAPTER XIII.

1777—Personal Experiences at Oriskany—Indian and Tory Barbarities.

Having had a general review of the Oriskany campaign, a few of the experiences and particulars of the patriot actors in that affair may be in order, particularly as they relate to the Palatine and Canajoharie men. Regarding details of the Oriskany conflict, Simms publishes the following experiences of those engaged:

"It is only in the minor events attending a battle, that the reader is made to realize its fullness and see its horrors, and that the reader may see this deadly conflict * * * some of its interesting scenes are here depicted.

"At the beginning of the Revolution, there dwelt in Fort Plain, two brothers named George and Robert Crouse. The former was a man of family, and his sons, Col. Robert and Deacon Henry Crouse, are well remembered in this community, where four sons of the latter still reside. [at the time Simms wrote these incidents.] Robert was a bachelor. Those brothers were remarkably large and well formed men, and would have served a sculptor as a model for a giant race. Robert was the tallest and came to be called a seven-footer, and is believed to have stood full six and a half feet in his boots, and well proportioned. His great strength became proverbial, and two anecdotes have been preserved in the memory of our venerable friend, William H. Seeber, going to prove it. In January, 1776, on the occasion of Gen. Schuyler's assembling troops at Caughnawaga, now Fonda, to arrest Sir John Johnson, the Tryon county militia were ordered thither by Gen. Tenbroeck of Albany, to whose brigade they then belonged. Nicholas Herkimer, then the senior colonel of Tryon county troops, assembled them as directed. The Tryon county militia became a separate brigade in September, 1776, with Col. Herkimer as its acting general, and he was, as stated elsewhere, later commissioned its brigadier general. While there the brigade was paraded on the ice in the river, and Robert Crouse was designated to bear the flag in saluting the generals. He waved it so easily and gracefully with one hand, when hardly another man present could have handled it with both hands, that not only the generals, but the entire assemblage was excited to admiration, and a significant murmur of applause was echoed from the hills hemming in the valley. Gen. Schuyler said to the officers near him, 'That man ought to have a commission,' and one is said to have been tendered him, which he declined. This incident probably accounts for the fact that Lieut. Sammons placed him among the officers killed at Oriskany. Henry Walrath, the strongest man by reputation in the Palatine settlements, came from Stone Arabia in the winter of 1775 and 1776, bringing a friend with him, as he told Robert Crouse, expressly to see which was the stronger man of the two. Said Crouse, 'Well, you go home and put 50 skipples of wheat on your sleigh, and I will put 50 skipples with it, and the strongest one shall have the 100 skipples'—75 bushels. The Stone Arabia bully never put in an appearance, which left Crouse the acknowledged champion. Robert Crouse was made a prisoner at Oriskany, and, as his friends afterward learned, by fellow prisoners who knew him, was most inhumanly murdered. Agreeable to the affidavit of Dr. Moses Younglove, who was also a prisoner from that battlefield, the Indians killed some of the prisoners at their own pleasure, and to his knowledge they tortured to death at least half a dozen. Of this number was Robert Crouse, who was the selected victim at one of their hellish orgies, as the late William Crouse, a nephew, learned subsequently by other prisoners who knew him. His remarkable stature possibly gave them a new idea of derisive torture, for, with their knives, they began by amputating his legs at the knee joints, and when accomplished they held him up on those bleeding limbs—derisively told him he was then as tall as those around him—and bade him walk. As his life was fast ebbing they sought other modes of torture. At length dispatching him they tore off and secured for market his reeking scalp. Whether they ate any of his flesh is unknown, but it is not improbable

they did as numbers of the Indians engaged in this contest had feasted on prisoners in earlier wars. Thus ignobly fell, not only the largest but one of the best men in the Mohawk valley."

Sam Crouse, a giant Fort Plainer, who died about 1890, probably inherited his enormous frame from these Revolutionary ancestors.

Captain Jacob Gardinier:—after being literally riddled with bullets and bayonets, crept into a cavity at the roots of a tree and, by the aid of his waiter, a German lad, who loaded his gun for him, his hand having been lacerated by a bayonet, he continued the fight shooting from that position an Indian who was dodging about to get a shot at an American officer. Of this brave militia captain, said the Rev. Johan Daniel Gros of Fort Plain, in a work published after the war on "Moral Philosophy:" "Let it stand recorded, among other patriotic deeds of that little army of militia, that a Jacob Gardinier, with a few of his men, vanquished a whole platoon, killing the captain, after he had held him for a long time by his collar as a shield against the balls and bayonets of the whole platoon. This brave militia captain is still alive and was cured of thirteen wounds."

George Walter, at Oriskany, was struck down with a severe bullet wound. Faint from loss of blood, he crept to a spring and slaked his thirst and revived. While watching the fight, an Indian lurking near discovered him and, running up, gave him a blow on the head with his tomahawk, and in another moment had torn off his reeking scalp. When found by his friends, some of his wounds were flyblown, but he recovered and lived until 1831, dying at a ripe old age. It is said that Walter, in telling of his experience, remarked: "Dat Indian tot I vash det, but I knows petter all de time; but I tot I would say nodding so as he would go off."

Captain Christopher W. Fox:—In the Palatine batallion of militia, there were three captains by the name of Fox, viz: Captain William Fox jr.,

Capt. Christopher P. Fox and Captain Christopher W. Fox. Probably they were all in the Oriskany battle and the last two named were quite surely there. Christopher W. was severely wounded in the right arm, which was partially dressed on the ground, where he remained with his men; and, discovering an Indian crawling from behind a tree in the direction of the enemy's encampment, grasping his sword in his left hand he said to some of his men: "You keep an eye on me for safety and I will kill an Indian." As he approached the savage, a mutual recognition took place. The Indian was a half-breed called William Johnson, and was a reputed son of his namesake, Sir William Johnson. He was down with a broken leg and begged for his life because he was wounded. "Ah," said the dauntless captain, directing the prostrate warrior to his crippled arm, "I am wounded too, and one of us must die." In an instant, with his left hand, he thrust the keen-edged sword through the Indian's body. This Captain Fox was wounded in the following fashion: He and a hostile Indian, under the cover of trees a few rods distant were, for some time, watching in a vain endeavor to get some advantage of each other; and, thinking to draw the Indian's shot, and win the game, Fox extended his hat upon his hand beside a tree to attract the savage's attention. The ruse succeeded and the Indian supposing the hat contained a head, fired on the target; but unfortunately Fox had a long arm and had extended it so far that the ball struck it and, dropping the hat, the hand fell limp at his side. The Indian, seeing the hat fall, no doubt supposed he had killed his man, but considered the hazard of securing a scalp too great to approach his victim. It was common practise to thrust out a hat on one's ramrod or a stick to draw an antagonist's charge, when fighting in the Indian fashion, but so reckless an act as that of this captain's seemed to merit the punishment. Fox became a major and resided after the war at Palatine Church. The following has

a direct bearing on the above:

"Recd., Williger, Oct. 16, 1779, of Christopher Fox, Esq., eight dollars in full for curing his arm of a wound received in the Oriskany fight, £ 3. 4. 0.
"Moses Younglove."

Abram Quackenboss:—The last syllable of this name is written boss, but pronounced bush. One of the earliest Low Dutch families to locate in the present town of Glen was that of Quackenbush, as the name is now written. One of Quackenbush's boyhood playmates, near the lower Mohawk castle at Fort Hunter, was an Indian called Bronkahorse, who was about his own age. Quackenbush was a lieutenant under the brave Capt. Gardinier. Among the followers of the Johnsons to Canada was his Indian friend, who also tried to get the white Whig to go with him, assuring him that he would have the same office in the royal army. Their next meeting was in the dodging, tree-to-tree fight at Oriskany. The lieutenant heard himself addressed in a familiar voice, which he recognized as that of his early Indian friend, now posted behind a tree within gunshot of the one which covered his own person. "Surrender yourself my prisoner and you shall be treated kindly," shouted the Mohawk brave, "but if you do not you will never get away from here alive—we intend to kill all who are not made prisoners!" The success of the enemy at the beginning of the contest made them bold and defiant. "Never will I become a prisoner," shouted back Quackenboss. Both were expert riflemen and now watched their chance. Bronkahorse fired first and planted a bullet in the tree scarcely an inch from his adversary's head, but he had lost his best chance, as the lieutenant sprang to a new position from which his adversary's tree would not shield him, and in the next instant the Indian dropped with a bullet through his heart.

The Seebers:—Major William Seeber, who lived next to Fort Plain and was then nearly 60 years old, was mortally wounded in the battle, where his son Audolph was slain and Capt.

Jacob H. fell with a broken thigh. Jacob cut staddles and attempted to withe them about his broken leg to enable him to escape, but could not stand upon it, and gave up, expecting to be slain. Henry Failing, an acquaintance, came to him and offered to remove him to greater safety, but Seeber declined, telling his friend to load his gun, take the remainder of his cartridges and leave him to his fate. He was afterward removed and died at Fort Herkimer. Failing was also severely wounded, but removed and recovered.

Garret Walrath, a soldier in the Canajoharie batallion, was at Oriskany and is said to have never feared flesh or the devil. In one of the terrible encounters in the early part of the engagement, he was made prisoner and pinioned and told to keep close behind an Indian, who claimed all his attention. He often purposely ran against his captor, whining and complaining that his arms were so tightly drawn back. * * * At this period not only the Indians but the whites, especially those accustomed to hunting, carried a sharp, well-pointed knife in a belt. Walrath * * * * cautiously grasped the handle of his knife and, watching his opportunity, in one of his stumbles over the heels of his captor, he adroitly plunged his knife into his body, and in the next instant he was a disembowled and dead Indian. The liberated captive, with his bloody knife in hand, cautiously sought his way back, and in an hour or two was welcomed by his surviving companions, who soon saw him armed again with a gun.

Col. Henry Diefendorf was a brave militia captain from the present town of Minden, where his descendants still reside. In the discharge of his duties, he was shot through the lungs, during the latter part of the engagement. Near him when he fell were William Cox, Henry Sanders and probably others of his company. He begged for water, and Sanders stamped a hole in the marshy soil and, as the water settled in it, he took off his shoe and in it gave the dying man a drink. Seeing by the smoke from whence the shot came that struck down his captain, Cox said: "Damn my soul, but I'll have a life for that one!" He ran to the tree before the foe could possibly reload his gun, where he found a large Indian down with a broken leg. As Cox leveled his rifle, the warrior threw up his hand and shouted: "Youker! you-ker!" which his adversary supposed was a cry for quarter. "I'll give you you-ker" said Cox as he sent a bullet through the Indian's head. He rejoined his comrades a few minutes later with the savage's gun.

Henry Thompson was a helper to the doughty Capt. Gardinier, who lived and had a blacksmith shop near the present village of Fultonville. Into Oriskany he followed his brave employer and, after the battle had raged for hours, he approached Gardinier and said he was hungry. "Fight away," shouted the captain. "I can't without eating," said the soldier. "Then get you a piece and eat," was the reply. He did so and sitting upon the body of a dead soldier, he ate with a real zest, while the bullets whistled about his head. His lunch finished, he arose and was again seen with renewed energy where peril was the most imminent.

Sir John Johnson married a daughter of John Watts of New York city and her brother, Stephen Watts, joined Johnson when he went to Canada. He was a British captain at Oriskany and, in making a deperate charge he was wounded and made a prisoner. As the Americans could not be encumbered with their wounded foes, he was left to his fate—and not despatched and scalped as were all wounded Americans found by the enemy. Being discovered by Henry N. Failing, a private soldier [from the present town of Minden] in the Canajoharie district batallion, he kindly carried him to a little stream of water that he might there slake his thirst and die more easily. To his thanks for the soldier's kindness he added the gift of his watch. Two days after, Capt. Watts was discovered by some straggling Indians looking for plunder, was taken to the enemy's camp, properly cared for and finally recovered.

Among the tragic incidents of Oriskany was one which happened at a tree afterward called "the bayonet tree." One of Herkimer's men was held up, dead or alive, and pinned to a tree several feet from the ground with a bayonet driven into the tree several inches. Here the body remained until it fell to the ground from decomposition. This bayonet was to have been seen in the tree for more than a quarter of a century and until the tree had grown so as to bury most of the blade.

Henry Thompson was not the only one of the patriots to satisfy his hunger during the battle. Adam Frank also opened his knapsack and sat down and made a hearty but hasty meal, after which he was heard to exclaim in German, "Jezt drauf auf die kerls!" —"Now we'll give it to them!"

Captain Andrew Dillenbeck of Stone Arabia, was the hero of a fight which resulted in his death. Tories of Johnson's Greens attempted to take him prisoner and, on Dillenbeck's saying he would not be taken alive, siezed his gun. Captain Dillenbeck wrenched it away and felled his enemy with the butt. He shot a second one dead, thrust a third through the body with his bayonet and then fell dead from a Tory shot.

Dr. Younglove, surgeon in the Tryon county brigade, was taken prisoner at Oriskany and, after his return to his Palatine home, made the following affidavit:

"Moses Younglove, surgeon of Gen. Herkimer's brigade of militia, deposeth and saith, that being in the battle of said militia on the 6th of August last, toward the close of the battle, he surrendered himself a prisoner to a savage, who immediately gave him up to a sergeant of Sir John Johnson's regiment; soon after which a lieutenant in the Indian department, came up in company with several Tories, when said Mr. Grinnis, by name, drew his tomahawk at this deponent and with a deal of persuasion was kindly prevailed on to spare his life. He then plundered him of his watch, buckles, spurs, etc., and other Tories, following his example, stripped him almost naked, with a great many threats, while they were stripping and massacreing prisoners on every side. That this deponent was brought before Mr. Butler Sen. (Col. John), who demanded of him what he was fighting for? to which deponent answered: 'He fought for the liberty that God and nature gave him, and to defend himself and dearest connexions from the massacre of the savages.' To which Butler replied: 'You are a damned impudent rebel!' and so saying immediately turned to the savages, encouraging them to kill him, and if they did not, the deponent and the other persons should be hanged on the gallows then preparing. That several prisoners were then taken forward to the enemy's headquarters with frequent scenes of horror and massacre, in which Tories were active as well as savages; and in particular one Davis, formerly known in Tryon county, on the Mohawk river. That Lieut. Singleton of Sir John Johnson's regiment, being wounded, entreated the savages to kill the prisoners, which they accordingly did, as nigh as this deponent can judge, about six or seven. That Isaac Paris was also taken that same road without receiving from them any remarkable insult, except stripping, until some Tories came up who kicked and abused him, after which the savages, thinking him a notable offender, murdered him barbarously. That those of the prisoners, who were delivered up to the provost guards, were ordered not to use any violence in protecting the prisoners from the savages, who came up every day with knives, feeling the prisoners to know which were fattest. That they dragged one of the prisoners out of the guard with the most lamentable cries, tortured him for a long time, and this deponent was informed, by both Tories and Indians, that they ate him, as appears they did another on an island in Lake Ontario [Buck's Island] by bones found there nearly picked, just after they had crossed the lake with the prisoners.

That the prisoners who were not delivered up were murdered, in considerable numbers, from day to day around the camp, some of them so nigh that their shrieks were heard. That Capt. Martin of the bateaux men, was delivered to the Indians at Oswego, on pretence of his having kept back some useful intelligence. That this deponent, during his imprisonment, and his fellows were kept almost starved for provisions, and what they drew were of the worst kind, such as spoiled flour, biscuit full of maggots, and mouldy, and no soap allowed or other method of keeping clean, and were insulted, struck, etc., without mercy by the guards, without any provocation given. That this deponent was informed by several sergeants orderly on St. Leger that twenty dollars were offered in general orders for every American scalp.

"Moses Younglove"

"John Barclay, Chairman of Albany Committee."

Lieut. Peter Groat and Andrew Cunningham, a neighbor, were captured at Oriskany and murdered at Wood creek, slices of their thighs being roasted and feasted upon by the savages with zest and mirth. Peter Ehle, a fellow prisoner, saw his comrades killed.

There were a few Oneidas with the provincials in this battle, among whom was the Indian interpreter, Spencer, who was killed. The Indians of the enemy suffered severely, being put forward early in the fight. The Senecas alone lost over 60 in killed and wounded, while the Mohawks and other tribes suffered severely. The fire of the patriots was fully as deadly against the Tories, their captains, McDonough, Wilson and Hare, lying dead on the field, with scores of men in Tory uniforms scattered around them. The great loss of the Indians has been made a pretext by English writers to justify the cruelties inflicted by them on their prisoners. Says the "Life of Mary Jemison" (the white woman), page 88: "Previous to the battle of Fort Stanwix, the British sent for the Indians (Senecas) to come and see them whip the rebels; and at the same time stated that they did not wish to have them fight, but wanted to have them just sit down, smoke their pipes and look on. Our Indians went to a man, but contrary to their expectations, instead of smoking and looking on, they were obliged to fight for their lives and, in the end, were completely beaten, with a great loss in killed and wounded. Our Indians alone had 36 killed and a great number wounded. Our town (Little Beard's Town) exhibited a scene of real sorrow and distress, when our warriors returned and recounted their misfortunes, and stated the real loss they had sustained in the engagement. The mourning was excessive, and was expressed by the most doleful yells, shrieks and howlings, and by inimitable gesticulations."

Here is an incident of the defense of Fort Schuyler, of a time probably after the Oriskany battle, from Judge Pomeroy Jones's "Annals of Oneida County":—"A sentinel, posted on the northwest bastion of the fort, was shot with a rifle while walking his stated rounds in the gray of the morning; the next morning the second met the same fate, on the same post; the crack of the rifle was heard but from whence it came, none could conjecture, and the alarm being given, no enemy could be discovered. Of course, on the third night this station was dreaded as being certain death and the soldier to whose lot it fell, quailed and hung back; but, to the surprise of the whole guard, a comrade offered to take his place and was accepted. Towards morning, the substitute sentinel drove a stake into the ground at the spot where his predecessors had been shot, on which he placed his hat and watch coat and with the help of a cord and a well stuffed knapsack, he soon had a very good apology for a portly soldier, who stood to the life at 'support arms,' with his trusty shining musket. Having thus posted his 'man of straw,' he quietly sat down behind the parapet closely watching through an embrassure for coming events. At early dawn, the well known report of the same rifle was heard, and the column of smoke ascending from the thick top of a black oak tree some 30 or 40 rods distant, showed the whereabouts of the marksman. The sergeant of the guard was soon on the spot and the commandant notified that the perch of the sharpshooter had been discovered. A four pounder was quickly loaded with canister and grape, and the sound of this morning gun boomed over the hill and dale in the distance, immediately succeeded by a shout from the garrison, as they beheld one of Britain's red allies tumbling head foremost from the tree top. On examining the counterfeit sentinel, the holes through the various folds of the knapsack were more than circumstantial evidence that the aim was most sure, and that, had the owner stood in its place, he would have followed to his account those who had preceded him there. It is hardly necessary to add that the sentinels on the northwest bastion were not afterwards molested."

It was hoped, by surviving friends in the valley below, that the troops advancing under Gen. Arnold to raise the siege of Fort Schuyler would be able to perform the melancholy task of burying the remains of our fallen soldiery at Oriskany. But, as over two weeks of excessively warm weather had transpired—it being then the 23d or 24th of August—decomposition had so rapidly taken place that the stench was intolerable, making it necessary for the health of the troops to give the field as wide a berth as possible.. So said James Williamson, who was a soldier under Arnold and who was on duty at Fort Stanwix. As the relieving American army force under Gen. Arnold approached Oriskany, evidences of its bloody onslaught greeted them. Here are some things which were noticed by Nicholas Stoner, a young musician in Col. Livingston's regiment, and copied from Simms's "Trappers:" Near the mouth of the Oriskany creek a gun was found standing against a tree with a pair of boots hanging on it, while in the creek

near, in a state bordering on putrefaction, lay their supposed owner. In the grass, a little way from the shore, lay a well dressed man without hat or coat, who, it was supposed, had made his way there to obtain drink. A black silk handkerchief encircled his head. John Clark, a sergeant, loosened it but its hair adhered to it on its removal, and he left it. He, however, took from his feet a pair of silver shoe buckles. His legs were so swollen that a pair of deerskin breeches were rent from top to bottom. On their way nine dead bodies lay across the road, disposed in regular order, as was imagined by the Indians after their death. The stench was so great that the Americans could not discharge the last debt due their heroic countrymen, and their bones were soon after bleaching on the ground. A little farther on an Indian was seen hanging to the limb of a tree. He was suspended by the traces of a harness, but by whom was unknown. Such were some of the scenes, a mile or two away, but, where the carnage had been greatest, they had to make as wide a circuit as possible. Not an American killed in that battle was ever buried.

Scalping was done to some extent by the American troops, but was not prompted by the hope of reward, as in the case of the Indians and Tories. "Scalps for the Canadian market" proved a source of revenue to the Indians, who took them to Montreal and redeemed them for cash, receiving payment for those of men, women and children alike. Lossing gives the following account of this diabolical practise: "The methods used by the Indians in scalping is probably not generally known. I was told by Mr. Dievendorff [who was scalped as a boy in Doxtader's Currytown 1781 raid and survived to an old age] that the scalping knife was a weapon, not unlike in appearance the bowie knife of the present day. The victim was usually stunned or killed by a blow from a tomahawk. Sometimes only a portion of the scalp (as was the case with Mr. Dievendorff) was taken from the crown and the back part of the head, but more frequently the whole scalp was removed. With the dexterity of a surgeon, the Indian placed the point of his knife at the roots of the hair on the forehead and made a circular incision around the head. If the hair was short, he would raise a lappet of the skin, take hold with his teeth, and tear it instantly from the skull. If long, such as the hair of females, he would twist it around his hand, and, by a sudden jerk, bare the skull. The scalps were then tanned with the hair on, and often marked in such a manner that the owners could tell when and where they were severally obtained, and whether they belonged to men or women. When Major Rogers, in 1759, destroyed the chief village of the St. Francis Indians, he found there a vast quantity of scalps, many of them comically painted with heiroglyphics. They were all stretched on small hoops." A remarkable phase of this unspeakable practise, is that a large number of the valley people who were scalped, recovered and lived to an old age. This was due to the hurried way in which many of the Indian attacks were made, so that the victims were stunned and not killed.

Col. John Butler had charge of the traffic in scalps with the Indians, during the Oriskany campaign, and probably later. Simms says "the usual bounty, after a time, was $8 for all, except those of officers and committeemen, which commanded from $10 to $20." That there was such a traffic in scalps has been denied by English writers but the fact seems substantiated by abundant evidence.

Undoubtedly the leading patriot in the valley at that time was Nicholas Herkimer, a resident of the Canajoharie district and in command of the Tryon county militia and of the forces at Oriskany. His father, Johan Jost Herkimer, had emigrated from the Palatinate about 1720 and settled on the Burnetsfield patent. At Fort Herkimer he established a trading place and later built a strong stone house which was stockaded and became the fort, bearing his name. Johan Jost Herkimer, legend says, was a man of mighty strength among a population of men of muscle. He knew the English and Indian languages, as well as his native German, and acted as interpreter between the English and Indians. He was concerned in the erection of Fort Stanwix and became a man of considerable property and died in 1775 at Fort Herkimer. His son, Nicholas, settled east of Fall Hill in the Canajoharie district and built there a substantial brick residence, in 1764, which is now standing. While at Fort Herkimer, Herkimer commanded that post during the two attacks of the French war, he then being a lieutenant of militia. His commission for this rank is now in the possession of a collateral descendant in San Francisco, while his brigadier-general's commission, from the New York provincial congress, hangs on the walls of a Fort Plain house. He was a member of the Tryon County Committee of Safety from Canajoharie district and colonel of the militia of that district, and colonel-in-chief of the county. In 1776 he was made a brigadier-general. He is described by one who saw him as a large, square built Dutchman and, contrary to many accounts which represent him as an old man at the time of the battle, family figures give his age at 49, and family tradition has it that he was then a sturdy, vigorous man, all of which is borne out by Oriskany events. Herkimer was a close friend of Brant and probably of other Mohawks, and was possibly the most influential Whig figure of the time in Tryon county. He served as chairman pro tem of the committee of safety and some of its papers and letters extant are signed by him. He seems to have been a man of sound sense, wise counsel and quick and effective action. His prestige was dimmed by the Tory action of his brother, Han Yost Herkimer, who was a militia colonel but ran away to Canada. Of his other brothers, only Capt. George Herkimer, an ardent Whig and scout officer, was with him at Oriskany, although other brothers were patriots with the exception of Han Yost. Undoubtedly Herkimer's strong Whig attitude and military ability had great effect in upholding the cause of independence in the county, particularly among the "Mohawk Dutch." His first wife was a sister of Peter S. Tygert and his second wife a daughter of the same. He left no children. Gen. Herkimer left an estate of 1,900 acres of land and willed his brother, George Herkimer, 500 acres and his homestead, where the latter was living in 1783, when Gen. Washington made his tour through the valley when he stopped here. The general in his will signed his name Nicholas "Herckheimer," although he varied it at other times. Herkimer's wound was not mortal but unskilful amputation of his wounded leg caused his death. It is said that the leg was sawed off short without tying the blood vessels up and the sturdy patriot slowly bled to death. When the leg was amputated two neighborhood boys buried it in the garden, and shortly after the General said to one of them: "I guess you boys will have to take that leg up and bury it with me, for I am going to follow it." The amputation was done by a young French surgeon with Arnold's expedition up the valley against the advice of the General's doctor, Dr. Petrie. Col. Willett called to see Herkimer soon after the operation and found him sitting up in bed and smoking his pipe. His strength failed toward night and, calling his family to his chamber, he read composedly the 38th psalm, closed the book, sank back upon his pillow and expired. The last three stanzas of this Psalm read as follows:

They also that render evil for good are mine adversaries; because I follow the thing that good is.

Forsake me not, O Lord; O my God, be not far from me.

Make haste to help me, O Lord my salvation.

Christopher P. Yates, who was a man of fine intellect and an efficient patriot, said of Herkimer: "I claim not for the General that he was versed in Latin or Greek, or in the philosophy of the German schools; but I claim for him, that no German immigrant was better read in the history of the Protestant reformation, and in the philosophy of the Bible than Gen. Herkimer."

Johan Jost Herkimer, the first of the family in the valley, left thirteen children—five sons and eight daughters, which gives an idea of the size of the valley families of the day. The marriages of the children of Johan Jost Herkimer gives an idea of the ratio of the Teutonic elements in the western Mohawk valley in the eighteenth century. Of these known marriages nine are with people of German ancestry, three with people of Holland blood and one (that of Hendrick Frey) with a person of Swiss descent.

Jurgh, Johan Jost, Madalana and Catharina Herkimer (or Erghemar) were patentees named in the Burnetsfield grant of 1725. Johan Jost was doubtless the progenitor of the family in America. Just who the others were, in relationship to him, is not definitely known. They are supposed to have come over in the Palatine immigration of 1722 and in this patent 100 acres was allotted to each of them on the south side of the river in the neighborhood that subsequently became known as Fort Herkimer. There is a tradition that Johan Jost carried a child and some of his chattels on his back from Schenectady to German Flatts. A family legend gives the story that on the first Herkimer's arrival at his future wilderness home, he asked permission, of his Indian neighbors, to build a cabin. They at first refused him, to Herkimer's great chagrin. At this time, these savages were busy trying to carry a dugout they had recently completed to the Mohawk. On account of its weight they were having difficulty in moving the canoe and asked the pioneer to help them. Motioning all the Mohawks to get on one end of the heavy boat, the stalwart German lifted the other end alone, and in this way the dugout was carried to the neighboring river. Astounded at the white man's great strength, the Indians at once gave Herkimer permission to build a cabin and cultivate the land.

Located amid a beautiful landscape, with the flatlands stretching away to the river and lofty Fall Hill in the background, the home of General Herkimer, in Danube, is a fine example of the Colonial Mohawk valley houses. Built of brick and finely finished, it is a monument to the solidity of character of the valley's early Teutonic settlers. It, in connection with the monument and the Herkimer family burial plot, has been, a number of times, the scene of patriotic gatherings. Here is located the first of the markers, which were put in position in the summer of 1912, to show the route of the valley militia in its march to the field of Oriskany. Capt. George Herkimer succeeded to the ownership of the house and its farm and, on his death, it passed to his son, Hon. John Herkimer, who occupied it until about 1815, when it passed out of the Herkimer family. Lossing, in 1848, writing of this place, says: "After breakfast I rode down to Danube, to visit the residence of General Herkimer while living and the old Castle church, near the dwelling place of Brant in the Revolution. It was a pleasant ride along the tow path between the canal and river. Herkimer's residence is about two and a half miles below Little Falls, near the canal, and in full view of the traveler upon the railroad, half a mile distant. It is a substantial brick edifice, was erected in 1764, and was a splendid mansion for the time and place. It is now owned by Daniel Conner, a farmer, who is 'modernizing' it, when I was there, by building a long, fashionable piazza in front, in place of the [former] small old porch, or stoop. He was also 'improving' some of the rooms within. The one in which General Herkimer died (on the right of the front entrance), and also the one, on the opposite side of the passage, are left precisely as they were when the general occupied the house; and Mr.

Conner has the good taste and patriotism to preserve them so. These rooms are handsomely wainscoted with white pine, wrought into neat moldings and panels, and the casements of the deep windows are of the same material and in the same style. Mr. Conner has carefully preserved the great lock of the front door of the 'castle'— for castle it really was in strength and appointments against Indian assaults. It is sixteen inches long and ten wide. Close to the house is a subterranean room, built of heavy masonry and arched, which the general used as a magazine for stores belonging to the Tryon County militia. It is still used, as a storeroom but with more pacific intentions. The family burying ground is upon a knoll a few rods southeast of the mansion, and there rest the remains of the gallant soldier, as secluded and forgotten as if they were of 'common mold.' Seventy years ago the Continental Congress, grateful for his services, resolved to erect a monument to his memory of the value of five hundred dollars; but the stone that may yet be reared is still in the quarry, and the patriot inscription to declare its intent and the soldier's worth is not yet conceived. Until 1847 no stone identified his grave. Then a plain marble slab was set up with the name of the hero upon it; and when I visited it (1848), it was overgrown with weeds and brambles. It was erected by his grandnephew, Warren Herkimer." In 1895, under the auspices of the Oneida Historical society, an imposing stone shaft was here erected to the memory of Herkimer, bearing the inscription "Vorwaert" (forward), his command to the militia, which started the march of the impatient men to the field of Oriskany.

A statue of Gen. Nicholas Herkimer was erected in the park at Herkimer in 1907 on the occasion of the celebration of the centennial of that village. It is an excellently modeled figure, cast in bronze, and represents the Oriskany leader, wounded and seated upon his saddle, pipe in hand, while he directs the battle. The action of the statue, pointing the way to victory, is vigorous and inspiring. The sculptor was Burr C. Miller of Paris, and the work is the gift to Herkimer of Warner Miller, former United States Senator from the state of New York, a resident of that town and father of the sculptor.

CHAPTER XIV.

1778—Indian Council at Johnstown, March 9—Manheim, Caroga, Springfield, Andrustown, German Flats Raids—Cherry Valley Massacre.

Early in 1778 the alarming news came to the valley that the western Indian tribes were to unite with the Mohawks. Cayugas, Onondagas and Senecas in a war upon the frontier, instigated by the Johnsons, Claus and Butler. Congress thereupon ordered a council held with the Six Nations at Johnstown in February and appointed Gen. Schuyler and Volkert P. Douw to conduct it together with a commissioner named James Duane, appointed by Governor Clinton. The Indians showed little interest in the conference and delayed coming until March 9. There were then present more than seven hundred of them, mostly friendly Oneidas and Tuscaroras and hostile Onondagas, with a few Mohawks, three or four Cayugas and not one of the Senecas, whose warriors outnumbered those of all the other Iroquois. Instead of attending the council the Senecas sent a message expressing surprise that they were asked to come while the American "tomahawks were sticking in their heads, their wounds bleeding and their eyes streaming with tears for the loss of their friends," meaning at the battle of Oriskany, which shows the extent of the damage the patriots inflicted on that fateful day.

The Oneidas and Tuscaroras expressed their allegiance to the United States and predicted the extinction of the hostile tribes. The rest of the Indians had little to say, excepting an Onondaga chief who hypocritically lamented the course of his tribe, laying it to the young and headstrong warriors. Nothing was effected by the

conference, except the satisfactory expression of allegiance on the part of the Oneidas and Tuscaroras. The commissioners closed the council by warning the hostile Iroquois to look to their behavior as the American cause was just or a terrible vengeance would overtake them. The Marquis de Lafayette, who was temporarily in command of the northern department was at the Johnstown council and considerably improved the frontier defences by ordering forts built at Cherry Valley and in the Oneida country, the three Schoharie forts garrisoned and armed and other border fortifications strengthened. Learning among other Tory activities, Col. Guy Carlton, nephew of the governor of Canada, was on a spying tour in the neighborhood, efforts were made for his capture, Lafayette himself offering a reward of fifty guineas for his arrest.

Irruptions of scalping parties of Canadian Indians and Tories began in the Mohawk valley about 1778 and continued up to 1783, when a peace treaty was signed. It is impossible to tell of each of these because they were so numerous, and records of all have not been preserved. One of the first, in the settlement of Manheim, occurred on April 3, 1778, under command of Captain Crawford, two weeks after the sacking of Fairfield, Herkimer county. About 50 Indians and Tories raided the Mohawk valley in the settlement of Manheim, near Little Falls. Among the Tories were L. Casselman, Countryman and Bowers, who had gone to join the British forces in Canada from the lower Mohawk. The marauders captured the miller, John Garter and his boy John and Joseph Newman and Bartholomew Pickert, who happened to be at the mill. At Windecker's place, James Van Slyck, his son-in-law, was sick in bed and, for a wonder, was unharmed by the savages. The prisoners made here and in the vicinity were John House, Forbush, John Windecker, a boy of 13; Ganet Van Slyck, another boy; John Cypher, Helmer, Jacob

Uher, George Attle. The two latter were rangers on a scout from Fort Snyder. Garter's mill was burned, but no other dwellings were destroyed and no one was killed. Four Whigs were captured in Salisbury, Herkimer county. The march to Canada was made through the snow and great hardships were suffered. Windecker's Indian captor proved very kind and carried him across several rapid streams on his back. Windecker said afterward, concerning their scarcity of food, that "An Indian would eat anything except crow." This raid was one of the earliest of the war and was not marked by the bloody ferocity which characterized the later ones.

The following, concerning the invasion of Ephratah in the Palatine district, in April, 1778, is abridged from Simms's "Frontiersmen of New York," Vol. II., pp. 146-151:

In 1773, 20 or more German families settled along Garoga creek in the present town of Ephratah and some at the present site of Kringsbush. These Germans were part of a shipload of immigrants, mostly from the district of Nassau near Frankfort-on-the-Main, which landed at Baltimore in 1773. Many of them settled in the Mohawk valley. The immigration from Germany, and even from Holland, into New York state was practically continuous from the time of first settlement up to the Revolution. On this voyage very rough weather was encountered on the Atlantic, the masts went by the board and the ship nearly foundered.

The settlement of Ephratah was so called after a place of that name in Germany. Prominent among these settlers was Nicholas Rechtor, whose father, Johannes Rechtor, came from Hesse in Germany and settled at Niskautau, six miles below Albany. These early Ephratah families all built log houses, except Rechtor, who put up a frame house and barn. Simms says this house was still standing (in 1882), "just back of a public house in Caroga, so called after the creek passing through it—the orig-

inal name still attaching to the settlement." Rechtor was located about three miles west of the stone grist mill Sir William Johnson had built for the use of that region which was then known as Tilleborough. Within a radius of five or six miles from Nicholas Rechtor's house the following were located: Jacob Appley, Jacob Frey, John Hurtz, Conrad Hart, John Smith, Henry Smith, John Cool, Jacob Deusler, Leonard Kretzer, Henry Hynce, Flander, Phye, John Spankable (now Sponable), John Winkle.

Among the settlers in the Kringsbush section were Matthias Smith, Leonard Helmer, Joseph Davis and his brother-in-law, John Kring, after whom the settlement was named.

In 1775, a small company of militia was organized among these settlers along the Caroga. The officers were Nicholas Rechtor, Captain; John Williams, George Smith, lieutenants; John Sholl, ensign. This company was in the Oriskany battle where Capt. Rechtor was thrown from and stepped on by his horse, disabling him.

About four in the afternoon of April 30, 1778, about 20 Indians and Tories invaded the Ephratah settlement. Most of the farmers were making maple sugar. Rechtor was drilling 20 men of his militia company about a mile from his home. Six of the enemy made their first appearance at the Harts' home and killed Conrad Hart, the father, and took captive his son Wilhelmus, a youth of 16. They plundered and burned Hart's building and from thence went to Jacob Appley's, where they destroyed all property. A daughter of Hart had, in the meantime escaped, at the time of the first attack, and ran to where the militia company was drilling. Instead of Rechtor and his men attacking the enemy in force they split up and ran singly or in small companies of three or four toward their homes. Jacob Appley, Daniel Hart and Peter Shyke went with Capt. Rechtor to his home.

The enemy had already reached Rechtor's. Here the savages, both Tory and Indian, found considerable plunder as the captain was well provided with the worldly goods for that time and locality. They were some time in packing up and Mrs. Rechtor, objecting to the wholesale looting of her household, was struggling with a big Indian over a long-handled frying pan. The Americans came up on the run and fired at the Indian. The shot struck the pan handle, glanced down and wounded the woman in the ankle. A general melee took place. Appley shot an Indian and was himself shot down. Shyke was severely wounded and Captain Rechtor was hit in the right arm. Helmus Hart came up with his hands bound, he having been tied to a tree when the Hart house was attacked. The Americans released his hands and he joined in the fight, which soon ended in the enemy running away.

At this time few of the settlers had been killed as they were in the sugar bush distant from their dwellings. Rechtor gathered all of his family (of seven children) that he could find and set out for Fort Paris, which he reached at midnight. The two youngest girls and the youngest boy could not be found in the bush, as they evidently feared Indians and would not venture forth even in reply to the calls of their parents. Appley was so severely wounded that he had to be left and, at his request, was propped up against the oven with a gun in his hand. Rechtor's little four-year-old boy Henry now came home and got himself some bread and milk and began eating it. Just then the savages came back. Appley shot and killed one and was himself killed and scalped and left with a bayonet sticking through his heart. The little boy Henry was killed and scalped and thrown into the creek. Here the dead little body was found next day, one hand still clutching the spoon with which he had been eating. The enemy's stay was short as they were gone when, shortly after, the two youngest Rechtor girls came out of the bush. Seeing Appley's dead body they ran in fright to their neighbor Hart's house. This they found burned and Hart dead and mangled and, so in

great fright, they ran back into the bush where they stayed all night. In the morning they found neighbors and were taken to Fort Paris, where they rejoined their family.

After leaving Rechtor's the enemy captured Peter Loucks, whom they took to Canada. A company of American soldiers, from Fort Paris, started in pursuit the next morning, May 1, 1778. They had Henry Flathead, a "friendly" Indian, for a guide. Coming upon the enemy's campfire this Indian gave a yell, probably to warn his red brethren. When the company came up meat was still cooking in the fire, but the enemy had vanished and could not be found.

At the time of the Ephratah invasion, two Indians of the raiding party shot and killed a girl named Rickard, as she was driving home cows near Fort Klock in the east end of the present town of St. Johnsville. Hearing the shot, George Klock came running out with his gun and as the Indians made for the girl's body to scalp it, he fired and they made for the woods and disappeared. Going north this pair of savages made John Smith a prisoner at Kringsbush and took him to Canada. He was a son of Matthias Smith, a veteran of Oriskany.

After the Ephratah raid most of the Whig families abandoned their homes, which were left standing by the Tories to afford themselves shelter on subsequent raids. Rechtor removed to his old home below Albany until after the war, when most of the surviving Ephratah settlers came back to their lands there. The raid along the Caroga was one of the first in the Mohawk valley attended with bloodshed.

On the day of the Ephratah raid a party of Senecas ravaged a portion of the Schoharie valley.

Joseph Brant and his warriors gathered at Oghkwaga early in 1778. This place is now Windsor, in Broome county.

Brant appeared at Unadilla in the spring of 1778 and Capt. McKean was sent by the people of Cherry Valley with a small force to reconnoitre the

Indian position. McKean injudiciously wrote Brant a letter violently denouncing him and asking him to come to Cherry Valley, with the taunting remark that there he would be changed from a "brant" to a "goose." Brant was enraged by this letter and answered it later with the Cherry Valley massacre.

Brant's first hostile movement of consequence, after his return to Oghkwaga in the spring of 1778, was to fall upon the little settlement at Springfield, at the head of Otsego lake. This was in the month of May and every house was burned but one, into which the women and children were collected and kept unharmed. Several men were captured and much plunder was taken but no one was murdered, probably because of no Tories being present.

At this same time, in May, 1778, Brant started out to destroy the Cherry Valley settlement. While reconnoitering the village from a distant hill he saw a company of boys drilling on the open space in front of the fort. He mistook these young patriots for soldiers and, thinking this post was strongly garrisoned, he deferred his attack until a later time. Drawing off his warriors he repaired to the deep glen northwest of the village to see if he could intercept any travellers along the road to the Mohawk and so pick up any information. Lieut. Matthew Wormuth, with a companion, started from Cherry Valley that evening to Fort Plain. The same day he had left Fort Plain to tell the Cherry Valley people that the militia would come up the next day, as Brant was known to be in the neighborhood. While Wormuth and Sitz, his companion, were riding along the edge of this glen, on their return to Fort Plain, Brant's warriors fired upon them, mortally wounding Wormuth and capturing Sitz. Lieutenant Wormuth was of Col. Klock's Palatine battalion, and that officer came up the next day with the valley militia, but Brant had fled and all that could be done was to take back Wormuth's body to Fort Plain, and thence to his father's home across the river in Palatine. Wormuth had been a personal friend of Brant, who expressed regret at the young officer's death.

————

In July Brant destroyed the little settlement of Andrustown, six miles southeast of German Flats, killing its inhabitants and driving away its live stock.

In the summer of 1778, Brant's long stay at Unadilla, without striking a blow on some of the exposed points of the frontier, excited suspicion among the inhabitants of the valley that he might be planning an attack on them, and a scouting party of four men was accordingly sent out to watch his movements. These rangers fell in with the enemy and three were killed. The fourth, John Adam Helmer, the famous scout, escaped and returned to German Flatts at sundown and gave the alarm that Brant and a large force would be upon the settlements in a short time. At nightfall the enemy, numbering about 300 Tories and 150 Indians, came to the outskirts of the settlements and stopped near the house of Brant's Tory friend, Shoemaker. Here the force remained until early morning. The settlers fled to Forts Dayton and Herkimer, taking with them their most precious belongings. Brant and his red and white warriors devastated the country in the vicinity of these forts, early the next day, and the whole valley thereabouts was illuminated with the light of burning houses, barns and crops. Only two or three persons were killed in this foray, but 63 dwellings, 57 barns, three grist-mills and two saw-mills were burned, and 235 horses, 269 sheep, 229 cattle and 93 oxen were taken and driven off by Brant and his raiders. This happened about Sept. 1, 1778. No scalps or prisoners were taken and the enemy ventured no attack on the forts.

In September, Col. Klock wrote to Gov. Clinton that 150 families were left destitute and homeless in the valley by the many Indian raids of 1778 up to that month.

Walter Butler had obtained a trans-fer from the Albany jail to a friendly Tory's house by feigning sickness. He intoxicated his guard and escaped. In November, 1778, he, together with Brant, fell upon the Cherry Valley settlement with a force of seven hundred Tories and Indians and killed 32 people and 16 soldiers of the garrison, looted the place, burned all the buildnigs and took captive most of the survivors. The women and children were allowed to return, with the exception of three women and their children, one of the women being murdered a day or two after the massacre.

At the time of the Cherry Valley massacre Lieut. Col. James Gordon of the Saratoga militia, is supposed to have been in command at Fort Plain and ordered Col. Klock's regiment and the company under Capt. Van Denbergh at Fort Plank to march to relief of Cherry Valley, where they arrived two hours after the enemy had gone. Some survivors from the afflicted district fled to Fort Plain for safety and many of them remained in its vicinity for the balance of the war.

Lossing gives an account of the Cherry Valley massacre, which we here abridge:

Colonel Ichabod Alden of Massachusetts, was in command of the fort and 250 men. On the 8th of November, he had received a dispatch from Fort Schuyler- saying his fort was about to be attacked, but treated it with unconcern and refused to allow the alarmed inhabitants to move into the fort or even leave their property there. However, Col. Alden sent out scouting parties. One of these, which went toward the Susquehanna, built a fire, went to sleep, and awoke prisoners of Brant and Butler. From them all necessary information was extorted. The next day the raiders camped on a lofty hill covered with evergreens, about a mile southwest of the village and overlooking the whole settlement. From that observatory they could see almost every house in the village. From the prisoners they learned that the officers were quartered out of the fort and that Col. Alden

and Lieut. Col. Stacia were at the house of Robert Wells, recently a judge of the county and formerly an intimate friend of Sir William Johnson and Col. John Butler. Early in the morning of Nov. 10, 1778, the enemy marched slowly toward the village. Snow had fallen during the night and the morning was dark and misty. A halt was made to examine the muskets, although the Indians, crazy for blood, could hardly be restrained. A settler on horseback, going toward the village, was shot, but, being only slightly wounded, galloped on and gave the alarm. The savages rushed in on the settlement. Wells's house was attacked and the whole family murdered together with Col. Alden, who escaped from a window but was struck down and scalped. The families of Mr. Dunlap, the venerable minister, and that of Mr. Mitchell were next almost wiped out, Little Aaron, a Mohawk chief, saving Mr. Dunlap and his daughter; 32 people, mostly women and children, and 16 soldiers were killed. The whole settlement was plundered and burned. The prisoners numbered nearly 40, and included the wife and children of Col. Campbell, who was then absent. They were marched down the valley that night, in a storm of sleet, and were huddled together promiscuously, some of them half naked and without shelter. The enemy, finding the women and children cumbersome, sent them all back the next day, except Mrs. Campbell and her children and her aged mother and a Mrs. Moore, who were kept as hostages for the kind treatment and ultimate exchange for the Tory family of Col. John Butler. Young Butler was the head and front of all the cruelty at Cherry Valley that day. He commanded the expedition and saw unmoved the murder of Mr. Wells, his father's friend, whom Brant hastened to save but arrived too late. Butler would not allow his rangers to even warn their friends in the settlement of approaching danger.

While Brant was collecting his troops at Oghkwaga the previous year, 1777, the strong stone mansion of

Samuel Campbell (colonel of the Canajoharie militia battalion) was fortified to be used as a place of retreat for the women and children in the event of attack. An embankment of earth and logs was thrown up around it, and included two barns. Small block-houses were erected within the enclosure. This was the only fort in Cherry Valley at this time. Mrs. Cannon, the mother of Mrs. Campbell, who was captured, was very old. On the retreat of the marauders, she was an encumbrance and a savage slew her with a tomahawk by the side of her daughter. Mrs. Campbell carried an eighteen-months old baby and was driven with inhuman haste before her captors, while they menaced her life with uplifted hatchets. Arriving among the Senecas, she was kindly treated and installed a member of one of the families. They allowed her to do as she pleased and her deportment was such that she seemed to engage the real affections of the people. Perceiving she wore caps, one was presented to her, considerably spotted with blood, which she recognized as belonging to her friend, Jane Wells. She and her children, from whom she was separated in the Indian country, were afterward exchanged for the wife and family of Colonel John Butler, then in the custody of the Committee of Safety at Albany. There are many well-authenticated instances on record of the humanity of Brant, exercised particularly toward women and children. He was a magnanimous victor and never took the life of a former friend or acquaintance. He loved a hero because of his heroism, although he might be his enemy, and was never known to take advantage of a conquered soldier. The challenge of Capt. McKean to Brant has been mentioned. After the Cherry Valley massacre, he inquired of one of the prisoners for Capt. McKean, who with his family, had left the settlement. Said Brant: "He sent me a challenge. I came to accept it. He is a fine soldier thus to retreat." The captured man replied: "Captain McKean would not turn his back upon an enemy when there was any probability of success." Brant said: "I know it. He is a brave man and I would have given more to take him than any other man in Cherry Valley; but I would not have hurt a hair of his head." Walter Butler ordered a woman and child to be slain in bed at Cherry Valley, when Brant interposed saying, "What, kill a woman and child! That child it not an enemy to the King nor a friend to congress. Long before he will be big enough to do any mischief, the dispute will be settled." When in 1780, Sir John Johnson and Brant led their raiding army through the Schoharie and Mohawk valleys, Brant's humanity was again' displayed. On their way to Fort Hunter an infant was carried off. The frantic mother followed them as far as the fort but could get no tidings of her child. On the morning after the departure of the invaders, and while Gen. Van Rensselaer's officers were at breakfast, a young Indian came bounding into the room, bearing the infant in his arms and a letter from Captain Brant, addressed to "the commander of the rebel army." The letter was as follows: "Sir—I send you by one of my runners, the child which he will deliver, that you may know that, whatever others may do, I do not make war upon women and children. I am sorry to say that I have those engaged with me who are more savage than the savages themselves." He named the Butlers and others of the Tory leaders. Brant hated the cowardly white Tory fiend, Butler, and objected strongly to serving under him in the Cherry Valley expedition. The Wells family were close friends of Col. John Butler, father of Walter Butler, and the murder of this family by Butler's raiders was particularly brutal. Mr. Wells was tomahawked by a Tory while kneeling in prayer. Jane Wells, his sister, who was a beautiful and accomplished woman, attempted to hide in a woodpile. An Indian caught her. He wiped his bloody scalping knife and sheathed it deliberately in view of the terrified woman. Then he leisurely took his tomahawk from his girdle and at this moment, a Tory, who had been a servant in the family, sprang forward and attempted to interfere but the savage thrust him aside and buried his hatchet in his victim's head. It is said that Colonel Butler, professedly grieved at the beastly murderous conduct of his son at Cherry Valley, remarked concerning the Wells family: "I would have gone miles on my knees to save that family, and why my son did not do it, God only knows."

Late in the fall of 1778, at the request of Sir John Johnson, the Canadian Governor-General Haldimand, sent fifty men to recover his and his father's papers which had been buried in an iron chest on the premises at Johnson Hall. They recovered the papers which were found to be practically worthless from dampness. A Tory, named Helmer, was captured.

The Saratoga and Oriskany campaigns have been summarized in the Oriskany chapter. The national events from the fall of 1777 through 1778 are summarized as follows: 1777, Oct. 4, American defeat at Germantown; winter 1777-8, American army in winter quarters at Valley Forge, Pa.; 1778, February, French recognize American independence and become allies of the colonies; 1778' June, British evacuate Philadelphia and indecisive battle of Monmouth follows; 1778, July, Wyoming, Pa., massacre of settlers by British and Indians under Col. Butler; 1778, Dec., Savannah, Ga., captured by British.

CHAPTER XV.

1779—Gen. Clinton at Canajoharie—Road Built to Otsego Lake—Guard on Otsquago Creek—Sullivan and Clinton Defeat Johnson and Brant.

To chastise the hostile Iroquois, Col. Van Schaick was sent from Fort Schuyler to make a descent on the Onondagas on April 18, 1779. The Indians fled and their three villages were burned. The Onondagas retaliated by a descent into the Schoharie valley where ten militiamen were killed.

In the spring of 1779 it was resolved to send a large American expedition into the Indian country to severely chastise the savages so as to discourage them from renewing their ravages. Gen. Sullivan was placed in chief command of the expedition, the plan of which was a combined movement in two divisions; one, from Pennsylvania under Sullivan, to ascend the Susquehanna, and the other from the north through the Mohawk valley to Otsego lake and the headwaters of the Susquehanna, under Gen. James Clinton. The campaign had been carefully worked out by Washington and experienced men called in council. Gen. Clinton's forces assembled at Schenectady and his supplies and military stores were sent up the Mohawk on batteaux to Canajoharie. These same boats were later transported to Otsego lake and used on his trip down the Susquehanna.

Clinton had a force of 1600 men and made his Mohawk rendezvous in the present village of Canajoharie, which must then have been a scene of great activity as well as the river upon which ordnance and supplies were brought in bateaux. In Canajoharie Clinton boarded with Johannes Roof, a pioneer settler of land at Fort Stanwix, which he abandoned on the approach of St. Leger and came to Canajoharie, there opening a tavern.

While Clinton was preparing for his overland journey at Canajoharie, the Otsquago road to Otsego lake from Fort Plain was guarded by two companies of infantry and one of artillery, with Fort Plain as their base.

John Fea, in his article on the "Indian Trails of the Mohawk Valley," says: "Upon the return of the Onondaga expedition, Clinton deployed two companies of infantry and one of artillery on the Otsquago road, west of Fort Plain. One of the companies was stationed at Camp Creek, near the present village of Starkville, at the confluence of the creek and the Otsquago. From this place the Indian trail from the Mohawk to Wa-ont-ha went southwestward. Lieutenant Van Horne, of Colonel Fisher's regiment, was in charge of the work of defense at this point, as it was expected that Brant would make a sortie from the west by the way of this trail, to harass the movement of Clinton's wagon train. During the stay at Camp Creek a corduroy road was made along the Otsquago creek on ground where the present village of Van Hornesville is located. The old roadway to Springfield at that time, went over the steep incline east of Van Hornesville. Clinton's troops made a new road over the 'pumpkin hook' district of about two miles in length to accommodate the carriage of his artillery. At the same time he was hewing a roadway through an unbroken forest from Seeber's Lane, southwest of Canajoharie creek, to the head of Otsego lake, a distance of about twenty miles. Over this road they transported 220 heavy batteaux and provisions for three months. June 17, 1779, he commenced the arduous task. He reached Springfield with all his luggage, June 30. At this place Clinton was joined by the troops that had been deployed at Otsquago." Eight horse wagons and oxcarts are said to have been used on this hard overland carry.

Clinton's united force soon reached the head of Otsego lake where they launched their bateaux and floated nine miles down its placid waters to its outlet at Cooperstown. It is said that there was not then a single house standing at that site. The passage down the lake was made on a lovely summer's day, and everything connected with it was so novel and picturesque that the scene was truly enchanting. On arriving at the foot of the lake, the troops landed and remained several weeks, until it was sufficiently raised by a dam constructed at the outlet, to float the fleet of 208 boats. When a sufficient head of water was thus obtained the boats were properly arranged along the outlet and filled with troops, stores and cannon. Then the dam was torn away and the flotilla passed down into the Susquehanna (a word signifying in Indian "crooked river"). It is said that, preparatory to opening the out-

let of the lake, a dam made by beavers, on one of the large inlets, was ordered destroyed. This was done but it was repaired by the little animals the next night. It had to be more thoroughly destroyed and a guard placed there all night to prevent its being rebuilt. While the army was quartered there two deserters were tried and one shot. The younger, a boy, was pardoned but the other, who had previously deserted from the British to the Americans and then deserted them, was shot. Said Clinton: "He is neither good for king or country— let him be shot." The flood from the opening of Clinton's dam destroyed the Indian's cornfields along the river banks, who, being ignorant of the cause of their loss, were astonished and alarmed.

Gen. Clinton's force formed a juncture with Sullivan's at Tioga on Aug. 22, and the united force moved up the Tioga and Chemung, destroying the Indians' growing crops. The force of 4600 Americans met the Tories and Indians under Johnson and Brant near the present city of Elmira on Aug. 29. A fierce battle ensued and was for long doubtful. The patriots' artillery under Proctor finally routed the enemy. The invaders rested that night and next day made a vigorous pursuit. The entire Indian country was ravaged and destroyed in a most thorough fashion. In revenge the savages retaliated upon the frontier settlements whenever opportunity offered.

While Clinton was waiting at Canajoharie for his troops and supplies to assemble, and also for the construction and delivery of bateaux, two Tories were there hung and a deserter shot. The Tory spies were Lieut. Henry Hare and Sergt. Newbery, both of Col. Butler's regiment. They were tried by a general court martial as spies and sentenced to be hanged, "which was done accordingly at Canajoharie, to the great satisfaction of all the inhabitants of that place who were friends of their country, as they were known to be very active in almost all the murders that were committed on the frontiers. They were inhabitants of Tryon county, had each a wife and several children, who came to see them and beg their lives." The foregoing quoted words are those of Gen. Clinton himself in a letter to his wife. At the time of the execution, Gen. Clinton rode up to Fort Plain and spent an hour or two with Dominie Gros, to avoid the importunity of the spies' friends who begged for their lives, and especially was this the case with Mrs. Hare. Hare and Newbury had left the Seneca country with 63 Indians and 2 white men, who divided them into three parties. One was to attack Schoharie, another party was to descend on Cherry Valley and the Mohawk river and the third party was to skulk about Fort Schuyler and the upper part of the Mohawk to take prisoners or scalps. Both had lived in the town of Glen and were captured there. A fifteen-year-old boy, named Francis Putman, captured Hare, who was delayed in his return to Canada by a sprained ankle. A party of Whigs under Lieut. Newkirk arrested New bury that night. It is said "they were enabled to find his house in the woods by following a tame deer which fled to it." The executions in Canajoharie took place on Academy hill. While Hare was in custody, at the request of Gen. Clinton, Johannes Roof asked the Tory if he did not kill Caty Steers at Fort Stanwix in 1777. "For you were seen with your hands in her hair," said Roof. Hare confessed that he had killed and scalped her.

Gen. James Clinton was born in Ulster county, New York, August 9, 1736. At the age of 20 (1756), he was a captain under Bradstreet in the attack on Fort Frontenac. In 1763 he commanded four companies in Ulster and Orange as protection against Indians. He, with his brother, George Clinton (governor of New York during the Revolution), early espoused the patriot cause. He was a colonel in 1775 and went with Montgomery to Canada. In 1776 he was a brigadier general and was in command, under Gov. Clinton, at Forts Montgomery and

Clinton when they fell into the hands of the enemy in 1777. He escaped and conjointly with Sullivan led the expedition against the Indians in 1779. During the remainder of the war he was connected with the Northern Department of the Army, having headquarters at Albany. He retired to his estate at Newburgh, after peace was declared, and died there in 1812, aged 75. He was the father of Dewitt Clinton, the eminent governor of New York and "father of the Canal system."

The state legislature on Oct. 23, 1779, levied a tax of $2,500,000, of which Tryon county's quota was $81,766. The quota of the Canajoharie district was $16,728. April 6, 1780, an other state tax of $5,000,000 was au thorized of which $120,000 was as signed to Tryon. The quota of the Canajoharie district was $28,000. Payment of these two taxes, levied inside of six months, must have been a con siderable hardship to the valley settlers at this time.

Colonel Visscher was in command at Fort Paris in Stone Arabia in November, 1779, having command of this section. While Visscher was on a visit to Fort Plank, a detachment of soldiers, from Col. Stephen J. Schuyler's regiment, located at Fort Paris, mutinied, knocked down the guards and started to desert. One of them was shot down and presumably the rest escaped. Capt. Jelles Fonda, in temporary command there, was courtmartialed and honorably acquitted. In December, at a conference, Colonels Visscher and Klock and Lieut. Col. Wagner dispersed a number of three months militia men, on account of the lateness of the season and the improbability of immediate invasions. This was done with the sanction of Gen. Ten Broeck and some of the garrisons were broken up for a time.

July 9, 1779, three Vols (now Folts) brothers and the wives of two of them, and a Mrs. Catherine Dorenberger, who had been a Hilts, went berrypicking up the West Canada creek, near Fort Dayton. A party of a dozen Indians and Tories discovered them. Two of the brothers and their wives escaped to the fort, although one of the women was wounded. Mrs. Dorenberger was overtaken and stabbed to death with a spear by her own brother, named Hilts, who was one of the guerilla party. He also tore off the scalp from her dead body. Joseph Vols was separated from the rest, but leveled his gun and fired at a party of nine who were pursuing him in a narrow path. He was so close that three Indians fell, two killed instantly and one mortally wounded. His gun was loaded with 21 buckshot. This is said to have been the best shot fired in Tryon county during the war. One Indian, in the race which followed, got up and wounded Vols with his tomahawk, but the Whig knocked his assailant down, stunned him with a blow of his gun and escaped, although wounded by several shots. Troops, hearing the firing, came up and the white and red savages fled. Conrad Vols, one of the brothers, was wounded at Oriskany two years before.

The national events of 1779 are herewith summarized: 1778-9, Col. Clarke conquers middle west from English by victories at Kaskaskia and Vincennes; 1779, July 15, Americans under Gen. "Mad Anthony" Wayne capture Stony Point on the Hudson; 1779, Aug. 29, Sullivan's and Clinton's patriot army defeat Indian and British force in battle of Chemung (at Elmira), Indian country subsequently devastated; 1779, September, Paul Jones, on American ship, Bon Homme Richard, defeats two British men-of-war; 1779, October, French and American attack on Savannah repulsed.

The lot of the soldier was not all one of warfare. In the midst of ever-present dangers, he took his holiday and his natural and robust pleasures with a carefree heart. An instance from Simms details a merrymaking of Revolutionary times: "In the fall of 1779,

there was a corn-husking at the residence of John Eikler in Philadelphia Bush. His house was some six miles east of Johnstown, and where John Frank formerly kept a tavern. Capt. John Littel permitted ten or a dozen young men of his company to go from the Johnstown fort to the husking, of which number was my [Simms's] informant, Jacob Shew. They went on foot from the fort to Eikler's. A lot of buxom maidens, corresponding in number, were already assembled from the scattered settlement on their arrival. As the night was a rainy one the corn was taken into the house to husk.

"In the protracted struggle for political freedom, many a lovely girl had to toil in the field to raise sustenance for herself and feebler friends, when the strong arms, on which they had before leaned, were wielding the sword or musket far away. As the husking progressed not a few red ears were found, imposing a penalty on the finder, and lucky indeed was the Son of Mars who canceled such forfeit, as he was brought in contact with the cherry lips of a blushing lass, who, although she may have said aloud the young rebel ought to be ashamed, secretly blessed the inventor of huskings. A part of the corn was risked and hung up under the roof on a lintel, which, to add variety to the entertainment, broke down under its accumulated weight, and came near entrapping one of the guests. After the corn was all husked and the eatables and drinkables—pumpkin pies and cider—were disposed of, the party had glorious times. But why specify at this late day the details of ancient sayings and doings? Suffice it to add, the rain came down in torrents, so as to prevent the guests from returning home; and after the midnight hilarity had stolen out through the crannies of the log dwelling, the guests—but how dispose of so many without beds? The husks were leveled down, and each took a soldier's lodge upon them; for the girls—heaven bless their memory —were the artless and true maidens of the times."

CHAPTER XVI.

1780 — May 21, Johnson's Johnstown Raid — August 2, Brant's Minden Raid.

After Sullivan's campaign the valley had comparative repose for a time. So far the lower Mohawk section had suffered little. Its men had gone forth to fight for the common defense and their numbers had been reduced by death and capture. They had received an influx of population from the defenseless people driven in from above, which, however, was no added protection.

May 21, 1780, Sir John Johnson entered Johnstown near midnight at the head of 500 Indians, Tories and British. He had crossed the country from Crown Point to the Sacandaga, a point from which an invasion was least expected, and stolen upon the settlement so quietly that the patriots were first warned of the enemy's presence by the beginning of the work of murder and destruction in their midst. The resident Tories, being in the secret and assisting the raiders, were exempt from injury. Johnson separated his men into two parties, one going through Johnstown and down the Cayadutta to the Mohawk, there to join the other division, which was to take a more easterly route to Tribes Hill. They were then to unite and ravage up the valley. The whole course of Sir John's eastern raiders was murderous and disgraceful. They murdered and scalped a Mr. Lodwick Putman and son, dragged Putman's son-in-law, Amasa Stevens, out of his house and killed him in the most brutal manner and then went on to the house of Gerret Putman, a stanch Whig, who had been marked as a victim but who had removed lately and rented his house to two Tory Englishmen. Ignorant of this the Tories and Indians broke into the house and murdered and scalped the two inmates before they had a chance to explain their situation. Henry Hansen was next murdered and his sons carried off prisoners. They next came to the house of Col. Visscher, whom Simms says

was a brave man in spite of the unfortunate panic retreat of his force at Oriskany. His two brothers were with him and they made a brave stand, fighting valiantly up the stairway and into their chamber, where they were stricken down and scalped and the house set on fire. Visscher was tomahawked, scalped and left for dead, but revived and lived many years. The, western division led by Sir John himself, went through Johnstown undiscovered by the Whig garrison of the fort which had formerly been the jail. This force captured Sampson Sammons and his three sons and, uniting with the eastern force, proceeded up the valley, burning every building not belonging to a Tory. The alarm, however, was getting abroad and the people had some chance to escape to the neighboring forts. Returning after a few miles foray to Caughnawaga they burned every building but the church and parsonage. Here in the morning an old man named Douw Fonda had been murdered. He was one of nine aged men, four over eighty, who were brutally killed and scalped on this raid. Sir John returned to Johnstown and recovered his buried plate and valuables and about twenty slaves. The plate and valuables filled two barrels. Toward night the militia began to gather under Col. John Harper and Johnson decided to get away, heading for the Sacandaga. The militia were in too small numbers to attack him but followed him several miles. Col. Van Schaick came up with 800 men in pursuit but too late to engage the guerillas.

While halting, on the day after leaving Johnstown, the elder Mr. Sammons (Sampson Sammons) requested a personal interview with Sir John Johnson, which was granted. He asked to be released, but the baronet hestitated. The old man then recurred to former times, when he and Sir John were friends and neighbors. Said he: "See what you have done, Sir John. You have taken myself and my sons prisoners, burned my dwelling to ashes, and left my family with no covering but the heavens above, and no prospect but desolation around them. Did we treat you in this manner when you were in the power of the Tryon County Committee? Do you remember when we were consulted by General Schuyler, and you agreed to surrender your arms? Do you then remember that you then agreed to remain neutral, and that, upon that condition, General Schuyler left you at liberty on your parole? Those conditions you violated. You went off to Canada, enrolled yourself in the service of the king, raised a regiment of the disaffected who abandoned their country with you, and you have now returned to wage a cruel war against us, by burning our dwellings and robbing us of our property. I was your friend in the Committee of Safety, and exerted myself to save your person from injury. And how am I requited? Your Indians have murdered and scalped old Mr. Fonda, at the age of eighty years, a man who, I have heard your father say, was like a father to him when he settled in Johnstown and Kingsborough. You cannot succeed, Sir John, in such a warfare, and you will never enjoy your property more." The baronet made no reply but the old gentleman was set at liberty.

Soon after this murderous raid of Sir John Johnson, Gen. Clinton ordered Col. Gansevoort to repair with his regiment to Fort Plain, to take charge of a large quantity of stores destined for Fort Schuyler and convoy the batteaux containing them to their destination. This caution was necessary to save the supplies from capture by the Indians. Most of the local militia accompanied Gansevoort's command.

Brant was again on the warpath, watching for a favorable moment to spring upon the unprotected inhabitants, and supplied the Tories with information of movements in the settlements. He was early aware of the departure of troops for Fort Schuyler and, when they had gathered at Fort Plain and started on their march of protection for the supplies going by river, on August 2, 1780, made a de-

scent on the Canajoharie district with a force of about 500 Indians and Tories, chiefly the former. There were several stockades in the neighborhoods desolated by the savages (for the Tories seem to have equaled the red men in their barbarity). Chief among them, however, was the principal fortification of Fort Plain. Here the garrison was insufficient, without help from the militia, to give battle to Brant's force and, as has been stated, the local troops were absent with Gansevoort's force. Brant evidently approached the Mohawk from the west by way of the Otsquago valley and his raiders in bands thoroughly devasted the Freysbush and Dutchtown roads.

The approach of the Indians was announced by a woman firing the signal shot from a Fort Plain cannon. The people were then busy with their harvesting, and all who were fortunate enough to escape fled to the fort, leaving their property to be destroyed. The firing of one signal shot indicated that the people were to flee to the nearest stockade, while two or three in quick succession ordered the settlers to seek safety by hiding in the bush or woods and told that the enemy was between them and the fort. Fifty-three dwellings were burned with their barns and buildings, 16 people were murdered and 50 or 60 captured. The Indians, knowing its weakness, rushed up within gunshot of Fort Plain, after ravaging the Dutchtown and Freysbush districts. Seeber's, Abeel's and other houses were burned and then the savages fired the Reformed Dutch church. The spire was adorned with a brass ball and the Indians, believing it to be gold, watched eagerly for it to fall. When at last it dropped, with the burning of the spire, they all sprang forward to seize the prize. This red hot ball of brass was responsible for many a blistered red man's hand. To make a show of force at Fort Plain, some of the women who had fled there, put on men's hats and carried poles, showing themselves just sufficiently above the stockade to give the savages the impression of militiamen. This ruse was evidently successful for, had Brant known how feebly the fort was defended he would probably have rushed this stockade, burned it and massacred its inmates.

The columns of smoke rising from the burning buildings were seen at Johnstown and were the first intimation of this latest incursion. The farmers left their harvest fields and joined Col. Wemple, marching up the river with the Schenectady and Albany militia, but they were not in time to check the work of destruction or cut off the retreat of the marauders. Colonel Wemple, who was thought to be more prudent than valorous on this occasion, only reached the desolated region in time to see the smoking ruins and rest securely in Fort Plain that night. The next morning some buildings, which had escaped the torch the day before were discovered to be on fire. Col. Wemple, on being notified of the fact, said that, if any volunteers were disposed to look into the matter, they might do so. Whereupon Major Bantlin, with some of the Tryon county militia, set out for the scene of the fire. It proved to have been set by a party of Brant's raiders who, as soon as discovered, fled to rejoin the main body. In a day one of the fairest portions of the valley had been desolated. The small forts which were demolished were not garrisoned and had been constructed by the people themselves. The inhabitants of the desolated region had protested against helping the government to keep open communication with Fort Schuyler, when there was constant need for the protection of their own district. The withdrawal of its militia and the consequent terrible result justified their worst apprehensions.

This raid which culminated around Fort Plain was one of the most destructive made during the war. Brant had with him Cornplanter and other distinguished chiefs. Col. Samuel Clyde sent Gov. George Clinton an account of this affair, evidently written from Fort Plain, as follows:

Canajoharie, Aug. 6, 1780.
Sir—I here send you an account of the fate of our district:

On the 2d day of this inst. Joseph Brant, at the head of four or five hundred Indians and Tories, broke in upon the settlements, and laid the best part of the district in ashes, and killed 16 of the inhabitants that we have found, took between 50 and 60 prisoners—mostly women and children—12 of whom they sent back. They have killed or drove away with them, upwards of 300 head of cattle and horses; have burned 53 dwelling houses, besides some outhouses, and as many barns; one very elegant church, and one grist mill, and two small forts that the women fled out of. They have burned all the inhabitants' weapons and implements for husbandry, so that they are left in a miserable condition. They have nothing left to support themselves but what grain they have growing, and that they cannot get saved for want of tools to work with and very few to be got here.

This affair happened at a very unfortunate hour, when all the militia of the county were called up to Fort Schuyler—Stanwix—to guard nine batteaux—half laden. It was said the enemy intended to take them on their passage to Fort Schuyler. There was scarce a man left that was able to go. It seems that everything conspired for our destruction in this quarter; one whole district almost destroyed and the best regiment of militia in the county rendered unable to help themselves or the public. This I refer you to Gen. Rensselaer for the truth of.

Brant, with subtle savagery, had thrown out a hint that he intended to take or destroy the supply flotilla on its way up the river. It was during this invasion that the Indians took the trader John Abeel, living at Fort Plain, and he was afterward liberated and sent back to his ruined home by his son Cornplanter, the Seneca chieftain. Parties of Indians at this time also made minor raids around Fort Herkimer and Fort Dayton, in the Schoharie valley and other sections.

————

Gyantwachia or Cornplanter, the Seneca chief, was associated with Brant in this Minden raid. He was a son of John Abeel, the Indian trader of Fort Plain, and the daughter of a Seneca chief. Although a half breed he was the leading man of his nation for a period of almost sixty years.

At the close of the Revolution, he was not only ready to bury the hatchet but to take sides in all future troubles with the Americans. He became the firm friend of Washington and was perhaps the only Indian war chief, in our borders, whose friendship for the United States was unshaken in the Indian difficulties existing from 1791 to 1794. In 1797 Cornplanter paid a visit to Washington at Philadelphia. He fixed his permanent residence on the Alleghany river in Pennsylvania, where he subsequently lived and died and where his descendants still reside. In 1802 Cornplanter paid a visit to President Jefferson. In the war of 1812 with England, the Seneca chief, then almost 70 years old, offered to lead 200 warriors with the American troops against the English. He was not allowed to do so but some of his nation were with the Americans in the war and rendered efficient service as scouts. His son, George Abeel, held a major's commission and led these red American soldiers. Cornplanter was about five feet, ten inches in height and a chief of fine bearing. He is said to have been a fine orator in the Indian way and, to further the interests of his people, made effective speeches before Washington and before the governor of Pennsylvania. The latter state gave him, in 1789, 1,300 acres of land and the national government paid him $250 yearly, in appreciation of his services rendered the country by keeping his own people in friendship with the United States. In 1866 the legislature of Pennsylvania erected a monument to Cornplanter at Jennesadaga, his village in Warren county in that state, and also published a pamphlet regarding his life and works. The inscription on the monument reads:

"Giantwahia, the Cornplanter.

"John O'Bail [Abeel], alias Cornplanter, died at Cornplanter town, February 18, 1836, aged about 100 years.

"Chief of the Seneca tribe, and principal chief of the Six Nations from the period of the Revolutionary war to the time of his death. Distinguished for talents, courage, eloquence sobriety, and love of his tribe and race, to whose welfare he devoted his time, his energies and his means during a long and eventful life."

Simms says the age given on this monument is wrong and that Corn planter was born about 1746 and was about 90 years old at the time of his death. His visit to Fort Plain in 1810 is treated of in a later chapter.

CHAPTER XVII.

1780, August 2—Incidents and Tragedies and Details of Brant's Minden Raid.

The Canajoharie district raid of August 2, 1780, by Indians and Tories under Brant, was made from the direction of the Susqehanna valley through the Otsquago valley and thoroughly ravaged the Dutchtown and Freysbush districts, culminating about Fort Plain. For that period, the portion of the Canajoharie district comprised in the town of Minden was thickly settled and the people fled to and crowded the forts which were so feebly defended on account of the withdrawal of the militia to convoy stores to Fort Schuyler. The maintenance of this latter exposed post, and the consequent splitting up of the defensive strength of Tryon county among so many forts, was doubtless the reason that so many terrible raids of the enemy devastated the valley, the hostile force escaping before the scattered garrisons and militia could unite for common defense.

In the Minden raid the raiders broke up into small bands, the more thoroughly to murder loot and burn. From Simms's account, it appears that the enemy remained in this section during August 2 and that night and the next day dispersed in small parties, probably toward the Susqehanna for the most part. This was done to evade pursuit by the militia then marching to Fort Plain and shows how difficult is was for the patriot Tryon county military authorities to check these forays and brings into prominence Willett's effective work in the following year, at the time of the two raids which ended in the American victories of Sharon Springs and Johnstown.

The Minden raid, in point of loss of life, prisoners taken and property destroyed takes rank as the most destructive which took place along the Mohawk during the Revolution. At German Flats, in September, 1778, 116 houses and barns were burned, but there was no loss of life with the exception of three rangers who were killed while scouting for Brant's force. It was due to the long heroic run of the noted scout Helmer to German Flats and his warning to the farmers that there was no further casualties. About the same number of barns and dwellings were burned in the Minden raid of 1780, but in addition 16 people were killed and 60 captured. The loss of stock and implements was a most serious one as it prevented the harvesting of crops and the Canajoharie district was one of the most fertile sections of the valley and was depended upon frequently for bread and foodstuffs by neighboring communities. Its defense of four forts had previously prevented its sacking, but its forts were useless without sufficient men and these were absent on the march to Fort Stanwix to convoy a comparatively trifling amount of stores.

In this chapter are narrated some of the personal experiences, tragedies and details of this hostile foray in Minden township. They show, as nothing else can, what these raids meant to the suffering valley people, just as the experiences of the patriot fighters at Oriskany display the horrors of Revolutionary warfare along the old New York frontier. They also give further information about the families about Fort Plain at that time and furnish some insight into the farm life of the period. They are summarized or copied from Simms's "Frontiersmen of New York."

John Rother, at this time, owned a grist mill and had a farm in the Geisenberg neighborhood. Daniel Olendorf was his miller. Rother owned a big dog which barked and gave warning of the approaching Indians, on Au-

gust 2. Rother seized his gun and ran for Fort Plank, more than a mile away, followed by his niece. His wife hid in a flax field. As the Indians approached the house the dog set upon them furiously and they stopped to shoot him, the reports arousing several settlers and warning them of danger. The savages plundered and burned the dwellings, the first they fired in that neighborhood. Rother and his niece were chased by one Indian. Not being able to keep up with her uncle, the girl kept falling behind and the Indian gaining. The panic-stricken girl shouted "Uncle, the Indian." Rother stopped and pointed his gun at the Indian who would stop or fall back. This was repeated a dozen times until the two fugitives reached the fort. Rother was afraid to fire for had he missed, both would have been tomahawked and scalped. His wife was not discovered by the savages and also escaped.

Joseph Myers lived four miles southwest of Fort Plain. On the day of the raid, he had gone to Fort Plank to make cartridges, leaving his wife and three children, aged three, five and seven years, at home. Evan, the only girl, was five. Myers had lost a limb and wore a wooden leg. The family lived a mile from the Rothers, before mentioned, and Mrs. Rother was known as the "Doctress," as she dispensed home-made German herb remedies. Mrs. Myers sent the two oldest children to get some salve for the youngest child's head. The oldest brother said he would carry the youngest on his back to the Rothers, let the "Doctress" apply the salve, and then carry him back. Evan was allowed to accompany them. When nearly half-way they heard a gun fired and seeing Indians around Rother's house, started to run home. The savages saw them and several chased them, one of them pinning the two little boys to the ground with a bayonet as they were running pick-a-back. Evan later thought she was not scalped as she did not cry. She was picked up in the arms of an Indian and the savages went to the Myers. Mrs. Myers, hearing the gun shot at Rother's, hid and saved her life. The buildings were plundered and burned. Evan was taken to Canada with other prisoners and, on account of her tender age, was borne on the back of an Indian most of the long, tiresome journey. On their arrival at the Indian village an Indian took the girl in his arms and whipped her. The little five-year-old was then put on a horse led by an Indian, to run the gauntlet. She was knocked off by blows several times and put on again and was considerably hurt but did not dare cry. She was then given an Indian dress and her cheeks painted. She quickly forgot her German tongue during her life with the Indians, who found such a small white child so much trouble that they finally delivered her at Montreal for a bounty. Here she soon forgot her Indian and learned to speak English. She was long in Canada before it was learned whose child she was as she had forgotten her own name. Peter Olendorf, who was captured in the same raid, readily guessed her parentage when she said her father had a wooden leg and lived not far from a fort. Mrs. Bartlett Pickard, with a nursing child, was captured in the vicinity of Myers, and later liberated by Brant and sent home. In order to take her home, Mrs. Pickard claimed Evan was her child but the Indians were not fooled and the pretence was of no use. Mrs. Pickard arrived at Fort Plain, three days after her capture, almost famished and then Mrs. Myers first learned the fate of her daughter. Mrs. Pletts, made a prisoner on the same day in Freysbush, brought Evan back with her, on her liberation from Canada, taking a motherly care of her for which, it is unnecessary to say, her parents were ever after grateful.

David Olendorf was at work with his wife in his barn. He was pitching wheat from his wagon and his wife was mowing it away, a duty that often devolved on women during the war. When he, before the muzzle of a gun, was ordered down from the wagon, she was not in sight and, upon being asked, Olendorf said there was no one else there. A suspicious savage said, "If any one else is in the barn call them out as we are going to burn it." True to their word they did burn it and, after it was set on fire, the woman was called down from the loft. The savages also burned and plundered the house. With other prisoners, the Olendorfs were started on the long journey to Canada, suffering severe privations on the way. Soon after their journey started the Indians asked Olendorf if he could run pretty well and he said "Yes." Thereupon they told him, if he could beat their best Indian runner, he would be set at liberty and this contest the white man easily won. He soon found out why his fleetness of foot had been thus tested, for he was securely bound every night during the rest of the journey. During the dreary march he incurred the displeasure of an Indian, who threw his tomahawk at Olendorf, the blade sticking in a tree behind which the white man sprang. An old savage saved his life. On reaching Canada Olendorf and his wife were separated and he was imprisoned. He then decided to enlist in the British service and desert to his countrymen at the earliest opportunity. While on his way to the New York frontier settlements, with a raiding party under Sir John Johnson, two prisoners were brought in. Olendorf, who was then a sergeant, overheard the men talk in German and he proposed to them for all three to escape. It became his official duty to post sentinels that night which favored his design and after stationing the most distant one he took occasion on his return to lop several twigs that he might pass behind the outer watchman unobserved. Securing provisions, he conducted the two men outside the camp at midnight. Observing great caution, part of the time crawling on their hands and knees, the three found the broken boughs and passed all the sentinels in safety. "Now if you know the way to the settlements, lead on for we have not a moment to lose," said Olendorf. One of the captives became pilot and in a few days the trio reached Fort Plain in safety, where they were joyously received by their friends, whom they forewarned of the enemy's approach.

Mrs. Olendorf, then with child, feared longer to remain in an Indian family to which she had been taken and, watching her opportunity when the family were all drunk, to which condition she had contributed as far as possible by freely passing the liquor, she fled for refuge to the residence of an English officer for protection. The family were at first afraid to conceal her, fearing the revenge of the savages. Her condition excited their pity and they concealed her in a closet, where the Indians failed to find her on their search. On the birth of her little son, two English gentlemen acted as sponsors, from whom she had a certificate of its birth. She was finally taken to Halifax, exchanged with other prisoners, and finally reached Fort Plain over a year after her capture. The boy born in captivity, Daniel Olendorf jr., became an inn keeper in Cooperstown and his brother Peter was an inn keeper at Fort Plain. Daniel Olendorf senior was one of the scouting party which shot Walter Butler the next year at West Canada creek.

Baltus Sitts, of the Geisenberg settlement, was at work in the fields with his wife and so escaped unseen, but his buildings were burned and plundered. Mary Sitts, nine years old, and her grandfather were captured. Sophia Sitts, a five-year-old, was taken by an Indian squaw in the apple orchard. After carrying the little prisoner on her back some distance, the squaw found it too hard and, setting the child on the ground, pointed to the house and told her to go back. The grandfather was taken to Fallhill where he was liberated at the intercession of the squaw named, who had doubtless received at some time some kindness or favor from the Sitts family. Mary Sitts was taken to Canada, adopted into an Indian family and ever after remained there. A few years later her father went after her and

found her, in everything but color, a veritable squaw. No persuasion could induce her to return and she later became the wife of an Indian, at whose death she married a white man and remained in Canada.

According to Simms, Sophia Sitts was living near Hallsville in 1882, being then at the age of 107 years. Simms says she then distinctly remembered her own and her sister's capture and says she was then five, placing her birth Oct. 6, 1774. This would make her the person living to the oldest known age in the history of the valley. In February, 1883, Mrs. Sitts was still living, being then 108 years old. There is no record of her death, to the writer's knowledge, but she probably passed away soon after. Few women are said to have done so much hard work in their lifetime as this centenarian and for many years she was considered one of the best binders ever seen in a wheat field. Sophia Sitts had three husbands, William Livingston, Joseph Pooler and Jacob Wagner.

Another similar case to that of Mary Sitts is that of Christina Bettinger, taken prisoner near Hallsville. Her father, Martin, was with the militia on the expedition to Fort Schuyler and her mother was taken prisoner, with six children, but was liberated after the party had gone a short distance. Among all the demoniac savagery, which loved to murder and torture human beings of the tenderest years and of tottering age and all the periods between, Brant's periods of clemency and humanity stand out peculiarly. He evidently protected his former friends as much as possible and he decried the fiendish savagery of Walter Butler and his like. There were other Indians somewhat like him. Christina Bettinger, 7 years old, was not at the house but was captured by another party and taken to Canada. She was not exchanged at the end of the war, and a few years later her father found her. He found her living among squaws and practically one of them. She was identified by the scar of a dog bite on her arm. She was given a small cake, baked and sent her by her mother, which touched her sensibility even to tears. She refused to return home and is believed to have married an Indian and, uncouth and uncivilized as she was, remained in her isolated wilderness adopted home. A family of Ecklers, residing near Bettingers, were also captured.

Three brothers, John, Sebastian and Matthias Shaul, then resided at Van Hornesville and were all captured and taken to Canada. Frederick Bronner, living nearby, secreted himself under an untanned cowhide, and so escaped capture. The women and children here were allowed to return home by Brant, shortly after. Jacob Bronner, George Snouts and Peter Casselman were captured by the enemy near Fort Plank. After the raid nine settlers without coffins were buried at this post.

The following is copied verbatim from Simms, as probably representative of family border experiences:

George Lintner was among the pioneer residents of that part of the Canajoharie settlements known as Geisenberg in the present town of Minden, four miles from Fort Plain. On the 2d day of August, Lintner went early in the day to Fort Plank, a mile or two distant, to perform some duty. At the end of only a few hours he learned from the signal guns of the neighboring forts, as also from the constant discharge of firearms, which he believed in the hands of the enemy, that the invaders of the territory were numerous and would doubtless find every habitation in the district. The arrival of Rother and his niece and probably other fugitives at this post, told him of the possible fate of his own family, but he dared not proceed thither alone and Fort Plank was too feebly garrisoned to afford a sallying party. His family consisted of a wife and five children, their ages ranging at about 15, 11, 8 and 6 years and an infant of a few months; and being now unable to afford them needed assistance caused him many an anxious thought and fearful foreboding. The names of these children in which their ages stand were, Albert, Elizabeth, John and Abram. During the forenoon, Mrs. Lintner and her children had heard the frequent discharge of guns in the neighborhood but did not suspect it proceeded from the enemy until noon, when they had seated themselves at the dinner table. The mother then began to feel disquieted and said: "My children we are eating our dinner here and the Indians might come and murder us before we are aware of it." As she said this she arose from the table and opened the door; and instantly she saw a sight that almost curdled the blood in her veins. Scarcely a mile distant she saw a thick cloud of smoke, and at once recognized it as coming from the roof of Rother's grist mill, while in the next moment she heard the discharge of several guns which the enemy had fired into a flock of sheep near the mill. Such omens could not be misconstrued, and snatching her infant child she fled from the house, followed by the other children, down a steep bank into the woods just beyond. Scarcely had they gained this covert when the Indians entered the house and found the table ready for dinner; and, not finding the family in the house, they fired into and then searched the bushes through which the family had passed a few minutes before. Their firing told the fugitives they had not fled one moment too soon. Dispatching the dinner so opportunely provided for them, they plundered and set fire to the house, and only remaining long enough to be sure it would burn, they left it to pay a similar visit to some other dwelling. After Mrs. Lintner had found a favorable place of concealment she discovered that Abram, her six-year-old boy, had become separated from the party, and although she felt a mother's anxiety for his safety, she dared not make a search for him. The lad found his way back to the house well on fire, evidently soon after the Indians left it and had sufficient presence of mind to pull the cradle out of doors. He remained about there all the afternoon and as night came on he dragged the cradle into a pig sty, still standing on the premises, in which he slept that night, too young to apprehend danger. The three oldest children, two boys and a girl, wended their way late in the day to Fort Clyde, which they reached in safety. Mrs. Lintner, with her infant child, remained that night under a hollow tree not far from her late home. A family dog was with her and several times in the evening its bark was answered by another which she supposed belonged to the enemy and which she feared might betray her hiding place. After a night of fearful solicitude, she made her way in safety to Fort Clyde, to find the children who had gained it the evening before. On the morning after he left his home of cheerful contentment, Lintner, having heard no alarm guns, ventured, as early as he dared to go, to learn the fate of his family. Finding his dwelling down, he approached its site with fearful apprehension, but, after careful examination of the debris in which he could find no charred remains, he became satisfied that the family had not been murdered in the house; and while still searching the premises, if possible to learn their fate, he discovered his little boy in an adjoining field following some cattle, evidently not knowing what else to do. He asked him where his mother and the other children were, when he began to cry, being unable to give any account of them except that they ran into the bushes back of the house. The father, having become satisfied that if the remainder of the family were not prisoners on the road to Canada, they might have reached Fort Clyde. Taking the hand of his little boy, thither he directed his steps; where to their great joy, the family were again united; when Mrs. Lintner, in German, expressed her gratitude as follows: "Obwhol wir nun Alles verboren haben ausser den Kleidern die wir auf den Liebe tragen, so fuhl ich mich doch reicher als jezmor in meinen Leben!" ("Now, although, we have lost everything but the clothes we have on, I feel richer than I ever did before in all my life!")

Within a short distance of Fort Ehle (a mile or more south of Canajoharie) Brant's raiders surprised and killed Adam Eights and took captive to Canada, Nathan Foster and Conrad Fritcher.

———

John Abeel was born in Albany about 1724. He was an Indian trader among the Senecas where he met the "beautiful daughter of a Seneca chief" and by her had a son who became the celebrated Cornplanter. He was forced by Sir William Johnson to give up his business among the Iroquois because his traffic in rum produced so much drunkenness and misery among them. In or shortly after 1756 he settled at the beginning of the Dutchtown road in the Sand Hill section and built himself a stone house. His grandson, Jacob Abeel, built here the present substantial brick house about 1860. John Abeel settled upon lands secured by patent to Rutger Bleecker, Nicholas Bleecker, James Delancey and John Haskoll, in 1729. They secured 4,300 acres in a body along the Mohawk on each side of the Otsquago and extending up the creek several

miles. In 1759 John Abeel married Mary Knouts. At the time of the Minden raid, Abeel was captured by the Indians. He was taken on the flats, between the house and the river. The family were preparing dinner and the table was set with food upon it, when an alarm gun at Fort Plain caused the women and children to run to that nearby shelter. Arriving at the Abeel house and finding a good dinner before them, the savages sat down and finished it. Some of the Indians brought out food and sat upon a wagon, which stood before the door to eat it. Henry Seeber, who was in the fort and had a good gun, took a shot at them although they were almost out of range. There was a commotion among them immediately and they scattered at once. Some of them fired the dwelling before leaving. As bloody rags were found about later it was evident that Seeber's bullet found a mark. It is believed that Cornplanter did not know of his father's captivity under several hours, when some war parties came together not very distant from the river. He had not been a prisoner long when he asked in the Indian tongue: "What do you mean to do with me?" This led at once to the inquiry as to his name and where he learned the Indian language. These things becoming known, among the savages, it was not long before Abeel was confronted by a chief of commanding figure and manner, who addressed him: "You, I understand, are John Abeel, once a trader among the Senecas. You are my father. My name is John Abeel, or Gy-ant-wachia, the Cornplanter. I am a warrior and have taken many scalps. You are now my prisoner but you are safe from all harm. Go with me to my home in the Seneca country and you shall be kindly cared for. My strong arm shall provide, you with corn and venison. But if you prefer to go back among your pale-faced friends, you shall be allowed to do so, and I will send an escort of trusty Senecas to conduct you back to Fort Plain." The chief's father chose to return, and early in the evening a party of Senecas left him near the fort. At the close of the war Abeel erected another house on the site of his burned dwelling. The trader had shown signs of insanity even prior to the war, and after that time, in one of his spells of insane anger, shot one of his negro slaves through the head, killing him. Neighbors went to arrest him but he seated himself in his door with his rifle and threatened to shoot the first one who attempted his arrest. At the first opportunity he was taken in charge but was not put on trial for the murder, as his unbalanced condition was so marked. As there were no asylums in those days, he was chained to the floor in a room of his own house. Abeel had periodical fits of being very ugly and troublesome and, on such occasions, he would clank his chain and continue a kind of Indian war dance nearly all night. He was handed his food through a small hole with a slide door cut in the wall. As he advanced in years and became enfeebled he was allowed to wander about his farm, and on one of his rambles, he was gored to death by a bull. His death was recorded by Rev. D. C. A. Pick of the Reformed Dutch church of Canajoharie (now Fort Plain), as follows: "John Abeel, gestorben den 1 December, 1794, alt 70; beerdigt den ejusd mensis anni alt in Michael."— John Abeel died 1 December, 1794, buried the 3, same week, same month and year; aged in the day of St. Michael 70 years.

One of the numerous small bands, into which Brant divided his force to make destruction more complete, visited the home of John Knouts in Freysbush. The site of the Knouts dwelling may still be seen in the apple orchard on the premises formerly owned by Josiah Roof. Here are also the graves of Mrs. Knouts and her children, slain by the Indians. Knouts was made here a prisoner and murdered on the way north after the savages left the settlement. When the Indians entered the house, Mrs. Knouts was busy outside it and hearing the

outcries of her children inside, she ran up just in time to see one of them tomahawked. While begging for her other children's lives, she was struck down and scalped with the other two children. Henry, a boy of eight or ten, was taken from the house, presumably by a Tory neighbor, around the corner and told to run for his life. This he did but was seen by an Indian, struck with a tomahawk, scalped and left for dead. On the day following a party went from Fort Clyde to bury these victims, when they found this little boy still alive and able to tell of the tragedy of the day before. He was an intelligent child and said he was running to get back of the barn and so into the woods. He said: "I should have escaped but an Indian met me between the house and the barn, who knocked me on the head with his hatchet and pulled out my hair," meaning that he had been scalped, of the details of which operation he was evidently ignorant. This brave little Knouts boy was taken to Fort Clyde and carefully treated and, after his wounds had nearly healed, he took cold and died. The mother was found lying in the dooryard with the three children murdered with her in her arms. Thus Indians sometimes disposed of their slain, before firing a dwelling, as supposed to strike the greater terror to living witnesses of their hellish cruelty. Her scalp was hanging on a stake, where the Indians had left it, evidently having forgotten it in their great haste to surprise other families. There is a tradition that the Indian who slew her took from her hand a ring having on it a Masonic emblem, discovering which he said: "Had I known the squaw had on such a ring, I would not have harmed her." It is needless to say the buildings on the Knouts place were burned and thus an entire family and their home were wiped out by almost incredible savagery. John Abeel, the Indian trader mentioned elsewhere, had married a Knouts girl, who was probably a relative of this family.

In the general destruction of the

Dutchtown settlements in Minden, to the surprise of everyone, the house of George Countryman remained unharmed, since it was well known that there was not a more staunch Whig in the neighborhood. The circumstance remained a mystery until the close of the war. He had a brother who had followed the Butlers and Johnsons to Canada, who was with the Minden marauders. He was a married man and, supposing his wife was at his brother's house, induced the raiders to spare it. After the war this brother in Canada wrote George Countryman that had be known at the time that his own wife was not in it, he would have seen that smoke with the rest.

The house of Johannes Lipe, very near Fort Plain, was saved from plunder and fire by the courage and presence of mind of his wife. She had been busy all the evening carrying her most valuable articles from her house to a place of concealment in the ravine nearby. The last time she returned she met two prowling Indians at the gate. She was familiar with their language and, without any apparent alarm, enquired of them if they knew anything of her two brothers who were among the Tories who had fled to Canada. Fortunately the savages had seen them at Oswegatchie and, supposing her to be a Tory likewise, they walked off and the house was spared.

The families of Freysbush who were accustomed to seek safety in Fort Clyde were Nellis, Yerdon, Garlock, Radnour, Dunckel, Wormuth, Miller, Lintner, Walrath, Lewis, Wolfe, Failing, Schreiber, Ehle, Knouts, Westerman, Brookman, Young, Yates and a few others. From the Knouts house the savages went to the home of Johan Steffanis Schreiber, who discovered them approaching and made his escape. They made prisoners of his wife and two or three small children and led them into captivity, a fact recorded on a family powder horn, which is now owned by the state.

Nancy Yerdon was married to George Pletts and lived on a farm owned in 1882 by Philip Failing. She had given

birth to twins a few months previous, one of whom had died, and had several other children. The family were living at Nancy's father's house, that of John Caspar Yerdon. On the day of the raid she went to the vicinity of a spring at some distance to dig potatoes for dinner, leaving her nursing child in a cradle in the house. While at work an Indian made her a prisoner and hurried her away to where other captives were being rounded up. The Yerdon house, for some reason, was not approached. After several small war parties were assembled, with their captives, a shower came up and the party took refuge behind a haystack. Here the savages conferred and decided to kill their prisoners if they had to abandon them. Mrs. Pletts, as the weather was warm, was clad only in an undergarment and a skirt, not even having on the accustomed short gown of that period, and thus scantily clad was compelled to travel all the way to Canada. The infant left in the cradle was named Elizabeth and grew up and married Henry Hurdick, who was a jockey on the local race-tracks of that day. Maria Strobeck, a "sprightly girl just entering her teens," was also captured with her father at a clearing where they had gone to get some ashes near the Failing farm in the vicinity of Mrs. Pletts, and went with the party as the latter did to Canada. On their way to Canada, Mrs. Pletts and the Strobeck girl, toward whom the former acted as a foster mother, were scantily fed. On her return, Mrs. Pletts told her friends that on their long, weary journey they came to a brook in which they caught several small fish which they ate raw, and, although they were wriggling in their mouths, they proved a luxury. On arriving in the Canadian country, they were taken into separate Indian families; and, finding many unclean dishes, Mrs. Pietts, who was a tidy woman, voluntarily scoured them clean and kept them so. This act very much pleased the Indians, who treated her afterward with marked kindness. She felt it still her duty to keep a parental eye on Miss Strobeck. Finding her romping with the young Indians, the married woman tried to persuade her to leave them, but "she was so happy with them she would give no heed to the counsel of Mrs. Pletts. Indeed she became so infatuated with the novelty of Indian life that she could not be persuaded to be included in the exchange of prisoners and did not return with Mrs. Pietts when she might. Some six or eight years after the war, her father journeyed to Canada and found her, but she could not be prevailed upon to return home with him; and it was supposed she subsequently took an Indian husband and remained there." While among the Indians, Mrs. Pletts was given a sewing needle, which she boasted of using for years after her return and which she prized very highly. Among the prisoners who came back from Canada were Mrs. Pletts and John Peter Dunckel. Years later, when they were well along in years and were then widow and widower, they concluded to unite their fortunes, and came on foot to Dominie Gros, who then lived in Freysbush. And so they were married and none of the ten grown-up children of the couple by former marriages, objected or ever considered this unconventional marriage of the old folks as a runaway match. It was an agreeable pastime for the young to hear this old couple relate stories of the war, their own perils included.

Mrs. Dyonisius Miller was made a prisoner in the Freysbush settlement. She had with her a small nursing child. She was placed on a horse, which was led by an Indian to Canada. Although the savages generally came down in large bodies, they usually returned in small parties; and prisoners taken near together often journeyed with different captives, some of them not meeting again until their return. As the party of which Mrs. Miller was one became straitened for food, she had but little nourishment for her infant child and, as it cried from weariness and hunger, an Indian more than once came back, hatchet in hand to kill it, but pressing it to her breast, she would not afford

him the desired opportunity. Indians dislike intensely the sound of a crying child. To save her darling, Mrs. Miller kept almost constantly nursing it or attempting to, until her breast became so sore as to cause her great agony. But she saved the life of the infant girl and brought it back safely to her old home, when released. This child, when grown to womanhood, married William Dygert.

Henry Nellis lived near Fort Clyde, upon whose land the post was erected, with his son, George H. Nellis. The latter became a general of militia and man of considerable prominence at a later day. On the day of the raid they both fled to the fort pursued by a party of Indians. At a shot the son caught his foot in some obstruction and fell, his father thinking him killed. The younger man jumped up and both got inside the stockade in safety. A bullet hole through the son's hat showed that the fall had saved his life..

Adam Garlock was riding his horse, when the beast scented the Indians, as horses frequently did in those days. Garlock, thus warned, saw a party of Indians approaching, wheeled his horse about and galloped in safety to Fort Clyde amid a storm of bullets. "This circumstance is said to have aided him in procuring a $40 pension, of which bounty he felt quite proud."

At this invasion of the enemy Elizabeth Garlock was scalped and left for dead on the river road above Fort Plain. She supposed the deed was done by a Tory named Countryman, who had been a former neighbor. He was painted as an Indian. Tories were often called "blue-eyed Indians." Elizabeth Garlock recovered and later married Nicholas Phillips and died at Vernon, N. Y., at the age of 80 years.

John, son of Thomas Casler, who was an early settler of Freysbush, was captured. On the way to Canada, the prisoners were bound to trees nights and one night the carelessness of the Indians set the leaves on fire. As the flames neared Casler, he called to the savages to release him. A Tory, in the raiding party, named Bernard Frey, who knew the prisoner well, said to the Indians, "Let the damned rebel burn up." The red men, however, were more humane and saved Casler. A night or two later Casler escaped and, rightly supposing the savages would search for him on the back track, he ran back a short distance and hid to one side of the route. Here he remained while his foes pursued him back and until their return. Then in safety he returned to the ashes of his home. Casler always said, in after life, that he would shoot Bernard Frey on sight, such was the feeling engendered among next-door neighbors around Fort Plain by this murderous warfare. Casler entertained no love for the Indians and, during a subsequent deer hunting trip, killed a red man on a Schoharie mountain.

Warner Dygert was murdered on his farm at the west end of the Canajoharie district. He was a brother-in-law of Gen. Nicholas Herkimer, and kept a tavern at Fall Hill. Dygert, with his son Suffrenas, started out to make a corn crib, carrying a gun as was the universal custom in those days. His movements were watched by four Indians. He set down his gun and, with his tinder box and flint, lit his pipe. Just then he was shot down and scalped. The little boy was taken to Canada, finally returning in the same party with Mrs. Pletts and Mr. Dunckel, before mentioned and other captives from the Canajoharie district. The younger Dygert finally removed to Canada.

Jacob Nellis of Dutchtown was journeying to Indian Castle on the day of the raid. He was shot down opposite East Canada creek. His father, who was called the oldest man of the name, saved himself by a ruse. As the Indians approached the house, the old man shouted at the top of his voice: "Here they are boys! March up! March up!" and the savages fled, fearing the house was fortified. A German doctor and his wife, named Frank, were killed in Dutchtown. Frederick Countryman was stabbed with a spear nineteen times and killed. Brant expressed regret at this and coming up and seeing the corpse made the typical Indian remark: "It is as it is, but if it had not been, it should not happen." An old man named House was captured and killed because the savages thought him too old to bother with on the Canadian march. A girl named Martha House was captured thinly clad and taken to Canada, reaching there after the long, hard journey in an almost naked condition. Her Indian captor treated her kindly. On her return she married a man named Staley, who had also been a Canadian captive.

Regarding Brant, during this raid the following comes from an early writer, Rev. Dr. Lintner, born in the locality and who knew the people and circumstances: "He [Brant] occasionally exhibited traits of humanity which were redeeming qualities of his character. On the evening of the day when the Canajoharie settlement was destroyed by the Indians, some 12 or 15 women were brought in as prisoners. Brant saw their distress and his heart was touched with compassion. While the Indians were regaling themselves over their plunder—dancing and yelling around their camp fires, Brant approached the little group of terror-stricken prisoners and said: 'Follow me!' They expected to be led to instant death but he conducted them through the darkness of the dreadful night to a place in the woods some distance from the Indian camp, where he ordered them to sit down and keep still until the next day, when the sun should have reached a mark which he made on a tree, and then they might return home. He then left them. The next morning, a little before break of day, he came again and made another mark higher on the tree and told them they must not set out till the sun had reached that mark; for some of his Indians were still back, and if they met them they would be killed. They remained according to his directions and then they safely returned to the settlement." The Rev. Mr. Lintner said in a historical address: "Much of the bitter feeling which existed in this country against the mother country, after the Revolution, was engendered by that inhuman policy which instigated the savages to make war upon us with the tomahawk and scalping knife. The bounty offered for scalps was horrible. It stimulated the savages to acts of barbarity and was revolting to the moral feelings and social sympathies of all civilized peoples."

There is at least one personal experience related of a soldier who probably accompanied Gansevoort's troops to Fort Schuyler, which expedition resulted in the Canajoharie district raid. In the spring of 1780 Jacob Shew went for one of "a class," as then termed, in Capt. Garret Putman's company, for the term of nine months, part of which time he was on duty at Fort Plank. The ranger service often called troops from one post to another. Shew was one of a guard of about a dozen men sent with a drove of cattle from Fort Plain to Fort Schuyler. While encamped near the village of Mohawk they were fired upon in the dark and several Americans were wounded. The fire was promptly returned and there was no reply from the enemy. Shew was also one of a guard sent up the Mohawk with several boats loaded with provisions and military stores. These boats, at that time, were usually laden at Schenectady and came to Fort Plain, where an armed guard was detailed to escort them up the valley. The troops went along the shore and at the rapids had to assist in getting the boats along, which were laid up nights, the boatmen encamping on the shore with the guard.

The tactics of these British and Indian raids was to destroy the supplies of Tryon county patriots and crumple back the frontier. During the whole war no deadlier blow, in this direction, was struck than that whose force centered in Minden around Fort Plain.

Fort Plain must have been a scene of tragedy enough to wring the stoutest heart. It was manned by a tiny garrison which feared, at any time, its utter annihilation and filled with men, women and children, all of whom had lost their homes and many of whom

mourned part or all of their families as dead or captured. Their grief was not mitigated by resentment toward the stupid act of the officials who had left unguarded one of the richest granaries of the opulent valley, to insure the safety of a few boat loads of provisions and supplies.

What was true of Fort Plain was also true of the other posts of the Canajoharie district, Forts Windecker, Plank and Clyde. Fort Willett was not then constructed. They were all crowded with the survivors of their neighborhoods. The Canajoharie district was thickly settled for that time and that portion of it comprised within the present town of Minden was particularly so, with its fertile Freysbush and Dutchtown sections. It was owing to the very complete chain of fortifications hereabouts that the greater part of the population escaped massacre. The people of Palatine also gathered in Fort Paris and Fort Kyser, and all up and down the valley, the population, left undefended by the absence of their military force, fled to neighboring forts. The fortified and palisaded farmhouses must almost have been crowded by a panic-stricken population and it was only these few well-defended places that escaped destruction.

Simms gives an account of the fortified houses of this section which are here summarized as follows:

In Canajoharie township: Fort Ehle; Van Alstine house (now called, for some unknown reason, Fort Rennselaer); Fort Failing.

In Palatine: Fort Frey, Fort Wagner, Fort Fox.

In St. Johnsville: Fort Hess, Fort Klock, Fort Nellis, Fort Timmerman, Fort House (a little below East Creek).

Simms gives no similar list of the Minden fortified houses.

William Irving Walter of St. Johnsville, in a letter to the Fort Plain Standard under date of December 19, 1912, says of the Minden raid:

"The raiders, after their work of massacre and rapine, camped at a ravine a little to the west of Starkville, still known locally as Camp Creek, where they intended to rest a few days and recruit for their long trip on the return." Brant's stay here was shortened by the approach of the militia, but at least part of his force was in the Minden vicinity two or three days. This shows the retreat of the Tory and Indian force to have been back up the Otsquago valley to the headwaters of the Susquehanna and from thence into the Iroquois country.

Simms says that Fort Plain became the headquarters of the neighboring valley forts in 1780. Whether it was such at the time of the Minden raid is not known. Here a military escort took charge of the convoys of supplies brought up the valley on flatboats, as before stated. This would necessitate a garrison larger than at the ordinary post and the American valley commander would naturally select the post, with the largest garrison and a central location, as his headquarters. Fort Plain was the most centrally located post in the valley and it was also the point where the guard for the boats was located, so that it is probable it was the headquarters on August 2, 1780.

Mrs. W. W. Crannell, an Albany writer, in her "Grandmother's Childhood Tales," gives a picture which might well pass and may well be that of a Minden family during the night of the raid of August 2, 1780. This account also gives a picture of a Mohawk valley farm house in the early nineteenth century and the whole is here included:

Seventeen miles from my own home in the county of Herkimer, was situated the old home in which my mother was born. With the exception of Santa Claus, there was nothing looked forward to so eagerly, or from which we anticipated so much pleasure as the semi-annual visit to this old homestead. After we left the main road, we drove along a private road or lane, that made its way from one main road to another; a sort of short cut of two or three miles, through the lands of several farmers whose houses were built, as the farmhouses of that period were wont to be, in the center of the

farm. When we reached the dooryard, we unbarred the gate and drove through a flock of hissing geese and quacking ducks, up to the back or porch door. The noise of the geese would call grandmother to the door, and her bright, cherry face, crowned with its wealth of snowy, white hair, would appear at the upper half of the door, which was flung open while her trembling fingers were unfastening the lower half. How well I remember the old house, with its porch or "stoop," through which we passed into the "living room." The red beams overhead were filled with pegs, upon which were hung braided ears of corn, stumps of dried apples, or other homely articles which had not been put in winter quarters yet. And then the fire-place—such corn and potatoes as we roasted in its ashes. How often we sat before its cheerful blaze and drank sweet cider and ate apples, while we listened to our elders' tales, until Morpheus wooed us to his embrace. And what fun it was to climb into bed. First to pull the curtains back, and then throw down the blue and white spread, the flannel and the linen sheets, all homespun. If it was cold, the warming pan was placed between the sheets, and then, getting upon a chair, we stept upon the chest near the bed, and with the aid of mother and a "one, two, three," in we went, down, down, down into the soft warm feather beds. Did we ever sleep such a sleep as that in after years?

But I digress; this is not what I set out to relate. When mother and aunts were out visiting the neighbors then grandmother (Nancy Keller), taking knitting, would sit down before the fire and talk of her girlhood.

"Those were hard and dreadful times," she would say. "Some of them I do not remember, as I was a baby when they transpired, but my mother (Moyer) told me that often she would wake up in the middle of the night and the sound of a horn, and a man's voice crying out 'To arms! to arms!' Father would run for his musket, and mother would take me in her arms and, with my two brothers clinging to her dress, start for her shelter in the woods. All the farmers had some place of safety for their families to run to in case of an alarm. Ours was a hollow place in the woods between some trees. It was just big enough for us to lie down in, and the boughs and underbrush at the sides had been arranged to hide it from the savage eye. One night we had gained the place in safety, our way to the woods being lighted by fires from burning hay-stacks and buildings. I had been ill and I moaned and cried, while my brothers lay down as close to mother's side as possible. All at once we heard soft foot falls on the leafy ground; then an Indian passed quickly with a lighted torch, then another and another; how many was never known for we could see them so plainly through the boughs placed over us, that we closed our eyes in fear and scarcely breathed. Yes 'we,' for I ceased crying and nestled close on mother's breast. How long did we lie there? We never knew. Measured by what we endured it was ages before we heard father's voice calling, 'All right, come out,' and what must mother have suffered? Every gun shot might be the death call of her husband; every footfall and quick passing shadow, be death personified for her. And when the footfall ceased near her hiding place and the shadow remained stationary, when one cry of the baby in her arms or the children at her side were messengers of instant and horrible death; when at last the shadow started and the feet gave a headlong bound, and a fearful whoop rang out upon the stillness about her; what wonderful control of her nerves she must have had, not to betray her presence by the least movement, and how well we learned, even to the baby to sustain a rigid silence."

CHAPTER XVIII.

1780—Johnson's Schoharie and Mohawk Invasion—Oct. 19, Battles of Stone Arabia and St. Johnsville—Van Rensselaer's Inefficiency—Enemy Escapes—Fort Plain Named Fort Rensselaer—Fort Plain Blockhouse Built—Fort Willett Begun.

In the fall of 1780, an invading force under Sir John Johnson, Joseph Brant and the Seneca chief Cornplanter, ravaged the Schoharie and Mohawk valleys. The battles of Stone Arabia and St. Johnsville were fought and the enemy escaped, after a defeat at the latter place. They would have been crushed or captured by a pursuing American force had it not been for the complete inefficiency of the militia commander, Gen. Robert Van Rensselaer. Practically every town of Montgomery county was concerned in this campaign, either being the scene of ravages by Johnson or the march of and battles of the patriot force. The object of this Tory and Indian raid, like all others, was to destroy completely the houses, barns and crops of all the Whigs along the Schoharie

and Mohawk. By destroying or plundering the country of all supplies the enemy hoped to weaken the resistance of the frontier. This raid was particularly destructive to the Schoharie country. It followed, within three months, Brant's terrible Minden foray of August 2, 1780. Thus did blow after blow fall upon the suffering but valiant people of the Mohawk.

At Unadilla, Brant and Cornplanter, with their Indians, joined Johnson and his force, which consisted of three companies of the Royal Greens, one company of German Yagers, 200 of Butler's rangers, a company of British regulars and a party of Indians. The total force must have approximated 800 men or more. Sir John and his army came from Montreal, by way of Oswego, bringing with them two small mortars and a brass three-pounder, mounted on legs instead of wheels and so called a "grasshopper." This artillery was mounted on pack horses.

The plan of the raiders was, upon reaching the Schoharie, to pass the upper, of the three small forts on that stream, by night and unobserved; to destroy the settlements between there and the Middle Fort and attack the latter in the morning. This plan was carried out October 16, the homes of all but Tories being burned. The Middle Fort was bombarded without effect and the enemy then moved down the Schoharie to Fort Hunter, making a feeble attack on the Lower Fort by the way.

All buildings and hay stacks belonging to Whigs were burned and their cattle and horses appropriated. One hundred thousand bushels of grain were thus destroyed and (says Beers) nearly 100 settlers were murdered. The Whigs were so roused over the destruction of their property that, after the enemy disappeared, they fired the buildings and crops of their Tory neighbors, which had been spared, and the ruin along the Schoharie was thus complete.

Ravaging the Schoharie valley, Johnson and Brant's Tory and Indian force moved north, down the Schoharie creek, and entered that part of its course which flows through Montgomery county. Johnson buried one mortar he had been using and his shells in a little "Vlaie" (natural meadow) in the town of Charleston. In 1857 some of these shells were plowed up. The Schoharie militia, under Col. Vrooman, followed Johnson's course toward the Mohawk, during which march the enemy took several prisoners and continued the looting and burning of houses and barns. Johnson and Brant gave Fort Hunter a wide berth, passing that fortification at a distance of half a mile. Here a Tory named Schremling, was scalped and killed (his political leanings not being known) and a number of women and children of the Schremling, Young and Martin families were captured.

An Indian and Tory detachment crossed the Mohawk to plunder and ravage the north side, while the main body continued westward through the town of Glen, on the south side highway, to a point, in the town of Root, a little east of the Nose, known on the Erie canal as the Willow Basin, and there encamped for the night. Nearly all the buildings, on both sides, along the Mohawk were burned and plundered from Fort Hunter to the Nose. On this march British regulars guarded the prisoners to prevent the Indians from murdering them. A little captive girl of ten years, Magdalena Martin, was taken up by Walter Butler and rode in front of him on his horse. The evening being very bitter, Butler let the little maid put her cold hands in his fur-lined pockets and thus they journeyed to the camping ground. One of the raiders asked Butler what he was going to do with the pretty girl. "Make a wife of her," was his quick reply. This small Revolutionary captive became the wife of Matthias Becker and the mother of ten children. She died in Fort Plain, at the home of her son-in-law, William A. Haslett, in 1862, in her 93d year. So closely are we unknowingly linked with the past that there may be those who read this page who personally knew this old lady, who, as a little girl, rode with Butler and warmed her hands in his

pockets on a chilly October night over a century and a quarter ago. And such a strange and wayward thing is the nature of man that we look with wonder at the picture of this Tory murderer of women and little ones cuddling a small rebel child to keep her from the cold.

The next morning at the Nose, learning that a force of Albany and Schenectady militia were coming after him, Johnson allowed Mrs. Martin and her children to return home, with the exception of her 14-year-old son.

News of the raid had reached Albany and the Schenectady and Albany militia quickly assembled and proceeded with great speed up the Mohawk to attack Johnson's men. Gen. Robert Van Rensselaer of Claverack, commanded the pursuit and he was accompanied by Gov. Clinton. On the evening of the 18th they encamped in the present town of Florida. From there Van Rensselaer sent word to Col. Brown at Fort Paris and to Fort Plain (probably directed to Col. John Harper). Brown was ordered to attack the enemy in the front the next morning, while Van Rensselaer's army fell on their rear.

On September 11, 1780, according to a state report, Col. Brown, at Fort Paris, had 276 men under him, and Col. John Harper (supposedly at Fort Plain then) commanded 146, and there were but 455 men to guard the frontier in the Canajoharie-Palatine districts. These troops were then under the command of Brigadier-General Robert Van Rensselaer. When Brown attacked Johnson at Stone Arabia he had but 200 American militiamen with him and it is probable the balance of the patriot force (then located at three posts) in this neighborhood were left to guard the forts or were on duty elsewhere. The Fort Plain soldiers joined Van Rensselaer's force as later noted. The valley people, warned of the enemy's approach, gathered in the local forts for safety and there were few or no casualties among them, after Johnson left Fort Hunter on his march westward.

On the morning of October 19, 1780,

Johnson's army crossed the Mohawk at Keator's rift (near Sprakers) and headed for Stone Arabia, leaving a guard of 40 men at the ford. At almost the same time Col. Brown paraded his men, to the number of 150 or 200, and sallied forth from Fort Paris to meet the enemy. The American commander, mounted on a small black horse, marched straight for the approaching foe. He passed Fort Keyser, where he was joined by a few militiamen, and met Johnson's army in an open field about two miles east by north of Palatine Bridge. Capt. Casselman advised Col. Brown, considering the overwhelming force and protected position of the enemy, to keep the Americans covered by a fence. Without his usual caution, Brown ordered an advance into the open, where his men were subjected to a heavy fire. The militia returned the fire, fought gallantly and stood their ground, although many of their number were being killed and wounded. Seeing he was being outflanked by the Indians, at about ten in the morning, Col. Brown ordered a retreat, at which time he was struck down by a musket ball through the heart. The pursuit of the enemy made it impossible for his men to bear off their commander's body and it was scalped and stripped of everything except a ruffled shirt. Thirty Americans were killed and the remainder fled, some north into the forest and some south toward the Mohawk and Van Rensselaer's army. Two of the Stone Arabia men took refuge in Judge Jacob Eacker's house and put up a defense until the Indians fired the building, after which the savages stood around and laughed at the shrieks of their burning victims. The enemy's loss was probably less than that of the Americans on this field.

The British regulars passed Fort Keyser without firing a shot. Capt. John Zielie, with six militiamen and two aged farmers, were at the portholes, with muskets cocked and hats filled with cartridges at their sides, but held their fire for fear of an attack which would mean annihilation. When the enemy were out of sight four of the militiamen from this post set out for the field of battle, found Col. Brown's body and bore it back in their arms to Fort Keyser.

The Tories, British and Indians after this ravaged, plundered and burned all through the Stone Arabia district, among other buildings, burning both the Reformed and Lutheran churches. Few, if any of the inhabitants were killed or captured as all had taken refuge in the forts or in the woods. After the burning and plundering, Johnson collected his men by bugle calls and the blowing of tin horns and pursued his way westward toward the Mohawk.

On the morning of the 19th, Gen. Van Rensselaer started his pursuit, from his Florida campground, at moonrise. He reached Fort Hunter before daybreak and was there joined by the Schoharie militia. Van Rensselaer came up to Keator's rift, shortly after Johnson had crossed. It was probably here that his force was joined by Col. Harper, Capt. McKean with 80 men (probably from Fort Plain) and a large body of Oneida Indians under their principal chief, Louis Atayataroughta, who had been commissioned a lieutenant-colonel by congress. Col. Harper, probably then in command at Fort Plain (as S. L. Frey locates him there in September), was in chief command of the Oneidas. Van Rensselaer's army was now double that of Johnson's. Here the American commander halted, perhaps deterred from crossing the ford by the small rear guard of the enemy which was stationed on the opposite bank. The firing at the Stone Arabia field, two miles distant, was plainly heard and here came fugitives fleeing from the defeated force, bringing news of the rout and of the killing of Col. Brown. One of Brown's men, a militia officer named Van Allen, promptly reported to Gen. Van Rensselaer, with an account of the action, and asked the latter if he was not going to cross the river and engage the enemy. The general replied that he did not know the fording place well enough. He was told that the ford was easy and Van

Allen offered to act as pilot. Thereupon Capt. McKean's company and the Oneidas crossed the river. Instead of supporting this advance party, in his promised cooperation with Col. Brown's men, it then being near noontime, Gen. Van Rensselaer now accompanied Col. Dubois to Fort Plain to dine with Gov. Clinton.

Gen. Van Rensselaer, after leaving Keator's Rift, ordered the company of Lieut. Driscoll and his artillery to Fort Plain, possibly anticipating an attack by Johnson in that quarter. He tried the ford opposite Fort Frey but found it impassable and ordered his men to cross at Walrath's ferry at Fort Plain. They, however, made the passage of the Mohawk at Ehle's rift, near what was later Ver Planck's and is now called Nellis's island. They stopped at the house of Adam Countryman on the Canajoharie side and here turned into the road which led to the ford, which existed in the river prior to the barge canal operations. This was later the Ver Planck and still later the Nellis farm. Here the American troops began the passage of the Mohawk while their general was wasting valuable time in a lengthy dinner at "Fort Plain or Rensselaer."

At Fort Plain, it is said, Col. Harper denounced Van Rensselaer for his incompetency and apparent cowardice and other officers joined in with Harper, while the Oneida chief called him a Tory to his face. About four o'clock Van Rensselaer rode back, through the present village of Fort Plain, to his men, who were as bitter against him as his officers were. Here he found that the remainder of his army had crossed the Mohawk at Ehle's rift (just below Fort Plain), in the extreme western end of the town of Canajoharie, on a rude bridge built upon wagons driven into the river. At length Van Rensselaer was stung into something like activity and, late in the afternoon, the pursuit was rapidly resumed (from the present village of Nelliston) up the north shore turnpike through the town of Palatine.

Sir John Johnson, seeing that he could not avoid an attack, threw up slight breastworks and arranged his forces in order of battle. This position was in the town of St. Johnsville, about one and one-half miles east of the eastern village limits of the village of St. Johnsville. The Tories and Butler's rangers occupied a small plain, partly protected by a bend in the river, while Brant with his Indians, concealed in a thicket on a slight elevation farther north, were supported by a detachment of German Yagers. It was near evening when the Americans came up and the battle commenced. Van Rensselaer's extreme right was commanded by Col. Dubois, and then came the Oneidas and the left was led by Col. Cuyler. As the Americans approached the Indians in ambush shouted the war-whoop. The Oneidas responded and rushed upon their Iroquois brethren, followed by McKean's men; the latter supported by Col. Dubois, whose wing of the battle was too extended to match the enemy's disposition of forces. Brant's savage band resisted for a time the impetuous charge, but finally broke and fled toward a ford, about two miles up the river. Brant was wounded in the heel but got away. Several were killed and wounded on both sides and the enemy everywhere gave way in great disorder and fled westward. It was now becoming so dark that the American officers feared their men would shoot each other and the general firing was discontinued, although the Oneidas, Capt. McKean's and Col. Clyde's men pursued and harassed the flying enemy, capturing one of their field pieces and some prisoners. Johnson's men, utterly exhausted from their prior marching and exertions, camped on a meadow, at a point on the river near the ford. Here he spiked and subsequently abandoned his cannon. At this time the Americans could have driven the enemy into the river and have captured or destroyed them. All accounts agree that the patriot troops were eager to get at the enemy but their spirit was of no avail owing to the weakness of their commanding officer.

Col. Dubois took a position above Johnson on the north side of the river to prevent the enemy's escape. Col. Harper's men and the Oneidas crossed to the opposite side and camped on the Minden shore, opposite Johnson's bivouac. Gen. Van Rensselaer ordered an attack at moonrise, giving orders that it was to begin under his personal supervision. He then executed the remarkable manoeuvre of falling back with the main body down the river three miles, where he went into camp for the night. Johnson's entire force, as subsequently shown, could have been easily captured at any time, as it was on the point of surrendering. Van Rensselaer failed, of course, to attack and, at moonrise, Johnson crossed the ford and escaped to the westward with his entire force, abandoning his cannon and 40 or 50 horses captured in the Schoharie valley, which were subsequently recovered by their owners. The next morning one of the enemy was killed and nine captured by seven men and a boy from Fort Windecker, some of them surrendering voluntarily on account of fatigue.

Gen. Van Rensselaer sent a message to Fort Schuyler for a force to proceed from that point to Onondaga lake to destroy Johnson's boats. Capt. Vrooman set out with 50 men, all of whom were captured by Johnson, through the treachery of one of Vrooman's party. The Oneidas and a body of the militia moved up the river after the retreating enemy, expecting Van Rensselaer to follow as he promised. Coming next morning upon the still burning camp fires of the enemy, the pursuing party halted, the Oneida chief fearing an ambuscade and refusing to proceed until the main body came up under Van Rensselaer. After following leisurely forward as far as Fort Herkimer, the Continental commander abandoned his weak pursuit and sent a messenger recalling the advance force.

The American army turned about face and marched back down the Mohawk. The garrisons returned to their posts and the militia to what shelters they had made or could make for themselves and their families, within the zones of protection afforded by these fortifications. The Schenectady and Albany militia continued on down the valley to their homes under the leadership of their thoroughly discredited commander.

This American army was one of the largest yet concentrated in the valley and probably was only equalled in numbers by that of Clinton which had encamped at Canajoharie the year before. The force that took the field on both sides at Klock's Field was the largest which arrayed itself for battle on any one Revolutionary field in the Mohawk country. About the same numbers were here engaged as at Oriskany (2,500), but at the action of St. Johnsville the clash took place on one battleground while Oriskany consisted of two fights several miles apart —the bloody struggle in the ravine and Willett's destructive sally from Fort Schuyler. Van Rensselaer's army had accomplished practically nothing and, moreover, had sat supinely by while Brown's heroic band was being scattered by the enemy. And all this lost opportunity and disgraceful record was due to the incapacity or cowardice of a general totally unfitted for military command. It was left for Willett, a year later, to show how effectively the valley Americans, when properly led, could beat off the Canadian invaders.

Time after time, up to the day of the Stone Arabia battle, the local patriot soldiers had attempted to grapple with their savage white and red invaders, only to see them slip away on each occasion, unharmed and unpunished. Now, after the enemy had been cornered at Klock's Field and could have been easily destroyed or captured, they had been practically given their liberty by Van Rensselaer.

The valley militia had flocked to the American standard, eager to strike a fatal blow at their hated foes. The patriot population and soldiers of the Mohawk must have been indeed disheartened, discouraged and disgusted at this fiasco of a campaign, which initially had promised complete American success.

Van Rensselaer's conduct was the worst display of inefficiency or cowardice seen in the valley, and perhaps anywhere, during the Revolution. An opportunity was lost of crushing completely the raiders and probably preventing future bloodshed and loss in the valley. Van Rensselaer was subsequently courtmartialed at Albany for his conduct but was acquitted, largely on account of his wealth and social position, it is said.

There was much scurrilous intrigue, dissension, bickering and petty jealousy among certain cliques of so-called patriots. The real American Revolutionary fighters were compelled to combat these vicious forces from within as well as the enemy. The acquittal of Van Rensselaer is an evidence that all Americans were not actuated by high-minded patriotism and strict justice, during the war of independence.

Had the Continental Revolutionary forces been composed exclusively of men like Washington and Willett the conflict would have ended within a year or two in complete American success. Not only did such patriots have to fight the early battles with raw, undisciplined and frequently unreliable troops, but they had to constantly combat an insidious Tory influence among the people and the effect of such inefficiency as that exemplified in Van Rensselaer and men of his ilk.

At this time, and until its discontinuance as an army post, the Minden fort was known both as Fort Plain and Fort Rensselaer, the latter being its official title, conferred upon it probably by Van Rensselaer himself; Fort Plain evidently being its popular name and the one which survived until a later date. This is treated in a subsequent chapter.

In S. L. Frey's article on Fort Rensselaer (Fort Plain) published in the (Fort Plain) Mohawk Valley Register of March 6, 1912, he says: "Gen. Van Rensselaer * * * was appointed to the command of some of the posts in this section in the summer of 1780,— Fort Paris, Fort Plank, Fort Plain and others. His headquarters were at Fort Plain. In the fall of that year he wrote to Gov. Clinton from Fort Plain, dating his letter 'Fort Rensselaer, Sept. 4, 1780.' This is the first time the name appears."

Van Rensselaer evidently gave his name to his headquarters post on his arrival there in the summer of 1780, which may have been in August after the Minden raid. At the time of the Stone Arabia battle, Col. John Harper was in command of Fort Plain (under Gen. Van Rensselaer, of course).

In the court martial of Gen. Van Rensselaer the designation "Fort Plane or Rensselaer" is frequently used in the testimony of the witnesses. In this evidence appears the names of the following as having been engaged in the valley military operations of the time of the Stone Arabia battle: Col. Dubois, Col. Harper, Major Lewis R. Morris, Col. Samuel Clyde (who commanded a company of Tryon county militia), Lieut. Driscoll and Col. Lewis, in whose quarters at "Fort Plane or Rensselaer," the commanding general went to dine.

———

The number of Oneidas engaged in the foregoing military operations is given as 200 warriors by one authority and 80 by another, the smaller figure probably being nearer the truth. During part, at least, of the war this tribe lived in, about and under the protection of Fort Hunter, their own country being too exposed to invasion. The Oneidas were generally loyal to the American cause and did good service for the patriots on several occasions—notably the campaign treated in this chapter, at Oriskany and at West Canada creek. As previously stated Col. John Harper was in command of these Indians, taking rank over their native chief.

———

After the Stone Arabia battle, some 25 or 30 Americans were buried in an open trench near Fort Paris. The situation is believed to have been a few rods southeast of the present schoolhouse. John Klock drew the bodies of Brown's men thither on a sled although there was no snow on the ground. They were buried side by side in the clothes in which they fell. Some others who were slain were interred elsewhere.

Col. Brown was buried in the graveyard near the Stone Arabia churches. Most of the Americans killed on this field were New England men, although local militiamen were also engaged. The loss of the enemy probably did not exceed half of the 40 or 45 patriots supposed to have been slain. On the anniversary of Col. John Brown's death in 1836, a monument was erected over his grave by his son, Henry Brown, of Berkshire, Mass., bearing the following inscription: "In memory of Col. John Brown, who was killed in battle on the 19th day of October, 1780, at Palatine, in the county of Montgomery. Age 36." This event was made a great occasion and was largely attended, veterans of the Stone Arabia battle being present. It is mentioned in a later chapter dealing with its period in Palatine.

After the Klock's Field battle some of McKean's volunteers came upon Fort Windecker, where nine of the enemy had been taken. On one of them being asked how he came there, his answer was a sharp commentary on the criminal inaction of General Van Rensselaer. The man, who was a valley Tory, said: "Last night, after the battle, we crossed the river; it was dark; we heard the words, 'lay down your arms,' and some of us did so. We were taken, nine of us, and marched into this little fort by seven militiamen. We formed the rear of three hundred of Johnson's Greens, who were running promiscuously through and over one another. I thought General Van Rensselaer's whole army was upon us. Why did you not take us prisoners yesterday, after Sir John ran off with the Indians and left us? We wanted to surrender."

It is reported that the Schoharie militia, engaged in this campaign, were short of knapsacks and carried their bread on poles, piercing each loaf and then spitting it on the sticks.

———

Col. John Brown was born in Sandersfield, Mass., in 1744. He was graduated at Yale college in 1771 and studied law. He commenced practise at Caughnawaga (Fonda) and was appointed King's attorney. He soon went to Pittsfield, Mass., where he became active in the patriot cause and in 1775 went to Canada on a mission to try to get the people there to join the American cause. He was elected to congress in 1775 but joined Allen and Arnold's expedition against Ticonderoga. He was at Fort Chambly and Quebec. In 1776 he was commissioned lieutenant-colonel. In 1777 he commanded the expedition against Ticonderoga and soon after left the service on account of his detestation of Arnold. Three years before the latter became a traitor Brown published a hand bill in which he denounced Arnold as a traitor and concluded: "Money is this man's god, and to get enough of it he would sacrifice his country." This was published in Albany in the winter of 1776-7, while Arnold was quartered there. Arnold was greatly excited over it and called Brown a scoundrel and threatened to kick him on sight. Brown heard of this and the next day, by invitation, went to dinner to which Arnold also came. The latter was standing with his back to the fire when Brown entered the door, and they met face to face. Brown said: "I understand, sir, that you have said you would kick me; I now present myself to give you an opportunity to put your threat into execution." Arnold made no reply. Brown then said: "Sir, you are a dirty scoundrel." Arnold was silent and Brown left the room, after apologizing to the gentlemen present for his intrusion. Col. Brown, after he left the army, was occasionally in the Massachusetts service. In the fall of 1780, with many of the Berkshire militia, he marched up the Mohawk river, his force to be used for defense as required.

Brown is said to have been a man of medium height, of fine military bearing and with dark eyes. He generally wore spectacles. His courage was proverbial among his men and in the Stone Arabia action seems to have run into recklessness, although, soldier that he was, he probably figured on holding the enemy at any cost until Van Rensselaer's large force could come up and, falling on the rear, crush them completely, which could have been readily accomplished by a skilful and determined commander. Col. Brown was immensely popular with his troops—with the militiamen from the valley as well as with the soldiers he commanded who were from his own state of Massachusetts.

Governor George Clinton visited Fort Plain on at least two known occasions. The first was during the Klock's Field operations and the second was when he accompanied Washington through the Mohawk valley in 1783. Clinton was a brother of Gen. James Clinton and an uncle of Dewitt Clinton, later the famous "canal Governor." He was born in Ulster county in 1739. In 1768 he was elected to the Colonial legislature, and was a member of the Continental congress in 1775. He was appointed a brigadier in the United States army in 1776' and during the whole war was active in military affairs in New York. In April, 1777, he was elected governor and continued so for eighteen years. He was president of the convention assembled at Poughkeepsie to consider the federal constitution in 1788. He was again chosen governor of the state in 1801, and in 1804. Afterward he was elected vice president of the United States and continued in that office until his death in Washington in 1812, aged 73 years.

In the fall of 1780 and the spring of 1781 the fortification of Fort Plain was strengthened by the erection of a strong blockhouse. It was situated about a hundred yards from the fort, commanding the steep northern side

of the plateau on which both block house and fort stood. The construction was of pine timber, 8x14 inches square, dovetailed at the ends, and Thomas Morrel of Schenectady, father of Judge Abram Morrel of Johnstown, superintended its erection. It was octagonal in shape and three stories in height, the second projecting five feet over the first, and the third five feet over the second, with portholes for cannon on the first floor, and for musketry on all its surfaces; with holes in projecting floors for small arms, so as to fire down upon a closely approaching foe. The first story is said to have been 30 feet in diameter, the second 40 and the third 50, making it look top heavy for a gale of wind. It mounted several cannon for signal guns and defense—one of which was a twelve-pounder—on the first floor. It stood upon a gentle elevation of several feet. This defense was not palisaded, but a ditch or dry moat several feet deep extended around it. The land upon which both defenses stood was owned by Johannes Lipe during the Revolution. It is said it was built under the supervision of a French engineer employed by Col. Gansevoort. The latter, by order of Gen. Clinton, had repaired to Fort Plain to take charge of a quantity of stores destined for Fort Schuyler, just prior to Brant's Minden raid of August 2, as we have seen. It was probably at this time its erection was planned. Ramparts of logs were thrown up around the defenses at the time of the blockhouse erection. Some little time after this, doubts were expressed as to its being cannon-ball proof. A trial was made with a six-pounder placed at a proper distance. Its ball passed entirely through the blockhouse, crossed a broad ravine and buried itself in a hill on which the old parsonage stood, an eighth of a mile distant. This proved the inefficiency of the building, and its strength was increased by lining it with heavy planks. In order to form a protection against hot shot for the magazine, the garrison stationed there in 1782 commenced throwing up a bank of earth around the

block-house. Rumors of peace and quiet that then prevailed in the valley, caused the work to cease. A representation of this blockhouse constitutes the seal of the village of Fort Plain. It was as much a part of the defensive works of Fort Plain as the stockaded fort and was of a more picturesque appearance and so was chosen for use on the seal.
chosen for the seal. A slight elevation marks its site at the present day 1913).

Fort Willett was begun in the fall of 1780 and finished in the spring of 1781.

———

There are extant few records of the garrisons which tenanted Fort Plain, for ten years or more, and also those of its adjoining posts. Some have been preserved by Simms and the gist of a few are here given:

In the summer of 1780, Captain Putman's company of rangers from Fort Plain started for Fort Herkimer. They stopped for the night at Fort Windecker and Cobus Mabee of Fairfield, was put on picket duty for the night outside the post. About midnight the guard saw a savage stealing up behind a rail fence. He deftly slipped his hat and coat over a stump and dropped down behind a nearby log and waited. The Indian came very near and at a short distance fired at the dummy man, drew his tomahawk and rushed up. But before he could sink it in the stump, Mabee shot him dead. The garrison, half dressed, rushed to arms and found their comrade had bagged a remarkably large Indian. As showing the crudity of the times, it is said the corpse lay unburied near the fort for some time and was made the butt of Indian play by the boys of Fort Windecker.

In the summer of 1780 the enemy was reported to be in the vicinity of Otsego lake and Capt. Putman led his company of rangers from Fort Plain to the lake, accompanied by a company of militia under Maj. Coapman, a Jerseyman. The route was from Fort Plain to Cherry Valley and from there to Otsego lake. Finding no signs of an enemy a return march was made to Cherry Valley and from there to the Mohawk. On the way back an argument arose as to relative physical superiority of the rangers or scouts and the militia. To prove which was the better set of men, a race was proposed to Garlock's tavern on Bowman (Canajoharie) creek. Major Coapman and Captain Putman were both heavy men and did not last long in the race of five or six miles, which soon started between the two rival companies. Putman's scouts were victorious and three of them, John Eikler, Jacob Shew and Isaac Quackenboss (a "lean man") distanced the militiamen and reached Garlock's pretty well played out. The soldiers were strung along the highway for miles in this run. "After the men had all assembled at the tavern, taken refreshments and the bill had been footed by Major Coapman, the party returned leisurely and in order to Fort Plain." It is a significant comment on the hardihood of the Revolutionary soldiers that they should find excitement in a five-mile run over a rough highway carrying their guns and packs.

Under date of April 3, 1780, Col. Visscher writes to Col. Goshen Van Schaick to order "some rum and ammunition for my regiment of militia [then stationed mostly in the Mohawk valley posts from Fort Johnson westward], being very necessary as the men are daily scouting."

———

A story is told of Fort Klock, in the present town of St. Johnsville, and near where the battle between Brant and Johnson's forces and Van Rensselaer's troops was fought. It probably relates to the time of this action although no date is given. A grandfather of Peter Crouse was one of the garrison of Fort Klock. Seeing a party of mounted English troopers passing, the militiaman remarked that he thought he could "hit one of those fellows on horseback." Taking careful aim he shot a British officer out of his saddle, and his frightened horse ran directly up to Fort Klock, where Crouse secured him. A number of camp trappings were fastened to the saddle, among which was a brass kettle. These articles became famous heirlooms in the Crouse family.

Elias Krepp, an old bachelor, was the miller of the grist mill. erected by Sir William Johnson, in the then Tilleborough at the now village of Ephratah. In 1780 a party of raiders burned the mill and took Krepp to Canada. After the war he returned and, with George Getman, went to the ruined mill and, from its walls, removed several hundred dollars in gold and silver which he had there hidden for safety.

The Sacandaga blockhouse (built 1779) was located two miles southeast of Mayfield and was a refuge for the few scattered families of the neighborhood and to defend Johnstown from surprise by way of the Sacandaga, a favorite route to the Mohawk for Canadian invaders. Its garrison being withdrawn, it was attacked by seven Indians in April, 1780, and successfully defended by one man; Woodworth, who, though slightly wounded, fought them off and put out fires they kindled. The savages fled to the forest and were followed by Woodworth and six militiamen on snowshoes a day or two later. The Americans came up with the savages and killed five of the party, returning with their packs and guns.

The chief national events of the year 1780 are summarized as follows: 1780, May 12, capture of Charleston, S. C., by British; 1780, August 16, American army under Gates defeated at Camden, S. C.; 1780, Sept. 23, capture of Major Andre of the British army by three Continental soldiers, Paulding, Williams and Van Wart, and subsequent disclosure of Arnold's treason, following his flight from his post at West Point on the Hudson.

CHAPTER XIX.

1781 — June, Col. Willett, Appointed Commander of Mohawk Valley Posts, Makes Fort Plain His Headquarters —Dreadful Tryon County Conditions —July 9, Currytown Raid—July 10, American Victory at Sharon—Fort Schuyler Abandoned.

Of the conditions in the Mohawk country at the opening of 1781, Beer's History of Montgomery County has the following:

"Gloomy indeed was the prospect at this time in the Mohawk valley. Desolation and destitution were on every side. Of an abundant harvest almost nothing remained. The Cherry Valley, Harpersfield, and all other settlements toward the headwaters of the Susquehanna, had been entirely deserted for localities of greater safety. Some idea of the lamentable condition of other communities in Tryon county may be obtained from a statement addressed to the legislature, December 20, 1780, by the supervisors of the county. In that document it was estimated that 700 buildings had been burned in the county; 613 persons had deserted to the enemy; 354 families had abandoned their dwellings; 197 lives had been lost; 121 persons had been carried into captivity, and hundreds of farms lay uncultivated by reason of the enemy.

"Nor were the terrible sufferings indicated by these statistics, mitigated by a brighter prospect. Before the winter was past, Brant was again hovering about with predatory bands to destroy what little property remained. Since the Oneidas had been driven from their country, the path of the enemy into the valley was almost unobstructed. It was with difficulty that supplies could be conveyed to Forts Plain and Dayton without being captured, and transportation to Fort Schuyler was of course far more hazardous. The militia had been greatly diminished and the people dispirited by repeated invasions, and the destruction of their property; and yet what information could be obtained indicated that another incursion might be looked for to sweep perhaps the whole extent of the valley, contemporaneously with a movement from the north toward Albany. Fort Schuyler was so much injured by flood and fire in the spring of 1781, that it was abandoned, the garrison retiring to the lower posts; and all the upper part of the valley was left open to the savages. [The Fort Schuyler troops went to Forts Dayton, Herkimer and Fort Plain.]

"Gov. Clinton was greatly pained by the gloomy outlook and knowing that Col. Willett was exceedingly popular in the valley, earnestly solicited his services in this quarter. Willett had just been appointed to the command of one of the two new regiments formed by the consolidation of the remnants of five New York regiments, and it was with reluctance that he left the main army for so difficult and harassing an undertaking as the defense of the Mohawk region. The spirit of the people, at this time lower than at any other during the long struggle, began to revive when Col. Willett appeared among them. It was in June that he repaired to Tryon county to take charge of the militia levies and state troops that he might be able to collect. In the letter to Gov. Clinton making known the weakness of his command, Col. Willett said: 'I confess myself not a little disappointed in having such a trifling force for such extensive business as I have on my hands; and also that nothing is done to enable me to avail myself of the militia. The prospect of a suffering county hurts me. Upon my own account I am not uneasy. Everything I can do shall be done, and more cannot be looked for. If it is, the reflection that I have done my duty must fix my own tranquility.'" Willett made his headquarters at Fort Plain, which continued to be the valley headquarters during the rest of the war. He had not been long at Fort Plain before his soldierly qualities and great ability as a commander were brought into play. Willett came to his valley headquarters in June and, in a month's time,

occurred the first raid he had to combat—that led by Dockstader.

The following is largely written from Simms's account of the Currytown invasion and Sharon Springs battle

1781, July 9, 500 Indians and Tories entered the town of Root on one of the raids that devastated Montgomery county the latter years of the war. Their commander was Capt. John Dockstader, a Tory who had gone from the Mohawk country to Canada. The settlement of Currytown (named after William Corry, the patentee of the lands thereabout) was the first objective of these marauders. Here a small block-house had been erected, near the dwelling of Henry Lewis, and surrounded with a palisade. At about ten in the morning the enemy entered the settlement. Jacob Dievendorf, a pioneer settler, was at work in the field with his two sons, Frederick and Jacob and a negro boy named Jacobus Blood. The last two were captured and Frederick, a boy of 14, ran toward the fort but was overtaken, toma hawked and scalped. Mrs. Dieven dorf, in spite of being a fleshy woman, made for the fort with several girl children and half a dozen slaves and reached it in safety, on the way breaking down a fence by her weight in climbing over. Peter Bellinger, a brother of Mrs. Dievendorf, was plowing and hearing the alarm, unhitched a plow horse and, mounting it, rode for the Mohawk and escaped although pursued by several Indians. Rudolf Keller and his wife happened to be at the fort, when the enemy appeared; Keller, Henry Lewis and Conrad Enders being the only men in the blockhouse at that time. Frederick Lewis and Henry Lewis jr. were the first to reach the fort after the invaders' appearance. Frederick Lewis fired three successive guns to warn the settlers of danger and several, taking the warning, escaped safely to the forest. Philip Bellinger thus escaped but was severely wounded and died with friends shortly after. Rudolf Keller's oldest son, seeing the enemy approach, ran home and hurried the rest of the family to the woods, the Indians entering the Keller house just as the fugitives disappeared into the forest. Jacob Tanner and his family were among the last to reach the block-house. On seeing the Indians coming, Tanner fled from his house, with his gun in one hand and a small child in his other arm, followed by his wife with an infant in her arms and several children running by her side holding onto her skirts. Several redmen with uplifted tomahawks chased the Tanner family toward the fort. Finding that they could not overtake them, one of the Indians fired at Tanner, the ball passing just over the child's head he carried and entering a picket of the fort. The defenders fired several shots at the savages and the fleeing family entered the block-house safely.

The Indians plundered and burned all the buildings in the settlement, a dozen or more, except the house of David Lewis. Lewis was a Tory and, although his house was set on fire, an Indian chief, with whom he was acquainted, gave him permission to put it out when they were gone. Jacob Moyer and his father, who were cutting timber in the woods not far from Yates, were found dead and scalped, one at each end of the log. They were killed by the party who pursued Peter Bellinger.

The lad, Frederick Dievendorf, after lying insensible for several hours, recovered and crawled toward the fort. He was seen by his uncle, Keller, who went out to meet him. As he approached, the lad, whose clothes were dyed in his own blood, still bewildered, raised his hands imploringly and besought his uncle not to kill him. Keller took him up in his arms and carried him to the fort. His wounds were properly dressed and he recovered, but was killed several years after by a falling tree. Jacob Dievendorf senior, fled before the Indians, on their approach and, in his flight, ran past a prisoner named James Butterfield, and at a little distance farther on hid himself under a fallen tree. His pursuers enquired of Butterfield what direction he had taken. "That way," said the prisoner, pointing in a different di-

rection. Although several Indians passed by the fallen tree Dievendorf remained undiscovered.

An old man named Putman, captured at this time, was too infirm to keep up with the enemy and was killed and scalped not far from his home.

The Currytown captives taken along by the enemy were Jacob Dievendorf Jr., the negro Jacob, Christian and Andrew Bellinger, sons of Frederick Bellinger, and a little girl named Miller, ten or twelve years old. Christian Bellinger had been in the nine month [militia] service. He was captred on going to get a span of horses, at which time he heard an alarm gun fired at Fort Plain. The horses were hobbled together and the Indians, with a bark rope, had tied the hobble to a tree in a favorable place to capture the one who came for them, who chanced to be young Bellinger. His brother (Andrew) was taken so young and kept so long—to the end of the war—and was so pleased with Indian life, that Christian had to go a third time to get him to return with him. Michael Stowitts (son of Philip G. P. Stowitts, who was killed on the patriot side in the Oriskany battle) was made a prisoner on the Stowitts farm, and is credited with having given the invaders an exaggerated account of the strength defending the fort, which possibly prevented its capture; but it is well known that even small defenses were avoided by the enemy, who did not like exposure to certain death.

On the morning of the same day of the Currytown raid (1781, July 9) Col. Willett sent out, from Fort Plain, Capt. Lawrence Gros with a scouting party of 40 men. Their mission had the double object of scouting for the enemy and provisions. Knowing that the settlements of New Dorlach and New Rhinebeck were inhabited mostly by Tories and that he might get a few beeves there, Gros led his men in that direction. Near the former home of one Baxter, he struck the trail of the enemy and estimated their number from their footprints at 500 men at least. Gros sent two scouts to follow the enemy and then marched his squad to Bowman's (Canajoharie) creek to await their report. The scouts came upon the enemy's camp of the night before after going about a mile. A few Indians were seen cooking food at the fires—making preparations, as the Americans supposed, for the return of their comrades who had gone to destroy Currytown. The two rangers returned quickly to Gros and reported their find, and the captain dispatched John Young and another man, both mounted, on a gallop to Fort Plain to inform Col. Willett. The commandant sent a messenger to Lieut. Col. Vedder, at Fort Paris, with orders to collect all troops possible, at his post and elsewhere, and to make a rapid march to the enemy's camp. Col. Willett detailed all the garrison of Fort Plain he could, with safety detach from that post, for the field. In addition he collected what militia he could from the neighborhood and set out. Passing Fort Clyde in Freysbush, Willett drafted into his ranks what men could there be spared and about midnight he joined Capt. Gros at Bowman's creek. The American force numbered 260 men, many of whom were militia. Col. Willett's battalion set out and, at daybreak, reached the enemy's camp, which was in a cedar swamp on the north side of the western turnpike, near the center of the present town of Sharon and about two miles east of Sharon Springs. This camp was on the highest ground of the swamp, only a few rods from the turnpike. On the south side of the road, a ridge of land may be seen and still south of that a small valley. By a roundabout march, Willett reached this little dale and there drew up his force in a half-circle formation. The men were instructed to take trees or fallen logs and not to leave them and to reserve their fire until they had a fair shot.

The enemy was double the number of the patriot force and stratagem was resorted to by the Fort Plain commandant. He sent several men over the ridge to show themselves, fire upon the raiders and then flee, drawing the foe toward the American

ranks. This ruse completely succeeded and the entire Tory and Indian band snatched up their weapons and chased the American skirmishers who fled toward Willett's ambuscade, Frederick Bellinger being overtaken and killed. The enemy was greeted with a deadly fire from the hidden soldiers and a fierce tree to tree fight began which lasted for two hours until the Tories and Indians, badly punished, broke and fled. John Strobeck, who was a private in Captain Gros's company and in the hottest part of the fight, said afterwards that "the Indians got tired of us and made off." Strobeck was wounded in the hip. During the battle, from a basswood stump, several shots were fired with telling effect at the patriots. William H. Seeber rested his rifle on the shoulder of Henry Failing and gave the hollow stump a centre shot, after which fire from that quarter ceased. About this time, it is said, the enemy were recovering from their first panic, learning they so greatly outnumbered the Continental force. A story is told that Col. Willett, seeing the foe gaining confidence, shouted in a loud voice, "My men, stand your ground and I'll bring up the levies and we'll surround the damned rascals!" The enemy hearing this, and expecting to be captured or slain by an increased American body, turned and ran. In the pursuit Seeber and Failing reached the stump the former had hit and found it was hollow. Seeing a pool of blood on the ground, Col. Willett observed: "One that stood behind that stump will never get back to Canada."

The enemy, in their retreat, were hotly pursued by the Americans, led by Col. Willett in person and so complete was the defeat of the raiders that Willett's men captured most of their camp equipage and plunder obtained the day before in the Currytown raid. Most of the cattle and horses the raiders had taken found their way back to that settlement. Col. Willett continued the pursuit but a short distance, fearing that he might himself fall into a snare similar to the one he had so successfully set for the enemy. The American force returned victorious to Fort Plain, immediately after the battle, bearing with them their wounded. Their loss of five killed and about the same number wounded was small and due to their protected position and the surprise they sprang on their foe.

The Indians, in their retreat from Sharon, crossed the west creek in New Dorlach (near the former Col. Rice residence) and made for the Susquehanna. The loss of the enemy was very severe—about 50 killed and wounded—and Dockstader is said to have returned to Canada (after one other engagement) with his force "greatly reduced." Two of the enemy carried a wounded comrade, on a blanket between two poles, all the way to the Genesee valley, where he died.

Five of Willett's men were killed, including Capt. McKean, a brave and efficient officer. He was taken to Van Alstine's fortified house at Canajoharie, which was on the then road from New Dorlach to Fort Plain, and died there the following day, after which he was buried in "soldier's ground" at Fort Plain; which was probably the burial plot about one hundred yards west of that post, remains of which are still to be seen. On the completion of the blockhouse, McKean's body was reburied on the brink of the hill in front of this fortification with military honors.

Among the wounded was a son of Capt. McKean, who was shot in the mouth. Jacob Radnour received a bullet in his right thigh which he carried to his grave. Like that Sir William Johnson got at Lake George, it gradually settled several inches and made him very lame. Hon. Garrett Dunckel was wounded in the head, "a ball passing in at the right eye and coming out back of the ear." Nicholas Yerdon was wounded in the right wrist, which caused the hand to shrivel and become useless. Adam Strobeck's wound in the hip has been mentioned. All three of the latter came from Freysbush and Radnour, Dunckel and Yerdon were in the Oriskany battle,

where Radnour and Yerdon were wounded. All these wounded were borne on litters back to Fort Plain and all recovered.

Finding their force defeated and having to abandon their prisoners in the flight, the Indians guarding them tomahawked and scalped all except the Bellinger boys and Butterfield. The killed at this time included a German named Carl Herwagen, who had been captured by the enemy on their return from Currytown to their camp the previous evening.

After the battle was over Lieut.-Col. Veeder arrived from Fort Paris with a company of 100 men, mostly from Stone Arabia. He buried the Americans killed in battle and fortunately found and interred the prisoners who were murdered and scalped near the enemy's former camp. The Dievendorf boy, who had been scalped, was found alive half buried among the dead leaves, with which he had covered himself to keep off mosquitoes and flies from his bloody head. One of Veeder's men, thinking him a wounded Indian, on account of his gory face, leveled his gun to shoot but it was knocked up by a fellow soldier, and the Currytown boy's life was spared for almost four-score years more. Young Dievendorf and the little Miller girl, also found alive, were tenderly taken back to Fort Plain, but the latter died on the way. Doctor Faught, a German physician of Stone Arabia, tended the wounds of both Jacob Dievendorf and his brother Frederick Dievendorf and both recovered. Jacob Dievendorf's scalped head was five years in healing. He became one of the wealthiest farmers of Montgomery county and died Oct. 8, 1859, over seventy-eight years after his terrible experience of being scalped and left for dead by his red captors on the bloody field of Sharon.

The battle of Sharon was fought, almost entirely, by men from the present limits of the town of Minden—the Fort Plain garrison, with additions from that of Fort Clyde, and the Minden militia. Some of the soldiers doubtless came from Forts Willett, Win decker and Plank. The Fort Paris company, as seen, did not get up in time to fight. The list of the Americans wounded at Sharon would indicate that the greater part of Willett's battalion were local men. Probably the men of the Mohawk formed a large percentage of the valley garrisons of that time. There was then little for the men of the Mohawk to do but to guard and fight and, between times, to till the fields which were not too exposed to the enemy's ravages. A considerable population must have clustered in and about the principal forts for protection.

Col. Marinus Willett, who made his headquarters at Fort Plain for the last three years of the war and who was connected with so many of the valley military operations and almost all the patriot successes in the valley, deserves mention here. He was a soldier of the highest qualifications, great courage and daring, a clever and fearless woodsman and an intrepid fighter in the open field. His quick, powerful, decisive blows, such as at Johnstown and Sharon Springs, conspired to end the raids from Canada which had devastated the valley. Marinus Willett was born in Jamaica, Long Island, in 1740, the youngest of six sons of Edward Willett, a Queens county farmer. In 1758 he joined the army, under Abercrombie, as a lieutenant in Col. Delaney's regiment. Exposure in the wilderness caused a sickness which confined him in Fort Stanwix until the end of the campaign. Willett early joined the Whigs, in the contest against British aggression. When the British troops in New York were ordered to Boston, after the skirmish at Lexington in 1775, they attempted to carry off a large quantity of spare arms in addition to their own. Willett resolved to prevent it and, although opposed by the mayor and other Whigs, he captured the baggage wagons containing the weapons, etc., and took them back to the city. These arms were afterwards used by the first regiment raised by the state of New York. He was appointed second captain of a company in McDougal's regiment and accompanied Montgomery's futile expedition against Quebec. He commanded St. John's until 1776. He was appointed lieutenant-colonel in 1777 and commanded Fort Constitution on the Hudson. In May he was ordered to Fort Stanwix, recently named Fort Schuyler, where he did such signal service. He was left in command of that fort where he remained until 1778, when he joined the army under Washington and fought with him at Monmouth. He accompanied Sullivan in his campaign against the Indians in 1779. Col. Willett was actively engaged in the Mohawk valley in 1780, 1781, 1782, 1783. So he spent at least four or five years in military service in the Mohawk valley. Washington sent him to treat with the Creek Indians in Florida in 1792 and the same year he was appointed a brigadier-general in the army which was intended to act against the northwestern Indians. He declined this appointment, being opposed to the expedition. Col. Willett was for some time sheriff and in 1807 was elected Mayor of New York city. He was president of the electoral college in 1824 and died in New York August 23, 1830, in the 91st year of his age. A portrait of Col. Willett hangs, among those of other former mayors, in the City Hall in New York and shows a face of much intelligence, power and forceful initiative. Marinus Willett was one of the men of iron who made the American republic possible. There are few natural leaders and he was one. Simms says Willett was a "large man." He was a direct descendant of Thomas Willett, who was a man of great ability and influence in the early years of New York province, and who was the first mayor of New York city after the Dutch rule, being appointed by Gov. Nicolls in 1665. Col. Marinus Willett had a natural son by a Fort Plain woman. This son he cared for and educated and later, when the son was a grown man, he returned to his birthplace and lived here and hereabouts for several years.

The following, concerning Willett, is taken from "New York in the Revolution:"

"Captain, Major, Lieutenant-Colonel, Colonel and Acting Brigadier Marinus Willett was a gallant officer. He held many commands and his promotion was rapid. In 1775-6 he was captain in Col. Alexander McDougal's regiment, 1st N. Y. Line. On April 27, 1776, the Provincial Congress recommended him to the Continental Congress for major of the same regiment. In November of the same year he was recommended for lieutenant-colonel of the 3d Line [regiment] and in July, 1780, he was made lieutenant-colonel commandant of the 5th regiment of the line. In 1781 as lieutenant-colonel he commanded a regiment of levies, [men drafted into military service] and in 1782 was made full colonel of still another regiment of levies. After the death of General Nicholas Herkimer, Colonel Willett commanded the Tryon County militia as acting brigadier-general." The regiment of levies, which Willett commanded in 1781 and which engaged in the Sharon and Johnstown battles, is mentioned in a later chapter dealing briefly with the Tryon county troops. It numbered 1008 soldiers, was largely composed of Mohawk river men, and probably formed all or part of the valley garrisons of the time when Fort Plain was the military headquarters of this section.

At German Flats, 1781, were several encounters. One of them was marked by great bravery on the part of Captain Solomon Woodworth and a small party of rangers which he organized. He marched from Fort Dayton to the Royal Grant for the purpose of observation. On the way he fell into an Indian ambush. One of the most desperate and bloody skirmishes of the war hereabouts then ensued. Woodworth and a large number of his scouts were slain. This was the same Woodworth who so valiantly defended the Sacandaga blockhouse, as told in a previous chapter. His company assembled at Fort Plain only a few days previous to the fatal action, which

took place at Fairfield. Some of his men were recruited from soldiers of the Fort Plain garrison whose time was soon to expire.

In this year also occurred the heroic defense by Christian Schell of his blockhouse home about five miles north of Herkimer village. Sixty Tories and Indians under Donald McDonald, a Tory formerly of Johnstown, attacked the place, most of the people fleeing to Fort Dayton. Schell had eight sons and two of them were captured in the fields while the old man ran safely home and with his other six sons and Mrs. Schell hade a successful defense. They captured McDonald wounded. The enemy drew off having 11 killed and 15 wounded. Schell and one of his boys were killed by Indians in his fields a little later.

Early in May, 1781, high water from the Mohawk destroyed a quantity of stores in Fort Schuyler. On May 12 this post was partially destroyed by fire. The soldiers were playing ball a little distance away and pretty much everything was burned except the palisade and the bombproof, which was saved by throwing dirt on it. This fire has been said to have been of incendiary origin having been started by a soldier of secret Tory sentiments. Samuel Pettit, who was then one of the garrison, in his old age, told Simms that the fire originated from charcoal used to repair arms in the armory. The post was abandoned and the troops marched down the Forts Dayton and Herkimer, which became now the most advanced posts on this frontier. Some of the Fort Schuyler garrison are said to have been removed to Fort Plain. After the abandonment of Fort Schuyler the principal Mohawk valley posts of Tryon county were, in their order from west to east, as follows: Fort Dayton (at present Herkimer), Fort Herkimer (at present German Flats), Fort Plain, Fort Paris (at Stone Arabia), Fort Johnstown, Fort Hunter. Fort Plain's central position probably influenced its selection as the valley American army headquarters.

Simms says that, in the spring of 1781, Col. Livingston, with his regiment of New York troops marched up the Mohawk valley to Fort Plain. No mention is made of further disposition of the troops, however. Possibly, these may have been part of "the reinforcements lately ordered northward" referred to by Gen. Washington in his letter of June 5, 1781, to Gov. Clinton. Washington advocated the concentration of these troops "on the Hudson and Mohawk rivers."

In the summer of 1781 Col. Willett went with a scouting party from Fort Plain to Fort Herkimer and on his return stopped at the Herkimer house. Here then lived Capt. George Herkimer, brother of the deceased General, who had succeeded to the Fall Hill estate. At this time a small body of Indians was seen in the woods above the house and Mrs. Herkimer went to the front door and stepped up on a seat on the stoop and, with her arm around the northwest post, she blew an alarm for her husband who with several slaves was hoeing corn on the flats near the river. Col. Willett came to the door and seeing the woman's exposed position shouted, "Woman, for God's sake, come in or you'll be shot!" He seized hold of Mrs. Herkimer's dress and pulled her inside the house and almost the instant she stepped from the seat to the floor a rifle ball entered the post—instead of her head—leaving a hole long visible. It is presumed that Willett's men quickly drove off the enemy as Captain Herkimer was not harmed.

In July, 1781, a party of 12 Indians made a foray in the Palatine district and captured five persons, on the Shults farm two miles north of the Stone Arabia churches. Three sons of John Shults—Henry, William and John junior, a lad named Felder Wolfe and a negro slave called Joseph went to a field to mow, carrying their guns and stacking them on the edge of the field, skirted on one side by thick woods. From this cover the Indians sprang out, secured the firearms, cap-

tured the harvesters and took them all prisoners to Canada. Upon the mowers not returning, people from the farm went to the field and found their scythes, but the guns were missing. These were the only evidences that the harvesters had been made prisoners. They remained in Canada until the end of the war.

CHAPTER XX.

1781—Oct. 24, Ross and Butler's Tory and Indian Raid in Montgomery and Fulton Counties—Oct. 25, American Victory at Johnstown—Willett's Pursuit, Killing of Walter Butler and Defeat of the Enemy at West Canada Creek—Rejoicing in the Mohawk Valley—Johnstown, the County Seat, at the Time of the Hall Battle, 1781.

Small guerilla parties continued to lurk around the frontier settlements during the remainder of the summer and early autumn of 1781. The vigilance of Col. Willett's scouts prevented their doing any great damage. The Tories, however, had lost none of their animosity against their former neighbors in the Mohawk valley, and in the late autumn of this year again took the field.

In October, 1781, occurred the last great raid, which took place during the war in the limits of western Montgomery or within present Montgomery and Fulton counties. The invaders were so severely punished by the valley troops under Willett, that it had a deterrent effect upon their further enterprises of this kind, at least in the neighborhood of Willett's headquarters at Fort Plain.

This last local foray was commanded by Major Ross and Walter Butler and consisted of 700 Tories and Indians and British regulars. Ross was afterward in command of the British fort at Oswego, when Capt. Thompson came from Fort Plain bearing to the enemy news of an armistice between England and the United States. Of this interesting journey, mention is made in a following chapter. Oct. 24, 1781, the enemy broke in upon the Mohawk settlements from the direction of the Susquehanna, at Currytown, where they had so ravaged the country a few months earlier. They burned no buildings as they did not wish their presence yet known to the neighboring militia. That same morning a scouting party went from Fort Plain towards Sharon Springs, there separating, all of them returning to their post except Jacob Tanner and Frederick Ottman, who set out for Currytown where Tanner wished to visit his family. Near Argusville they came in touch with the enemy, who were approaching the Mohawk by the southwest route. The two American scouts ran down Flat creek and, throwing away their guns and knapsacks, escaped and spread the alarm. At the Putman place (Willow Basin, in the town of Root below the Nose), they came upon a funeral party attending services over the remains of Frederick Putman, who had been killed by the enemy while hunting martin up Yatesville creek. Thus warned, the party broke up and its members fled for safety and to warn others.

The enemy in force, to the number of 700, went from Argusville to Currytown, plundering houses on their way but avoiding the little fort at that place. From Currytown they made for the Mohawk and there came upon and captured the two scouts, Tanner and Ottman, Rudolf Keller and his wife, Michael Stowitts and Jacob Myers, all returning from the Putman funeral, and later took John Lewis near the river. Mrs. Keller was left near Yatesville (now Randall) by the intercession of a Tory nephew. Half a dozen other women just previously taken were also left here, among them Mrs. Adam Fine and a girl named Moyer. The invaders after this did not encumber themselves with any more women prisoners on this raid. Myers was an old man and, on the forced and terrible march which followed the Tory defeat at Johnstown, he could not keep up with the party and was killed and scalped.

Leaving the Yatesville neighborhood, Major Ross led his party on the south side down the Mohawk, taking

the new road recently laid over Stone Ridge, into the present town of Glen. On the ridge, they came at twilight to the Wood home, and took there John Wood captive. Here Joseph Printup, a lieutenant of militia, was at his son's (William I. Printup) house, as were also Jacob Frank, John Loucks and John Van Alstyne, neighbors. Printup had been cleaning his gun and, as he reloaded it, said: "Now I'm ready for the Indians." Almost at the same instant the advance party was seen approaching the house. Frank and Loucks ran for the woods, Loucks being shot down and scalped and Frank escaping. Printup fired on the advance party. An Indian put his gun to the patriot's breast, but a Tory friend of Printup's, with the Indians, struck the gun down and the Whig lieutenant was hit in the thigh. The Tory interfered and saved Printup's life and then he was made a prisoner. Several times, during the following march the lieutenant was saved from the Indians' tomahawks by his friend of the enemy. Printup suffered agonies on the way but finally got to Johnstown, where an old Scotch woman, Mrs. Van Sickler (probably the wife of Johnstown's first blacksmith and also Sir William's), interceded for him and he was left at her house. From here he returned to Stone Ridge and was finally cured of his wounds. At the time of his capture Van Alstyne was also made prisoner and he helped Printup along the road. According to the Indian custom, had he not been able to keep up, he would have been at once scalped and killed.

Jacob, a brother of the former Van Alstyne, was taken shortly after as was Evert Van Epps. John C., a son of Charles Van Epps, spread the alarm on horseback down the river, and the inhabitants fled to safety in the woods. At Auriesville Printup told John Van Alstyne to escape if he could and the latter promptly ran for liberty up the ravine. The enemy continued on to Yankee Hill, in the town of Florida, fording the Schoharie at its mouth. Captain Snook sent Conrad Stein to warn the settlers hereabouts, who mostly escaped.

On the morning of October 25, 1781, the invading party broke camp, forded the Mohawk, entered the town of Amsterdam and headed for Johnstown, small parties of Indians meanwhile raiding the country in every direction. Houses were burned belonging to farmers by the name of Wart, Henry Rury, Captain Snook, John Stein, Samuel Pettingill, William De-Line, Patrick Connelly, George Young and several others in the neighborhood. A man named Bowman was killed and scalped.

The raiders crossed the Mohawk near Stanton's Island, below Amsterdam. Here they burned the houses of Timothy Hunt and Nathan Skeels, Soon after the Tory main body went over the ford a Whig named Ben Yates, came up on the south bank and saw an Indian on the opposite shore. "Discovering Yates and, doubting his ability to harm him, he turned 'round and slapped his buttocks in defiance. In the next instant, a bullet, from the rifle of Ben, struck the Indian, and the former had only to ford the river to get an extra gun and some plunder made in the neighborhood."

That same morning Capt. Littel led a scouting party from the Johnstown fort to learn the enemy's whereabouts. Five miles east of Johnstown they came upon Ross's advance party. Here Lieut. Saulkill, of the scouts, was killed and the rest of the party fled and later were in the ensuing battle. At Johnstown, Hugh McMonts and David and William Scarborough were killed by the raiders.

As soon as the news reached Col. Willett at Fort Plain, he started to the rescue with what men he could hastily collect. Marching through the night he reached Fort Hunter the next morning (October 25, 1781), but the enemy had already crossed the river and directed their course toward Johnstown, plundering and burning right and left. Willett's force lost some time in fording the Mohawk which was not easily passable at this point, but this accomplished, the pur-

suit was vigorously prosecuted and the enemy were overtaken at Johnstown.

Col. Willett had but 416 men, and his inferiority of force compelled a resort to strategy in attacking. Accordingly Col. Rowley, of Massachusetts, was detached with about 60 of his men and some of the Tryon County militia to gain the rear of the enemy by a circuitous march and fall upon them, while Col. Willett attacked them in front. The invaders were met by Col. Willett near Johnson Hall and the battle immediately began. It was for a time hotly contested, but at length the patriot militia, under Willett, suddenly gave way and fled precipitately, before their commander could induce them to make a stand. The enemy would have won an easy and complete victory had not Col. Rowley at this moment, attacked vigorously upon their rear and obstinately maintained an unequal contest. This gave Col. Willett time to rally his men, who again pressed forward. At nightfall, after a severe struggle, the enemy overcome and harassed on all sides, fled in confusion to the woods, not halting to encamp until they had gone several miles. In the engagement the Americans lost about 40; the enemy had about the same number killed and 50 taken prisoners. This American victory was won on the nothwest limits of the present city of Johnstown and near Johnson Hall, where a monument marks the field.

A young patriot, named William Scarborough, was among the garrison at the Johnstown fort at the time of this action, left it with another soldier named Crosset, to join Willett's force. They fell in with the enemy on the way, and Crosset, after shooting one or two of the latter, was himself killed. Scarborough was surrounded and captured by a company of Highlanders under Capt. McDonald, formerly living near Johnstown. Scarborough and the Scotch officer had been neighbors before the war and had got into a political wrangle, which resulted in a fight and the beating of the Highland chief. Henceforward he cherished a bitter hatred toward his adversary, and finding him now in his power, ordered him shot at once. His men refusing the murderous office, McDonald took it upon himself, and cut the prisoner to pieces with his sword.

Capt. Andrew Fink of Palatine, was also in the Johnstown battle. During the action near the Hall, the British took from the Americans a field-piece, which Col. Willett was anxious to recover. He sent Capt. Fink with a party of volunteers, to reconnoitre the enemy and if possible, get the lost cannon. Three of the volunteers were Christian and Mynder Fink, brothers of the captain, and George Stansell. While observing the movements of the enemy from the covert of a fallen tree, Stansell was shot down beside his brave leader with a bullet through his lungs, and was borne from the woods by Han Yost Fink. Strengthening his body of volunteers, Capt. Fink again entered the forest. The cannon was soon after recaptured and, it being near night and the enemy having fled, Willett drew off his men and quartered them in the old Episcopal church at Johnstown, gaining entrance by breaking a window.

The day after the battle, Col. Willett ordered Capt. Littel to send a "scout" (scouting party as then called) from Fort Johnstown to follow the enemy, discover its direction and to report the same. Captain Littel had been slightly wounded in the Hall battle but took with him William Laird and Jacob Shew and set out after the enemy. (Shew was on service in many of the neighborhood posts, Fort Plain included, and is responsible for much of the information Simms used regarding local events).

The enemy camped the first night near Bennett's Corners, four miles from the Hall, and the following day, striking the Caroga valley, went up that stream and went into camp for the night (Oct. 26, 1781) half a mile beyond the outlet of Caroga lakes. The next day Littel's scouting party came up and warmed themselves at Ross's deserted camp fires. After further observing the enemy's trail

Littel became satisfied that they would go to Canada by way of Buck's Island. His party lodged in the woods, near Ross's last camp, and returned to Fort Johnsown next day, from whence Peter Yost was sent on horse, with messages to Col. Willett at Fort Dayton, to which post he had advanced.

Ross's party meanwhile was heading for West Canada creek. The retreating Tories and Indians struck the most easterly of the Jerseyfield roads (leading to Mount's clearing), followed it several miles and encamped for the night on what has since been called Butler's Ridge, in the town of Norway (Herkimer county), half a mile from Black creek.

Early the next morning (Oct. 26, 1781) Willett started his pursuit. He halted at Stone Arabia, and sent forward a detachment of troops to make forced marches to Oneida lake, where he was informed the enemy had left their boats, for the purpose of destroying them. In the meanwhile he pushed forward with the main force to German Flats, where he learned the advance party had returned without accomplishing their errand. From his scouts of the Johnstown fort party, he also learned that the enemy had taken a northerly course to and along the West Canada creek. With about 400 of his best men, he started in pursuit in the face of a driving snow storm.

The route of the pursuing band of Americans was as follows: From Fort Dayton up West Canada creek, crossing it about a mile above Fort Dayton, going up its eastern side to Middleville, from there up the Moltner brook to the Jerseyfield road leading to Little Falls; striking the Jersey field road northeast of present Fairfield village, following it up and camping at night a mile or two from the enemy's position.

Willett's camp was in a thick woods on the Royal Grant. He sent out a scouting party under Jacob Sammons, to discover the enemy. Sammons found them a mile or so above and, after reconnoitering their position, returned and reported to Col. Willett that the enemy were well armed with bayonets.

The American officer gave up the plan of a night attack upon them and continued his pursuit early the next morning (Oct. 28, 1781), but the enemy were as quick on foot as he. In the afternoon he came up with a lagging party of Indians, and a short but sharp skirmish ensued. Some of the Indians were killed, some taken prisoners and others escaped. Willett kept upon the enemy's trail along the creek, and toward evening came up with the main body at a place called Jerseyfield, on the northeastern side of West Canada creek. A running fight ensued, the Indians became terrified, and retreated across the stream at a ford, where Walter Butler, their leader, tried to rally them. In this action it is said 25 of the enemy were killed and a number wounded. A brisk fire was kept up across the creek by both parties for some time. Butler, who had dismounted, left cover and took some water out of the creek with a tin cup. He was in the act of drinking it when he was seen by two of the American pursuing party—Anthony, an Indian, and Daniel Olendorf, a man from the present town of Minden. They both fired at once at Butler, who fell wounded in the head. The savage then threw off his blanket, put his rifle on it and ran across the stream to where Butler lay in great pain, supporting his head on his hand. Seeing the Indian brandishing his tomahawk, the Tory raised his other hand saying, "Spare me—give me quarters!" "Me give you Sherry Valley quarters" replied the red man and struck Butler dead with his weapon, burying it in his head. Just as the Tory captain fell, Col. Willett came up on the opposite side of the creek. Olendorf told him where Butler lay and the American commander together with Andrew Gray of Stone Arabia and John Brower, forded the stream and came upon the scene just as Anthony was about to take his dead victim's scalp. Col. Lewis, the Oneida chief with the American party here came up also and Anthony asked permission to scalp the fallen Tory. The red officer asked Willett if he should permit it. Col. Willett replied: "He belongs to your party, Col. Lewis," whereupon the chief gave a nod of assent and the reeking scalp was torn off the quivering body of the man who had incited his savages to inflict death and the same bloody mutilation on the bodies of scores of men, women and children.

Anthony stripped Butler and returned across the creek to Olendorf. Here the savage put on the red regimentals and strutted about saying: "I be British ofser." "You a fool," remarked Olendorf and told the Indian that if he was seen in Butler's uniform he would be instantly shot by mistake. The savage thereupon hurriedly shed his victim's clothes.

Butler's body was left where it fell, and the place was afterwards called Butler's Ford. The pursuit was kept up until evening, when Willett, completely successful by entirely routing and dispersing the enemy, stopped and started on his return march.

The sufferings of the retreating force of beaten Tories and Indians, on their way to Canada, must have been many and acute. The weather was cold and, in their hasty flight, many of them had cast away their blankets to make progress more speedy. The loss of the Americans in this pursuit was only one man; that of the enemy is not known. It must have been very heavy. Colonel Willett, in his despatch to Governor Clinton observed, "The fields of Johnstown, the brooks and rivers, the hills and mountains, the deep and gloomy marshes through which they had to pass, they alone can tell; and perhaps the officers who detached them on the expedition."

On account of the inclement weather and the lack of provisions, Willett and his force returned to Fort Dayton, after abandoning the chase of the badly beaten enemy. Here the people had gathered together and prepared a feast for the victorious American soldiers and their able commander. And the occasion was also one of great rejoicing over the death of Butler, from whom the people of Tryon county had suffered so much.

The news of the Johnstown and West Canada creek victories and the death of Butler was spread through the valley at about the same time as the tidings of the surrender of the British army under Cornwallis at Yorktown. That great event did not give any more joy to the people along the Mohawk than the welcome assurance that the fiend Butler had been wiped out in the vigorous pursuit by Willett and his fighting men. Willett's return to his headquarters at Fort Plain must have been in the nature of a triumphal march and he probably was there heartily greeted by the much tried people of the Canajoharie and Palatine districts.

The battle of Johnstown was fought by the garrisons of the Fort Plain headquarters and its adjacent posts, by what local militia could be quickly gathered, and probably some men from Fort Hunter and Fort Johnson and with the aid of the Johnstown garrison. The picked force Willett took up West Canada creek doubtless included some of the scouts or militia posted at Fort Herkimer and Fort Dayton. So this campaign takes on a particular local interest as, although the battle of Johnstown and the skirmish at West Canada creek were fought outside of the Canajoharie and Palatine districts, the great majority of the forces there engaged were from the Fort Plain valley headquarters and the posts within a five-mile radius of it. This, as has been before mentioned is true of the Sharon Springs battle as well. So, like the greater action of Oriskany, these Revolutionary Tryon county conflicts are of much local interest because so large a proportion of the American soldiers engaged came from the Canajoharie and Palatine districts of which Fort Plain was the center, even though the scenes of battles were outside of them.

Three of the late Revolutionary actions—Stone Arabia, St. Johnsville and Sharon Springs, occurred within the Canajoharie and Palatine districts and the two former within the present lim-

its of the towns of Palatine and St. Johnsville. The battle of Johnstown has been stated to have been the last action of the Revolution on record and fittingly terminated in an American victory.

————

The Mohawk Valley Democrat (Fonda), in its issue of Feb. 27, 1913, printed a statement of Philip Graff, a Mohawk valley soldier who took part in the West Canada creek skirmish and was present at the death of Walter Butler. This document has been in the possession of the Sammons family for over a century. Graff's account differs somewhat from Olendorf's, but both are probably true, the confusion of the battle preventing both from seeing all its incidents individually. The Graff statement follows in its original form:

"In October 1781, I was inlisted in the state troops for four months and was then stationed at fort Herkimer in a company of Capt. Peter Van Ranselaer and Leut. John Spencer. Some time in November after Col. Willett had a battle with Major Ross at Johnstown he arrived at Fort Herkimer. Our company then was ordered to join with Col. Willett's men and with them we crossed the river from the south to the north side the next morning; we were marched to the north through the Royal Grants and encamped in the woods, made fire; some snow had fell that day. The next morning by daybreak we marched on to the enemy about one and came with the rear of the enemy, took some prisoners and Lieut. John Rykeman, several of their horses with blankets and provisions and packs on—we then pursued the enemy on to Jersey Field and in coming down a hill to the creek, we received a very strong fire from the enemy who had [crossed] the west Canada creek, which was returned from Willett's men with spirit. The enemy on the west side of the creek and Willett's men on the east side. One of the Oneida Indians having got near the creek saw Major Butler look from behind a tree to Willett's men at the east, took aim at him and shot him through his hat and upper part of his head. Butler fell, the enemy run, the Indian run through the rest of the Indians and [an] advance immediately followed when Indian who shot Butler arrived first having noticed particular where Butler fell; he was tottering up and down in great agony, partly setting, looking the Indian in the face when the Indian shot him about through the eye brow and eye and immediately took his scalp off. The Oneida Indians then mostly got up and give tremendous yell and war hoop, immediately striped Butler of all his close, left him naked laying on his face. The Indian walked forward (the rest followed) with the scalp in his hand; came to the guard called out, 'I have Butler's scalp,' struck it against a tree, 'take the blood' [evidently addressing] Lieut. Rykeman who was in the guard, [and] struck it at his face [saying] 'Butler's scalp, you Bogen.' Rykeman drew his head back and avoided the stroke. I saw two [of] his sergeants and little farther saw another of the enemy shot through the body. Butler was killed about 11 o'clock. We pursued the enemy until evening and returned the morning, past Butler again in the position we left him the day before. I believe he never was buried."

Some incidents of the West Canada creek pursuit follow:

Soon after crossing West Canada creek, some of Willett's men found a little five-year-old girl beneath a fallen tree, crying piteously. She had been made a prisoner and left by the Indians in their flight. The militiamen comforted her and took her back to her valley home. The weather at this time was very severe and the sufferings of the enemy and their prisoners were intense.

A militiaman named Lodowick Moyer, who was in the American pursuit, said that "ice was forming in the creeks and, in crossing them, the soldiers took off their pantaloons (note the 'pantaloons') and thought the ice would cut their legs off." They were gone four days on two days rations.

He said "the enemy left a wounded Tory behind after the West Canada creek skirmish, who had been wounded at the Hall battle. Col. Willett sent him back down the creek on a horse, with someone to care for him. He died on the way and was buried under a fallen tree. Col. Willett was as kind as he was brave."

Simms says: "The prisoners captured by Major Ross and party suffered much on their way to Canada from the cold, being 17 days journeying to the Genesee valley, during which time they were compelled to live almost entirely on a stinted allowance of horse-flesh. Some of the prisoners wintered in the Genesee valley and were taken to Niagara the following March. Keller, one of the Currytown prisoners, on arriving at Niagara was sold, and one Countryman, a native of the Mohawk valley and then an officer in the British service was his purchaser." He was sent successively to Rebel Island (near Montreal), to Halifax, Nova Scotia, and finally to Boston, "where he was exchanged and left to foot it home without money, as were many [liberated] prisoners during the war. They were however, welcomed to the table of every patriot on whom they chanced to call and suffered but little by hunger. Keller reached his family near Fort Plain, whither they had removed in his absence, Dec. 24, 1782. Van Epps, a fellow prisoner, reached his home [in Glen] about 18 months after his capture and the rest of the prisoners, taken that fall [1781], returned when he did or at subsequent periods, as they were confined in different places."

Johnstown, the scene of the foregoing battle, was begun by Sir William Johnson in 1760. At the time of the battle of Johnstown, in 1781, it consisted, besides Johnson Hall, of a court house and jail (both erected in 1772), a stone Episcopal church (built in 1771), a few taverns and stores and a small number of dwellings, some of which had been built by Sir William. After Sir John Johnson's flight to Canada in 1776, the patriot committee had the stone jail converted into a fort, further strengthening it with a palisade and block-house. The Johnstown fort, Fort Johnson, Fort Hunter, Fort Paris, Fort Plain, Fort Clyde, Fort Plank, Fort Willett and Fort Windecker were the chief fortifications in the present limits of Montgomery and Fulton counties during the Revolution. With the addition of Forts Dayton and Herkimer (in present Herkimer county) and Fort Schuyler (abandoned in 1781, and in present Oneida county) they formed the defenses of the valley and this part of the Revolutionary New York frontier. Six of these nine Fulton and Montgomery army posts were within the limits of the present Minden and Palatine townships.

On June 26, 1872, at Johnstown, was held the centennial celebration of the erection of the court house and the jail which was the Johnstown fort of the Revolution. Gov. Horatio Seymour was the chief speaker. A portion of his address follows:

The edifice and its objects were in strange contrast with the aspect of the country. It was pushing the forms and rules of English jurisprudence far into the territories of the Indian tribes and it was one of the first steps taken in that march of civilization which has now forced its way across the continent. There is a historic interest attached to all the classes of men who met at that time [the laying of the corner stone of the court house in 1772]. There was the German from the Palatinate, who had been driven from his home by the invasion of the French and who had been sent to this country by the Ministry of Queen Anne; the Hollander, who could look with pride upon the struggles of his country against the powers of Spain and in defense of civil and religious liberty; the stern Iroquois warriors, the conquerors of one-half the original territories of our Union, who looked upon the ceremonies in their quiet, watchful way. There was also a band of Catholic Scotch Highlanders, who had been driven away from their native hills by the harsh policy of the British government, which sought by such rigor to force the rule of law upon the wild clansmen. There were to be seen Brant and Butler and others, whose names, to this day, recall in this valley scenes of cruelty, rapine

and bloodshed. The presence of Sir William Johnson, with an attendance of British officers and soldiers gave dignity and brilliancy to the event, while over all, asserting the power of the Crown, waved the broad folds of the British flag. The aspects of those who then met at this place not only made a clear picture of the state of our country, but it came at a point of time in our history of intense interest. All, in the mingled crowd of soldiers, settlers and savages, felt that the future was dark and dangerous. They had fought side by side in the deep forests against the French and Indian allies; now they did not know how soon they would meet as foes in deadly conflict.

———

In the fall of 1781, Conrad Edick was captured by a party of seven marauding Indians in the neighborhood of Fort Plank, in the present town of Minden. They hurried off into the wilderness and at nightfall stopped at an abandoned log house to stay there for the night. The party made a fire, as the weather was cold, and ate a scanty supper. After this the savages sat about on the cabin floor and discussed the poor success of their expedition, lamenting the lack of spoil and prisoners they had secured. They determined to hold a pow wow in the morning, kill and scalp their prisoner and return to the vicinity of the Mohawk to secure more plunder and prisoners if possible. Edick, unbeknown to them, understood the Mohawk dialect, and was harrowed to thus learn his fate. When the Indians lay down to sleep, their prisoner was placed between two of the red men and tied to them by cords passing over his breast and thighs. Sleep was out of the question for the agonized white man, as he lay trying to figure out some plan of escape. His restless hands felt about the debris on the floor and came in contact with a bit of glass, to his great joy. Assuring himself that his savage bedfellows slept soundly, he found he could reach his bindings with his hands and cautiously severed those which were fastened to his chest and then the ones about his legs. He knew the Indians had left a large watch dog on guard outside the door and he had also noticed, on his captive journey the preceding day, a large hollow log in the woods nearby. From the door he made a break for the forest and the dog at once chased him . barking . loudly. Before Edick reached cover 100 yards away, the Indians woke, grasped their rifles and pursued. As he neared the edge of the woods they fired at the fleeing prisoner but Edick luckily stumbled and the volley went over his head. Jumping up he ran among the trees until he found the hollow log and crawled inside. The Mohawks and their dog made a search for their escaped captive but the animal proved poor on the scent and did not discover Edick's hiding place. The savages sat down on the very log in which the white man was concealed and discussed their prisoner's escape. They decided he had climbed a tree or that "the devil" had spirited him away. As it was nearing morning the party resolved to eat and follow their plan of the night before to return and plunder along the Mohawk. One Indian went to a neighboring field and shot a sheep which they dressed. Then the savages built a fire against the same log in which Edick was hidden and proceeded to cook their mutton. The white man suffered tortures from the heat and smoke and stuffed parts of his clothing and some leaves into the crannies of the log to keep the fire out. He controlled his tortures of mind and body and desire to cough on account of the smoke, knowing he would be instantly killed if discovered. When the cooking was finished, his miseries gradually subsided with the dying fire. The savages, after their breakfast, left one of their number on guard to keep a lookout for their lost prisoner and started on their new foray. Often during the morning the Indian sentinel sat or stood on Edick's log. Not hearing the savage's movements for some time, the white man ventured to creep out of his hiding place. Not seeing the savage, Edick ran for his life and eventually reached Fort Plank in safety. Conrad Edick, after this terri-

ble experience, lived to a ripe old age, dying at Frankfort, N. Y., 1846, aged about 80 years, which would make him under 20 at the time of the above exciting affair. Ittig was the original German for the name Edick.

————

In the latter part of October, 1781, four patriots were captured in the Sharon neighborhood by Indian marauders. Christian Myndert abandoned his home there in the fall of 1781, on account of the several Indian forays in that neighborhood. He returned with Lieut. Jacob Borst of Cobleskill, Sergeant William Kneiskern and Jacob Kerker, all armed, to fix his buildings for the winter. After the work the party went to the house, built a fire and warmed themselves, setting their guns in a corner of the room. Six Indians, commanded by a valley Tory named Walrath, broke into the room, seized the guns and captured the entire party, carrying them off to Canada. They were subjected to such cruelties in the Indian country that Borst died at Niagara.

————

Following are the principal national occurrences of the year 1781 summarized: 1781, Jan. 17, Americans under Morgan destroy British force at Cowpens, S. C.; 1781, March 1, Articles of Confederation (adopted 1777) between the thirteen states finally go into effect; 1781, March 15, indecisive battle at Guilford Court House, S. C., between British under Tarleton and Americans under Greene; 1781, April 25, defeat of Greene's army at Hobkirk Hill, near Camden, S. C.; 1781, Sept. 6, Benedict Arnold, in command of a British force, burns and plunders New London, Conn., while his associate officer, Col. Eyre, takes Fort Griswold and massacres half the garrison after the surrender; 1781, Sept. 8, battle at Eutaw Springs, S. C., with advantage with the Americans; 1781, Oct. 19, surrender of the British army, under Cornwallis, to Washington at Yorktown, Va.

CHAPTER XXI.

1782—Last of the War in the Valley—
Rebuilding and Repopulation—Tory
and Indian Raid at Fort Herkimer—
Tories—Gen. Washington at Schenectady.

The following chapter deals with
the year 1782 and 1783 as relating to
the Canajoharie and Palatine districts
and Tryon, later Montgomery county.
As there were no hostilities to speak
of in those years in this immediate
section, the valley began to rapidly
build up again. Families returned to
their burned homes. The whole section had been razed of dwellings by
the raiding parties of the enemy but
houses and barns were now reared
and, with rumors of peace in the
air, the valley was rapidly repopulated in these two years. When Washington came to Fort Plain in 1783 much
of the marks of war along the Mohawk
had vanished. In 1782, and even in
1783, small scalping parties of Indians
committed occasional murders and
depredations and in 1782 the Herkimer settlements were destructively
visited but the Canajoharie and Palatine districts were comparatively free
of further hostilities, except in a small
way. This was largely due to the
efficient protection afforded by Col.
Willett and his garrisons.

In February, 1782, the Tryon county
court of general session indicted 41
persons for their Tory proclivities, on
the charge of "aiding, abetting, feed-
ing and comforting the enemy." Molly
Brant was one of those indicted. In
February, 1781, this court indicted 104
Tryon county Tories on this charge.
In October, 1781, 16 more were so
charged. Among the 163 persons
indicted many bore the names of Mohawk valley German and Dutch pioneer families. Simms says, "Indeed
we may say that thus very many of
the German families of New York became represented in Canada, and are
so to this day."

The Tories were not allowed to return without vigorous protests. Peter
Young of the town of Florida, living
at Young's lake (a small pond near
Schoharie creek) was an ardent
patriot. He married a Serviss girl,
whose family were Tories. At the
close of hostilities two of Young's
brothers-in-law made Mrs. Young a
visit. Young came in on them and ordered them back to Canada at the
point of a musket and they promptly
took up their return journey.

Christopher P. Yates wrote a letter
to Col. H. Frey dated Freyburg, March
22, 1782. He said among other things:
"We have already had three different
inroads from the enemy. The last was
at Bowman's kill, [Canajoharie creek]
from whence they took three children
of McFee's family."

1782, July 26 and 27, occurred Capt.
Crysler's last Tory invasion of the
Schoharie country at Foxescreek and
in the Cobleskill valley, which was the
final incursion in that quarter.

One of the last Indian murders of
the Revolution, within the present
limits of Fulton and Montgomery
county was that of Henry Stoner of
Fonda's Bush, later Broadalbin, in
1782. He was an old patriot and was
struck down and tomahawked in his
fields. His son, Nick Stoner, the famous trapper, attacked the Indian
murderer of his father with an andiron
in a Johnstown tavern after the war.
Strange to say young Stoner was im
prisoned for this affray in which he
laid out several savages, but was
shortly after released from the Johns
town jail.

In July, 1782, all the buildings on the
south side of the Mohawk in the German Flats section, except Fort Herkimer and the Johan Jost Herkimer
house, were destroyed by a force of 600
Tories and Indians. The night before
the mill at Little Falls had been burned by the raiders. One man was killed
in attempting to escape to Fort Herkimer and another was caught, tortured and killed near that post, the
Indians hoping his cries would draw
a party from the fort and so weaken
it that they could make a successful
attack. The garrison's hot fire kept
off the enemy. Two soldiers in the
fort were hit and killed and a number
of the invaders are presumed to have

been killed and wounded. The valley of the Mohawk was not again visited by any serious raid during the remainder of the war. The conflict had not entirely ceased in other quarters but there was a general subsiding of hostilities here. Toward the close of 1782, the British commander-in-chief directed that no more Indian expeditions be sent out, and those on foot were called in.

———

The following account shows the resourcefulness and reckless daring of one, at least, of the Tories of the valley: Among the Mohawk valley refugees in Canada was John Helmer, a son of Philip Helmer, who lived at Fonda's Bush. Having returned to that settlement he was arrested and imprisoned at Johnstown. The sentinel at the jail one day allowed Helmer to take his gun in hand to look at it, as the prisoner expressed admiration for it. Helmer, with the weapon, intimidated the guard and escaped again to Canada. With charcteristic recklessness, he returned later to recruit British soldiers among his Tory neighbors and was again captured and jailed at Johnstown. Fortunately for the venturesome Tory, a sister of his had a lover among the garrison stationed at the jail, which was then also a fort; and he not only released Helmer but with another soldier set out with him for Canada. The two deserters were shot dead by a pursuing party and Helmer, although severely wounded by a bayonet thrust, escaped to the woods. Later he was found half dead and was returned to the jail for the third time. His wound, having healed, he again escaped and reached Canada after almost incredible sufferings. Here he remained and made his home after the war. Among the Tory fighters seem to have been many of reckless valor, although their most typical leader, Walter Butler, died the death of a coward after a record unequalled for bloody and inhuman crimes, showing that a craven heart and a murderous hand go together. The spirit animating the Tory fighters

seems to have been absolutely different from that of the Americans. Believing that the cause of the king was just, they resorted to every diabolical device to murder and intimidate the Whig population of the valley. The more violent their crimes, however, the harder did the provincials stand their ground. Many of the Tories were more savage than the Indians, as Brant affirms and their murderous cruelty toward the women and chil dren, as well as men, who were for merly their neighbors, almost surpass belief. They seem to have been as ready with the scalping knife as the Indians and were constantly inciting their savage allies to the utmost barbarities. In contrast to this attitude, that of the Whig population of the valley was marked. Much as the Tory soldiers were hated, their women and children who were left behind were not injured or maltreated in a single known instance, and the Tory prisoners taken were treated with the utmost justice. The intense hatred of England, which prevailed in the valley after the Revolution, was due as much to Tory barbarities as to the murders and tortures perpetrated by the Indians. American justice combined with American brawn, won in this horrible struggle against white and red savagery, but the bitter passions engendered by this civil war along the Mohawk endured for years afterward.

It was the Tory methods of warfare, particularly as shown on the frontier of New York, that so thoroughly embittered American sentiment against England, a feeling that existed in varying degree for the greater part of a century after the close of the Revolution. Warfare, based upon the murder of women and children and the destruction and looting of property can never stand high in the eyes of civilized people. Tory and Indian murders, barbarities and scalpings combined with the Revolutionary use of hired foreign troops, such as the Hessians, were the causes which tended to divide the two great branches of the

English speaking peoples during the greater part of the nineteenth century. It is probable that the actions of many of the Tryon county Tories, during the war for liberty, were actuated by the thought of gain. In case the British cause had triumphed the patriots' lands would doubtless have been confiscated and given to the Tories in proportion to their Revolutionary "services." This would be rendered easier by the wholesale murder of the "rebel" population and it was probably such a policy that induced the fiendish methods of the Tory invaders and their Indian allies.

There is abundant evidence that the valley Tories were promised the "rebels'" lands if they would fight for King George. Sir John Johnson was particularly lavish with these promises to his followers from the Mohawk valley. It is said that two Tryon county Tories, then serving under Sir John, began an argument as to which should have the rich lands of Lieut.-Col. Wagner in Palatine. It ended in a rough and tumble fight which laid the two warriors up for several days.

It is a fitting place here to refer to the difficulty experienced in the foregoing Revolutionary chapters in naming, as a whole, the forces invading the valley. They are generally spoken of as the "enemy" or the "raiders" or some such term, for the simple reason that they cannot be referred to as "English" or "British," because they were composed of such vary elements. were composed of such verying elements. British, Tories, Indians and Germans composed the army under St. Leger and under Sir John Johnson at Stone Arabia and St. Johnsville and in almost every other case of battle and invasion. The Americans looked upon the British use of Indians in the conflict as a brutal, uncivilized proceeding and England's further employment of Hessian troops was a still further cause of the just hatred of our countryman against Britain. True, America had many friends in England but the ruling party countenanced the savagery referred to and brought about a deplorable state of affairs in the after relations of the two countries.

———

Philip Helmer had had a love affair with a maiden of the Palafter district. Johannes Bellinger, a Whig, lived just above Fort Hess, in the town of St. Johnsville, and had six daughters, with one of whom the lively Tory, Philip Helmer, was enamored. He was of course forbidden the Bellinger place and consequently formed a plot to kidnap his sweetheart, Peggy by name. Taking a party of Indians he set out for Bellinger's but, evidently fearing the savages would do harm to the family, he gave the alarm at Fort Hess and a party of volunteers set out to ambuscade the red men. On their approach, one of the militia became excited and shouted: "Boys, here they are," and the Indians turned and fled, one of their number being shot down and killed. It is said that this double-turncoat, Helmer, married Peggy Bellinger after the war.

Another account says that Tories and Indians of the guerilla party intended carrying off the Bellinger girls as concubines for themselves, leaving Helmer entirely out of the deal. Learning of this he turned informer as related.

———

The reunions of valley families with members who had been captured during the Revolution, furnish countless dramatic incidents. One of these has a homely smack of early farm life. Leonard Paneter was captured in the present town of St. Johnsville, when he was but eight years old, and taken to Canada. On his release from captivity a year later he was sent to Schenectady with others who had been taken in the valley and who were now exchanged and free to return to their Mohawk homes. Young Paneter's father sent an older son down to Schenectady to bring the boy back. Here he found a number of lads drawn up in line waiting for parents or relatives to identify them. The boys did not at once know each other but Leonard upon seeing the horse that carried his brother, remembered it at once, and the brothers were soon reunited. and happily on their way, probably both riding the old nag homeward.

In the summer of 1782, Gen. Washington was at Albany and was invited to visit Schenectady by its citizens. He accepted and rode there from Albany in a carriage with Gen. Schuyler on June 30, 1782. Washington walked with his hat under his arm in a long procession which served as his escort a considerable distance. A public dinner was given the commander-in-chief at the tavern kept by Abraham Clinch, who was a drummer boy under Braddock. Being acquainted with the adventures and sufferings of Col. Visscher, who then lived in Schenectady, Washington expressed surprise that the noted Tryon county militia officer had not been invited, and sent a messenger for him. Visscher was a man of spirit, but somewhat retiring. He was found in his barn doing some work, which he left with reluctance. Presenting himself to Washington the latter gave him marked attention and seated Visscher next himself at the dinner. A number of Tryon militia officers were there present. Visscher, it will be remembered, was in chief command of the neighboring posts, with headquarters at Fort Paris in Stone Arabia, in 1779, and later was scalped by Indians but recovered, as previously related. He also commanded the unfortunate rear guard at Oriskany but was himself a man of utmost bravery.

During this Schenectady visit, it is related, Washington was walking about the streets of that city with a citizen named Banker, a blacksmith. An old negro passing took off his hat and bowed respectfully to the general, a salutation which Washington politely returned. His Schenectady companion expressed surprise, saying that slaves were not thus noticed in the valley. Washington replied: "I cannot be less civil than a poor negro." Washington on this Schenectady journey also visited Saratoga Springs and vicinity.

CHAPTER XXII.

1783—February 9, Col. Willett's Attempt to Capture Fort Oswego—Privations of the American Troops on the Return Trip.

One of the last military enterprises (and possibly the very final one) on which Colonel Willett set out from Fort Plain was the attempt to capture the important British fortification of Oswego in February, 1783. This, as per Washington's report to congress, was an expedition in which a force of 500 Americans were engaged under Willett. They were troops of the New York line and part of a Rhode Island regiment and were all probably then stationed at the valley posts of which Fort Plain was the headquarters, and it was doubtless here that the planning and final preparations, for the Oswego expedition, were made. Of this little known enterprise, one of the last of the Revolution, Simms has the following:

"Said Moses Nelson, an American prisoner there [at Oswego] in the spring of 1782, when the enemy set about rebuilding Fort Oswego, three officers, Capt. Nellis, Lieut. James Hare, and Ensign Robert Nellis, a son of the captain and all of the forester service had charge of the Indians there employed. [These Tory Nellises may have been of the Palatine Nellis family.] Nelson and two other lads, also prisoners, accompanied this party which was conveyed in a sloop, as waiters. About 100 persons were employed in building this fortress, which occupied most of the season. The winter following, Nelson remained at this fort and was in it when Col. Willett advanced with a body of troops, February 9, 1783, with the intention of taking it by surprise. The enterprise is said to have been abortive in consequence of Col. Willett's guide, who was an Oneida Indian, having lost his way in the night when within a few miles of the fort. The men were illy provided for their return—certain victory having been anticipated—and their sufferings were, in consequence, very severe. This enterprise was un-

dertaken agreeable to the orders of
Gen. Washington.

"Col. Willett, possibly, may not have
known, as well as Washington did, that
Fort Oswego had been so strongly
fitted up the preceding year and consequently the difficulties he had to encounter before its capture. Be that as
it may, the probability is, that had the
attack been made, the impossibility of
scaling the walls would have frus-
trated the design, with the loss of
many brave men. The fort was surrounded by a deep moat, in which were
planted many sharp pickets. From the
lower part of the walls projected down
and outward another row of heavy
pickets. A drawbridge enabled the inmates to pass out and in, which was
drawn up and secured to the wall
every night. The corners [of the fort]
were built out so that mounted cannon commanded the trenches. Two of
Willett's men, badly frozen, entered
the fort in the morning, surrendering
themselves prisoners, from whom the
garrison learned the object of the enterprise. The ladders prepared by
Willett to scale the walls were left on
his return, and a party of British soldiers went and brought them in. Said
the American prisoner Nelson, 'The
longest of them, when placed against
the walls inside the pickets, reached
only about two-thirds of the way to
the top.' The post was strongly garrisoned and it was the opinion of Nelson that the accident or treachery
which misled the troops was most
providential, tending to save Col. Willett from defeat and most of his men
from certain death."

John Roof of Canajoharie, who was a
private in this ill-fated expedition, told
Simms that so certain was Willett of
success that insufficient provisions
were taken along for the journey out
and back to the valley. There were
several dogs with the American troops
at the start and these were killed on
the out trip, as their barking, it was
feared, would betray the expedition to
the enemy. On the wintry trip back
the suffering and famished soldiers
were glad to dig these animals out of
the snow and eat them. The return of

the Americans to the valley forts must
have been a trip of great privation.

Gen. Washington reported the fail
ure of Willett's attempt on Oswego to
the President of Congress, February
25, 1783, as follows:

"Sir—I am sorry to acquaint your
Excellency—for the information of
Congress—that a project which I had
formed for attacking the enemy's fort
at Oswego—as soon as the sleighing
should be good, and the ice of the
Oneida lake should have acquired sufficient thickness to admit the passage
of a detachment—has miscarried. The
report of Col. Willett, to whom I had
entrusted the command of the party,
consisting of a part of the Rhode
Island regiment and the State troops
of New York—in all about 500 men—
will assign reasons for the disappointment."

Washington further said that, although the expedition had failed, "I
am certain nothing depending upon
Col. Willett, to give efficiency to it,
was wanting."

CHAPTER XXIII.

1783—April 17, Messenger From Gen.
Washington Reaches Fort Plain Giving News of End of Hostilities—
April 18, Captain Thompson's Journey to Oswego With a Flag of Truce.

In April, 1783, Captain Alexander
Thompson made a journey from "Fort
Rennselaer" (Fort Plain) to the British
post of Oswego to announce the for-
mal cessation of hostilities between
England and the United States of
America. He kept a record of his trip
and this journal was given to Simms
by Rev. Dr. Denis Wortman, long a
pastor of the Reformed church at Fort
Plain. It is headed, "Journal of a tour
from the American Garrison at Fort
Rennselaer in Canajoharie on the Mohawk river, to the British Garrison of
Oswego, as a Flagg, to announce a
cessation of hostilities on the frontiers
of New York, commenced, Friday,
April 18, 1783."

This journal recounts a wilderness
journey made within a year of a century and a half after the trip of the

Dutch traders through the Canajoharie district, narrated in the first
chapter. Traveling conditions along
the route seem to have been similar
even at this later date. It also details
a tour over a historic route of traffic
of which the Mohawk was an important part, and a great highway so vital
to the Canajoharie and Palatine dis-
triet people. The details narrated give
vividly, moreover, a characteristic picture of wilderness travel and life at
that day. Thus, aside from its interest in relation to the news of peace
in the Mohawk valley and its revela-
tion of the importance of old Fort
Plain, it is given due place here.

This diary belonged (in 1880) to
Mrs. Thomas Buckley of Brooklyn, a
granddaughter of its Revolutionary
author. We have seen that the name
of Fort Plain had been changed to
Fort Rensselaer, in honor of Gen. Van
Rensselaer, who had proved so lacking
during the Stone Arabia and Klock's
Field battles. This name it retained
officially to the end of the war. Simms
has summarized Captain Thompson's
record as follows:

"On the first of January of this year
(1783), Capt. Thompson, as his journal shows, was appointed to the artillery command of several posts of
the Mohawk valley, which he names as
follows: Fort Rensselaer, Fort Plank,
Fort Herkimer and Fort Dayton. Fort
Rensselaer—another name for Fort
Plain—being, as he says, the headquarters for the river forts, he thought
proper to have his own quarters near
those of the commanding officer [Col.
Willett], so as to furnish from his own
company detachments as required.

"On the 17th of April—only a little
over two months after Col. Willett's
attempt to surprise Fort Oswego—an
express arrived at Fort Plain, from
Washington's headquarters, to have an
officer sent from thence with a flag to
Oswego to announce to that garrison
(from whence many of the Indian
depredators came) a general cessation
of hostilities, and an impending peace.
"Major Andrew Fink, then in command at Fort Plain [under Col. Wil-
lett], committed this important and

hazardous mission to Capt. Thompson.
His companions were to be four, a
bombardier of his own company, a
sergeant of Willett's militia, and a
Stockbridge Indian, and his guide and
interpreter were to join him at Fort
Herkimer. All things were to be ready
for an early start on the morning of
the 18th, but, when the nature of his
mission became known along the valley, many, having lost friends whose
fate was unknown, desired a chance to
send letters by the flagbearer; and the
start was thus delayed until 11 o'clock,
at which hour numerous packets and
letters were collected to be sent to
friends in Canada. To some inquirers
he said on his return, his mission
proved to be one of joy, to others one
of sadness; 'as the veil of mysteries
had not been lifted.

"A flag of truce having been made
by securing a white cloth to the head
of a spontoon [a short spear much used
on this frontier] to be borne by the
sergeant, he left the fort with the
flag man in front of him and the ar-
tilleryman and the Indian in his rear.
He started with a pack horse which
he discreetly left at Fort Herkimer.
The novelty of his mission drew a
great crowd together and he was accompanied several miles by a caval-
cade of officers, soldiers and citizens.
He went up the river road on the
south side of the Mohawk and spoke
of passing Fort Windecker (near Mindenville), and the Canajoharie or Upper Mohawk castle (now Danube,
where the Mohawks' church still
stands), arriving at Mr. Schuyler's
house at the foot of Fall Hill about 3
p. m., where he and his party were
presented an excellent dinner. Leaving Schuyler's at 4 o'clock he passed
over Fall Hill and arrived at Fort
Herkimer at sunset. At this garrison,
Capt. Thompson found David Schuyler, a brother of the man he had dined
with, who became his guide and interpreter. Eight days' rations were put
into knapsacks, and one short musket
was concealed in a blanket, with which
to kill game, if by any means their
provisions failed. On Saturday morning, April 19, in a snow storm, this

party of five set out on their wilderness journey, still on the south side of the Mohawk. They met several hunting parties and made their first halt opposite 'Thompson's place, above New Germantown,' now in the town of Schuyler. A few miles above they fell in with a party of ten families of Indians on a hunting excursion and learned how forest children lived. Here his men, instructed by their Indian companion, soon erected a wigwam for the night in the, following manner: Two stakes,, with crotches at the upper end, were set upright about ten feet apart, upon which they placed a pole. Then they covered the sides with bark resting the top against the pole with the bottom on the ground, so as to leave a space about twelve feet wide. The gables were also covered with bark; a fire was made in the middle of the structure, and a small hole left in the top for the smoke to pass out, and when some hemlock boughs had been cut for their beds, the wigwam was completed. Such a structure the Indians would construct in an incredibly short space of time, where bark was handily obtained. In such rude huts, many a hunter or weary traveler has found a good night's rest.

"The next morning the journey was resumed on the Fort Stanwix road, and at 10 o'clock he passed the ruins of Old Fort Schuyler of the French war (now Utica). On Capt. Thompson's arrival at the 'Seekaquate' creek (Sadaquada or Saquoit creek), which enters the Mohawk at Whitestown, he found the bridge gone. Soon after passing this stream, he said he ascended 'Ariska (Oriskany) Hill,' which he observed 'was usually allowed to be the highest piece of ground from Schenectada to Fort Stanwix.' Says the journal: 'I went over the ground where Gen. Herkimer fought Sir John Johnson; this is allowed to be one of the most desperate engagements that has ever been fought by the militia. I saw a vast number of human skulls and bones scattered through the woods.' This was nearly five and a half years after the battle. He halt-

ed to view the ruins of Fort Stanwix [Fort Schuyler] and those of St. Leger's works while besieging the fort and, passing along the site of Fort Bull, on Wood creek, at the end of a mile and a half, he encamped for the night, erecting the usual Indian wigwam. The night was one of terror, as the howling of wolves and other animals prevented much sleep, but, keeping up their fires, the beasts were kept at bay.

"Monday morning, on arriving at Canada creek, a tributary of Wood creek, two trees were felled to bridge the stream. A mile and a half below he left the creek and ascended Pine Ridge, where he discovered in his path a human footprint made by a shoe, which indicated a white wearer. On arriving at Fish creek, he halted to fish but with poor success. He had purposed to cross the creek and pursue his way to Oswego on the north side of Oneida lake, striking Oswego river near the falls, but, learning from his Indian (who had recently been on a scout to the Three Rivers) that he had seen three flat-bottomed boats with oars, and as the ice had recently left the lakes and thinking they might still be there, he changed his course for Wood creek, and striking it at a well-known place, called 'The Scow,' he sent the Indian and sergeant to search for the boats and to return the same evening. The three remaining at 'The Scow' were soon searching for material for a cabin, but neither bark nor hemlock could be found and, as it was fast growing dark, they collected what logs and wood they could to keep up a good fire which was started. At eight o'clock it began to rain terribly and in two or three hours the fire was put out. As the boat seekers did not come back that night it became one of great anxiety and discontent.

"The men returned after daylight and reported a serviceable boat without oars, which they had launched and towed round the edge of the lake and left at the royal block house, known as Fort Royal, at the mouth of Wood creek. No time was lost in reaching the boat, which was found to leak badly. They caulked it as best they could with an old rope. From a board oars were soon made, a pole raised and blankets substituted for a sail with bark halliards. Having everything aboard, they moved into Oneida lake (20 miles long) with a favorable but light wind. It was deemed prudent to run across the lake to Nine Mile Point, on the north shore, but before reaching it two men were kept constantly bailing. The boat was again repaired and put afloat, sailing from point to point. As night approached the crew landed half way down the lake, where they improvised a cabin with a good fire to dry their clothes. The night was pleasant but the howling of wild beasts again terrific.

"On Wednesday, the 23d [of April], a beautiful day, the party were early on the move, and, from the middle of the lake, Capt. Thompson said he could see both ends of it, and enjoyed one of the most beautiful views imaginable. There were several islands on the western side of the lake covered with lofty timber, while back of the Oneida castles the elevated ground made a very beautiful prospect. After about eight miles sail, he heard a gun, evidently fired by an enemy, but, to avoid observation, he sailed along the shore until he was opposite 'Six Mile Islands,' as the two largest islands in the lake, lying side by side, are called. He went ashore, where a fire was kindled and a good dinner enjoyed; after which he again dropped down the lake, passed Fort Brewerton, and entered the Oneida river. Here he found a rapid current in his favor and the river, the most serpentine of any stream he had ever been on, abounding at that season with immense numbers of wild fowl, especially of ducks of many varieties. He saw many flocks of geese, but he would not allow the old musket to be fired, lest a lurking scout might be attracted to his position. He continued his course down the river, sometimes on the Onondaga side, and at others on the Oswego side.

"About two miles from Three Rivers (nearly 20 miles from Oneida lake), he discovered a party of Indians, in three canoes, coming up the river near the same shore. On seeing his boat, they gave a yell and paddled to the opposite shore; they landed, drew their canoes out of the water, ascended the bank and took to trees [not having presumably made out the flag of truce]. When the flag was opposite, they hailed in Indian and in English, which last was answered. When assured that the captain had a flag of truce, the Canadians asked him to come ashore. Four Indians then came out from behind trees and beckoned him to land. He did so and was conducted into the woods. His men also landed and the Indians drew his boat well on shore. He was brought into the presence of two white men and an old Indian, who were seated on the ground. One of them told Capt. Thompson his name was Hare, a lieutenant of Butler's rangers, and that he had just started on an enterprise to the neighborhood of Fort Plain. Thompson assured the lieutenant that all hostilities had ceased on the warpath, and that his mission was to convey such intelligence to the commanding officer at Oswego. When assured that all American scouts had been called in, after several consultations, the war party (consisting of one other white man and eight Indians—all being painted alike) concluded to take Thompson to the fort, saying, if the measure proved a finesse, they had him sure. He was conducted back to his boat, to the great relief of his friends who were exercised by thoughts of treachery, and, with a canoe on each side of the boat and one behind it, the flotilla passed down the river, Lieutenant Hare taking a seat with Captain Thompson in his boat. The party glided down past the Three Rivers [the junction of the Oneida and Seneca rivers with the Oswego], about three miles below which they landed and encamped for the night, constructing two cabins, one of which Lieut. Hare, Capt. Thompson and two Indians occupied, the remainder of both parties using the other.

"Early Thursday morning, Lieut Hare sent one of his canoes to Oswego to inform the commander of the approaching flag, and, soon after sunrise, they all embarked down the rapids which increased as they approached the falls [of the Oswego]. On arriving there they drew the boats around the carrying place, and safely passing the rifts below, they stopped within a mile of Lake Ontario where they were hailed by a sentinel on shore to await orders from the commandant of the fort [Major Ross]."

Thompson was conducted blindfolded into the fort, hearing the drawbridge over the trench let down, the chains of which made a remarkable clattering. In the fort his blindfold was removed and he delivered his message to Major Ross, who received him very courteously, the latter inviting him to sit down to a dinner of cold ham, fowl, wine, etc., while the major looked over the papers. Major Ross had, within a fortnight, received orders from Gov. Haldimand of Canada to strengthen his fortifications for American invasion and was greatly surprised at the news Thompson had brought. However, Ross pledged his honor that all his scouts would be at once called in and ordered the sloop Caldwell (mounting 14 guns) to Fort Niagara to spread the news of the armistice. The curtains, which had been put up at the windows looking out on Lake Ontario, were now drawn and Major Ross asked his guest to look out and see the Caldwell departing on her errand of peace. The view from the window opening out upon the wide sunlit waters of the lake was a delightful one. Ross regretted that he could not conduct the American captain about the British works. The matter of American prisoners in Canada was brought up and Major Ross said information about them would be forthcoming as soon as possible, in the meantime receiving a list of those made in Tryon county during the war, and the messages Thompson brought. Ross said it was impossible for any officer to control the savages when on excursions and he really believed many cruel

depredations had been committed by them on the frontiers which were known only to the Indians. He had exerted himself to prevent the murdering of prisoners and said "but the utmost effort could not prevent them from taking the scalps of the killed." The major said that he was very happy that such an unnatural war was ended, adding however that war created the "soldier's harvest." Ross was much upset to learn that the entire state of New York, including Oswego and Fort Niagara, were to be ceded to the United States in the treaty of peace then under consideration.

Captain Thompson was introduced to a number of British officers and treated with great courtesy, having however a verbal tilt with Capt. Crawford of Johnson's Greens (who invaded the Mohawk valley in 1778). Says the journal: "This person comes under that despicable character of a loyal subject. He appeared to be really ignorant of the cause he fought for, and had the wickedness to observe that he had made more money in the British service in the war than he would have made in the American service in 100 years." Captain Thompson replied that "American officers fought for principle, not money."

Major Ross wished to send Thompson back up the Oswego river and through Oneida lake to Wood creek in his own barge, but the American captain said he desired to return, by land on the west side of the Oswego to see the country, and politely refused the courteous offer. The Indians at Oswego had heard a rumor that "all their lands were to be taken from them and that they were to be driven to where the sun went down." They had threatened the life of the American messenger and were in an ugly mood. Capt. Thompson was given a list of the valley American prisoners then in Canada that evening. The patriot captain, for his own and his comrades' safety, deemed it best to depart at once and thanking Major Ross for his courteous treatment, he was again blindfolded and led outside the fort down to his companions at the river edge at 11 o'clock on Sunday evening, April 27. He took back with him a 14-year-old American boy who had been captured near Fort Stanwix. Here the journal ends. Major Ross had promised to send a detachment of British troops back with the American party over the most dangerous part of their journey and it is probable he did so. The patriots, retracing their former steps, arrived at Fort Plain once more, having completed satisfactorily their important mission.

After Capt. Thompson's return, Fort Plain must have been the Mecca of people from all over the Mohawk valley who came to learn of friends or relatives captive in Canada.

Thus from Fort Plain was spread the first news of approaching peace through the valley and to the British foe on the borders of New York state.

CHAPTER XXIV.

1783—July, Washington's Tour of Mohawk Valley and Visit to Otsego Lake—His Letters Concerning Trip —Stops at Palatine, Fort Plain, Cherry Valley and Canajoharie—Col. Clyde—Final Records of Fort Plain or Fort Rensselaer—Last Revolutionary Indian Murder in Canajoharie District.

In the spring of 1783, an order for the cessation of hostilities between Great Britain and the United States was published in the camp of the latter, but an army organization was kept up until fall. As the initiatory step to his contemplated tour of observation in central New York, Gen. Washington wrote to Gen. Philip Schuyler, from his Newburgh headquarters, July 15, 1783, as follows:

"Dear Sir:—I have always entertained a great desire to see the northern part of this State, before I returned Southward. The present irksome interval, while we are waiting for the definite treaty, affords an opportunity of gratifying this inclination. I have therefore concerted with Geo. Clinton to make a tour to reconnoitre those places, where the most remarkable

posts were established, and the ground which became famous by being the theatre of action in 1777. On our return from thence, we propose to pass across the Mohawk river, in order to have a view of that tract of country, which is so much celebrated for the fertility of its soil and the beauty of its situation. We shall set out by water on Friday the 18th, if nothing shall intervene to prevent our journey.

"Mr. Dimler, assistant quartermaster-general, who will have the honor of delivering this letter, precedes us to make arrangements, and particularly to have some light boats provided and transported to Lake George, that we may not be delayed upon our arrival there.

"I pray you, my dear sir, to be so good as to advise Mr. Dimler in what manner to proceed in this business, to excuse the trouble I am about to give you, and to be persuaded that your kind information and discretion to the bearer will greatly increase the obligations with which I have the honor to be, etc."—Sparks Life, 8, 425.

On July 16, Washington wrote the president of congress as to his intended trip. He returned to his headquarters at Newburgh, August 5, 1783, and on the following day, August 6, wrote to the congressional president a brief record of his journey. After speaking of his return, which was by water from Albany to Newburgh, he says:

"My tour, having been extended as far northward as Crown Point, and westward to Fort Schuyler [Stanwix] and its district, and my movements having been pretty rapid, my horses, which are not yet arrived, will be so much fatigued that they will need some days to recruit, etc." In another letter, of the same date, he refers further to his tour in these words: "I was the more particularly induced by two considerations to make the tour, which in my letter of the 16th ultimo, I informed Congress I had in contemplation, and from which I returned last evening. The one was the inclination to see the northern and western posts of the State, with those places which have been the theatre of important military transactions; the other a desire to facilitate, as far as in my power, the operations which will be necessary for occupying the posts which are ceded by the treaty of peace, as soon as they shall be evacuated by the British troops." He had his eye upon Detroit as a point to be looked after and wanted some of the well-affected citizens of that place to preserve the fortifications and buildings there "until such time as a garrison could be sent with provisions and stores sufficient to take and hold possession of them. The propriety of this measure has appeared in a more forcible point of light, since I have been up the Mohawk river, and taken a view of the situation of things in that quarter. * * * I engaged at Fort Rensselaer [Fort Plain] a gentleman whose name is Cassaty, formerly a resident of Detroit and who is well recommended, to proceed without loss of time, find out the disposition of the inhabitants and make every previous inquiry which might be necessary for the information of the Baron on his arrival, that he should be able to make such final arrangements, as the circumstances might appear to justify. This seemed to be the best alternative on failure of furnishing a garrison of our troops, which, for many reasons, would be infinitely the most eligible mode, if the season and your means would possibly admit. I have at the same time endeavored to take the best preparatory steps in my power for supplying the garrisons on the western waters by the provision contract. I can only form my magazine at Fort Herkimer on the German Flats, which is 32 miles by land and almost 50 by water from the carrying place between the Mohawk river and Wood creek. The route by the former is impracticable, in its present state, for carriages and the other extremely difficult for bateaux, as the river is much obstructed with fallen and floating trees, from the long disuse of the navigation. That nothing, however, which depends upon me might be left undone, I have directed 10 months provisions for 500 men to be laid up at Fort Herkimer,

and have ordered Col. Willett, an active officer commanding the troops of the state [evidently meaning state troops in this locality], to repair the roads, remove the obstructions in the river, and, as far as can be effected by the labors of the soldiers, build houses for the reception of the provisions and stores at the carrying place [Fort Schuyler] in order that the whole may be in perfect readiness to move forward, so soon as the arrangement shall be made with Gen. Haldemand [governor general of Canada.]"

October 12, 1783, Washington wrote to the Chevalier Chastelleux, as follows: "I have lately made a tour through the Lakes George and Champlain as far as Crown Point. Thence returning to Schenectady, I proceeded up the Mohawk river to Fort Schuyler and crossed over to Wood creek, which empties into the Oneida lake, and affords the water communication with Ontario. I then traversed the country to the eastern branch of the Susquehanna, and viewed the Lake Otsego; and the portage between that lake and the Mohawk river at Canajoharie. Prompted by these actual observations, I could not help taking a more extensive view of the vast inland navigation of these United States, from maps and the information of others, and could not but be struck by the immense extent and importance of it, and with the goodness of Providence, which has dealt its favors to us with so profuse a hand. Would to God we may have wisdom enough to improve them. I shall not rest contented till I have explored the western country, and traversed those lines or a great portion of them, which have given bounds to a new empire. But when it may, if it ever shall happen, I dare not say, as my first attention must be given to the deranged situation of my private concerns, which are not a little injured by almost nine years absence and a total disregard of them, etc., etc."

Simms publishes the following account of Washington's visit to Fort Plain, during his trip through this section:

"The reader will observe by Washington's correspondence that he made the northern trip by water to Crown Point, but from Schenectady to Fort Stanwix [Schuyler], or rather its site, on horseback. The tour of inspection, as shadowed in his letters, is devoid of all incident, and whether or not he halted at Fort Plain on his way up is uncertain; but as he speaks last of going to Otsego lake, it is presumed he made no halt at the river forts going up, nor is there any account of his visiting Johnstown in his tour, but it is reasonable to conclude that he did. He did not mention Fort Plain, but it is well known that he was there, giving it another name [Fort Rensselaer]. Arriving in this vicinity [on July 30, 1783], said the late Cornelius Mabie, who was thus informed by his mother, he tarried over night with Peter Wormuth, in Palatine on the late Reuben Lipe farm, the former having had an only son killed, as elsewhere shown, near Cherry Valley. It was no doubt known to many that he had passed up the valley, who were on the quivive to see him on his return, and good tradition says that, in the morning, many people had assembled at Wormuth's to see world's model man, and to satisfy their curiosity, he walked back and forth in front of the house, which fronted toward the river. This old stone dwelling in ruins, was totally demolished about the year 1865.

"We have seen that Washington found Col. Willett in command at Fort Herkimer [then together with Fort Dayton, the most advanced frontier posts in the state], at which time Col. Clyde was in command of Fort Plain. Just how many attended his Excellency through the Mohawk valley, is not satisfactorily known. His correspondence only names Gov. George Clinton. Campbell in his 'Annals' says he was accompanied by Gov. Clinton, Gen. Hand and many other officers of the New York line. The officers making the escort were no doubt attended by their aids and servants. Whether any other officer remained with Washington at

Wormuth's over night is unknown. It is presumed, however, the house being small and the fort only a mile off, that his attendants all went thither, crossing at Walrath's Ferry, opposite the fort, some of whom returned in the morning to escort the Commander-in-Chief over the river. [July 31, 1783] A pretty incident awaited his arrival on the eminence near the fort. Beside the road Rev. Mrs. Gros had paraded a bevy of small boys to make their obeisance (her nephew, Lawrence Gros, from whom this fact was derived, being one of the number). At a signal, they took off and swung their hats, huzzaed a welcome and made their best bow to Washington, when the illustrious guest gracefully lifted his chapeau and returned their respectful salutation with a cheerful 'Good morning, boys!' Immediately after, he rode up to the fort where he received a military salute from the garrison.

"I suppose Washington to have been welcomed within the large blockhouse, and on introducing the guest to its commandant, Gov. Clinton took occasion to say to him: 'Gen. Washington, this is Col. Clyde, a true Whig and a brave officer who has made great sacrifices for his country.' The General answered warmly, 'Then, sir, you should remember him in your appointments.' From this hint, Gov. Clinton afterward appointed him sheriff of Montgomery county. Gen. Washington dined with Col. Clyde, after which, escorted by Maj. Thornton, they proceeded to Cherry Valley, where they became the guests over night, of Col. Campbell, who had returned not long before and erected a log house. Burnt out as the Campbells had been, their accommodations were limited for so many people, but they were all soldiers and had often been on short allowance of 'bed and board' and could rough it if necessary. Besides, it is possible other families had returned to discover their hospitality for the night. They found themselves very agreeably entertained, however. Mrs. Campbell and her children had been prisoners in Canada. In the morning, Gov. Clinton, seeing several of her boys, told Mrs. Campbell, 'They would make good soldiers in time.' She replied she 'hoped their services would never be thus needed.' Said Washington, 'I hope so too, madam, for I have seen enough of war.' One of those boys, the late Judge James S. Campbell, was captured so young and kept so long among the Indians that he could only speak their language when exchanged. After breakfast the party were early in the saddle to visit the outlet of Otsego lake, and see where Gen. James Clinton dammed the lake, just above its outlet, to float his boats down the Susquehanna, to join in Sullivan's expedition. The party returned the same evening to Fort Plain, via the portage road opened by Clinton to Springfield from Canajoharie, and the next day, as believed, they dropped down the valley."

On reaching Canajoharie, August 1, 1783, Washington and his company were received by Col. Clyde, who had ridden down from Fort Plain in the morning to receive the commander's party on its return from Otsego lake. After the destruction of Cherry Valley in 1778, Clyde removed his family to the neighborhood of Schenectady, where they remained until the close of hostilities. One account says that, at this time (August, 1783) they had removed to the Van Alstine stone house, in the present village of Canajoharie. Here, it is said, Washington and his party were the guests of Col. and Mrs. Clyde at dinner on August 1, 1783. Part or all of the distinguished party probably returned to spend the night at Fort Plain, where there were accommodations.

Undoubtedly crowds of valley people gathered at points where Washington stopped on his trip. A considerable assemblage of patriots must have been present at Fort Plain on this eventful long ago midsummer day. There had been no severe raids in the Canajoharie and Palatine districts in two years. The much tried people were rebuilding their homes, those who had removed to safer localities were returning to their abandoned farms,

and, with the assurance of peace, new settlers were already coming in.

Mr. S. L. Frey gives the following list of names of persons who probably accompanied General Washington into the Mohawk valley in 1783: Gov. George Clinton, Gen. Hand, Mr. Dimler (assistant quartermaster), Col. David Humphries, Hodijah Baylies, Wm. S. Smith, Jonathan Trumbull jr., Tench Tilghman, Richard Varick (recording secretary), Benjamin Walker, Richard K. Mead, David Cobb, and many officers of the New York line.

We see, from the foregoing letters of Washington, that at Fort Plain [Fort Rensselaer] the commandant of the army of the United States engaged "a gentleman whose name is Cassaty" (a sketch of whom appears later) as his personal emissary to Detroit to observe the conditions at that important post on the lakes, preparatory to its American occupation. So that it becomes evident that two messengers at Washington's orders, left Fort Plain in 1783 on momentous errands for the British lake posts of Oswego and Detroit.

––––––

Col. Samuel Clyde, then in command at Fort Plain, was born in Windham, Rockingham county, New Hampshire, April 11, 1732, his mother's name being Esther Rankin. He worked on his father's farm until 20, when he went to Cape Breton and labored as a ship carpenter, from whence he went to Halifax and worked on a dock for the English navy. In 1757 he came to New Hampshire and raised a company of batteaux men and rangers, of which he was appointed captain, by Gen. James Abercromby, said company being under Lieut. Col. John Bradstreet. This commission was dated at Albany, May 25, 1758. He marched his company to Albany and to Lake George where he fought in the battle of Ticonderoga, when Gen. Howe was slain and the British defeated. Clyde was afterward at the capture of Fort Frontenac, and, returning from the campaign to Schenectady, in 1761, he there married Catherine Wasson, a niece of Matthew Thornton, a signer of the Declaration of Independence. Judge Hammond, who knew Mrs. Clyde, wrote of her in 1852 as follows: "Mrs. Clyde was a woman of uncommon talents, both natural and acquired, and of great fortitude. She read much and kept up with the literature of the day. Her style in conversing was peculiarly elegant, and at the same time easy and unaffected. Her manner was dignified and attractive. Her conversation with young men during the Revolutionary war, tended greatly to raise their drooping spirits, and confirm their resolution to stand by their country to the last." Not a few noble women of the frontiers thus made their influence felt in the hour of need.

In 1762 Clyde settled at Cherry Valley and while here he was employed, about 1770, by Sir William Johnson to build the church for the use of the Indians at the upper Mohawk castle in the present town of Danube. At the beginning of the country's trouble with England, a company of volunteers was raised in Cherry Valley and New Town Martin for home protection, of which Samuel Clyde was commissioned its captain by the 40 men he was to command, and John Campbell, jr., was chosen lieutenant and James Cannon ensign. Among the names of the volunteers voting for these officers appears that of James Campbell, afterwards colonel. Capt. Clyde's commission was dated July 13, 1775. Oct. 28, 1775, the state provincial congress commissioned him as a captain and adjutant of the first (Canajoharie) regiment of Tryon county militia. Sept. 5, 1776, he was commissioned second major of the first (Canajoharie) regiment commanded by Col. Cox.

After the battle of Oriskany and death of Gen. Herkimer, many of the officers of the brigade wanted Major Clyde to consent to accept the office of Brigadier-General, whose appointment they would solicit. To this he would not accede, as other officers in the brigade outranked him and he would not countenance an act that would originate jealousies, however well merited the honors might be. It has ever surprised the student that Gen. Herkimer's place remained unfilled during the war. That the eye of the army was fixed upon Major Clyde for this honorable promotion is not surprising when we come to know that of all men in that bloody ravine, no one better knew his duty or acquitted himself more valiantly than he. He was in the thickest of the fight, and in a hand to hand encounter was knocked down by an enemy with the breech of a gun, while in another he shot an officer whose musket he brought from the field to become an heirloom in his family. Besides Gen. Herkimer slain, and Brigade Inspector Major John Frey a prisoner, he is believed to have been the only man at Oriskany who ranked as high as a captain in the French war, which doubtless had something to do with the confidence reposed in him.

After Cherry Valley was destroyed in 1778, Col. Clyde removed with his family to the neighborhood of the Mohawk where he lived six or seven years, at least part of the time in the Van Alstine house in the present village of Canajoharie.

June 25, 1778, Major Clyde was appointed lieutenant-colonel of the Canajoharie regiment, James Campbell then being colonel. His commission as such passed the secretary's office with the signature of Gov. George Clinton, March 17, 1781. That Clyde was acting colonel of this regiment long before the date of his commission as lieutenant-colonel, there is positive evidence. The acting colonels of the Tryon county militia in May, 1780, so recognized by the government at Albany, were Cols. Klock, Visscher, Clyde and Bellinger. Col. Clyde seems to have been on duty every summer in the bounds of his regiment until the close of the war. As colonel of the Canajoharie district regiment, he would naturally have been, as he was, on duty at its principal fortification, Fort Plain, during Washington's visit in 1783. On the organization of the state government in 1777, he was a member of the legislature. March 8, 1785, true to Washington's pertinent suggestion at Fort Plain, he was commissioned as sheriff of Montgomery county by Gov. Clinton, which office he discharged with conscientious fidelity. It is said he frequently swam his horse across the Mohawk at flood tide at Canajoharie in order to attend court at Johnstown.

Simms says: "After the destruction, in 1778, of Cherry Valley, Col. Campbell made his home at Niskayuna and is not remembered to have taken any part in military affairs [in this vicinity] after that date." It is doubtless true that, although he held a lieutenant-colonel's commission, Samuel Clyde was recognized by the Albany military authorities and the Tryon county militia as colonel of the Canajoharie regiment, which Clyde says was "the best regiment of militia in the county." Col. Clyde was the leading figure in militia affairs in the district of Canajoharie during the years 1779, 1780, 1781, 1782 and 1783. He died in Cooperstown Nov. 30, 1790, aged 58 years.

The Cassaty whom Washington "engaged at Fort Rensselaer" as his emissary to Detroit. was Colonel Thomas Cassaty. He married Nancy, a daughter of Peter Wormuth and a sister of Lieut. Matthew Wormuth, who was shot by Brant near Cherry Valley in 1778. Cassaty was living near or at his father-in-law's when Washington stopped there (in Palatine near Fort Plain) during his valley tour of 1783. This probably readily led to his engagement in the service mentioned. Colonel Cassaty as a boy and young man was stationed at the British post of Detroit, where his father, James Cassaty, was a captain in the English service. At the outbreak of the Revolution the two Cassatys, both American born, sided with the colonists. The commandant of Detroit denounced Capt. James Cassaty and in the altercation young Thomas Cassaty, then a youth of seventeen, shot down the British officer. He then fled into the Michigan woods and escaped. He lived with the Indians and there is one report which says he was the father

of the noted chief, Tecumseh. Toward the end of the war he appeared in the Mohawk valley. Colonel Cassaty died at Oriskany Falls, Oneida county, 1831, aged about 80 years, leaving two sons and five daughters. After the Detroit affray, Capt. James Cassaty was confined in a Canadian dungeon for three years.

It will be noted that Washington speaks of Fort Plain as "Fort Rensselaer," this being the name it bore in the last four years of the Revolution —it being named for the Gen. Van Rensselaer, whose conduct was so dubious when there at the operations of 1780, ending at Klock's Field.

As previously shown, at the court martial of Gen. Van Rensselaer in Albany for dereliction in the campaign of 1780, witnesses referred constantly to "Fort Rensselaer or Fort Plain" or vice versa.

Dr. Hough published some years ago, an account of the Klock's Field campaign and the subsequent court martial of Gen. Van Rensselaer, showing that the latter officer writing from Fort Plain—a name which had been established for years—dated his papers at "Fort Rensselaer;" anxious, as it would seem, to have this principal fort take his own name. It is believed that never before that time it had ever been called by any other name than Fort Plain. About three years later General Washington was here and dated his correspondence from "Fort Rensselaer," and others probably did so, unaware that the name of the fort had been changed. The following document, from the papers of the late William H. Seeber, shows how the vanity of the inefficient soldier had temporarily affected the name Fort Plain:

"By virtue of the appointment of his Excellency, George Clinton, Esq., Governor of the State of New York, etc., etc.

"We do hereby, in pursuance of an act entitled an act to amend an act, entitled an act to accommodate the inhabitants of the frontier, with habitations and other purposes therein mentioned, passed the 22d of March, 1781 —Grant unto William Seeber, Peter Adams, George Garlock and Henry Smith, license and liberty to cut and remove wood or timber from the lands of John Laile (or Lail), George Kraus, John Fatterle, John Plaikert, Wellem (William) Fenck, George Ekar, John Walrath and Henry Walrath, lying contiguous to Fort Plain, being a place of defense, for fuel, fencing and timber for the use of the first above mentioned persons.

"Given under our hands at Canajoharie, this 8th day of November, 1782.

Christian Nellis,

M. Willett,

Commissioners."

This instrument was drawn up in the handwriting of Squire Nellis and taken to Col. Willett to sign. In the handwriting of the latter and with the ink of his signature, Willett crossed off the word "Plain" and interlined the name "Rensselaer." Simms says: "It seems surprising that Col. Willett, who so disapproved of changing the name of Fort Stanwix, should have connived at changing the name of Fort Plain; and it can only be accounted for by presuming that he was thereby courting the influence of wealth and position." The foregoing quotation does not coincide with Willett's sturdy character, and it seems entirely probable that Van Rensselaer had succeeded in having his name adopted, at least for the time, as the official designation of Fort Plain.

The foregoing chapter is taken entirely from Simms's "Frontiersmen of New York," with some few additions.

S. L. Frey says, in his interesting paper on "Fort Rensselaer," (published in the Mohawk Valley Register, March 6, 1912):

"In 1786, Capt. B. Hudson was in command of the place, taking care of the stores and other government property. As this is the last time that 'Fort Rensselaer' is mentioned as far as I can find, I give a copy of an old receipt:

Fort Rancelair, Aug. 22d, 1786.
State of New York, Dr.
To John Lipe, Senior.

For Timber Building the Blockhouse, for fire wood, Fancing & Possession of the Place by the Troops of the United States Under the Command of Colonel Willet one hundred & fifty Pounds, being the amount of my Damage.

his
John X Lipe.
mark

Witness Present
B. Hudson.

From this it will be seen that Johannes Lipe had not been paid for his timber, used in the blockhouse six years before. Following this receipt is a note by Rufus Grider, the former antiquarian of Canajoharie:

"Copy of a paper found and obtained on the Lipe Farm, where Fort Plain and Fort Rensselair was located. The present owners are the descendants of the Lipe who owned it during and after the Revolution; the ownership has not gone out of the family.

R. A. Grider.

June 17, 1894."

Mr. Frey continues: "We thus have a continuous mention of 'Fort Rensselair,' as another name for Fort Plain, from Sept. 4, 1780, to Aug. 22, 1786. It would be well if the old Revolutionary families in the vicinity would examine any paper they may have relating to that period; possibly we might find that 'Fort Rensselair' is mentioned after 1786."

———

Thus we are able to trace the history of the Fort Plain fortifications through a period of ten years of important service. Although the fort and blockhouse probably stood for some years after 1786, reference to Fort Plain, after that date, implies the Sand Hill settlement (which took its name from the fort) and the later village which thus became known during the construction of the Erie canal. The name has thus been in existence for a period of almost 140 years. How long Fort Plain or Fort Rensselaer continued to exist as an army post after 1786 is not now known.

———

The accounts to follow deal with western Montgomery county and with the settlement adjacent to Fort Plain, known as Sand Hill and Fort Plain and a continuation of the record of life and events, in the old Canajoharie and Palatine districts, until about 1825, when the old settlement ceased to be important and the new canal town which sprang up adopted the honored name of Fort Plain. For convenience the end of the second series of sketches is put at 1838, the date of the severance of Montgomery and Fulton counties. Washington's visit to Fort Plain properly marks the end of the first series of chapters of the story of old Fort Plain.

The last victims of savage marauders near Fort Plain were Frederick Young and a man named House, of the town of Minden. They were in a field when a small party of Indians shot them both down. Young was not killed and when an Indian stooped over to scalp him, the victim seized the knife, the blade nearly severing his fingers. Both were scalped but Young was found alive and taken to Fort Plank, where he died before night. The two Minden men were shot within sight of the fort but the Indians got away before the patriot militia could assemble to engage them. This event happened in 1783, eight days after the inhabitants had news that peace had been ratified, and it is probable that the savages had not heard of this.

One of the first murder trials in the Johnstown jail after the war was that of John Adam Hartmann, a Revolutionary veteran, for killing an Indian in 1783. They met at a tavern in the present town of Herkimer, and the savage excited Hartmann's abhorrence by boasting of murders and scalpings performed by him during the war, and particularly by showing him a tobacco pouch made from the skin of the hand and part of the arm of a white child with the finger nails remaining attached. Hartmann said nothing at the time and the two left the tavern on their journey together, traveling a road which led through a dense forest. Here the savage's body was found a year later. Hartmann was acquitted

for lack of evidence. He had been a ranger at Fort Dayton. On a foray, in which he killed an Indian, at almost the same instant, he was shot and wounded by a Tory. Hartmann was a famous frontiersman and had many adventures. He was a fine type of the intrepid soldiers in the tried and true militia of Tryon county.

Following are the principal events of 1783 summarized: The treaty of peace with Great Britain, acknowledging the independence of the United States of America was signed in Paris, Sept. 3, 1783; 1783, Nov. 25, "Evacuation Day," British left New York and an American force under Gen. Washington and Gov. Clinton entered New York city, shortly after which Washington bade farewell to his officers at Fraunce's Tavern in that city and left for Mount Vernon, Md., his journey through New Jersey, Pennsylvania and Maryland being a triumphial tour; 1783, Dec. 23, Washington resigned his command of the American army to congress at Annapolis, Md.

CHAPTER XXV.
1775-1783—Review of Mohawk Valley Events—Tryon County Militia Records — Territory Covered in These Sketches.

With this chapter are concluded the first two periods of the history of the middle Mohawk valley—that of settlement and that of the war of the Revolution. At almost every point this story touches that of the nation. Just as Walt Whitman sings of man as representative of the race and the race as the single man multiplied, so, in this history of the Mohawk country, we see the growing nation and in viewing the land of America we get a diminished yet clear prospect of our own valley. Thus while following the current of local life and events we are borne along as well on the great stream of national life.

In the foregoing chapters, mention has been made of the connection of the men of the Mohawk country with the decisive event of the Revolution—

the success of the Americans in the 1777 campaign against Burgoyne and St. Leger. A further instance of the vital interlocking of our story with that greater one of the United States, is evidenced in that thrilling first encounter of the Iroquois with the French power, represented by Champlain and his Canadian savages. The shots fired by the Frenchman into the ranks of the red men of the Five Nations gave us these United States, for it made the Iroquois enemies of the French power forever. They formed a bulwark against the encroachment of the Gallic dominion and may, at that early date, have prevented France from conquering the greater part of the thirteen colonies. Thus it is that the shot of an arquebus, on the shore of a lonely lake, or the death struggle of a few hundred farmers in a forest fight, may settle the destinies of a nation. A further instance of past conditions affecting the present is evidenced in the state of New York, the boundaries of which were largely determined by the Dutch settlements along the Hudson and the territory occupied by the Five Nations. It has also been stated that the successful example of the Iroquois confederacy had a considerable influence in formation of the United States of America.

The Revolutionary record of Tryon county, besides detailing the defense against British invasion of the New York frontier, is concerned with two great national military movements of the war—the vital defeat of Burgoyne at Saratoga (to which the successful defense of Fort Schuyler contributed) and the Sullivan and Clinton invasion of the Indian country, in connection with which occurred the march of the New York detachment of the American army along the Mohawk to Canajoharie, the rendezvous there, the cutting of a road through the wilderness to Otsego lake and the subsequent unique march thither of Clinton's force, convoying the river flatboats with their supplies, loaded on eight-horse wagons and oxcarts. This campaign was one of the most noteworthy of the war and the Mohawk valley side

of it seems to have never received the full and proper presentation that it merits.

The Tryon county infantry and militia, as has been shown, had been instrumental in the American success of the Saratoga campaign. Creasy calls this one of the fifteen decisive battles of the world (up to 1855) and mentions the British checks at Fort Stanwix (Schuyler) and at Bennington as strongly influencing the final defeat of Burgoyne and the British army. Of this historically great battle Lord Mahon wrote:

"Even of those great conflicts, in which hundreds of thousands have been engaged and tens of thousands have fallen, none has been more fruitful of results than this surrender * * at Saratoga."

The victory at Stillwater was decisive not only in ensuring American independence but it eventually brought about American predominance over the western hemisphere. To this great world result the men of the Mohawk contributed, at Oriskany and Fort Schuyler, as much as if they had fought on the field of Stillwater itself, where some of them were also engaged.

The record of the Mohawk country garrisons and the militia of Tryon county is one of the best of the American soldiery of the Revolution. Wherever the Tryon county men met the enemy on anything like equal footing they had beaten them. Under good leaders like Willett they had proved the best of rangers and line of battle men. The feats of scouts like Helmer and Demuth are fit subjects for song and legend, and the deeds of the American man behind the gun, on the fields of Tryon county, make stories which will hold the interest of Mohawk valley folk for centuries to come.

It would be interesting if the composition of the different Tryon county garrisons, throughout the Revolution, could be known. Future research may show them, and it may be here mentioned that the history of the Mohawk valley during the war for independence should be made the subject of a comprehensive work, treating the matter in complete form. It furnishes as interesting material as that of any region of similar extent within the limits of the original thirteen colonies.

Occasional glimpses have been caught, in the foregoing chapters of the garrisons and the commanders of the army posts of present western Montgomery county—Fort Plain, Fort Paris, Fort Windecker, Fort Willett, Fort Plank, Fort Clyde. We know from the frequent recurrence of the names of families then resident along the Mohawk, in the accounts of the Revolutionary movements of the Tryon county American forces, that the patriot army in the Mohawk country was always largely composed of local men. They are frequently spoken of as militia but their years of service made them as efficient as regulars, and they were such in every sense especially during the latter years of the war.

We have records of Tryon county men who were engaged in many of the military movements hereabouts during the Revolution. There were undoubtedly scores who fought at Oriskany who took part in all of the later conflicts. This was especially true of the Palatine and Canajoharie district men, as their territory was the scene of most of the important events after Oriskany. We have one record of a Canajoharie district man who took part in the first and last Revolutionary military movements in the Mohawk valley. This was John Roof jr., who fought at Oriskany in 1777 and went with Willett on the expedition to Fort Oswego in 1783. He was probably in military service, in the intervening years and there were scores like him. At the end of hostilities, about 1782, these Tryon county soldiers entered upon the reclamation of their farm lands and the rebuilding of their homes as vigorously as they had opposed the motley savages employed by England to ravage their country during the six years from 1777 to 1782.

That the valley Revolutionary soldiers of Tryon county were men of the greatest physical hardihood is plainly evident. Proof of this is seen in the many instances of their long marches over rough ground and, at the end of these "hikes," frequently the infantry went into battle. In 1780, Van Rensselaer's army, from the neighborhood of Albany, marched to Keator's rift at Sprakers, a distance of over fifty miles, and at the close of their second day in Montgomery county, after marching over ten miles more, went into action at Klock's Field. On this day, from the time they left their camping ground in the town of Florida, they covered thirty miles and fought a battle as well. On the evening of the day of the appearance of Ross and Butler and their raiders (Oct. 24, 1781), Colonel Willett and his four hundred fighters, from Fort Plain and the neighboring posts, marched through the night to Fort Hunter (a distance of twenty miles), reaching there the next morning, October 25. After a strenuous time crossing the Mohawk, the Americans made a further journey of nine or ten miles, when they went into action and won the victory of Johnstown. They had tramped thirty miles and won a hard victory in a night and a day. After a day's rest, the troops continued the pursuit of the beaten enemy to Jerseyfield on West Canada creek, where they killed Butler and many of his band and scattered Ross's force completely. On their return to Fort Dayton, they had covered over 60 miles of ground under winter condi tions, suffering great hardships, and had performed this feat in four days on two days rations. The Fort Plain soldiers in this campaign, covered 150 miles from their start until the time they returned to their barracks. The great physical vigor of the men of the Mohawk country is also shown in the amusing incident of the footrace between a company of scouts and a company of infantry, on the Freysbush road, while on the march back to Fort Plain. It is to be regretted that conditions which produced such men of iron in the valley could not have continued to give us men of equal vigor.

Besides this evidence of the generally fine physical condition of the valley Americans, the previous chapters have given abundant proof of the individual military valor and physical prowess of men like Herkimer, Clyde, Dillenbeck, Willett, Stockwell, Gardinier, Helmer, Demuth, Crouse, Vols, Woodworth, and a host of others.

Some years ago the state of New York published part of its Revolutionary records in a volume entitled "New York in the Revolution." This is a roster of the regular troops and militia raised in New York during the war of independence and includes the Tryon county militia. Many of the names are misspelled but this roll of the local militia forms a record of the families settled in the country of the Mohawks at the time of the Revolution. Regarding the Tryon county list, State Historian James A. Holden, says: "I am doubtful as to how many of the men served in more than one regiment or capacity. The names are apt to be doubled, as the terms of enrollment were very lax and a man might be on more than one regiment roll at a time, as I am informed. However the number given is approximate and can be so stated in your work." In the publication referred to the enrolled men's names are given. No date is attached to any of the lists. Below is summarized the numbers of each organization together with its officers, from the county of Tryon:

Tryon County Brigade of Militia:

First Regiment (Canajoharie district). Officers: Colonel, Samuel Campbell; colonel, Ebenezer Cox (killed at Oriskany); lieutenant-colonel, Samuel Clyde; major, Abraham Copeman; major, Peter S. Dygert; adjutant, Jacob Seeber; quartermaster, John Pickard; surgeon, Adam Frank; surgeon, David Younglove. Summary: Staff, 9; line, 38; men, 552; total, 599. Col. Clyde was acting colonel after 1778.

Second Regiment (Palatine district). Officers: Colonel, Jacob Klock; lieutenant-colonel, Peter Wagner; major, Christian William Fox; major, Christopher Fox; adjutant, Samuel Gray; adjutant, Andrew Irvin; quartermaster, Jacob Eacker; surgeon, Johann Georg Vach. Summary: Staff, 8; line, 43; men, 615; total, 666.

Third Regiment (Mohawk district). Officers: Colonel, Frederick Visscher (Fisher); lieutenant-colonel, Volkert Veeder; major, John Bluen (Bliven?); major, John Nukerk; adjutant, Peter Conyn; adjutant, John G. Lansing jr.; adjutant, Gideon Marlatt; quartermaster, Abraham Van Horn; quartermaster, Simon Veeder; surgeon, John George Folke (Vach?); surgeon, William Petry. Summary: Staff, 12; line, 62; men, 651; total, 725.

Fourth Regiment (German Flats and Kingsland). Officers: Colonel, Peter Bellinger; adjutant, George Demuth; quartermaster, Peter Bellinger. Summary: Staff, 3; line, 20; men, 415; total, 438. The foregoing list of staff officers for this fourth regiment is, of course, incomplete.

Fifth Regiment (Schoharie valley?). There is no list of men given. John Harper was colonel.

Battalion (company?) Minute Men. Officers: Colonel, Samuel Campbell; captain, Francis Utt; lieutenant, Adam Lipe; lieutenant, Jacob Matthias; ensign, William Suber (Seeber?). Summary: Staff, 1; line, 4; men, 60; total, 65. Col. Campbell removed to Niskayuna, below Schenectady, in 1779 and had no share in Tryon county military matters after that date.

Battalion Rangers (Scouts), First Company: Captain, John Winn; lieutenant, Lawrence Gros; lieutenant, Peter Schremling. Second company: Captain, Christian Getman; lieutenant, James Billington; lieutenant, Jacob Sammans (Sammons?). Third company: Captain, John Kasselman; lieutenant, John Empie; ensign, George Gittman (Getman). Summary: Officers, 9; men, 155; total, 164.

Associated "exempts." Captain, Jelles Fonda; lieutenant, Zephaniah Batchellor; lieutenant, Abraham Garrason; ensign, Samson Sammon (Sampson Sammons); ensign, ——— Lawrance. Summary: Line, 5; men, 159; total, 164. These were invalids or men beyond the age of military service (then about 60 years) who were organized for defense, while the active men were absent on military duty. They could be called upon in case of great emergency.

The total of the Tryon county militia foots up 2,830 men. This does not include the fifth regiment which evidently came from the Schoharie valley and of which there are no records in "New York in the Revolution." This is not a chronicle of the Schoharie valley (a separate region), but only of the land of the Mohawk or the central Mohawk river section, and the Schoharie valley is only treated where it passes through present Montgomery county or where it affects this story.

In 1781 Colonel Willett was in command of a regiment of "levies" at Fort Plain as aforementioned. These were men drafted into service, and included many men from the settlers along the Mohawk. A list of these levies is given in "New York in the Revolution," which is here summarized as follows: Officers: Colonel, Marinus Willett; lieutenant colonel, John McKinstry; major, Andrew Fink (major of brigade); major, Lyman Hitchcock (muster master); major, Josiah Throop; major, Elias Van Bunschoten; adjutant, Jelles A. Fonda; adjutant, Pliny Moore; quartermaster, John Fondey (Fonda); quartermaster, Matthew Trotter; quartermaster, Jacob Winney; paymaster, Abraham Ten Eyck; surgeon, Calvin Delano; surgeon. William Petry; surgeon's mate, George Faugh; surgeon's mate, Moses Willard; chaplain, John Daniel Gros (pastor of the Canajoharie district Reformed Dutch church at Fort Plain). Summary: Staff, 17; line, 75; men, 916; total, 1,008. These men were probably distributed among the principal valley posts and acted in conjunction with the Tryon county militia. This regiment may have done duty in the valley a large part of the last three years of the war. On page 68 of "New York in the Revolution" is recorded a regiment of "levies" of which Col. John Harper was commandant. On page 77 is given another of which Col. Lewis Dubois was in command. The Revolu-

tionary records are frequently fragmentary and incomplete and, as before stated, there is no date given with each roll so that it is impossible to tell at just what period of the war the different bodies listed were engaged. It may be that they include all the men enrolled in each militia organization throughout the war, or even all the men liable for military duty in each district.

In consideration of all the Revolutionary history in the chapters foregoing it must be remembered that the events recorded all occurred in the great county of Tryon, of which Johnstown was the civic center and Fort Plain the military headquarters, during the last four years of the war— 1780, 1781, 1782, 1783.

It will be noted that all the Mohawk valley military actions, with the exception of Oriskany and West Canada creek, occurred within a fifteen mile radius of Fort Plain, and this is the region especially considered in all the chapters of this work, comprising as it did the Mohawk river sections of the Canajoharie and Palatine districts of Tryon, later Montgomery county.

This history, also, in full detail, covers the middle valley country occupied by the Mohawks, during the greater part of the historical period and in which their settlements were located exclusively during the last century of their valley tribal existence. Here much Indian life was centered, all of which is of great interest to the student of Indian lore and which would fill a considerable volume. At Indian Hill, on a branch of the Otsquago south of Fort Plain, are found some of the earliest Indian remains in eastern New York. This interesting spot is considered in a later chapter on the town of Minden. The Mohawk valley, from the Schoharie river to Fall Hill, seems to have been the home of the Mohawks from the earliest historical times. However, the seats of their castles and villages were frequently changed within this territory. The river section between Fall Hill and the Noses has been called Canajoharie by the Mohawks, evidently from the earliest times.

Their later chief villages, as shown in the foregoing chapters, were at Fort Hunter and Indian Castle. This river country occupied by the Mohawks is here treated in detail historically as well as the Canajoharie and Palatine districts. So that "The Story of Old Fort Plain," is, in truth, a history of old Tryon and Montgomery county, of the country of the Mohawk Iroquois (from the time of its discovery) which is also the middle Mohawk valley, of the Canajoharie and Palatine districts and the five western towns of present Montgomery county, as well as the "Story of Old Fort Plain." It is all of these because the stories of them are so interwoven that it is better to here present the whole fabric to the view of the reader than it is to tear it apart and attempt to show the different threads separately.

In a general way, also, the history of the valley, within a radius of fifty miles of Fort Plain, is treated during the first three periods of its history (from 1616 to 1838). This enables the reader to gain a clearer idea of the life and events of the smaller area aforementioned, which is considered in great detail and from every viewpoint.

The foregoing chapters offer an opportunity of close acquaintance with many actively connected with the thrilling events of the Revolution and with the life of the times. It is probable that mention has been made in this work, of the majority of families or heads of families in the Canajoharie and Palatine districts. The beginnings of human things are extraordnarily interesting to human beings and, in the chapters dealing with the first three periods of the history of the country of the Mohawks, we see the individuals themselves, who make up the local communities and live again with them their lives of peace or war on the hills and in the vales of this fair northland country.

The growing population makes it impossible to consider individuals, in this local record, after the end of the third period of Montgomery history (1838) and, after that date, the valley hereabouts is treated historically and in a general way without reference to people individually, except where the mention of names is absolutely necessary to the continuity of the story.

The succeeding chapters cover the third and fourth periods of the history of the country of the Mohawks, in its relation to the old Canajoharie and Palatine districts, whose river sections are now largely comprised within the present limits of the five western towns of Montgomery county. Here we see a similar linking together of local with national history in the matter of the valley's highways and waterways. The Mohawk route to the west, by its natural formation, was and is probably the most important in the eastern states. It was largely through it that the tide of westward emigration flowed and through it east traded with the west from the earliest times. Its highways and great railroads follow the old Indian trails and the Barge canal, in its eastern section, covers largely the exact route from the Hudson to the Great Lakes, followed by the Indian canoe and the Mohawk flatboat. The Erie and the subsequent railroads, made the nation, the state, the metropolis and the valley great, populous and rich in material things, as it is today. On the completion of the Erie canal, the trade and traffic it brought, to and through New York, raised it from a secondary to a first position among the states and its metropolis quickly became the largest city in the western hemisphere.

Rich in material things our valley is indeed today, according to modern ideas, albeit it is poorer far in its natural resources than it was when the Dutch made their first settlements in its eastern part two centuries and a half ago. It is for the men of today and of the future to conserve the natural wealth remaining and to bring back, as much as possible, that which has been lost and wasted—particularly the health-giving and soil-preserving forest.

THE STORY OF OLD FORT PLAIN

(SECOND SERIES 1784-1838)

CHAPTER I.

1784-1838—Mohawk Valley After the Revolution — Constructive Period — Montgomery County and its Divisions—Towns and Their Changes.

The Revolutionary struggle had well-nigh destroyed the one-time prosperous farming community along the Mohawk and in its adjacent territory. This section had been more harried, by the enemy and their red allies, than any other part of the thirteen colonies. Raid after raid had swept down from Canada over the fair valley, burning, plundering, and murdering. Stoutly had the sturdy people fought back their dreadful foe. The savage enemy had been again and again beaten back from the Mohawk, but the bloody contest had left the population greatly depleted and the farm land in ruin and rapidly going back to the wilderness from which it had been wrested. Those of faint heart and of Tory leanings had fled the country and the patriot families who were left were often sadly broken. Numbers of defenseless women and little children had been struck down by the savage tomahawk and the bones of the men of Tryon county whitened the fields where battle and skirmish had been bitterly fought. The bravery of the women, and even the children, of the patriot families, amid the bloody scenes of the Revolution, had been remarkable in the extreme. Terrific as had been the murderous destruction, along the Mohawk, yet a wonderful rejuvenesence and rapid growth were to follow. The years ensuing were ones of great development of the farmlands, increase of population and steps, for the furtherance of transportation and commerce, which were eventually to make the Mohawk valley one of the greatest arteries of trade and traffic in the entire world.

Toward the close of the war, Col. Willett sent to Gen. Washington a lengthy statement of the condition of affairs in Tryon county, from which it appears that, whereas at the opening of the struggle the enrolled militia of the county numbered not less than 2,500, there were then not more than 800 men liable to bear arms, and not more than 1,200 who could be taxed or assessed for the raising of men for the public service. To account for so large a reduction of the Tryon people, it was estimated that, of the number by which the population had been decreased, one-third had been killed or made prisoners; one-third had gone over to the enemy; and one-third for the time being, had abandoned the country. Beers's history says:

"The suffering of the unfortunate inhabitants of the Mohawk valley were the measure of delight, with which they had hailed the return of peace. The dispersed population returned to the blackened ruins of their former habitations, rebuilt their houses and again brought their farms under cultivation. With astounding audacity, the Tories now began to sneak back again and claim peace and property among those whom they had impoverished and bereaved. It was not to be expected that this would be tolerated. The outraged feelings of the community found the following expression at a meeting of the principal inhabitants of the Mohawk district, May 9, 1783:

"Taking into consideration the peculiar circumstances of this county relating to its situation, and the numbers that joined the enemy from among us, whose brutal barbarities in their frequent visits to their old neighbors are too shocking to humanity to relate:

"They have murdered the peaceful husbandmen, and his lovely boys about him unarmed and defenceless in the field. They have, with malicious pleasure, butchered the aged and infirm; they have wantonly sported with the lives of helpless women and children, numbers they have scalped alive, shut them up in their houses and burnt them to death. Several children, by the vigilance of their friends, have been snatched from flaming buildings; and though tomahawked and scalped, are still living among us; they have made more than 300 widows and above 2,000 orphans in this county; they have killed thousands of cattle and horses that rotted in the field; they have burnt more than two million bushels of grain, many hundreds of buildings, and vast stores of forage; and now these merciless fiends are creeping in among us again to claim the privilege of fellow-citizens, and demand a restitution of their forfeited estates; but can they leave their infernal tempers behind them and be safe or peaceable neighbors? Or can the disconsolate widow and the bereaved mother reconcile her tender feelings to a free and cheerful neighborhood with those who so inhumanly made her such? Impossible! It is contrary to nature, the first principle of which is self-preservation. It is contrary to the law of nations, especially that nation which for numberless reasons, we should be thought to pattern after. * * * * * It is contrary to the eternal rule of reason and rectitude. If Britain employed them. let Britain pay them. We will not; therefore, 'Resolved, unanimously, that all those who have gone off to the enemy or have been banished by any law of this state, or those, who we shall find, tarried as spies or tools of the enemy, and encouraged and harbored those who went away, shall not live in this district on any pretence whatever; and as for those who have washed their faces from Indian paint and their hands from the innocent blood of our dear ones, and have returned, either openly or covertly, we hereby warn them to leave this district before the 20th of June next, or they may expect to feel the just resentment of an injured and determined people.

"'We likewise, unanimously desire our brethren in the other districts in the county to join with us to instruct our representatives not to consent to the repealing any laws made for the safety of the state against treason, or confiscation of traitors' estates, or to passing any new acts for the return or restitution of Tories.'

" By order of the meeting.

" 'Josiah Thorp, Chairman.' "

Notwithstanding these sentiments of the Whigs, numbers of Tories did return and settle among their old neighbors. The Mohawk lands, which were considerable before the war, were confiscated and the tribe were granted homes in Canada, as has been stated in the sketch of Brant.

During the revolution, the English governor, in honor of whom Tryon county was named, rendered the title odious by a series of infamous acts in the service of the Crown, and the New York legislature, on the 2d of April, 1784, voted that the county should be called Montgomery, in honor of Gen. Richard Montgomery, who fell in the attack on Quebec, early in the war. At the beginning of the Revolution, the population of the county was estimated at 10,000. At the close of the war it had probably been reduced to almost one-third of that number, but so inviting were the fertile lands of the county, that in three years after the return of peace (1786) it had a population of 15,000. Doubtless many of these were people who had deserted their valley homes at the beginning of hostilities and who now returned to settle again among their patriot neighbors who had borne the brunt of the struggle, and who had so nobly furthered the cause of American rule. By 1800 the population of present Montgomery county can safely be estimated at 10,000, almost entirely settled on the farms.

The boundaries of the several counties in the state were more minutely defined, March 7, 1788, and Montgomery was declared to contain all that part of the state bounded east by the counties of Ulster, Albany, Washington and Clinton and south by the state of Pennsylvania. What had been districts in Tryon county were, with the exception of Old England, made towns in Montgomery county, the Mohawk district forming two towns, Caughnawaga north of the river and Mohawk south of it. The Palatine and Canajoharie districts were organized as towns, retaining those names. Thus after an existence of sixteen years, principally during the Revolutionary period, the old Tryon districts experienced their first change.

The presence of the warlike Mohawks and their use as allies on the frontier, had saved the valley savages their lands until about the year 1700. Notice has been made of the Dutch, German and British immigration after that date into the Mohawk valley. With the virtual breaking down of the Iroquois confederacy on account of the Revolution, their wide lands were thrown open for settlement and, after 1783, another and greater tide of immigration set in along the Mohawk.

The war had made people of other states and of other sections of New York familiar with Tryon county. Sullivan and Clinton's campaign, in the Iroquois country, had particularly revealed the fertility of the western part of the state, and a tide of emigration thither set in at the close of the war, mostly by way of the Mohawk valley. The river had been the first artery of transportation and traffic. Now it began to be rivaled by turnpike travel. Later water travel was to resume first place after the digging of the Erie canal, afterward to be again superseded by land traffic when the railroads began to develop. All of these were to make eventually the Mohawk valley the great road and waterway it is today.

Immigration to western New York led to the formation from Montgomery, Jan. 27, 1789, of Ontario county, which originally included all of the state west of a line running due north from the "82nd milestone" on the Pennsylvania boundary, through Seneca lake to Sodus Bay on Lake Ontario. This was the first great change in the borders of Tryon or Montgomery county (which had been of larger area than several present-day states) since its formation seventeen years before. Other divisions were to come rapidly. In 1791 the county of Montgomery was still further reduced by the for-

mation of Tioga, Otsego and Herkimer. The latter joined Montgomery county on the north as well as the west, the present east and west line, between Fulton and Hamilton, continued westward, being part of their common boundary, and another part of it a line running north and south from Little Falls, and intersecting the former "at a place called Jersey-fields." Of the region thus taken from Montgomery county on the north, the present territory of Hamilton was restored in 1797, only to be set apart under its present name, Feb. 12, 1816. April 7, 1817, the western boundary of Montgomery was moved eastward from the meridian of Little Falls to East Canada creek, and a line running south from its mouth, where it still remains. This divided the territory of the old Canajoharie and Palatine districts between two counties, after this region had formed part of Tryon or Montgomery county for a period of forty-five years, which was undoubtedly that of its greatest growth as well as covering the thrilling Revolutionary period. It also, for the first time, made an unnatural and artificial demarcation of the Canajoharie region, known as such north and south of the Mohawk since the dawn of history. The line between Montgomery and Schenectady has always been part of the boundary of the former, having originally separated it from Albany county. The formation of Otsego county, Feb. 16, 1791, established the line which now separates it and Schoharie from Montgomery. The latter took its northern boundary and entire present outline on the formation of Fulton county in 1838, which will be considered later. Thus the present Montgomery is the small remainder of a once large territory and bears that region's original name. It also contains the greater part of the territory immediately along the river, of three of the five districts which originally composed Tryon and Montgomery county. These three districts were Canajoharie, Palatine and Mohawk, and are all names of present-day townships of our county, which were portions of the original districts. It is in the lands along the Mohawk river, contained in these old districts, where the principal part of the population was gathered at the close of the Revolutionary war.

The three towns of Montgomery which formed part of the Canajoharie district were set apart on the following dates: Minden 1798, Root 1823 (formed partly from the old Mohawk and old Canajoharie districts). Canajoharie, part of the original district of that name set apart in 1772. The town of Palatine is the remaining portion of the original Tryon county district of that name. The town of St. Johnstriet, was set apart on the formation of Fulton county in 1838. In 1793 Caughnawaga was divided into Johnstown, Mayfield, Broadalbin and Amsterdam, and Mohawk into Charleston and Florida, their dividing line being Schoharie creek. In 1797 Salisbury, now in Herkimer county, was taken from Palatine and in 1798 part of Canajoharie went to form Minden.

An eighteenth century writer gives us a good view of the valley during the decade after the Revolution in a "Description of the Country Between Albany and Niagara in 1792," from Volume II. of the "Documentary History of New York." It follows verbatim.

"I am just returned from Niagara, about 560 miles west of Boston. I went first to Albany, from thence to Schenectady, about Sixteen miles; this has been a very considerable place of trade but is now falling to decay: It was supported by the Indian traders; but this business is so arrested by traders far in the country, that very little of it reached so far down: it stands upon the Mohawk river, about 9 miles above the Falls, called Cohoes; but this I take to be the Indian name for Falls. Its chief business is to receive the merchandise from Albany and put it into batteaux to go up the river and forward to Albany Such produce of the back country as is sent to market. After leaving Schenectada, I

travelled over a most beautiful country of eighty miles to Fort Schuyler, where I forded the Mohawk. This extent was the scene of British and Savage cruelty during the late war, and they did not cease, while anything remained to destroy. What a contrast now!—every house and barn rebuilt, the pastures crowded with Cattle, Sheep, etc., and the lap of Ceres full. Most of the land on each Side of the Mohawk river, is a rich flat highly cultivated with every species of grain, the land on each side rising in agreeable Slopes; this, added to the view of a fine river passing through the whole, gives the beholder the most pleasing sensations imaginable. I next passed through Whitestown. It would appear to you, my friend, on hearing the relation of events in the western country, that the whole was fable; and if you were placed in Whitestown or Clinton, ten miles from Fort Schuyler, and see the progress of improvement, you would believe it enchanted ground. You would there view an extensive well built town, surrounded by highly cultivated fields, which Spot in the year 1783 was the 'haunt of tribes' and the hiding place of wolves, now a flourishing happy Situation, containing about Six thousand people—Clinton stands a little South of Whitestown and is a very large, thriving town."

This writer also says that "after passing Clinton there are no inhabitants upon the road until you reach Oneida, an Indian town, the first of the Six Nations; it contains about Five hundred and fifty inhabitants; here I slept and found the natives very friendly." He also writes, "The Indians are settled on all the reservations made by this State, and are to be met with at every settlement of whites, in quest of rum."

On Dec. 2, 1784, a council was held at Fort Schuyler between the Six Nations and American representatives. Gov. Clinton, Gen. Lafayette and other distinguished men were present. Brant was displeased with the Iroquois situation, their lands having been ceded to the United States by the treaty of peace. Red Jacket was for war with the new nation while Cornplanter was for peace. Under certain conditions, the Six Nations were allowed to retain a portion of their old lands, with the exception of the Mohawks who had permanently settled themselves in Canada. After the multitude of whites and Indians had enjoyed a great feast (due to the wise forethought of Gov. Clinton), a foot race took place, in which each of the Six Nations was represented by one competitor. Gov. Clinton hung up a buckskin bag, containing $250, on a flag staff at the starting point on the bank of the Mohawk. This was a race of over two miles and was won, amid great excitement by a mere lad of the Oneida tribe, named Paul, who ran the great champion of the Mohawks off his feet and distanced the rest of his competitors. Gov. Clinton presented little Paul the prize and heartily congratulated him. Thus ended the last council of the Six Nations in the Mohawk valley, exactly a century and a quarter after the first held at Caughnawaga between the Iroquois and the Dutch in 1659.

Following is a short sketch of the Revolutionary patriot for whom this county was named: Richard Montgomery was born in the north of Ireland in 1737. He entered the British army at the age of 20 and was with Wolfe at the storming of Quebec. Although he returned, after the French war, he had formed a liking for America and, in 1772, came back and made his home at Rhinebeck on the Hudson, where he married a daughter of Robert B. Livingston. He sided with the patriots at the outbreak of the Revolution and in 1775 was second in command to Schuyler in the expedition against Canada. The illness of Schuyler caused the chief command to devolve upon Montgomery and in the capture of St. John's, Chambley and Montreal and his attack cn Quebec, he exhibited great judgment and military skill. He was commissioned a major general before he reached Quebec. In

that campaign he had every difficulty to contend with—undisciplined and mutinous troops, scarcity of provisions and ammunition, want of heavy artillery, lack of clothing, the rigor of winter and desertions of whole companics. Yet he pressed onward and in all probability, had his life been spared, would have entered Quebec in triumph. In the heroic attack of the Americans on this stronghold, Dec. 31, 1775 (during a heavy snowstorm), Montgomery. was killed and his force defeated. Congress voted Montgomery a monument, by an act passed Jan. 25, 1776, and it was erected on the Broadway side of St. Paul's church in New York. It bears the following inscription: "This monument is erected by order of Congress, 25th of January, 1776, to transmit to posterity a grateful remembrance of the patriot conduct, enterprise and perseverence of Major-General Richard Montgomery, who, after a series of successes amid the most discouraging difficulties, fell in the attack on Quebec, 31st December, 1775, aged 37 years."

In 1818 his remains were brought from Quebec and buried under this memorial.

General Montgomery left no children, but his widow survived him more than half a century. A day or two before he left his home at Rhinebeck for the Canadian campaign, the general was walking on the lawn in the rear of his brother-in-law's mansion with its owner. As they came near the house, Montgomery stuck a willow twig in the ground and said, "Peter let that grow to remember me by." Lossing says it did grow and that when he visited the spot (in 1848) it was a willow with a trunk at least ten feet in circumference.

The following is a summary of the principal Mohawk valley events of the period covered in this chapter (from 1784 to 1838), prepared with especial reference to the Canajoharie and Palatine districts and the five western towns of Montgomery county:

1784, last council of the Iroquois in the valley (with Gov. Clinton at Fort

Stanwix); 1789, first cutting up of Montgomery to form Ontario county in 1789; 1790, legislative appropriation of £100 to erect a bridge at East Creek, opening up a period of bridge building in the valley; 1792, incorporation of Inland Lock and Navigation Co. to improve the Mohawk; 1794, Johnstown academy formed; 1795, Union college, Schenectady, incorporated, formerly Union academy, 1785; 1798, Schenectady incorporated as a city; 1800, charter granted for construction of Mohawk turnpike from Schenectady to Utica; 1808, first survey for Erie canal; May and September, 1812, Mohawk valley regiments garrison Sacketts Harbor and take part in repulse of British there in 1813; July 4, 1817, beginning of Erie canal work at Rome, N. Y.; 1819, business part of Schenectady burned; 1819, first canal boat launched at Rome to run between Rome and Utica; 1821, navigation on the Erie between Rome and Little Falls, canal boats using the river from there to Schenectady; 1823, canal open to Spraker's Basin on the east end; Oct. 26, 1825, start of Clinton's triumphal tour on the completed Erie canal from Buffalo to Albany and from thence, by the Hudson, to New York; 1827, slavery finally abolished in New York state; 1831, building of the Albany and Schenectady railroad; 1836, completion of the Utica and Schenectady railroad; 1836, removal of · the Montgomery county court house from Johnstown to Fonda (Caughnawaga); 1838, separation of Fulton from Montgomery county.

———

The chief national events of the formative period between 1784 and about 1840, which has been treated somewhat locally in the foregoing chapter are as follows:

1787, September, Constitution of the United States framed by state delegates at Philadelphia; 1788, July 26, New York state ratifies Constitution, being the ninth state so to do and putting it into effect; 1789, April 6, Washington inaugurated first president in New York city (then national capital), John Adams, vice president; 1790, .Philadelphia becomes national capitol until 1800; 1792, Washington re-elected president, John Adams, vice president; 1795, invention of the cotton gin by Eli Whitney of Savannah, Ga.; 1796, John Adams elected second president, Thomas Jefferson, vice president; 1799, Dec. 14, Washington's death; 1800, Washington city becomes national capital; Thomas Jefferson elected third president, Aaron Burr, vice president; 1803, cession of French Louisiana territory (1,171,931 square miles) to United States for $15,000,000; 1804, Thomas Jefferson re-elected president, George Clinton (former governor of New York) vice president; 1807, Clermont, first steamer, runs from New York to Albany; 1808, James Madison elected · fourth president, George Clinton re-elected vice president; 1812, James Madison re-elected president, Elbridge Gerry, vice president; 1812, June 18, second war (of 1812) declared by congress against England; 1813, British repulsed from in front of Sackett's Harbor, N. Y.; 1813, Harrison defeats British force and Indian force under Tecumseh; 1813, Sept. 10, Perry's American fleet captures British squadron on Lake Erie; 1814, July 25, battle of Lundy's Lane in Canada on the Niagara fron tier; 1814, August, British army burns the Capitol and White House at Wash ington; 1814, September, McDonough's American fleet destroys British fleet on Lake Champlain at Plattsburgh, N. Y., and American force checks British army there preventing invasion of New York; 1814, Dec. 24, peace of Ghent signed; 1815, Jan. 8, defeat of British by Jackson's army before New Orleans, La.; 1816, first tariff, with protection as its aim, enacted; 1819, first ocean steamer, "Savannah," crosses Atlantic from Savannah to Liverpool, England, in twenty-two days; 1820, first struggle between slave and free states over the Missouri Compromise act; 1823, "Monroe doctrine" first propounded by President Monroe in his annual message to congress; 1824, John Quincy Adams elected sixth president, John C. Calhoun, vice president; 1827, first U. S. railway from Quincy, Mass., quarries to tidewater (built to transport granite used in construction of Bunker Hill monument); 1828, Andrew Jackson elected seventh president, John C. Calhoun re-elected vice president; 1831, Cyrus McCormick operates first successful mowing machine at Steele's Tavern, Va.; 1832, South Carolina passes Act of Nullification of national (high) protective tariff of 1832; 1832, Andrew Jackson re-elected president, Martin Van Buren elected vice president; 1832, first American sewing machine made by Walter Hunt of New York city; 1830-5, first threshing machine made at Fly Creek, N. Y., not perfected there until 1840; 1836, Martin Van Buren elected eighth president, Richard M. Johnson, vice president; 1836, first model of telegraph instrument made by Samuel F. B. Morse of New York city; 1837-1842, years of financial depression; 1839, first photographs from life made by J. W. Draper of New York city; 1840, invention of baseball by Abner (afterward General) Doubleday, a schoolboy at Cooperstown, N. Y.

CHAPTER II.

1784-1838 — People and Life in the Mohawk Valley—Dress—The Revolutionary Houses — The Mohawk Dutch—English Becomes the Popular Tongue—Rev. Taylor's Journey in 1802—Valley Sports—Doubleday's Invention of Baseball—Last of the Mohawks in the Valley—The Iroquois Population in 1890 and the Mohawks in Canada.

The history of the Mohawk valley from 1784 to 1838 is one of great development and progress. Immigration poured into and through the valley, and consequently steps were taken for the bettering of transportation facilities, in the improvement of Mohawk river navigation and of the highways and in the building of bridges. The clearing of the land made the forest recede far back from the river except in scattered woods, and, toward the

end of this important period, the valley began to assume its present day aspect. Settlements were made farther and farther away from the Mohawk and rough highways to them were opened up. Logging was an important industry. Towns began to spring up along the course of the river or to develop from the hamlets and little villages already there located. Manufacturing began and factories were established. Schools and churches were built everywhere. Newspapers were started and the whole complicated fabric of modern civilization was woven from the crude materials of a frontier civilization. Human life in the valley changed from its early strong simplicity to that of today, with its advantages and disadvantages. Albany was the metropolis for Central New York, while Schenectady was the most important town in the valley until the close of this period when Utica outstripped it. The cities and villages of the present were, almost without exception, in existence at the end of this time. Johnstown continued the county seat during this half century. Toward the close of this chapter of the valley history came the epochal events of the construction of the Erie canal and the railroad, the latter of which may be said to end this historical period and usher in that of today.

The steam engine had been perfected in England early in the eighteenth century but it was not in general use in the Mohawk valley until the nineteenth century. Water power was generally utilized for manufacturing purposes and this is the reason of the early growth of factory towns like Little Falls and Amsterdam, which used the power of the Mohawk and the Chuctanunda. Almost every stream, with sufficient fall and volume of water, had its power utilized. The principal water courses in western Montgomery county, used for milling and manufacturing purposes were Zimmerman's creek in St. Johnsville, Caroga and Knayderack (Schenck's Hollow) in Palatine, Yatesville (Randall) and Flat Creek (Sprakers) in

Root, Canajoharie in Canajoharie and the Otsquago in Minden.

This period also marked the passing of slavery in the Mohawk valley, it being finally abolished in the state of New York in 1827. This would have ordinarily occasioned disturbance in valley labor conditions as some farmers had had a score of black slaves. The emancipation had probably been discounted and many slaves had been previously voluntarily freed by their masters. It is remarkable, considering the evidently large number of slaves here a century ago, that the colored population of the valley is no larger today than it is.

The time was also one in which the apprentice system flourished and orphan children, and others, were frequently bound out as apprentices until they attained their majority, being virtually under the control of their guardians (except in cases where the legal ties were dissolved by law) until the minors attained their majority.

In a general way this was a period of great evolution, in which was finally produced the valley as we know it today. The life of the people of the Mohawk country is here considered, with reference to their dress (a matter of undoubted importance historically) their home and daily life, their character and changing language and their pastimes and sports. When history is truly written we shall all see the people's life of the past days pictured as well as the movements of the chief actors in the great and changing drama.

The river traffic, highway and canal building, and other items of the life of this period, are dealt with in later chapters. These include churches, militia, war of 1812, bridges, railroad building and other valley features of the years from 1784 to 1838.

The period from 1784 to about 1800, which is partly considered in this chapter, was one of great transition in the dress of the people. Its most distinguishing mark in that respect was the adoption, for general use of trousers or pantaloons, which supplanted the "small clothes" dress of men about the beginning of the nineteenth century. Mrs. John Adams, wife of the later president who was then minister to England, commented, in 1784, in one of her interesting letters, on the fact that dress and fashion seemed less regarded in London than in the American cities. True, to the majority of Tryon county people, fashionable dress was of little concern as this was a frontier and farming country, but rich apparel was no stranger to them, having been seen at civil and military functions in Johnstown and other valley points and at Schenectady and Albany. The advent of Washington's staff in his tour of the valley and stops at Fort Plain and Fort Herkimer in 1783 must have been a brilliant spectacle, which undoubtedly brought out all the good clothes in Tryon county. Gen. Washington was most punctilious and careful in matters of dress, his attitude, in his own words, being that "orderly and handsome dress was imperative for men in office and authority, that they and the nation should stand well in the eyes of other peoples, that they should impress the simpler of their own folk."

Robert W. Chambers, the well-known novelist, is a resident of Fulton county, living at Broadalbin in what was the Mohawk district of Tryon. His novel "Cardigan" deals, in its early pages, with life at Johnson Hall. It suggests that, at the military and civic functions at the Tryon county seat, the dignitaries, officials, officers and their ladies there assembled must have rivalled the rainbow in the kaleidoscopic brilliancy of their rich attire. In 1780 when John Hancock was inaugurated governor of Massachusetts he wore a scarlet velvet suit which is still preserved in the Boston State House. His dress "on an important occasion when he desired to make an impression and yet not to appear over-carefully dressed," was thus described by a contemporary: "He wore a red velvet cap within which was one of fine linen, the last turned up two or three inches over the lower edge of the velvet. He also wore a blue damask gown, lined with velvet, a. white stock, a white satin embroidered waistcoat, black satin smallclothes, white silk stockings and red morocco slippers." Many of the portraits and descriptions in Mrs. Earle's "Two Centuries of Costume in America" bring vividly before us the life of the time and its American people. Tasteful and beautiful are many of the gowns of the fine ladies of the time. some of whom are radiantly lovely themselves. The men pictured therein show frequently strong well-modeled features of an American type which today is found only occasionally. Readers interested in this and the colonial period should study Mrs. Alice Morse Earle's "Home Life in Colonial Days," which gives a vivid insight into the life of both times.

Cleanliness was a not uncommon virtue of the Americans of that day. Dr. Younglove was the Palatine physician who was a surgeon with Herkimer's regiment. As we have seen he was captured by the British at Oriskany and taken to Canada. One of his chief complaints, during his early captivity, was as to the lack of soap and other means of keeping clean. English travelers of the time commented on the general neatness and cleanliness of American women, which would suggest a not similar condition existing in Europe. These same foreigners of the time found grounds for criticism in the riot of extravagance of dress and living which pervaded the "upper" classes of society in the American cities. The Count de Rochembeau asserted that the wives of American merchants and bankers were clad to the top of the French fashions and another French critic deplored it as a great misfortune that, in republics, women should sacrifice so much time to "trifles." Franklin warned his countrymen against this wave of reckless expenditure and Washington, who in his younger years was most careful about his rich and correct dress, later wore, as an example, home-reared and native made cloth. His wife was attired in domestic products, and

we find her knitting and netting, weaving cloth at home, using up old materials.

In the few growing villages along the Mohawk and among a comparatively small number of well-to-do families in Tryon county this passion for rich attire probably existed, but the Mohawk valley Dutchman and his household needed none of Franklin's warnings against extravagance. While a few families of means and luxurious tastes affected the rich fashions of the day, the mass of the valley people dressed simply, as farmer folk generally do the world over. The short working skirt for women probably persisted and the change from breeches to trousers but little affected the Mohawk farmer, for the buckskin leggings of the frontier were nothing but a form of trousers and nether garments reaching. below the knee had always been worn by workingmen and farm laborers, and by gentlemen for rough and ready wear. For farm laborers, these were frequently of coarse tow and were called "tongs," "skilts," overalls, pantaloons or trousers. One writer, speaking of farm workers and their "pants" of a period prior to the Revolution, says: "They wore checked shirts and a sort of brown trousers known as skilts. These were short, reaching just below the knee and very large, being a full half yard broad at the bottom; and, without braces or gallows, were kept up by the hips, sailor fashion." Mrs. Earle says: "It is plain that these skilts or tongs were the universal wear of farmers in hot weather. Tight breeches were ill adapted for farm work."

Trousers, or pantaloons, were evidently also the country dress or rough and ready wear of eighteenth century gentlemen. Young Major Andre was reputed one of the dandies of the British army in America but, at the time of his capture (perhaps in the disguise of a patriot country merchant) he wore "a round hat, crimson coat (such as was worn by English and American gentlemen) with pantaloons and vest of buff nankeen," and riding boots. President John Adams also makes mention of his wearing "trousers" about his farm. It is also probable that trousers or pantaloons were worn by soldiers during the Revolution, at least by the Continental militiamen. During the pursuit of Ross and Butler up West Canada creek in October, 1781 (as stated in a previous chapter), it is said the American soldiers took off their "pantaloons" to ford the icy creeks. This is on the authority of one of their number. The word "pantaloons," however, as used here may refer to either breeches or trousers.

Women's costume in 1784 varied from the plain, simple, somewhat full skirted dress of the housewife to the thousand frivolities of the fashionable society of the American cities. Velvets, silks, and laces in every variety of brilliant color were used by both men and women. About 1800 came the change to the simpler dress for men of today, although for full dress occasions knee breeches continued to be worn by some men until about 1830, and a few old gentlemen clung to this fashion of their youth even after that period.

Visitors to New York city, who are interested in the life of the people at the period covered by this chapter, will find the Governor's room in the City Hall a most interesting place. Here are portraits of many state notables from the early days of the colony until the middle of the nineteenth century, affording a vivid insight into the life and changes of those times. Three of Fort Plain's distinguished visitors are present—Washington, Governor Clinton and President Van Buren. Horatio Seymour of Utica and Joseph C. Yates of Schenectady, Mohawk valley governors, are also here, as is Bouck, the Schoharie governor. Washington and Clinton are depicted in buff and blue continental regimentals, perhaps of the very style they wore during their Mohawk valley trip and Fort Plain visit of 1783. Most interesting is the study of the changing costume of these dignitaries. Colonial and Revolutionary military dress was frequently a resplendent affair and so continued to be until after the war of 1812. Mor-

gan Lewis, who was governor of the state 1804-7, is shown here, in a portrait of 1808, in a uniform of yellow and black with a maroon sash, Wellington boots, highly decorated long sabre, and white gloves. He has a military coat of black velvet, edged with gold braid and lined with crimson satin.

Governor Joseph C. Yates is represented in a superb full-length portrait painted by the New York artist, John Vanderlyn, in 1827. He is depicted in black full dress, with knee breeches, black stockings and pumps. Governor Yates was a member of the well-known Yates family of Schenectady and Yates county is named for him. He was born in 1768 and died in 1837, and was a founder of Union college, first mayor of Schenectady in 1798, and governor 1823-5.

Governor Dewitt Clinton was also painted in 1827 in the same style costume with the addition of a black cloak with a red lining. Both Yates and Clinton, although past middleage, make a brave showing in this attire and it seems incredible that men of taste and fashion should have dropped such a dignified and stately full dress for that which Martin Van Buren wears in a portrait dated 1830. Here we have the dress suit of the nineteenth century with a few differences of cut and the funny pantaloons which make malformations of Van Buren's legs compared with the underpinning of Yates and Clinton. And so went out the knee breeches and entered the era of the stove-pipe hat. Students of such things say man's dress both reflects the spirit of the times and also influences it. Truly it seems to have indeed done so and particularly at the end of this post-Revolutionary period of fifty years. While the costume of 1913 may not be as resplendent as that of 1784, it has features of comfort lacking at the earlier time. In America the wearing of underclothes is now well-nigh universal and these garments were unknown, except in winter, in Revolutionary days. Underwear manufacture is a feature of Mohawk valley industry.

Valley homes and life after the war are vividly pictured in the following from "Beer's History (1878)." This was written of the town of Florida, but applies equally to the other Montgomery county towns as well:

"With the opening of the nineteenth century we seem to come a long step toward the present. It seems a great milestone in history, dividing a fading past from the fresher present. The long, doubtful struggle with England had resulted in a dearly bought, dearly prized peace, with its beautiful victories. Local tradition has not yet lost the memory of the suffering that followed the infamous raid of Butler and Brant through this neighborhood in 1780; and still treasures tales of hairbreadth escapes of families that found darksome homes in the cellars of their burned dwellings, of the fearful hushing of children, lest their voices should betray the places of concealment, of the hiding of plate and valuables, tea kettles freighted with spoons being hid in such haste as to defy future unearthing. * * But at last 'the land had rest.' The red man, once sovereign lord, had disappeared; the powerful Johnson family was exiled, its homes sequestered and in other hands. Sturdy toil and earnest labor won their due return and thrift and competency were everywhere attested by hospitable homes and well stored barns. Albany was the main market for the products, wheat forming the most considerable item. School houses and churches now dotted the landscape, and busy grist and saw mills perched on many streams. The Dutch [and German] language was much spoken, but many Connecticut and New England settlers never acquired it, and theirs [eventually] became the common tongue.

"Not alone have the 'blazed' or marked trees and saplings, which indicated the lines of roads or farm boundaries, long since decayed, but 'block house' and log cabin have also disappeared, and it may be doubted if five specimens of these early homes can now be found within the bounds of Florida. Yet still there live those who can remember the old-fashioned houses. Says Mr. David Cady:

"We have seen the type and warmed ourselves at the great hospitable fireplace, with crane, pothooks and trammels, occupying nearly the side of the room; while outer doors were so opposed that a horse might draw in the huge log by one entrance, leaving by the other. Strange, too, to our childish eyes, were the curious chimnies of tree limbs encrusted with mortar. The wide fireplace was universal; the huge brick oven indispensable. Stoves were not, though an occasional Franklin was possessed. The turkey was oft cooked suspended before the crackling fire; the corn baked in the low coal-covered bake kettle, the potatoes roasted beneath the ashes, and apples upon a ledge of bricks; nuts and cider were in store in every house. As refinement progressed and wealth advanced, from the fireside wall extended a square cornice, perhaps six feet deep by ten feet wide, from which depended a brave valance of gay printed chintz or snowy linen, perchance decked with mazy net work and tassled fringe, wrought by the cunning hand of the mistress or her daughter. These too have we seen. Possibly the household thrift of the last [eighteenth] century was not greater than that of the present time, but its field of exertion was vastly different. The hum of the great and the buzz of the little spinning wheel were heard in every home. By the great wheels the fleecy rolls of wool, often hand carded, were turned into the firm yarns that by the motions of deft fingers grew into warm stockings and mittens, or by the stout and clumsy loom became gay coverlet of scarlet, or blue and white, or the graver 'press cloth' for garb of women and children, or the butternut or brown or black homespun of men's wear. The little wheel mainly drew from twirling distaff the thread that should make the 'fine, twined linen,' the glory and pride of mistress or maid, who could show her handiwork in piles of sheets, tablecloths and garments. Upon these, too, was often

lavished garniture of curious needlework, hemstitch, and herringbone and
lacestitch. Plaid linseys and linen
wear were, too, fields for taste to dis-
port in, while the patient and careful
toil must not go unchronicled that
from the wrecks of old and worn out
clothes produced wondrous resurrec-
tion in the 'hit-or-miss' or striped rag
carpet, an accessory of so much comfort, so great endurance, and often so
great beauty.

"Horseback was the most common
style of traveling. The well-sweep or
bubbling spring supplied the clear,
cold water. Such was the then, we
know the now. In modes of life, in
dress and equipage, in social and political habits, in locomotion, in com-
forts, in commerce, one needs not to
draw the contrast; more wide or
striking it scarce could be."

Mr. Cady has most pleasingly described the old log cabin homes, but
we must remember that much that he
details of them was also true of the
stone and brick houses which were
built up along the Mohawk, almost
from the first advent of the white settlers. The century or more following
the initial settlements was marked by
the erection of strong, well-made
houses and barns, which might well be
adapted for present day construction.
When stone was easily obtainable, as
in the Palatine and parts of the Canajoharie districts, fine, solid, comfortable farm dwellings were built which
seem to reflect the simple, solid, honest character of the Mohawk valley
men of German and Dutch ancestry
of the time. While the "Mohawk
Dutchman" has been criticised, justly
or unjustly, for penury, lack of enterprise and progressiveness and other
failings, he seems to have possessed
the sterling virtues of horse sense, justice, honesty, toleration, self restraint
and, greatest of all, pertinacity. All
these qualities are so well exemplified
in the greatest American of the time—
Washington—of a different blood.
These same traits seem to reflect
themselves in the structures built by
the men of the Mohawk from 1784 to

1838. There are many examples lining the river's course on both highways and in the villages. The Frey
house (1800) in Palatine Bridge is an
example of the stone construction,
while the Groff house (typical of that
fine old Schenectady Dutch style) and
the public library (1835) on Willett
street, Fort Plain, are examples respectively of brick and wood building
of the period under consideration. The
old Paris store or "Bleecker house,"
in Fort Plain, is another interesting
specimen of early valley building. The
reason the middle and upper Mohawk
valley have so few pre-Revolutionary
buildings is that these were destroyed
in the raids from 1778 to 1782.

These same human qualities enumerated have continued to make the "Mohawk Dutch" such an important part
of the valley's population, probably
the largest element even at this day.

It has been authoritatively stated
that the Teutonic is the largest single
racial factor in our country. It has
never been exploited like the Puritan
strain has in history and literature
but it is none the less important on
that account. Wherever the Teutonic
race settled it did its work well as did
other peoples of America. Of its original locations, the Dutch settlements of
New Jersey and the Hudson and Mohawk valleys and the German settlements of Pennsylvania and the Hudson, Mohawk and Schoharie valleys are
of prime historical importance. As
has been previously mentioned, these
two elements (the Dutch and the German) were much intermingled and always have been.

At the beginning of the Revolution,
it may be roughly estimated, that, in
the entire valley, one-half the population was of German blood, one-quarter of Holland descent (including populous Schenectady county) and one-
quarter of other racial elements, or in
other words, three-quarters "Mohawk
Dutch." This supposition is borne out
somewhat by the "Oriskany roster"
and similar records of the time. After
the Revolution, with growing immigration, the Teutonic element somewhat
decreased, but the majority of the

families of a great part of the valley possess some strain of this sterling blood. And the spirit of toleration and restraint inherited from these early Teutonic settlers is a valued heritage of the valley people of today. Possibly the Holland Dutch element was greater than in the foregoing estimate. There is no means of accurately telling, but the guess may stand for Tryon county alone.

There were then present other equally sterling racial elements, notably Irish, Scotch, Welsh and English, but these were not of such numerical strength as the Teutonic in the formative period of the valley and did not consequently affect the course of life and events to the same extent as did the latter, so generally predominant in the early years. Today the British element (inclusive of the four peoples mentioned) is present in much greater proportion than in colonial and Revolutionary times. However in the towns of Montgomery county, aside from the city of Amsterdam, the opinion is worth venturing that the old "Mohawk Dutch" stock still constitutes a majority of the population. This is particularly true of the country sections and of the five western towns. In the list of premium winners at the Fort Plain street fair of 1912, two-thirds of the names published were of this typical valley, original Teutonic stock. The foregoing racial discourse will have served its purpose if it indicates that we must consider New York, New Jersey and Pennsylvania history (and that of other great regions where non-British elements largely located) in an entirely different light from that of the Puritan settlements of New England or the cavalier's Virginia and Maryland. These latter (especially New England) seem to have been historically exploited to the slighting of other equally important colonial centers of life. This country is not a second England, or even an enlarged New England, but a new nation, made up of many elements, although dominated by one great cohesive national idea, and largely differing in racial ancestry in different areas. Historically these race and national elements must be duly considered to give a clear understanding of certain periods, but we are today all Americans—and Americans alone—regardless of the original stock from which we sprang.

The period under consideration marked the passing of German in the western and Dutch in the eastern valley as the predominant tongues. The change was gradual. Dominies, who, at the close of the war preached, in the churches, several sermons in German or Dutch (or both) to one in English, after 1800 were discoursing more in the latter than in the former tongues. German and Dutch were still spoken in 1838 but then English had long been the popular language. The old "Mohawk Dutch" still lingers as a subsidiary speech to a limited extent.

For the most part the men of this period (from 1784 to 1838) led lives of hard work in the open air, and were consequently sturdy. Factory life was a negligible quantity, even toward the end of this time, and the town population was small in comparison with the people who were on the farms. Agricultural conditions and work gradually improved and approached the more advanced methods of the present, although doubtless not specialized as now. In most sections, the farming population, at the end of this period, was larger than it is at the present time (1913). The country was what might be called a natural country and human life was consequently natural and not lived under such artificial conditions as now. The great health-giving and soil-preserving forest still occupied considerable stretches of country and furnished hunting and fishing for the male population. There were farms, forests and watercourses and no huge cities, with their big factories and indoor life, to tend toward the deterioration of the valley's people.

With none of the present-day agricultural machinery, such as the reaper and thresher, the men of that day were compelled to do themselves the hard work of the farms and also of the towns. Consequently they had sturdy bodies, and so did the women and their children, as well—and no people can have a better asset. The women were probably generally good housewives, who gave their daughters thorough training in the work of the household, and who took the same pride in a well-kept house as their husbands did in a well-managed, productive farm. Aimless discontent seems to have been markedly absent and the women of the time were evidently lacking in sexless prudery and priggishness. The natural ardors of youth seem not to have been then considered evidences of depravity, and early marriages and large families were the rule. There was no need of sending the little child, of that day, to kindergarten for pretty nearly every farm and town house was a kindergarten in itself. It is said that never, in any nation's history, has there been such a record of population increase as in the American states from their settlement up to the time of the great invasion of foreign immigrants about 1840, when this natural national growth began to slacken and approach the present (1913) stationary position among the purely American element of the population (let us say among families who settled here prior to 1840). If this trend should unfortunately continue the Revolutionary American stock is bound to die out or become at most a negligible national quantity.

It is not to be inferred from the foregoing that 1784 or 1838 is superior to 1913 as a period of human life. In comfort, sanitation, kindliness and toleration we are ahead of the earlier time. Both times have something that each lack by themselves.

During the time of this chapter, the tavern continued, as before and during the Revolution, a center of social and political life. Here were held dances, banquets, meetings and elections. "Trainings" of the militia and horse races brought out the people as at present county fairs. An agricultural association was formed in Johnstown

and county fairs were held there about the middle of this period.

The work and government of the valley, after the conflict for independence, were in the hands of the patriot Revolutionary warriors. They assumed the direction of county affairs, without change—the form of government of old Tryon being much like that of the Montgomery county which it became. Later the sons and grandsons of Revolutionary sires took up their share of work and politics and at the close of this after-war period (in 1838) there must have been but comparatively few of the men of '76 left.

———

Rev. John Taylor's journal of 1802, written during his journey up the Mohawk valley, gives us a sketch of the people and country hereabouts at that interesting time, also an insight into the crude farming methods then prevailing. Parts of his diary relating to this section are as follows:

"July 23, 1802—Tripes (alias Tribes) Hill, in the town of Amsterdam, county of Montgomery. * * * This place appears to be a perfect Babel as to language. But very few of the people, I believe, would be able to pronounce Shibboleth. The articulation, even of New England people, is injured by their being intermingled with the Dutch, Irish and Scotch. The character of the Dutch people, even on first acquaintance, appears to be that of kindness and justice. As to religion, they know but little about it, and are extremely superstitious. They are influenced very much by dreams and apparitions. The most intelligent of them seem to be under the influence of fear from that cause. The High Dutch have some singular customs with regard to their dead. When a person dies, nothing will influence ye connections, nor any other person, unless essentially necessary, to touch the body. When the funeral is appointed, none attend but such as are invited. When the corpse is placed in the street a tune is sung by a choir of persons appointed for the purpose—and continue singing until they arrive at the grave; and after the body is deposited, they have some remarks made, return to ye house and in general get drunk. 12 men are bearers—or carriers—and they have no relief. No will is opened or debt paid until six weeks from ye time of death.

"27th—Left Amsterdam and traveled 5 miles to Johnstown—a very pleasant village—containing one Dutch presbyterian chh and an Episcopalian. The village is tolerably well built. It is a county town—lies about 4 miles from the River and contains about 600 inhabitants. In this town there is a jail, court house and academy. About ¾ths of a mile from the center of the town we find the buildings erected by Sir William Johnson." Mr. Taylor also continues as follows:

"Johnstown, west of Amsterdam on the Mohawk—extent [the town] 11 by 8 miles. It contains one Scotch Presbyterian congregation, who have an elegant meeting house, Simon Hosack Pastor of the Chh, a Gent. of learning and piety, educated at Edinburgh. This is a very respectable congregation. The town contains an Episcopal congregation, who have an elegant stone church with organs. John Urquhart, curate. Congregation not numerous. There is also in this town one reformed Dutch chh. Mr. Van Horn, an excellent character, pastor. A respectable congregation. Further there is one large Presbyterian congregation—vacant—the people [of this congregation] principally from New England.

"Palatine, west of Johnstown and Mayfield; extent 15 by 12 miles [then depleted in size from 1772]. A place called Stone Arabia is in this town and contains one Lutheran Chh and one Dutch reformed Chh. Mr. Lubauch is minister of the latter and Mr. Crotz of the former. Four miles west of Stone Arabia, in the same town of Palatine, is a reformed Lutheran Chh to whom Mr. Crotz preaches part of the time.

"After leaving this town [Johnstown] I passed about ten miles in a heavy timbered country with but few inhabitants. The soil, however, appears in general to be excellent. The country is a little more uneven than

it is back in Amsterdam. After traveling ten miles in a tolerable road, I came to Stonearabe (or Robby as the Dutch pronounce it). This is a parish of Palatine and is composed principally of High Dutch or Germans. Passing on 4 miles, came upon the river in another parish of Palatine, a snug little village with a handsome stone Chh [Palatine Church]. Having traveled a number of miles back of the river, I find that there is a great similarity in the soil, but some difference in the timber. From Johnstown to Stone Arabia, the timber is beech and maple, with some hemlocks. In Stone Arabia the timber is walnut and butternut. The fields of wheat are numerous and the crop in general is excellent. In everything but wheat the husbandry appears to be bad. The land for Indian corn, it is evident from appearance is not properly plowed—they plow very shallow. Neither is the corn tended—it is in general full of weeds and grass and looks miserably. Rie is large. Flax does not appear to be good. Whether this is owing to the season or the soil, I know not. Pease appear to flourish—so do oats; but the soil, I believe, is too hard and clayey for potatoes—they look very sickly. I perceive as yet, but one great defect in the morals of the people—they are too much addicted to drink. The back part of Montgomery [now Fulton] county consists of some pine plains; but in general the lumber is beach and maple. A good grass and wheat country."

Like many after war times, the close of the Revolution ushered in an era of recklessness and license. Gambling, extravagance, horse-racing, drunkenness and dueling were forms of its evidence. The duel was a recognized and tolerated method for the settlement of private grievances at the beginning of the nineteenth century. The Roseboom-Kane affair at Canajoharie is treated in a later chapter relative to that town. Another duel caused great public excitement in New York city and state in the first year of the nineteenth century. The principals were Philip Hamilton, son of Alexander Hamilton, and George J. Eacker, who had come to New York from his home in the town of Palatine a few years before. The latter was the son of Judge Eacker of Palatine and a nephew of General Herkimer. Eacker studied law, was admitted to the bar and became associated in a law firm with Brockholst Livingston, after his arrival in the city. He was a friend and admirer of Aaron Burr and a Jeffersonian in politics. Party feeling ran very high and Eacker became embroiled with the Federalists of which party Alexander Hamilton was a national and state leader. In 1801 Eacker delivered the Fourth of July oration in New York city, and seems to have thereby incurred the enmity of the Hamiltons and their party. Nov. 20, 1801, Eacker and his fiancee (a Miss Livingston) occupied a box at the John St. theatre, and he was there insulted by Philip Hamilton (then in his twentieth year), son of Alexander Hamilton, and by young Hamilton's friend Price. The talk between them, in Eacker presence, ran somewhat as follows: "How did you like Eacker's sour krout oration on the Fourth of July?" The answer placed it in a very low scale. "What will you give for a printed copy of it?" "About a sixpence" was the reply. "Don't you think the Mohawk Dutchman is a greater man than Washington?" "Yes, far greater," etc., etc. Eacker resented this abuse and a duel with Price followed at noon, Sunday, November 22, at Powle's Hook. Four shots were exchanged between the principals without result, when the seconds intervened. A second duel with young Hamilton took place the following day, Monday, November 23, at three in the afternoon at the same place, in which Eacker shot Hamilton through the body at the first fire and the unfortunate young man died the next day. It is a curious commentary upon the position dueling occupied, in the estimation of men of the time, that Alexander Hamilton held no grievance against the slayer of his son, and Joseph Herkimer of Little Falls,

observed to a friend that he "never witnessed more especial compliments or respectful greetings pass between lawyers than did between Gen. Hamilton and Eacker after his son's death." Eacker died in 1803 of consumption and Alexander Hamilton was himself killed in a duel with Aaron Burr in 1804. George J. Eacker was a prominent militiaman and volunteer fireman of New York city at the time of his early death.

————

Among the valley sports, after as before the Revolution, the chief seem to have been horse racing, foot racing and ball.

We have the following somewhat amusing anecdote concerning the meddling of the clergy with the sports of the people. At a race on the Sand Flats at Fonda, the German minister of Stone Arabia thought it his duty to protest against race track gambling, which was the cause of much iniquity, so he rode there in his chaise with that intent. Arriving at the grounds he had barely commenced his protest against the evils of the race course, when a wag, who knew the parson's horse had been in a former similar race, rode up saying: "Dominie, you have a fine horse there" and, touching both horses smartly with his whip, shouted "Go!" and both animals and drivers started off toward the minister's home at a racing clip. Several voices were heard shouting, "Go it, dominie, we'll bet on your horse." Before the reverend gentleman could pull up his nag both horses had sped a long way and the Stone Arabia clergyman, realizing the force of his remarks had been unavoidably broken, kept on to his home and was never again seen at a race course.

Trivial as certain of these accounts and anecdotes may appear they give us an insight and understanding of the people's character and daily life in the early days of the valley, which no citation of mere events and figures, however correct, can picture. They bring up visions like looking on a camera obscura, filled with the moving figures and backed by the unfamiliar scenes of a day long passed.

Here is appended a hand bill of races in Palatine forty years after the Revolutionary period. However the character of the pre-Revolutionary races was, without doubt, similar and it will give us an idea of what was the major sport and recreation of our valley ancestors:

"Second Day's Purse, $50—

"To be given to the jockey rider, running two mile heats, winning two heats out of three; free for any horse, mare or gelding in the United States.

"The third day a new SADDLE and BRIDLE, to be given to the jockey rider running one mile heats, winning two heats out of three; free for any three-year-old colt in the United States.

"Likewise on the last day, a BEAVER HAT, worth $10, to be given to the jockey footman running round the course in the shortest time. To start at four o'clock, p. m., on the last day's running.

"On the first Tuesday in November next, races will commence on the flats of George Waggoner in Palatine. The purses as above, except the hat.

"October 4, 1819.
                    "A SPORTSMAN."

The foot race did not take place as a Palatine contestant was sick, and a purse of $30 was made up for a quarter-mile foot race. William Moyer, a tailor, and John K. Diell represented the town of Canajoharie and one Waggoner and an unknown man were the champions of Palatine. The tap of a drum started them, as was usual then, and Diell won the sprint by six feet. The time was 58 seconds, which was very fast considering the track and the fact that there were no spiked shoes in those days.

In 1824 a footrace took place in the village of Canajoharie for a purse of $1,000, the runners being David Spraker of Palatine and Joseph White of Cherry Valley. The distance of ten rods was marked off on Montgomery street and the contestants were started by David F. Sacia. Spraker won the prize and the race by three feet. This race was a topic of general conversation for a half century afterward.

Games of ball had been popular sport with the soldiers of the Revolution. We read that the garrison was playing ball when Fort Schuyler took fire. This was probably then as later the game of "town ball." There were four bases in that game, but, instead of touching the runner to put him out, the rule required that he must be hit with a thrown ball. There were no basemen. This game survives, in the rules of our national sport, in that a baserunner who is hit by a batted ball is out.

The modern game of baseball was invented by a schoolboy of the old Canajoharie district, Abner Doubleday, who originated it at Green's school in Cooperstown, during the Harrison presidential campaign of 1840. This is so near to the time dealt with in this chapter that it is given place here, particularly as Cooperstown was for years so closely connected with Fort Plain, the latter village being its outlet to the Mohawk valley, by way of the Otsquago, all the towns along which route made Fort Plain their trade center, particularly before the days of the railroads.

In 1840, a great crowd had gathered at Cooperstown for a picnic and political meeting, during the excitement of this famous campaign. Of course the boys of the neighborhood of the school mentioned were present in large numbers. Young Doubleday (who later became a U. S. army general) had been working for some time on a game, based on "town ball," for the boys to play at the picnic. American boys of that time were vastly interested in all games requiring agility, quick thinking and athletic prowess and Doubleday's game took hold like wildfire. The New York Evening World, in June, 1908, had the following regarding this truly historic event:

"Young Doubleday was also fond of town ball, but he saw the opportunity to make the game more scientific and for several nights he worked on a new set of rules and a diagram of the field.

"When the boys assembled that afternoon Doubleday gathered them around and explained as well as he could, the points of the new game. He decided that there must be four bases ninety feet apart, and the boys immediately began to refer to the game as 'baseball.' The name stuck.

"The rules made by Gen. Doubleday specified that the ball should be made of rubber and yarn and covered with leather. It must weigh about five ounces and must not be more than nine inches in circumference. The weight of the ball and the size of the hand were taken into consideration in determining these measurements. The bat was to be of round wood, and to be used with both hands. In town ball the bat was frequently used with one hand.

"The next thing for the inventor was to determine the distance between the bases. After several experiments it was found that a man would have to hustle to run 42 [walking] paces or about 90 feet before a ball of those dimensions could be returned after having been driven to the outfield. Thus it was that 90 feet was fixed as the distance between the bases. A proof of Doubleday's wonderful judgment is the fact that, to this day, the ball is 'five ounces, 9 inch' and the distance between the bases is 90 feet. The underlying principles of baseball have not been changed one iota since 1840.

"The batters immediately began to study means by which they could drive the ball so as to easily make the 90 feet. But there were two sides to that proposition and the fielders learned to handle the ball faster so as to affect the batsmen. The American boy is naturally inventive and for 70 years he has worked, both at the bat and in the field, to overcome the problem which was created by Doubleday's measurements. That constant effort has made baseball the great national pastime of America."

All American boys should take pride in the fact that the leading athletic game of North America was invented and virtually perfected by a Cooperstown schoolboy.

The Mohawk valley has produced a number of ballplayers of exceptional ability. A St. Johnsville man is today (1913) with the New York National League team as an outfielder and a Palatine (Nelliston) native is manager of the Brooklyn National League team, after a long and successful career as shortstop with three championship league teams— New York, Brooklyn and Chicago. This player, W. F. Dahlen, started his career on the famous old Institute (C. L. I.) school team of Fort Plain.

General Abner Doubleday was born at Ballston Springs, Saratoga county, June 26, 1819; graduated at West Point in 1842. He became a captain of the U. S. army in 1855 and was one of the garrison of Fort Sumter in 1861. He was made a brigadier-general of volunteers Feb., 1862, and a major general in Nov., 1862. Doubleday was in the battles of Manassas, South Mountain, Antietam, Chancellorsville and at Gettysburg commanded the First Corps in the first day's battle after the death of Gen. Reynolds. He was breveted a major-general of the U. S. army and became colonel of infantry in 1867; retired 1873; died 1893. Gen. Doubleday published "Reminiscences of Forts Sumter and Moultrie" (1876), and "Chancellorsville and Gettysburg" (1882).

────────

The historical time covered in this chapter witnessed the complete disappearance of the Mohawk Iroquois from his old valley hunting grounds. At the close of the Revolution a few friendly or neutral Mohawks and a small number of individuals of other tribes remained along the river. There was a violent but natural prejudice against all Indians, on the part of the white population, which caused many of these natives to move to Canada or other friendly neighborhoods. By 1840, it is probable that the last of these remaining valley savages had died out. As has been previously noted the majority of the Mohawks left the valley with the Johnson family, at the beginning of Revolutionary hostilities, and settled in Canada, on the Grand river. Here they were granted lands and many of them have become prosperous farmers. The Mohawks and Oneidas have increased greatly in number and prospered while other Iroquois tribes have diminished.

According to the U. S. census of 1890 the total Iroquois population of North America was 45,000, a large proportion of the Indian inhabitants. This included, besides the Six Nations, the Cherokees who numbered 28,000 and is the largest tribe of Iroquois blood, numbering twice as many individuals as the New York state Iroquois or the Six Nations. The Wyandots, also of the same American Indian stock, numbered 689. In the census of 1890, the Mohawk population includes those of that tribe living at Caughnawaga and Lake of Two Mountain, Quebec, and at Grand River, Ontario, and the Mohawk, Oneida and Huron mixed-bloods living at St. Regis, and those living on other reservations. The great majority are, of course, resident in Canada. In 1890 the numbers of the Six Nations were as follows: Mohawks, 6,656; Oneidas, 3,129; Senecas, 3,055; Cayugas, 1,301; Onondagas, 890; Tuskaroras, 733. Total, 15,664. This is about what the New York state Iroquois population was at the time of the Dutch settlement. From a small tribe the Mohawks have risen to the greatest in numbers, while the Senecas, once the first, and numbering as many as the other five tribes combined, have shrunk so that they now are third in rank in population. The success of the Mohawks on their Canadian lands would suggest that the Indian, under proper conditions, can make a place for himself in civilized society.

CHAPTER III.

1689-1825—Western Montgomery County and the Palatine and Canajoharie Districts Townships — Life, Trade, Schools, Development.

This is the first of two chapters dealing with Western Montgomery county and treats of the period from settlement in 1689 to 1825, but principally of the time from 1784 to 1825. The second chapter, in the third series, gives the record from 1825 to 1913.

The succeeding descriptions are intended to portray the state and growth of trade, traffic and commerce in the five west end towns of Montgomery county from their settlement until about the building of the Erie canal. The history of these towns is divided into four periods: of settlement, 1689-1774; Revolution, 1774-1783; agricultural and highway and river traffic development, 1784-1825; development of commerce, manufacturing and towns, 1825-1913. The beginnings of things are always interesting and will be found particularly so in these instances. Names and personalities are treated which, in later accounts, must be disregarded on account of the great growth of the population. While, prior to the advent of the Erie canal, we can deal with individuals, in our later accounts the people must be treated in classes or as a whole. The 10,000 people in the Mohawk valley and that of its tributary Schoharie, at the time of the formation of Tryon county in 1772, have grown to between four hundred thousand and a half million of human beings. In the five west end towns of Montgomery where, in 1772, there were probably two or three thousand white people there are today approximately eighteen thousand.

Dutchtown and Freysbush were the first Minden sections settled and here schools were first established by the German settlers. There was some instruction given also at the Reformed Dutch church at Sand Hill. The ceremonies at this house of worship in honor of the memory of Washington in Dec., 1799, is treated in a separate chapter which describes this church as one of the five Revolutionary churches of Western Montgomery county. The church and the tavern were the centers of social life in the eighteenth century in the valley. The militia trainings, the part the men of the Mohawk played in the war of 1812, the improvement of and traffic on the

Mohawk, highway development and the inn life along the Mohawk turnpike, the construction of the canal and the railroad, the change of business center from Sand Hill to Prospect Hill, and other features of the life of this period, in Minden, Western Montgomery county and the Mohawk valley, are all given space in succeeding chapters.

The greater part of the following is from Beer's History of Montgomery and Fulton counties:

Small stores were established in the different Mohawk valley German settlements soon after they were planted. They contained small stocks of such goods as their white neighbors must, of necessity, have and certain kinds which their traffic with the Indians called for; the latter consisting of firearms, knives, hatchets, ammunition, trinkets, brass and copper kettles, scarlet cloth, rum and tobacco. These, with a few other articles, were bartered for furs to great advantage, at least; of the early white storekeepers, who were German or Dutch for the most part.

The first store, in the town of Minden, was established near the Sand Hill church by William Seeber, a German, at the place where for years (the late) Adam Lipe resided. His store was opened about 1750 and he traded here during the French war. As we have seen he died here of a wound received at Oriskany, over four months after that battle in which his two sons were also killed.

John Abeel settled at Fort Plain about the middle of the eighteenth century, shortly after Seeber opened his store. He probably traded here also, to what extent is not known. As the father of Cornplanter, the Seneca chief, his story is told in a former chapter.

A few of the trading places were general stores on a considerable scale and such a one must have been that of Isaac Paris jr., during the short time he traded at Fort Plain. The size of his store shows that he did a large business for the eighteenth century.

Isaac Paris jr. seems to have followed Seeber, having erected his store in 1786, this being what is now known as the Bleecker house. Here he resided and traded several years, dying at an early age. Conrad Gansevoort came from Schenectady in 1790. He married Elizabeth, a daughter of John Roseboom, who also moved up from Schenectady and settled below Canajoharie. Gansevoort built a dwelling with a store in it on a knoll at the foot of Sand Hill, on the farm where the late Seeber Lipe lived. This house is still standing, just this side of the Little Woods creek, on the extreme western edge of Fort Plain. It has been converted into a double dwelling. Shortly before 1810 Gansevoort retired from business and returned to Schenectady. He had been a successful merchant and was a man much respected in the township. The elevated road across the flats from the river ferry met the south shore highway just in front of Gansevoort's store and about the year 1800 and shortly before old Fort Plain or Sand Hill must have been a lively little hamlet.

Three Oothout brothers, Garret, Jonas and Volkert, came from Schenectady about the advent of Conrad Gansevoort. They erected a large two story building, some fifty feet long, for a store with a dwelling in its easterly end. It stood on the river road, just west of the Sand Hill settlement, about one and a quarter miles west of the present center of Fort Plain. "Of the Oothout firm, it is remembered that Garret, the oldest and who was a bachelor, was blind, but remarkably shrewd with a sense of feeling so keen that he could readily distinguish silver coins, so that no one could pass a ten-cent piece on him for a shilling or a pistareen for the quarter of a dollar." For a number of years, Gansevoort and the Oothouts had quite a large trade, the latter firm wholesaling to some extent. Both of these firms purchased considerable wheat, as no doubt their neighbor Paris did while in trade, which they sent to Albany, by way of Schenectady, on the river in their own boats.

Abram Oothout was a younger brother and with his wife, Gazena DeGraff, settled on a farm adjoining the store. In the dwelling, known later as the Pollock house, his daughter Margaret was born in 1811. She later became the second wife of Peter J. Wagner.

Robert McFarlan appears to have been the next merchant to come to old Fort Plain, having removed here in 1798 from Paulet, Vt. He was "a remarkably smart business man," and established his store on the opposite side of the road from the church. He married a daughter of Major Hause, of the neighborhood, "which proved a stroke of good policy, since he not only got a good wife but also the trade of her host of relatives and friends. He also ran an ashery near Hallsville in connection with his Sand Hill store. McFarlan at once became active in the affairs of the section, filling the positions of justice of the peace and colonel of the militia." He is said to "have been not only a fine looking but a very efficient officer. One of the few remaining gravestones in the old Sand Hill cemetery is one bearing the inscription 'In memory of Robert McFarlan, Esq., who departed this life July 14, 1813, in the 49th year of his age.' "

In 1806 a bridge was erected across the Mohawk river at the "'island," near old Fort Plain, superseding the ferry which was located just below. This was an important event for this locality and was duly celebrated. This structure, together with the one built at Canajoharie in 1803, were at that time the only bridges over the river between Schenectady and Little Falls. The matter of bridges is treated later.

About the year 1808, when Conrad Gansevoort returned to Schenectady, Henry N. Bleecker, a young man from Albany, who had long been his clerk, succeeded him in his business. At the end of a few years he returned and went to Canajoharie and there married Betsey, a daughter of Philip R. Frey and granddaughter of Col. Hendrick Frey. She "is said to have been the prettiest of three fine looking sis-

ters." Here Bleecker settled and died at an early age on the Frey farm. David Lipe and Rufus Firman succeeded Bleecker and are supposed to have been the last merchants to occupy the Gansevoort store.

A year or two after the death of McFarlan, John A. Lipe and Abraham Dievendorff began to trade in the McFarlan building. They soon separated and Henry Dievendorff joined his brother Abraham in trade at this store. Lipe fitted up a store on the same side of the street but closer to the church, which his son, Conrad Lipe, occupied until the year 1819, when he died, his father continuing the business for some time after. A postoffice was established at Sand Hill in 1816, with Conrad Lipe as postmaster, and as, at that time, there were three or four merchants located there, the only church in Canajoharie or Minden near the river, and a bridge across the Mohawk, the settlement must have been a place of considerable life for the period.

About 1820, the Dievendorff brothers erected a store near the Erie canal which was then being constructed, hoping to be benefited by the canal trade. This building stood near the premises, formerly occupied by William Clark on Upper Canal street. It was a long, yellow two-story building, the upper floor being used for a public hall. Preaching was held in this room and it was also the scene of dances and other social occasions. One of these was the marriage of the Peter J. Wagner aforementioned to Margaret Oothout in 1823. In connection with their business, the Dievendorffs ran a distillery. They failed and were succeeded by David Dievendorff, a son of Henry, who had long been a clerk for his father and uncle. He also failed. About 1828, as the business part of the young village was destined to be lower down, the Dievendorff block was removed to the site of the present brick stores occupied by H. E. Shinaman and Lipe & Pardee. John R. Dygert and John Roth succeeded the Dievendorff Bros. in the Sand Hill section and after a little

time Solomon H. Moyer bought out
Roth. A few years later Dygert &
Moyer removed to a store erected by
Dygert at the canal bridge, where
Wood, Clark & Co. were in business
for so many years and which is now
occupied by William Linney. Many
of the Sand Hill or old Fort Plain
buildings have been destroyed by fire
or demolished within the last quarter
century (prior to 1913).

Before 1805 it is said there were
few buildings on the site of the present village of Fort Plain. It must be
remembered that several of the buildings aforementioned, including the
fort and blockhouse, were within the
present limits of the village at its
western end. Isaac Soule kept a tavern here as early as 1804. In 1805 Joseph Wagner settled on a farm, occupying a large part of the site of present Fort Plain, and in 1806 he put up
a small public house which was kept
as such until 1850. It then became a
residence and is still standing and
owned by Andrew Dunn. In 1807 Dr.
Joshua Webster and Jonathan Stickney, settlers who came here from New
England, built a tannery on the east
side of the old Otsquago creek channel. This was constructed from the
material in the old Governor Clarke
mansion which had long been abandoned and had the reputation of being
a "haunted house." John C. Lipe opened a store in Soule's tavern in 1808,
there also being a tailor shop in the
building. Dr. Webster was the first
physician, having come here in 1797
from Scarboro, Maine. Peter J. Wagner was the first lawyer and he also
represented old Montgomery county in
congress. Before and shortly after the
completion of the Erie canal many business houses were established in Fort
Plain and when the village was incorporated in 1832 practically the entire business of old Fort Plain or Sand
Hill had removed to the present center.
The first hatter in the present village
was William A. Haslet, who established a store in 1826. Harvey E. Williams opened the first hardware store
in 1827. S. N. S. Gant established the
Fort Plain Watch Tower, the first

newspaper, in 1828. This became, by
various changes The Mohawk Valley
Register. Numerous other professional
and business men established themselves in Fort Plain in the five years
after the completion of the Erie canal
in 1825.

John Warner came into Freysbush
as a successful Yankee schoolmaster,
and, about 1810, he opened a store. In
1825 he built the store (now occupied
by the Co-operative store), which was
the second store devoted to dry goods
in Fort Plain. Henry P. Voorhees had
built the first in 1824 on the bank of
the creek. This building formed the
back part of what was for a long
period the Lipe and Mereness crock-
ery establishments. In those days before aqueducts were in use on the
canal, the creek water was dammed
back, and, on a bridge over the Otsquago, the canal horses drew the
boats across the creek. This set back
the water up the channel of the stream
and canal boats then unloaded mer
chandise and grain on the docks (re
mains of which may be seen) at the
back of the Main street stores.

Robert Hall moved from Washing
ton county about 1800 and followed the
trade of a pack peddler through the
Mohawk valley. He settled about 1810
at the site of Hallsville, which bears
his name. He, with two men named
John White and Cooper, built a store
and tavern. Later Hall bought out his
partners and continued the business
alone. He had an extensive business,
at one time having four stores running in the county, besides a brewery, an ashery and distillery, and he
also owned a grist mill in Herkimer
county. General trainings were frequently held at his place and elections
were held at the tavern. Hall served
in the war of 1812 as captain and was
stationed at Sackett's Harbor during
the war. During the early part of 1800
bands of Mohawk Indians frequently
camped at this place. Robert Hall was
a member of the state legislature and
was interested in the establishment of
the Fort Plain National bank.

Whipping posts and stocks were not
only to be seen in nearly every town

in New England at the beginning of the nineteenth century, but also in all the older settlements of New York. They were designed to punish petty thefts, for which from ten to fifty lashes were inflicted, according to the magnitude of the crime and its attendant circumstances. They were probably in use at Amsterdam, Caughuawaga, Stone Arabia and Herkimer and they are known to have been located at Johnstown, Fort Hunter, Freysbush and old Fort Plain or Sand Hill. The Freysbush post stood on the site of the cheese factory. One of the last punishments of that kind in this section was meted out to Jacob Cramer at the Freysbush post. John Rice, a constable of the then town of Canajoharie, gave the culprit thirty-nine lashes on his bare back for stealing a wash of clothes. This custom of punishment has long been obsolete, but there seemed to have been times when immediate penalty for petty offenses, inflicted in this way, saved a bill of expense if it did not actually lessen crime.

In 1810 the Seneca chief Cornplanter, son of John Abeel of Sand Hill, paid a visit to his relatives at Fort Plain and to the scenes of the murderous Indian raid in which he had been engaged with Brant some thirty years before. Simms gives the following account of this event:

"The Hon. Peter J. Wagner, a grandson on the mother's side of John Abeel, well remembers a visit of Cornplanter to his relatives at Fort Plain. He places the visit in the fall of about 1810. The noted chieftain then came here, in his native dress of feather and plume, on his way to Albany, attended by several other Indian chiefs. The party was first entertained at the house of Joseph Wagner, the father of informant, whose wife was a half-sister of the distinguished chief, who received at her hands that kind and courteous attention which his reputation'justly entitled him to expect. The distinguished guests also found the fatted calf prepared for them at Nicholas Dygert's; his wife being a sister of Mrs. Wagner [and a half-sister of

the Seneca chief]. Indeed, they were made to feel equally at home at Jacob Abeel's, at the homestead—his father, John Abeel having then been dead more than a dozen years. His widow was living with her son and exerted herself to make her home one of comfort and hospitality for the red men. These guests were here several days, and Cornplanter was so handsomely treated by his kinsfolk, that he must have carried home a grateful recollection of his visit. He was then judged nearly six feet high and well proportioned. He appeared in attire and ornament as the representative man of his nation, and well did he sustain the role of his national reputation. Many people in this vicinity then saw the celebrated Cornplanter, who never gave his white relatives cause to blush for any known act of his life, and his visit has ever been treasured as a bright spot in the memory of his friends."

———

The following relates to life, trade and the general early development of the townships of Canajoharie:

Johannes Roof had kept a tavern at Fort Stanwix and, when that post was threatened by St. Leger in 1777, he moved down the Mohawk to Canajoharie where he also conducted a public house during the Revolution and for some years thereafter. When the army under Clinton rendezvoused here, preparatory to crossing to Otsego lake, Gen. James Clinton boarded with Roof. The accommodations of the tavern were rather meagre, but ale, spirits, sauerkraut, Dutch cheese, bread and maple sugar generally abounded. A more modern tavern was later erected in front of the stone inn. It was called the "Stage House" and had a coach and four horses painted on its front. It was kept in 1826 by Reuben Peake and later by Elisha Kane Roof. The stages ran to Cherry Valley and originally had two horses. In 1844, four-horse stages, carrying mail and passengers, began running to Cherry Valley and Cooperstown, leaving the Eldridge house daily. This line was kept up for about twenty years. Washington is said to have stopped at Roof's house in 1783. It was of stone rubble work 22x38 feet and a story and a half high, with gable end to the public square. This building was bought of Henry Schremling by John (Johannes) Roof. Martin Roof, a brother of Johannes, was a druggist at an early day in Canajoharie and one of its first postmasters, also an acting justice of the peace. It is said that the Roofs were so prominent here that at one time the early settlement was called Roof's village. They kept tavern here until after 1795. When Roof came here in 1777 it is said there were not more than half a dozen houses on the site of Canajoharie village.

Henry Schremling conducted a grist mill near the site of Arkell & Smiths' dam, in the latter part of the eighteenth century. The first grist mill on Canajoharie creek was erected by Gose Van Alstine about 1760. It was a wooden building and stood on the east bank of the stream about 30 rods from the end of the gorge leading to the falls. From here, near the original "Canajoharie," or the big pothole in the creek's bed, the water is said to have been conveyed to it in a race course. About 1815 the mill burned down and Mrs. Isaac Flint, who, among the ignorant, weak-minded and superstitious, was considered a witch, was accused of setting it on fire. Learning that she was in danger of being arrested, she hung herself. Nathaniel Conkling, an uncle of Senator Roscoe Conkling, was the coroner who called the inquest. Instead of the poor victim of superstition it is probable that a relative of the mill owners was the culprit. The old stone miller's dwelling which adjoined the mill was after occupied as Lieber's cooper shop for the manufacture of flour barrels, and was also burned in 1828.

In 1817, a short distance below this site, a stone mill was erected by Goertner and Lieber. At this place they also had a sawmill, distillery, fulling mill and carding machine. For some time a large business was done here, including much of the milling for the towns of Palatine, Root and Charleston as well as Canajoharie. In 1838 these mills were burned and never rebuilt. Henry Lieber and his brother, John, on coming to America at the beginning of the nineteenth century were sold into servitude to pay their passage from Germany—a custom long in vogue and of which many immigrant people without means availed themselves. Henry Lieber, on becoming his own master, first learned the weaver's trade, and then became a pack peddler. He next had a small store in Freysbush, then one in Newville and then became established in trade at Canajoharie, just before the advent of the canal.

The second grist mill on Canajoharie creek was built about 1770, by Col. Hendrick Frey, from whom Freysbush took its name and who was a noted Tory during the Revolution. This place was known as the Upper Mill and was forty or fifty rods from the Van Alstine mill. It stood at the base of the high land on the west side of the stream near the mouth of the gorge. Col. Frey was an extensive landholder and, in disposing of farms in Freysbush, he stipulated that the buyers should have their milling done at his mill. Near it was his stone dwelling, where he lived during the war. Henry Frey Cox inherited this property, in 1812 from his grandfather, Col. Frey, and with it about 750 acres of land mostly heavily timbered. Much of this timber John A. Ehle, who erected a store house, sawmill and dry dock below Canajoharie village, on the canal at its completion, sawed up and took to tidewater in boats of his own construction; thus, for several years, giving employment to a large number of men.. The Upper Mill property became the property in 1828 of Harvey St. John and Nicholas Van Alstine and for several years they manufactured flour for the New York market, working up most of the wheat raised in this and several adjoining towns. The property passed through a good many hands until 1849 when the mill was burned down and never rebuilt, and the stone house was burned only eight days after the mill.

The first trader after the war, in the present town of Canajoharie, was William Beekman, who located near Van Alstine's ferry, a mile east of (present) Canajoharie village in 1788. In a few years he moved to Sharon and became the pioneer merchant of that town. On the organization of Schoharie county in 1795 he was appointed the first judge of the common pleas bench, which position he held for nearly forty years. He was succeeded in his business at Canajoharie by Barent Roseboom & Brothers, John and Abraham. Philip Van Alstine later became sole partner with Barent Roseboom, the firm occupying a store on the east side of Canajoharie creek, and within the present village limits, which then contained scarcely a dozen houses.

The Kane brothers, seven in number, came into Canajoharie very soon after the advent of Beekman, probably about 1790, and at first established themselves in business in the old stone dwelling of Philip Van Alstine, which was erected about 1750 and later became known as Fort Rensselaer. It is still standing and tradition has it that Washington was here on his valley trip in 1783. The firm was known as John Kane & Brothers, but whether all of them were interested is not known. They were a family of smart young men and soon made their store the leading one in this section, so that, for a time, much of the trade of the Herkimer county settlements centered here. These brothers were John, Elias, Charles, Elisha, Oliver, James and Archibald. Before long they built a stone dwelling with an arched roof at Martin Van Alstine's ferry, a mile east of Canajoharie. This ferry had been in operation some time before the Revolution. At this place James and Archibald Kane continued to trade until about 1805. Probably no business firm in the valley ever before became so widely known. In 1799 their purchases of potash and wheat amounted to $120,000. On leaving Canajoharie these famous brothers separated widely, John going to New York, Elias

and James to Albany, Elisha to Philadelphia, Oliver to Rhode Island, Charles to Glens Falls and Archibald to Hayti, where he married a sister of the black ruler of the country and where he afterward shortly died. The Kane dwelling came to be called the "round top," as it had a hip in its roof, which was covered with sheet lead. A little canal which led from the Kane store to the river was long visible.

The war of the Revolution, as all wars do, inaugurated a dissolute period of drinking, gambling and horse-racing, which lasted for years and was at its height at the time of the Kanes. Their house became the rendezvous for card players and a quarrel over stakes occurred on one occasion, resulting in a duel, April 18, 1801, in the small pine grove on the hill west of the Kane house. Barent Roseboom wounded Archibald Kane in the right arm. Dr. Webster of Fort Plain was Kane's surgeon and charged him 10s—$1.25—for each of his half-dozen visits but one for which the charge was 8s. The doctor lived four miles from his patient and the moderateness of his charges is said to have been characteristic of the man.

About 1805 Henry Nazro had a store in the present limits of Canajoharie village. In a few years he was succeeded by Abram Wemple, a good business man and a captain of a company of militia cavalry. He is reputed to have been a "tall, handsome, and resolute officer, and died, greatly lamented, about 1815." His father was with him in business in "the yellow building" vacated by Barent Roseboom. Joseph Failing succeeded as storekeeper in this place, when Wemple moved his business across the creek, in a new store which he built. Usher joined Failing and in 1817 one of the numerous fires, which afflicted Canajoharie in the nineteenth century, wiped out the old Roseboom store in which they were doing business. Failing also kept a tavern here. The Abram Wemple store was occupied in 1826 by the somewhat eccentric Dick Bortle. Here at his opening he fixed up a lot of bottles with colored liquids to make a notable liquor show and here he kept a saloon. "He drew an easy fiddle bow, spun an inimitable yarn, and could gracefully entertain any guest from a beggar to a prince."

James B. Alton, came from Ames and kept a store and public house but failed before the Erie canal was completed. In 1821 Herman I. Ehle began business and in 1824 erected his store on the canal. Henry Lieber established himself here about 1822 and, in connection with his mills did a considerable business. He built several canal boats for his own traffic and one, the "Prince Orange," was the first of the class called lake boats constructed in this part of the state. It was built in 1826 and was launched at the site of the brick brewery and malt house built by Lieber in 1827. This building went in the great fire of 1877. One of the industries of this period, removed to Canajoharie from Palatine Bridge, was a furnace for plow and other castings, the firm being Gibson, Johnson & Ehle. Herman I. Ehle, with whom the historian J. R. Simms, later of Fort Plain, was for two years a clerk and afterward a partner, was for a number of years known as one of the best dry goods dealers in Central New York. John Taylor moved to Canajoharie, as a partner of Ehle in 1827. Edward H. Winans was in business in the village then. The above comprises what is known of the business life of Canajoharie village at about the eventful and trade booming period of the construction of the Erie canal.

Canajoharie's first physician was Dr. Jonathan Eights, who removed to Albany before 1820. To represent the legal profession, the village had in its earliest days Roger Dougherty and Alfred Conkling, father of Senator Roscoe Conkling, and a little later, Nicholas Van Alstine, a native of the locality.

The first school in the present town of Canajoharie, stood on Seebers Lane, a mile and a half southwest of Canajoharie village, and the district was styled "No. 1, in and for the town of Canajoharie" when the common school system was adopted.

About 1797 a grist mill, a sawmill and a wheelwright's shop were set in operation at Ames in the town of Canajoharie. A pottery and nail factory followed. Russell and Mills were the first merchants of Ames, beginning business about 1800.

Jacob Ehle and James Knox, his brother-in-law, settled at Mapletown, in Canajoharie township, in 1791, paying $2.62½ per acre for their lands. Mr. Ehle built his house on the old Indian trail from Canajoharie to New Dorlach. (Sharon Springs) and, in clearing his lands he left all the promising hard maple trees. This "sugar bush" gave the settlement its name.

Marshville, in the town of Canajoharie, was the site of a sawmill built at an early day by one of the Seeber family. Stephen and Henry Garlock later operated this property. At this place one Joe Carley did the horse and ox shoeing for a large circle of the country, being near the main route to Cherry Valley. Carley flourished after the war of 1812, during the "shinplaster" period. Some sheep were stolen from a farmer named Goertner and the thief was traced to a nearby dwelling, where bones and horns were found under a floor. Shortly after manu script shinplasters appeared purport ing to be issued by "The Muttonville Bank, Joe Carley, President" and "pay able in good merchantable mutton." Hence came the name "Muttonville," by which the little hamlet is some times called.

The following gives an idea of how matters stood with the smaller farmers and poorer classes of this section at about the year 1800. Beer's History tells of an interview with Mrs. Bryars of Ames, whose family were early settlers of that place. "In her mother's time, the neighbors would live for six weeks in succession without bread, subsisting upon potatoes, butter and salt. Barns were so scarce that grain had to be hauled many miles to be threshed; hence farmers put off the job until they had finished sowing their winter grain, living without breadstuffs rather than lose the time necessary for threshing. Mrs.

Bryars was married in petticoat and short gown and Mr. Bryars in linen pantaloons [and it is presumed a coat and shirt]; neither wore shoes or stockings. Philip Button of Ames, says that his grandfather, Jonah Phelps, cleared the place where Button lives and that he used to carry his grist on his back two and a half miles to Sharon Springs. He made his first payment ($10) on his place by burning potash. Mr. Button's great-grandfather, Benjamin Button, was for five years a soldier in the American army of the Revolution. Being granted a furlough of three days he walked seventy miles between sunrise and sunset to his home. He remained there one day and walked back to his regiment the next."

The town of Root is today a beautiful and fertile agricultural section. Business and trade have always taken second place to the important work of farming. Its business development occurred mostly at and after the building of the Erie canal which is the limit of the period of trade growth we are considering.

Before the canal period, John Mc-Kernon had established a store in Currytown. He retired from this business and about 1820 was engaged in the work of building a bridge across the Mohawk in this town at the point now known as Randall.

A mill was built before this date on Yatesville creek (the Wasontha). About a mile below Rural Grove, occurs what is known as Vrooman's Falls, a perpendicular cataract of about twenty-five feet, which, when the stream is in full flow, is a most attractive spectacle. Here stood Vrooman's grist mill and his name has been perpetuated in the natural water power that turned his mill wheel. The building was carried off bodily by a flood in 1813 and dashed to pieces against a large elm.

Only the half of the town of Root, west of the Big Nose, was in the old Canajoharie district, but the whole town is included in the accounts in these sketches.

Palatine is the oldest section settled by whites in old Tryon county. Hendrick Frey located in the wilderness at now Palatine Bridge in 1689, as before stated and here came the Palatine immigrants at some time about 1711 or 1712. Minden seems to have been settled in the Dutchtown and Freysbush sections a few years after, in 1720, and St. Johnsville about that time or a few years later. Canajoharie, Danube, Root and Manheim were then colonized by Germans and a few Dutch within a comparatively short time. Prior to the Revolution, there were storekeepers or traders as they were called in the Palatine settlements. The latter town has always been a strictly agricultural community. Fox's mills on the Caroga were burned in the Stone Arabia raid of 1780. Major Schuyler rebuilt mills on this stream about 1784. Major Jellis Fonda had a mill on the Canagara creek, near the present county home (the old Schenck place). About 1800, on the improvement of the Mohawk (north shore) turnpike, many taverns sprang up in Palatine, along this route, which formed a considerable industry. The first postoffice in the town was established at Palatine Church in 1813. It is said that, during the war of 1812, when a person wished to send a letter to a valley friend or relative with the American army at Sackett's Harbor, he left it at any hotel on the turnpike. The landlord would then hand it to any teamster going that way, "who would carry it as far as he went on the road, and then pass it to another of his craft and in that way it would [possibly] eventually reach its destination." The first brewery in Palatine was erected about 1800 by a German named Moyer. It was situated about a mile north of Stone Arabia and was in operation only a few years.

In regard to the schools of Palatine, Beer's History says: "Until after the close of the Revolutionary war German was the prevailing language and, probably without an exception, the schools prior to that date were taught in the German tongue.

Soon after the restoration of peace, people from New England began to settle here, followed immediately by the innovation of the 'Yankee schoolmaster.' Among the early teachers of English schools in the town were John Martin and men named Crookenburg and Mackey. The former [Martin] taught in the vicinity of Oswegatchie about 1795 and a building was subsequently erected for his school. It was' finished with living apartments in one end and a school room in the other. He was succeeded by his son in the early nineteenth century. Mackey taught about 1795 near Stone Arabia and Crookenburg kept school near Palatine Church."

The first school commissioners and inspectors of schools were elected, in accordance with a new act of the legislature in April, 1813. They were Abraham Sternburgh, Henry J. Frey and John Quilhart, commissioners; and John J. Nellis, John I. Cook, Richard Young, Jost A. Snell and Harmanus Van Slyck, inspectors. The town was first divided into school districts—eleven in number, Dec. 7, 1814, by David T. Zielley, Andrew Gray and Chauncey Hutchinson, school commissioners. In the spring of 1815, a redivision was made, creating in all seventeen districts. It will be remembered that at that time (and until the formation of Fulton from Montgomery county in 1838) Palatine embraced the present town of Ephratah. There are now twelve well-apportioned districts, a few of which are fractional, and eleven schoolhouses within its limits.

A union academy, the first within the present boundaries of Montgomery county, was established at Stone Arabia and incorporated by the Regents of the University, March 31, 1795, as "The Union Academy of Palatine." The only records obtainable relating to this institution, are in connection with the Reformed church of that place. At a meeting of the consistory, held January 24, 1795, composed of Rev. D. Christian Peck, pastor; Henry Loucks and Christian Fink, elders and John Snell and Dietrich Coppernoll, deacons, it was "resolved that the five acres of church land of the Reformed Dutch church of Stone Arabia, which are not given to the present minister as a part of his salary, shall be given and presented to the use and benefit of the Union Academy to be erected at Stone Arabia." On the 14th of November, 1795, the board of trustees, through their president, Charles Newkirk, asked and obtained permission from the consistory of the Reformed church to occupy their school house (which appears to have been a part of the parsonage which had been used for school purposes), for one year for the use of the academy.

John Nifher was probably its first principal and its teacher of English. The academy building was a two-story frame structure, erected by subscription and completed in 1799. Its site was immediately opposite the Reformed church. Fire destroyed it about 1807 and it was never rebuilt.

Directly after the Revolution, probably in the summer of the years between 1784 and 1786, Molly Brant, with two of her grown up children, came down from Canada to recover property willed them in Philadelphia Bush. One of the children was George Johnson, who was of a dark complexion and the other was the wife of Dr. Carr, late a surgeon in the British army. They all visited Major Philip Schuyler at Palatine Church, where he was erecting mills on Caroga creek, Fox's mills there having been burned by the enemy. Mills were rebuilt on the opposite side of the creek. Maj. Schuyler was one of the commissioners appointed to look after such claims as those of Molly Brant and her children. The heirs were too young to forfeit their inheritance and recovered pay for lands now in Mayfield and Perth. While at Schuyler's, the party conversed in the Mohawk dialect, except Dr. Carr. Mrs. Schuyler, when night came on, was quite perplexed to know how to dispose of her guests, as the carpenters and millwrights were occupying all of her beds. Molly Brant set her at ease by assuring her that they would care for themselves and spreading their blankets on the floor, they camped down in true Indian style, to Mrs. Schuyler's great relief.

In 1784, Moses Van Camp worked for Garret Walrath, who had a blacksmith shop in Palatine about half a mile westward from the Fort Plain depot and near the ferry of that day. While trying to drive away some Indians, who were stealing Walrath's potatoes, one of the savages threatened Van Camp with a knife whereupon the blacksmith killed him with a hammer. The Palatine man narrowly escaped a tomohawk hurled at him, by a brother of his victim, at Fort Stanwix a year or two later.

In 1836 a monument was erected over the grave of Col. Brown in Stone Arabia by his son, Henry Brown of Berkshire, Mass., and on the 19th day of October, 1836, a meeting was held at the burial place in honor of the event and of the patriot's memory. A large assemblage was present and included some veterans of the Stone Arabia action. A sermon was preached by Rev. Abraham Van Horne of Caughnawaga, and a patriotic address was delivered by Gerrit Roof of Canajoharie (a grandson of Johannes Roof, the Revolutionary patriot). In a portion of his speech Roof addressed the veterans as follows:

"I see before me a little remnant of those intrepid spirits who fought in the memorable engagement of October 19, 1780. Fifty-six years ago this day you battled with greatly superior numbers, consisting of British regulars, loyalists and savages. Venerable pa triots, we bid you welcome this day! In the name of your country, we thank you for the important services you rendered in the dark hours of her tribulation. Be assured they will be held in grateful remembrance while the Mohawk shall continue to wind its course through yonder rich and fertile valley. They will be the theme of praise long after the marble, erected this day to the memory of your brave commander, shall have crumbled to dust. Fifty-six years ago, this day, these hills resounded with the din of

arms and the roar of musketry. Look yonder! The field—the field is before us—the field on which the heroic Brown poured out his life's blood in defense of his country. You fought by his side. You saw him as he fell, covered with wounds and with face to the foe. * * * His was that bravery that quailed not before tyranny, and that feared not death. His was the patriotism that nerves the arm of the warrior, battling for the liberties of his country, and leads him on to the performance of deeds of glory."

———

The town of St. Johnsville was settled about 1725. It was part of Palatine until 1808 and its early history, both as to events and commerce, is largely that of the older town. The first settlement at the village of St. Johnsville was made in 1776 by Jacob Zimmerman, who built the first grist mill in the town soon after. George Klock built another in 1801. David Quackenbush erected the third grist mill in 1804. This became later the Thumb iron foundry and the saw and planing mill of Thumb & Flanders. In 1825 James Averill built a stone grist mill and distillery. Christopher Nellis kept a tavern at St. Johnsville in 1783 and a store in 1801. The foregoing are the industries that the writer has knowledge of which were located at St. Johnsville prior to the completion of the Erie canal in 1825.

Henry Hayes taught a German school at an early day and Lot Ryan, an Irishman, taught the first English school in 1792.

———

Danube and Manheim were included in Western Montgomery county up to 1817. They were and are agricultural towns. The development of Dolgeville came at a period later than that herein described. In 1817 the eastern boundary of Herkimer county was moved from Fall Hill to East Creek and the old Canajoharie and Palatine districts towns were divided between two counties.

CHAPTER IV.

The Five Revolutionary Churches of Western Montgomery County—Other Revolutionary Churches in Montgomery and Fulton Counties and in Danube and Manheim.

The first Reformed Dutch church of Canajoharie (now the Reformed church of Fort Plain) was erected in 1750 on Sand Hill, a little above the Abeel place, on the Dutchtown road. The Germans who, about 1720, settled the town of Minden, at first located principally in the Dutchtown section. The road through that section led down to the river at Sand Hill where there was a ferry. The road across the flats (raised several feet to make it passable in times of flood), to this crossing of the Mohawk, is still plainly visible. At this central point would be a natural gathering place of the people and here the German frontiersmen erected the first known house of worship in the Canajoharie district. Of this church, Rev. A. Rosencrantz was the pastor for the first eight years. This building was of wood and stood in a sightly spot on the westerly side of the Dutchtown road, in front of the burial ground still to be seen (1913), surrounded by its dying grove of ancient pine trees. As previously told the church was burned in the Indian raid of 1780, after which services were held in a barn that stood on the old William Lipe farm in a ravine, through which the road ran from the river ferry up the hill to the gate of old Fort Plain. This old barn was torn down and a new one erected on its site in 1859. An old dwelling standing below it was over a century old when it was demolished in 1875 to give place to the present one of brick. These buildings, with several others, were so near the fort that the enemy never ventured to injure them. Another one so protected was an old house which was torn down by Harvey E. Williams when he built the present large brick dwelling on upper Canal street about 1870.

A new church edifice, erected on the site of the old one at the close of the war, was also constructed of wood, and was a large and well proportioned building, with a small half-round pulpit having a short uncushioned bench for its seat that would accommodate only one sitter; while over the dominie's head was a dangerous looking sounding board. The church had a gallery on three sides and was topped by a steeple without a bell. It was built by contract by Peter March for £1,000 ($2,500 at that time). A lightning rod on the building having become broken, it was struck during a storm and considerable damage was done.

General Washington died Dec. 14, 1799, and his death was solemnly observed at this church, as at many others throughout the land. As a number of days was then necessary to spread the news of important events throughout the land, the funeral ceremonies did not take place until the latter part of December, 1799. The weather was cold, but there was little snow on the ground and the gathering of people was immense. The church was beautifully decorated with evergreens and crepe and was literally packed with an interested audience. The Rev. Isaac Labaugh officiated and his discourse was afterward published. Led in a procession was a caparisoned horse with holsters upon the saddle, to which was also attached a pair of boots, indicating the loss of a soldier. This was the custom at the funeral of an officer, or cavalryman. Where the procession formed is not known but probably at the tavern of Nicholas Dygert, then located next beyond the Christian Bellinger place, westward of the church. This was perhaps the most important and imposing observance of Washington's death witnessed in the Mohawk valley, and not a few were there assembled who saw the national leader on his visit to Fort Plain in the summer of 1783, sixteen years before, when his excursion extended to Fort Schuyler and up the Otsquago valley to Cherry Valley and from thence to the foot of Otsego lake at the present site of Cooperstown.

Following the first pastor of the first Reformed Dutch church of Canajoharie, Rev. A. Rosencrantz, came Rev. Ludwig Luppe, Rev. Kennipe, Rev. J. L. Broeffle, Dr. John Daniel Gros (1776 (?)-1788), Rev. A. Christian Diedrich Peck (1788 to 1796), Dr. John Daniel Gros (1796 to 1800), Rev. Isaac Labaugh (from 1800 to 1803 pastor of the Reformed churches of Fort Plain, Stone Arabia and Sharon), Rev. J. I. Wack (1803 to 1816). Dominie Kennipe was mercilessly beaten one day, as he was riding along the river, by his fellow traveler, a hard man named Diel. "The minister would not prosecute but appealed to God, and, strange to say, both men died on the same night." Dominie Peck is described as "a portly man, an amateur equestrian, who left behind him the reputation of an unsurpassed orator." Great congregations thronged to hear him. Dr. Gros was "a man of considerable learning who had been professor of moral philosophy in Columbia college," New York city. Dominie Wack was an army chaplain in the war of 1812 and "a man of commanding personal appearance." The Reformed church at Sand Hill ceased to exist when the church society moved to its present site in Fort Plain and erected a church in 1834. This event practically marks the end of Sand Hill or old Fort Plain, the new canal town of that name taking up its story.

The Reformed church of Stone Arabia was the oldest church west of Schenectady, having been formed by Rev. John Jacob Ehle in 1711. Ehle was Reformed minister for this section and his services were conducted in German. A log church was first erected about 1711 on the lot now occupied by the Lutheran church. In 1733 the joint Lutheran and Reformed societies erected a frame church where the Reformed house of worship now is located. A disagreement arose as to the denomination of the new church and the Lutherans withdrew to the log church. Dominie Ehle was followed by Rev. Johannes Schuyler (1743-1751), Rev. Armilo Wernig (1751-1758), Rev.

Abraham Rosencrantz (1759-1769). Rev. Mr. Rosencrantz at first preached only at Schoharie and Stone Arabia, but later had charge also of the Reformed churches of Canajoharie (at Fort Plain), St. Johnsville and German Flatts, supervising, in that way, the religious instruction of almost the entire western Mohawk valley population of the Reformed faith. His salary at Stone Arabia was £70 annually, paid promptly as the receipts show, and from all the churches his salary must have been considerable for that time. He came to this country from Germany when a young man and married a sister of General Herkimer. He later settled at German Flats, where he died in 1794 and was buried under the Reformed church there. From 1769 to 1787 Stone Arabia church seems to have been without a pastor, although supplied occasionally by Dominie Gross of the Fort Plain church and by Dominie Rosenkrantz. The Stone Arabia Dutch Reformed church as well as that of the Lutherans was burned by the Tory and Indian force under Johnson and Brant, Oct. 19, 1780. After the Revolution a frame building was erected. In 1788 Rev. D. C. A. Peck was called and a new stone church was built at a cost of $3,378, which was considered at that time the best church building west of Schenectady. It is today the best and most interesting example of the eighteenth century Mohawk valley church architerture in this section. Philip Schuyler was the master mechanic. The workmen were boarded near by, the women of the church taking turns cooking for them. The Rev. Mr. Peck preached here in the German language only but kept the records in English. In 1797 he was called to German Flats and went from there to New York, where he fell dead in the street in 1802. In 1799 the adjoining parsonage was built and Rev. Isaac Labaugh of Kinderhook became pastor in connection with the Fort Plain church. It is significant of the trend of those times and also of the racial strains in the old Palatine district at this period that the consistorial minutes show

Dominie Labaugh was to preach in three different languages as follows: "He shall preach two sermons in the German languages, then one in English, then two again in German, then one in Low Dutch." In 1803 this order was changed to two sermons in English instead of one, which is also significant of the growth of the English language and its attendant institutions and customs in this midsection of the Mohawk valley. Rev. J. J. Wack preached here in German and English from 1804 to 1828, also ministering to the Fort Plain church at the same time. His salary was $200 from each church, $1 for each marriage or funeral, and 50 cents for each infant baptism. Rev. Isaac Ketcham (1830-1836) and Rev. B. B. Westfall (1838-1844) were succeeding pastors. Under the latter the church was repaired and a new bell procured. This church at its formation in 1711 was the only one in a district where eight Reformed churches are now.

The Stone Arabia Lutheran church dates from the separation of the united Reformed and Lutheran societies in 1733. Rev. William Christian Buckmeyer came here from Loonenburg on the Hudson and was the first pastor. Succeeding him were Rev. Peter Nicholas Sommer (1743), Rev. Frederick Rees (1751), Rev. Theopilus England (1763), Rev. Frederick Reis (1773), Rev. Philip Grotz (1780). It was during Dominie Grotz's labors, in 1792, that the present frame Lutheran church was built at Stone Arabia. Rev. Peter Wilhelm Domier came here from Germany and was pastor from 1811 to 1826, when he returned to his native country. All these pastors had preached in German and the first dominie to have services in the English language, as well, was Rev. John D. Lawyer, who was here from 1827 to 1838.

Sir William Johnson, in a characteristic letter dated April 4, 1771, to the Rev. Dr. Auchmutty, writes as follows: "I desired our friend, Mr. Inglis [the Rev. Theopilus England, pastor of the Lutheran church of Stone Arabia from 1763 to 1773] to mention a Circumstance concerning Religion here that I think you ought to know. The Lutheran minister at Stoneraby has lately in a voluntary Manner without any previous Arguments to induce him thereto desired to take orders in the Church of England, and what is much more Strange, It is the desire of his Congregation that he should do so. The great difficulty is That, they will be without a Minister during his absence, and that it will be attended with an expence which from their great Occonomy, they do not chuse to Incurr, Especially as they have some Charitable Establishments amongst themselves that are chargeable. If * * * * it Could be Carried through without making much noise, It would add the Majority of Inhabitants of a very fine Settlement to the Church, and as they are Foreigners must strengthen their allegiance to the Gov't." Dr. Auchmutty replied from New York favorably to the change of denomination but whether from the "great Occonomy" of the church forbidding them to send their minister to England for ordination, or for some other reason, nothing seems to have come of the proposal.

The "Palatine Evangelical Lutheran Church" edifice, at Palatine Church, is the oldest church building now standing within the limits of Montgomery and Fulton counties. It was also the first church structure in the Palatine or Canajoharie districts to be fittingly built of a permanent material such as the stone of which it is constructed. Others were mostly of clapboards at that time. It was erected in 1770 of stone by the generous donations of a few individuals. Peter Wagner and Andrew Reber contributed £100 each. Johannes Hess and six Nellises, namely, William jr., Andrew, Johannes, Henry, Christian and David each gave £60, while the building of the spire, which seems to have been an after consideration, was paid for by the Nellis family exclusively. This church, unlike most others in the valley, was not destroyed by the British raiders of the Revolution, for the reason, it is supposed of the Tory proclivities of one or more of the Nellis family. It remained as originally built for a century, when it was remodeled and repaired at a cost of $4,000 and in the fall of 1870, on its one hundredth anniversary, a large celebration and fair was held, at which Gov. Seymour delivered an appropriate address. Many later celebrations have been held here and the church has been restored. In its early history, this society seems never to have had any independent church organization but was supplied by ministers from other churches, principally the Lutheran church of Stone Arabia.

As early as 1756 a Reformed church was erected in the eastern part of the town of St. Johnsville by Christian Klock. The Rev. Mr. Rosenkrantz was the first preacher and John Henry Disland the second. This structure was torn down in 1818 and a church was erected in the present village. This was replaced in the latter nineteenth century by the present substantial brick church edifice.

Mason's History says of St. John's Reformed church of St. Johnsville: "The name St. Johnsville was unquestionably derived from St. John's Reformed church, erected in 1770 and moved to the village in 1804 * * * The Reformed church of St. Johnsville is one of the oldest religious societies in the Mohawk valley, its history dating back to the middle of the eighteenth century. The present handsome brick edifice was built in 1881. * * * The church received the name of 'St. John's Dutch Reformed' during the latter part of the eighteenth century, and reliable records indicate that the church title suggested a name for the village. This fact has been substantiated in a great degree by Rev. P. Furbeck, who devoted a great deal of attention to the subject. The Rev. Abram Rosenkrantz, who first ministered to the Dutch Reformed church, was a historic character, as was also his successor, Rev. John Henry Dyslin. The latter was born in Burgdorf, Can-

ton Berne, Switzerland, and was appointed by the 'high German authorities of Palatine district, Canajoharie Castle' to the church, July 13, 1788."

It is only the province of this sketch to treat of the churches which were in existence in the five west end towns of Montgomery at the time of the formation of the Canajoharie and Palatine districts of Tryon county in 1772. Their story is continued until about the end of the story of Old Fort Plain, which may be put at 1834, when the Reformed church of Fort Plain withdrew from its old home in the Sand Hill section and erected a new church at its present Fort Plain site. These details throw light on the life of the people, during this changeful period, at the end of the eighteenth and the beginning of the nineteenth century. Shortly after this time, church societies of other denominations were formed in great numbers in the five towns under consideration.

In 1794 a Free Will Baptist church society was formed several miles west of Ames, in the township of Canajobarie, and in 1796 it was removed to that settlement. This was the first known religious organization in that town. Its present church at Ames was built in 1832.

So far as known there was no church in the present village of Canajoharie, prior to the Revolution, the first house of worship, in that settlement, being a union church which was built in 1818. Rev. George B. Miller, a Lutheran, was the first settled preacher. He had many difficulties to contend with, among them being that of having to be his own chorister. In this musical capacity he had to compete with the bugles played on the line and packet boats in the summer of 1826, the first year of through canaling. The canal had been dug so near the church as to leave barely room for the tow path. These instruments were even sounded before the open windows in prayer time and it was not until an appeal was made to the state authorities that this nuisance was broken up. Mr. Miller was pastor for nine years and later died at Hartwick seminary, of which he was long principal. Before the erection of this union church, the people in the present township of Canajoharie probably attended the Stone Arabia or Fort Plain churches. After the organization of the Reformed church in 1827 other church societies soon were formed in the village of Canajoharie

In the town of Root a Dutch Reformed church was organized at Currytown about 1790 and a church was built and dedicated in 1809, which was remodeled in 1849 and the spire rebuilt. This was the first church society in Root and the only one in existence before 1800.

Mention has been made of the Indian Castle (Danube) church, erected by Sir William Johnson in the western part of the Canajoharie district about 1760, largely for the use of the Mohawks then residing there. It is said that Samuel Clyde, later colonel of the Canajoharie battalion or regiment of militia, superintended its construction.

Lossing writes of the church at Indian Castle, which with the Herkimer house, constitute an interesting pair of pre-Revolutionary objects of the town of Danube and of the old Canajoharie district. "The Castle church, as it is called—the middle one of the three constructed under the auspices of Sir William Johnson—is still standing (1848), two and a half miles below the Herkimer mansion. It is a wooden building, and was originally so painted as to resemble stone. Its present steeple is not ancient, but the form is not unlike that of the original. Here the pious Kirkland often preached the Gospel to the heathen, and here Brant and his companions received lessons of heavenly wisdom. The church stood upon land that belonged to the sachem, and the house of Brant, where Christian missionaries were often entertained before he took up the war hatchet, stood about seventy-five rods northward of the church. Bricks and stones of the foundation are still to be seen in an apple orchard north of

the road, and the locality was well defined, when I visited it, by rank weeds, nowhere else in the field so luxuriant."

Previous mention has been made of the stealing of the bell of the "Castle church" by hostile Indians during the Revolution. The savages probably intended to take this souvenir of their old house of worship to install in a new Indian church in Canada. The marauders forgot to secure the clapper and its clanging roused the German patriots of the neighborhood, who sallied forth and recovered the bell and returned it to its place.

The "old yellow church" is situated in the western part of Manheim about three miles northerly from Little Falls at what was formerly known as Remensneider's Bush, almost on the line between the town of Little Falls and Manheim, where there was a considerable settlement at the time of the Revolution. Here was a mill and a block house and this was the scene of the raid in April, 1778. At this church are buried 35 Revolutionary patriot soldiers.

Before the war of independence a Reformed Dutch church was organized in Manheim and a building erected. The Manheim Reformed church was burned during the Revolution and rebuilt soon after. This building remained standing until 1850 when the present new frame edifice took its place. Rev. Caleb Alexander, who made a tour of the valley in 1801, wrote: "Between Fairfield and Little Falls is a Dutch settlement called Manheim, rich farms, a meeting house and a minister." This is the only Revolutionary church society in the town of Manheim.

Aside from the five Revolutionary churches of western Montgomery mentioned in the foregoing, the other sectarian buildings or societies of that time, within the present limits of Montgomery and Fulton counties, are noted as follows: Queen Anne's Chapel at Fort Hunter was erected about 1710, the year before the building of the fort. Beer's (1878) History says: "The liberality of Queen Anne caused the erection and endowment of a chapel and manse. The manse is still standing in sturdy strength. It is a two-story stone building, about 25 by 35 feet, and is, perhaps, the oldest structure in the Mohawk valley, west of Schenectady [county line]. * * * This chapel contained a veritable organ, the very Christopher Columbus of its kind, in all probability the first instrument of music of such dignity in the wilderness west of Albany. Queen Anne in 1712 sent as furniture for the chapel a number of silver dishes and a quantity of church furnishings and supplies (including bibles) for this chapel and for missionary use among the Mohawks and Onondagas. This chapel was destroyed by the building of the Erie canal." At the time of the building of Queen Anne's chapel the Dutch Reformed and Episcopal denominations supported missions or missionaries among the Iroquois tribes.

A mile east of Minaville in the town of Florida (in which Fort Hunter is also situated) a Reformed church was erected before 1784.

The Caughnawaga Reformed Dutch church was built in 1763 at the eastern end of Caughnawaga (Fonda) in the present town of Mohawk. It was a stone structure and served the people of its neighborhood until 1842 when its congregation removed to worship in a church nearer the railroad station. In 1868 this noted building was torn down.

An English church (which became the present St. John's Episcopal) was built of stone in Johnstown in 1771, by Johnson, and is mentioned in preceding chapters. In 1836 this structure was burned and in 1837 a new church was erected. Sir William Johnson gave his Lutheran and Presbyterian neighbors glebes of 50 acres each and their church societies, at least, were in existence prior to the Revolution. These are the only Revolutionary church societies of Fulton county.

The foregoing shows the following five churches or church societies in existence in western Montgomery county, before or during the Revolution: Three Reformed churches at Stone Arabia, Fort Plain, St. Johnsville; two Lutheran churches at Stone Arabia and Palatine Church. In the Canajoharie and Palatine districts were seven churches—four Reformed churches at Stone Arabia, Fort Plain, St. Johnsville and Manheim; two Lutheran churches at Stone Arabia and Palatine Church and one Episcopal or Union church at Indian Castle, Danube. In Montgomery county were eight Revolutionary churches—five Reformed churches at Stone Arabia, Fort Plain, St. Johnsville, Caughnawaga (Fonda) and Minaville; two Lutheran churches at Stone Arabia and Palatine Church and one Episcopal church at Fort Hunter. In Fulton county were three Revolutionary church societies— Episcopal, Lutheran and Presbyterian. In Fulton and Montgomery counties (or old Montgomery county prior to 1838) were eleven church societies at the end of the Revolution. All of these are in existence, with the exception of the Episcopal church at Fort Hunter, which was destroyed by the building of the Erie canal, as previously stated.

Hon. Francis Granger, postmaster-general under Gen. W. H. Harrison, has left an account of a Sunday at the old Caughnawaga Reformed Dutch church, which deserves a place here as illuminating the life of the times. A condensation of his narrative follows:

" * * * Loads of the worshippers were coming in from the country. As fast as the women alighted from the sheepskin-bottomed chairs which formed the seats in the wagons, the men, after providing for their teams, repaired to a neighboring bar-room. Gravely, as befitted the day, each ordered a drink. Having drained his glass, the thirsty Christian thrust his hand deep in his pocket and drew forth a long, narrow leather wallet, with a string woven in the neck, rolled up around the coin which it contained. Taking the purse by the bottom and emptying the cash into his left hand he selected a sixpence and laying it before the landlord, poured back the remainder into the depths of the wallet, folded it carefully up, restored it to his pocket, and returned to the church. Thither Mr. Granger also betook himself. An officious usher took him in charge, and, shutting him up in one of the high-partitioned box pews, which occupied most of the floor, left him to pursue his meditations. The most noticeable feature of the odd interior of the building was the pulpit, which was a little five-sided coop, perched aloft on a slender support, reached by the narrowest of stairways, and canopied by a sounding board that completely roofed it over. On the wall, on either side of the pulpit, hung a pole several feet in length, suspended by an iron hoop or ring, from which also depended a little bag with a bell at the bottom. In due time the clergyman entered, and, mounting the slender stairway, seated himself in his little domain, which barely contained him. From his fresh and rubicund face, it would almost seem that his parishioners were countenanced by him in their matter of their Sunday morning dram. Here, thought the visitor, observant of his glowing features, was a light of the church set in a Dutch candlestick and covered with an umbrella, to prevent any untimely extinguishment. The congregation entered heartily into the singing, and Mr. Granger thought it might be good worship, though sad music. At the proper stage, the ushers, taking down the scoop nets from beside the pulpit went fishing expertly among the worshipers for a collection, tinkling the little bells appended, as if to warn them to be ready with their change. There was need of notice, for getting at the coin was the same deliberate operation as at the tavern. There was the diving for the purse, the unrolling and emptying of the contents; but the observer noted that the burgher's eye scanned his palm for a penny instead of a sixpence. When they had gone the round of the house, the collectors took their turn at the performance, seeming to hear the Head of the Church saying, as of old 'Bring me a penny.'

The dominie had got well into his sermon, in a commonplace way, before he saw Mr. Granger. Then, at the sight of a well-dressed and intelligent stranger in the house, he perceptibly roused himself, and became really eloquent. At the close of the service he had an interview with the visitor, who assured him, in all sincerity, that he was never more interested in a sermon in his life."

CHAPTER V.

The Mohawk River and Watershed— History and Topography.

This is the first of five chapters dealing with the Mohawk river, its valley and watershed and with water traffic on the Mohawk through its valley. This chapter treats of the Mohawk, its geological history, its topography and geography. The following chapter deals with early traffic on the Mohawk, including the years from 1609 to 1825. Subsequent ones will treat of the Erie canal 1825-1913, the Barge canal, and of the geology of the central Mohawk river section, particularly that between Fall Hill and the Noses. This latter is from the pen of Abram Devendorf and forms chapter VII. of the third series of these papers. Attention is called to the accompanying map which gives a birds-eye view of the Mohawk watershed, the names of all except the first and second class tributaries being omitted for the sake of clearness.

The Mohawk valley forms a most important region of the Hudson river watershed. As it is the site of the eastern section of the Barge canal, the water supply of the Mohawk watershed is a subject of the greatest importance. The valley of the Mohawk breaks through the Atlantic states mountain system and forms a natural road and waterway between tidewater and the Great Lakes. Its position in this respect is unique and makes it a link in a great chain of land and water communication, running from the sea far into the middle and northwestern portions of North America. The Mo-

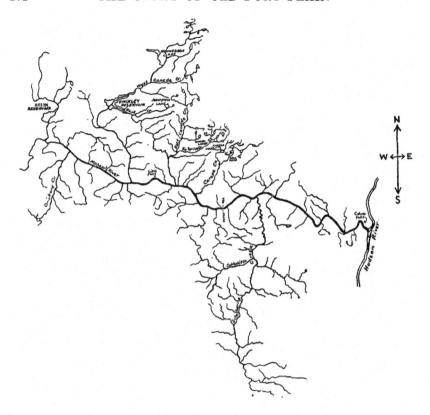

THE MOHAWK RIVER, ITS VALLEY AND WATERSHED.

THE NAMES OF ITS FIRST AND SECOND CLASS AFFLUENTS ARE GIVEN TO AID THE READER IN
LOCATING THE DIFFERENT STREAMS AND REGIONS OF THE WATERSHED.

hawk river basin takes natural importance as the seat of the life of the
Mohawk tribe of the great Iroquois
confederacy; as a place, in the seventeenth and eighteenth centuries, of
interesting settlement by Dutch, German and British; as the scene of vital
and terrible Revolutionary warfare,
and as a region of highway, waterway, railroad, industrial, town and
agricultural development. All these
are treated in separate chapters of
this work.

The Mohawk river rises in the southern part of Lewis county and flows
about 135 miles to its junction with
the Hudson at Troy. Its course is in a
generally easterly direction. The

stream has two tributaries of the first
class—the West Canada and Schoharie
creeks. The West Canada rises in the
Adirondacks in Herkimer and Hamilton counties and has a course of about
sixty miles to its junction with the
Mohawk at Herkimer. The Schoharie
rises in Greene county, among the
Catskills, about seventy miles or more
to the south of its confluence with the
Mohawk at Fort Hunter. It was
through this valley, from the Hudson,
that the first Palatines came to Palatine on the Mohawk, settling the Schoharie valley on the way. The Schoharie valley is a beautiful and important region of the Mohawk valley,
whose history, however, is only con-

sidered very generally in this publication.

The Oriskany, entering the Mohawk at Oriskany, the East Canada creek entering at East Creek station and the Caroga (also written Garoga) joining its parent stream at Palatine Church, may be considered second class tributaries. The Oriskany rises in Madison county and the East and Caroga creeks have their headwaters on the edge of the Adirondack region,—the East creek in Herkimer, Hamilton and in the Canada lakes of Fulton county and the Caroga in the lake region of Fulton county formed by headwaters of East creek just mentioned and its own headwaters—the Caroga lakes, Peck's Pond and minor ponds.

A rough classification of the Mohawk's third class tributaries comprise the following: Nine Mile creek, Saquoit, Nowadaga, Otsquago, Canajoharie, Flat creek, Cayadutta, North Chuctanunda, South Chuctanunda, Alplauskill. The greater part of these important tributaries, both of the first and second class, enter the Mohawk in Montgomery county. In the central section of the Mohawk basin, which is considered particularly in these chapters, the southern rim of the watershed lies much nearer to the river than the northern. In the valley country from Ilion to Fultonville, the southern rim lies about fifteen miles or less from the river while the northern is from two to three times that distance from the Mohawk. The Adirondack region covers a large part of the northern edge of the watershed. The headwaters of the Schoharie lie in the Catskill country. The Mohawk watershed was, three hundred years ago, part of the great eastern forest, and two-thirds of it has been denuded by the European colonists. Much of the farm lands are fertile—some of them very fertile.

The Oneida lake watershed lies to the west of the Mohawk headwaters and the Black river valley to the north. The Oneida lake waters continue the Mohawk waterway westward to Lakes Ontario and Erie and the Black river forms a water and highway to northern New York and the St. Lawrence. The Mohawk's "parent" valley—the Hudson—borders the northeastern and eastern sides while the Susquehanna bounds the southwestern limit of the Mohawk basin. The Delaware head waters lie close to those of the Schoharie. The foregoing gives a general view of the Mohawk and its watershed. The following matter covers the subject in greater detail.

The story of the Mohawk river is the history of civilization in America. Its chronicle is of interest to a great region of territory of North America, as it is the chief link between the Great Lakes and the ocean. Together with Oneida lake and the Oswego river, it connects the tidewaters of the Hudson with the great inland seas. These latter today carry an enormous commerce which should find a great part of its outlet through the Barge canal, which follows the Mohawk river in its eastern course. With progress in canalization it may be that a canal will eventually join the Great Lakes, by way of the Lake of the Woods to Lakes Winnipeg and Winnipegosis in Canada. This would make a territory immediately contributory to these great waterways of an area equal to about one-third of the United States, and a much greater region would indirectly contribute to its commerce. It would extend from New York city up the Hudson, through the Mohawk river, Oneida lake and Oswego river to Lake Ontario, to Lake Erie, through Lakes Huron and Superior to the outlet of Rainy Lake, through that lake and the river of the same name into the Lake of the Woods, in Canada, and thence into Whitemouth river, into Winnipeg river, into Lake Winnipeg (tapping the Red River of the North running down into the Dakotas), into Lake Manitoba, into Lake Winnipegosis and there joining the great Saskatchewan river, and, by way of Lake Winnipeg, reaching many more waterways of the Canadian northwest, which drain practically that entire great granary of North America. This waterway would reach, from the sea into the interior, four thousand miles and has long been projected. The present Great Lakes—Barge canal—Mohawk river—Hudson waterway has a length of about fifteen hundred miles or more, and taps a great part of industrial America. This route would be impossible without the break, in the Eastern States mountain system, through which the Mohawk flows from a point very close to the watershed of Lake Ontario to sea level at Troy. Thus the history and development of this important link in this inland waterway is of interest to people along the whole route, as, without the Mohawk, this line of transportation would be non-existent.

The Laurentian hills of Quebec province and the Adirondack region comprise some of the oldest land surfaces of the world. Of the latter the Mohawk valley now forms the greater part of the southern border, the hills north of the river in Montgomery county being the first foothills of the Adirondack mountains. When the Adirondack region rose from the ocean, the southern shore was approximately along the northern border of Fulton county and many of the streams now flowing from the north into the Mohawk were rushing mountain torrents which fell from those barren heights into the sea at the shore line mentioned. Some of these were probably the West and East Canada and the Caroga creeks and some others mentioned later. The Mohawk valley was then under the ocean and its rise and emergence from the waters of the sea came at a later date.

After this emergence but before the "birth" of the Mohawk, this region was part of the slope from the Adirondack mountains to the sea, which then flowed along the southern borders of New York during the carboniferous era. Some of the then streams of this drainage slope are supposed to have been the West Canada creek, East Canada creek, Garoga, Cayadutta, North Chuctanunda and Sacandaga.

The Mohawk river dates its geological history from the end of the coal period, when occurred the elevation of the Appalachian range of mountains. This uplift (according to S. L. Frey, in his interesting "Story of Our River") extended through New York state and included Ohio, Indiana, Illinois and Wisconsin and, in consequence, the Great Lakes were formed, with their drainage outlet probably by way of the Illinois river at that time. The Cherry Valley hills were part of this uplift and in this way the Mohawk valley was made between that range of low mountains of which they are a part and the Adirondack highlands.

Mr Frey says: "At the time of the disturbance [raising of the Appalachian range] there had been two important uplifts running north and south at right angles to the Cherry Valley hills. These are called by geologists 'the uplifts of the Mohawk,' one at the Noses and the other at Little Falls. When, therefore, the water could no longer flow south, on account of the hills, or east, on account of the uplifts, it gathered until the basins filled, when all to the east of Little Falls discharged over the top of the uplift at the Noses, and all, to the west of the barrier [Fall Hill] at Little Falls ran west and emptied into the Great Lakes basin. Thus was the Mohawk river formed, a part of it running east and a part west. This condition probably prevailed for a very long period, the river wearing its way into the soft and fissile shale." Here we see the eastern of these early "lakes of the Mohawk," covering a large part of what the Mohawks termed Canajoharie and which was later the Canajoharie and Palatine districts, with which we are dealing in this narrative.

As the ages rolled by, the lowering of the temperature in North America (attributed to a variety of causes) produced the glacial period, during which this part of the continent was covered by an ice sheet (5,000 feet thick in places) as far south as central New Jersey. The glacier, in its southern march, reached the Mohawk valley and the river, which then ran in a deep channel. Says Mr. Frey:

"The ice filled this deep depression, and, turning eastward, followed the course of the river, grinding and grooving and tearing the rocks at the sides and bottom. Of course the uplift at Little Falls was greatly lowered; but it was at the uplift at the Noses that there seems to have been the hardest struggle, and the most enormous amount of grinding and erosion. The glacier seems to have been held back by the peculiar configuration of the hills, at a point just west of Sprakers Basin. The result was the scooping out of a deep trough in the rock, beginning at Gros's rift. This grew deeper as it goes east, the sides of the excavation slope up to the banks and cliffs on each side, and the rock is now buried under deposits of soil and sand, of gravel, boulders and hardpan. The village of Canajoharie (that is the business part of it) stands on a deposit of this character fifty feet in depth. As we go eastward the excavation in the rock grows deeper and deeper and the steep hills seem to surround a great basin and to close the valley. * * * The age of ice lasted long, but it came to an end at last. As the climate grew warm again the ice melted and great floods poured out at the foot of the glacier and, held by the high ridge at the south and by the ice wall at the north, gathered into great lakes. The most northern one, which has been called Lake Agassiz, was where the Red River of the North is and was 600 miles long. The other, called Lake Iroquois, occupied the Great Lakes basin. It is probable that the former discharged into the latter and the outlet, as long as the glacier blocked the St. Lawrence, was by way of the Mohawk valley [to the Hudson valley and the ocean], although there may have been one or two other outlets toward the southwest. But the most of it ran east to the Hudson and was our river on an immense scale. [Here we have the original Great Lakes to the sea waterway through the Mohawk valley.] * * * This great flow of water finished the work of the glacier, made the rounded hills that we see; and the worn, rocky cliffs, finished the cutting of a channel through the uplifts at Little Falls and the Noses, and made an easy grade for canals and rail roads and boulevards." With the continual gradual recession of the ice sheet to the north, the waters of the Great Lakes made their outlet to the sea through the St. Lawrence river. The Mohawk then drained only its own watershed and shrank to its present course. When the forest was here it probably carried a larger volume of water than at present, with its watershed largely denuded.

The total area of the actual Mohawk valley watershed is 3,485 square miles, which is roughly 8 per cent or about one-fourteenth of the state's area.

This Mohawk drainage territory is comprised in the following counties with a very rough estimate of the number of acres in each drained by the Mohawk and its tributaries: Lewis, 20,000; Oneida, 500,000; Madison, 5,000; Herkimer, 500,000; Hamilton, 150,000; Montgomery 250,000; Otsego, 5,000; Fulton, 225,000; Schoharie, 400,000; Delaware, 5,000; Greene (headwaters of Schoharie river), 150,-000; Albany, 30,000; Saratoga, 30,000. This makes thirteen of the state's sixty-one counties, some part of which forms a portion of the Mohawk watershed. Of these thirteen counties, Montgomery is the only one whose territory is entirely within the limits of the Mohawk river drainage system.

The western part of Oneida county is drained by the Oneida lake watershed, while the extreme southern section belongs to the Susquehanna valley, and the extreme northeastern lies in the Black river watershed. The upper portion of Herkimer county (in the Adirondack forest section) is drained by the Black river, and the extreme south lies in the Susquehanna valley. The eastern part of Fulton county belongs to the upper Hudson system, being watered by the Sacandaga and its tributaries. The southern part of Schenectady county drains into the Hudson and a small portion of western Schoharie county is in the Susquehanna valley.

The Mohawk drains a country of high rolling hills, rising into mountains on several of its divides from other adjoining basins. In the central Mohawk region, which is the one under consideration in this work, the edges of the watershed rise to summits of over 2,500 feet on the north and south margins. The divide which separates the Big Sprite (branch of the East creek) and the headwaters of the Caroga from the Sacandaga valley, has summits of the following elevations: In the town of Bleecker, Fulton county, Pigeon Mt. 2,700, Pinnacle 2,514, Shaker Mt. 2,500; in the town of Caroga, Fulton county, adjoining Canada lakes, Pine Mt. 2,200, Camelhump 2,278 and 2,265, Sheeley Mt. 2,120; in the town of Stratford, Fulton county, West Rooster Hill, 2,240. Hills of from five to over eight hundred feet elevation rise from the Mohawk flats themselves. In western Montgomery county, the highest of these is Getman Hill (sea elevation, 1,140 feet and 838 feet above the Mohawk). This summit is almost in the point where the town lines of St. Johnsville, Ephratah and Oppenheim join and is part of the ridge that occupies the northern horizon as seen from old and new Fort Plain. Probably the highest hill rising directly from the Mohawk river flats is Yantapuchaberg, on the south side of the river between Amsterdam and Schenectady. This mountain has a sea elevation of 1,385 feet and rises about 1,150 feet above the Mohawk. Old Yantapuchaberg is one of the most beautiful hills in the Mohawk valley, or anywhere else, with its wooded slopes rising to a forest crested summit. It is an object of the traveler's interest on the Central railroad opposite. Summits, equal in height to those in the Fulton county lake region rise in the Cherry Valley hills on the central southern rim of the watershed.

The Mohawk river bed falls from a sea elevation of 420 feet at Rome to 184 feet at Crescent in Saratoga county. From there the river drops, by Cohoes falls and rapids, to sea level at Troy. In Montgomery county the river elevations vary from 302 feet at St. Johnsville and Fort Plain to 255 feet at Amsterdam. The Mohawk, for over sixty years prior to 1913 was paralleled by canals the greater part of its length. Black River canal follows the course of the east upper head branch of the Mohawk and the main stream from near Boonville to Rome, a distance of over twenty miles, and from Rome to Cohoes the Erie canal follows the river for over 100 miles. The Barge canal largely follows the Mohawk's course from Rome to Cohoes.

It must be remembered that the name Mohawk valley applies to the entire watershed of this important river—to the headwaters of the Schoharie in the Catskills and the lake sources of the West Canada, East Canada and Caroga creeks in the Adirondacks just as much as to the Mohawk itself, along which main stream, the greater part of the population of the Mohawk basin is located and where the major items of human life and activity have had their scene and enactment.

The lakes of the Mohawk basin are confined to the north central rim of the watershed and to the headwaters of the West Canada, East Canada and Caroga creeks. The majority of these lakes and ponds lie in northern Fulton county and include the Canada and Caroga lakes and Peck's pond and its tributary lakes or ponds. Two small lakes or ponds, one at the headwaters of Oriskany creek and the other at the source of the South Chuctanunda are the only ponds of a size worthy of mention on the south side of the Mohawk watershed. Honnedaga Lake, one of the headwater lakes of the West Canada, is the largest and Canada, Caroga, Peck and Jerseyfield lakes are of the second class and about the same area. According to the maps, Honnedaga lake is about four miles long and a mile wide. Canada lake is about two miles long and a half mile wide. The Barge canal reservoirs, Hinckley and Delta, are the largest lakes in the Mohawk watershed although they are, of course, artificial.

Under the heading "A brief topography of the Mohawk valley," Simms writes as follows: "The Mohawk river rises in Lewis county, about 20 miles to the northward of Rome, [near a place called Mohawk Hill] arriving at which place it takes an easterly course, and, at a distance of about 135 miles from its source, enters the Hudson between Troy and Waterford. Its source is near Black river, which, running northwesterly, empties into Lake Ontario. Wood creek also rises northwesterly from Rome and, at a point two miles distant from the bend of the Mohawk, [the old carrying place between Wood creek and the Mohawk] it finds a westerly course into Oneida lake, which discharges into Oswego river and runs into Lake Ontario at Oswego. The Mohawk has two prominent cascades to interrupt its navigation—the Cohoes Falls, not far from its mouth with 70 feet fall, requiring six deep locks on the Erie canal to overcome the ascent, and the Little Falls [also called Canajoharie Falls in the early days], so called as compared with the Cohoes, having a fall of 42 feet, the canal descending 40 feet in a single mile by five locks, averaging about eight feet lift. The mountain barrier at this point through which the water furrowed its way in the long ago, affords some of the most romantic scenery in Central New York. The river in its course through Oneida, Herkimer, Montgomery and Schenectady counties, passes through some of the richest bottom lands or river flats to be found in any country.

"For nearly two centuries the Mohawk was navigated above Schenectady by small water craft, mostly batteaux, [flatboats] around which danced the red man's canoe; but it was always interrupted by the Little Falls, some 58 miles above, which necessitated a carrying place of a mile; and, at a later period, when the waters of Wood creek and Oneida lake were utilized, a carrying place of two miles was established between that creek and the Mohawk, so that boats from Schenectady went to Oswego and back, at first to convey Indian goods and military stores. For the benefit of young readers I may say that, at carrying places, both cargo and boat had to be taken from the water and conveyed around the obstruction by land—usually by teams and extra hands; quite constantly employed—of course, to be relaunched and reloaded to pursue its onward course.

"After the Revolution which had familiarized the whole country with the rich lands of western New York, from which the Indians had mostly been driven by their sympathy with Britain, many citizens from New England—not a few of whom had been soldiers—removed thither, especially to Ontario county. * * * Some of these settlers moved up the Mohawk valley with ox-teams and covered wagons, while others journeyed in boats from Schenectady, their cattle being driven along the river roads. Parties by water were often composed of several families, to aid each other at the carrying places, as also to guard against any and every danger. The valley soon became a thoroughfare for thousands passing through it, and the travel has gone on increasing, with improved facilities, until millions by rail are now speeding along, where thousands sought their way by river craft and private conveyances or, a little later, by canal craft and stages. The world, at times, now seems hurrying to and fro through the valley.

"The Mohawk valley is not only wonderfully beautified but its fertility is greatly increased by the numerous tributaries, large and small, entering the river upon both shores, which afford advantageous mill-sites for hundreds of mills and manufactories, employing the labor of many thousands of operatives."

Regarding Wood creek, which was formerly connected by a canal with the Mohawk at Rome, Spafford wrote in 1824, as follows: "Wood creek of the Oneida lake, long so famous for its navigation, on which millions of property have been wafted and large armies—a little stream over which a man may almost step—deserves notice for its historic importance in days of yore, the rather as it now is lost sight of and will soon be forgotten, merged in the glories of the Erie canal."

Simms gives a list of the tributaries of the Mohawk of which the following are the principal, with the points at which they enter the river. Commencing at Rome, on the south side of the Mohawk, descending the valley are the following: Oriskany at Oriskany; Saquoit, near Whitesboro; Furnace creek at Frankfort; Steele's creek at Ilion; Nowadaga (also called Inchunando, Conowadaga) at Indian Castle; Otsquago at Fort Plain; Canajoharie at Canajoharie; Plattekill or Flat creek at Sprakers; Wasontha (Yatesville) at Randall; Oghrackie or Arieskill at Auriesville; Schoharie river at Fort Hunter; Tuechtanonda, or Little Chuctanunda or South Chuctanunda at Amsterdam (south side); Cowilla, opposite Cranesville; Zantzee, near Hoffman's Ferry; Plotterkill, a little distance below; Bennekill, just above Schenectady; Donker's Kill between Schenectady and the mouth of the Mohawk.

Beginning on the north side and going down the river from Rome are the following tributary streams: No. 6, Mile creek, two and a half miles from Rome; No. 9 Mile creek, seven miles from Rome; Rasceloth or Sterling creek in the town of Schuyler; Teughtaghnarow or West Canada creek, below Herkimer; Ciohana or East Canada creek. at East Creek (called also Gayohara); Crum Creek; Fox's creek, [or Timmermans creek] at Upper St. Johnsville; Zimmerman's creek at St. Johnsville; Mother creek, between St. Johnsville and Palatine Church; Caroga at Palatine Church; Kanagara [or Knayderack] at the county home [Schenck's]; Cayadutta at Fonda; Dadanoscara at DeGraff's; Kayaderosseros at Fort Johnson; Chuctanunda, or North Chuctanunda, at Amsterdam; Eva's Kill at Cranesville; Lewis Kill and Vertkill, above Schenectady; Alplauskill and Anthonykill, between Schenectady and Troy.

The foregoing treats of the geological history and topography of the Mohawk and its valley. The following chapter tells of early navigation on the river, which formed such an important feature of life along the Mohawk during the two centuries from 1609 to 1825.

CHAPTER VI.

1609-1795—Traffic and Travel on the Mohawk River—Canoes, Dugouts, Skiffs, Batteaux—Carries at Little Falls and Wood Creek—1792, Inland Lock Navigation Co.—1795, Canals and Locks at Little Falls, German Flats and Rome—Schenectady and Durham Boats and River Packets—1821-1825, Mohawk Part of Erie Canal System—1825, Erie Canal Supersedes River as Valley Waterway.

This is the second chapter dealing with the Mohawk river. It is also the first chapter dealing with transportation and commerce along that stream, either by land or water. This chapter, concerning Mohawk river traffic from 1609 to 1825, is to be followed by others treating of bridges, turnpikes, Erie canal, railroads, Barge canal, etc., making in all seven or eight sketches on this subject. Even Atwood's aeroplane journey over the course of the Mohawk might fittingly be included in this chronicle of three centuries of traffic and travel through the valley. Persons interested in this subject separately can follow the story in the chapters aforementioned as they are published in their chronological order, just as the same procedure may be carried out in the consideration of the chapters dealing with the Mohawk river, as suggested in the last chapter. Agriculture, manufacturing and transportation are said to form a triangle comprising the business life of a country or region. The following opens up the interesting subject of transportation in the Mohawk valley during three centuries.

The first settlers of New York in the Hudson valley adopted water transportation as the forests were generally impassable, except over the Indian trails. Travel by water or on foot were the first methods used in the Mohawk valley. The history of transportation along the Mohawk may be epitomized in the following methods of freight and passenger carriage: Man carriage, canoe, dugout, skiff, flatboat, raft, skates, snowshoes, saddle-horse, pack-horse, oxcart, sled, chaise, coach, sulky, wagon, covered big (Conestoga) wagon, stage coach, large river boat, buggy, canal boat, canal packet boat, railroad coach, railroad freight car, steam tug, horse car, steam launch, steam yacht, bicycle, electric trolley car, automobile, motor bus, motor truck, motor cycle, motor boat, motor tug, aeroplane, canal barge.

Mohawk river traffic may be briefly summarized as follows: The Mohawk Indians, living on the river shores and frequently changing their habitations from the south to the north side and back again, used bark canoes and dugouts to traverse the river. These were doubtless also used by the first white explorers and traders. After Schenectady was settled, in the lower Mohawk valley in 1661, probably the flat-bottomed "scow skiff," propelled by oars, made its appearance. From this was evolved the larger flat or flatboat or batteau, propelled by oars, poles and sails. These boats were in use by traders, settlers and soldiers to carry goods, farm produce and war material until after the Revolution. They carried from one to two tons, their size being determined by the fact that they had to make two land carries on the river trip. The Inland Lock Navigation Co. was formed in 1792 and the building of locks and canals, at Little Falls, German Flats and Rome in 1795 made larger boats possible. The Durham and Schenectady boats of ten tons burden, made their appearance, poles and sails being the propelling forces employed by the Mohawk sailors of a century ago. The smaller batteaux also continued in use. From 1795 to 1825 the river was a lively line of traffic, even passenger packets being in use. From 1821-1825 the Mohawk was utilized as a part of the Erie canal system and when the canal had been dug from Rome to Little

Falls, the canal boats entered the river at the latter place and continued their journey to Schenectady on the Mohawk. Later when the canal was finished from Rome to Sprakers boats left the canal near the Noses and continued on by the river to their destination at Schenectady. In 1826 Erie navigation began and the Mohawk ceased to be used as a trade route. Many of the river boatmen and some of their craft, however, continued their work on the new canal, which eclipsed the river until these latter days of the Barge canal.

———

From the days of the Mohawk canoes and dugouts and those of the first Indian traders, the river was the artery of trade between the east and the far west. From Albany to Schenectady was a portage and also around the Cohoes falls. From these points the boats called batteaux or flatboats soon came into use by the white settlers and traders. The river was followed to Little Falls where there was another carry by land around the rapids, although these were sometimes shot by venturesome boatmen on the down trip when the river was swollen. At Wood creek was a third carry from the Mohawk. Canals were built at Little Falls and Wood Creek in 1795.

Before this at Little Falls sleds and wagons were used to carry the batteaux around the portage. These batteaux were flat-bottomed scows of sufficient dimensions to carry several tons and were propelled by setting poles which were kept for sale at convenient points along the river. With backs to the prow the batteaux men thrust the poles to the river's bed and, bearing hard upon them and walking aft, laboriously pushed the boat against the current. A sort of harmony of movement was secured by the captains by the cries, "Bowsmen up!" and "Second men up!" Steering was done with a tiller oar. Such was the mode of transporting merchandise and Indian commodities to and from the west for nearly two centuries; and such, too, the method of transporting munitions of war during the Revolution. Much of the material used in building defenses like Fort Plain was brought up this way and convoying batteaux flotilla containing war supplies was frequently part of the duties of the militia and regulars located here and in surrounding districts. Revolutionary captains in the batteaux service were in 1832 made entitled to the same pensions as captains in the Continental army.

Small batteaux, known in those times as three-handed and four-handed boats, were in early use on the Mohawk. They were so called because three or four men were required to propel and care for them. Passing the carry at Little Falls in early days, the boats proceeded to Fort Stanwix where the carry was made to Wood creek, whence they floated into and through Oneida lake and the Oswego river to Oswego where they entered Lake Ontario. From Oswego to Niagara, then a place of much importance, merchandise was transported in the same boats or aboard sloops. This was the water route to the west until the completion of the Erie canal in 1825.

The earliest boatmen were troubled by the Indians who took toll for the navigation of the river and who were particularly threatening and rapacious at the Wood creek carry. The rifts in the river offered a serious menace to this form of transportation and wrecks and drownings were not infrequent. On the down trip the flood times were welcomed as overcoming this trouble and this must have been a favorite time for making the journey east. On the up trip over the rifts the polemen were assisted by men on shore with ropes. Rude sails were also used during favoring winds and sails, oars and poles were the three methods of propelling the white man's boats on the Mohawk for two centuries.

It was not until 1800 that the turnpikes were improved sufficiently to compete with the Mohawk in matters of transportation, and the river, at the Revolutionary period, was the main artery of traffic and remained so for some time. Schenectady then was a lively river port and important town to the Mohawk valley people.

The first rift or rapids, above Schenectady, was met with, at a distance of six miles, and was called Six Flats Rift. Proceeding west in order came Fort Hunter rift, Caughnawaga rift at Fultonville, Keator's rift at Sprakers, the greatest in the river, having a fall of ten feet in a few rods; Brandywine rift at Canajoharie, short but rapid; Ehle's rift, near Fort Plain; Kneiskern's rift, a small rapid near the upper Indian Castle and a little above the river dam; the Little Falls, so called in contradistinction to the great Falls at Cohoes; Wolf's rift, five miles above the falls.

At Fort Plain, a bend in the river opposite the house of Peter Ehle from whom the rift took its name was known as Ehle's crank; and opposite the residence of Nicholas Gros, a little below, another turn in the river was called Gros's crank.

At the Little Falls, a descent of 40 feet in half a mile, boats could not be forced up the current and it became a carrying place for them and merchandise, which were transported around the rapids, usually on the north shore, at first on sleds and later on wagons with small wide rimmed wheels. The water craft were then relaunched and reloaded and proceeded on their western journey. On such occasions, one of the party usually stayed with the goods deposited above while the team returned for the boat.

The difficulties of forcing the boats over the rifts of the Mohawk increased with their size. As many as twenty men, pulling with ropes on the bank and pushing with poles on the boat, were sometimes unable to propel a single boat over Keator's rift. Black slaves, owned by settlers near the rapids, were frequently employed in this occupation.

An early traveler writes as follows of this waterway: "The Oniada Lake, situated near the head of the River Oswego, receives the waters of Wood Creek, which takes its rise not far from the Mohawk River. These two lie so adjacent to each other that a junction is effected by sluices at Fort Stanwix. * * * * Here [Little Falls] the roaring rapids interrupted all navigation, empty boats not even being able to pass over them. The early portage, of one mile here in sleds over the swampy ground, has been described as it was in 1756, when enterprising Teutons residing here transferred all boats in sleds over marshy ground which 'would admit of no wheel carriage.' * * * Later on, about 1790, we find that the Germans' sleds were out of use and that boats were transferred on wheeled vehicles appropriately fashioned to carry them without damage to their hulls. No great boats could be transferred by such means; this fact had a tendency to limit the carrying capacity of Mohawk batteaus to about one and a half tons." Johan Jost Herkimer, father of Nicholas Herkimer, was a pioneer in this carrying business at "The Falls" and here laid the foundation of a considerable fortune.

Washington mentions the advantages of the Mohawk valley waterway and after the Revolution efforts were made to improve it and many plans were put forward, some bearing a rude resemblance to the present barge canal dams. To this end the Inland Lock Navigation company was incorporated March 30, 1792, Gen. Philip Schuyler being elected its president. Locks and canals were built at Little Falls, at Wolfs Rift at German Flats, and at Rome, connecting with Wood Creek. These canals were constructed about 1795, prior to which time there were carries at Little Falls and Wood Creek. These river locks and canals continued in use until 1825, the year of the opening of the Erie canal.

After the river improvements were made the Durham boat was substituted for the unwieldly batteaux. The Durham boat was of ten or fifteen tons capacity and had sharpened bows. Cleats were along the sides to give the polemen's feet better purchase and a small caboose was the crew's storehouse and the cooking was done on shore, where fuel was plenty. It is related that one of these boats left Utica in the morning and reached Schenectady on the evening of the same day, which was considered a record trip. The expense of transportation from Albany to Schenectady was 16 cents per 100 pounds. From Schenectady to Utica, 75 cents and from Utica to Oswego $1.25, making a through rate of $2.16 per 100 pounds. This would give $43.20 per ton as the freight rate between Schenectady and Oswego, less than 200 miles. In 1913 the rate per ton by lake boats from Buffalo to Duluth, about 700 miles, was 39 cents.

The river improvements and cost of transportation made the enterprise un profitable and the company sold out to the state in 1820. With the building of the Erie canal the traffic boat men disappeared from the Mohawk. It is probable that at Fort Plain was a landing for batteaux, during the life time of the post, and afterward for the larger boats. Possibly the Otsquago was here deep where it traversed the level flatland for a half mile and bat teaux may have been able to penetrate its still waters up to the Clarke house and Paris store.

Along the river road, near some of the rapids, were public houses, a good share of whose custom came from the boatmen. As near these runs as possible, boats often tied up for the night and here a lot of old Mohawk sailors had jolly times. Jost Spraker's tavern, at Keator's rift, was one of those. Another riverman's favorite tavern was the old Isaac Weatherby house at Brandywine rift, situated a mile below Palatine Bridge, and below the junction of the Oswegatchie and the river roads.

Accidents, drownings and wrecks were many. Two which occurred near Fort Plain, shortly before the Erie was opened, are described by Simms as follows: "Ezra Copley in 1823 ran a Durham boat on a rock in Ehle's rift, below the Fort Plain bridge. It was loaded with wheat in bulk, was stove and filled with water. The wheat was taken to Ehle's barn and dried, the boat was repaired, reloaded and went on its destination. One of the best of this class of craft, known as the 'Butterfly,' was descending the river, swollen by floods, when the steersman lost control of it and it struck broadside on one of the stone piers of the Canajoharie bridge and broke near the centre. The contents of the boat literally filled the river for some distance and three hands were drowned. The body of one, named Clark, was recovered twelve miles below at Fultonville. The steersman retained his hold on the long tiller (some 20 feet long) and reached shore about a quarter mile below the bridge. Most of the flour on the boat was saved along the river. The owner of the craft, a man named Meyers, had the boat's fragments taken to Schenectady and rebuilt. After this it was taken through the newly completed Erie canal to Cayuga lake. Here, while making a trip loaded with gypsum, it sank and its owner was drowned. Thus ended the unfortunate 'Butterfly,' one of the last of the freight craft that sailed the Mohawk." Many of the river boats probably found early use on the Erie canal, after 1825. In the last few years (1821-1825) of canal construction the Mohawk was used in connection with the completed portions of the Erie canal for the transportation of canal boats from the west to Schenectady and vice versa, notably from Little Falls and later from Sprakers, to Schenectady.

Several large rowboats, constructed especially to carry twenty passengers each, from Utica to Schenectady, and tastefully curtained, were in use on the Mohawk at about 1800. They were called river packets.

Christian Schultz, who journeyed on the river in 1807, spoke of there being three kinds of boats on the Mohawk—the Schenectady boats being preferred, which carried about ten tons when the river would permit. He said they usually progressed 18 to 25 miles per day up the stream by sails and poles. These boats, modeled much like the Long Island round-bottomed skiffs, were 40 to 50 feet in length and were steered by a large swing oar of

the same length. When the wind favored they set a square sail and a top sail. He was informed that one "galley," the "Mohawk Register," had gone at the rate of six miles an hour against the stream and he adds: "During this time, believe me, nothing could be more charming than sailing on the Mohawk." They did not often have a favorable wind and the curves in the river rendered the course of a boat irregular and the use of sails precarious, on which account their chief dependence was upon their pike poles, which it required much experience to use to advantage.

Of the poles and the manner of using them on the river boats, Mr. Schultz gives the following account: "These poles are from 18 to 22 feet in length, having a sharp pointed iron with a socket weighing 10 to 12 pounds affixed to the lower end; the upper has a large knob called a button mounted upon it, so that the poleman may press upon it with his whole weight without endangering his person. This manner of impelling the boat forward is extremely laborious, and none but those who have been some time accustomed to it, can manage these poles with any kind of advantage. Within the boat on each side is fixed a plank running fore and aft with a number of cleats nailed upon it, for the purpose of giving the poleman sure footing and hard poling. The men, after setting the poles against the rock, bank or bottom of the river, declining their heads very low, place the upper end or button against the back part of their shoulder, then falling on their hands and toes creep the whole length of the gang boards and send the boat forward at considerable speed. The first sight of four men on each side of the boat, creeping along on their hands and toes, apparently transfixed by a huge pole, is no small curiosity; nor was it until I perceived their perseverance for 200 or 300 yards, that I became satisfied they were not playing some pranks.

"From the general practise of this method, as likewise from my own trials and observations, I am convinced that they have fallen upon the most powerful way possible to exert their bodily strength for the purpose required. The position, however, was so extremely awkward to me, that I doubt whether the description I have given will adequately describe the procedure. I have met with another kind of boat on the river, which is called a dorm or dorem; how it is spelled I know not. [This was the Durham boat and the third boat to which he alludes was the batteau, propelled by oars.] The only difference I could observe in this [the Durham] from the former one, is that it is built sharp on both ends, and generally much larger and stouter. They likewise have flats [scows] similar to those seen on the Susquehanna, but much lighter built and larger. On all these they occasionally carry the sails before mentioned.

"The Mohawk is by no means dangerons to ascend, on account of the slowness of the boat's progress; but as it is full of rocks, stones and shallows, there is some risk of staving the boat and, at this season [probably midsummer], is so low as to require the boat to be dragged over many places. The channel, in some instances, is not more than eight feet in width [the boats were long and narrow], which will barely permit a boat to pass by rubbing on both sides. This is sometimes caused by natural or accidental obstructions of rocks in the channel, but oftener by artificial means. This, which at first view would appear to be an inconvenience, is produced by two lines or ridges of stone, generally constructed on sandy, gravelly or stony shallows, in such manner as to form an acute angle where they meet, the extremities of which widen as they extend up the river, while at the lower end there is just space enough left to admit the passage of a boat. The water being thus collected at the widest part of these ridges, and continually pent up within narrower limits as it descends, causes a rise at the passage; so that where the depth was no more than eight inches before, a contrivance of this kind will raise it to twelve; and strange as it may appear, a boat drawing fifteen inches will pass through it with safety and ease. The cause is simply this: The boat, being somewhat below the passage, its resistance to the current is such as to cause a swell of four or five inches more, which affords it an easy passage over the shoal."

The reader must remember that at this time, the waters of the Erie then having their channel in the Mohawk, the river was of considerable more volume than it was after the building of the canal.

This writer says that the Mohawk might be considered 100 yards in width with extremely fertile banks. He speaks of passing through eight locks at Little Falls, whereas two of these were at Wolf's rift, several miles above. He said the Mohawk afforded very poor fishing, since at the end of nine days he had only caught a "poor cat fish, no longer than a herring." He visited Utica, which then had 160 houses, and Whitestown.

Of Rome he says: "Rome * * * is near the head of the Mohawk. The entrance into this village is through a handsome canal about a mile in length. It is here that the Mohawk is made to contribute a part of its stream towards filling Wood creek, which of itself is so low in dry seasons as to be totally insufficient to float a boat without the aid of the Mohawk. Rome, formerly known as Fort Stanwix, is delightfully situated in an elevated and level country commanding an extensive view for miles around. This village consists of about 80 houses, but it seems quite destitute of every kind of trade, and rather upon the decline. The only spirit which I perceived stirring among them was that of money digging, and the old fort betrayed evident signs of the prevalence of this mania, as it had literally been turned inside out for the purpose of discovering concealed 'treasures.'"

In descending Wood creek he passed through a range of five canal locks. He spoke of the rate of toll as being too high. He said the toll, in passing the eight locks at Little Falls, was

$2.25 per ton of merchandise, and the toll on the boat was from $1.50 to $2.62½ each boat. The toll was at a still higher rate to pass through the Wood creek locks, being $3.00 per ton on the goods and from $1.50 to $3.50 on the boats.

In 1807, at the time of Mr. Schultz's trip up the Mohawk, he passed the following towns to which is added a rough estimate of their population at that time: Schenectady, several thousand; Amsterdam, 150; Caughnawaga (Fonda), 200; Canajoharie, 200; Fort Plain, 200; Little Falls, 300; Herkimer, 300; Utica, 1,200; Whitestown; Rome, 500. Johnstown, only three miles from the Mohawk, had probably 600 and was the third town in importance in the valley. Montgomery county, in 1807 and up to 1817, extended westward from the Schenectady county line to Fall Hill. Schenectady was the most important town in the state west of Albany in 1807.

The Rev. Mr. Taylor, previously alluded to, gives an interesting account of the Little Falls locks and the Little Falls country itself in 1802: "Passing on from Manheim, we found the mountains drawing to a point upon two sides of the river. When we come to the river there is only a narrow pass for about three-fourths of a mile between the river and the foot of the rocks. When we come to the Falls the scene which it presents is sublime. We now enter Herkimer county—a small village of the town of Herkimer, called Little Falls, by which the canals pass, which were constructed in [17]95. The length of the canal is three-fourths of a mile. There are six locks. The appearance of the falls is sublime. The village is built upon a ledge of rocks. It promises fair to be a place of business as to trade, as all produce of the Royal grants will naturally be brought here to be shipped. They have a new and beautiful meeting house, standing about 40 rods back on the hill, built in the form of an octagon. I am now, July 27 [1802], about 30 rods from fall mountain on the south. Between this and the mountain is the Mohawk, and a bridge over

it, in length about 16 rods. Between this and the bridge is the canal. On the right about 40 rods are the falls, or one bar of the falls in full view. The falls extend about three-fourths of a mile. Upon the whole, the place is the most romantic of any I ever saw; and the objects are such as to excite sublime ideas in a reflecting mind. From the appearance of the rocks, and fragments of rocks where the town is built, it is, I think, demonstratably evident that the waters of the Mohawk, in passing over the fall, were 80 or 90 feet higher, in some early period, than they are now. The rocks, even a hundred feet perpendicular above the present high water mark, are worn in the same manner as those over which the river passes. The rocks are not only worn by the descent of the water, but in the flat rocks are many round holes, worn by the whirling of stones—some even 5 feet and 20 inches over. If these effects were produced by the water, as I have no doubt they were, then it follows as a necessary consequence, that the flats above and all the lowlands for a considerable extent of the country, were covered with water, and that here was a lake—but the water, having lowered, its bed, laid the lands above dry."

In regard to the foregoing speculations of the Rev. John Taylor the following from the Fort Plain Standard of August 1, 1912, is of interest:

"The Mohawk valley, and especially that section of it at Little Falls, is a classic example among geographers. Not only is the Little Falls gorge the only low pass over the Appalachian Highlands between Canada and Alabama through which easy access is made from the Atlantic to the West, but is is also an extremely interesting place in itself. The Mohawk river at one time had its source at Little Falls while a westward flowing stream ran from that point to where now is Lake Ontario. During the glacial period the gorge was partly scooped out by ice, then for a time, while the St. Lawrence river was obstructed by ice, the Great Lakes had their outlet through the Mohawk valley instead of the St. Lawrence and Little Falls rivalled Niagara. Today the evidences of the work of ice and water, and also of far more ancient earthquake and volcanic action, are to be seen in unusual clearness at the Little Falls gorge." This item was anent the visit to Little Falls of leading geographers of the world in 1912.

The batteaux and boats of the Mohawk were the natural predecessors of the Erie packets and canal boats, the Central freight car, coach and Pullman and the 3,000 ton barge. To the Mohawk and the utilization of its stream for transportation, is due much of the subsequent development of the communities along its banks and of New York state in general.

CHAPTER VII.

1609-1913—Mohawk Valley Transportation — Indian Trails — Horse and Cart Roads, Highways (1700-1800) —Turnpikes and Mohawk Turnpike (1800-1840) — County Roads (1840-1885)—Bicycle Routes (1885-1900)— Automobile Roads (1900-1913) — Weed's 1824 Stage Coach Journey on the Mohawk Turnpike.

This chapter, dealing with the Mohawk valley highways, is the second one describing transportation in the Mohawk valley. The first, published just before this one, covered traffic on the Mohawk river. Others follow treating of bridges, the Erie canal, railroads and the Barge canal. The highways are the most important and basic element in the matter of transportation, and their history and the life on the Mohawk thoroughfares are therefore of prime interest to all the valley inhabitants.

The early highways and rude roads of our valley generally followed the Indian trails. These trails were good, though only two or three feet wide and "in many places, the savages kept the woods clear from underbrush by burning over large tracts." All streams had to be forded, except where the few ferries were, and these fords often determined the location of roads. Trees were felled across narrow streams to make footbridges and the colonial governments frequently ordered these made. "When new paths were cut through the forests, the settlers 'blazed' the trees, that is they chopped a piece of bark off tree after tree, standing on the side of the way. Thus the 'blazes' stood out clear and white in the dark shadows of the forests, like welcome guide-posts, showing the traveler his way."

The Indian trails covered eastern New York and connected the various Iroquois villages with each other or led to hunting and fishing grounds (like the Otsquago and Caroga trails) or into or towards these grounds and the countries of the enemies of the Mohawks and their brother tribes— such as the trail which ran from Canada to the Sacandaga and through Johnstown, Stone Arabia and Palatine to the ford at the mouth of the Caroga, there connecting with the Otsquago trail. The explorers, soldiers, traders and "wood-runners" used these Indian trails and the first white settlers utilized them as roads as a matter of course, because, like the buffalo trails of the great west, they connected the most important points and watercourses and lakes by the shortest and easiest routes. These western buffalo trails were also Indian trails and are now trunk line railroads. So the trails naturally became the first valley highways and most of the more important of these today are the Indian trails, enlarged, improved, straightened and graded. Of those of western Montgomery county are the north and south shore Mohawk turnpikes, the old Caroga road leading to the Caroga, Canada and other lakes of northern Fulton county and into the Adirondack country, the Canadian trail aforementioned leading from Lake George through Johnstown and Stone Arabia to the mouth of the Caroga, and the Otsquago valley road beginning at the other side of the Caroga ford and running to Otsego lake, the headwaters of the Susquehanna and into the Iroquois country.

Over the old Indian valley trails

or on the river came the first Dutch explorers and traders with their Iroquois guides and helpers and the early French explorers and priests with their Algonquin aids and guides. Following them came the Dutch, German and British settlers carrying their goods on their backs, on packhorses or in oxcarts or horsecarts—many of their fellow pioneers toiling painfully up against the current of the river in flatboats to their new homes in the Mohawk wilderness. Still later with the settlement and clearing of farms, these hardy men widened and cleared the trails and blazed new ones over which they transported farm and forest produce in their rude wooden sleds and carts. Probably the first valley cartroad was the one between Albany and Schenectady after the settlement of Schenectady in 1661.

Prior to 1800, and even later, these farm carts and wooden sleds were made on the farm. Just as all food and raw materials (such as hemp, flax, wool, etc.) were grown by the husbandman on his own lands, so was everything he and his family used made there. This necessitated an endless round of toil on the farm, from sunrise until after sunset all the year round excepting part of Sundays, but it made the farmer self-supporting, self-sufficient and independent of the world outside his own personal domain. Each farm was a kingdom unto itself. Every homestead had its carpenter's room or bench, just as it had its soap kettle, cheese room and smoke house (and occasional ice house), and all tools, implements, vehicles and rude farm machinery were made on the farm by the farmer himself. The nearest blacksmith shop supplied the necessary ironwork.

Later the valley trails, or the cartroads they were turned into, were used by the American and British troops and their baggage trains during the Revolution. Following their gradual improvement and the great immigration and traffic following the war for independence came the turnpikes, coincident with the building of bridges. Probably by 1800 the majority of our Mohawk valley highway system had been constructed, but it had for its basis the old Indian trails of the Mohawks. None of these improvements such as highways and bridges came of themselves but were the result of the strenuous work of the early valley men.

After 1783, it was found necessary to improve transportation facilities in the Mohawk valley to accommodate its population and the tide of emigration pouring through it to the west. Roads were improved, bridges constructed and taverns built or remodeled from farmhouses on the lines of travel. New towns and counties were also formed as told in prior chapters.

In April, 1790, the state legislature voted "£100 for the purpose of erecting a bridge across the East Canada creek, not exceeding three miles from the mouth thereof, upon the road from the Mohawk river to the Royal Grant." In 1793 commissioners were appointed by the legislature with directions to build "a bridge over the East Canada creek, nearly opposite Canajoharie Castle, on the public road leading from Tribes Hill to the Little Falls."

About 1790 stages made weekly trips in the valley and daily trips after the completion of the Mohawk turnpike. The completion of the Schoharie bridge at Fort Hunter and the construction of the Great Western turnpike from Albany westward marked the year 1798. This route connected with the Mohawk at Canajoharie by stages which ran from Roof's tavern where the Hotel Wagner stands.

The most important of all the valley roads are north and south shore turnpikes which traverse the shores of the Mohawk for a distance of about ninety miles between Schenectady and Rome. In future days these will be splendid highways and are today most important roads, the north shore or Mohawk turnpike being one of the historic roads of North America and an important part of the trunk highway between New York and Buffalo, largely paralleling the Central railroad system, trolley systems and the Barge canal. Chapter V. of this work gives a French account of these two river highways in 1756, covering the distance mentioned from Rome to Schenectady.

Prior to 1800 the south shore road seems to have been the more important but since that time the north shore or Mohawk turnpike has been the major one. Over the Mohawk turnpike vast quantities of crops, raw material and merchandise were transported in the half century comprised in the latter years of the eighteenth and early part of the nineteenth centuries. It has figured as a Mohawk Indian trail (until 1700), cart and horse path (1700-1750), wagon and stage road (1750-1836), freight wagon turnpike (1800-1840), bicycle and automobile touring route (1890-1913) and has a future, among other things, as a freight and passenger motor car line. It is paralleled (1913) throughout by the New York Central railroad and by trolley lines from Rome to Cohoes, with the exception of a gap between Little Falls and Fonda, which doubtless will be connected ere long. The Mohawk turnpike shares, with the Mohawk river and the early Erie canal the glory of having been one of the valley travel routes' by way of which hundreds of thousands of the ancestors of the present day westerners made their way to new homes, prior to the building of the railroads and even for a number of years thereafter.

The building of bridges over the East and West Canada creeks in 1793 made the north shore road the favorite valley route, and the next forward step was the improvement of this Mohawk turnpike from Schenectady to Utica. The charter for its construction was granted April 4, 1800.

Seth Wetmore, Levi Norton, Ozias Bronson, Hewitt Hills and three others were the first board of directors. This road was also called the Albany turnpike.

The Mohawk turnpike connected at Schenectady with the Mohawk and Hudson turnpike to Albany, the two forming a continuous trade route over one hundred miles in length from Albany and the Hudson valley to Rome and thence to the Great Lakes and western New York and the Great West.

"The charter of the Utica and Schenectady Railroad company, granted in 1833, required it, before beginning transportation, to purchase the rights of the Mohawk Turnpike Co. and to assume the responsibilities of the latter. One of these responsibilities was that of keeping the turnpike in repair. It was provided however that the railroad company might abandon the turnpike, giving notice to the commissioners of highways, and after such notice it should be kept in order in the same manner as other highways. The railroad company for a time took toll on the turnpike and kept it in repair, but subsequently removed the gates and became responsible for the maintenance of only a part of the old highway."

With the opening of the Erie canal in 1825, traffic on the Mohawk turnpike began to diminish as the freight wagons could not compete with the canal boats during the summer months. Probably they had a considerable use for a number of years, on the north turnpike in winter and on other Mohawk valley roads, to the north and south, all the year round. The stages continued to largely carry the valley passenger traffic, sharing it with the Erie canal packets in the summer months until after the building of the Utica and Schenectady railroad in 1836. This railroad, like any other railroad, was and is merely a highway with an iron bed carrying, by mechanical motive power, greatly enlarged editions of the turnpike stages and freight wagons. Stages continued in use on other Mohawk valley roads until the present day.

The legislature in 1802 authorized the opening of certain roads in the state, and in pursuance of this act, the highway called the State road, leading from Johnstown in a northwestern direction to the Black River country, was opened. It was subsequently much used while that part of the country was being settled by emigrants from the east.

The improvement of the road, leading from Schenectady to Utica along the south side of the Mohawk was deemed expedient, and commissioners were appointed in 1806 to direct the work, their instructions being to strighten the existing road and open it to a width of fifty feet. The towns through which it passed were required to repair and maintain it if their population was not too small.

The following from Simms's "Frontiersmen of New York," gives a good picture of the Mohawk turnpike and life thereon during the early nineteenth century:

"While the Mohawk was literally filled with boats of different kinds—for nearly every family living upon its banks had some kind of one—and Schenectady was a live town for receiving and dispatching freight on and off them—large wagons were used in competition with them in the transportation of merchandise and produce to and from western New York. The produce—wheat, whiskey and potash—came to Albany, from whence merchandise was returned. These wagons, covered with canvas, and drawn by three to eight horses, were seen in numbers on the western and Mohawk turnpikes. The leaders usually had a little bell fastened upon the headstall. Mr. Alonzo Crosby, long superintendent of the eastern part of the western turnpike, counted up to 50 or more taverns between Albany and Cherry Valley, in the distance of 52 miles. Palatine Church, a hamlet at that time of some importance on the Mohawk turnpike, was 61 miles from Albany, the inns in that distance also averaging one to every mile. Indeed, innkeepers were neighbors on those roads for a hundred miles to the westward of Albany. At this period tavern keeping was a lucrative business, especially for the houses prepared with inclosed sheds and good stabling.

"The horses before these wagons, which, at times, had a hundred or more bushels of wheat on, never trav-eled out of a walk. At the period of their use, brakes were unknown in descending hills, but a heavy iron shoe was used on the six-inch tire, which could be thrown from the wheel at the foot of a hill by a spring managed by the foot of the driver. The teamsters usually went on foot, whip in hand, and their constant travel had worn a good foot-path along each side of the road, near the fence, a hundred miles from Albany. The horses were seldom stabled nights, but had an oilcloth covering and were fed from a box or trough carried along and attached to the pole, which could not fall to the ground. The rear of the wagon was ornamented with a tar bucket and a water pail. The wagons were painted blue or slate color, and the covering remained white. A small box was secured upon one side or end of the wagon, containing a hammer, wrench, currycomb, etc. Those wagons paid no toll as they filled the ruts made by farm wagons. Some of the teams were driven by a single line on the forward nigh horse, and occasionally a postillion was seen on the nigh wheel horse; but those large Pennsylvania horses were so well trained as to be dexterously managed with a long leathern whip. When it was heavy traveling, those monster wagons progressed but a few miles in a day, sometimes being two weeks in going from Albany to Geneva, Canandaigua or Rochester. Freight or merchandise west was, at first, one dollar a hundred from Albany to Utica. Although there were so many taverns on the road, still so numerous were the teams that, at times, one of a party in company was mounted and sent forward before night to secure accommodations with a good wagon-yard inclosure.

"From two to ten of these large wagons were sometimes seen in company, some of them carrying from three to four tons. The horses were usually fat. Some carried a jack-screw for raising an axle to take off a wheel; but this was seldom done, as a hole for pouring in tar or grease was made for the purpose. In ascending hills, the wagon was blocked at intervals with a stone, carried by the teamster behind it. After those mammoth wagons were supplanted by the Erie canal, several of them might have been seen about the old Loucks tavern, [in Albany] as also at Paul Clark's inn in the southwest part of Albany, where some of them rotted down.

"On the Mohawk turnpike, as remembered by Andrew A. Fink, George Wagner and others, were the following inn-keepers from Herkimer (80 miles from Albany) descending the valley. They may not be named in the order in which they stood: John Rasback, John Potter, Heacock; across West Canada creek, Nathaniel Etheridge, Upham, James Artcher, a teamster married one of his daughters. This inn had a peculiar sign. On one side was painted a gentleman richly clad and elegantly mounted on horseback with this motto, 'I am going to law.' On the reverse side was a very dilapidated man on a horse, the very picture of poverty, saying, 'I have been to law.' [Continuing the list] John McCombs, Warner Dygert; at Little Falls, John Sheldon, Carr, Harris, Major Morgan; below the Falls, A. A. Fink. From Fink's to East Creek is five miles, and in that distance were 13 dwellings, 12 of which were taverns occupied as follows: Bauder; William Smith, his sign had on it an Indian chief; John Petrie, Henry Shults, James Van Valkenburgh, Lawrence Timmerman, John Wagner, Owens, Nathan Christie, Esq., David Richtmyer, Frederick Getman, James and Luther Pardee; below East Creek, John Stauring, Van Dresser, James Billington, John Bancker, Michael U. Bauder, Yates, Jacob Failing, a favorite place for large wagons; Zimmerman, Joseph Klock, Christian Klock, Daniel C. Nellis, John C. Nellis, Brown, Gen. Peter C. Fox, at Palatine Church; George Fox, John C. Lipe, George Wagner, Charles Walrath, Harris, Weaver, Richard Bortle, Nicholas Gros, Samuel Fenner, an old sea captain who spun his skipper's yarns to customers; Jacob Hees, who also had a boat and lumber landing at Pal-

atine Bridge; Josiah Shepard, a stage house; Weatherby, Jost Spraker, John DeWandelaer, now Schenck's place near the Nose; Frederick Dockstader, kept many large wagons; Connelly, Fred Dockstader, 2d, who had a run of double teams; Gen. Henry Fonda at now village of Fonda; Giles Fonda, Pride, Hardenburgh, Conyne, Lepper; in Tribes Hill, Kline, Putman, Wilson; Guy Park, a favorable place for large wagons, kept at one time by McGerk; Col. William Shuler at Amsterdam; below were Crane of Cranesville, Lewis Groat, Swart and others on this part of the route not remembered. At Schenectady are recalled, Tucker, Jacob Wagner, Shields, while the names of two others are forgotten, —one of them had a house in Frog Alley, which was burned by the slacking of lime. Between Schenectady and Albany were, Havely, Brooks, Vielie. The Half-way house was a stage house and kept by Leavitt Kingsbury, which became noted for its delicious coffee.

"In the period of wagon transport when hay was $20 a ton, innkeepers had one dollar a span for keeping horses over night; and when hay was $10 a ton they had 50 cents a span, or one shilling a pound for hay. In spring and fall it was a common sight to see ten or fifteen horses drawing a single wagon from its fastness in the mud. The first load of hemp from the west, said Fink, was a five horse load from Wadsworth's flats in the Genesee valley.

"Some of the teamsters were at different times on both (the Mohawk and the western) turnpikes. Freight from Albany to Buffalo was at first $5 per hundred weight, but competition at one time brought it down to $1.25. The teamsters on these turnpikes were as jovial and accommodating set of men, as ever engaged in any vocation, seldom having any feuds or lasting difficulties. Said Mr. Fink, in 1805-6 when Oneida and adjoining counties were receiving many of their pioneer settlers, New England people came prospecting on horseback, with well-filled saddle-bags and portmanteaus, and he often had 30 or 40 in a single night to entertain at his house below Little Falls."

This was the day of the stage coach also and the Mohawk turnpike presented a spectacle of life and bustle as it shared with the Mohawk river the traffic of the valley. This was particularly so during the years from 1800 to the building of the Erie canal in 1825.

The earliest authentic town record of Palatine, now in existence, is that of a meeting of the commissioners of excise, held May 3, 1803, for the purpose of granting licenses to innkeepers. The number thus licensed will give an idea of the teaming and travel through the Palatine district, before the days of railroads or canals or even the completion of the Mohawk turnpike. The commissioners of excise were Jacob Ecker, Henry Beekman and Peter C. Fox who swore to an oath, before Justice of the Peace John Zielley, that "we will not on any account or pretense whatever, grant any license to any person within the said town of Palatine, for the purpose of keeping an inn or tavern, except when it shall appear to us to be absolutely necessary for the benefit of travelers." Jost Spraker, Henry Cook, Andrew J. Dillenbeck, John F. Empie, Peter W. Nellis and 47 others (51 in all) were granted licenses. The sum paid by each was from $5 to $6.50, according to location, amounting in the aggregate for that year to $258.50.

The Mohawk turnpike was the scene of much military activity during the years of 1812, 1813 and 1814, caused by the movement of New York troops going to defense of the frontier (in the second war with Great Britain) and their return at the close of hostilities. It shared this military traffic with the Mohawk river.

After the railroad trains on the Utica and Schenectady road (forerunner of the New York Central), started running up and down the valley, the Mohawk turnpike ceased to be a line of bustling activity and important traffic route, being used only for local and farm wagon freightage. On the valley roads about 1880 appeared riders on the high bicycle and a few years later the serviceable "safety" came into use and a veritable "bicycle craze" was inaugurated which lasted until about 1900, after which time the cheap and useful "wheel" took its rightful place as a means of transport. After 1895 appeared the "bicycle's son"—the automobile, and the future of our highways lies largely in their use as automobile freight and passenger roads—this use probably always to be supplemented by the farm horse and wagon. Coeval with the appearance of the bicycle and automobile came the trolley car, whose lines parallel the valley roads in many places and which will undoubtedly form a traffic system, together with the railroads, the Barge canal and good highways, that will give wellnigh perfect transportation facilities to the Mohawk valley. The proper building of lasting highways is now one of the most important features of traffic in the Mohawk region as well as in New York state. Today we see regular lines of motor buses carrying passengers and motor trucks carrying freight running between different points in the valley. This is borne out by the following paragraph from the Fort Plain Standard of June 19, 1913:

"The Fort Plain and Cooperstown Transportation Co. will start a passenger, freight and express business between this village and Cooperstown July 1. Motor busses will be utilized."

This is doubly interesting as it was only a few months previous to this that the Cooperstown-Fort Plain stage route was abandoned after a duration of probably a century or more over this historic route to the Susquehanna valley.

The interest in automobiles and the automobile interests were largely responsible for the good roads movement but the motor car has been its own enemy in that the suction of the rubber tires destroys the surface of what were once considered fine roads. Better materials will doubtless be found adapted to automobiles and all other vehicles, but in the meantime much money has been wasted. Writing on this subject S. L. Frey has said: "The automobile road between Albany and Buffalo runs through Montgomery county for thirty miles. It has for a foundation the solid strata of the Silurian rocks and the stone bed of the old Mohawk turnpike. It passes through a country of granite boulders, gneiss, sandstone, limestone, all kinds of ledges, cliffs and quarries, and yet $20,000 [cost] a mile. And the grade some two feet to the mile with no hills!"

The north shore turnpike is about forty miles long through Montgomery. Mr. Frey's article suggests that the Mohawk valley, with its abundance of stone supply, is an ideal region for the construction of ideal roads. Doubtless they will come in time. At present (1913) the automobile traffic is enormous, particularly in summer. An average of a car every two minutes has been noted, during a period of several hours over the old Mohawk turnpike and the cars come from every part of the country.

The New York Times of July 20, 1913, published a description of the automobile route from New York to Canada by way of the Hudson and Mohawk valleys. The itinerary in part, is here given, thus describing the Mohawk turnpike from Schenectady to Rome in 1913. This is one of the most important highways of the United States today just as it was one of the most noteworthy stage and freight wagon lines a century previous:

"From Albany, owing to the poor condition of the direct route, it is advisable to go by way of Loudonville and Latham's Corners, then over the Troy-Schenectady State road to Schenectady, whence good macadam leads through the beautiful Mohawk valley, passing Scotia, Hoffmans, Amsterdam, Fort Johnson, Tribes Hill and Fonda. The road is under construction from Fonda to Palatine Bridge, and a detour is advisable over a good but narrow country road on the south side of the river. A good State road is followed from Palatine Bridge through Nelliston, St. Johnsville, Little Falls, Herkimer and Mohawk, and thence

through Ilion, Schuyler and Deerfield to Utica. The scenery through the Mohawk valley leaves little to be desired.

"On the other side of Utica the route leads through Rome, Camden, Williamstown, Richland, Mansville and Adams to Watertown. This route offers better road conditions than that through Boonville and Copenhagen." The route continues from Watertown to Ogdensburg and across the St. Lawrence river to Canada.

The New York Sun, in July, 1913, published an automobile itinerary from New York to Cooperstown. It describes the route and road conditions of the north shore Mohawk turnpike, from Schenectady to Nelliston and the Otsquago valley road from Fort Plain to Otsego lake, in 1913, and may be interesting to future readers. It is here reprinted as follows: "Leaving Albany the run is over a rough macadam and then poor dirt to Schenectady. Excellent macadam is then followed through Fonda. A picturesque alternate from Schenectady to Amsterdam is that via Mariaville. Although a little longer than the first route, the scenery is enjoyable and the roads are of good macadam. Between Fonda and Palatine Bridge the going is not of the best. Construction work is going on, but the road is passable, although very heavy in wet weather. A continuous panorama of beautiful views on this drive will more than recompense one for the discomforting road conditions. From Palatine Bridge [through Nelliston and Fort Plain] the roads are of good macadam and brick to about one mile before reaching Starkville, where a fairly good dirt road is encountered and followed through Van Hornesville to Springfield Centre. To Cooperstown from Springfield Centre good roads are found. First a dirt road is followed which offers good going in dry weather. The balance to Cooperstown is macadam with some badly worn stretches. The run down the west side of Otsego lake is replete with excellent scenery, affording splendid views of the lake."

This Fort Plain-Springfield-Coop-erstown road is a historic one, devel-oping from a Mohawk trail, Revolu-tionary road, stage and freight traffic route to the automobile highway of today. Mention has been made of the unique geographical position of the Mohawk valley in its being the only natural break through the Applachian range to the west in the Middle Atlan-tic states. The Otsquago valley occu-pies a similar position in the southern central Mohawk basin, as it is a natural break and easy grade leading from the Mohawk river to the Susque-hanna watershed.

The following from the Beers his-tory of Montgomery county was writ-ten by Thurlow Weed, for many years a power in Whig and Republican poli-tics in New York state and editor of the Albany Journal. It was evidently written in 1870 and recounts the inci-. dents of a stage coach trip on the Mo-hawk turnpike in 1824, a year before the completion of the Erie canal and in the heyday of Mohawk valley coach-ing days. Although Mr. Weed, writ-ing almost a half-century after his trip, makes many errors in the loca-tion of stage houses, etc., yet his nar-rative gives a suggestive picture of stage coach and freight-wagon days along the Mohawk in the early years of the nineteenth century. Mr. Weed's and other writings of the period, show that, while Conestoga was the true name of the great freight wagons and the stout breed of horses which drew them, yet they were generally known in the valley and in New York state as Pennsylvania wagons and horses. The part of the sketch of travel on the Mohawk turnpike by Thurlow Weed, printed herewith, covers that historic highway from Fall Hill through Mont-gomery county. His narrative deals entirely with the year 1824, except where he says "Judge Conkling is now (1870) the oldest surviving New York member of congress from this dis-trict." This Judge Conkling of Cana-joharie, was the father of U. S. Sena-tor Roscoe Conkling, who became as much of an influence in the machin-ery of New York state politics as Thurlow Weed himself had been.

The proper location of the points mentioned by Mr. Weed in his jour ney, in their order from west to east, are as follows, according to Simms: East Creek, Couch's stage house; St. Johnsville, Failing's tavern; between Canajoharie and Sprakers (south side of river), Kane's store; Sprakers, Spraker's stage house; near Tribes Hill, Conyne's tavern; Fort Johnson, at Fort Johnson. Of these, Mr. Weed correctly located only Couch's tavern and Fort Johnson. His account follows:

"From Little Falls we come after an hour's ride to a hill by the bank of the river, which, several years before, Gen. Scott was descending in a stage when the driver discovered at a sharp turn near the bottom of the hill a Pennsylvania wagon winding its way up diagonally. The driver saw but one escape from a disastrous collision, and that to most persons would have appeared even more dangerous than the collision. The driver however, having no time for reflection, instantly guided his team over the precipice and into the river, from which the horses, passengers, coach and driver, were safely extricated. The passengers, following Gen. Scott's example, made the driver a handsome present as a reward for his courage and sagacity.

"We dine at East Canada Creek, where the stage house, kept by Mr. Couch, was always to be relied on for excellent ham and eggs and fresh brook trout. Nothing of especial in-terest until we reach Spraker's, a well known tavern that neither stages nor vehicles of any description were ever known to pass. Of Mr. Spraker, senior, innumerable anecdotes were told. He was a man without education, but possessed strong good sense, consider-able conversational powers, and much natural humor. Most of the stories told about him are so Joe-Millerish that I will repeat but one of them. On one occasion, he had a misunderstand-ing with a neighbor, which provoked both to say hard things of each other. Mr. Spraker having received a verbal hot shot from his antagonist, reflected a few moments and replied, 'Ferguson, dare are worse men in hell dan you;" adding after a pause, 'but they are chained.' * * * * * * * *

"At Canajoharie a tall handsome man with graceful manners, is added to our list of passengers. This is the Hon. Alfred Conkling, who in 1820 was elected to congress from this district, and who has just been appointed judge of the United States District Court, for the Northern District of New York, by Mr. Adams. Judge Conkling is now (in 1870) the oldest surviving New York member of congress. In passing Conyne's hotel, near the Nose, the fate of a young lady who 'loved not wisely but too well,' with an exciting trial for breach of promise, etc., would be related. Still further east we stop at Failing's tavern to water. Though but an ordinary tavern in the summer season, all travelers cherish a pleasant remembrance of its winter fare; for leaving a cold stage with chilled limbs, if not frozen ears, you were sure to find in Failing's bar and dining-rooms 'rousing fires;' and the remembrance of the light lively 'hot and hot' buckwheat cakes, and the unimpeachable sausages, would renew the appetite even if you had just risen from a hearty meal.

"Going some miles further east we come in sight of a building on the west side of the Mohawk river, and near its brink, the peculiar architecture of which attracts attention. This was formerly Charles Kane's store, or rather the store of the brothers Kane, five of whom were distinguished merchants in the early years of the present century. They were all gentlemen of education, commanding in person, accomplished and refined in manners and associations. * * * Here Commodore Charles Morris, one of the most gallant of our naval officers, who in 1812 distinguished himself on board the United States Frigate 'Constitution' in her engagement with the British frigate 'Guerriere' passed his boyhood. In 1841, when I visited him on board of the United States seventy-four gun ship 'Franklin,' lying off Annapolis, he informed me that among

his earliest recollections, was the launching and sailing of miniature ships on the Mohawk river. On the opposite side of the river, in the town of Florida, is the residence of Dr. Alexander Sheldon, for twelve years a member of the legislature from Montgomery county, serving six years as speaker of the house of assembly. The last year Dr. S. was in the legislature, one of his sons, Milton Sheldon, was also a member from Monroe county. Another son, Smith Sheldon, who was educated for a dry goods merchant, drifted some years ago to the city of New York, and is now the head of the extensive publishing house of Sheldon & Co., Broadway.

"The next points of attraction were of much historical interest. Sir William and Guy Johnson built spacious and showy mansions a few miles west of the village of Amsterdam, long before the Revolution, in passing which, interesting anecdotes relating to the English Baronet's connection with the Indians were remembered. A few miles west of Sir William Johnson's, old stagers would look for an addition to our number of passengers in the person of Daniel Cady, a very eminent lawyer, who resided at Johnstown, and for more than fifty years was constantly passing to and from Albany. At Amsterdam, Marcus T. Reynolds, then a rising lawyer of that village, often took his seat in the stage, and was a most companionable traveler."

Mr. Simms, commenting on this sketch, indorses the author's reference to circumstances "which compelled the male passengers at times to get out into the mud, and with rails appropriated from the nearest fence, to pry the wheels up so that the horses could start anew. Two miles an hour was not unfrequently, in the spring and fall, good speed at certain localities."

Correcting Mr. Weed's errors, as to locality, Mr. Simms says: "Conyne's hotel was three miles east of Fonda (he says near the Nose; if so there may have been two keepers of the same name), and * * * Failing's tavern was at St. Johnsville, and some twelve miles to the westward of the Nose, and more than twenty miles to the westward of Conyne's. At Palatine Bridge was one of the most noted stage houses in the valley. It was built and first kept by Shepherd, and afterwards by the late Joshua Reed, and was as widely and favorably known as any other public house within fifty miles of it."

For a clear and comprehensive description of old turnpike days, travel and vehicles, the reader is advised to consult Alice Morse Earle's "Home Life in Colonial Days."

CHAPTER VIII.

1793-1913 — First Bridges in Middle Mohawk Valley and Montgomery County—Celebration at Opening of Fort Plain Bridge, July 4, 1806—Fort Plain Free Bridge, 1858.

This is the third chapter on Mohawk valley transportation. The two prior ones were on river and turnpike traffic. Those to follow relate to Erie canal, railroads and Barge canal and Atwood's aeroplane flight.

The increase of population in Tryon, now Montgomery county, following the Revolutionary war, and the increase in traffic along the Mohawk necessitated improvements in river navigation and in the highways, as has been noted in preceding chapters. Great numbers of new settlers were journeying through the valley to points in the middle west, aside from those who were coming into the Mohawk valley and into western and northern New York to permanently locate. The fords and ferries on the Mohawk and its contributory creeks had been the only and difficult means of crossing these streams, during the eighteenth century which was the period of first settlement and development. The greatly increased traffic necessitated the construction of bridges and the building of these was one of the marked features of the life along the Mohawk at the beginning of the nineteenth century.

A list of the important bridges and the dates of their construction in the eastern part of the Mohawk valley follows:

East (Canada) creek, 1793; Schoharie creek at Fort Hunter, 1798; Schoharie creek at Mill Point, 1800; Little Falls (prior to), 1802; across the Mohawk at Canajoharie, 1803; Fort Plain (Sand Hill), 1806; Schenectady, 1810; Fonda (Caughnawaga), 1811; Amsterdam, 1823; Yosts, 1825 (carried away by ice shortly after); Fort Hunter, 1852; St. Johnsville, 1852.

These cross-overs were all wooden structures and these picturesque bridges have all been replaced by those of modern iron construction. The last of the old-timers to go was that at St. Johnsville, and many of them had formerly been undermined and carried away by ice during the Mohawk spring freshets. Each had its toll-keeper and the quaint list of tolls, in well-painted characters, which stood at the west side of the East Creek bridge was long of interest to later-day travelers.

The first important structure spanning a stream within the present limits of Montgomery and Fulton counties was the bridge at East (Canada) creek. In April, 1790, the state legislature voted "one hundred pounds for the purpose of erecting a bridge across the East Canada creek, not exceeding three miles from the mouth thereof, upon the road from the Mohawk river to the Royal Grant." In 1793, commissioners were appointed by the legislature to build "a bridge over the East Canada creek, nearly opposite Canajoharie Castle, on the public road leading from Tribes Hill to the Little Falls," also over West Canada creek.

In 1798 a very important bridge was built on the south shore turnpike over the Schoharie creek at Fort Hunter. The improvement of the Mohawk (north shore) turnpike from Schenectady to Utica, about 1800, necessitated the erection of other structures across streams, which had formerly been forded by travelers.

The first bridge across the Mohawk was probably the one at Little Falls noted by Rev. John Taylor in his diary of his valley tour of 1802. This was six-teen rods long, and it is mentioned in a former chapter of this work on Mo-hawk river traffic.

The second bridge over the Mohawk river in the valley seems to have been the one erected at Canajoharie in 1803, by Theodore Burr of Jefferson county. This was popularly called a bow bridge and consisted of a single arch 330 feet long. It fell in 1807 with a crash that was heard for miles. In 1808 a second bridge was built which was carried away in the spring freshet of 1822. David I. Zielley, a Palatine farmer, built a third bridge which "went out" with the ice in 1833, and Simms says "its destruction was a most splendid sight from Canajoharie, as the writer well remembers." A new bridge was built by August, 1833, which remained in use in part up to recent years. The Canajoharie bridge was rebuilt in 1913.

The third bridge to be completed and used across the Mohawk was that built at the lower end of "the Island," which lies in the Mohawk at the northern limits of Fort Plain. This structure consisted of two bridges with several rods of the roadway of the island intervening between them— the shorter one on the western shore and the longer one on the eastern side of the island. The Mohawk here runs north and south and the main channel was on the east side of the island. The Minden exit was near the store of James Oothout, the early Minden tradesman.

This was officially called the "Montgomery bridge," but came to be called in the neighborhood, "Oot-hout's bridge." The commissioners for its erection were James Beardsley of East Creek, Col. Charles Newkirk and Col. Peter Wagner of Palatine Church, for the east side, and Messrs. Oothout, Gansevoort, Dygert, Arndt and Keller for the west side. Beards-ley, himself a millwright, was its con-tractor and Philip Washburn, who had worked under Burr, who built the Canajoharie bridge, was boss carpen-ter under Beardsley. These twin bridges, like many such early struc-tures were of wood, not covered and rested upon wooden- piers or supports. The toll house was upon the Fort Plain side of the river. The timber for the "north bridge" (as generally called) came mostly from the Wag-ner farm, while that for the "south" bridge came from Snellsbush. Al-though the river runs north and south from Palatine Church to Canajoharie, the river sides are generally called north and south sides as in the rest of the valley where the course of the Mohawk is generally east and west. After the Canajoharie bridge fell in 1807 it was the only bridge across the Mohawk in the present county until the new one at Canajoharie was built. James Beardsley of East Creek was one of the Fort Plain bridge commis-sioners because at that date (1806 and until 1817) Montgomery county ran west to Fall Hill.

Simms says that the completion of Fort Plain bridge "was celebrated with no little pomp on the 4th of July, 1806, and took place on the north [east] bank of the river not far from the bridge. Gen. Peter C. Fox, in full uniform and mounted upon a splendid gray horse, was grand marshal on the occasion, and had at his command a company of artillery with a cannon, and Capt. Peter Young's well-mounted cavalry. The latter company is said to have trotted across the bridge to test its strength, and a severe one that would naturally be. Besides several yoke of oxen were driven over it to obtain a still further proof of its com-pleteness, while a cannon blazed away at one end of it. Some one delivered an oration on this occasion. A dinner was served at the public house of the elder George Wagner to the multi-tude, who looked upon the completion of this enterprise as a marked event— and, indeed, such it was, for the ser-vices of ferrymen who had pulled at the rope for years, a little below, were now at an end and the delay and dan-ger of crossing by ferriage was obvi-ated.

"Methinks I can now see the table on which this dinner was served, groaning under the burden of good eatables; its head adorned with a good sized pig roasted whole—a sight yet common fifty years ago, but now seldom seen at the festive board. This Wagner place is the present [1882] homestead [now burned] of the old innkeeper's grandson, Chauncey Wagner. This remarkable bridge celebration was kept up three successive days, the parties dancing each night at the Wagner tavern, where Washburn and his hands boarded.

"When this bridge was erected, nearly all there was of Fort Plain—which took its name from the [former] military post nearby—was in the vicinity of this bridge. True, Isaac Paris had a few years before been trading at the now Bleecker residence in the present village, and Casper Lipe had another store for a time near the creek bridge; but besides the Oothout store, Conrad Gansevoort had one half a mile below at Abeel's; while on the hill near the meeting house, Robert McFarlan was then trading—besides there were several mechanics within the same distance, all of whom are said to have done a prosperous business. * * * The ice took off the northern or principal structure of the Island Bridge in April, 1825, after it had served the public for nineteen years."

At that time a growing, lively little village was on the present site of Fort Plain and had entirely usurped in importance the old Sand Hill section. Consequently the next bridge was built at the present river bridge site and was opened for carriages, January 1, 1829. This was a substantial covered bridge, like many similar structures in the valley at that day. The bridge stock of the Island Bridge company had not been a profitable investment and stock in the new bridge company was not greatly sought after. This bridge went out in the spring "high water" of 1842 and lodged on Ver Planck's (now Nellis) island and on the Gros flats. A new bridge was built in the summer of 1842 and lasted until the spring of 1887, when the ice broke down the abutments, during the spring flood

and carried the bridge away. The present iron structure which replaced it is said to be the longest single span iron bridge of its type in Central New York.

A free bridge, across the Mohawk at Fort Plain was projected in 1857 and work on an iron bridge, to stand just north of the present one, was begun in the same summer. Before the masonry was completed the work was stopped by an injunction, which delayed its completion until the summer of 1858 when the bridge was opened absolutely free to the public and the covered bridge company thereby ceased taking toll. Litigation over the two bridges between the two companies finally resulted in the free bridge people obtaining possession of the old bridge at a serious loss to the stockholders interested in the latter. The iron bridge was finally disposed of and the proceeds used to raise and put into condition the covered bridge which continued to be free to the public. The late William Aplin says that, about the middle of the nineteenth century, the farmers of this neighborhood used to utilize a large door in the bridge for the purpose of dumping the manure from their farms into the Mohawk! Thus have farmers and farming methods changed between that time and this.

Says Simms: "The Fort Plain free bridge movement had a direct tendency to make nearly all the other bridges on the river free bridges; the time having arrived when the enterprise of the country demanded the measure. In 1859 an act was passed to erect a free bridge at Canajoharie or compel the sale of the old one—to be made free—which result followed."

In 1825, it has been previously noted a bridge across the Mohawk was erected between Yosts, at the western end of the town of Mohawk and Randall, in the eastern end of the town of Root. This was shortly after swept away by ice. In 1852 a bridge was built across the Mohawk at St. Johnsville, on the site of the present structure, thus completing the three bridges which span the river in western Montgomery county.

A feature of bridge building on the Mohawk is today (1913) the bridges erected by the state in connection with the Barge canal locks. These may be utilized by the towns, on which they abut, constructing proper approaches. In western Montgomery county these locks and bridges are at Fort Plain, Canajoharie and Yosts (Randall). The Amsterdam bridge was rebuilt in 1913.

It is difficult today to realize the importance of the erection of the first bridges to the valley people. It meant greater trade and intercourse among themselves and with the outside world and the construction of an important bridge was invariably followed by an increased population center at one or both ends of the structure. Communities like Fort Plain and Canajoharie, which have been deprived of their bridges, can thoroughly realize the importance of such viaducts of traffic and transportation and the necessity for the permanence of their construction and efficiency of their upkeep. Good roads and good bridges go together as prime essentials for civilized agricultural regions.

CHAPTER IX.

1812—The Militia System—Trainings— War With England—The Mohawk Valley Militia.

After the Revolutionary war was crowned by peace, the men of America kept up their military training and the militia system arose, under which martial exercise was regularly practised. The officers and men supplied themselves with their necessary military arms and outfit, and this system continued for over a half century after the close of the war for independence.

Beers's History says: "This militia consisted of all the able-bodied white male population, between 18 and 45. State officers, clergymen and school teachers were exempt from such duty. Students in colleges and academies, employes on coasting vessels, and in certain factories, and members of fire companies were also exempt, except in case of insurrection or invasion. Persons (like Quakers) whose only bar to military service was religious scruples could purchase exemption for a set sum paid annually. The major-general, brigade-inspector and chief of the staff department, except the adjutant and commissary generals, were appointed by the Governor. Colonels were chosen by the captains and subalterns of the regiments, and these latter by the written ballots of their respective regiments and separate battalions. The commanding officers of regiments or battalions appointed their staff officers. Every non-commissioned officer and private was obliged to equip and uniform himself, and perform military duty for 15 years from enrollment, after which he was exempt except in case of insurrection or invasion. A non-commissioned officer could get excused from duty in seven years, by furnishing himself with certain specified equipment, other than those required by law. It was the duty of the commanding officer of each company to enroll all military subjects within the limits of his jurisdiction, and they must equip themselves within six months after being notified.

"On the first September Monday of each year, every company of the militia was obliged to assemble within its geographical limits for training. One day in each year, between Sept. 1 and Oct. 15, at a place designated by the commander of the brigade, the regiment was directed to assemble for general training. All the officers of each regiment or battalion were required to rendezvous two days in succession, in June, July or August, for drill under the brigade inspector. A colonel also appointed a day for the commissioned officers and musicians of his regiment to meet for drill, the day after the last mentioned gathering being generally selected. Each militiaman was personally notified of an approaching muster by a non-commissioned officer bearing a warrant from the commandant of his company;

or he might be summoned without a warrant by a commissioned officer, either by visit or letter. A failure to appear, or to bring the necessary equipment, resulted in a court-martial and a fine, unless a good excuse could be given. Delinquents who could not pay were imprisoned in the county jail. When a draft was ordered for public service it was made by lot in each company, which was ordered out on parade for that purpose."

"General training" was a great holiday for everybody in the neighborhood where it was held. The militiamen and their wives and families (and particularly the small boys) together with the "exempts" turned out and made an enjoyable and festive day of it. The place of meeting and the extent of the parade grounds were designated by the commanding officer. The sale of liquor on the ground could only be carried on by the consent of the same official, but total abstinence seldom seems to have been the rule on this eventful day. The flats near Fort Plain were favorite places for "general training."

The first company of cavalry organized in this part of the Mohawk valley took in a large district of country and was raised and commanded by Capt. Hudson (a merchant of Indian Castle, and probably the Capt. B. Hudson, who commanded Fort Plain in 1786) early in the nineteenth century. Peter Young of Fort Plain, became its second captain, and he was succeeded by Capt. Wemple (of Canajoharie). At his death Jacob Eacker of Palatine, became captain, and on his resignation Nicholas N. Van Alstine commanded. As he was not the unanimous choice of the company, which was then a large one, his selection led to a division into two companies, that on the north side of the Mohawk being commanded by Barent Getman. In 1836, the major general of the second division of militia was an Amsterdam man bearing the singular name of Benedict Arnold. Aaron C. Whitlock of Ephratah was brigadier-general in the same division.

At the time of the War of 1812, the state of New York, along the Canadian frontier, was largely a wilderness and transportation thence was slow and laborious. The slightly improved Mohawk river was the only route, except the valley highways, for the westward conveyance of cannon. This heavy ordinance was loaded on Durham boats and so sent up the river. April 10, 1812, congress authorized a draft of 100,000 men from the militia of the country to prosecute the war with England; 13,500 of these were assigned as the quota of New York. A few days later the detached militia of the state was arranged in two divisions and eight brigades. The fourth brigade comprised the 10th, 11th and 13th regiments in the Mohawk valley and was under the command of Gen. Richard Dodge of Johnstown, a veteran of the Revolution (and a brother-in-law of Washington Irving). These troops went to the front and returned largely by the north and south shore turnpikes.

Says Beers: "The embargo act was extensively violated and much illicit trade carried on along the Canadian frontier, smugglers sometimes being protected by armed forces from the Canadian side. To break up this state of things and protect the military stores collected at the outposts, a regiment of valley militia, under Col. Christopher P. Bellinger, was stationed in May, 1812, at Sackett's Harbor and other points in Northern New York. These on the declaration of war in the following month (June, 1812) were reinforced by a draft on the militia not yet called into service. The Montgomery county militia responded promptly to the calls for troops to defend the frontier, and were noted for their valor and patriotic zeal, submitting without complaint to the various privations incident to the march and camp. A detachment of them under Gen. Dodge arrived at Sackett's Harbor, Sept. 21, 1812, and the general took command at the post. During the two succeeding years, the militia and volunteers from the Mohawk valley were on duty all along the frontier. When the term of service of any company or regiment expired it was succeeded by another. Many of the garrison of Sackett's Harbor, when it was attacked by the British, May 24, 1813, were from this section. That place was an important depot of military stores, a large amount of which was destroyed by the garrison, in fear of its falling into the hands of the British, who, however, were finally repulsed.

"The house in the town of Florida, later owned by Waterman Sweet, was kept as a hotel by one Van Derveer, during the war of 1812, and was a place of drafting militia into the service.

"At Canajoharie, a recruiting rendezvous was opened by Lieut. Alphonso Wetmore and Ensign Robert Morris of the Thirteenth regiment, both residents of Ames, who raised two companies which were ordered to the Niagara frontier in time to take part in the first events of importance in that quarter. The Thirteenth suffered severely at the battle of Queenstown Heights, Ensign Morris and Lieut. Valleau being among the killed and five other officers severely wounded. After that engagement operations were for some time confined to bombardment across the Niagara river from the fortifications at [Fort] Niagara and Black Rock [now part of Buffalo]. At the latter point Lieut. Wetmore lost his right arm by a cannon shot. He was subsequently promoted to the offices of major and division paymaster."

At the time of the publication of Beers's History in 1878, a goodly number of the Montgomery and Fulton veterans of 1812 still survived. They are therein mentioned as follows: Moses Winn, Minden, in his 88th year (his father was a captain in the Revolution and sheriff of the county after the war); George Bauder, Palatine, in his 92d year; John Walrath, Minden, nearly 82; William H. Seeber, Minden, about 86; Peter G. Dunckel, Minden, about 84; Henry Nellis, Palatine, about

84; John Casler, Minden, nearly 86; Abram Moyer, Minden, about 84; Cornelius Clement Flint, Minden, about 84; Benjamin Getman, Ephratah, 86; Henry Lasher, Palatine, 88; Pythagoras Wetmore, Canajoharie, 80; John Eigabroadt, St. Johnsville, about 82. In the eastern part may be mentioned: J. Lout, Mohawk; David Ressiguie, 94; Amasa Shippee, Capt. Reuben Willard, Northampton. It is only a few years ago (from the date of this writing, 1912) that the great public funeral occurred in New York of Hiram Cronk, the last survivor of the War of 1812, and a resident of the Mohawk valley throughout his life, his death occurring near Utica. At the time of the war of 1812, it should be remembered that Montgomery and Fulton were one county—Montgomery. Its western limit was a line running north and south from Fall Hill.

One of the leading figures in the 1812 militia of the old Canajoharie district was Major John Herkimer, son of Capt. George Herkimer and nephew of General Nicholas Herkimer. At that time the river section of the district was divided into the towns of Minden and Canajoharie, and Major Herkimer was a resident of that western portion of Minden which later, in 1817, became Danube, when it was included in Herkimer county. He occupied the Herkimer homestead until 1817. John Herkimer represented Montgomery county in 1799 in the state assembly. March 13, 1813, he was commissioned a major in Col. Mill's New York volunteer regiment. Major Herkimer was in the battle at Sackett's Harbor, when Col. Mills was killed. Herkimer was a leading anti-Clintonian and was a member of congress in 1822, where he voted for John Quincy Adams in the electoral college deadlock which threw the election into congress. He was a Herkimer county judge and was generally known as Judge Herkimer.

CHAPTER X.

1817-1825—Construction of Erie Canal — Clinton's Triumphal Trip — Fort Plain's Celebration.

This chapter on the Erie canal is the fourth chapter describing transportation in the Mohawk valley. Former ones dealt with Mohawk river traffic, valley highways and bridges. Those following the present one treating of the Erie canal concern railroad building, the Barge canal and the first aeroplane flight by Atwood, in all seven chapters on Mohawk valley traffic conditions. The Erie canal is supplied with water from the Mohawk river and thus is closely connected with that stream.. This is therefore the fourth chapter relative to the Mohawk. The first described the Mohawk river and its valley, the second considered Mohawk river traffic, the third treated of river and other bridges, the present and fourth covers the Erie canal and the fifth will be on. the Barge canal and the sixth will consider the geology of the middle Mohawk valley.

Canal construction in the United States in the early nineteenth century was part of that great movement for the improvement of transportation which followed the war for independence and began almost immediately at the conclusion of peace in 1783. As a general rule, turnpike and bridge building inaugurated this movement, followed by canal and railroad construction in the second and third decades of the nineteenth century. The first American canal of importance was the Lehigh, completed in 1821, running 108 miles from Coalport, Pa., to Easton, Pa. The second was the Champlain canal, completed in 1822, and running 81 miles from Whitehall, N. Y., to Watervliet, N. Y. In discussing the Erie canal we consider one of the most important trade routes and canals of the world.

The construction of Erie canal from 1817 to 1825 gave the greatest impetus to the development of population, trade and commerce in the Mohawk valley that it has ever experienced. Certain towns and villages owe their location and growth almost entirely to "Clinton's ditch" and are therefore Canal towns. In Montgomery county, Fort Plain, Canajoharie and Fultonville belong to this class. In the heyday of canaling these were among the most important canal towns on the Erie between Utica and Schenectady. Fort Plain was then as at present (1913) the largest town in the 40-mile strip between Little Falls and Amsterdam, and Canajoharie, with its dry dock and boat building works, was equally important.

The project of a continuous waterway from the Hudson to .the Great Lakes had been . agitated ever since the days of the earliest settlement of New York state and the Mohawk river-Wood creek-Oneida lake-Oswego river route is the parent of the Erie canal and was in use as the water route (with the carry at Wood creek) from the Hudson to Lake Ontario for two centuries before the completion of the Erie canal. Washington, on his tour of the valley in 1783, was greatly impressed by the water communications of the regions, as is shown in a prior chapter.

The incorporation of the Inland Lock Navigation Co. in 1792 was the first step toward canalizing this Mohawk river to the lakes route, which, had previously been traversed exclusively by canoes, dugouts and flatboats. This company was not successful as has been shown and sold out to the state in 1820.

Mrs. Earle, in her work, "Home Life in Colonial Days," states that the Hudson-to-the-Great Lakes canal project was proposed in the New York provincial assembly as early as 1768.

While the Erie canal was doubtless the outcome of the public-spirited efforts of a number of the state's most progressive and far-seeing citizens, it is true that particular credit for the inauguration of the enterprise is due a few moving spirits. The "Live Wire," a publication issued by the Buffalo Chamber of Commerce, devoted its issue of August, 1913, to the Barge canal with incidental allusion to its predecessor, the Erie. It stated that the Erie canal was generally called the "Grand Canal" during its period of construction. The periodical mentioned gives great credit for New York state taking up the construction of the waterway to Jesse Hawley, a resident of Ontario county. On Jan. 14, 1807, he published an article in the Pittsburgh "Commonwealth" urging the building of the Albany to Buffalo canal, under the signature "Hercules." He was at that time temporarily living in Pittsburgh. The "Live Wire" says that prior to this time no one had printed a word or spoken a word in public in favor of this measure. On Hawley's return to his previous home in Ontario county, New York, he published a series of fourteen articles in the "Ontario Messenger" (also known as the "Genesee Messenger"), a newspaper issued at Canandaigua. These papers constituted a complete exposition of the whole subject, setting forth the advantages of the work, describing the canals of Europe, comparing the Erie canal scheme with them and estimating the cost—which estimate closely approximated the actual expense of the canal afterward built. It is interesting to note that the initial measure taking up the subject of the public work, was introduced into the state assembly by Judge Forman, from the then great county of Ontario, where Hawley resided and where his views were published.

At Schenectady in 1803, Gouverneur Morris suggested to Simeon DeWitt, state surveyor, a project for conveying the water of Lake Erie direct to the Hudson, by means of a canal so constructed as to preserve a continuous fall to the high lands bordering on the river, which should be surmounted by the use of locks. The surveyor-general, in common with most of those to whom the scheme was mentioned, regarded the project as visionary. He so represented it to James Geddes, a surveyor of Onondaga county. Geddes, on reflection, decided it practical. The proposition was first brought before the legislature by Joshua Forman, member from Onondaga, Feb. 4, 1808.

A committee was appointed to investigate the subject and reported in favor of an examination of the route (both from Oneida lake to Lake Ontario and from Lake Erie eastward to the Hudson). This was made by the aforementioned James Geddes, who made a favorable report to the committee. A further survey was made in 1810 and the cost of the canal estimated at $5,000,000. The length of the canal was estimated at 350 miles and the cost of transportation at $6 per ton. Appeals for help from the national government having failed, the canal commissioners were, by the legislature, authorized to obtain a loan of $5,000,000, and procure the right of way.

Further progress was prevented by the War of 1812, but toward the close of 1815 the project was revised. In spite of much opposition, the efforts of the canal champions both in and out of the legislature (especially Dewitt Clinton), procured the passage of an act Apr. 17, 1816, providing for the appointment of commissioners to take up the work. The following formed this board: Dewitt Clinton, Stephen Van Rensselaer, Samuel Young, Joseph Elliott and Myron Holles. Clinton was president. The plan of a continuous slope from Lake Erie, first proposed, was abandoned by the commission, and that of following the undulations of the surface adopted. Five millions was again estimated as the full cost of construction. April 15, 1817, an act prepared by Clinton was passed, in the face of great opposition, authorizing the commencement of the actual work. The canal project had always been considered by many a ruinous experiment and "lamentations were frequently heard on the miseries of an overtaxed people and their posterity." Says Beers:

"The canal was divided into three sections, from Albany to Rome, Rome to the Seneca river, and thence to Lake Erie. Charles C. Broadhead was engineer in charge of the eastern division, Benjamin Wright of the middle division and James Geddes of the western. The canal was planned to be

40 feet wide at the surface, 28 at the bottom and the depth of water to be four feet. The locks were 90 feet long and 12 wide in the clear. The commissioners were authorized to borrow, on the credit of the State, sums not exceeding $400,000 in any one year. Nearly $50,000 had been spent in exploration and surveys on the work before ground was broken." These figures seem insignificantly petty compared with the vast sums that have since been frequently wasted on so-called public improvements.

Ground was broken at Rome, July 4, 1817, in the presence of DeWitt Clinton, the canal's greatest champion, who was then governor of New York and the canal commissioners. John Richardson held the plow in opening the first furrow. "It was more than two years before any part of the line was ready for use. On the 22d of October, 1819, the first boat was launched at Rome to run to Utica for passenger use. It was called the 'Chief Engineer;' was 61 feet long, seven and one-half feet wide; had two cabins, each 14 feet long, with a flat deck between them, and was drawn by one horse. The next day [Oct. 23, 1819], the commissioners and some of the most prominent citizens of Utica embarked there for the return trip to Rome and set off with a band playing, bells ringing, cannon thundering and thousands of spectators cheering from the banks. "On the 21st of July, 1820, tolls were first levied, the rates being fixed by the commissioners; the amount received that year [in the short stretch then in use] was over $5,000, taken by six collectors. The canal was used between Rome and Little Falls in the autumn of 1821, the contractor at the latter point availing himself of the unprofitable labors of the Inland Lock Navigation Co. (previously referred to); and the portion east to the Hudson was under contract. Meanwhile the river floated the canal boats from Little Falls to Schenectady. The Mohawk valley, below the former point, was thoroughly explored under the supervision of Benjamin Wright, chief engineer, and the intended direct line,

from Schenectady to the Hudson river near Albany, was abandoned in favor of the course of the Mohawk river [from Schenectady to Cohoes]. The accuracy of the engineering work on the line was considered wonderful, in view of the fact that the engineers, Wright and Geddes, had had no previous experience of the kind, having been only land surveyors before their employment on this great work.

"In the spring of 1823, the canal was open uninterruptedly from Sprakers [thus including most of the line through the five western towns of Montgomery county] to the western part of the state and in September following [Sept., 1823] the St. Johnsville feeder was completed. The spot at the 'Nose,' however, was still unfinished, and, at that point, merchandise was transferred to river boats past the unfinished section.

"In the latter stages of the great work unexpectedly rapid progress was made, its success being now assured, and on the 26th of October, 1825, the finishing touch had been given and the canal was thrown open to navigation throughout, by the admission of water from Lake Erie at Black Rock [Buffalo]. The length of the canal was 363 miles, and its initial cost $7,143,780.86. Its completion was celebrated with unbounded joy which found expression in extraordinary civic and military ceremonies, and all the festivities that a proud and happy commonwealth could invent.

"On the morning of Oct. 26 [1825], the first flotilla of boats, bound for New York from Lake Erie, entered the canal at Buffalo carrying the Governor and Canal Commissioners [in the packet, 'Seneca Chief']. Their departure was the signal for the firing of the first of a large number of cannon stationed within hearing distance of each other along the whole line of the canal and the Hudson river and at Sandy Hook, by which the momentous news of the opening of through travel at Buffalo was announced at the Hook in an hour and twenty minutes. One of the signal guns stationed at Sprakers Basin was fired by the

Revolutionary veteran Goshen Van Alstine [living on Canajoharie creek during the war]. The official voyagers were everywhere greeted with enthusiastic demonstrations."

In New York harbor Clinton poured water, carried from Lake Erie, into the waters of the Atlantic commemorating thereby the joining of the two bodies by way of the Erie canal,' and the great voyage was over. Sketches of canal scenery were stamped upon earthenware and various implements in commemoration of the great achievement. Albany was reached Nov. 2, 1825, where a great celebration took place. The gubernatorial party arrived at New York, Nov. 4, where was held a great public demonstration in celebration of the event. The trip from Buffalo to Albany had occupied seven days.

"As at first constructed, the canal passed through instead of over the streams which it had to cross, especially in the Mohawk valley, their waters being raised to its level as near as possible by means of dams. This gave a surplus of water in certain localities, and afforded some fine milling privileges. One of this sort was furnished below Canajoharie creek, where John A. Ehle built a sawmill to avail himself of it. To carry the water through a stream of any size required, upon both shores of the latter, guard locks with gates, which could be closed during freshets. Considerable difficulty was frequently experienced at such places by a long string of boats accumulating on each side of the stream where, at times, they were delayed for several days, during which their crews came to be on familiar and not always friendly terms. Such delays were sometimes caused by a freshet in the creek injuring the dam. The passage of the first boat across a creek, on the subsidence of high water, was a marked event, sometimes drawing a large crowd of people together to witness it. The first thing was to get the boat within the guard lock and close the gate behind it. Then with a strong team, sometimes doubled, the feat was undertaken [the

horses traveling over on a towing bridge over the dam]. The greatest difficulty was experienced at Schoharie creek, that being so large; and on the parting of a towline midway of the stream, in several instances, boats were borne by an aggravated current over the dam and into the river, occasionally with loss of life. In such cases the boats had to go to Schenectady before they could get back into the canal. The passenger packet boats had the precedence in passing locks, and it was readily conceded at creek crossings in freshet times." Such crossings were located on the Otsquago at Fort Plain, on the Canajoharie at Canajoharie, on Flat creek at Sprakers, and on Yatesville creek at Yatesville (now Randall).

At the outset the canal was the fashionable avenue of western travel, as well as a highway of commerce. The packets were elegantly furnished, set excellent tables and far outstripped the freight boats in speed, by their comparative lightness and their three-horse teams. The canal accordingly furnished the natural route of Lafayette in his grand tour of this part of the country in 1825. At the crossing at Schoharie creek, Lafayette's packet was delayed and it was there boarded by Thomas Sammons who was engaged in boating on the Erie canal. When Marquis de Lafayette was on a military errand at Johnstown, during the Revolution, he was there entertained by Jacob Sammons, a brother of Thomas, who had leased Johnson Hall from the Committee of Sequestration. Here Thomas Sammons had repeatedly met the French nobleman. In his cabin the Marquis greeted Sammons most cordially, asking after his Johnstown host (who had died since that time). The eminent Frenchman held the boat until his interview was ended, when Sammons and his son (who told this anecdote) stepped ashore both proud and happy over their courteous reception. Lafayette's packet was decorated with streamers and evergreens, even the harness of the horses bristling with flags. At all stops, locks and crossings, he was greeted by cheering crowds and we may well assume that such were present at the locks and creek crossings of western Montgomery county aforementioned.

The canal early became taxed beyond its capacity, and its enlargement became a necessity. By legislative act of May, 1835, the canal commissioners were authorized to make its enlargement and to construct double locks as fast as they deemed advisable. Under this act the enlargement was begun and carried on, with more or less activity, for a quarter of a century before it was completed throughout. In this reconstruction the canal was carried over the cross streams by aqueducts. It was reduced in length to 350 miles, and increased in breadth to 70 feet at the surface and 52½ feet at the bottom, while the depth of water was increased from four feet to seven feet. The cost of this enlargement was over $30,000,000. In 1896 and 1897, under an appropriation of $9,000,000, further enlargement was made. The water depth was increased (at least in part) to nine feet, and locks accommodating two boats were installed. From being the main central New York artery of freight traffic, commerce on the canal has dwindled to a small figure. Where formerly the docks of the canal towns were scenes of bustling activity they are now deserted. Such a state of affairs is due to the inability of the canal boats of 250 tons to successfully compete with the constantly increasing carrying capacity of the railroads. The railroads soon put the canal packets out of business but there are yet those who remember well this convenient, picturesque and pleasant (if somewhat slow) method of travel prior to the middle of the nineteenth century. Attention is called to Lossing's mention, in a later chapter of his trip by packet boat on the canal from Fort Plain to Fultonville in 1848. The Erie canal, particularly in its earlier years, was a favorite route of travel by emigrants going to the west.

Down to 1866, the construction, enlargement and improvement of the Erie and Champlain canals (the latter requiring but a small part of the whole amount) had cost no less than $46,018,234; the repairs and maintenance had cost $12,900,333, making a total expense of $58,918,567. On the other hand, the receipts for tolls on the Erie and Champlain canals had then amounted to $81,057,168, leaving a balance in favor of these canals of $22,138,601. The cost of other canals reduced the direct profit on the canal system of the state to a trifle, although the indirect profits have been enormous.

Future readers will ask, "What was the motive power and manner of boating on the old Erie canal?" The boats were at first drawn by one horse or mule. As they increased in size two or three horses or mules were used on one boat. The canal craft also went in pairs, threes and fours, sometimes two being lashed together and one or two others being in tow. These tows frequently had four horse or mule teams. Occasionally three or four boats went through towed by a tug. Steam canal boats have also been common. These generally formed the second boat of a pair, lashed bow and stern, and towed one or two others. Lake boats, which could journey from lake ports west of Buffalo through to New York, were seen in considerable numbers at times. Their use made the expense of breaking bulk at Buffalo unnecessary. All these double boats had to be unlashed before entering the locks, prior to the lock enlargement of the canal improvement of 1898. From Albany down these craft made the trip to New York in great tows or lashed flotillas, towed by one or two tugs.

Accidents of various sorts on the Erie have been common—leaks and banks giving way forming the principal source of trouble. Horses or mules frequently fell into the water, but were generally rescued. The canal banks were of riprap on the tow path side, except in towns where they were of stone. Here was generally located an incline up which horses were taken who had tumbled into the canal. Drownings were frequent about the locks.. One of the most remarkable accidents. on the canal occurred at Fort Plain in 1896, when an omnibus filled with passengers went through the River street bridge into the canal. All the people were rescued with great difficulty and the state was compelled to pay damages to a considerable amount. An iron lift bridge succeeded this weak structure, there being two located within the limits of Fort Plain.

Canal grocery stores were a feature of the Erie in its prime, these being located near the locks. The Erie waterway has always provided occupation for a considerable number of people, along its route, they being employed as lock and bridge tenders, bank watches, state (repair) scow hands, etc.

In western Montgomery county locks on the Erie canal are located at Mindenville, St. Johnsville, Fort Plain and Sprakers. At Mindenville also is located a feeder from the Mohawk river. On the northern limits of Fort Plain is what is generally called "the wide waters," a basin about a fifth of a mile long and over 100 feet wide. Bridges over the Erie canal average about one per mile.

One of the features of Erie canal transportation, since the latter part of the nineteenth century, has been the transit, during the summer months, of pleasure boats running from the Hudson river and southern and eastern points to the Thousand Islands and the Great Lakes. This has been a particularly large item of traffic since the introduction of the gasoline motor boat. The craft vary from a row-boat size to large yachts which test the capacity of the locks. The trip through the Erie canal and the Mohawk valley has been a pleasing feature of summer outings to thousands of Americans from the country over.

The Erie canal, after a life of almost a century since its first boat ran from Rome to Utica, is soon to give way to the vastly more efficient Barge canal. What disposition will be made of its bed by the state of New York is not known. At this time it is interesting to recall the picture of the for-. mer activity along its course, its picturesque packets and the bustle and life that it brought to the canal towns to which it gave birth. Those who love the scenery along the valley will soon miss from the view the twin courses of the Mohawk and the Erie canal winding their glittering way through the landscape.

––––––

The State Engineer's department has furnished the following regarding the Erie canal: The boats used on the Erie canal between 1817 and 1830 measured 61x7x3½ feet and had a capacity of 30 tons. Between 1830 and 1850 boats of 75x12x3¼ feet were used. These had a capacity of 75 tons. From 1850 to 1862 the boats were 90x15x3½ feet in size and had a capacity of 100 tons. After 1862 the boats were increased to 98x17½x6 feet with a capacity of 240 tons. This is the boat still in use (1913). Until the Barge canal is completed boats of greater size cannot be used.

The records of tonnage are not available prior to 1837. In that year the Erie canal carried 667,151 tons. In 1850 the tonnage was 1,635,089. In 1875 it was 2,787,226. Although the tonnage records do not go back of 1837 the records of tolls collected are available since 1820. In 1825 the amount collected on the Erie canal was $492,-664.23. In 1850 they were $2,933,125.93. In 1875 they were $1,428,078.25. Tolls were abolished on the canals in 1882. For several years prior to that date tolls had been decreased, although the amount of freight carried had increased or remained about the same. The year 1880 was the season of greatest tonnage on the Erie canal, 4,608,651 tons having been carried. In 1910 the tonnage was 2,023,185.

The arbitrary selection of certain years does not give a very good idea of the growth of canal traffic. The records are contained in a convenient form for reference in a history of the canals which was published by the state a few years ago. It is entitled "History of the Canal System of the State of New York, together with Brief Histories of the Canals of the

United States and Canada." At pages 1062 and 1064 of the second volume of this work appears the tables from which the above is quoted. The reader is referred to this work for a fuller account of the state's waterways.

In the foregoing paragraphs the tonnage of different years on the Erie is given among them that of 1910. The following gives the tonnage of the principal canals of the world for the year 1910, with the exception that the figures for the Kaiser Wilhelm canal are those for 1909: Sault Ste. Marie (between Lakes Superior and Huron), 36,395,687; Suez, Mediterranean and Red Seas, 23,054,901; Kaiser Wilhelm (Baltic and North Seas, Germany), 6,-267,805; Manchester (England), 5,-000,000; Erie, 2,023,185. The importance of our American inland waterways is easily seen by reference to the figures for the Sault Ste. Marie and the fact that its tonnage is fifty per cent greater than that great waterway of all the nations—the Suez canal. The Sault Ste. Marie is one of the links in the great chain of waterways of which the Barge canal will form a part.

Following are the principal canals of New York, in the order of their completion together with statistics pertaining to each. Attention is called to their general low cost of construction:

Champlain (Whitehall, N. Y., to Watervliet, N. Y.), built 1822; length 81 miles; locks, 32; depth, 6 feet; cost, $4,044,000. This was the second important canal completed in the United States.

Erie (Albany, N. Y., to Buffalo, N. Y.), built 1825; length, 387 miles; locks, 72; depth, 7 feet; cost, $52,540,800. The Erie is and has always been the most important canal of its type (aside from ship canals) in the world.

Oswego (Oswego, N. Y., to Syracuse, N. Y.), built 1828; length, 38 miles; locks, 18; depth, 7 feet; cost $5,239,-526.

Cayuga and Seneca (Montezuma, N. Y., to Cayuga and Seneca lakes, N. Y.), built, 1839; length 25 miles; locks, 11; depth, 7 feet; cost, $2,232,632.

Black River (Rome, N. Y., to Lyons Falls, N. Y. Formerly boats went from the latter point to Carthage, N. Y., on the Black River), built, 1849; length, 35 miles; locks, 109; depth, 4 feet; cost, $3,581,954.

These waterways have played a great part in the development of the country. Those of New York state were all part of one scheme of water transit and many of them are utilized in the Barge canal system. In this way they are and have been important to the dwellers in the Mohawk valley through which the Erie and the Barge canal flow. The future of transportation lies largely in utilizing waterways and the lines of the old canals hence deserve the attention of the reader.

———

Following are statistics relative to some of the other important canals of North America, outside New York state. The general subject of water traffic is worthy of consideration as some of these old and abandoned canals may, in the future, form part of a North American great inland system of waterways, including those of New York state and the Mohawk valley.

Lehigh (Coalport, Pa., to Easton, Pa.), built, 1821; length, 108 miles; first large American canal to be completed. Schuylkill (Mill Creek, Pa., to Philadelphia, Pa.), built, 1826; length, 108 miles. Welland (present ship canal from Lake Erie to Lake Ontario), first completed in 1833, since enlarged and further enlargement contemplated; length, 27 miles; locks, 26; depth, 14 feet; cost, $27,264,802. Miami and Erie (Cincinnati, O., to Toledo, O.), built, 1835; length, 274 miles. Ohio (Cleveland, O., to Portsmouth, O.), built, 1835; length, 317 miles. Pennsylvania (Columbia, Northumberland, Wilkesbarre, Huntingdon, Pa.), built, 1839; length, 193 miles. Illinois and Michigan (Chicago, Ill., to LaSalle, Ill.), built, 1848; length, 102 miles. Chesapeake and Ohio (Cumberland, Md., to Washington, D. C.), built, 1850; length, 184 miles. Illinois and Mississippi (around rapids at Rock River, Ill., connecting with Mississippi), built, 1895; length, 75 miles.

Celebrations of the opening of the Erie canal were not alone confined to the villages along its banks but were held in many enterprising communities all over the state. The New York authorities ordered all the artillery of the state to be out on Oct. 26, and fire a salute and where villages had military organizations there was generally some celebration or parade.

At Cooperstown a splendid celebration took place with Col. G. S. Crafts as marshal. Major Benjamin's corps of artillery fired a salute from the summit of Mount Vision. A feu-de-joie by Capt. Comstock's company of light infantry followed the salute, which was succeeded by proceedings in the Episcopal church where an address was delivered by Samuel Starkweather, Esq. A public dinner was served at Major Griffith's hotel, where patriotic toasts washed the dinner down.

At Fort Plain (then a village of not more than 200, including Sand Hill) the event of the opening of the Erie canal was fittingly observed. Says Simms:

"The substantial citizens of the neighborhood assembled on the day [Oct. 26, 1825] of general festivities on the canal and celebrated the marked event. A long procession headed by Dr. G. S. Spalding as marshal and led with martial music marched from the public house of mine host, Joseph Wagner, to Sand Hill where, near the church a six pound cannon heralded the event of the day [Clinton's entering the canal at Buffalo] in thunder tones abroad. The patriotic crowd is said to have proceeded to the hill and back two and two, and it is probably well that some of them did so. A report of this celebration, published in the Johnstown 'Republican' soon after, says: 'An address with an appropriate prayer was pronounced in Washington Hall [which was in an upper room of the Warner store] to a crowded audience, by Rev. John Wack, who did much honor to his head and heart. After the address the company partook of a collation prepared by Mr.

Joseph Wagner. Dr. Joshua Webster acted as president and Robert Hall, Esq., as vice-president. The festivity of the day terminated with a ball in the evening.'

"The sumptuous dinner at this first Wagner House (said Simeon Tingue, then its hotel clerk) was spread the entire length of the ball-room. This house stood on the north side of the guard lock, and is now owned by Andrew Dunn. After discussing the merits of a good dinner numerous toasts were washed down by good liquor, which as was soon apparent was freely used by all present. Remembered among those at the table were several [by the name of] Fox, Gros, Wagner, Hackney, Marvin, Ferguson, Adams, Cole, Belding, Mabee, Diefendorf, Crouse, Lipe, Dygert, Ehle, Nellis, Abeel, Seeber, Verplanck, Washburn, Moyer, Casler, Clum, Failing, Roof, Firman, Langdon, Warner, Cunning and others. A more jovial or free-from-care set of men were never assembled in Minden. Here is a glance at the toasts. First came thirteen regular toasts and the eleventh was as follows: "Constitution of the United States—'And the rain descended and the floods came and the winds blew and beat upon the house, and it fell not for it was founded upon a rock.'" Nine cheers. The twelfth was "Education" and drew out six cheers, while the thirteenth upon the "Canals of New York" was followed by twelve cheers. Of the nineteen good volunteer toasts recorded, I think every mover but one has gone to his rest— the exception is Hon. Peter J. Wagner, now (1882) past 87; and here is his sentiment: "Liberty of the Press —The armed neutrality of a powerful Republic. Here no Harrington is denounced as a bloodstained ruffian—no Galileo doomed to languish and pine within the cells of an accursed Inquisition." Mr. Wagner had more to do with preparing the toasts than any other man. As the guests grew hilarious, W. P. M. Cole, a witty Yankee teacher, jumped upon the table, which was a temporary one resting upon sawhorses. Many dishes were yet upon the table when down it went and all on it upon the floor. And, after the guests left the hall, lucky was it if they all got home before dark.

"It was expected that the boat [Seneca Chief, bearing Gov. Clinton and suite to tidewater] would arrive on the evening of 'Monday, October 31 [1825], possibly heralded by stages, anticipating which event a large concourse of people gathered from a distance of several miles around. Preparations had been made to proclaim the event by erecting two long poles on Prospect Hill, each with half a barrel of pitch on top with cords to hoist lighted shavings to ignite them. A cannon was also placed between them. To herald the event James A. Lee, a constable, was sent on horseback to Countryman's lock, some miles above; and, to spread the tidings, two young men—Rugene Webster and Solomon Norton—were delegated to Abeel's tavern half a mile west, to 'telegraph' with a musket from that point. Headquarters were at the new store of Warner, then directly above the guard lock, the windows of which were illuminated. It was eleven o'clock at night when the mounted express reached Abeel's, where was also a jolly crowd. Norton fired the overloaded musket and experienced its fearful rebound, to be followed by the thunder of the 32 pound signal gun.

"In a very few minutes the beacons were on fire and war's mouthpiece on the hill heralded the approach of the Seneca Chief. Gov. Clinton—with a waiter by his side holding a lamp—as the boat, towed by three horses, ran in by the store, came on deck. Limping a little, rubbing his eyes and looking up at the light, seeming in the clouds, he exclaimed in admiration of the view, "My God! what is that?" His wonder was how the light could be burning so far heavenward. The truth was the night was dark and foggy, obscuring the bold bluff on which the light was burning more than a hundred feet above his boat—a scene calculated to astonish any beholder not knowing the circumstances. But the visit must be brief, and every eye of the hundreds present (whether Clintonians or not) desired to see the projector of 'Clinton's Ditch,' and somebody must say something. John Taylor, an Irish schoolmaster—sometimes witty and always garrulous—stepped upon the bow of the boat and said (not knowing what else to say) "Gov. Clinton, this is my friend, John Warner's store." Poor Taylor, in attempting to regain the shore, fell into the canal but * * * he was rescued without injury. Later in life it was his fate to be drowned in the canal. Lawrence Gros, who was just then commencing trade as a partner of Warner in his new store, and Dr. Webster were possibly the only ones present who could claim a personal acquaintance with the Governor; and so desirous was Col. Crouse, and perhaps others, for an introduction to his Excellency, that they stepped on board and, entering the cabin, rode down to the lock one-quarter of a mile below. It is presumed that the Governor discovered that some of his guests had, in waiting, kept their spirits up in a manner often resorted to at that period. Martial music attended the boat down to the lock and, as the Fort Plain guests stepped on shore, the band struck up 'Yankee Doodle,' when Gov. Clinton, from the deck, swung the crowd an adieu with his hat, entered the cabin with Canal Commissioner Bouck and others, and the Seneca Chief moved forward."

———

DeWitt Clinton, the "father" of the Erie canal and the virtual builder of "Clinton's Ditch," was born in Deer Park, Orange county, March 2, 1769. He was a son of Gen. James Clinton, of the Sullivan and Clinton expedition to the Indian country in 1779, and who made Canajoharie his rendezvous in the Mohawk valley prior to his overland trip to join Sullivan. Gov. George Clinton (who was at least twice at Fort Plain) was his uncle. His mother's name was Mary DeWitt of the New York Dutch family of that name. He graduated at Columbia college in New York city in 1786, studied law and in 1790 became private secretary to his uncle, Gov. Clinton. He was "a man of ardent temperament, dignified manners, inclined to reserve and of noble personal appearance." He was elected as a Republican or Anti-Federalist to the New York assembly in 1797 and to the State Senate in 1798, and soon became his party's most influential leader in New York. In 1801 he was elected to the United States Senate. In 1803 he was appointed by the Governor and council, Mayor of New York, which office he held, by successive reappointments, until 1814. He served as Lieutenant-Governor from 1811-1813 and in 1810 was chairman of the canal board. In 1812 he was nominated for President of the United States by the party opposed to President Madison's war policy, receiving 89 electoral votes (including those of New York), but was not elected. In 1815 he framed and presented to the state legislature a memorial advocating the construction of the Erie canal (which was ordered in 1817). He was elected governor of New York almost unanimously in 1817 and in 1820 re-elected (over Daniel D. Tompkins), during his terms being president of the board of canal commissioners. He declined a renomination in 1822 and in 1824 was removed as a canal commissioner. In the fall of 1824 he was again elected governor by a large majority, making the triumphal tour of the Erie canal in celebration of its opening, October, 1825. He was re-elected in 1826 and died in Albany before completing his term, Feb. 11, 1828, aged 58 years.

CHAPTER XI.

1831-1836 — First Valley Railroads — The Mohawk and Hudson (1831), Utica and Schenectady (1836), New York Central (1853), New York Central and Hudson River Railroad (1869), Fonda, Johnstown and Gloversville (1870), West Shore Railroad (1883) — First Freight Business — Trolley Lines.

This description of railroad building in this locality is the fifth chapter on transportation in the Mohawk valley.

Prior ones have covered the subjects of Mohawk river traffic, turnpike construction and travel, river and other bridges and Erie canal. Others to follow, handling the same subject, concern the Barge canal and Atwood's St. Louis to New York flight—seven chapters in all. Turnpike construction marked the first years of the nineteenth century, canal construction was a feature of the opening years of that century's third decade and railroad building marked the early years of the fourth decade—all of these improvements in national transportation and traffic being rendered necessary by the opening up of new country, the increase in population, trade, manufactures and agriculture.

A steam railway engine was patented by Richard Trevithick in 1802 and 1804 in England. This was tried out first on the highways but later used on colliery railways with a speed no greater than that of horse hauling. In 1814 Stephenson produced an engine with a speed of six miles an hour. Railroad rails came into use on colliery horse railways in 1790. The first steam colliery railroad of any length (37 miles) was the Stockton and Darlington railway opened in England in 1825. The first American railway was that from the granite quarries of Quincy, Mass., to tidewater (5 miles), built to supply the granite for Bunker Hill monument. This was completed in 1827. The Delaware and Hudson built 16 miles of coal mine railway, to the head of its canal of that name, in 1828. By 1830, the Baltimore and Ohio had 60 miles of a 250-mile railroad completed and the Mohawk and Hudson had laid 12 miles of its 16-mile line from Albany to Schenectady. The South Carolina R. R., Camden and Amboy, Ithaca and Owego and the Lexington and Ohio were all under construction in 1830. The Mohawk and Hudson was the first and the Utica and Schenectady the second link in the great railroad system operated at present (1913) by the New York Central railroad. Most of these early railroads used horse power at first.

Within a decade or two after the

Erie canal was completed, and equipped with boats for passenger and freight traffic, it was threatened with eclipse by the building of railroads. The first of these in New York state, to be chartered by the legislature, was the Mohawk and Hudson River Railroad company, for a railroad to run from Albany to Schenectady. This was the pioneer railroad in the state and is said to have been the second of any importance in the country. It was finished in 1831 and was rudely built and equipped. The rails were similar to those later used for horsecars, and at first horses furnished the only motive power, except that, at the summits of the higher hills, stationary engines were located to draw up and let down the cars by ropes. The passenger cars were modeled after the stage coach of the day, being hung on leather thorough-braces and having seats both inside and out. A lever attached to the truck was operated by downward pressure as a brake. The first locomotive (used in the first year of travel) was made at West Point, N. Y., and was named "Dewitt Clinton." This first engine used wood for fuel and, on its earlier trips, liberally besprinkled the outside passengers with live cinders, and they were often busy beating out the incipient fires thus started on their clothing.

The advantages of steam railroads being here practically seen, other lines were immediately projected and applications for charters made. Among them was the Utica and Schenectady, connecting those cities and covering a distance of about 80 miles. With its parent road, the Mohawk and Hudson, it made a line almost 100 miles long and so traversed the greater part of the Mohawk valley.

In 1836 the Mohawk and Hudson railroad, from Albany to Schenectady, covered 15 of the 100 miles of railroad then in operation in this state. A contemporary writes, in 1836, of it and its extension (the Utica and Schenectady road then nearly completed), as follows: "This road, the importance of which entitles it to a conspicuous station among the many improvements of the age, is designed to form no in considerable link in the extensive chain of communication between the western world and the tide waters of the Hudson. Passing through a country famed for its fertility of soil and its exuberance of agricultural productions, the route can scarcely fail of presenting some features to the contemplation of the most fastidious traveler. With the Mohawk river almost constantly in view, as it majestically sweeps onward in its course, confined on either side by a succession of lofty and precipitous hills, the eye of the amateur may frequently discern landscapes comprising almost every variety of picturesque and scenic beauty."

Says Beers's History of 1878: "It was not to be supposed that Schenectady would long remain the terminus of a road pointing up the Mohawk valley toward the growing west. Enterprising men soon resolved on its extension among the thriving villages created by the tide of westward emigration, and in 1833, a charter was granted for the construction of the Utica and Schenectady Railroad. The original capital of the company, $2,-000,000, more than sufficed for the building and equipment of the road, and the enterprise proved conspicuously successful. [It usurped the north shore Mohawk turnpike in places, which, in those sections, had to be reconstructed further away from the river.] The first board of directors consisted of Erastus Corning, John Townsend, Lewis Benedict, James Porter, Alonzo C. Page, Tobias A. Stoutenburgh, Nathaniel S. Benton, Nicholas Deveraux, Henry Seymour, Alfred Munson, James Hooker, John Mason and Churchill C. Cambreling. Erastus Corning was first president; James Porter, secretary; William C. Young, chief engineer, and on the completion of the road superintendent; Gideon Davidson, commissioner. One of the provisions of the charter was that each county through which the road passed must be represented by one or more of its citizens on the board of directors. Under this regulation, Tobias A. Stoutenburgh was chosen from Montgomery county. The original charter also fixed the maximum fare at four cents a mile, and required the company to sell out to the state after ten and within fifteen years if the state desired to purchase.

"The work of construction went on with rapidity, and, on the 1st of August, 1836, the road was opened for the conveyance of passengers. That August day was an event in the valley, both in itself and in its foreshadowings. The long excursion train was packed with delighted passengers, and each station furnished yet other crowds seeking places in the overflowing cars. The train made slow progress, but eager and curious eyes watched the iron monster that puffed its murky breath and hissed through its brazen throat.

"At this time the idea of carrying freight was not entertained. The charter forbade it, consequently no preparations for the transmission of merchandise had been made by the company. The desire of the superintendent seemed to be to confine the business of the road to the carrying of passengers. The occasion for handling freight, however, of course, arose on the closing of the canal in 1836. On the very day that frost stopped navigation in that year, a German family, wishing to convey their effects from Palatine Bridge to Schenectady, were permitted to ship them on a car, and this, it may be said, was the beginning of the way freight business of the Central railroad. The conductor in this case, having no tariff of rates to guide him, made the rather exorbitant charge of $14. The legislature, in 1837, authorized the company to carry freight and subsequently made the regulation, allowing passengers to have a specified amount of baggage carried free of charge. The first freight cars were called 'stage wagons.'" [The modern T rail was invented by Col. Robert Stevens of New Jersey, in 1830. Steel rails were first used in 1857 in England. The first iron rails were but three feet long.]

"Improvements were made in track and rolling stock at an early day in the history of the Utica and Schenectady road. We have said that the rails were originally like those of later street railroads—namely sticks of timber, with bands of iron, spiked upon them, called 'strap rails.' The irons had a tendency to work loose at the ends and turn up, forming what were called 'snake heads,' which were ready, on catching the bottom of a car, to spear the passengers or throw the train from the track. [Solid iron rails accordingly superseded them.] The first improvement in passenger cars consisted in building frame bodies, somewhat ornamented, and placing them on four-wheeled trucks. Each car was divided by partitions into three compartments, seating eight persons apiece and entered by a door on either side. The conductor traversed a plank running along the side of the car, and, holding on to an iron over the door of each section, reached in for the fare. [This arrangement was somewhat on the style of passenger coaches on English roads. In 1831 the first American style passenger coach (with doors at each end) was used and this style soon supplanted the English type in North America.]

"At first no time tables governed the running of the trains. One would leave Utica at a specified hour, each week-day morning, and get to Schenectady when it could, returning on the same plan. For a long time, after the completion of the road, there were few station agents, and freight conductors had to hunt up patrons at each stopping place, where merchandise was to be left, and collect the charges. Freight trains ran about eight miles an hour, passenger trains about 20 or less. Time and experience gradually brought order and exactness into every department of the business on this line and it enjoyed unexampled prosperity.

"In the spring of 1853, the legislature passed an act for the consolidation of roads, then in operation (and some only projected) between Albany and Buffalo, to form the New York Central. This was effected a few weeks later. The new company had a capital of $23,085,600. The Utica and Schenectady was, of course, one of the roads absorbed by it. One of the original directors, who remained as such up to the time of the consolidation, states that, at that time, 'the stock capital of the company was $4,500,000, on which the shareholders received 50 per cent premium in six per cent bonds of the consolidated company, equal at par to $2,475,000; and how much of the two-and-a-half millions increase was made up by extra dividends in the old company, and how much of the surplus has been and will be paid by the trustees to the shareholders of the company, I need not name to make good the assertion that the Utica and Schenectady Company has turned out the most successful of modern railway enterprises.' The growth of business on this road is evidenced by the fact that its second track was laid before it became part of the New York Central.

"The ambition of each railway mag nate, as the actual and prospective greatness of the West became appar ent, was the control of a through line from the seaboard which could make sure of its share of the transportation for the great grain regions and popu lous cities so rapidly developing. Cornelius Vanderbilt's first step in this direction was the consolidation for 500 years of the Hudson River Railroad with the New York Central, which took place under an act passed by the legislature in May, 1869, the line taking the name of the New York Central and Hudson River Railroad. The immense business of the transportation of freight commanded by this road required that its freight trains should have tracks to themselves, and made it at once necessary and profitable to double the already large capacity of the line from Buffalo to Albany, where much of its traffic was diverted toward New England. This was aecomplished by the construction of third and fourth tracks between those cities, which were completed in the autumn of 1874.

"The almost incalculable advantages to be derived from railroad facilities are offered at their best to the inhab itants of the Mohawk valley. The creation of points of sale and shipment for agricultural products in creases the value of farm property, and Montgomery county everywhere shows in its rich, well-cultivated farms and fine buildings, the benefits of home markets and the highest facilities for transportation. The villages, which by the Central Railroad are placed within an hour and a half of Albany and six or seven of New York, are far more nearly equal to those cities in their advantages as homes than they could be without it, while possessing their own class of attractions and thus are assured of a solid growth and development. To arrest or seriously delay the conveyance of what now comes and goes so promptly by mail and express would be to take away much of what constitutes civilization, and remand the community thus afflicted to comparative barbarism."

The first stations on the Mohawk and Schenectady Railroad, in the five western towns of Montgomery county, were located at Sprakers, Palatine Bridge-Canajoharie, Fort Plain, Palatine Church and St. Johnsville. That at Palatine Church was subsequently dropped. St. Johnsville was long an important station of the Central road, having a railroad restaurant and coal pockets. Little Falls was an important point and Fonda also, as here connections were made north after 1870.

The stations on the West Shore road in Montgomery county are in the eastern part, Amsterdam, Fort Hunter, Fultonville, and in the five western towns are Randall, Sprakers, Canajoharic, Fort Plain, St. Johnsville and Mindenville (flag station). The full list of stations on the Central in Montgomery county, from east to west, are Amsterdam, Fort Johnson, Tribes Hill, Fonda, Yosts, Sprakers, Palatine Bridge-Canajoharie, Fort Plain-Nelliston, St. Johnsville. Some of the fastest trains in the world run over the Central. The passenger and freight service is enormous and a train is almost always in sight from Prospect

Hill, Fort Plain. The Central is one of the few four-track roads in the world.

The building of the West Shore railroad cut through and seriously injured the business section of Canajoharie. Fort Plain was at first similarly threatened, as the original plans called for a railroad running along the east side of Canal street throughout the village. The most strenuous efforts of leading and influential Fort Plain citizens were required to bring about a change of plans in the early 80s, and the present course of the railroad, on the flats through the village limits a distance of a mile and a half, was adopted. The opening of the West Shore in 1883 was marked by a terrible collision of trains, with loss of life, at Diefendorf Hill, just west of Fort Plain. A local train, running west from Canajoharie to Syracuse in the morning and returning in the evening, has been known as the Canajoharie local, almost since the inauguration of service over the road.

The West Shore road and the Central entered into a fierce rate competition, shortly before the West Shore's absorption by the Central, which brought the passenger rate down to a cent a mile for a short period. The passenger fare is now (1913) two cents per mile on both roads as it is generally on most New York state railroads. Freight rates have shown a decline since the inauguration of freight service in the valley in 1836, as previously referred to. The average rate per ton per mile was 0.74 cents in 1891. The West Shore was bought by the Central about 1895 and is today (1913) used almost exclusively as a freight branch of the N. Y. C. & H. R. R.R. system. The passenger train service has been cut down to a few local and through trains daily, the north shore railroad, the Central, handling most of the passenger traffic. The West Shore takes its name from its occupancy of the west shore of the Hudson, the Central occupying the east shore. Through the Mohawk valley the West Shore R.R. follows the south shore of the Mohawk river and the Central the north bank. In the six miles from Canajoharie to Palatine Church the West Shore is truly on the west shore of the Mohawk, as the course of the river in that distance is generally northwest and southeast. The West Shore was built by Italian labor. As the Erie canal was largely dug by Irishmen, so it is probable that the Utica and Schenectady was constructed by that race as its construction followed the canal within fifteen years.

The carrying capacity of both passenger coaches and freight cars has constantly increased together with the drawing power of the locomotives, since the first days of railroading. This was the cause of the gradual decline of canal business—the limited possibilities of transportation on this waterway finally being unable to meet railroad competition except on certain classes of freight.

In the United States (1913) freight cars are 30 to 36 feet long, with two four-wheeled trucks, and weigh from 20,000 lbs. to 30,000 lbs. and carry 40,000 to 60,000 lbs., the combined weight of the larger cars and burden being 45 tons. European freight cars are only 12 to 18 feet long, with four wheels, weigh 11,000 to 18,000 lbs., and carry 18,000 to 23,000 lbs. Steel is now (1913) supplanting wood in the construction of both passenger and freight cars in the United States. This has been true of trolley car construction for a number of years past. An interesting comparison is afforded by the fact that one 1,500 ton Barge canal barge will carry a load as large as 50 biggest freight cars can haul. Tandem barges, or one 3,000 ton barge, will equal a 100-car train in carrying capacity.

American locomotives and passenger cars are heavier and more powerful than European types. European passenger cars are (1913) from 26 to 56 feet long, while the American ones are 80 feet long, in the largest cars, and are wider, higher and of generally stronger and heavier construction. Nine to twelve car American express trains weigh from 350 to 500 tons, while in Great Britain ten to fifteen car express trains weigh 270 tons at the most. The heaviest New York Central locomotive (1913) weighs 135 tons, with a "tractive effort" of 31,000 pounds. The largest American locomotive yet produced weighs 308 tons with a "tractive effort" of 111,000 pounds. Passenger train speed on the Mohawk section of the Central has been registered exceeding 68 miles per hour.

The railroad mileage of the United States was 2,816 in 1840, 30,600 in 1860 and 177,753 in 1893, when the world's railroad mileage was 405,000. Half the railway mileage of the world is in North America, including the United States, Canada and Mexico. The United States's mileage was 240,000 in 1910, of which 25,000 miles was included in the "Vanderbilt" or New York Central group of roads, the third largest system in the country.

The building of the Fonda, Johnstown and Gloversville Railroad (1870) with extension to Northville (1875) and the construction of the West Shore railroad (finished 1883) completed the construction of steam railroads at present operating within the limits of old (Fulton and) Montgomery county. · The future usefulness of iron track railways, for local passenger and freight service, seems to lie in the electric trolley service and such a road is already in use between Schenectady, Amsterdam, Johnstown and Gloversville and Fonda, in the east end of the county, and one is projected, from Little Falls, via St. Johnsville, to Johnstown, with a spur connecting with Nelliston, Fort Plain and Canajoharie, which will undoubtedly in time be continued down the valley making a connecting link in the electric trolley line from Buffalo to New York city. Trolleys parallel the railroads in the Mohawk valley from Rome to Little Falls and from Fonda to Cohoes. At Schenectady there are trolley connections with Albany and with the upper Hudson valley.

A railroad through the Otsquago valley connecting the Mohawk valley at Fort Plain with the upper Susquehanna valley at Richfield Springs and Cooperstown has long been projected.

A meeting to promote this enterprise was held in Fort Plain as early as 1828. The Fort Plain and Richfield Springs Railroad company was formed about 1885. Later Boston capitalists became interested, right of way was secured, and a roadbed was constructed over a large part of the line, beginning at the base of Prospect Hill, Fort Plain. The enterprise failed financially about 1895. At one time the project contemplated uniting the proposed railroads with the "dead ends" of railroads at Cooperstown, Cherry Valley and Richfield Springs. Connection between the Mohawk and Susquehanna valleys was made about 1905 by the trolley line running from Herkimer through Mohawk and Richfield Springs to Oneonta with a branch to Coopers town.

One of the leading railroad men of the mid-nineteenth century was Webster Wagner of Palatine Bridge, whose name is closely associated with the early development of sleeping and drawing room railroad coaches. He was a member of the Palatine Wagner family which located about 1720 in Palatine township, on the farm now (1913) owned by Charles D. Smith, about two miles west of Fort Plain. Webster Wagner was born in 1817 at Palatine Bridge, where he became ticket and freight agent on the Schenectady and Utica railroad in 1843. He later handled grain and farm produce and while in this business, he conceived the idea of building sleeping cars. A company was formed and four cars were built at a cost of $3,200 each. Berths were provided for the sleepers, each having a pair of cheap blankets and a pillow. These cars began running on the New York Central, Sept. 1, 1858, during the presidency of Erastus Corning. Trouble with the ventilation of the cars hampered the success of the project at first. The ventilators, being opposite to the sleepers, made it dangerous to leave them open at night while, with them closed the air was suffocating. To obviate this trouble, in 1859, Mr. Wagner invented the elevated car roof, placing ventilators in the elevation, which proved successful and greatly improved the air in the coaches. This improvement was shortly after generally adopted for all types of passenger railroad cars. During the Civil war these sleeping coaches cost to produce from $18,000 to $24,000 each. In 1867, Wagner invented and put in operation his first drawing room or palace car, the first ever seen in America, which at once became so popular as to secure him a fortune. Wagner palace and sleeping cars came into general use. Pullman introduced a similar type into Europe, and about 1890, the Wagner and Pullman companies were consolidated under the name of the Pullman company. In 1871, Webster Wagner was elected to the assembly and to the state senate in 1872, 1874, 1876, 1878. He met a tragic death in a terrible railroad accident on the Central road at Spuyten Duyvil in 1882, when he was burned to death in one of his own drawing room cars. Mr. Wagner's full name was John Webster Wagner, he being named after his father's physician, Dr. John Webster, according to Mason's History.

The present chair, buffet, sleeping, combination, dining, and observation coaches of steel construction are all later developments of the original sleeping car first put in operation by Webster Wagner on the New York Central railroad in 1858. The first rude sleeping coach was run on the Cumberland Valley Railroad (Pennsylvania) in 1836.

CHAPTER XII.

1836, Fonda Made County Seat of Montgomery County — New Court House Built at Fonda—Dissatisfaction in Northern Montgomery—1838, Fulton County Created From Northern Montgomery County.

It must be remembered that in all the foregoing reference to Montgomery county (up to 1838), it included Fulton county as well. This was indeed a noble county and it is to be regretted that it was thus cut in two.

This final division of Montgomery took place 222 years after LaCarnon, the French Canadian priest, first entered the Mohawk country, 149 years after Hendrick Frey made the first recorded white settlement in the county, and 127 years after the Palatines located in Stone Arabia. The towns of the present county, including the five western ones of Minden, Canajoharie, Root, Palatine and St. Johnsville assumed their present territorial boundaries (except Canajoharie and Minden as later noted). A long period of development (from the ending of the Revolution) had been completed and the present day era was ushered in.

Old Montgomery county (including its northern region, present Fulton county, and its southern section, present Montgomery county) was a natural division of territory. It largely embraced the Mohawk watershed from East Creek to the Schenectady line, with the exception that it did not include the Schoharie valley on the south. Prior to 1817, when the present towns of Danube and Manheim were taken from it and added to Herkimer county, western Montgomery county included the old Canajoharie country and its succeeding districts of Palatine and Canajoharie.

In 1836 when the county seat was moved to Fonda from Johnstown the latter place had been the Montgomery capital for a period of 64 years, dating from the establishment of Tryon county in 1772. So long in fact had these two artificial divisions, of what is naturally one region, been associated that we still speak of "Fulton and Montgomery county" as though they were yet one, and the two are often linked together in the consideration of history, politics, agriculture, industry and other phases of human life and society.

This division was due to the fact that the county seat was removed to Caughnawaga (Fonda) in 1836 and the people of Fulton county, resenting this, obtained the erection of the then Montgomery county into two separate divisions (Fulton and Montgomery) by act of the legislature in 1838; and

Johnstown again became a county seat—that of the new county of Fulton. This removal was the result of the building of the Utica and Schenectady railroad, which made the central town of Fonda very accessible to the other river towns of the county, while it left Johnstown three miles away and without railroad communication until the completion of the Fonda, Johnstown and Gloversville railroad in 1870. Other causes conduced to this change, in the governing town of the county, which resulted in the unfortunate dismemberment of old Montgomery. Fonda took its name from the Fonda family, which largely owned the land upon which it was built. It was not then an incorporated village and did not become one until 1851. Regarding this subject, the Mohawk Valley Democrat (Fonda) published in its issue of August 15, 1912, the following from the pen of Washington Frothingham of the county seat:

"Fonda is the only village in the Mohawk valley which originated in a land speculation. In 1835, or a little later, John B. Borst of Schoharie, visited this neighborhood and planned a new place to supersede Caughnawaga and to become the capital of Montgomery county. What is now Fonda consisted then of a tavern, a few houses, a fulling mill and a small store. The surrounding lands were owned by the Fonda family, which obtained a liberal price. [from Borst] The Central railroad (then only the Utica and Schenectady) was nearly finished and Borst gave it land for its station at his new village; but a bolder plan was to have the county seat removed from Johnstown. Only after a great effort he succeeded. He gave the plot known as 'the park' to the railroad company and also gave to the county the land occupied by the jail and court house, an area of four acres. Lots were offered at $50 to $100 and both houses and stores were built, and to boom the place, a grand hotel was erected. In this way Fonda, as they named the new settlement, was made the county capital and started with much promise. Yet, notwithstanding

all their push, the scheme did not succeed [financially] and Borst and his associates were bitterly disappointed. Johnstown was much distressed over the loss of the public buildings, but a new county [Fulton] was soon formed, and the records were all copied, down to the creation of Fulton county, so the loss was not deeply felt. The hard feelings of its loss have now passed away and the two places are now on better terms than ever being connected by two railroads and a macadam road."

Prior to Borst's land scheme the village had existed in the Dutch hamlet of Caughnawaga, on the site of an Indian village. It is not improbable, prior to the boom of Johnstown caused by Sir William Johnson's removal there in 1762, that Caughnawaga may have been the largest center of white population in present Fulton-Montgomery county, little hamlet though it was. Prior to the Revolution it was a center for public gatherings, for social intercourse, politics and sports—such as horse racing, a track being there located. Caughnawaga still exists as the eastern end of Fonda.

Says Beers: "The projectors of the village of Fonda conceived that the prospects of their enterprise would be brightened by making the embryo city the capital of Montgomery county. A petition for the removal of the county buildings was accordingly presented to the legislature in 1836. The immediate vicinity of the Mohawk was by this time so thickly inhabited that the old county seat was not central to the population of the county, and it was left comparatively out of the world by the construction of the Utica and Schenectady railroad. The petition made a persuasive showing, on a statistical basis, of what proportion of the inhabitants would be accommodated by the proposed change; and an act authorizing the erection of a court house and jail at Fonda was passed during the session in which it was presented. The commissioners appointed to locate the buildings and superintend construction were Aaron C. Wheelock, Henry Adams and Howland Fish. The act required them to raise and pay into the treasury of the county $4,500, as a preliminary step, and procure a site of at least three acres for the new county buildings. The comptroller was authorized, on receiving a bond from the county treasurer, to loan the county the sum required [for the erection of the buildings] from the common school fund, to be repaid at any time, or times (within five years), that the supervisors might decide upon. Under these arrangements, the court house and jail were built in 1836. The removal of the county seat from Johnstown was naturally very unsatisfactory to the northern portion of the county, and resulted in the division of Montgomery two years later." The old court house still stands and is a building possessed of a simple and pleasing exterior, in a somewhat classic style of architecture. A new court house has been erected in a locality removed from the noise of the Central trains which pass immediately in front of the older building. It is interesting to note in the foregoing that the change to Fonda and the building of the original Central railroad are coincident in point of time—1836.

In 1836, Montgomery county (then including Fulton) contained 585,000 acres of land; the value of its real estate was $3,753,506 and the personal estate $647,899. The county taxes were $19,289.66 and the town taxes $13,023.00.

There were then four academies in the county, located at Amsterdam, Kingsborough, Johnstown and Canajoharie. The county contained 8 woolen factories, 13 iron works, 5 paper mills, 62 tanneries, 8 breweries, 274 saw mills, 74 grist mills, 31 fulling mills, 29 carding machines, 4 oil mills.

The following newspapers were issued: The Johnstown Herald, The Montgomery Republican, at Johnstown; The Northern Banner, at Broadalbin; The Intelligencer and Mohawk Advertiser, at Amsterdam; The Montgomery Argus, at Canajoharie; The Fort Plain Journal, at Fort Plain; The Garland (semi-monthly) and the Christian Palladium (semi monthly), at Union Mills.

The following are some of the officials of Montgomery (including Fulton) county, in 1836, before its division: Elijah Wilcox, collector of canal tolls at Fultonville; John Livermore, one of the canal superintendents of repairs; David Spraker of Canajoharie, one of the four senators from this, the fourth, district, embracing Saratoga, Washington, St. Lawrence and Montgomery counties; Henry V. Berry of Caughnawaga (Fonda), Joseph Blair of Mills' Corners, Jacob Johnson of Minaville, members of assembly; Abraham Morrell, David Spraker, masters and examiners in chancery; Abram Morrell, first judge of the court of common pleas; Samuel A. Gilbert, John Hand, Henry J. Dievendorff, David F. Sacia, judges of the court of common pleas; Michael Kettle, Johnstown, sheriff; Tobias A. Stoutenburgh, Johnstown, surrogate; Charles McVean, Johnstown, district attorney; Joseph Farmer, Johnstown, county treasurer; Matthias Bovee, Amsterdam, member of congress. Benedict Arnold of Amsterdam, was major general of the second division of cavalry and Aaron C. Whitlock of Ephratah, brigadier general in the same division of this branch of the state militia.

In the county there were 40 lawyers, 44 physicians and 28 clergymen, not including the Methodists (for some reason not enumerated in the list from which this is taken).

Since this division of 1838, the present ten towns of Montgomery have retained boundaries given them then, with the exception of the subtraction of the Freysbush district from Canajoharie and its addition to Minden in 1849. This county dismemberment made the towns of Amsterdam, Mohawk and St. Johnsville very narrow in width from north to south, in some places their northern boundaries being within two miles of the river and even a trifle less. The southside townships were, of course, in nowise affected.

At this important period there were,

in the county four villages—Johnstown, incorporated 1808; Canajoharie, incorporated 1829; Amsterdam, incorporated 1830; Fort Plain, incorporated 1832. The population of Johnstown was (1836) 1200 to 1500 and of Fort Plain about 400. No data exists on the population of the other two. Johnstown had 600 in 1802 and in 1844 had 250 dwellings. In 1804 Amsterdam had 100, about equally divided between Dutch and other elements, and in 1813 it had 150. Its growth thereafter was very rapid, outstripping the other villages in a few decades. Gloversville had a dozen houses in 1830. It was incorporated in 1851. Fultonville was incorporated in 1848; Fonda, in 1850 (probable population, 400); St. Johnsville, 1857 (with a population of 720).

In 1836 the population of Montgomery county was almost entirely rural, as will be seen from the figures of village population then. Most of its people were located on the farms, and engaged in agriculture.

So much for the noble old county of Montgomery, which had had an eventful existence with Fulton as part of it for two-thirds of a century. From the Montgomery county of 1784, embracing half the state, it finally assumed territorial borders which make it one of the smallest in area of New York's 62 counties.

———

Mr. Frothingham, who wrote the foregoing concerning Fonda, is the well-known clergyman and writer of Fonda, now (1913) 92 years of age. He was a boy of four when flatboats, on the Mohawk, and huge freight wagons, on the Mohawk turnpike, still carried the bulk of the through freight through the valley, prior to the open-

ing of the Erie canal in the fall of 1825. He was a youth of fifteen when the first railroad train ran in the valley and was a young man of seventeen when Fulton was sundered from Montgomery county. Mr. Frothingham has seen most of the changes which have taken place, in customs, life and transportation in this section from the early pioneer days. He edited Mason's History of Montgomery County, published in 1892, and has written much concerning valley historical matters.

———

Fulton county was named from Robert Fulton, whose success in promoting steam navigation was at that time (1838) still fresh in the public memory. Robert Fulton was born at Little Britain, Lancaster county, Pennsylvania, in 1765. He became a miniature and portrait painter and practised his art in Philadelphia, New York and London. In England he turned his attention to inventing, producing several mechanical contrivances. At this time he became interested in canal navigation and improvement. Later in Paris he brought out a submarine torpedo boat, which was rejected for use by the French, British and United States governments. In 1803 Fulton built a steamboat on the Seine in Paris. In 1807 he launched the steamboat Clermont on the Hudson in New York, which made a successful trip to Albany, and which may be said to have solved the problem of steam navigation. Fulton built many steamboats, ferryboats, etc., and in 1814 constructed the U. S. steamer, "Demologos" (later called Fulton the First), which was the first war steamer built. Robert Fulton died in New York in 1815, aged 50 years.

THE STORY OF OLD FORT PLAIN

(THIRD SERIES 1838-1913)

CHAPTER I.

1838-1913 — Montgomery County, Topography, Population and History— Farm Statistics and Amsterdam Industrial Statistics—Fulton County, Herkimer County and Mohawk Valley Statistics.

The following or third series of chapters treats of Montgomery county and the middle Mohawk valley during the years from 1838 (the date of separation of Fulton from Montgomery county) until the present day (1913):

Montgomery county of today consists of the ten townships of Amsterdam, Mohawk, Palatine, St. Johnsville, Minden, Canajoharie, Root, Glen, Charleston, Florida. The towns along the north side of the Mohawk river from east to west are Amsterdam, Mohawk, Palatine, St. Johnsville, while the south shore towns from east to west are Florida, Glen, Root, Canajoharie, Minden. The town of Charleston is the only one in the county which does not abut on the river as it lies directly south of the town of Glen. Glen and Charleston lie on the west shore of the Schoharie creek while Florida is on the east side, these three towns being the ones in Montgomery along which this picturesque stream flows, finally emptying into the Mohawk at Fort Hunter between the towns of Florida and Glen. The Schoharie is the chief tributary of the Mohawk.

The important creeks in the county flowing into the Mohawk are, on the north shore beginning at the west: East Canada, at East Creek; Crum creek, one-half mile east of East Creek; Timmerman, at Upper St. Johnsville; Zimmerman's, at St. Johns-

ville; Caroga, at Palatine Church; Knauderack, flowing through Schenck's Hollow, past the county home; Cayadutta, at Fonda; Danoscara, at Tribes Hill; Kayaderosseras, at Fort Johnson; Chuctanunda, at Amsterdam; Evaskill, at Cranesville.

From west to east, on the south shore, are the Otsquago, at Fort Plain; Canajoharie, at Canajoharie; Flat creek, at Sprakers; Yatesville creek, at Randall; Allston, at Stone Ridge; Auries, or Ochraqua, at Auriesville; Schoharie, at Fort Hunter; South Chuctanunda, at Amsterdam (south side); Cowilla, opposite Cranesville. Persons interested in Montgomery, its life and history would do well to procure a map of the county.

The boundaries of Montgomery county are north, Fulton; east, Saratoga and Schenectady; south, Schenectady, Schoharie, Otsego; west, Herkimer.

In reference to its geology the following is briefly summarized from Mason's: Gneiss is found in patches, its principal locality being near the Nose on the river. Resting upon it are heavy masses of calciferous sandstone, mostly on the north side and trending northward into Fulton county. Next above the sandstone are the Black River and Trenton limestone, not important as surface rocks but furnishing valuable quarries of building stone. Hudson river group slates and shales extend along the south side of the county and are found in a few places north of the river. Drift and boulders abound. A deep, rich, vegetable mould forms the soil of the alluvial plains or "flats" along the river. On the uplands is mostly a highly productive, sandy and gravelly loam. The land is generally adapted to agriculture and especially dairying, which forms a leading feature of Montgomery farm activities. Traces of coal, lead and silver are found in Montgomery county rocks.

The country is one of rolling hills for the most part, although in some parts, back from the river, it is only gently undulating. Much of it is broken and somewhat precipitous in parts, particularly along the banks of the streams. The picturesque Canajoharie creek gorge is a miniature canyon with walls 100 feet high in places. There is much natural beauty throughout the county, which is to be expected of a county 33 miles long and lying along the Mohawk, famed as traversing a most picturesque valley. There are beautiful falls on the Canajoharie, a mile south of the village of that name and on Flat creek, a mile south of Sprakers. There are sulphur springs in almost every township.

The views from some of the hilltops are always extensive and often inspiring. From some heights foothills may be seen which lie at the edge of the great Adirondack forest, which also, at one time, covered Montgomery county extensively, with the exception of the vlaies or natural meadows. The following are the elevations of the highest points of land, above sea level as given on the map issued by S. Conover of Amsterdam: Minden, at Salt Springville, 986; Canajoharie, at Mapletown, 1213; Root, two miles southeast of Lykers, 1310; Glen, two miles south of Glen village, 1200; Charleston, Oak Ridge, near Oak Ridge settlement, 1446; Florida, two miles southwest of Minaville, 1203; Amsterdam, in the east central part, 700; Mohawk, Van Deusen Hill, 1029; Palatine, Rickard's Hill in north part, 1029; St. Johnsville, Getman hill on the north line in the east end, 1140. Oak Ridge, 1446 feet, in Charleston, is the highest point on the south side and also in Montgomery county. It is 11 miles from the Mohawk. Getman Hill, 1140 feet, in St. Johnsville township, is the highest northside point and is less than three miles from the river. Sub-

tracting the river bed sea elevations (302 feet at Fort Plain, 278 feet at Fonda and 267 feet at Amsterdam), will give the height of the hills above the Mohawk. The best and most characteristic valley views are to be obtained on the hills, back from the Mohawk river.

The area of Montgomery county is about 385 square miles and the soil is in general fertile, that on the "flats" being a particularly rich loam.. The 43d parallel of north latitude cuts directly through the center of St. Johnsville and the county lies between the 74th and 75th degree meridians westward from Greenwich, England, and 2 and 3 degrees east of Washington. It is bounded on the north by Fulton, on the east by Saratoga and Schenectady, on the south by Schoharie and Otsego and on the west by Herkimer county. It is 33 miles long and 15 miles wide at the point of the greatest breadth at Randall. Yosts is almost exactly in its center lengthways.

Aside from the ten towns, it contains the city of Amsterdam and the villages of Hagaman and Fort Johnson in Amsterdam town and the villages of Fonda in Mohawk town, Palatine Bridge and Nelliston in Palatine town, St. Johnsville in St. Johnsville town, Fort Plain in Minden town, Canajoharie in Canajoharie town, Fultonville in Glen town. It also has the following unincorporated places or neighborhood centers:

In Minden:— Mindenville, Minden, Hallsville, Brookmans Corners, Salt Springville, Freysbush.

In Canajoharie:—Sprout Brook, Van Deusenville, Buel, Marshville, Ames, Waterville, Mapletown.

In Root:—Sprakers, Randall, Flat Creek, Browns Hollow, Lykers, Currytown, Rural Grove, Stone Ridge.

In Glen:—Glen, Auriesville, Mill Point.

In Charleston:—Charleston Four Corners, Charleston, Oak Ridge, Carytown, Burtonsville.

In Florida:—Fort Hunter, Minaville, Miller Corners, Scotch Bush, Scotch Church.

In Amsterdam:—Cranesville, Manny Corners.

In Mohawk:—Tribes Hill, Berryville, Yosts.

In Palatine:—McKinley, Stone Arabia Four Corners, Stone Arabia, Three Points, Wagners Hollow, Palatine Church.

In St. Johnsville:—Upper St. Johnsville.

The following regards the civil government of Montgomery, the same as that of other New York counties. It forms, of course, part of a state senatorial and part of a national congressional district, their boundaries varying at different times. It is an assembly district and is represented by one assemblyman at Albany.

The strictly county officers, with their terms of office in years, are: Sheriff, 3; county judge, 6; surrogate, 6; county clerk, 3; treasurer, 3; district attorney, 3; four coroners, 4; superintendent of poor, 3; two district school commissioners (one for five west towns and one for five east towns, exclusive of the city of Amsterdam), 3. A county highway superintendent, two commissioners of elections and a sealer of weights and measures are appointed by the board of supervisors. For lists of Montgomery county officers see Beer's History of Montgomery and Fulton Counties (1878) and Mason's History of Montgomery County (1892).

The town officers are with their terms of office in years: Supervisor, 2; town clerk, 2; four justices of peace, 4; three assessors, 4; one or three highway superintendents, 2; overseer of poor, 2; collector, 2; three auditors, 2; not more than five constables, 2; a board of health composed of the town board and a health officer (appointed).

The usual village officers are president, board of trustees, boards of sewer and water commissioners, clerk, treasurer, collector, police officers and street commissioner.

The history of Montgomery county from 1838, the date of separation of Fulton 'and Montgomery counties, covers the Civil war period and is one of : agricultural development and change, of the great increase and development of the villages and the county's city, Amsterdam, and the remarkable growth of manufacturing industries in all the population centers of importance. Hops, which were long raised in the southern section of the Montgomery, are but little cultivated on account of the lack of reliability as to crop and because of the competition of the Pacific slope. The same is true of broom corn which was so long a principal crop on the river flatlands and which stimulated the building of broom factories in almost all the river towns. The county has also largely become a dairying section instead of one where general crops (and wheat largely) were raised 75 years ago. There is but little lumbering done as the available timber is largely gone and areas must be replanted to protect the soil and the flow of the watercourses. Fruit growing is of increasing importance and much fine poultry is raised both for market and for breeding. Hay, oats and corn are the three most important crops.

A large and interesting volume could be made of the present industries of old Montgomery (including present Fulton) county. To the north of us in Fulton there is lumbering and Gloversville (with Johnstown) is the glove manufacturing center of the United States. Amsterdam has carpet works of great size and capacity and "Amsterdam rugs" are sold everywhere in enormous quantities. The same is true of many other county manufactures. Barkley's Geography of Montgomery County, published in 1892, gives the following as the natural and manufactured products of Montgomery, to which additions have been made to bring the list up to date.

Agricultural:—Cattle, horses, sheep, swine, wool, hides, lumber, butter, cheese, wheat, corn, oats, hay, rye, buckwheat, potatoes, flax, hops, beans, apples, pears, plums, grapes, honey, alfalfa, eggs, poultry, vegetables and garden truck.

Mineral:—Limestone, clay and sand. Lead ore in small quantities has been found on the banks of Flat creek in

Root, and gold, copper, zinc and lead had been obtained in non-payable amounts from the banks of East Canada creek in the town of St. Johnsville. Limestone is found in abundance in the towns or Amsterdam, Florida, Mohawk, Root, Canajoharie, Palatine and St. Johnsville. It was largely used for building in the earlier days and made handsome houses.

The manufactures of 1913 by towns are as follows:

Amsterdam town and city:—Carpets, rugs, knit goods, brooms, springs, linseed oil, boilers, paper boxes, silk, beer, malt, waterwheels, caskets, paper, cigars, clothing, soda water, bricks, wooden building material (sash, doors, blinds, etc.), lumber.

Canajoharie:—Paper bags, food products, beer, flour, feed, cider, wagons.

Charleston:—Wagons, sleighs, flour, feed, cotton yarn, lumber, cider, wine.

Florida:—Brooms, wagons, sleighs, cultivators, wine.

Glen:—Silk goods, poultry coops, brooms, stoves, lumber, cider, waterwheels, castings, flour, feed.

Minden:—Knit goods, paper boxes, furniture, broom machinery, flour, feed, cider, pickles, hose bands, wagons, silk goods, toy wagons, cabinets, corn huskers, milk products, broombands, cigars.

Mohawk:—Knit goods, paper, wagons, soda water, flour, feed, tile, cider.

Palatine:—Condensed milk, candy, milk products, straw board, vinegar, cider.

Root:—Wagons, lumber, cider.

St. Johnsville:—Agricultural machinery, threshing machines, pianos, piano actions, fifth wheels, wagons, sleighs, knit goods, condensed milk, carriage forgings, cider, flour, feed, lumber, bricks, piano players.

The chief events in the history of Montgomery county of the period being considered are: 1838, division of Montgomery and Fulton counties; enlargement of the Erie canal, begun in 1835; formation of Montgomery County Agricultural society, 1844; Civil war and enlistment of Montgomery county men, 1861-5; completion Fonda, Johnstown and Gloversville railroad, 1870;

West Shore railroad completed, 1883; Amsterdam becomes a city, 1885; electric road connects Schenectady, Amsterdam, Fonda, Johnstown and Gloversville, 1905; commencement of Barge canal work, 1905; electric power plant established at Ephratah, using waters of Pecks Pond and Garoga lakes and transmission line run to Fort Plain, 1911; 1911, Atwood's aeroplane flight through the Mohawk valley on his St. Louis to New York air trip. He landed at Nelliston and remained over night at Fort Plain.

An agricultural fair was held in old Montgomery county at Johnstown, as early as Oct. 12, 1819, by a society organized in that year. Fairs have been held in most of the years succeeding this date. In 1865, the Fulton County Agricultural society bought 18 acres near Johnstown for a permanent fair ground. In recent years the fair has been discontinued and the grounds sold for building lots.

The growth of agricultural societies, as relating to Montgomery, finds a fitting place here. There are two of these in the county, the Montgomery County Agricultural society, holding annual fall exhibitions and races at Fonda on its fair grounds, and the Fort Plain Street Fair association (mentioned elsewhere) holding an annual September fair on the brick pavements of Fort Plain.

In 1793 the Society for the Promotion of Agriculture, Arts and Manu factures was established, and in 1801 this body, for convenience of action, divided the state into agricultural districts, each consisting of a county. A secretary was appointed in each district, whose duties were to convene the members of the society within the county, learn the state of agriculture and manufactures therein and report to the president of the society. Shortly after this time, premiums were offered for the best specimens of home made cloth, and were awarded partly by the general authority of the society and partly by county judges appointed by it. By an act of legislature; in 1819, for the improvement of agriculture, a board of officers was created and an appropriation made for two years, which was to be distributed among the different counties of the state for the advancement of agriculture and domestic manufactures, on the condition that the counties themselves subscribed an equal sum, but this was carried out but little by the counties and no permanent result came of it. The present State Agricultural society was formed in 1832. No state appropriation was made for it until 1841, when measures were taken for raising funds and holding annual fairs. In the spring of 1841, $40,000 was appropriated, partly to the state society and partly for division among the counties in proportion to their representation in the assembly.

It was under this act that the Montgomery County Agricultural society was organized. Pursuant to a notice by the county clerk, a meeting was held Sept. 20, 1844, at the Fonda court house. The committee on nominations reported the following, which were adopted: President, Tunis I. Van Deveer; vice-presidents, Joshua Reed, Peter H. Fonda; secretary, John Frey; treasurer, John Nellis; board of directors, Amsterdam, Benedict Arnold; Charleston, Robert Baird; Canajoharie, Jeremiah Gardner; Florida, Lawrence Servoss; Glen, Richard Hudson; Minden, Barney Becker; Mohawk, Lyndes Jones; Palatine, William Snell; Root, George Spraker; St. Johnsville, John Y. Edwards. A committee was appointed to draft a constitution and report it at a subsequent meeting, which all desirous to promote the interests of agriculture, manufactures and rural arts, were earnestly invited to attend.

Oct. 13, 1844, the organization was completed and arrangements made for the first fair which was held at the court house, Nov. 11, 12, 1844. The receipts came to $471,50 and the expenses $462. The fair was held at the court house for the three following years (1844, 1845, 1846), the annual receipts averaging about $250. In 1847 the fair was held in Canajoharie. The next four were held at the court house in Fonda, the tenth (in 1853) at Fort Plain, in St. Johnsville in 1854 and at

Canajoharie in 1855. Since then it has been held annually at Fonda, that place having been fixed upon as the permanent locality in 1863. In 1860 the constitution and by-laws were adopted, the officers to be a president, two vice-presidents, a secretary and a treasurer, an executive committee of three, a board of directors consisting of three members from each town of the county. All of the officials' terms were one year. Membership for one year was put at 50 cents and persons could become life members on payment of $10. The annual meeting is held on the evening of the first day of the fair and officers are then elected to become active the following New Year.

In 1863 the society purchased its present grounds in Fonda, a field of 13 acres, formerly belonging to the Van Horne family. The fair of 1864 was held on these new grounds and proved the most successful up to that date, the receipts being over $2,000—double those of any previous year. In 1872 further buildings were put up and other improvements effected. In 1876, the grandstand was built, and, as it was centennial year, an unusually attractive show was made in all departments and a great variety of sports and races took place. The receipts were $3,800. A street carnival feature has since been added to the "Fonda fair." There are many other agricultural societies in the county, formed for social or business purposes.

Montgomery county, like every other section of the country, suffered terribly from the Civil war. Its men responded in numbers to the call to arms and hundreds lie buried on southern battle fields or in the burial grounds of their home neighborhoods. A dreadful sorrow filled the valley and houses were numberless where a father, husband or son had gone to the front never to return alive.

The completion of the Fonda, Johnstown and Gloversville railroad in 1870 was a county event of importance. In 1875 it was extended to Northville.

The construction of the West Shore railroad (completed 1883) proved a great stimulus to Montgomery towns on the south shore. It has stations at Amsterdam, Fort Hunter, Auriesville, Fultonville, Randall, Sprakers, Canajoharie, Fort Plain, Mindenville. For a time there was great competition between the two roads and the new West Shore (so named from running on the west side of the Hudson) made business very lively. The competition resulted in a cut rate of one cent a mile which prevailed for awhile through the valley. The West Shore finally failed and was absorbed by the New York Central and is now used principally as a freight route.

The following newspapers are published in Montgomery county: Amsterdam Recorder, Amsterdam Sentinel, Mohawk Valley (Fonda) Democrat, Montgomery County Republican (Fultonville), Canajoharie Radii, Canajoharie Courier, Hay Trade Journal (Canajoharie), Fort Plain Standard, Mohawk Valley Register (Fort Plain), Fort Plain Free Press, St. Johnsville News, St. Johnsville Enterprise.

The following newspapers are published in Fulton county: Gloversville Herald, Gloversville Leader, Johnstown Democrat.

The Mohawk valley has been the scene of considerable change in its population, although not to the same extent as other parts of the United States of America. The rural population of Montgomery and parts of Fulton is probably largely identical with that of a century ago and it is probable that much of this farm population is no greater in certain localities than in 1812, and in some sections even less. It is in the cities and towns that the greatest population changes have occurred and these largely coincide with the conglomerate urban people of the rest of the United States. In the valley, however, there is generally a substratum of the original white population in the cities and larger villages. With the exception of the city of Amsterdam the county of Montgomery has a population throughout very similar to that here present in the early part of the nineteenth century or before the division of Montgomery and Fulton counties in 1838. This is largely due to the fact that there has been no great incentive to immigration into the county since then, with the exception of the industrial opportunities offered by the east end city. It is probable that certain early elements which came into the valley after the Revolution have largely decreased—such as the New England, which we read of so largely at that time and whose restlessness (its greatest weakness) induced these Yankees to again take up a western hegira. The early men of this region not only largely developed it but have themselves scattered all over the country and Mohawk valley names may now be found from the Mohawk river to San Francisco bay. New York city had, for a number of years, a Montgomery County society, which numbered 200 members and held annual dinners.

The valley has witnessed and participated in that great urban growth and development which was a leading characteristic of national life in the nineteenth century. This has not only brought in un-American peoples but has, by its indoor life and sedentary work, markedly depreciated the vigor of the original Mohawk valley stock.

Recent years in Montgomery county have been marked principally by the great development of manufactures, highway improvements, electric trolley road building, utilization and transmission of electric power, free rural mail delivery, city and village improvement, and the construction of the Barge canal which is to replace the Erie.

It has been a peaceful time, broken only by the Spanish war of 1898 which called to the service a few men of Montgomery. In a general way, it is the industrial development, the solution of social and economic problems, the improvement of rural communication, the development of rural life and the improvement in agriculture which immediately concern the people of Montgomery county.

The towns along the Mohawk, including those in Montgomery county, are so situated that it is probable they will experience a gradual but sure growth into cities, some of considerable size. Their location on the Barge canal and two lines of railroad is the main cause of this development, com bined with their situation in a rich agricultural territory with foodstuffs raised at their very doors and serving as markets for the farming country for miles around. The gradual growth of these Mohawk river centers has been largely composed of the original population and without a great access of an undesirable foreign element. There have been exceptions to this rule, but it is to be hoped that such conditions will prevail, thereby avoiding many of the evils which have followed the undesirable and rapid growth of cities in other sections of the country. The development of Schenectady, from the quiet Dutch town of 1880, with a population of less than 15,000, to the great manufacturing center of 1910 with 72,000 people, has been the one marked exception to the gradual growth of the other river towns. In a lesser way the building up of Amsterdam in the same period, is also noteworthy. Its population of 31,267 in 1910 made it the third city, in point of size in the Mohawk valley and was more than half of the Montgomery county population of 57,567. Amsterdam's growth is entirely responsible for the increase of the county's population in recent years and it is probable that the rest of Montgomery's population has decreased in the past fifty years. With the growing demand for foodstuffs and their increasing price, a growth in the agricultural population can be looked for, particularly in sections so favorably situated as to markets and transportation as the townships immediately adjacent to the Mohawk river. So that with growing towns and demand for agricultural products, combined with the good land available, it is reasonable to suppose the already large Mohawk valley population will be much greater in the years to come —a population which may easily comprise a million people in time. This is, of course, provided that the water supply of the valley is conserved by reforestation, dams, etc. No section can

grow beyond its water supply. The rainfall of the Mohawk basin has been steadily decreasing for a century.

The area of Montgomery county is 254,720 acres. That of Fulton county is 330,240 acres. The area of old Montgomery county, which included these divisions prior to 1838, was 584,960 acres. Root is the largest town of Montgomery county and St. Johnsville is the smallest. With the figures at hand it is impossible to give the area of each township. Root, Florida and Minden are the three largest towns. However the size of townships or counties means little as they are only imaginary divisions.

The census department at Washington has kindly furnished figures for this work relative to the population of Montgomery county. In 1790 the population of Montgomery was 18,261. In 1850 (after the detachment of Fulton county) the population was 31,992; 1860, 30,866; 1870, 34,457; 1880, 38,315; 1890, 45,699; 1900, 47,488; 1910, 57,567.

The 1910 population by towns is as follows: Amsterdam, including Amsterdam city, 34,341; Canajoharie, 3,-889; Charleston, 900; Florida, 1,904; Glen, 2,002; Minden, 4,645; Mohawk, 2,488; Palatine, 2,517; Root, 1,512; St. Johnsville, 3,369.

The populations of the villages and city are as follows: Amsterdam city, 31,267; Fort Plain, 2,762; St. Johnsville, 2,536; Canajoharie, 2,273; Fonda, 1,100; Hagaman, 875; Fultonville, 812; Nelliston, 737; Fort Johnson (incorporated 1909, formerly Akin), 600; Palatine Bridge, 392.

The incorporation of the villages of Montgomery county took place as follows: Canajoharie, 1829; Amsterdam, 1830; Fort Plain, 1832; Fultonville, 1848; Fonda, 1850; St. Johnsville, 1857. Since the latter date the villages of Hagaman, Palatine Bridge, Nelliston and Fort Johnson have been incorporated.

There are several population centers in the county which include two or more incorporated or unincorporated places. With the best census figures and estimates at hand the total population of these centers, which virtually form single communities, are as follows: Amsterdam - Hagaman - Fort Johnson-Rockton, 33,792; Fort Hunter-Tribes Hill, 1,000; Fonda-Fultonville, 1,912; Canajoharie-Palatine Bridge, 2,665; Fort Plain-Nelliston, 3,499

The variation of population in the different townships is shown in the following figures. From a study of these it is shown that the rural population has steadily declined since 1850 while the towns have increased. While the decline of the number of people in the agricultural sections seems to be still going on, it is not probable that it will long continue. On the other hand an increase of the farming population may be looked for in the future. The town populations by censuses follow:

Amsterdam, 1850, 4,128; 1880, 11,170; 1910 (including Amsterdam city, except the south side fifth ward in the town of Florida, formerly Port Jackson), 31,962.

Canajoharie, 1850, 4,097; 1880, 4,294; 1910, 3,889.

Charleston, 1850, 2,216; 1880, 1,334; 1910, 900.

Florida, 1850, 3,571; 1880, 3,249; 1910, (including former Port Jackson village, or Amsterdam city fifth ward), 4,283.

Glen, 1850, 3,043; 1880, 2,622; 1910, 2,002.

Minden, 1850, 4,623; 1880, 5,100; 1910, 4,645.

Mohawk, 1850, 3,095; 1880, 2,943; 1910, 2,488.

Palatine, 1850, 2,856; 1880, 2,786; 1910, 2,517.

Root, 1850, 2,736; 1880, 2,275; 1910, 1,512.

St. Johnsville, 1850, 1,627; 1880, 2,002; 1910, 3,369.

According to the foregoing every town in the county has lost in population, from 1850 to 1910, except Amsterdam and St. Johnsville.

The census of 1910 places the population of Montgomery county at 57,567 and that of Fulton county at 44,534. The combined population of Fulton and Montgomery counties is 102,091. The total number of farms in the two counties is 4,221, with a total agricultural production valued at $6,707,681 in 1909. The combined value of goods manufactured in Montgomery and Fulton counties in 1909 is roughly estimated at $50,000,000.

For this work it is impossible to obtain figures of manufactures, as relating to New York state, by counties so details regarding such production is lacking for Montgomery and Fulton counties. The number of all farms in Montgomery county in 1910 was 2,189 as against 2,407 in 1900. In Fulton county there were 1,932 farms in 1910 and 2,234 in 1900.

The following interesting information regarding the condition of agriculture in Montgomery county is furnished by the census of 1910:

Population (1910), 57,567; population in 1900, 47,488.

Number of all farms, 2,189; number of all farms in 1900, 2,407.

Color and nativity of farmers—Native white, 1,883; foreign-born white, 306.

Number of farms, classified by size—Under 3 acres, 17; 3 to 9 acres, 148; 10 to 19 acres, 126; 20 to 49 acres, 191; 50 to 99 acres, 514; 100 to 174 acres, 888; 175 to 259 acres, 249; 260 to 499 acres, 52; 500 to 999 acres, 3; 1,000 acres and over, 1.

Land and farm area—Approximate land area, 254,720 acres; land in farms, 234,041 acres; land in farms in 1900, 236,934 acres; improved land in farms, 195,262 acres; improved land in farms in 1900, 202,394 acres; woodland in farms, 25,002 acres; other unimproved land in farms, 13,777 acres; per cent of land area in farms, 91.9; per cent of farm land improved, 83.4; average acres per farm, 106.9; average improved acres per farm, 89.2.

Value of farm property—All farm property, $15,460,547; all farm property in 1900, $12,929,081; per cent increase, 1900-1910, 19.6; land, $6,303,804; land in 1900, $5,941,600; buildings, $5,517,979; buildings in 1900, $4,608,840; implements and machinery, $1,120,835; implements, etc., in 1900, $769,990; domestic animals, poultry and bees, $2,-517,929; domestic animals, etc., in 1900, $1,608,651.

Per cent of value of all property in—Land, 40.8; buildings, 35.7; implements and machinery, 7.2; domestic animals, poultry and bees, 16.3.

Average values—All property per farm, $7,063; land and buildings per farm, $5,401; land per acre, $26.93; land per acre in 1900, $25.08.

Domestic animals (farms and ranges)—Farms reporting domestic animals, 2,099; value of domestic animals, $2,399,736.

Cattle—Total number, 36,537; dairy cows, 22,804; other cows, 1,640; yearling heifers, 3,629; calves, 6,725; yearling steers and bulls 1,134; other steers and bulls, 605; value, $1,234,434.

Horses—Total number, 7,639; mature horses, 7,221; yearling colts, 327; spring colts, 91; value, $1,065,093.

Mules—Total number, 5; mature mules, 4; yearling colts, 1; value, $655.

Swine—Total number, 9,098; mature hogs, 4,944; spring pigs, 4,154; value, $74,709.

Sheep—Total number, 3,902; rams, ewes and wethers, 2,108; spring lambs, 1,794; value, $24,746.

Goats—Number, 21; value, $99.

Poultry and Bees—Number of poultry of all kinds, 143,302; value, $102,959; number of colonies of bees, 3,615; value, $15,234.

Number, acreage and value of farms classified by tenure, color and nativity of farmers and mortgage debt by counties: April 15, 1910:

Farms operated by owners—Number of farms, 1,446; number of farms in 1900, 1,550; per cent of all farms, 66.1; per cent of all farms in 1900, 64.4; land in farms, 139,760 acres; improved land in farms, 115,923 acres; value of land and buildings, $7,117,522. Degree of ownership: Farms consisting of owned land only, 1,341; farms consisting of owned and hired land, 105. Color and nativity of owners: Native white, 1,226; foreign-born white, 220.

Farms operated by tenants—Number of farms, 719; number of farms in 1900, 819; per cent of all farms, 32.8; per cent of all farms in 1900, 34.0; land in farms, 89,673 acres; improved land in farms, 75,378 acres; value of land and buildings, $4,347,361. Form of tenancy: Share tenants, 458; share-cash tenants, 12; cash tenants, 241; tenure not specified, 8. Color and nativity of tenants: Native white, 635; foreign-born white, 84.

Farms operated by managers—Number of farms, 24; number of farms in 1900, 38; land in farms, 4,608 acres; improved land in farms, 3,961 acres; value of land and buildings, $356,900.

Mortgage debt reports—For all farms operated by owners: Number free from mortgage debt, 849; number with mortgage debt, 588; number with no mortgage report, 9. For farms consisting of owned land only: Number reporting debt and amount, 506; value of their land and buildings, $2,268,987; amount of mortgage debt, $878,719; per cent of value of land and buildings, 38.7.

Live stock products (1909)—Dairy products: Dairy cows on farms re-porting dairy products, 22,128; dairy cows on farms reporting milk produced, 19,314; milk produced, 11,123,057 gallons; milk sold, 10,288,208 gallons; cream sold, 3,377 gallons; butter fat sold, 449,839 pounds; butter produced, 236,592 pounds; butter sold, 155,301 pounds; cheese produced, 950 pounds; cheese sold, 900 pounds; value of dairy products, excluding home use of milk and cream, $1,299,769; receipts from sale of dairy products, $1,277,634. Poultry products: Number of poultry raised, 159,955; number of poultry sold, 64,106; eggs produced, 916,984 dozens; eggs sold, 651,515 dozens; value of poultry and eggs produced, $315,758; receipts from sale of poultry and eggs, $199,250. Honey and wax: Honey produced, 123,366 pounds; wax produced, 1,478 pounds; value of honey and wax produced, $13,759. Wool, mohair and goat hair: Wool, number fleeces shorn, 1,685; mohair and goat hair, number fleeces shorn, 8; value of wool and mohair produced, $3,185.

Domestic animals sold or slaughtered (1909)—Calves, number sold or slaughtered, 16,515; other cattle, number sold or slaughtered, 4,442; number horses, mules and asses and burros sold, 352; number swine sold or slaughtered, 1,582; receipts from sale of animals, $265,270; value of animals slaughtered, $156,419.

Value of all crops and principal classes thereof and acreage and production of principal crops, 1909:

Value of all crops, $2,673,527; cereals, $756,512; other grains and seeds, $3,078; hay and forage, $1,433,171; vegetables, $204,201; fruits and nuts, $101,027; all other crops, $175,538.

Selected crops—Cereals: Total, 42,071 acres; 1,282,282 bushels. Corn, 10,003 acres; 398,357 bushels. Oats, 25,507 acres; 726,120 bushels. Wheat, 312 acres; 7,893 bushels. Barley, 284 acres; 7,233 bushels. Buckwheat, 5,470 acres; 133,434 bushels. Rye, 486 acres; 8,967 bushels. Other grains: Dry peas, 21 acres; 422 bushels. Dry edible beans, 103 acres; 875 bushels. Hay and forage, 86,409 acres; 130,173 tons. All tame or cultivated grasses, 82,109 acres; 94,777 tons. Timothy alone, 23,867 acres; 26,937 tons. Timothy and clover, mixed, 51,322 acres; 58,529 tons. Clover alone, 5,411 acres; 6,951 tons. Alfalfa, 201 acres; 490 tons. Millet or Hungarian grass, 289 acres; 572 tons. Other tame or cultivated grasses, 1,019 acres; 1,298 tons. Wild, salt or prairie grasses, 10 acres; 10 tons. Grains cut green, 92 acres; 131 tons. Coarse forage, 4,198 acres; 35,253 tons. Root forage, 2 tons. Special crops: Potatoes, 2,007 acres; 193,644 bushels. All other vegetables, 1,021 acres. Hops, 209 acres; 148,329 pounds. Number maple trees, 9,470;

maple sugar made, 294 pounds; maple syrup made, 2,941 gallons.

Fruits and Nuts—Orchard fruits: Total number trees, 97,906; 140,105 bushels. Apples, 77,804 trees; 131,264 bushels. Peaches and nectarines, 309 trees; 226 bushels. Pears, 5,159 trees; 2,742 bushels. Plums and prunes, 9,001 trees; 4,411 bushels. Cherries, 5,561 trees; 1,447 bushels. Quinces, 37 trees; 4 bushels. Grapes, 8,612 vines; 81,787 pounds. Small fruits: Total, 89 acres; 117,489 quarts. Strawberries, 21 acres; 45,515 quarts. Raspberries and loganberries, 38 acres; 45,454 quarts. Nuts, 2,700 trees; 42,530 pounds.

Selected farm expenses and receipts, 1909:

Labor: Farms reporting, 1,659; cash expended, $372,973; rent and board furnished, $153,487. Fertilizer: Farms reporting, 868; amount expended, $32,-960. Feed: Farms reporting, 1,378; amount expended, $184,083. Receipts from sale of feedable crops, $411,442.

Number and value of domestic animals not on farms April 15, 1910:

Inclosures reporting domestic animals, 1,182; value of domestic animals, $387,155. Cattle: Total number, 210; value, $8,999; number of dairy cows, 154. Horses: Total number, 2,103; value, $371,169; number of mature horses, 2,089. Mules and asses and burros: Total number, 19; value, $4,-420; number of mature mules, 18. Swine: Total number, 241; value, $2,409. Sheep and goats: Total number, 19; value, $158.

The total value of all the products of Montgomery county farms, including dairy, poultry, eggs, honey and wax, wool, domestic animals sold and slaughtered, and all crops (exclusive of lumber) was $4,727,687 in 1909.

While the census statistics of manufactures for the counties of New York state are not available, those for its cities of over 10,000 population are given. Of the class of (41) cities, between ten and fifty thousand inhabitants, Amsterdam leads in the number of its people engaged in industry—10,776. It has 97 industrial establishments and produced $22,449,000 worth of manufactures in 1909 against $10,-643,000 in 1899, or an increase of over 100 per cent in ten years.

It is probable that the total manufactures of Montgomery county exceed $28,000,000 annually.

The following figures are given relative to Fulton county's agricultural interests. They will form an interesting table in comparison with the first one published relative to Montgomery, whose farming statistics are given in full. It has been the aim, in this work, to still consider Fulton and Montgomery counties (old Montgomery county) as one civil section. The Fulton county farming figures follow:

Population, 44,534; population in 1900, 42,842.

Number of all farms, 1,932; number of all farms in 1900, 2,234.

Color and nativity of farmers: Native white, 1,795; foreign-born white, 134; negro and other non-white, 3.

Number of farms, classified by size: Under 3 acres, 12; 3 to 9 acres, 101; 10 to 19 acres, 122; 20 to 49 acres, 305; 50 to 99 acres, 514; 100 to 174 acres, 628; 175 to 259 acres, 179; 260 to 499 acres, 60; 500 to 999 acres, 3; 1,000 acres and over, 8.

Land and farm area—Approximate land area, 330,240 acres; land in farms, 205,845 acres; land in farms in 1900, 208,687 acres; improved land in farms, 98,781 acres; improved land in farms in 1900, 115,213 acres; woodland in farms, 69,219 acres; other unimproved land in farms, 37,845 acres; per cent of land area in farms, 62.3; per cent of farm land improved, 48.0; average acres per farm, 106.5; average improved acres per farm, 51.1.

Value of farm property—All farm property, $6,808,265; all farm property in 1900, $5,834,750; per cent increase, 1900-1910, 16.7; land, $2,659,010; land in 1900, $2,603,800; buildings, $2,549,-545; buildings in 1900, $2,066,850; implements and machinery $465,742; implements, etc., in 1900, $331,420; domestic animals, poultry and bees, $1,-133,968; domestic animals, etc., in 1900, $832,680.

Per cent of value of all property in—Land, 39.1; buildings, 37.4; implements and machinery, 6.8; domestic animals, poultry and bees, 16.7.

Average values—All property per farm, $3,524; land and buildings per farm, $2,696; land per acre, $12.92; land per acre in 1900, $12.48.

Domestic animals (farms and ranges)—Farms reporting domestic animals. 1,741; value of domestic animals, $1,079,357.

Cattle—Total number, 16,096; dairy cows, 9,835; other cows. 990; yearling heifers, 1,608; calves, 2,896; yearling steers and bulls, 385; other steers and bulls, 382; value $486,396.

Horses—Total number, 4,064; mature horses, 3,851; yearling colts, 198; spring colts, 15; value, $543,860.

Mules—Total number, 8; mature mules, 7; yearling colts, 1; value, $1,735.

Asses and burros—Number, 2; value, $425.

Swine—Total number, 4,344; mature hogs, 2,519; spring pigs, 1,825; value, $38,471.

Sheep—Total number, 2,027; rams, ewes and wethers, 1,290; spring lambs, 737; value, $8,413.

Goats—Number, 15; value, $57.

Poultry and Bees: Number of poultry of all kinds, 67,193; value, $49,239; number of colonies of bees, 1,265; value, $5,372.

Fulton county's farms produced in 1909, products of the following value: Dairy products, $437,818; poultry and eggs, $150,387; honey and wax, $3,169; wool and mohair, $1,542; domestic animals sold, $96,404; domestic animals slaughtered, $89,873; all crops, $1,200,- 801. Total value of Fulton county farm production for 1909 (exclusive of lumber), $1,979,994.

Fulton county has the city of Gloversville (first incorporated as a village in 1851), with a population (1910) of 20,642, and the city of Johnstown (first incorporated as a village in 1808), with a population (1910) of 10,447. They are so closely joined that they may justly be considered one population center of over 31,000. Northville (population, 1,130) and Mayfield (population, 509) are the two other incorporated places of Fulton county.

Gloversville has 6,604 persons engaged in industry (mostly glovemaking), 187 establishments, with products of a value, for 1909, of $14,171,000, a great increase over 1899 when approximately $9,000,000 of manufactures were produced. Johnstown has 3,009 persons engaged in industry (largely glovemaking), 138 establishments and a manufactured product, for 1909, of $6,574,000 against approximately $5,- 000,000 in 1899. Johnstown and Gloversville together, produced $20,745,000 worth of goods in 1909, which included practically all the manufactures of Fulton county.

Following is a brief resume of 1909 agricultural statistics for Herkimer county:

Population, 56,356. Number of farms, 1910, 3,092. Number of farms, 1900, 3,227. Native white farmers, 2,769. Foreign born farmers, 322.

Land area, 933,760 acres. farm lands (acres), 371,969. Improved farm lands, 258,595. Farm woodland, 76,385. Other unimproved farm land, 36,989.

Value of domestic animals, $3,631,- 865. Cattle, 64,914. Dairy cows, 40,423. Horses, 8,213. Swine, 9,754. Sheep, 2,957. Poultry, 134,528. Colonies of bees, 2,179.

Value of dairy products, $2,199,633. Value of poultry and eggs, $290,047. Value of honey and wax, $8,976. Value of cut of wool and mohair, $2,825. Receipts from sale of animals, $467,399. Value of animals slaughtered, $176,655. Value of all crops produced, $2,847,042. Total 1909 farm production of Herkimer county (lumber excluded), $5,992,- 577.

Herkimer county is the leading dairy county of the Mohawk valley in proportion to its improved farm acreage, although Oneida county with an acreage of 800,000 and 6,929 farms, leads in total value of all dairy and other farm products, and is therefore the first (in 1910) agricultural county of the six Mohawk valley counties.

Herkimer county has one city, Little Falls (incorporated 1895), with a population of 12,273. It has 4,211 persons engaged in industry in 55 establishments and in 1909 produced $8,460,000 worth of manufactures. Herkimer county has the important sister villages of Herkimer, Mohawk, Ilion and Frankfort (virtually one community, with a population of about 20,000) and the lively village of Dolgeville, in the town of Manheim on East creek. The total manufacturing product value yearly for Herkimer county may exceed $25,000,000.

———

Let us turn from the dry bones of these statistics to a charming view of the farming country of Montgomery and the valley of the Mohawk. It is from the pen of Mrs. A. D. Smith and formed part of a sketch published in the Fultonville Republican, Dec. 5, 1912, entitled "A Ramble—Visit to a Colonial House." The building described is. the frame house erected in 1743 by John Butler, father of the notorious Walter Butler of Revolutionary infamy, located about a mile northeast of Fonda. The prelude to the sketch mentioned is here reproduced:

"On one of the recent Indian summer days we chanced to walk over Switzer hill, turning our glances backward now and then to take in the remarkable panorama to the south—the distant hills, bathed in azure, the broad meadows, the populous settlements, the cattle grazing, the husbandman bending over his plow, the historic Mohawk moving, in its sinuous pathway, on toward the ocean, the mystical autumn light over the rare scene. Close at one side was the ravine with babbling brook; the great pines to our right, sighing and moaning, making music all the day. Charmed with the beauties of the scene, in our heart we uttered a silent prayer and thereby were refreshed from within as well as from without. We saw on every hand preparations for the winter season, the golden risks of corn, the barrels of ruddy apples, great piles of cabbages, golden pumpkins, casks of sweet cider, fresh from the mill, flocks of chickens, broods of turkeys ready to be sacrificed for the national feast. And we said, fortunate the man who lives much in the open, close to nature, breathes the pure air and works with the mystical forces of the earth with God as an ally. The farmer learns a powerful lesson in faith and strength."

According to the United States census of 1910, the six Mohawk valley counties comprise an area of 2,861,440 acres divided as follows: Oneida, 800,000; Herkimer, 933,760; Montgomery, 254,720; Fulton, 330,240; Schenectady, 131,840; Schoharie, 410,880. It is estimated that this area of the Mohawk valley counties was divided in 1910, about as follows: Improved farm land, 1,350,000 acres; unimproved farm land, 260,000 acres; town sites, 100,-000 acres; waste land or land occupied by industries, railroads, etc., outside towns, 100,000 acres; forest and farm woodland, 1,050,000 acres. In these six counties were 18,457 farms, on which there were 14,034 operating owners, the remainder being leased. There was a marked decrease in farms in all these six Mohawk counties from 1900 to 1910, and there was a similar decrease in acreage of improved farm land in all the six counties except Oneida. In the six counties combined the improved farm land acreage decreased from 1,515,745 acres in 1900 to 1,351,461 acres in 1910, showing that much land is reverting to widerness. Most of the farm lands are fertile—the Mohawk flats being reputed to be among the richest lands of the world. Dairying is the leading agricultural industry. Hops are grown to a lessening extent in the southern watershed and poultry, fruits and market gardening are increasingly important farm features of the valley. .

The six Mohawk valley counties have the following population: Oneida, 154,157; Herkimer, 56,356; Montgomery, 57,567; Fulton, 44,534; Schenectady, 88,235; Schoharie, 23,855. Total, 424,704 (census, 1910). That of New York state (1910), was 9,113,614, so that the population of the Mohawk watershed counties was, in 1910, .0467 of that of the state or a little less than one-twentieth.

The towns are located almost exclusively on the Mohawk river; 310,-000 of the 425,000 population of the watershed being so located in centers of 1,000 and over; in centers of from 250 to 1,000, 35,000; farm population, 80,000. A large part of this population is descended from the pre-Revolutionary Dutch, German and British settlers of the Mohawk basin. At the beginning of the Revolution the population of the Mohawk valley was about 20,000 whites and 1,000 or more Iroquois.   •

Seventeen towns, of over 1,000 population, line the Mohawk, from its souce to its outlet into the Hudson. On its tributary streams are seven more, making twenty-four in the Mohawk watershed. From the source of the Mohawk to Rome (a distance of twenty miles), the largest town is

West Leyden with 600 population. According to the census of 1910, the population of the towns mentioned, from Rome eastward, was as follows: Rome, 20,497; Oriskany, 1,200; Waterville on Oriskany creek, 1,410; Clinton, on Oriskany creek, 1,236, Whitesboro, 2,375; New Hartford, 1,195, and New York Mills, on Saquoit creek, 2,600; Utica, 74,419; Frankfort, 3,303; Ilion, 6,588; Mohawk, 2,079; Herkimer, 7,520; Little Falls, 12,273; Dolgeville, on East Canada creek, 2,685; St. Johnsville, 2,536; Fort Plain, 2,762; Canajoharie, 2,273; Fonda, 1,100; on the Cayadutta, Johnstown, 10,447; Gloversville, 20,642; on the Schoharie, Cobleskill, 2,086; Middleburg, 1,114; Amsterdam, 31,267; Scotia, 2,957; Schenectady, 72,826; Cohoes, 24,709. A great variety of manufactures is produced in these centers, most of which are strictly manufacturing towns, although all are more or less, centers of trade for their tributary agriculture districts.

Manufacturing was generally begun in the valley population centers from 50 to 100 years ago. Their industries comprise a great range of goods, some of which have long been made in the valley and are identified with its growth. The knit goods industry is the leading one. Some of the other Mohawk valley manufactures are white goods, arms, typewriters, woodwork, house and office furniture, dairy machinery and goods, agricultural machinery, piano actions, paper bags, broom machinery and articles, food products, milk products, gloves, carpets and rugs, locomotives, electrical machinery and manufactured goods, paints, oils, varnishes, wagons, flour, feed, lumber, paper.

CHAPTER II.

1848—Trip of Benson J. Lossing from Currytown to Sharon Springs, to Cherry Valley, to Fort Plain—Revolutionary Scenes and People Then Living.

Benson J. Lossing has the following account of a trip in 1848 around about Fort Plain, published in his "Pictorial Field Book of the Revolution" (1850),

in which he covers thoroughly the Revolutionary news, happenings and personages of the Mohawk valley. Much of this volume was gathered while the author was visiting around and in Fort Plain, which he made his headquarters for gathering data. The condensed Revolutionary biographies in this work were largely compiled or taken from the Field Book. It covers a journey from Currytown to Cherry Valley, by way of Sharon Springs, and from Cherry Valley to Fort Plain.

After referring to the Currytown raid and massacre of 1781, Lossing says that after Lieut. McKean was buried near the Fort Plain blockhouse, it was afterward called Fort McKean in his honor. Referring to the massacre by the Indians of the prisoners taken at Currytown, he says:

"At the time of the attack the Indians had placed most of their prisoners on the horses which they had stolen from Currytown and each was well guarded. When they were about to retreat before Willett, fearing the recapture of the prisoners and the consequent loss of scalps, the savages began to murder and scalp them. Young Dievendorff (my informant) leaped from his horse and, running toward the swamp, was pursued, knocked down by a blow of a tomahawk upon his shoulder, scalped and left for dead. Willett did not bury his slain but a detachment of militia, under Col. Veeder, who repaired to the field after the battle, entombed them, and fortunately discovered and proceeded to bury the bodies of the prisoners who were murdered and scalped near the camp. Young Dievendorff, who was stunned and insensible, was seen struggling among the leaves and his bloody face being mistaken for that of an Indian, one of the soldiers leveled his musket to shoot him. A fellow soldier, perceiving his mistake, knocked up his piece and saved the lad's life. He was taken to Fort Plain, and, being placed under the care of Dr. Faught, a German physician of Stone Arabia, was restored to health. It was five years, however, before his head was perfectly healed; and when I saw him (August,

1848), it had the tender appearance and feeling of a wound recently healed. He is still living (1849) and, in the midst of the settlement of Currytown, which soon arose from its ashes, and is a living monument of savage cruelty and the sufferings of the martyrs for American liberty.

"Toward evening we left Currytown for Cherry Valley, by way of Sharon Springs. The road lay through a beautiful though very hilly country. From the summits of some of the eminences which we passed the views were truly magnificent. Looking down into Canajoharie valley, from the top of its eastern slope, it appeared like a vast enameled basin, having its concavity garnished with pictures of rolling intervales, broad cultivated fields, green groves, bright streams, villages and neat farm houses in abundance; and its distant rim on its northern verge seemed beautifully embossed with wooded hills, rising one above another in profuse outlines far away beyond the Mohawk. We reached the Springs toward sunset, passing the Pavilion on the way. The Pavilion is a very large hotel, situated upon one of the loftiest summits in the neighborhood, and commanding a magnificent view of the country. It was erected in 1836 by a New York company and is filled with invalids and other visitors during the summer. The springs are in a broad ravine, and along the margin of a hill, and near them the little village of Sharon has grown up. Our stay was brief—just long enough to have a lost shoe replaced by another upon our horse, and to visit the famous fountains—for, having none of the 'ills which flesh is heir to' of sufficient malignity to require the infliction of sulphereted or chalybeate draughts, we were glad to escape to the hills and vales less suggestive of Tophet and the Valley of Hinnom. How any but invalids, who find the waters less nauseous than the allopathic doses of the shops, and, consequently are happier than at home, can spend a 'season' there, within smelling distance of the gaseous fountains, and call the sojourn 'pleasure,' is a question that can

only be solved by Fashion, the shrewd alchemist, in whose alembic common miseries are transmuted into conventional happiness. The sulphereted hydrogen does not infect the Pavilion, I believe, and a summer residence there secures enjoyment of pure air and delightful drives and walks in the midst of a lovely hill country.

"It was quite dark when we reached Cherry Valley, eight miles west of Sharon Springs. Cherry Valley derived its name from the following circumstance: Mr. Dunlap, [the venerable pastor whose family suffered at the time of the massacre of 1778], engaged in writing some letters, inquired of Mr. Lindesay [the original proprietor of the soil] where he should date them, who proposed the name of a town in Scotland. Mr. Dunlap, pointing to the fine wild cherry trees and to the valley, replied 'Let us give our place an appropriate name and call it Cherry Valley,' which was readily agreed to. This village lies imbosomed within lofty hills, open only on the southwest, in the direction of the Susquehanna, and, as we approached it along the margin of the mountain on its eastern border, the lights sparkling below us like stars reflected from a lake, gave us the first indication of its presence. In the course of the evening we called upon the Honorable James Campbell, who at the time of the destruction of the settlement in 1778, was a child six years of age. He is the son of Col. Samuel Campbell, already mentioned [colonel of the Canajoharie district battalion at Oriskany] and father of the Honorable William W. Campbell of New York city, the author of the 'Annals of Tryon County,' so frequently cited. With his mother and family, he was carried into captivity. He has a clear recollection of events in the Indian country while he was a captive, his arrival and stay at Niagara, his subsequent sojourn in Canada, and the final reunion of the family after an absence and separation of two years. The children of Mrs. Campbell were all restored to her at Niagara, except this one. In June, 1780, she was sent to Montreal, and there she was joined by her missing boy. He had been with a tribe of the Mohawks and had forgotten his own language, but remembered his mother and expressed his joy at seeing her, in the Indian tongue. Honorable William Campbell, late surveyor general of New York, was her son. She lived until 1836, being then 93 years of age. She was the last survivor of the Revolutionary women in the region of the headwaters of the Susquehanna. The residence of Hon. James S. Campbell, a handsome modern structure, is upon the site of the old family mansion, which was stockaded and used as a fort at the time of the invasion. The doors and window shutters were made bullet proof, and the two barns, that were included within the ramparts, were strengthened. The present pleasant dwelling is upon the northern verge of the town, on the road leading from Cherry Valley to the Mohawk [at Fort Plain].

"In a former chapter we have noticed that Brant's first hostile movement after his return from Canada and establishment of his headquarters at Oghkwanà [in 1778] was an attempt to cut off the settlement of Cherry Valley, or at least to make captive the members of the active Committee of Correspondence. It was a sunny morning, toward the close of May [1778] when Brant and his warriors cautiously moved up to the brow of a lofty hill on the east side of the town to reconnoitre the settlement at their feet. He was astonished and chagrined on seeing a fortification, where he supposed all was weak and defenceless, and greater was his disappointment when quite a large and well-armed garrison appeared upon the esplanade in front of Col. Campbell's house. These soldiers were not as formidable as the sachem supposed, for they were only half grown boys, who, full of the martial spirit of the times, had formed themselves into companies, and, armed with wooden guns and swords, had regular drills each day. It was such display on the morning in question that attracted Brant's attention. His

vision being somewhat obstructed by the trees and shrubs in which he was concealed, he mistook the boys for full grown soldiers and, considering an attack dangerous, moved his party to a hiding place at the foot of the Tekaharawa Falls, in a deep ravine north of the village, near the road leading to the Mohawk. The Tekaharawa is the western branch of Canajoharie or Bowman's Creek, which falls into the Mohawk at Canajoharie, opposite Palatine. In that deep, rocky glen, 'where the whole scene was shadowy and dark even at mid-day,' his warriors were concealed, while Brant and two or three followers hid themselves in ambush behind a large rock by the roadside, for the purpose of obtaining such information as might fall in his way.

"On the morning of the day, Lieut. Wormuth, a promising young officer of Palatine, had been sent from Fort Plain to Cherry Valley with the information, for the committee at the latter place, that a military force might be expected there the next day. His noble bearing and rich velvet dress attracted a great deal of attention at the village; and, when toward evening, he started to return accompanied by Peter Sitz, the bearer of some dispatches, the people in admiration looked after him until he disappeared beyond the hill. On leaving he cast down his portmanteau, saying, 'I shall be back for it in the morning.' But he never returned. As the two patriots galloped along the margin of the Tekaharawa Glen, they were hailed, but, instead of answering, they put spurs to their horses. The warriors in ambush arose and fired a volley upon them. The lieutenant fell and Brant, rushing out from his concealment, scalped him with his own hands. Sitz was captured and his dispatches fell into the hands of Brant. Fortunately they were double, and Sitz had the presence of mind to destroy the genuine and deliver the fictitious to the sachem. Deceived by these dispatches concerning the strength of Cherry Valley, Brant withdrew to Cobleskill and thence to Oghkawaga, and the settlement was saved from destruction at that time. Its subsequent fate is recorded in a previous chapter.

"Judge Campbell kindly offered to accompany us in the morning to 'Brant's rock.' This rock which is about four feet high, lies in a field on the left of the road leading from Cherry Valley to the Mohawk, about a mile and a half north of the residence of Judge Campbell. It is a fossiliferous mass, composed chiefly of shells. Behind this rock, the body of Lieut. Wormuth, lifeless and the head scalped, was found by the villagers, who heard the firing on the previous evening. Judge Campbell pointed out the stump of a large tree by the roadside, as the place where Lieutenant Wormuth fell. The tree was pierced by many bullets, and Judge Campbell had extracted several of them when a boy.

"Having engaged to be back at Fort Plain in time next day to catch the cars for Albany at 2 o'clock, and the distance from the 'rock' being twelve miles over a rough and hilly road, an early start was necessary, for I wished to make a sketch of the village and valley, as also of the rock.

"At early dawn, the light not being sufficient to perceive the outline of distant objects, I stood upon the high ridge north of the village, which divides the headwaters of the eastern branch of the Susquehanna from the tributaries of the Mohawk. As the pale light in the east grew ruddy, a magnificent panorama was revealed on every side. As the stars faded away, trees and fields, and hills and the quiet village arose from the gloom. The sun's first rays burst over the eastern hills into the valley, lighting it up with sudden splendor, while the swelling chorus of birds and the hum of insects broke the stillness; and the perfumes of flowers arose from the dewy grass like sweet incense.

"On the north the valley of the Canajoharie stretches away to the Mohawk twelve miles distant, whose course was the mountain toward the Susquehanna marked by a white line of mist that skirted the more remote hills; and on the south Cherry Valley extends down

proper, and formed the easy warpath to the settlement at its head from Oghkwaga and Unadilla. From the bosom of the ridge whereon I stood, spring the headwaters of the eastern branch of Susquehanna and those of Canajoharie. I had finished the sketch here given [in the Field Book] before the sun was fairly above the treetops and, while the mist yet hovered over the Tekaharawa we were at Brant's rock, within the sound of the tiny cascades. There we parted from Judge Campbell and hastened on toward Fort Plain, where we arrived in time to breakfast and to take the morning train for Albany."

CHAPTER III.

1861-1865 — Montgomery and Fulton County Men in the Civil War—115th, 153d and Other Regiments and Companies With Montgomery and Fulton County Representation—1912, 115th and 153d Celebrate 50th Anniversary of Mustering in at Fonda.

The part the men of Montgomery and Fulton counties played in the great and lamentable war of the rebellion was one of honor and the record of those men who went to the front from the valley deserves a full and complete narrative which the present work will not allow. It is to be hoped that the soldiers of '61-'65 of Montgomery and Fulton will some day have their story told at length in a suitable publication. Their deeds deserve such a narrative and it should be written now while the veterans of that terrible struggle are still with us and can supply that personal note in such a story which is so essential to such a tale.

Included in this suggested record should be noble work the union women of America performed in the service of their country during the Rebellion. The women of Montgomery and Fulton counties were well to the forefront in this regard, not only making supplies and clothing for the union soldiers and hospital supplies, but serving, at the front and elsewhere, as nurses, exposed to danger and disease. The part these noble women played should be included in every comprehensive chronicle of the Civil war.

From Montgomery and Fulton counties 1930 men are known to have gone into the Union armies. These are the soldiers whose names are given in the works mentioned. There were probably others from these counties who engaged in the service of their country but of whose county address no record was made. It is probable that the quota of the two counties was fully 2,000 fighters in the federal forces— undoubtedly the figure was greatly in excess of this. Montgomery county was represented in twenty Civil war organizations. Montgomery and Fulton counties furnished over fifty men to each of nine regiments.

For a somewhat detailed account of Montgomery and Fulton Civil war history the reader is referred to Beers's History of Montgomery and Fulton Counties (1878), under the headings "Montgomery County in the Civil War —History of the 115th New York Volunteer Infantry;" History of Montgomery County, Chap. XXV; and "Fulton County's Record in the War for the Union, History of the 153d New York Volunteers," History of Fulton County, Chap. III; also to "History of Montgomery County" (Mason, 1892) edited by Washington Frothingham, under the heading "Montgomery County during the Rebellion" (Chap. XV.). Beers's History gives the known names of the Civil war soldiers who went to the front from the two counties and their home addresses when known. Mason's has a similar list.

The Civil war history of Montgomery is very closely associated with that of Fulton county. Two regiments of New York volunteer infantry were largely raised in these two counties— the 115th and 153d. In the 115th, 583 men came from the two counties combined and, in the 153d, 598 soldiers represented Montgomery and Fulton counties. Following is a list of the Civil war organizations in which these two divisions (comprising old Montgomery county) were principally rep-

resented, together with the number of men from each and their combined totals for the two counties:

115th N. Y. Vols., Montgomery, 421; Fulton, 162. Total, 583.

153d N. Y. Vols., Montgomery, 329; Fulton, 269. Total, 598.

13th Regiment Artillery, Montgomery, 33; Fulton, 71. Total, 104.

16th Regiment Artillery, Montgomery, 36; Fulton, 8. Total, 44.

2d Regular Cavalry, Montgomery, 6; Fulton, 31. Total, 37.

Other Civil war military organizations receiving recruits from Montgomery were as follows, together with the number of men enlisted from the county: Co. K, 1st Artillery ("Fort Plain Battery"), 65; Co. E, 43d infantry, 69; Cos. B and D, 32d regiment, 130.

Commands other than the above to which Fulton contributed, with the number of recruits from that county, follow: 77th Infantry, 101; Co. I, 10th Cavalry, 92; 97th N. Y. volunteers, 53; Co. D, 93d regiment, 51.

The known men enlisted in all union Civil war commands from Montgomery county came from the towns of Montgomery county in the following proportion: Amsterdam, 115; Canajoharie, 93; Charleston, 34; Florida, 66; Glen, 101; Minden, 103; Mohawk, 122; Palatine, 75; Root, 42; St. Johnsville, 72. This list gives the addresses of only 810 of the 1,095 men known to have gone to the Civil war from Montgomery county. Hence it does not pretend to show the total number from each town.

Of the 810 soldiers whose town addresses are given in Beers's (1878) and Mason's (1892) histories, as coming from Montgomery county, 365 came from the five western towns and 445 from the five eastern towns. This is in no way an attempt to give an estimate of the number of union soldiers of Fulton and Montgomery counties and only recapitulates the figures given in Beers's and Mason's histories.

The staff officers of the 115th regiment were as follows: Colonel, Simeon Sammons, Mohawk; Lieut. Col., E. I. Walrath, Syracuse; Lieut. Col., Geo.

S. Batcheller, Saratoga; N. J. Johnson, Ballston (commanded regiment in May, 1864); major, Patrick H. Cowan, Saratoga; surgeon, C. McFarland; surgeon, R. E. Sutton, Saratoga; assistant surgeon, Samuel W. Peters; 2d assistant surgeon, Hiram W. Ingerson, Fonda; adjutant, Thomas R. Horton, Fultonville; quartermaster, Martin McMartin, Johnstown; chaplain, S. W. Clemens; captains, Co. A, Garret Van Deveer, Fonda; Co. B, John P. Kneeskern, Minden; Co. D, Sidney D. Lingenfelter, Amsterdam; Co. E, William H. Shaw, Mayfield; Co. I, Ezra E. Walrath, Syracuse; Co. K, William Smith, Amsterdam.

The staff officers of the 153d New York volunteer regiment were as follows (no addresses are given in Beers's): Colonel, Duncan McMartin, resigned April 25, 1863; colonel, Edwin P. Davis, mustered out with regiment, Oct. 2, 1865; Lieut. Col., Thomas A. Armstrong, resigned, Feb. 18, 1863; Lieut. Col., W. H. Printup, resigned Nov. 17, 1863; Lieut. Col., Alexander Stram, discharged Jan. 4, 1865; major, Edwin P. Davis, promoted to colonel Mar. 26, 1863; major, Alexander Strain, promoted to Lieut. Col., Dec. 1, 1863; major, Stephen Sammons, resigned Aug. 27, 1864; major, George H. McLaughlin, promoted to Lieut. Col., Jan. 26, 1865; major, C. F. Putnam, died, Savannah, Ga., Sept. 9, 1865; adjutant, Stephen Sammons, promoted to major Dec. 2, 1863; adjutant, Abram V. Davis, mustered out with regiment Oct. 2, 1865; quartermaster, D. C. Livingston, resigned Aug. 22, 1863; quartermaster, John D. Blanchard, mustered out with regiment; surgeon, H. S. Hendee, resigned Feb. 8, 1864; assistant surgeon, J. L. Alexander, resigned Aug. 19, 1863; assistant surgeon, N. L. Snow, promoted to surgeon Apr. 14, 1864; assistant surgeon, J. Sweeney, mustered out with regiment; chaplain, J. Henry Enders, mustered out with regiment; captains: Co. A, David Spaulding, Johnstown; Co. B, Robert R. Meredith, Mohawk; Co. C, W. H. Printup; Co. D, J. J. Buchanan; Co. E, Jacob C. Klock, Fonda; Co. F, Isaac S. Van

Woerts, Fonda; Co. G, George H. McLaughlin, Fonda.

Company K, 1st Artillery. Enrolled at Fort Plain. Officers: Captain, Lorenzo Crounse; 1st lieutenant, S. Walter Stocking; 2d lieutenant, Angell Matthewson; 1st sergeant, George W. Fox; quartermaster sergeant, William J. Canfield; sergeant, Mosher Marion; 1st corporal, Phelps Conover; 3d corporal, Aden G. Voorhees; 4th corporal, Gottlieb Ludwig; 6th corporal, William E. Smith; 7th corporal, Horatio Fox; 8th corporal, Henry Tabor; bugler, George W. Beardsley; artificer, Clark Burtiss; wagoner, Martin Sitts.

Company E, 43d Infantry. Enrolled at Canajoharie: Captain, Jacob Wilson; 1st lieutenant, Hiram A. Winslow; 2d sergeant, Thomas Avery; 3d sergeant, Frank Shurburt; 4th sergeant, J. W. Hagadorn; 5th sergeant, Jackson Davis; 1st corporal, John D. Dain; 2d corporal, William F. Ward; 3d corporal, Cornelius Van Alstyne; 5th corporal, Christopher Richards; 6th corporal, Martin O'Brien; musicians, Charles Marcy, William Flint.

Officers Co. F, 97th Regiment, N. Y. Vols.: Captain, Stephen G. Hutchinson, Lassellsville; 1st lieutenant, E. Gray Spencer, Brocketts Bridge; corporal, Olaf Peterson, Lassellsville; corporal, Augustus Johnson, Brocketts Bridge; corporal, Wallace McLaughlin, Lassellsville; corporal, Henry Fical, Lassellsville; corporal, William B. Judd, Brocketts Bridge; musician, Henry F. Butler, Lassellsville; musician, George F. Dempster, Lassellsville.

Co. I, 10th Cavalry, was recruited principally from Mayfield and Broadalbin, in Fulton Co. David Getman, Mayfield, was captain and Stephen Dennie was 1st lieutenant and Charles H. Hill, 2d lieutenant.

Co. K, 77th N. Y. Infantry, was recruited almost exclusively from Gloversville. Captain, Nathan S. Babcock; 1st lieutenant, John W. McGregor; 2d lieutenant, Philander A. Cobb.

Co. D, 93d Regiment Infantry was recruited largely from Northampton, Fulton county. Captain, George M. Voorhees; 1st lieutenant, Henry P.

Smith; 2d lieutenant, Philemon B. Marvin, all of Northampton.

A goodly proportion of Co. F, 2d Regiment Cavalry, came from Mayfield, Fulton county. Captain, W. H. Shaw; 1st lieutenant, D. Getman; 2d lieutenant, J. L. Haines, all of Mayfield.

The following, from Beers's (1878) History of Montgomery and Fulton Counties, gives a sketch of the 115th New York Volunteer Regiment: 583 men from Fulton and Montgomery county were enrolled in the 115th:

In writing the history of the 115th N. Y. Volunteer Infantry, we record the acts of a noble body of men, whose deeds are already written in blood and inscribed high up in the roll of Fame. This regiment was raised in the counties of Saratoga, Montgomery, Fulton and Hamilton, and mustered into the United States service on the 26th day of August, 1862, by Capt. Edgerton, U. S. A., at Fonda, the place of rendezvous of the regiment.

With ten hundred and forty enlisted men, the regiment broke camp at Fonda on the 29th day of August, 1862, and was forwarded to the seat of war as soon as possible, arriving at Sandy Hook, Md., on the Baltimore and Ohio R.R., on the 1st of Sept., where the regiment was furnished with arms, but very little ammunition. It then moved to Harper's Ferry, Va., where it was assigned to guard duty along the Shenandoah Valley R.R., with headquarters at Charlestown, Va.

The regiment performed guard duty faithfully, until a few days before the surrender of Harper's Ferry, when it and others were ordered to concentrate at that place. On the way to the Ferry James English, a member of Co. D, was wounded in the hand, by the accidental discharge of a musket, necessitating amputation at the wrist; he was the first man wounded in the regiment. On arriving at, or near Harper's Ferry, the regiment was encamped on Bolivar Heights, in the rear of the village. From this point it performed picket duty, and while so engaged, John Hubbard, of Co. A, was wounded by a guerilla. On the 12th, Companies E and A were ordered to report to Col. Tom Ford, in command of Maryland Heights, and upon doing so, were ordered to proceed up the Potomac, to the old "John Brown" school-house, and form a skirmish line from the river as far up the mountain as possible, the left resting on the river.

Early the next morning the two companies were ordered back to Ford's headquarters, and from there to Elk Ridge, at the Lookout, on the highest peak of the mountain. Here for the first time members of the 115th regiment met the enemy in deadly combat. After several hours fighting, and holding their position, the two companies were ordered to evacuate the place, and report to Gen. Miles' headquarters, which they did very reluctantly, and not until they had received the third order. Company E had one man wounded. About this time Company K moved up, and in a few minutes its captain was carried to the rear, having been wounded in the thigh by a minie-ball. Upon nearing the foot of the mountain, at what was known as Maryland Heights, Companies E and A met the remainder of the regiment, who congratulated them upon their safe return.

The regiment returned to camp on Bolivar Heights. The troops were kept moving to and fro until the morning of the 15th, when General Miles made one of the most cowardly and disgraceful surrenders recorded in the annals of American history. Eleven thousand men, armed and equipped in the best style, with plenty of ammunition, holding one of the most defensible positions in the United States, were ignominiously surrendered, instead of aiding to surround Lee's, Longstreet's, Hill's and Jackson's corps where there was no possible way of escape. Thus the Union army was reduced, and eleven thousand as good fighting men as ever shouldered a musket were doomed to bear the taunts of their enemies, at home and abroad, as "Harper's Ferry cowards." But every regiment that was obliged to participate in that farce, and whose honor was sold by the commanding officer, has, upon bloody fields, won bright laurels, and vindicated its soldierly character. By the good graces of the rebel generals, who had the captured army as an "elephant on their hands," the prisoners were paroled the next day, and allowed to depart in peace, which they did with sorrowing hearts.

The regiment returned to Annapolis, Maryland, and thence went to Chicago, where it went into camp on the Cook county fair ground, which was called "Camp Tyler," after the general in command of the troops around the city. During the stay of the 115th in Chicago its duties were about the same as those of troops in garrison, but the men were allowed rather more liberties than regular soldiers on duty. While at Chicago, the weather being very bad most of the time, and the men not on fatigue duty enough to give them healthy exercise, malarial fever caused the death of quite a number.

About the 20th of November, 1862, the regiment was ordered to proceed to Washington. The capital was reached about the 23d, and at the same time the soldiers of the 115th were exchanged and marched over to Arlington Heights. There they were supposed to go into winter quarters, but by the time quarters were built the regiment was ordered out again, and kept in motion between Arlington, Fairfax, Hunter's creek, Alexandria and Yorktown, where it embarked on the steamer "Matanzas," January 23d, 1863, and arrived at Hilton Head, S. C., Department of the South, about the 26th of January.

Here the regiment was divided into detachments for post, camp and outpost duty. Companies E and D were detailed to garrison Battery Mitchell, an outpost on Scull creek. Company B was stationed at Saybrook, and other companies at different points on and around Hilton Head Island, until the 28th of May, when the different detachments were relieved and the regiment was again a unit at Hilton Head. On the 2d of June, Companies E and B were, by order of General Chatfield, detailed for special field duty, and went with other troops up May river, S. C., and burned the town of Bluffton. About the 27th of June the regiment was moved to the city of Beaufort, S. C., some twelve miles up Beaufort river, where it went into camp. After remaining here a while and suffering severely from malaria, incident to the dull routine life of the camp, the regiment was again divided into detachments and sent to do outpost and picket duty on Beaufort, Port Royal and other islands adjacent to them.

On the 20th of December the regiment embarked on transports for the old camp at Hilton Head, where it was attached to Gen. T. Seymour's "illstarred" Florida expedition. The force left Hilton Head on the 5th of February, 1864, reached Jacksonville on the evening of the 7th, and occupied the city without opposition. During the night of the 8th the expedition reached Camp Finnegan, about twelve miles from Jacksonville, capturing a battery of six guns, a quantity of small arms, etc., and a large amount of provisions, upon which the boys feasted until next day, when, with well filled haversacks, they moved toward Tallahassee, reaching and occupying Baldwin without opposition, and reaching Barber's Plantation during the night. The next day the troops advanced to Sanderson's Station, where they burned the railroad depot filled with corn, and several resin and turpentine manufactories, and tore up considerable railroad track, burning ties and other property belonging to

the rebels. By order of Gen. Seymour, the army fell back to Barber's Plantation and remained there until the 19th.

During this time the 115th, a part of the 4th Massachusetts cavalry and a section of the 3d R. I. F.ying Artillery were ordered to proceed to Callahan, a station on the Fernandina and Cedar Keys railroad, and capture whatever they might find, which was one pony, seven bushels of sweet potatoes, and one or two Florida hogs, of the kind that need to have knots tied in their tails to prevent their getting through cracks. Returning to camp, weary, footsore and hungry, the boys of the 115th were allowed to rest about one day, when the whole command broke camp early on the morning of the 20th, for the disastrous field of Olustee, known by the rebels as Ocean Pond.

Upon arriving on the field the order of battle was formed, with the 115th on the extreme right of the infantry line, and the troops ordered to move forward, which they did with a steadiness that showed the 15,000 rebels that they had work to do. Upon arriving on a rise of ground between where the line was formed and the rebel position, the advancing force received a murderous fire, at which the colored troops on the extreme left broke very badly. The white troops upon the left began to double up on the 115th, but order was soon restored. About this time the rebels made a charge upon the Union right, which was repulsed by the 115th, who sent the enemy back over their works with heavy loss. The combat continued to rage with fury until the supply of ammunition on both sides gave out, and, night coming on, both parties were willing to call it a drawn battle; but Gen. Seymour, by ordering a retreat, gave the rebels to understand that he abandoned the contest. Upon this occasion Gen. Seymour took occasion to publicly compliment the 115th, giving it the honor and praise of saving his little army from total annihilation, and naming it the "Iron-hearted Regiment." The regiment lost over one-half its number in killed, wounded and missing. Col. Sammons was wounded in the foot at the commencement of the battle. Capt. Vanderveer was mortally wounded, and died in a few days. Lieuts. Tompkins and Shaffer were killed, besides many of the best non-commissioned officers and men.

On leaving Olustee the expedition retraced its steps toward Jacksonville, where the 115th did picket and camp duty until February 9th, when the force embarked on transports for Palatka, Fla., about one hundred miles up the St. John's river from Jacksonville. Here the troops rested, and nothing of interest transpired. On the

14th of April they again embarked on transports for Hilton Head, S. C., making a few hours' stop at Jacksonville, and arriving at their destination on the evening of the 16th. On the 18th the regiment sailed for Gloucester Point, Va., reaching that place on the 21st, and was attached to the 10th army corps. On May 4th it was attached to the Army of the James, under Gen. B. F. Butler. The army moved up the James river to Bermuda Hundred, and on the 7th of May the 115th participated and suffered severely in the ill-fated battle of Chesterfield Heights, Va., losing about eighty in ; killed, wounded and missing. From this time to the 16th of May the regiment was marching, fighting, picketing, etc. On the morning of that day the disastrous battle of Drury's Bluff was fought, and the 115th regiment again brought into requisition under the immediate supervision of Gen. Adelbert Ames, who complimented it for its bravery and skilful movements, which saved Butler's army from total rout.

On the 17th the regiment went into camp at Hatcher's Run. From this time it was on picket duty all the time to the 28th, when it marched to City Point, and embarked on board the steamer "De Molay," for White House, Va., landing there on the 31st, at 4 p. m. The 115th took up the line of march for Cold Harbor, Va., reaching that place June 1st, at 3.30 p. m., and immediately, with the rest of the brigade, charged the enemy's works, this regiment capturing two hundred and fifty men with their arms and equipments. Here the regiment was again complimented for bravery by Gen. Devens.

From that time to the 12th, the regiment was under a continuous fire day and night. During the night of the 12th it marched for White House Landing, which place was reached at 6 a. m., of the 13th. Next day the regiment embarked for City Point, landed at Powhattan, on the James, and marched the rest of the way. On the 23d it moved up in front of Petersburgh, Va. From this time the regiment was in the trenches before Petersburgh, to July 29th, when Gen. Turner's division, to which the 115th was attached, moved to the left, to assist Burnside's ninth corps in the explosion of the mine, and charge upon the enemy's works. This occurred at 5 o'clock, on the morning of the 30th of July. Here, again, the 115th displayed its courage and cool bravery by standing as a wall of fire between the advancing Rebels, and the partially demoralized 9th corps, and was again complimented by both Gens. Burnside and Turner.

From Petersburgh the regiment marched to near City Point, and then to Bermuda Hundred, losing several men by sun stroke, as the weather was extremely hot, and the roads dry and dusty. Up to this time the regiment had been under fire for thirty-seven days, and needed rest, which was had at Hatch's farm, until, on the evening of the 13th of August, the regiment broke camp and marched to Deep Bottom, on the north side of the James river, which was reached at 7 o'clock a. m., on the 14th. That day and the next were occupied in marching and countermarching. On the 16th the enemy were found strongly posted at Charles City Court House, where fighting began at once and continued until the evening of the 18th, when the 115th was deployed and covered the retreat of the Union forces. In this affair the regiment lost eighty-four killed, wounded and missing.

On the 20th it returned to the old camp at Bermuda, with only one hundred and twenty men fit for duty. Comparative rest was the happy lot of the decimated regiment until the 28th, when it marched to Petersburgh again and occupied the trenches in front of that city. The regiment had a little rest, doing only trench and camp duty until the 28th of September, when it broke camp and marched to the north side of the James. On the 29th the 115th participated in the capture of two redoubts on Chaffin's farm, known by some as Spring Hill. Here the losses of the regiment were very severe, among the dead being the loved and lamented Capt. W. H. McKittrick, of Co. C. During this engagement in charges, countercharges, victories and repulses, the enemy lost three times the number that the 115th did.

From this time to October 27th, the regiment was doing picket duty most of the time. On that day a reconnoissance was made in force on the Darbytown road, in front of Richmond, the 115th taking a prominent part in charging the rebel works, and losing quite heavily. Among the number killed was Sergeant Ide of Company F, the idol of his comrades. Returning to camp, the regiment had five days comparative rest. On the 8th of December, the 115th embarked on the propellor "Haze," and participated in the abortive attempt to capture Fort Fisher, N. C. In the afternoon of December 30th, the regiment debarked at Jones' Landing, on the James river, Va., and just after dark was again in the old camp on Chafin's farm.

On January 4th, 1865, the 115th again embarked on board the propellor "De Molay," on its second expedition against the keystone of the confederacy. The whole force was under command of Gen. Alfred H. Terry. The troops landed at Flay Pond battery, a short distance north of Fort Fisher, on the 13th at 9 a. m. The 115th lost but two or three men in landing. At 3 p. m. of the 15th, the grand charge was made upon the fort, the 115th bearing a noble part in its capture, and being again complimented by General Terry, also by Gen. Ames, who knew something of its fighting qualities while in the army of the James. The loss to the regiment was about 70, and among the killed was Lieut. S. S. Olney, of Co. F, whose loss to the regiment and company could not be made good. At about 8 o'clock, on the morning of the 16th, one of the magazines of the fort exploded, killing and wounding more of this regiment than the fighting of the day before.

From this time to the surrender of Johnson's rebel army, the 115th was continually employed in fighting, marching, picket and guard duty, until it reached Raleigh, N. C., where it was assigned to "safe guard" duty in the city, from April 23d to June 17th, when it was mustered out of service. On the 19th, the regiment left Raleigh for Albany, N. Y., where it was paid off by Paymaster C. F. Davis, on the 6th of July, 1865, there being something less than two hundred of the original members. Upon leaving the U. S. service, the men quietly returned to their homes and former vocations, and to-day the old 115th N. Y. Volunteer Infantry is represented in nearly every state in the Union, and almost every calling in life. However humble or exalted they may now be, if you speak of the camp, the bivouac, the fatigue, the march, the picket, the fight, and the camp fires of years gone by, their eyes will kindle, and at the fireside they fight their battles o'er and o'er, until one could almost hear the roar of musketry, and the bursting of shells. But we must stop, for we can add nothing to the laurels already wreathed around the brow of one of the best of our country's defenders, the 115th Regiment, New York Volunteer Infantry. It only remains to add the following list of battles which were participated in by the regiment, or a part of it:

Maryland Heights, Sept. 13, 1862.
Bolivar Heights, Va., Sept. 15, 1862.
West Point, Va., Jan. 8, 1863.
Jacksonville, Fla., Feb. 7, 1864.
Camp Finegan, Fla., Feb. 8, 1864.
Baldwin, Fla., Feb. 9, 1864.
Sanderson, Fla., Feb. 11, 1864.
Callahan Station, Fla., Feb. 14, 1864.
Olustee, Fla., Feb. 20, 1864.
Palatka, Fla., March 10, 1864.
Bermuda Hundred, Va., May 5, 1864.
Chesterfield Heights, Va., May 7, 1864.
Old Church, Va., May 9, 1864.
Weir Bottom Church, Va., May 12, 1864.
Drury's Bluff, Va., May 14, 1864.

Proctor's Creek and Port Walthall, Va., May 16, 1864.
Cold Harbor, Va., June 1, 1864.
Chickahominy, Va., June, 1864.
Petersburgh, Va., June 23, 1864.
Burnside Mine, Va., July 30, 1864.
• Deep Bottom, Va., Aug. 16-18, 1864.
Fort Gilmer, Va., Sept. 29, 1864.
Darbytown Road, Va., Oct. 27, 1864.
Fort Fisher, N. C., Dec. 25, 1864.
Fort Fisher, N. C., Jan. 15, 1865.
Fort Anderson, N. C., Feb. 19, 1865.
Sugar Loaf Battery, N. C., Feb., 20, 1865.
Wilmington, N. C., Feb. 22, 1865.

The 115th brought out of the war six flags, which Col. Sammons, in behalf of the regiment, presented to the state. The national ensign, a gift of the ladies of the XVth Senatorial district, Aug. 20, 1862, showed service, the staff and three-fifths of the flag being gone. The regimental banner, presented by the state authorities while the regiment was at Fonda, of silk, with eagle and shield in the center, the national motto in a scroll beneath, and thirty-four stars in the field above, bearing the inscription, "115th N. Y. Vol. Regiment Infantry," came out rent in the center and torn from side to side. A second and similar regimental banner survived in better condition, and with it was a new national flag inscribed with the names of the regiment's battles; also two guidons of bunting. These flags were turned over to the adjutant general. They are represented by Lieut. Col. N. J. Johnson, and are carried by Sergt. James English, who lost an arm while supporting them in the field.

———

Beers's History has the following regarding the 153d New York Volunteers. 598 Montgomery and Fulton county men were enlisted in the 153d, the largest number from these twin counties in any Civil war organization:

The 153d Regt. N. Y. State Vols. was raised in 1862 under the second call of President Lincoln, for 300,000 men. Seven of its companies were from the counties of Fulton, Montgomery and Saratoga, the other three from Clinton, Essex and Warren. The regiment was mustered into service at Fonda, Oct. 18th, 1862, and left for Virginia the same day. On arriving at Washington, Oct. 22d, it was at once ordered to Alexandria, Va., and there encamped. While here the regiment attained a high degree of discipline through the efficient attention of Col. McMartin and his officers. The men, however, suffered considerably from typhoid pneumonia, measles and smallpox. Col. McMartin was at length compelled to resign through an accident and failing health. By his generous and impartial conduct he had won the hearts of his officers and men, and they bade him adieu with deep regret. Col. Armstrong also resigned, and Maj. E. P. Davis was promoted to the colonelcy of the regiment.

At that time Alexandria was a vast depot of military stores. Its fortifications were considered of but little avail if the enemy should make a sudden dash upon the town under cover of night. The troops were often aroused from their slumbers and formed in line of battle, across the different roads leading to the city, remaining under arms till dawn, to repel any attack. For fourteen consecutive nights this regiment lay behind temporary barriers of quartermasters' wagons, in the open.air, expecting the enemy.

On the 20th of July, 1863, the regiment was ordered to Capital Hill barracks, Washington. Its duty here was guarding the depot of the Baltimore and Ohio railroad, examining travelers' passes, patrolling the city, convoying troops to the front, and prisoners to Point Lookout, and guarding Contraband Camp, Central Guardhouse, Carroll and Old Capital Prisons. Surgeon Hendee and Quartermaster Livingston resigned while here, and Dr. Snow, 1st assistant, became surgeon.

On the 20th of February, 1864, the regiment embarked on the steamer Mississippi for New Orleans, where it arrived February 28th, landing at Algiers, opposite that city, and occupying the Belleville Iron Works. Thence it proceeded by rail, March 3d, to Brashaer, 80 miles distant. Crossing Grand Lake at Bashaer, the troops marched up the beautiful valley of the bayou Teche. On the 5th, they arrived at Franklin, and reporting to Gen. Franklin, were assigned to the 1st brigade, 1st division, 19th army corps. On the 15th they were again on the move toward Alexandria, on the Red river, arriving there March 24th, where they found Gen. Banks awaiting them. On their way thither Joseph Hawkins, of Co. K, died of exhaustion.

On the 28th of March they left Alexandria for Shreveport, 170 miles distant, which was in possession of the enemy. Gen. Lee led the cavalry division, the 13th corps followed, then the 1st division of the 19th corps, next the 13th and 19th corps trains with ten days rations. The 1st brigade of the 19th army corps, to which the regiment was assigned, was commanded by Gen. Dwight, and consisted of the 29th, 114th, 116th and 153d N. Y. regiments. The country now supplied the entire army with beef, vast numbers of cattle being secured daily. After a march of 36 miles the army came to Pleasant Hill, and halted for the train to come up.

On the 8th of April, the 153d regiment was detailed to guard the division train, and consequently, in rear of the army. On that day the cavalry and 13th corps, being in advance, were met by the enemy at Sabine Cross Roads, and being overpowered by superior numbers, fell back in confusion. Gen. Emery, apprised of the disaster in front, drew up his (1st) division at Pleasant Grove, three miles below Sabine Cross Roads. The rebels, pressing the retreating forces, at length charged upon Emery with great impetuosity. For an hour and a half he gallantly resisted their repeated onsets, until darkness put an end to the conflict. The Union troops continued on the battlefield until midnight, when they were ordered back to Pleasant Hill, this regiment covering their retreat. The next morning the enemy, having discovered their retreat, followed them to Pleasant Hill. Our troops took position to resist the onset. At length the enemy drove in their skirmish line and made an attack in force on their left. Five times they charged on the 1st brigade, and were as often driven back. This was the first battle in which this regiment had taken part. In his report of it, Col. Davis says: "My men behaved nobly, and I attach much credit to the noble manner in which my line officers acted. Lieut. Col. Strain, Maj. Sammons and Adjut. Davis rendered me valuable assistance in keeping my line together and maintaining my position." For three hours the conflict raged, when, night coming on, the work of death ended. Our troops lay on their arms in line of battle all night, but the enemy, taking advantage of the darkness, had removed. On account of the scarcity of water and rations the army began to retreat, April 10, toward Grand Ecore, a small town on a bluff of the Red river. This place was reached the following day.

Gen. Dwight now became chief of staff to Gen. Banks, and Col. Beal, of the 29th Maine, was assigned to the 1st brigade. April 23d the army left Grand Ecore. As it moved out the town was fired. This was said to be the work of a rebel, and done to apprise the enemy of the army's departure. After a forced march of 40 miles, the force went into camp, at midnight, near Cloutierville, but at 4 o'clock the next morning was again on the way to Cane River Crossing. This place was in possession of the rebel general Bee, with 4,000 men, who were fortifying Monet's Bluff, which commands it. At this point the situation of the army was indeed critical. The enemy was closely pursuing them in the rear; Gen. Bee, strongly fortified, was in front; Cane river on the right, and a dense swamp and forest on the left. The 1st brigade was thrown forward into a wood, which the enemy began to shell; as they fired too high, however, they did but little injury. At length our forces made a simultaneous attack. The enemy replied with great vigor to our batteries, but Birge carried the Bluff and forced them to retreat. Our troops now being ordered to cross the river, the 2d Vet. Cavalry, the 116th and 153d pressed forward and were among the first to occupy the heights.

The Union troops continued their retreat toward Alexandria, the base of supplies, which place they reached on the 25th of April, and encamped near our gunboats and transports. Here they remained until the 13th of May, when they again took up their march, now toward the Mississippi, the fleet leaving at the same time. As the troops left Alexandria a fire broke out in such a way as to make it impossible to prevent a general conflagration. There was some skirmishing by the troops on this march, and once they met the enemy in force. It was on this route that the Battle of Mansura occurred, but it was fought principally with artillery on the Union side.

On the 17th of May the army reached the Atchafalaya river near Simsport, where the transports were found awaiting it. The river, 600 feet wide at this point, was bridged with 19 transports fastened together, and on the 19th the troops and trains passed over. On the 22d they reached Marganzia Bend on the Mississippi. Here the 153d suffered much through sickness and death. On the 1st of July the 153d and 114th regiments took the steamer Crescent for New Orleans, where they arrived on the 2d, and the following day moved down the river under sealed orders. They soon learned they were destined for Fortress Monroe. Arriving there, they were at once ordered to report in Washington, which they reached July 11th, 1864. The 153d took position in the rifle pits beyond Fort Saratoga. At this time Gen. Early was foraging in Maryland, menacing Washington, and causing our troops considerable uneasiness.

This regiment, with the 6th and 19th corps, under command of Gen. Wright, were at length sent, with other troops, in pursuit of Early. After moving from place to place for several days, they at length settled temporarily at Harper's Ferry, August 5th. On the 7th of August Gen. Sheridan was placed in command of the "Middle Department," composed of the late departments of West Virginia, Washington and Susquehanna. On the 10th of August, 1864, the army began its

march up the Shenandoah Valley, passing from town to town, and occasionally making short stops. While camping at Charlestown, Cadman, of Company A, and Charles Thornton, of Company H, of the 153d regiment, while making some purchases for the mess at a farm house near by, were captured by guerillas. In the melee the latter was killed; the former was taken to Richmond and confined in Libby Prison. Both were highly esteemed. Leaving Charlestown, the army returned to Harper's Ferry, camping on the ground twice before occupied. On the 28th of August the force was ordered up the valley. Again marching or countermarching, skirmishing with or pursuing the enemy, or being pursued by him, was the order of the day. It soon became apparent, however, that the army was about to make a determined advance. On the 18th of September all surplus baggage was sent to the rear, and early the following morning the force was in motion.

Early held the west side of the Opequan creek. Sheridan was in his front and on his right. The cavalry had driven the enemy and cleared the passage of the Opequan. This was now forded by the infantry, who advanced along the turnpike through a deep ravine about a mile in length. Early had hoped to prevent their entering this ravine, but in this he failed. It now remained for him to seize the upper opening and prevent our troops from forming in line of battle; or, failing in this, he hoped after the Union troops had formed to mass his whole strength against them, and by holding the gorge to cut off their retreat.

The battle of Opequan creek or Winchester, was fought to gain possession of this ravine, the key to Winchester. At ten o'clock a. m., the 6th corps left the ravine, and filing to the left, advanced on the open plain in two lines of battle, the first of which carried one of the enemy's rifle pits. The 19th corps closely followed the 6th, Gen. Grover's division joining them on the right. Dwight's division, to which the 153d belonged, was sent as Grover's support. While their brigade was forming, it received repeated volleys from the enemy, who were behind and protected by a ledge of rocks. The burden of the conflict in the early part of the day came upon the 19th corps and Rickett's division of the 6th corps, who for hours held the approaches to the ravine—while the 8th corps was swinging around the enemy's flank—Early, in the meantime, having massed his forces against them. At 3 o'clock, the cavalry, with the 8th corps, charged the enemy's left flank. The entire army now advanced. The wood in which the enemy had concentrated was quickly carried, and the foe fled from it in great haste, leaving behind their guns and accoutrements. The retreat soon became a disastrous rout. The enemy fled through Winchester in confusion. Col. Davis, of this regiment, was in command of the 1st brigade. In the hottest of the fight, he was at the front cheering his troops. At one time he seized one of the regimental color standards, and bearing it aloft, pressed forward, inspiring his men with new enthusiasm.

The victory was complete. It was believed that the 19th corps suffered most severely in this battle, having lost 1940 in killed and wounded. Capts. DeWandelaer and Jacob C. Klock, of this regiment, were found in the house of a rebel Congressman. Capt. Klock was severely wounded. He was, however, enabled to return to his home in St. Johnsville, where, after being promoted major, he died, Oct. 4, 1864. Post Klock, No. 70, G. A. R., of Fort Plain, N. Y., was named in honor of this gallant officer. After the battle of Opequan creek or Winchester, the enemy were pursued 8 miles south, to Fisher's Hill, where they were found strongly fortified between two mountain ranges. From this stronghold they were completely routed on the 22d, giving Sheridan possession of Fisher's Hill, the most formidable natural barrier in the valley. . Following up this victory, the Union forces pursued the enemy night and day, harassing and driving them through Woodstock, Mt. Jackson, Mt. Crauford and Staunton to Waynesborough, destroying flouring mills and vast quantities of grain.

While in the valley 22 of the men were captured by Moseby. Seven of them he decided to hang, because Custer had executed seven of his guerillas at Fort Royal. The number having been selected by lot, it was ordered that they be put to death half a mile west of Berryville. Four of the condemned escaped, yet not until they had been severely wounded; the other three were hanged. One of these was a member of the 153d.

On the 30th of September, the troops started down the valley, and on the 10th of October crossed Cedar creek and encamped. October 18th the 1st and part of the 2d division proceeded on a reconnoisance, nearly as far as Strasburg. They found the rebels encamped here, and also discovered that the enemy were again strongly entrenched at Fisher's Hill.

On the 15th Sheridan made a flying visit to Washington, leaving Gen. Wright, of the 6th corps, in command. Early, aware of Sheridan's absence, and having been reinforced by Longstreet's corps, attacked our army in force at daybreak on the 19th. The 8th corps was surprised and driven back in confusion. The 6th and 19th corps were soon ordered to retire from the position. The enemy captured our guns and turned them upon our soldiers, who checked this onset and then fell back. Sheridan, returning from Washington and learning of the disaster hastened to his army, which had retreated several miles. He at once formed a line of battle, and as he dashed along the ranks, said: "Never mind, boys, we'll whip them yet." The air was rent with responsive cheers from his men. At one o'clock the pickets of the 19th corps were vigorously attacked and driven in by the enemy. Our line now pressed forward on a double quick and soon received a severe fire, but continued steadily to advance, when the enemy opened fire upon the right flank, the line swinging to the right to meet it. It was soon found that the rebels were retreating to the left, when the line was immediately turned in that direction, and the enemy were driven in confusion from behind a temporary breastwork. Their retreat now became a rout, and was followed up by our troops, until they retook the breastworks from which they had been driven in the morning, the 153d regiment being among the first to occupy the works. Following the pursuit almost to Strasburg, the Union forces encamped, and on the 21st returned to their old quarters near Cedar creek. Col. Davis, of the 153d, was made Brigadier General by brevet for his bravery at this battle.

On the 9th of November, the army left Cedar creek and encamped near Newtown. Here the troops remained until December 29th, when they broke camp and marched to Stevenson's depot, the terminus of the Harper's Ferry and Winchester railroads; here they began to erect winter quarters near the depot in a grove of oak and black walnut. On the 23d of March, 1865, this regiment was sent across to Snicker's gap, but returned the following day without adventure. At midnight, April 9th, the booming of cannon announced the surrender of Lee. April 11th the regiment moved to Summit Point, and on the 20th they left this place by cars for Washington. While passing Harper's Ferry, Fink, of Company C, was killed. On the following day this regiment encamped near Fort Stevens, at Washington, and took part in the grand review of veterans at that place, April 23d and 24th.

On the 6th of June, 1865, the 153d embarked on the steamer Oriental, for Savannah, Georgia, where it arrived on the 13th. Colonel—now Brig.-General by brevet—Davis was in command of the city, which this regiment now guarded. Dr. A. L. Snow was here promoted Brigade-Surgeon, and was afterward assigned the position of health officer of the district and city of Savannah.

Major Charles F. Putnam, died here, after a severe but brief illness. This brave officer had been with the regiment from the first. On the 9th his remains were borne by his comrades to the beautiful Laurel Grove cemetery. They were brought north at the time of the return of the regiment, and interred in the cemetery at Fultonville, near his former home. Adjutant A. V. Davis was now promoted to the rank of major, an honor richly merited.

On the 5th of October, this regiment took the steamer "Emilie" for the north by the way of Hilton Head, which place was reached the same day. On the 7th the 153d left by the steamer "McLellan" for New York, arriving there on the 10th of October, and on the 11th took the "Mary Benton" for Albany. Here a large number of the sick were taken to the "Ira Harris" hospital. Of them twelve or fourteen died, several at Albany, the others after reaching their homes. On the 16th of October, 1865, the men were mustered out of the service and paid off.

The two guidons of the regiment, of white silk, with "153" in the centre, were presented by Mrs. Joseph Strain, at Albany, and carried through the campaign in the southwest. The regimental banner is of blue silk, bearing the arms and motto of the United States and the legend "153d N. Y. Vol. Regiment Infantry."

Beers has the following reference to the 97th Regiment New York Volunteers. 53 Fulton county men were enrolled in the 97th:

The 97th Regiment New York Volunteers, was organized in Booneville, N. Y., under command of Col. Chas. Wheelock, and was mustered into the service February 18th, 1862. The regiment left Booneville for Washington March 12th, but remained in Albany for one week, and only arrived in New York March 18th, where the troops received the Enfield rifled musket. The 97th arrived in Washington March 20th. In May the regiment was assigned to Gen. Duryee's brigade, Gen. Rickett's division, and was under Gen. McDowell's command during the advance in the Shenandoah Valley, in June, 1862.

The regiment was in ten battles and suffered great loss, being reduced to less than 100 effective men before the close of the war. During the months of September and October, 1863, it received a large number of conscripts. The regiment was attached to the 2d brigade, 2d division, 1st army corps, in December, 1863. It took part in the following engagements: Cedar Mountain, August 9, 1862; Rappahanock Station, August 23, 1862; Thoroughfare Gap, August 28, 1862; second Bull Run, August 30, 1862; Chantilla, September 1, 1862; South Mountain, Md., September 14, 1862; Antietam, Md., September 17, 1862; first Fredericksburg, December 13, 1862; Chancellorsville, Va., May 1, 1863; Gettysburg, July 1-3, 1863.

The following is a list of engagements participated in by Co. I, 10th N. Y. Cavalry, which was recruited mainly from Mayfield and Broadalbin, Fulton county. 92 Fulton county men were enrolled in this organization:

Louisa Court House, Va., May 4, 1863; Brandy Station, Va., June 9, 1863; Aldie, Va., June 17, 1863; Middleburg, June 19, 1863; Upperville, Va., June 20, 1863; Gettysburg, Pa., July 2 and 3, 1863; Shepherdstown, Va., July 16, 1863; Sulphur Springs, Va., October 12, 1863; Little Auburn and Brestoe Station, October 14, 1863; Mill Run, Va., November 24, 1863; The Wilderness, Va., May 5, 6, 7 and 8, 1864; Ground Squirrel Church, Va., May 11, 1864; Defences of Richmond, Va., May 12, 1864; Hanover Town, Va., May 28, 1864; Cold Harbor, Va., June 1, 1864; Trav —— Station, Va., June 11, 1864; White House Landing, Va., June 22, 1864; St. Mary's Church, Va., June 24, 1864; Gravel Church Hill, Va., July 28, 1864; Lee's Mills, Va., July 30, 1864; Deep Bottom, Va., August 14 and 15, 1864; Fisher's Hill, Va., August 18, 1864; Weldon Rail Road, Va., August 21, 1864; Ream's Station, Va., August 23, 1864; Vaughn Road, Va., September 30 and October 1, 1864; South Side Rail Road, Va., October 27, 1864; Despritanna Station, Va., November 18, 1864; Stony Creek, Va., December 1, 1864; Belfield Station, Va., December 9, 1864; Janett's Station, Va., December 10, 1864; Dinwiddie Court-House, Va., March 31, 1865; grand cavalry charge, Sailor's Creek, Va., April 6, 1865; Jettersville, Va., April 5, 1865; Fannville, Va., April 7, 1865; Appomattox Station, Va., April 9, 1865.

Co. K, First Light Artillery, was known as the "Fort Plain Battery" because it was recruited at Fort Plain in the fall of '61. It was mustered in at Albany, Nov. 20, 1861. Its service began at Washington and in May, 1862, at Harpers Ferry it joined the Second brigade, Siegel's division. It was with the Twelfth corps after June 26, 1862;

until May 12, 1863, when it was transferred to the reserve artillery where it
remained until March, 1864. It was
later connected with the Twenty-sec-
ond corps in the defense of Washington. Battery K was mustered out at
Elmira, N. Y., June 20, 1865. It then
being under command of Capt. Stocking. Mason's History says, "the service of the First was light artillery
and by batteries in the Army of the
Potomac, also in the Army of Virginia,
of the Cumberland, and of Georgia,
and was of such a detached character
that the official record of battles of the
Fort Plain Battery cannot be separated
from those of other batteries of the
regiment." Capt. Lorenzo Crounse,
who commanded Co. K when it was
mustered in, later became governor of
Nebraska. Most of the men of this
organization came from Fort Plain
and the adjoining country, and the
company numbered 65 men on mustering in.

The Thirty-second regiment was recruited under one of the first calls for
troops. It was organized in New York
city and was mustered into service,
for two years, May 31, 1861. On the
expiration of this term, the three-year
men were transferred to the 121st
New York. Company B was recruited
at Canajoharie and Company D at Amsterdam, but the names of these volunteers are missing; but they are estimated as numbering about 130 men.
This regiment served for several
weeks at Washington and Alexandria,
after being mustered in. It was then
attached to the Army of the Potomac
until it was mustered out June 9,
1863. Following is a summary of the
battles of the Thirty-second: Fairfax Court House, July 17, 1861; Black-
burn's Ford, July 20, 1861; Bull Run,
July 21, 1861; Munson's Hill, Aug. 25
and Sept. 28, 1861; Anandale, Dec. 2,
1861; West Point, Va., May 7, 1862;
Seven Days' battles, June 25-July 2,
1862; Gaines' Mill, June 27, 1862; Garnett's and Golding's farms, June 28,
1862; Glendale, June 30, 1862; Malvern
Hill, July 1, 1862; Crampton Pass,
Sept. 14, 1862; Antietam, Sept. 17,

1862; Fredericksburg, Dec. 11-15, 1862;
Franklin's Crossing, April 29 and May
2, 1863; Marye's Heights and Salem
Church, May 3-4, 1863.

The Forty-third New York was organized and mustered into service at
Albany in September, 1861, for three
years service. It was known variously
as the "Albany and Yates Rifles" and
"Vinton Rifles." It saw hard service
and bore an honorable part in the
campaigns of the Army of the Potomac. Co. E of this regiment was recruited at Canajoharie, that company
numbering 70 volunteers, at the time
of mustering in. The 43d served at
and near Washington until Oct. 15,
when it became part of Hancock's brigade, Smith's division, Army of the
Potomac. May, 1862, it was made
part of the first brigade, second division, sixth corps, and later was in the
"Light Brigade" at Chancellorsville. It
later formed part of the third brigade, second division, sixth corps, under command of Col. Charles A. Milli
kin, being mustered out of service at
Washington, June 27, 1865. Its list of
battles follows: Vienna and Flint
Hill, Feb. 22, 1862; Siege of Yorktown,
April 5 and May 4, 1862; Lee's Mills,
April 16 and 28, 1862; Williamsburg,
May 5, 1862; Seven days' battle, June
25 to July 2, 1862; Garnett's Farm,
June 27, 1862; Garnett's and Golding's
Farms, June 28, 1862; Savage Station,
June 29, 1862; White Oak Swamp
Bridge, June 30, 1862; Malvern Hill,
July 1, 1862; Sugar Loaf Mountain,
Sept. 10-11, 1862; Crampton Pass,
Sept. 14, 1862; Antietam, Sept. 17,
1862; Fredericksburg, Dec. 11-15,
1862; Marye's Heights and Salem
church, May 3-4, 1863; Deep Run
Crossing, June 5, 1863; Gettysburg,
July 1-3, 1863; Fairfield, Pa., July 5,
1863; Antietam and Marsh Run, July
7, 1863; near Lietersburg, July 10,
1863; Funkstown, July 11-13, 1863;
Williamsport, July 14, 1863; Auburn,
Oct. 13, 1863; Rappahannock Station,
Nov. 7, 1863; Mine Run Campaign,
Nov. 26 and Dec. 2, 1863; Wilderness,
May 5-7, 1864; Spottsylvania Court
House, May 8-21, 1864; Piney Branch

Church, May 8, 1864; Landron's Farm, May 10, 1864; the Salient, May 12, 1864; North Anna, May 22-26, 1864; Tolopotomy, May 27-31, 1864; Cold Harbor, June 1-12, 1864; before Petersburg, June 18, July 9 and December, 1864, and April 2, 1865; Assault of Petersburg, June 18-19, 1864; Weldon railroad, June 21-23, 1864; Fort Stevens, July 12-13, 1864; Charlestown, Aug. 21, 1864; Opequan Creek, Sept. 13, 1864; Opequan, Sept. 19, 1864; Fisher's Hill, Sept. 22, 1864; Cedar Creek, Oct. 19, 1864; Petersburg Works, March 22, 1865; Appomattox campaign, March 28 and April 9, 1865; Fall of Petersburg, April 2, 1865; Sailor's Creek, April 6, 1865; Appomatox Court House, April 9, 1865.

The Thirteenth Heavy Artillery had 33 Montgomery county and 71 Fulton county men in its ranks or 104 in all. It was mustered in by companies the latter part of 1863 and early part of 1864. The official record of the battles of the Thirteenth is as follows: Before Petersburg and Richmond, May 5 and 31, 1864; before Peterburg, June 15, 1864; assault on Petersburg, June 15 and 17, 1864; Swift Creek, Oct. 7, 1864; Day's Point, Nov. 14, 1864; Fort Fisher, Dec. 25, 1864, Jan. 15, 1865; fall of Petersburg, April 2, 1865.

In the Sixteenth Heavy Artillery were 36 men from Montgomery and 8 from Fulton, a total of 44. The Montgomery men came from the towns of Minden, St. Johnsville and Canajoharie and were enrolled in Companies F and H. The Sixteenth was mustered in at Elmira and left the state in detachments, the local companies going in January, 1864. The regiment was recruited in New York city by Col. Joseph J. Morrison, its commanding officer. The regiment served as heavy artillery and infantry at Fortress Monroe, Yorktown and Gloucester Point, later being divided and sent on detached service. It was mustered out at Washington, Aug. 31, 1865.

On Monday and Tuesday, August 26 and 27, 1912, was held the fiftieth an-

niversary and the thirty-first annual reunion of the 115th and 153d New York Volunteer Regiments at Fonda, N. Y. This historic occasion, for the counties of Montgomery and Fulton, is reported as follows in the Mohawk Valley Democrat, Fonda, August 29, 1912:

Fifty years ago today Fonda sent forth the first fully organized regiment from this congressional district to defend the flag of our Union, to maintain our country as one undivided whole, and to uphold the constitution of the founders of our government which declares that before the law all men are free and equal.

The outbreak of the Civil war found the political situation in Montgomery county to be much the same as in other sections of the state, and while at times there were murmurings and dissatisfaction, they were not of such character as to cause general alarm.

During the course of the war Montgomery county furnished men for twenty different regiments, although in several of them the representation was quite small. In May, 1861, the 32d was accepted and of the several companies B was recruited at Canajoharie and D at Amsterdam. The 42d regiment was despatched in September, 1861, and Canajoharie furnished the greater portion of Co. E. This was one of the hardest fighting regiments in the Army of the Potomac.

The 115th contained more Montgomery county recruits than any to which the county contributed and was raised at a time when the government was in great need of volunteers during the trying summer of 1862. Companies A, B, D, G, H, I and K contained men from this county, forming almost half of the entire regiment. The regiment was mustered into service at Fonda on August 26, 1862, by Captain Edgerton of the regular army and broke camp on August 29, 1862.

The 153d regiment was recruited soon afterward, seven of its companies being from this and Fulton counties, the Montgomery county men being mostly in companies B, C and E. It also was mustered into service at Fonda, which took place on October 14, 1862.

The regimental organizations of these two commands have for the past thirty years held annual reunions in various places in this congressional district, but they have always held them at separate times and in different localities.

This year being the fiftieth anniversary of their departure for the seat of war it was agreed to hold a joint reunion here, the place that they were mustered into the service. It was very fitting that Fonda should be selected for their semi-centennial and the people here have shown their appreciation of the honor by the splendid reception accorded them. Veterans have been looking forward to this for a year and some of them traveled long distances to participate in the event. Several came from Iowa and Comrade M. B. Foote of Hastings, Neb., was in California when he received his notice and started at once across the continent, arriving here Monday morning. Others came from Wisconsin and Ohio.

The festivities commenced on Monday evening, when an association camp fire was held by Co. C of the 115th regiment, but was broadened by invitation to include not only the 115th and 153d regiments, but also the public. This was held in the old court house hall, which was artistically draped with the national colors. At the back of the rostrum were hung the portraits of Col. Simeon Sammons and Garret Van Derveer, captain of Co. A, both of the 115th; also that of Colonel Edwin P. Davis of the 153d regiment. In the northwest corner a tent was stretched and beside it was an old camp kettle and a stack of arms. Comrade James E. Reid of Boston presided over the meeting.

Most interesting exercises were held here, including experiences given by comrades.

The hall was packed with people, at least 500 being present, and many were turned away as it was impossible for them to gain admittance.

On Tuesday the general reunion of the two regiments occurred. The meeting at 9 a. m. was called to order by A. H. Mills, chairman of the citizens' committee. The Rev. Washington Frothingham made the opening prayer. The address of welcome was delivered by Harry Y. MacNeil, president of the village, who extended the veterans a most hearty and cordial greeting. This was responded to by Comrade James E. Reid for the 115th and by Comrade C. B. Clute for the 153d. After this the two regiments separated and held their organization meetings in executive session.

At one o'clock the two regiments formed into line and preceded by the veteran drum corps marched to the Reformed church, where the members of the D. A. R. served a bountiful and delicious dinner.

After refreshments the visitors were conveyed in autos to the grave of Col. Sammons, about a mile north of the village, where he lies buried on the ancestral family farm which he owned during his lifetime and has been in the family for several generations and is still occupied by them. At the time of the Revolution it was occupied by Sampson Sammons and his sons, who were sturdy and uncompromising patriots, the father being a member of the Committee of Safety, a most honorable and at the same time dangerous office to hold. This spot is only a short distance from the old camp ground where the two regiments were mustered into service. It was called Camp Mohawk.

One of the most interesting features of the celebration was the stirring old time music furnished by the veteran drum corps, which included all the familiar airs of fifty years ago. Adam Young of Fonda was one of the snare drummers. The others were all from this county and were 70 years or more of age. During the afternoon while the St. Johnsville band was giving a concert in the park the drum corps filled the waits with the inspiring martial music of war times.

About 350 people partook of the refreshments and all pronounced them most delicious.

The veterans have gone to their several homes, but it is doubtful if age will ever dim the recollection of their semi-centennial at Fonda in 1912.

Exactly 100 members of the 115th Regiment answered to roll call at this their fiftieth anniversary and thirty-first reunion. Forty-two of the 153d answered to roll call at Fonda, 142 veterans being present for both regiments out of the 1181 that are known to have gone to the front from Montgomery and Fulton counties.

Since the foregoing chapter was written (in which reference was made to the lack of published experiences of Civil war soldiers from the Mohawk valley) two valley newspapers have started interesting publications regarding personal descriptions and impressions of local veterans written by them on the field during the Rebellion.

The Mohawk Valley Register is at present (October, 1913) republishing letters from the field, written fifty years ago by Lieut. Angell Matthewson of Co. K, First Light Artillery (known as the Fort Plain Battery), to the Register, of which he was then one of the editors and proprietors. These are very interesting and particularly so to readers of western Montgomery county, many of whom are relatives or friends of the local members of this famous military organization. Mr. Matthewson died in 1913.

The Herkimer Citizen has been

printing, for eight months (since January, 1913) letters and diaries, written by members of the 34th New York. This was a Herkimer county regiment, five of its companies having been recruited from that county. It was mustered in June 15, 1861, and mustered out June 30, 1863. The 34th was in fierce fighting during McClellan's advance on and retreat from Richmond in the summer of '62 and particularly distinguished itself in a famous charge at Fair Oaks which is said to have won the battle for the federal forces. On June 17, 1863, the regiment was given a great ovation on its return to Herkimer county at Little Falls. It had three colonels, Ladue, Suiter and Laflin. Col. Suiter was in command during the fighting before Richmond in which the regiment lost very heavily, and Col. Laflin was in command of the regiment at the time of its famous reception by the citizens of Little Falls. At this time the staff officers were: Colonel, Byron Laflin; lieutenant-colonel, John Beverly; major, Wells Sponable; adjutant, John Kirk; quartermaster, Nathan Easterbrooks; surgeon, S. F. Manley; assistant surgeon, J. Hurley Miller; chaplain, S. Franklin Schoonmaker.

The letters and journals of the Herkimer county boys in this famous body, which the Citizen has published, form most absorbing reading and give a graphic picture of the soldier's life from the private's point of view. This is particularly true of Private W. J. McLean, who wrote a diary of his life and the army's movements, battles and retreats, in the campaign of the Army of the Potomac during 1862, before Richmond. Both these Civil war publications (those of the Register and the Citizen) deserve permanent preservation as they give an insight into the miseries of war and the life of the soldier, such as the regular histories absolutely fail of providing.

Sept. 17, 1913, at Herkimer, during appropriate public exercises, the colors of the 34th Regiment were presented to the Herkimer Historical society by James Suiter, life president of the 34th Regiment association and son of Col. Suiter. They had been preserved for nearly fifty years by Major Wells Sponable of the 34th, who turned them over to Mr. Suiter shortly before his death in 1911. A reunion of the 34th was held at Herkimer on the same date (Sept. 17, 1913) and over thirty veterans of the organization were present, this year being the fiftieth anniversary of the mustering out of the regiment. Among the old soldiers, who answered the roll call, were several whose letters and diaries, written on the field when young men half a century ago, have made such entertaining reading in the Herkimer Citizen for the past few months. Mr. McLean, the author of the diary mentioned was one of these. This reunion was held on the fifty-first anniversary of the battle of Antietam, Md., in which the 34th bore a gallant part in the repulse of the Confederates from Union soil. This was the bloodiest single day's fighting of the Civil war and the 34th lost heavily. Other regiments in which Herkimer county was represented were the 81st, 97th and 121st.

In July, 1913, was held the fiftieth anniversary of the battle of Gettysburg on the field of action, which is said to have defeated the Confederacy.

Fifty thousand veterans attended this historic event, a number of them going from the Mohawk valley. A great many of old boys in grey took part in this reunion, which is said to have marked the absolute and final reunion of the north and south. A similar anniversary was held at Chickamauga in September, 1913 (in what was once rebel territory), largely participated in by blue and gray veterans who fought on that bloody battleground.

Colonel Angell Matthewson was born in Pulaski, Oswego county, New York, June 8, 1837, and received his education in the academy of that town. When only 15 years of age he commenced working at the printer's trade in the office of the Pulaski Democrat. At 21 he was foreman of the job department of the Daily Palladium in Oswego, and a year later was city editor of the same paper. In 1859 he became associated with the Morning Herald office of Utica, N. Y., and went shortly after to Fort Plain, N. Y., where he became proprietor of the Mohawk Valley Register. In 1861 he enlisted in the Union army and raised a company in his home town in New York, of which he became second lieutenant. Lorenzo Crounse, afterwards governor of Nebraska, was captain of the same company. This company rendezvoused at Elmira, in September, 1861, where it was attached to the First New York Light Artillery, as Battery K of that regiment. May 18, 1861, Lieutenant Matthewson was appointed post adjutant at Camp Berry, Washington, D. C.

May 30, 1862, at Bolivar Heights, near Harper's Ferry, with a single piece of artillery, he routed the enemy's sharp shooters, and engaged a four-gun battery for half an hour, handling his gun with such judgment and skill that the only damage sustained was the disabling of one of the wheels of the gun carriage by a solid shot from the enemy, while the enemy's loss, as reported by Major Gardner of the Fifth New York Cavalry, was seven killed and upwards of 50 wounded. For his services on this occasion, he was appointed ordinance officer on the staff of Major-General Franz Sigel, June 7, 1862, and afterwards served in the same capacity on the staffs of Generals Cooper and Augur. November, 1862, he was promoted to first lieutenant and assigned to duty with Battery D of his regiment. May 23, 1863, he was appointed adjutant of his regiment and May 25 was appointed acting assistant adjutant-general of the Artillery Brigade, First Corps, Army of the Potomac, which position he held one year. July 1, 1864, he was promoted to captain of his company for meritorious service at North Anna River, Va., May 22, 1864, where he was shot through the thigh with a minnie ball, while in command of Battery D and fighting almost a forlorn hope. He was in service until the end of the war, three years and nine months, and was mustered out

at Elmira, N. Y., June 17, 1865. He was engaged in the following battles: Harper's Ferry, Cedar Mountain, Rappahannock Station, Fredericksburg, Chancellorsville, Gettysburg, Mine Run, Wilderness, Spottsylvania, North Anna River, Siege of Petersburg, Weldon Railroad, Hatcher's Run and Lee's surrender at Appomattox Court House.

After the close of the war Colonel Matthewson returned to Fort Plain, where he continued to engage in the newspaper business and also purchased the Canajoharie Radii, which he conducted for a number of years. In 1868 he was nominated and elected on the Democratic ticket to the lower house of the New York legislature from Montgomery county and served in that capacity for two years. At the close of his service in the legislature he determined to go west and disposed of his newspaper interests in New York. When he reached Kansas City he was offered the position of city editor of the Kansas City Journal, but from friends in New York he had heard of the founding of a new town by the name of Parsons, and determined to go to the place in the up-building of which he subsequently became such a powerful factor.

When Colonel Matthewson was east in 1912, he visited the old Gettysburg battlefield, where he had served so brilliantly as a captain in the Union army, and walked over the field with a guide, an old veteran of the battle, and came to a spot where the guide said: "Here is where a battery of Union artillery was posted to shell the Confederate ranks. They were firing too high and their shells went wild, doing absolutely no good whatever. A Confederate battery was turned on them, however, and commenced to wreak havoc among the Union forces stationed here. About that time a young captain in the Union army came up, relieved the officer in charge of the battery, telling him his aim was poor, ordered the direction of the guns lowered and with telling and accurate aim silenced within a few minutes the Confederate battery which was doing so much damage to our forces."

"Do you know who that captain was?" asked Colonel Matthewson.

The guide replied that he did not.

"I was the man," modestly admitted the Colonel.

And the monument that marks the battlefield contains the name of Angell Matthewson in commemoration of his valiant service to the Union cause at that great battle.

Colonel Matthewson died at his home in Parsons, Kansas, Jan. 15, 1913, after a long, useful and successful career both as soldier and citizen.

Col. Simeon Sammons, colonel of the 115th New York regiment during the Civil war, was born in the town of Mohawk in 1811. He was the son of Hon. Thomas Sammons, who was a Revolutionary soldier and patriot and who collected the celebrated "Sammons papers," frequently referred to and some of which are reprinted in this work. Thomas Sammons was for two terms a member of congress. Sampson Sammons was the grandfather of Col. Sammons and had charge of Johnson Hall, under the Tryon County Committee, during the Revolution. Col. Sammons was educated at Johnstown Academy and later held a commission in the militia. He was chosen colonel of the 115th, August, 1862, and was twice wounded during his service. After the war Col. Sammons was elected to the New York assembly for one term and also filled the office of harbor master of the port of New York. He died in 1881, aged 70 years.

CHAPTER IV.

1892, Barge Canal Recommendation of State Engineer Martin Schenck—1900, Report of the Greene Canal Commission, Barge Canal Survey—1903, Passage of $101,000,000 Barge Canal Act—1905, Work Begun on Champlain Canal Section—Locks Widened to 45 Feet—Features of the Mohawk River Canalization.

I have lately made a tour through the Lakes George and Champlain as far as Crown Point. Thence returning to Schenectady, I proceeded up the Mohawk river to Fort Schuyler and crossed over to Wood creek, which empties into the Oneida lake, and affords the water communication with Ontario. I then traversed the country to the eastern branch of the Susquehanna, and viewed the Lake Otsego, and the portage between that lake and the Mohawk river at Canajoharie. Prompted by these actual observations, I could not help taking a more extensive view of the vast inland navigation of these United States, from maps and the information of others, and could not but be struck by the immense extent and importance of it, and with the goodness of Providence, which has dealt its favors to us with so profuse a hand. Would to God we may have wisdom enough to improve them.—From a letter to Count Chastelleaux written by General Washington, after his journey up the Mohawk river in 1783. (See Chapter XXIV, First Series.)

This present chapter describes the New York state Barge canal, now (1913) nearing completion, and is the sixth chapter treating of transportation in the Mohawk valley. Prior ones have covered Mohawk river traffic, highways, bridges, Erie canal and railroad building. The seventh and last sketch regarding valley transportation methods will be the one describing the first aeroplane flight over the course of the Mohawk. This is also the fifth chapter in the series which considers the Mohawk river in its various features. This series has comprised the following subjects: Mohawk river and valley, Mohawk river traffic, river and other bridges, Erie canal, Barge canal.

The Barge canal is the most important engineering work in all the world's history, not in the working difficulties encountered (which may be at their utmost in the Panama canal) but in the population concerned, in volume of available trade, and in future possibilities, in which the Barge canal promises to far surpass any waterway or land trade route now or ever in existence, not excepting the Panama or the Suez canals. The greatest wonder connected with the whole work of the Barge canal is not its immense importance to half the hundred million people of North America but the fact that it has been practically completed at this time (1913) with hardly a single proper exposition of the importance of the work for the enlightenment of the people of the United States, with the single exception of the very interesting exploitation of the matter in the "Live Wire" of August 1, 1913, published by the Buffalo Chamber of Commerce, from which verbatim extracts are made in this chapter. There are millions of people in the United States who have never heard of the Barge canal, whereas the Panama enterprise is known practically to the entire population. More people of this country, and of the entire region of North America, will receive greater benefits from the Barge canal than from the waterway which bisects the Isthmus of Panama.

This paramount importance of the Barge canal to all the people of the middle west, the northwest and the eastern states and Atlantic seaboard, can be proven by reference to the tonnage figures of the Sault Ste. Marie canal (between Lakes Superior and Huron) and that of the Suez canal. In 1910, the "Soo" passed a tonnage of 36 million while the Suez reported 23 million tons. Much of the Great Lakes traffic must find its outlet by way of the Barge canal and there is every indication that its tonnage figures will equal and probably greatly surpass those of the Sault Ste. Marie.

If Elkanah Watson was the "father" of the old improved Mohawk waterway of 1796 and Jesse Hawley was the "father" of the Erie canal of 1825, because their writings and activities were the first powerful means of furthering these projects, then the honor of being the "parent" of the Barge canal belongs to a Mohawk valley man and a native of Montgomery county— Martin Schenck. He is entitled to this distinction for the same reason as Watson and Hawley are entitled to theirs. His was the first public and definite proposal for a canal of the Barge canal type, made in his report of 1892, when Mr. Schenck was state engineer and surveyor. Martin Schenck was born at the old Schenck place near the mouth of Knauderack creek, which runs through Schenck's

Hollow, just west of the north side "Nose", in the town of Palatine.

In this place it is well to state that Watson and Hawley were but two of many men who had advocated a lakes to-the-sea waterway (by way of the Mohawk valley) from the earliest days of the colony. They take their distinction from the fact that they were the first to put their plans before the public in a practical, concrete form, just as Martin Schenck was the first to advocate publicly a Barge canal of a definite type, allied to the present undertaking. Hawley, Geddes and Forman were all instrumental in the initial advancement of the Erie (or Grand) canal project, probably in the order named. Clinton did not take hold until the plan had already assumed a definite form, but his political power was one of the main causes for the act authorizing the canal work, and he, to a certain extent, deserves the title of the "father of the Erie canal." The whole question of the originator of the canal idea has been threshed out for a century. The fact of the matter is that there have been hundreds of influential New York state men who have aided the cause of state waterways from the days of the Inland Lock Navigation company. No one man is entitled to the sole credit of an idea so long in the minds of many men, but the canal projectors mentioned have well-earned distinction on account of their public labors mentioned.

The Barge Canal Bulletin, under date of August, 1909, carried an article on "The Evolution of the Barge Canal," which described the efforts of the friends of the canals in behalf of the improvement and efficiency of the state waterways, from the completion of the Erie in 1825 to the successful culmination of their efforts in securing the legislative enactment of the Barge canal acts. The essay mentioned contains the following:

"The first official presentation, of what is practically and distinctively the form of the present thousand-ton Barge canal, seems to have been contained in the annual report for 1892, of State Engineer and Surveyor .Martin Schenck, who said: 'The practical canal of the future, connecting Lake Erie and the Hudson river, ought to be one capable of bearing barges, 250 feet in length by 25 feet breadth of beam, of a draft not to exceed 10 feet, and of such a height that the great majority of bridges, that should span the canal, might be fixed structures instead of drawbridges. With the proposed canal (which could be built for a reasonable sum), bearing barges towed in fleets, each boat carrying 50,000 bushels of wheat, New York would be enabled to hold her commercial supremacy against all comers for many years to come.' "

While Mr. Schenck's plan was not immediately adopted yet it probably blazed the way for the Barge canal, the initial legislative measures for the construction of which were adopted eleven years later in 1903. The legislature, of the same year in which Mr. Schenck wrote his "Barge canal message," provided for a constitutional convention, which, among its other duties was to consider amendments relative to canal improvement. The constitutional convention met in 1894 and among its amendments was one providing that the canals might be improved in such manner as the legislature should provide by law. This was carried at the election of 1894, and was generally considered as a public mandate to the legislature to undertake the improvement of the New York state canals. The amendment became operative Jan. 1, 1895, and the legislature of that year passed an act authorizing the deepening of the Erie and Oswego canals to 9 feet and the Champlain canal to 7 feet. The project was a failure, the appropriation of nine million dollars being insufficient for the work and charges of graft and swindling were rife at the time.

On March 8, 1899, Gov. Roosevelt appointed a committee of citizens, headed by Gen. Francis V. Greene, who were to consider the whole state canal question and report on the same. The "Barge Canal Bulletin" says: "The date of this appointment marks the

real beginning of the Barge canal enterprise as we know it today." Early in 1900 this committee reported, after a thorough study of the entire problem. They emphatically recommended that the canals should not be abandoned (a policy which was advocated by many citizens of the time) but proposed the enlargement of the Erie, Champlain and Oswego canals—the Erie to a size suitable for 1,000-ton barges and the Champlain and Oswego to a 9 foot depth—practically the same recommendations that Mr. Schenck had made eight years before. This would allow of the use of boats on the Erie 150 feet long, 25 wide, drawing 10 feet of water. The locks were to be 310 feet long by 28 feet wide, with 11 feet of water on the sills. The route followed closely the line of the present Barge canal construction. Upon the submission of this report the legislature appropriated $200,000 for Barge canal surveys and estimates. Data had been gathered shortly before, over much of the proposed route, by the U. S. Deep Waterway Survey and this was available and hastened the preliminary work. The report of the survey was submitted to the legislature, March 15, 1901. Conflicting interests deferred legislative action until 1903, when a bill appropriating $82,000,000 was introduced, providing for the improvement of the Erie canal, Oswego canal and the Champlain canal. The estimate of cost was later raised to $100,592,993 and the bill as revised was submitted to the people at the election of 1903 and was carried. This law, with its subsequent amendments, came to be known as the $101,000,000 Barge canal act of 1903, and under its provisions the Barge canal is now under construction. Says the Barge Canal Bulletin:

"In brief, the act provided for the issuance of eighteen-year bonds for canal improvement to the amount of not exceeding $101,000,000, not more than $10,000,000 to be issued within two years after passage of the act. A general annual tax of twelve-thousandths of a mill was authorized for each million of dollars in bonds outstanding in any fiscal year. The State Engineer and the Superintendent of Public Works were directed to begin improvements to the canals upon the basis of a channel 75 feet in width on the bottom, 12 feet of water and at least 1,128 square feet of water cross-section, except at aqueducts and through cities and villages, where the width might be reduced and the cross-section of water modified as deemed necessary by the State Engineer, with the approval of the Canal Board. In rivers and lakes the channel was to have a minimum bottom width of 200 feet, a minimum depth of 12 feet and at least 2,400 square feet of water cross-section. The locks were to be 328 feet long by 28 feet wide in the clear, and with 11 feet of water on the miter-sills.

"Routes to be followed and details of construction were fixed. In general the route of the Erie was by way of the Hudson river from Troy to Waterford; thence by a new channel to the Mohawk above Cohoes falls, and up the canalized Mohawk to Rome, with a few diversions to the existing canal; thence down the valley of Wood creek, across Oneida lake, down Oneida river to Three River Point and up Seneca river to the mouth of Crusoe creek; thence by a new route to the existing canal at Clyde, whence the line of the existing canal was to be followed generally to the Niagara river at Tonawanda, and by this river and Black Rock harbor to Lake Erie. All work was to be by contract and provisions for the condemnation of necessary lands and for the sale of abandoned portions of the canal were made. An Advisory Board of five expert civil engineers and a Special Deputy State Engineer were authorized. The criticisms of the various commissions, that were appointed to consider canal affairs after the 1895 improvement, were heeded in part by vesting most of the responsibility for the work in the State Engineer, giving him authority over the preparation of plans and the supervision of construction, including both engineering and inspection." It will be noted that the foregoing route

utilizes the natural waterways of the Mohawk and Oswego river valleys (joined by the Wood creek line) over two-thirds of the route. The Mohawk river section comprises a third of the Erie route of the Barge canal system.

"Since the passage of the act of 1903, a score or more amendatory provisions have been made, many of which refer to its financing or to matters of administrative detail. One only have we space to speak of here—the widening of the locks in 1905 to 45 feet. This could be done without greatly increasing the cost, and would permit the passage of lake boats carrying 2,600 tons. The advantages of this great increase in carrying capacity of barges of forty-three feet beam over those of twenty-seven feet, the fact that Canadian canals now possess locks forty-five feet in width by four teen feet depth on miter-sills, and the further fact that more than three fourths of the entire Barge canal route is through canalized natural waterways of sufficient width to enable boats of this beam to pass each other, were cogent reasons why this change was made.

"It would be obvious that in an undertaking of this character and magnitude, a vast amount of preliminary work in the way of surveys, borings, soundings, studies, plans and maps would be required. This preliminary work was soon under way, but it was not until April, 1905, that actual construction was begun, upon the Champlain division, quietly and without any of the ceremonies usual to such an occasion."

This, in brief is the history of the inception of the Barge canal idea, its consideration and public adoption and the commencement of work. It may be briefly summarized as follows: 1892, State Engineer and Surveyor Martin Schenck's annual message and report advocating a Barge canal; 1899, March 9, Gov. Roosevelt appoints canal investigating committee; 1900, canal committee reports and recommends canal enlargement; 1900, New York legislature appropriates $200,000 for preliminary surveys; 1901, March 15, report of canal survey made to legislature; 1903, $101,000,000 Barge canal act of 1903, providing for the Barge canal improvement of the Erie, Oswego and Champlain canals; 1905, beginning of Barge canal work on the Champlain division. The state engineers, in charge of this work since its commencement, have been 1903-1904, Edward A. Bond; 1905-1907, Henry A. Van Alstyne; 1908, Frederick Skene; 1909-1910, Frank M. Williams; 1911-1914, John A. Bensel.

The Barge canal through New York state largely supplants and parallels the present Erie. Through the valley it follows largely the course of the Mohawk and the old trade route from Albany to Oswego and the great lakes.

In the section especially covered in this historical narrative and within the limits of Montgomery county, locks on the canal are located as follows: Amsterdam, Fonda, Yosts, Canajoharie, Fort Plain, St. Johnsville, Little Falls. Terminal docks are projected at Amsterdam, Fonda, Canajoharie, Fort Plain, St. Johnsville, Little Falls. All the towns along the Barge canal become ports of both the Atlantic ocean and the Great Lakes. This was true only in a smaller degree of the "canal towns" of the Erie. It is fitting that the Mohawk valley, the first white settlers of which were natives of Holland—the great canal county—should be occupied by a section of the world's greatest canal.

The following is here reprinted from a pamphlet entitled "The New York State Barge Canal" by State Engineer J. A. Bensel, published in 1912. Some of these facts were included in the chapter on the Erie canal but it is nevertheless printed here complete as follows:

To understand the canal enlargement which New York state is now engaged in, a brief glance at the history of canal-building in the state is needed. The first work of interior waterway improvement was performed by two private companies, chartered in 1792. By the end of the eighteenth century they had completed most of their works. About 1808 agitation for state-built canals was begun. In 1817 the work of construction was commenced, the main branch being completed in 1825. Within the next decade several lateral canals were built. This period was closely followed by the first enlargement of three of the chief canals—a work protracted through many years and not completed till 1862. Then followed some two decades of little activity, during the latter part of which several of the lateral branches were abandoned. In 1884 the period of later improvements was begun by a series of lock-lengthenings, which continued for about ten years. The last decade and a half has witnessed the undertakings of two enlargements, the latter of which is the work now in progress—the Barge canal.

During the history of its canals New York state has opened 1,050 miles of navigable waterways, including a hundred miles of interior lake navigation. In addition there are nearly 500 miles of lake and river navigation along the Canadian and Vermont borders, and 150 miles on the Hudson river. Some 350 miles of these canals have been officially abandoned, while about 50 miles more have fallen into disuse. The work of improvement now going on, known as Barge canal construction, consists of the enlargement of four of the existing canals, large portions of the channels, however, being relocated. On one of these canals this is the second enlargement since its original building, on two this is the third enlargement, while on the other branch it is the fourth.

The four canals being improved are: (1) The Erie, or main canal, which stretches across the state from east to west, joining the Hudson river and Lake Erie; (2) the Champlain, which runs northerly from the eastern terminus of the Erie and enters the head of Lake Champlain; (3) the Oswego, which starts north, midway on the line of the Erie, and reaches Lake Ontario; (4) the Cayuga and Seneca, which leaves the Erie a little to the west of the Oswego junction and extends south, first to Cayuga lake and then to Seneca lake.

The original Erie canal was begun in 1817 and finished in 1825. It had a bottom width of 28 feet, a width at water-surface of 40 feet and 4 feet depth of water. The first enlargement was made between 1836 and 1862. At that time the section of waterway was 70 feet at water-line, 52½ or 56 feet at bottom, according to slope of sides, and 7 feet deep. The second enlargement was begun in 1896, when a depth of 9 feet was attempted, but this work was completed only at disconnected localities.

The original Champlain canal, begun in 1817 and finished in 1823, had widths of 26 and 40 feet, respectively, at bottom and water-surface, and 4 feet depth. In 1860 widths of 35 and 50 feet, respectively, at bottom and water-line, and a depth of 5 feet were authorized. In 1870 increased widths of 44 and 58 feet, respectively, and a depth of 7 feet were ordered by the legislature. This improvement, however, was not completed. The enlargement of 1896-8 called for a depth of 7 feet, but this work also was not completed.

The original Oswego canal, which was begun in 1825 and finished in 1828, had the same dimensions as the original Champlain, namely, 26 and 40 by 4 feet. The first enlargement was started in 1852 and completed in 1862, and gave a channel of the same size as the Erie at that time—52½ and 70 by 7 feet. The second enlargement, that of 1896-8, was also similar to that of the Erie, a depth of 9 feet being attempted, but the work was never wholly completed.

The original prism of the Cayuga and Seneca canal, which was constructed between 1826 and 1828, was the same in size as the Erie, 28 and 40 by 4 feet. The first enlargement, accomplished from 1854 to 1862, was also similar to that of the Erie—52½ and 70 by 7 feet. This branch did not share with the other three in the enlargement of 1896-8.

The dimensions of the present enlargement, or Barge canal improvement, are the same for all four branches of the system. Briefly it may be stated that the law requires a channel at least 75 feet wide at the bottom and having 12 feet of water. In rivers and lakes the width is 200 feet, and 72 per cent of the length of the whole system is in river or lake channel. The locks are 328 feet long between gates, 45 feet wide, and have 12 feet of water over the sills.

These few pages cannot give any detailed account of route or of structures. The description might be extended indefinitely, for there is much of interest to be found throughout the 440 miles of construction and the 350 miles of intervening lakes or adjoining rivers.

In general it may be stated that the Barge canal project is largely a river canalization scheme. Previous state canals have been chiefly independent, or artificial channels, built in several instances on cross-country locations. Now, however, the route returns to the natural watercourses. The bed or the valley of the Mohawk is utilized from the Hudson to the old portage near Rome. Then Wood creek, Oneida lake, and Oneida, Seneca and Clyde rivers are used, carrying the channel to the western part of the state, where the streams run north and the alignment of the old channel is retained

for the new canal. The other branches of the Barge canal occupy natural streams throughout most of their lengths.

The accompanying statistical tabulation gives some of the leading facts concerning the Barge canal:

(As certain plans are still under consideration, the following figures are subject to change. All canals are meant, unless otherwise specified.)

Erie branch, length of canal, not including Hudson and Niagara river termini, 323.2 miles. Erie branch, number of locks, 35. Oneida lake, not included in above mileage, no improvement needed, about 19 miles. Spurs to Erie branch (Syracuse and Rochester harbors), 10.26 miles. Champlain branch, length of canal, 61.5 miles. Champlain branch, number of locks, 11. Oswego branch, canal, 22.8 miles. Oswego branch, number of locks, 7. Cayuga and Seneca branch, length of canal (including spurs at heads of lakes), approximate, 27.3 miles. Cayuga and Seneca branch, number of locks, 4. Cayuga and Seneca lakes, portions needing no improvement and not included in above mileage, 65 miles. Width of channel, land line, earth section, bottom, minimum, 75 feet. Width of channel, land line, earth section, water-surface, 123 to 171 feet. Width of channel, land line, rock section, bottom, minimum, 94 feet. Width of channel, river line, bottom, generally, 200 feet. Depth of channel, land line and minimum river line, 12 feet. Locks, length between gates, 328 feet. Locks, available length, 310 feet. Locks, width of chamber, 45 feet. Locks, depth of water on sills, 12 feet. Dams, new, 28. Dams, old, with new crests, 6. Dams, old, used without change, 5. Bridges, 199. Boats, capacity, utilizing full lock width, about 3,000 tons. Boats, capacity, built for two to pass in most restricted channel and for two, traveling tandem, to be locked at one lockage, about 1,500 tons. Authorization of work (Erie, Champlain and Oswego canals), chapter 147, laws of 1903. Authorization of work (Cayuga and Seneca canal), chapter 391, laws of 1909. Appropriation (Erie, Champlain and Oswego canals), $101,000,000. Appropriation (Cayuga and Seneca canal), $7,000,000. Construction work begun (Champlain canal), April 24, 1905. Construction work begun (Erie canal), June 7, 1905. Excavation, preliminary (1903) estimate, not including work for dams, bridges, highway, railway, and stream changes and other small items (Erie, Champlain and Oswego canals), 132,225,800 cubic yards. Excavation, contract plans (Erie, Champlain and Oswego canals), approximate, 105,000,000 cubic yards. Excavation, contract plans (Cayuga and

Seneca canal), approximate, 9,100,000 cubic yards. Concrete, preliminary (1903) estimate (Erie, Champlain and Oswego canals), 3,243,100 cubic yards. Concrete, contract plans (Erie, Champlain and Oswego canals), approximate, 2,600,000 cubic yards. Concrete, contract plans (Cayuga and Seneca canal), approximate, 150,000 cubic yards.

In the summer of 1913, a party composed of representatives of the Buffalo Chamber of Commerce made a tour of the Barge canal in company with State Engineer John A. Bensel and some of his official staff. The record of this very interesting trip was embodied in the August (1913) issue of the "Live Wire," a periodical put out by the Buffalo institution mentioned. The number was profusely illustrated with views of the canal. This publication is particularly interesting considering the remarkable fact that this great engineering work—the Barge canal—has received but trifling publicity from the papers of the state during its construction. The great lake metropolis of Western New York appreciates the tremendous advantages that will accrue to it from the canal and its men of business showed their foresight and intelligence in making the trip referred to. Not only Buffalo but the whole east and even the world at large must feel the trade, business and commercial impetus of the Barge canal. But New York state is bound to be the greatest gainer by this public work, which is justly entitled to the name of "the Grand Canal"—a title the people along the Erie canal gave to that waterway during its period of construction.

State Engineer John A. Bensel, in a recent article on this subject, points out that about 71 per cent of the territory of the state lies within 50 miles of the Barge canal, that three-quarters of the population of the state live within two miles of the new waterway, and that the Barge canal goes through the most thickly-populated section in the United States.

The "Live Wire" gives the following interesting comparisons between the Barge canal and the Panama canal:

Barge canal—540 miles long; total lockage lift, 1,050 feet; dams, 39; locks, 57 lift, 2 guard and 9 smaller locks; number of structures, between 350 and 400; cost, $127,800,000; built by state with a population of 9,000,000; excavation, estimated total, 114,100,000 cubic yards; concrete, estimated total, 2,750,000 cubic yards; excavation to January 1, 1913, 78,428,286 cubic yards; work begun, April 24, 1905.

Panama canal—50 miles long; total lockage lift, 170 feet; dams, 4; locks, 6 pairs; number of structures, 12 locks, 1 spillway and 4 dams; cost, $375,000,000; built by United States with a population of 90,000,000; excavation, estimated total, 203,710,000 cubic yards; concrete, estimated total, 5,000,000 cubic yards; excavation to January 1, 1913, 188,280,312 cubic yards; work begun by Americans, May 4, 1904.

"Buffalo Live Wire" of August, 1913, covered the whole subject of the Barge canal, describing the central line from Buffalo to Waterford on the Hudson, the Cayuga and Seneca branch, the great reservoirs, the Oswego branch and the Champlain section. After dealing with this great work westward of Rome, the Barge canal work in the Mohawk valley was treated—covering the ground from Rome to the Hudson. Much of this concerns the territory covered in these chapters—the middle Mohawk valley.

One of the Gargantuan tasks of the Barge canal work was the relocating of the New York Central railroad systems through Rome. The tracks and appurtenances were literally picked up and carried a distance of three miles and replaced, the total expense involved being about $1,000,000. In the doing of this work the New York Central built three new bridges and raised high, new embankments for its new line.

In the publication referred to the Delta and Hinckley reservoirs are described as follows:

The total length of the Delta dam is 1,100 feet, the length of the spillway being 300 feet. The maximum height of masonry above rock is 100 feet, and the approximate height of overfall (pool to crest) 70 feet. The masonry material used in this dam totaled 90,-000 cubic yards. The contract price for the entire work, including altera-tions was $940,840. Details of con-struction included canal relocation for nearly two miles; a flight of lift locks three lifts of 20.6 feet each; one lift lock with a lift of 12.1 feet, and a re-inforced concrete aqueduct, trunk, about 208 feet long.

Other figures generating new ideas concerning the bigness of the Delta dam include statements to the effect that the area of watershed served by this dam totals 137 square miles. The capacity of the reservoirs at crest level is 2,750,000,000 cubic feet. The maxi-mum depth at crest level is 70 feet, while the average depth at crest level is 23 feet. In the construction of this dam the village of Delta was wiped out and 295 buildings were removed; ten miles of highways were submerg-ed and seven locks and one aqueduct were destroyed. The maximum flood at the Delta dam is more than 8,000,-000 cubic feet per second, while the maximum regulated flood is 2,600 cubic feet per second.

The Hinckley dam, like the Delta dam, is located in Oneida county, a few miles distant from Trenton Falls. It is much larger than the Delta dam and its construction gives to the state a lake nine miles in length or one-third again as big as the one at Delta. [The Delta dam is on the upper Mo-hawk river, about five miles north of Rome. The Hinckley reservoir at Hinckley, on the West Canada creek, about twenty-five miles north of Her-kimer. Other reservoirs of this type are contemplated in the Mohawk val-ley—probably on the Schoharie or East Canada creeks. The Hinckley reser-voir is located both in Oneida and Herkimer counties.]

In quantity of material used in the construction of these two tremendous dams there are surprisingly large fig-ures, as indicated above. Take the masonry material alone. It totals up-wards of 200,000 cubic yards, which if loaded into ordinary dump wagons, would present a picture something like this: By the time the first team reached either the Delta or Hinckley dams, the last wagon would be just starting out of Charleston, South Caro-lina. Or, if the procession were start-ing from the west, the last wagon would be at Springfield, Illinois, when the first wagon was dumped.

The following from the Buffalo "Live Wire," of August, 1913, gives a good description of the Barge canal work along the Mohawk river from Albany to Utica:

One does not have to be an engineer, an architect, nor yet a builder to ap-preciate the many striking features of this portion of the canal work. It is fraught with romance at almost every point. It is tinged with history all along the valley of the Mohawk. The old and the new intermingle, and there is always something to study accord-ing to the manner in which one's mind inclines.

Considering merely the work itself, four striking features of engineering accomplishments stand out promi-nently from the mass of detail in-volved in the building of this section of the canal. These features include lock and dam construction, the prin-ciple of movable dams, the canalizing of the Mohawk river, and land cuts.

Starting at the Hudson river end of the section, the first piece of lock and dam construction encountered is the lift from the Hudson river level to the level of the Mohawk, a distance of 184 feet, or 14 feet more than the entire lift in the entire Panama canal. This 184-foot lift is overcome by a series of five locks which replace 16 small locks that are required to make the same lift on the old canal. A great saving in time of lockage has been made here, for it will be possible for barges to go through the new locks in about one hour and 35 minutes, as against 8 hours required to lift through the 16 old locks.

At the entrance to the Mohawk river (or land line level) two immense dams have been constructed. The first of these is known as the Crescent dam and the second as the Vischer's Ferry dam. The Crescent dam is the more impressive of the two and, as its name implies, is constructed in the form of a half-circle intersected on one end by a large island. The dam is complete except for five openings, which still remain to be closed and which cannot be finished until pending litigation in which the state is involved with toll bridge companies is settled, or until the legislature enacts proposed laws which will make it possible to complete this work. In the meantime an injunction stops further proceed-ings.

Some idea of the size of Crescent dam may be obtained when it is stated that the total length of the structure is 1,922 feet, with a radius of 700 feet. The height of crest above top of apron is 39 feet. The width on the base is 42 feet and one-half inch. The width on top is 11 feet, five inches. The rise of the pool is about 27 feet, and the width of the apron 40 feet. The total amount of concrete used in the construction of the dam was 54,360 cubic yards, and the contract price for the work was $466,438.78. The dam forms a lake which varies in depth from 15 to 45 feet, and has a width of from one-half mile to two miles, extending as far up stream as Vischer's Ferry dam, about 10 and one-half miles distant.

A fine power house has been built at this dam which furnishes electric power for the five locks known as the Waterford Flight, the most distant of these locks being fully two miles from the dam. One gets some idea here of the immensity of the floods along the Mohawk river. Last spring, despite the fact that the flood waters were able to discharge through the five big openings left in the dam, the space proved insufficient and the flood poured over the top of the dam structure.

The Vischer's Ferry dam forms a lake varying in depth from 12 to 36 feet, and having a varying width of from one-half to one and a quarter miles. The lake is about 11 miles long. This dam is complete and in operation and as soon as the openings left in the Crescent dam can be completed it will be possible to use the new Barge canal from Schenectady to the Hudson river.

The contract price for the Vischer's Ferry dam was $518,149.65. The total length of the dam is nearly 2,000 feet. The width of the base is about 40 and one-half feet, and the width on top nearly 11 and one-half feet. The height of the crest above top of apron is 36 feet, and the total width of the apron is 38 feet. A total of 57,750 cubic yards of concrete was used in this dam.

The construction of the locks and dam at Vischer's Ferry and Crescent was very difficult due to the floods and because of the need to maintain navigation on the present Erie canal.

From Schenectady westward there are eight movable dams which are of a type of construction that forms various pools to Little Falls. These movable dams are raised out of the river in winter and leave the stream in its natural state, so that the dam does not interfere in any way with the floods. One of the largest of these dams may be seen at Amsterdam. It is 750 feet long and consists of three spans, each of them 250 feet long. This structure alone cost $800,000.

Pictures are printed in the August, 1913, (Buffalo) "Live Wire" of the movable dams and bridges at Amsterdam and Fort Plain. The Fort Plain bridge has two spans of 250 feet each, being 500 feet in length. This was the first dam and bridge of its type completed in the valley. The eight movable dams and locks in the river westward from Schenectady to Little Falls (a distance of about 60 miles) are at

the following locations: Rotterdam Junction, Cranesville, Amsterdam, Tribes Hill, Yosts (Randall), Canajoharie, Fort Plain, St. Johnsville.

Some of the most impressive work along the entire canal system may be seen at Little Falls. The cut made here is a veritable monster of rock excavation, the rock being igneous in character and unusually hard. This excavation, however, does not represent the principal difficulty in the work here encountered. The problem rather hinges on the fact that the West Shore and New York Central railroads, the canal itself and the Mohawk river all come together at this point in a narrow gorge, the situation being further complicated by the presence of mills and other industrial plants in the gorge. Two old locks now being operated here will simply be covered with water and wont even be pulled out, because when the waters are let in there will be ample depth over them. The new water level will be 20 feet above that of the present Erie canal water surface.

The highest lift lock ever constructed in the world has been built at Little Falls. It has a total lift of 42 and one-half feet, which is exactly one fourth of the entire lift of the entire Panama canal.

The total cost of the work at Little Falls, including lock construction, was $950,000.

Having mastered marshes and quick sand and built the prism of the canal across gorges and along lines highly elevated above the surrounding country, the problem confronting State Engineer John A. Bensel at Scotia, N. Y., seemed simple at first. It appeared to be a mere detail, although a large one, of the general task of canalizing the Mohawk river, and on the surface apparently all that was called for was the construction of a lock and dam. When test pits were sunk, it revealed an entirely different state of affairs, for it was found necessary to sink caissons in order that the underflow of water in the river might be cut off. This work, which is always dangerous, was rendered more so by the fact that some of the caissons had to be sunk 82 feet below the surface of the river. A short time before the chamber members inspected the work, two men lost their lives in one of the caissons.

The construction work involved in the building of the eight movable locks and dams built incidental to the canalizing of the Mohawk included foundations of varied character, some on rock, others in hardpan and lighter material, making it necessary, where the lighter material was encountered, to enclose the entire structure with sheet piling.

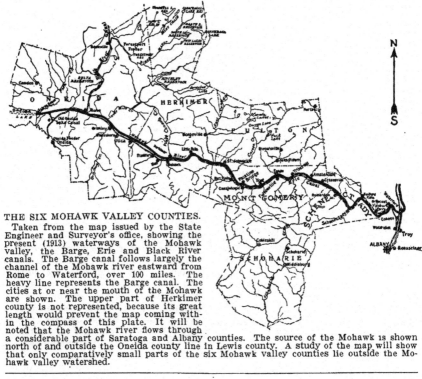

THE SIX MOHAWK VALLEY COUNTIES.
Taken from the map issued by the State
Engineer and Surveyor's office, showing the
present (1913) waterways of the Mohawk
valley, the Barge, Erie and Black River
canals. The Barge canal follows largely the
channel of the Mohawk river eastward from
Rome to Waterford, over 100 miles. The
heavy line represents the Barge canal. The
cities at or near the mouth of the Mohawk
are shown. The upper part of Herkimer
county is not represented, because its great
length would prevent the map coming within the compass of this plate. It will be
noted that the Mohawk river flows through
a considerable part of Saratoga and Albany counties. The source of the Mohawk is shown
north of and outside the Oneida county line in Lewis county. A study of the map will show
that only comparatively small parts of the six Mohawk valley counties lie outside the Mohawk valley watershed.

At Rocky Rift Feeder, Crescent and
Herkimer, three guard gates have
been built in order to confine the floods
in the Mohawk river. These gates are
the highest on the entire Barge canal
system, their height being 24 feet.
Sometimes the building of a lock involves other tasks of considerable
magnitude. This was the case at
Sterling Creek, where it was necessary
to build a railroad bridge of very
heavy type for the main line of the
New York Central incidental to the
work of building the lock.

In the canalizing of the Mohawk
river from Crescent dam to Schenectady, a very small amount of excavation was required, inasmuch as the
two large dams forming the two lakes
already referred to gave sufficient
depth for navigation. In the canalizing work various kinds of material
were encountered, such as fine sand,
hardpan and rock. Where the rock
was encountered it was very difficult
to carry on the work, due to the numerous floods for which the Mohawk
river is noted. In various places along
the river, at this season of the year,

one sees the river bed exposed, the
bottom being rock worn smooth by
the rush of waters, and it does not
require a vivid imagination to picture
the spring floods tearing along the
unobstructed bed of the stream on
such a bottom and sweeping everything before it.

The fine sand also presented serious
problems because it was always necessary to maintain channels, an exceedingly difficult task in soil of such
character. However, all these difficulties have been overcome and the
entire canalizing work is under contract and will be completed in order
to turn navigation through the new
Barge canal in 1915.

The excavation at this time [1913]
has been finished from Rotterdam to
Amsterdam, a distance of 10 miles.
The excavation has also been completed from about half way between
Tribes Hill and Fonda to Canajoharie,
about 15 miles in all. From Fort Plain
to about one and one-half miles west
of St. Johnsville, excavation has also
been completed. From St. Johnsville
to Sterling Creek the excavating is

about 90 per cent finished, and from Sterling Creek to Utica the canal prism has been completed.

Taking into consideration that no excavating will be necessary above the two large dams, the canalizing of the Mohawk river is about 80 per cent finished in length.

From the Hudson river to the Mohawk at Waterford, the canal prism is constructed in a new location. This stretch includes the five locks known as the Waterford Flight, already referred to as a lift which, in itself, is 14 feet higher than the total lift of the entire Panama canal. This exceptionally high lift was necessary in order that the canal might pass around Cohoes falls and the dam at Cohoes. In the vicinity of the Rocky Rift Feeder, another line will be necessary for the purpose of overcoming the slope in the Mohawk river and the Rocky Rift Feeder dam, which stores water for the maintenance of the present canal.

At Little Falls the new construction follows the same lines as those of the old canal. This is a land line constructed for the purpose of passing around the falls at Little Falls.

From Herkimer east another land line is provided for, the object being to overcome the slope in the Mohawk river. This is an exceptionally difficult piece of work in view of the fact that navigation must be maintained in the old canal.

From Sterling Creek west, the work is similar as from Herkimer east, and for the same reason—namely, that the slope in the Mohawk river must be overcome.

In the vicinity of Little Falls, contracts still remain to be let for the making of connections with the Mohawk river above and below Little Falls. The reasons for not placing this work under contract at this time are that this will have to be the last piece of construction work between Little Falls and the Hudson river, the old canal being destroyed just east of Little Falls lock and the water surfaces at this location will be materially changed.

All of the main structures between Waterford and Utica have been completed with the exception of the lock and dam at Scotia, where the work is progressing in a very satisfactory manner.

It is expected that all the Barge canal work on this portion of the system will be advanced to such a stage that navigation will be turned through the new canal in May, 1915.

The state engineer's report for 1913 contains the following: "The Barge Canal Terminal Law provides that the section of the present [1913 Erie] canal system, from Rome to Mohawk, shall be maintained as a part of the Barge canal terminal system, but no provision is made for funds to construct the necessary junction locks at Rome and Mohawk." The report contains a map showing the portions of the old Erie canal cut off from the present Barge canal. The report continues: "It is evident that the question as to what disposition shall be made of those portions of the canals so cut off should be one for the consideration of the present [1913] legislature." The report shows that there is a constitutional provision prohibiting the sale of canal lands but they have nevertheless been sold by the state, in the past, after they have been abandoned for canal purposes. The state engineer suggests proper legislation to dispose of abandoned canals and canal lands, which do not enter into the present and projected enlarged canal system of the state, and also an enactment to provide for the locks aforementioned at Rome and Mohawk. In case of these locks, being constructed a stretch of the old Erie canal, about 25 miles long, will remain in use and this will probably be all that will be left of the Mohawk river section of the old Erie canal. The disposition of the rest of the canal bed and adjacent lands in the Mohawk valley is a present day [1913] subject of speculation.

By chapter 190 of the laws of 1911, the state engineer was directed to make a survey for the ultimate purpose of improving the Black river for navigation between the state dam at Carthage and Sacketts Harbor on Lake Ontario. A full description of this route is in the 1913 report aforementioned. A summary of the cost of this waterway construction is $16,300,-000, for a canal having prism and locks of the same size as the Barge canal improvement. It is not impossible that the Black river and canal may be similarly canalized in the future and that picturesque and once important old trade route will come into its own once more, after years of disuse. This would form an important link in the future great waterways of the state and would connect with the Barge canal at Rome.

The carrying capacity of the Barge canal may be clearly appreciated when the fact is considered that one 1,500 ton barge will carry a load equal to that of the average 50-car freight train of the present day (1913). A 3,000 ton barge, or two 1,500 ton barges running tandem, have a cargo tonnage equal to that of a 100 freight car train. It is probable that the railroads have approached their extreme capacity as freight carriers, as regards the load per train under present conditions. Therefore it seems that the Mohawk waterway has a great future as a carrier of slow freight. It would be indeed interesting to know just what the situation will be a century hence with regard to the rival abilities of the railroads and the Barge canal as freight carriers. The writer believes the carrying capacity of the Barge canal may be still further increased, if conditions demand it. To provide a depth of water, which may be necessary for present and future waterway, needs that the greatest care should be taken of the water supply of the Mohawk watershed; reforesting barren wastes where possible to provide woods to hold the water in the soil and also in the provision of a more than ample reservoir system.

The Barge canal dredges have in many sections covered the Mohawk's banks high with spoil from the river bottom. It is suggested here that this ugly condition be done away with and the river banks strengthened by the planting of shrubbery and trees along the entire river course. The disfigurement of a stream, as world-noted for its beauty as the Mohawk, is not to be taken lightly and the state should endeavor to retain as much of its attractiveness as possible. Formerly the shores were lined with beautiful trees and the replanting of them will renew the river's charm as much as possible and strengthen the banks against the wash of the current.

It seems appropriate that the Mohawk should be the location of one of the world's greatest canals, inasmuch as the eastern end of its valley was settled by people from Holland, the country which may be fittingly termed the "mother of canals." Of the Mohawk valley section of the Barge canal, western Montgomery county forms almost the center.

In 1912 and 1913 inquiries, as to the safety of the Hinckley Barge canal reservoir, were made of the office of the State Engineer and Surveyor. The villages of Poland, Newport, Middleville and Herkimer all lie in the West Canada creek valley, in which is located the Hinckley reservoir. These four villages all joined in a request for information as to the safety of the Hinckley dam in 1913. A special report was made by State Engineer Bensel on the subject, which showed unusual precautions for the safety of this structure had been taken, which should guard it against any damage from even the greatest floods. The subject suggests that an inspection of all storage reservoirs on the Mohawk and its tributaries should be made annually by the proper parties.

Some opposition to the Barge canal has been offered by people who hoped to see a ship canal supplant the Erie. It seems to be the consensus of expert opinion that such a waterway is impracticable. However conditions change and it is not improbable that the Barge canal will prove to be a step toward a greater waterway, perhaps a century hence, which will connect the Hudson with the Great Lakes by way of the Mohawk river, Oneida lake and river and the Oswego river to Lake Ontario and thence to Lake Erie and westward by means of a canal around Niagara Falls. The carrying capacity of both railroads and Barge canal will probably soon be overtaxed by the east and west freight traffic.

At last the people of New York state are taking an advanced and enlightened position in regard to the great transportation advantages of their natural waterways and their present development brings out strongly the keen insight and knowledge of the possibilities of inland waterway traffic displayed by Washington in the extract from his letter which heads this chapter and which was written anent his visit to the Mohawk river section of the present Barge canal.

Martin Schenck, who, as state engineer in his report of 1892, first publicly proposed the Barge canal, was born on the Schenck farm at Schenck's Hollow, in the town of Palatine, near the Nose, where the Montgomery county home is now located. The first Schenck (Peter) came to Long Island, in New York state, in 1650, from Holland. A descendant, Ralph Schenck, moved to Johnstown during the Revolution. He was an active patriot and soldier, serving at Monmouth and Cowpens, among other fields, and held the rank of lieutenant. His son William bought the Jelles Fonda place from John DeWandelaer at the mouth of the Kanagara or Knauderack, which later became known as Schenck's and Schenck's Hollow. Major Jelles Fonda had here a store and a mill and a fine brick house (said to have been one of the best in the valley), all of which property was burned by Johnson in his first raid of 1780. William Schenck here had a grist mill, saw mill, fulling mill, plaster mill, cider mill, blacksmith shop and cooper shop in the early nineteenth century, making it a place of considerable importance. Here, about or before 1830, he built a fine brick house, which is now the main building of the Montgomery county home, the farm having been acquired by the county about 1900. The Schenck place is one of the most noted of the historic farms and dwellings along the Mohawk, being a large, well kept place, situated amidst beautiful surroundings. It, however, has the unenviable reputation of being located on the banks of a stream, which is one of the few haunts of rattlesnakes in the valley.

Benjamin Schenck, son of William Schenck, was the father of Martin Schenck, who was born at the Schenck place in 1848. He studied civil engineering at Union college and became engaged in railroad and general engineering and contracting work. In 1874 he was elected to the assembly from Montgomery county. He was later an engineer employed in West Shore railroad construction and in 1883 became connected with the canal department. In 1892 Martin Schenck was elected state engineer and surveyor and served as such until 1894.

CHAPTER V.

1911, August 14-25, Atwood's 1,266-Mile Flight From St. Louis to New York—Flies 95 Miles From Syracuse to Nelliston, August 22 and Stays Overnight at Fort Plain—Flies 66 Miles From Nelliston to Castleton, August 23, With a Stop in Glen for Repairs—"Following the Mohawk."

This chapter, relative to the first aeroplane flight through the Mohawk valley, is the seventh and last chapter treating of valley transportation. The others have covered early Mohawk river traffic, bridges, turnpike travel, Erie canal, railroads and Barge canal.

In 1911 Harry N. Atwood made a flight by aeroplane from St. Louis to New York, a distance by air of 1,266 miles. It was an epoch-making event in the history of aviation and formed a fitting chapter in the long record of travel and transportation along the Mohawk, for Atwood followed our river in his air journey through this part of the state. Birds of passage follow the same route from lakes to coast and in the summer of 1912 the writer saw three gulls flying westward over the river from the porch of the Haymarket club fronting the river and north of Fort Plain. This is a sight which has been noted frequently and it was fitting that the first bird man who flew over Central New York should follow the same air path. The St. Louis-New York flight up to date (1913) remains one of the most noteworthy accomplishments of aviation the world over. Atwood had flown from Boston to Washington, June 30-July, 1911, and this was, up to that time, the longest cross country air journey made in the western hemisphere, eclipsing Curtiss's great flight down the Hudson from Albany to New York, the previous year, 1910.

Harry N. Atwood left St. Louis August 14, 1911, and reached Chicago, 283 miles away in 6 hours and 32 minutes, the same day. He made Buffalo, August 19, and his flight through New York state with the distances and the places he reached each day are as follows: August 20, Buffalo to Lyons, 104 miles; August 21, Lyons to Belle Isle (near Syracuse), 40 miles; August 22, Belle Isle to Fort Plain, 95 miles; August 23, Fort Plain to Castleton (on the Hudson), 66 miles; August 24, Castleton to Nyack, 109 miles; August 25, Nyack to New York, 28 miles. Duration of flight, 12 days. Net flying time 28 hrs., 53 min. Average speed 43.9 miles per hr. Air distance covered, 1,266 miles.

The following is from the Fort Plain Standard of August 24, 1911.

With the ease, grace and confidence of a huge eagle, from out of the western sky Tuesday evening came young Atwood, the St. Louis-to-New York aviator, and it was the good fortune of Nelliston and Fort Plain to get for nothing that for which many cities paid big money—the presence of the foremost bird-man of them all so far as long flights in a short time is concerned. The sight afforded as Atwood came within the vision of the thousands watching intently for him—at first little more than a speck surrounded by a whirl—was one that will never be forgotten by those who witnessed it. Steadily drawing nearer and nearer, for a time coming as straight as the proverbial gun-barrel, and then suddenly shifting to his right, but only for a brief period, the bold but cautious aviator seemed to be searching for a safe place to land. Suddenly resuming his course, somewhat south of east, he dashed over the mill portion of Fort Plain and over the Mohawk river, spied the vacant lot in the rear of the E. I. Nellis homestead, Nelliston. and alighted like a graceful, high-flying bird desirous of spending the night in seclusion and in comfort.

All this happened from shortly before 7 o'clock Tuesday evening, Aug. 22, 1911 (screw the date to your mind). when Atwood was first discovered by the thousands watching and waiting for him, until exactly 7 o'clock, when he alighted safe and sound at the point mentioned. And it was certainly a novel, thrilling, never-to-be-forgotten sight to behold man and machine come from out of the sky—a phenomenon—and a few moments later, through landing, shift himself into a mere human being exciting wonderment by the aid of mere man's cleverness.

With a wild rush many of the thousands who had long waited for Atwood, expecting only to see him pass over Fort Plain, hastened to the scene of the landing, and the shouts of people, mingled with the noise of automobiles, motorcycles, clatter of hoofs and rumbling of wagons, quickly caused that which was apparently chaos and pandemonium.

The surging, seething mob soon surrounded man and machine, and he, coolest of the wild assemblage, made every effort (and with success) to save his biplane from damage. Atwood begged, expostulated and warned and was quickly aided in his efforts by men who realized the all but helpless predicament in which the aviator, far from police protection, found himself through the intense enthusiasm of the admiring but rash, thoughtless thousands. But all's well that ends well, for despite the eagerness of the crowd, no damage was caused to the biplane.

After assuring himself that the machine was safe and in good hands, Atwood was brought to Hotel Greeley by autoist Harold Gray, and from the time the car left the Nellis aviation field until the wash-room of said hotel was reached, Atwood was cheered, shouted at and greeted with yells of admiration and encouragement from lusty thousands. And then (prosaic mortal that he is) he ate a hearty supper heartily! And all the time people, and then more people, were arriving in front of Hotel Greeley, and the big crowd included the Old band, and the J. J. Witter Fife, Drum and Bugle corps. Noise? That isn't quite the word, but it will suffice.

When the cause of it all felt sufficiently rested and refreshed, he was escorted from the Greeley grill room to Canal street by Postmaster Scott and was cheered, cheered and then cheered, and then introduced to the crowd, after which came a modest, well-put, brief expression of thanks for the cordial greeting. And then the Old band turned loose "Come Josephine in My Flying Machine." Rather pat, that Old band, eh?

When he could break away without causing displeasure, Atwood, with others, returned to the Nellis lot, located the biplane carefully for the night, and then came back to Hotel Greeley, where the aviator retired about midnight, after leaving a call for 5.30.

Atwood came from Little Falls to Fort Plain, 16 miles, in 18 minutes.

The daring aviator was in constant demand for interviews, via the telephone, and to the Albany Knickerbocker Press he said:

"I arrived in Fort Plain at 7 o'clock this evening from Amboy, which place I left at 5 o'clock. For the last five miles of the flight I was watching for a decent landing place, and Fort Plain looked good to me. I have been used better by the people here than at any place on the flight."

When Atwood landed the first person his eyes encountered was a boy, to whom he put this:

"Where the devil am I?"

"In the Nellis pasture," came the startling response from the startled lad.

Just the least bit indefinite, that, to a stranger dropping out of the clouds after flying nearly 100 miles.

Cheerfully responding to the first knock on his door yesterday morning, Atwood, after breakfasting, was again taken to the Nellis lot by Harold Gray, and after carefully ascertaining that all was well, made a get-away at 7.25, the journey being preceded by two circles, made high in the air, that added to his reputation for cleverness and generosity and astounded the hundreds of awed spectators, who all but breathlessly stared after the daring aviator till staring was useless—he was out of sight, but not out of mind!

Atwood arrived at his Wednesday morning destination, Castleton, 70 miles from here, at 9.15. Slow going, which is explained by the following from last night's Amsterdam Recorder: "Members of Minch's band, bound for the Sunday school picnic at Charleston Four Corners, had the pleasure of meeting Atwood while on their way south. The aviator was obliged to land in consequence of a leaking gasoline tank and alighted easily, on the Jay Blood farm, in the town of Glen, about a mile northeast of Glen village. He used a shoestring in making repairs. The stop, which necessitated a delay of about 20 minutes, was witnessed by the bandmen, who, it may be remarked, also stopped that length of time. Bandmaster Conrad Minch and his associates hastened to the field to greet the daring birdman and lend such assistance as they could, and many of the residents of the neighborhood also gathered about the machine, which came down in a small gulley. When repairs had been made the Amsterdam musicians, all of whom had shaken hands with Atwood, assisted with willing hands to move the biplane to a more elevated position, from which the aviator speedily rose and after circling about in gratitude

for the assistance given him, resumed his flight eastward. Atwood said that there had been a leakage of gasoline from the time he passed Palatine Bridge and declared that his mechanic should not have permitted his commencing the flight with the machine in the condition it was. Atwood told those with whom he conversed that because of the haze he had floated away from the Mohawk valley and asked how far he was from the river. When told that it was about two miles away Atwood responded, 'Well, that isn't far. I will soon get back to it.' "

"The Making of an Aviator" was the title of a very interesting paper contributed to the Saturday Evening Post (Dec. 7, 1912) by Harry N. Atwood. In it, under the subheading of "Following the Mohawk" he described his journey, in the air largely over the valley, from Syracuse to Fort Plain, although he does not mention the place or Nelliston by name. This sketch forms one of the most interesting documents of flying yet published and the Mohawk valley part is here reprinted:

"The great future of the aeroplane—its coming necessity to mankind and its marvelous possibilities—was impressed upon my mind most strongly one night when I was making a leg of my flight between the cities of St. Louis and New York. Owing to the inclemency of the weather I had been obliged to remain upon the ground until late in the afternoon. I was located in a little valley in the hills just outside the suburbs of Syracuse. In accordance with my customary schedule I desired to cover at least a hundred miles more toward my destination. At sunset the disturbing wind elements suddenly died out and I immediately prepared for flight. Ten minutes later and the smoke of the city of Syracuse was fast becoming a speck in the western horizon.

"I shall never forget that beautiful evening. The Mohawk river lay beneath me; but, as it wound in and out between the hills, I would leave its course for a few minutes at a time and pick it up again at another point. Twilight set in and the valley and the river became very indistinct. The tops of the hills and the mountains, however, stood out clearly in the waning light.

"One by one I could make out the lights of the farmhouses, thousands of feet beneath me in the valley; and they seemed to increase in number in exactly the same manner as the stars above me increased in number.

"Finally the Mohawk became shrouded in darkness, and it was only when passing over a lighted village or town that I was able to distinguish anything. I felt as if I were in a dream.

"I gazed into the dark depths and wondered what sensation the mortals down there were experiencing as I roared over their communities! I did not experience any inability to keep my equilibrium, but I did experience a peculiar sense of giddiness, which was probably due to the unusual surroundings. Mile after mile I flew, high over the valley, marveling at the wonders of the situation and forgetting that sooner or later I should be obliged to make a landing. This realization came to me very forcibly when I discovered that it was almost impossible to make out even the tops of the mountains. Then I selected the first hill I came to and began circling round it in long spirals, gradually coming to it closer and closer. Finally discovering an opening among the trees, I dropped into it safely. [At Nelliston, opposite Fort Plain.]

"It seems to me that this experience alone demonstrates very clearly the possibilities and the adaptability of aviation to almost every type of mankind.. The only feature about it that can be criticised or questioned is the fact that it is accompanied by considerable danger; but it will not take long for human ingenuity to eliminate this one and only obstacle."

CHAPTER VI.

Geological Review of the Middle Mohawk Valley by Abram Devendorf— Lake Albany Covering the Old Mohawk Country of Canajoharie, From Little Falls to the Noses—The Glacial Period—Surface Indications.

In a foregoing chapter some mention has been made of the topography and geological history of the Mohawk river and its valley. The following chapter on the geology of the middle valley deals with the subject in detail and much of the interesting surface indications of past glacial and water action. It covers especially the old Mohawk region of Canajoharie (later the Palatine and Canajoharie districts), the lower levels of which were at one time covered by the waters of "Lake Albany." This chapter has been kindly written for this work by Abram Devendorf of the town of Minden, formerly postmaster of Fort Plain and an authority on the geology of the valley. The reader is referred to any good text book for the geological terms used and a proper understanding of the different rock strata.

The Mohawk river flows through one of the most ancient valleys on this planet. It was once a mighty stream which conveyed the waters of the Great Lakes into the ocean at some point near Schenectady. The ocean then extended up the Hudson valley north and probably included Lakes George and Champlain. Between Schenectady and Albany is a delta deposited there by the waters of the Mohawk. The finer material was carried along and formed the clay beds at Albany and farther south. During pre-glacial times this river was a chain of lakes with outlets at the Noses near Sprakers and at Little Falls.

This valley divides the eastern part of New York state into two dissimilar sections, viz: The Adirondacks on the north and a dissected plateau on the south. During the pre-Cambrian period the rock formations of the Adirondacks were deposited by the sea on a floor of older rocks the nature of which have never been determined unless we infer that they were similar to the dikes and intrusions found at

Little Falls and at several places in the Adirondack region.

The rocks in the Adirondacks are the oldest sedimentary rocks on the earth's surface, indicating that this region, including the Mohawk valley, was below sea level at different times and it is mere conjecture from what source this material came to cover the old floor which may have been in a semi-fluid state except that the entire state and the country beyond was covered by the waters of a shoreless ocean with currents that carried the sediment possibly from many directions and deposited this material on the original foundation.

A similar condition existed in the Mohawk valley except volcanic activity was not as severe as it was farther north, and if the structure of the original floor could be ascertained it would be found that it is not as crystalline as it is in the northern part of the state. The length of time required for such a deposition has never been deciphered; it is evident however that it involved a prodigious length of time. The Mohawk valley was simply the border land of the Adirondacks and too remote from the heart of that region, where igneous action was greatest, to receive but a slight effect from this volcanic activity.

At some later date there was a general upheaval not only of the Adirondacks but also of the Mohawk valley until these two sections became a dry land area and remained so for many ages. During this time the broken surface from the upheaval, was worn down by the erosive agencies and the sediment carried by the Mohawk river down to the sea. Igneous activity in the northern part of the state continued during this period forming fissures and great dike openings which were filled with lava from the reservoirs of molten matter underneath. The elevation of the Adirondacks must have been several hundred feet, if not two to three thousand feet, above sea level. The long protracted erosion wore down the mountains and hills to mere stumps leaving a low altitude. While the last finishing touches of ero-

sion were given to the Adirondack region the sea began to encroach on this area from the north and continued until the Mohawk valley was again under water. The first deposit from this subsidence formed the Potsdam sandstone in the northern part of the state and is entirely lacking in this county except one or two fringes along the Fulton county border which bear a resemblance to that found in St. Lawrence county. The inference is that the ocean had not yet enveloped this entire area but was gradually encroaching over all the Adirondacks and the Mohawk valley. The Potsdam sandstone, a valuable building stone quarried largely in St. Lawrence county, is composed of coarse sand and gravel deposited in shallow water in which strong currents operated to remove the mud. During the Potsdam period Montgomery county was above sea level, but subsidence continued until this county was again under water. For some reason now the character of the deposit changes. Instead of a pure sandstone like the Potsdam, the formation is a dolomite or calciferous sandrock or, as it is now called, Beekmantown limestone. This rock is a peculiar formation not like ordinary open sea deposits but more like an inland sea deposit, the nature of which is not exactly understood. It is the first sedimentary deposit on the old land surface in the Mohawk valley. This formation contains but few fossils. Animal and plant life existed only in meager quantities. The lower layers are nearly barren of fossils but the upper layers are fucoidal and somewhat changed in structure and character indicating a transition to another period and a formation entirely different in composition—a lime stone, highly fossiliferous and marine in nature and known as the Trenton. Of this series the Lowville or birdseye is a very valuable quarry stone, thick bedded and abounding in calcite filled tubes, which adds to the looks of the stone when dressed.

The Trenton beds were deposits from clear water and from an open sea which probably existed south and east of this continent. Some of the beds of this series were deposited in shallow water and abound in shells.

Toward the close of the Trenton fine muds began to be washed into the previously clear sea producing a series of alternating limestone and shale bands and later continuously giving rise to the fine muds of the Utica formation. This was followed by a change of life. New species appear and the old become extinct. This change however, was gradual and required an immense length of time. What currents brought this muddy water into the clear sea which existed during Trenton times is an unsettled question, but it probably came from the ocean that covered this continent to the westward and southward.

Following this period of Utica slate formation came a movement of disturbance and uplift of the region of the Adirondacks and the Mohawk valley as far west as Rome, but the remainder of the state remained submerged and continued so until the last layer of the Helderberg was deposited. Then the sea receded westward and the Helderberg mountains arose from the sea. It is probable that during this upheaval the faults at Little Falls, East Creek, St. Johnsville, the Noses and at Hoffmans were formed. The uplift at Little Falls at that time was several hundred feet and at the Noses not so much. The escarpment at either of these places was sufficient to dam the waters of the Mohawk and form the Utica and Albany lakes. This time probably is coincident with the upheaval of the Taconic range of Massachusetts and a period of great earthquakes which shook the valley and distorted the rocks in every direction.

The Chazy limestone which overlies the Calciferous or Beekmantown in the Champlain valley is entirely absent in the Mohawk valley. Its absence may be accounted for from the fact that there was an uplift of this region at the close of the Calciferous period and the beginning of the Trenton. This uplift was only slight but sufficient to stop deposition in the valley.

Then subsidence began and continued without interruption during the Trenton and Utica periods.

The only exposure of the pre-Cambrian rocks is at the Noses. It is a variety of syenite called quartzose gneiss and is the bed rock on which was laid the Calciferous sandrock instead of the Potsdam sandstone which underlies the Calciferous in other localities. On the south side of the river a short distance below Sprakers is a fine exposure of the Calciferous containing layers of dolomite, calcite and drusy cavities. The upper strata have plenty of fucoidal cavities filled with calcite similar to the lower beds of the Trenton.

From the time of the last deposit of the Utica shales to the glacial period involves an immense length of time and during this time great changes were taking place. The Helderberg series were deposited, also the Onondaga, Hamilton, Portage and Chemung groups—strata that measure several thousand feet in thickness and which required millions of years to deposit.

When the Helderbergs emerged from the sea and the waters of the ocean were thrown back the agitation in the valley must have been immense. At this period the Mohawk valley, the northern and eastern part of the state must have been elevated several hundred feet higher than it is now as the Hudson river channel extended at least 50 miles farther south and the whole state must have been a barren waste, except what was covered by water. But previous to this period, or during the time the Utica slate was deposited, some geologists claim that a continent existed, occupying the area of the north Atlantic, from which the muds came to make the deposit of the Utica and Hudson river shales. No land animals existed until centuries after and the same is true of plant life except the growth of lichens and mosses which began to cover the barren rocks.

The glacial period dates back many thousand years. Some geologists say at least 50,000 years and others think a longer period elapsed. How long this condition persisted, how many times the ice came and went over the immediate region we do not know. There is no way to get at the time even approximately. The gorge of the Niagara river and the gorge on the Mississippi river at St. Antony's Falls furnish data for an approximate estimate, but the length of time that the northern part of this continent was covered by ice and snow is very uncertain, except that it must have been centuries. This ice sheet, that moved in a southeast direction, must have been a mile in thickness and in its movement, which was very slow, it filled valleys, scooped out lakes and tore down mountains. The first glacial sheet that covered this state as far south as the southern tier of counties and which plowed out the Finger lakes of the western part of the state and Otsego lake and changed the water courses of many streams, came from the Labrador district. It is probable as this ice sheet moved over the Adirondacks into the valley that it divided at Little Falls. Part of it moving west and the remainder came down the Mohawk valley to the Hudson river. From the moraines strung along Lake Ontario and Lake Erie in Ohio and the terraces formed by Lake Warren, which covered the northwest, and Lake Iroquois, which extended some 30 or 40 miles farther east and south than the present Lake Ontario, would indicate that there were three glacial periods or at least three recessions. The Wisconsin glacier, which covered the Great Lakes, extended far over the western part of the state. Previous to this time a river drained the area now occupied by Lake Erie and extended along the south shore of the present Lake Ontario, either after or before the tilting of this continent which sent the waters of these lakes into the Mississippi river by way of Chicago. Geologists say that in about 3,000 years the same condition will again exist and the waters of all the lakes above the Falls instead of flowing down the St. Lawrence valley will find their way into the Mississippi valley, and the great cataract at Niagara will no longer exist.

Before the glacial period the rock barrier at Little Falls was the divide between Hudson and St. Lawrence waters and later this barrier formed a lake which extended probably as far west as Rome. The West Canada creek and other side streams filled this depression with detritus carried down from the north and south, forming a delta which blocked the river for miles above the barrier at Little Falls. About four miles south of Little Falls is a low pass that leads from the valley to Newville and down the Nowadaga creek to Indian Castle which may have been the ancient course of the river previous to the glacial period. The upheaval of the rock barrier occurred after the Utica slate deposit, due to a fault that extends far north but disappears a short distance south of the river in the town of Danube. This rock barrier must have been 600 feet high, at least high enough to hold back the waters of the Mohawk, which found an outlet by way of Newville. During glacial times the ice wore away the softer rocks down to the crystallines and the river assumed its ancient channel.

The Labrador sheet of ice closed the St. Lawrence river and held back the waters of the Great Lakes and extended nearly to the southern boundaries of this state and over all of New England, and after the ice, in its last northerly retreat, uncovered the Mohawk valley but still lay across the St. Lawrence, the drainage of the Great Lakes passed to the sea by way of the Mohawk, the eastern end of the lake in the Ontario basin being at Rome. The present river is but an insignificant stream compared to the mighty river that carried the waters of the Great Lakes to the sea through the Mohawk valley. The depth of water in this stream estimated from the terraces lining the valley was from 25 to 30 feet above the present flood plain.

It is probable that during this epoch the cold was not continuous. That there were intervals of warmth that caused the glacier to recede and afterward advance again is evident from the different lines of deposit left by the recession. The length of time that the glacial sheet covered New York state, or existed within the area of the United States, is entirely problematical. At least several thousand years elapsed before the climate became normal as at the present time. What caused this climatic change is an open question and the different theories advanced by geologists and astronomers hardly account for such a phenomenal climate. Some astronomers claim that in the course of time the same condition will recur.

The polar axis describes a circle in the heavens in about 25,800 years and at the present time the North Pole points within one and one-half degrees to the Polar star. In about 12,500 years the polar axis will point to the constellation Lyra, and 2,000 years later to the star Alpha in the handle of the dipper (Ursa Major). Some claim that this change in the earth's axis may produce a change of climate owing to the procession of the equinoxes which is caused by the change in the polar axis of the earth.

The elevation theory advanced by some geologists seems more plausible as there are plenty of evidences that this continent was several thousand feet higher than it is at present. The Cretaceous sea which covered the western and southwestern states and extended eastward to the Appalachian range was the last important or extensive body of water that covered this continent and, at the close of this period, this continent became elevated to such a height as to produce a frigid climate. The Mississippi valley was simply a depression through which the waters of what are now the Great Lakes flowed to the southern sea. During this period of elevation the Mississippi river wore out a channel 1,000 to 1,500 feet deep, which since has been filled by silt and debris brought down by the river. This ancient channel, which was at one time a canon, extends some 40 miles into the Gulf of Mexico.

Another theory is that the Gulf stream, which originates in the equa-

torial regions, may have taken a different course. It is known that The Japan current in the Pacific, as it swings southward from the Aleutian Islands along the coast of America, modifies the climate of Washington and Oregon, and the warm waters of the Gulf Stream temper the climate of England, which is north of the 51st parallel and nearly on a line with Labrador. If, by some seismic disturbance, the Isthmus of Darien should sink below sea level and the Gulf Stream as it swings around through the Carribean sea and enters the Gulf of Mexico should instead pass into the Pacific ocean, England would be as cold as Labrador and New York state nearly as cold, and it is probable that the inland states would be as arid as the plains east of the Rocky mountains. It is the moisture of the Gulf Stream which is carried far inland by the south and east winds which gives the middle states a moist climate.

The ancient terraces are still to be seen along the valley. Two are quite distinct and the traces of the third are found at some places. In Fort Plain, the Institute hill and Prospect hill undoubtedly were parts of the upper terrace, and West street is about on the same horizon of the second terrace. At Mindenville the third or lower terrace is plainly visible. These terraces show the different levels of the Albany lake which extended from the escarpment at the Noses to the uplift at Little Falls, and the different levels of the Mohawk river during the time that it was carrying the waters of Lake Iroquois to the sea.

The glacier, as it came from the Adirondacks and swung around into the valley at Little Falls, carried with it the loose material torn from the archean rocks of the north and the softer shales and limestones lying nearer the valley and deposited this glacial drift along the river and as far south, in this vicinity, as the southern part of this county. The softer rocks as the Utica slate, Trenton and Calciferous were ground up by the ice sheet and were left as a mantle covering the land, making the different soils which were afterwards modified by other agencies. The glacier that moved down the valley and across it left all along drumlins and lateral moraines. Some of these moraines were altered by water. The finer material was carried along and deposited as clay and sand beds. Going south of this county we find a different class of boulders which indicates another stream of ice different from that which went down the valley and left a different soil in the southern part of Canajoharie, Root and Glen.

Fort Hill, one mile west of St. Johnsville, is a deposit of altered drift carried there by the East Canada creek and the river. There are layers in this deposit where the gravel and sand are cemented together in a solid mass from the acids and carbonates carried down from the crystalline rocks and limestones. The drumlin, or possibly a moraine, along the state road between the two villages is of the same origin. A great deal of this material brought down by the East Canada creek was deposited on the south side of the river. The finer sediment was carried along farther east and formed the sand and clay beds of Mindenville and St. Johnsville.

The streams that empty into the Mohawk river on the south side of the river are not as glaciated as those coming from the north. Garoga creek is lined by lateral moraines. This stream during glacial time was several times larger than it is as present and during the long period that has elapsed since it was filled with ice it has worn a very deep channel and carried this erosive material down to the river to help build up islands and fill the river channel. There is no doubt that the clay and silt beds along the West Shore railroad and the clay beds of Institute hill (Fort Plain) were deposited there by the Garoga creek.

Prospect hill (Fort Plain) is a very interesting formation. It has a bold front on two sides and is a remnant of a much larger deposit which filled or at least covered the plain on which Fort Plain is located. Its outward appearance looks like a delta, a fluvile deposit by the Otsquago creek and the Mohawk river. But it is not, neither is it a drift deposit from the glacier that came down the valley from the north, as its composition is alluvium with some sand and small stones from nearby formations mixed with the crystallines from the north. It is probable that during this time, the glacier coming down the Otsquago valley made this deposit while the valley was covered with ice. This drumlin or terminal moraine extends but a short distance down the valley. Outside Fort Plain, on the Starkville road and on the Green farm, is a terminal moraine lodged there by the ice but which has been altered somewhat from the different courses that the stream has taken during the centuries since the glacial period. The Otsquago valley was once filled by ice and water as far south as Starkville. The terraces along the line indicate the height of water at that time and are quite distinct all along. In and along the creek and in the stone walls along the Starkville road can be found boulders of different sizes, from the crystalline rocks of the Adirondacks, carried across the river and deposited there as the ice melted. We find Gabbros, Diorites, Syenites and Anortisites torn loose from the quarries in the north and carried across the river probably over the ice. In the creek, near the Van Slyke saw mill, is a large syenite boulder worn round and smooth from the long distance which it traveled. Its home undoubtedly was near Lassellsville, where we find the same formation from whence it was torn and, in its travels, it was ground to its present dimensions.

The terraces along the Otsquago valley show the height of water of the Albany lake. It is not so many centuries ago that this lake disappeared. It is probable that the early Aborigines knew of it and according to a tradition which has been handed down one day the Great Spirit became angry and swept across the lake and tore away the barrier at the Nose to appease his wrath. After the ice lobe had melted in this valley the waters of the Great

Lakes continued to flow through the valley, as the St. Lawrence was still ice bound and continued so for a great many years. It was during this time that the gorge below Sprakers was worn through, and also the barrier at Little Falls was worn through. The glacial drift strung along the valley and the deposits which partially filled the Albany and Utica lakes formed an abrasive material and was more effective to wear away these barriers than the glacial ice.

The flood plain of the present Mohawk river is at least 15 feet above the old river bed which has been filled in by the debris brought down by the river and its tributaries. The Mohawk flats is a deposit by the river in times of floods of alluvium very rich in vegetable humus, which has made these flats famous for the growth of cereals and grass. The depth of this deposit varies from 6 to 10 feet in thickness and required centuries to form.

At the close of the glacial period and during the early part of the Pleistocene period, a large part of this continent was depressed 1,500 or 2,000 feet and, in emerging, remained for a long period at 400 or 500 feet below its present level. All those parts, therefore, which have now an elevation of less than that amount, were beneath the waters of the ocean. The glacier left a mantle over the land of fine material, interspersed with boulders, which was modified by other agencies into the present soil. During this long period rivers and smaller streams had been operating to carry the sediment and other material from the hills down to the valleys, and had dug out deep channels by the abrasive materials carried along by the rapid currents. Partly in the village of Canajoharie, is a deep canon worn through the drift and the Utica slate by the waters of Bowman's (Canajoharie) creek, which came from a lake of water that covered the flat lands in the valley from Ames westward and which received the drainage from the Sharon and Cherry Valley hills. Near Marshville, along the state road, is a licustrine deposit of clay deposited there by the still waters of a pleistocene lake which emptied into Bowman's (Canajoharie) creek.

Finally, it was during this period that the huge animals, like the mastadon and a species of elephant, existed and roamed over the northern part of the United States, from the Hudson valley to the Rocky mountains. According to tradition, the Indians saw living mastodons, which is undoubtedly true. The climate was supposably the same as today, on the general average. It is probable however, that the polar current, which has a westerly tendency into the Gulf of St. Lawrence, may have chilled the waters that covered parts of New England and Canada. On the other hand, it is probable that the Gulf Stream flowed over the lower parts of the southern states, which would have a tendency to counteract the cold from the polar current. The changes of that period were similar to the changes which we observe today and which will continue in the future. The process of elevation and depression is very slow and it will require thousands of years to make a noticeable change in the general features of the Mohawk valley.

Abram Devendorf.

Fort Plain, April 24, 1913.

CHAPTER VII.

Western Montgomery County Schools —Supt. Alter's 1912 Report.

The school districts in western Montgomery are divided among the towns as follows: St. Johnsville, 4; Canajoharie, 12; Minden, 17; Palatine, 11; Root, 13. Superintendent N. B. Alter of this district, has kindly furnished this work with the following abstract of his 1912 report:

The District Superintendent of Schools for the first district of Montgomery county has completed making the abstracts from the trustees' reports for that district. Following is a report of the school conditions in that district. The figures include all of the schools.

There are fifty-seven school districts in this supervisory district and the schools are housed in fifty-eight buildings—the village of St. Johnsville having two buildings. Forty-eight of these buildings are frame buildings, five are brick and five are stone. All of the buildings are of the old type except eleven. The total value of the school house sites was placed at $14,030. There are only ten districts that own sites which are as large as they should be. The value of the school buildings and furniture is fixed at $145,339. The apparatus is valued at $4,781 and the libraries at $12,267. All other property, including text books owned by the school, is valued at $2,210. There are 15,892 volumes in the school libraries, 991 being added last year.

One hundred and eight teachers were required to look after the educational interests of the children. They held the following credentials: One State certificate, three College Graduate certificates, two College Graduate Limited certificates, five College Professional certificates, five College Professioual Limited, twenty-eight Normal diplomas, twenty-two Teachers' Training Class certificates and forty-four Commissioner's certificates. There was also one temporary certificate for part of the year. District number 2 in the town of Minden, in addition to maintaining a home school, also contracted with the village of St. Johnsville for a part of the pupils in that district. There were seventeen men teachers and ninety-five women teachers employed in the schools during the year.

The law specifies that the schools shall be in session at least thirty-two weeks. Nineteen out of the fifty-seven schools were satisfied with the minimum requirement. However, the average term for the district was 175 days.

Another provision of the law is that a census of all of the children between the ages of 5 and 18 must be taken during the last week in August. According to figures submitted by the trustees there were 2,558 children of school age in the supervisory district the first of September, 1911. The registration figures, which are absolutely correct, show that there were 2,640 children in attendance during the year. In addition to this there were 59 registered who were over 18. Of course, some of those registered might have been registered in other districts during the year. The fact remains, nevertheless, that the census was not taken in many of the districts. The average daily attendance was 1,942, for pupils between 5 and 18 and 43 for pupils over 18.

The District superintendent made 263 official visits to the teachers under his supervision; 103 trees were planted on the school grounds; 72 school record certificates were issued. Eight arrests were made in connection with the Compulsory Education law. One was committed to a truant school.

All of the schools carried a balance over to the last school year of $5,348.01. Twelve thousand, six hundred and fifty dollars was received from the state for teachers' wages, $667.51 for libraries and apparatus, $1,522.53 for tuition of academic pupils and $813.46 academic fund for quota and attendance; $89.26 was deducted from the teachers' wages for the teachers' retirement fund; $514.16 was received from individual pupils for tuition and $55,866.09 was raised by tax; $3,608.01 was received from all other sources. The village of Canajoharie had the highest tax rate —$12 per thousand of valuation. While district number 2, town of Minden, had the lowest, $2.73. We might add that this district does not own the site where the school house stands.

Wages were paid to teachers as follows: Principals received $7,750; men teachers, $4,835; women teachers, $42,479.82.

Other expenses were as follows: Libraries, $1,002; text books, $102.34; apparatus, $330.59; furniture, $501.92; repair, insurance, etc., $3,745.40; bonded indebtedness, principal, $2,000; interest, $777.20. Only two districts now have outstanding bonds. Two thousand, four hundred and ninety-eight dollars and eighty cents was spent for janitors' wages; fuel, light, etc., cost $5,171.66; stationery and supplies, $636.99; attendance officers for three schools, $155. The towns pay the attendance officers for the common school districts. Some of the Union Free schools have their janitors act as attendance officer and have reported the cost in with the janitors' wages. Incidental expenses claimed $2,598.34. A balance of $6,659.55 remains.

Only two districts have libraries of 50 volumes or less; 14 between 50 and 100 volumes; 25 with 100 to 200 volumes; 11 have from 200 to 500 volumes; one has between 500 and 1,000 volumes and four have over 1,000 volumes in their school libraries. Every district has a school library.

The average school term in the district was 175 days. There was an average of 26 pupils to a teacher. There was an average daily attendance per teacher of 18. The per cent of daily attendance based on total enrollment was 69.5 per cent. The cost per pupil based on the average daily attendance was $37.50. The average weekly salary per teacher (this takes in the principals, some of whom receive as high as $40 per week) was $14.19. The average yearly salary was $509.86. The lowest salary paid was $304.

It is a commonly accepted fact that the country boy and girl longs for the time when the country may be left behind and the joys of the city be realized. Why? There must be a lack of attraction to draw the best that is produced in the country cityward. Country life must be made more attractive. The hard-headed farmer must realize that the place to start creating this attractiveness is in the country school. More money must be spent for country schools and this money must be spent in a better way. It is time for the people in the country to stop grumbling about taxes and get to work and place their school buildings in such shape that they will compare favorably with their own homes. Think of storing coal and wood in the front hall of a home! Country folk do not even criticise storing fuel in the front hall of a school building. There are no high school tax rates in Montgomery county!

The District Superintendent asked a trustee to repair a leaking roof—he has a child in the school. He put it off until after his fall work was finished. It seems to me that it must be uncomfortable to say the least, to have to sit in a school room that is apt to drip water upon the student.

The District Superintendent has asked every trustee in his district to buy slate blackboards for the schools. One finally agreed to paint the old boards at a cost of four dollars when eight dollars would have bought a permanent board. In justice to the progressive trustees of the first district, it may be added that twelve out of forty-seven not having slate boards have recently put in slate. There are more to follow.

Think of the farmer boys and girls who are sent away from home for better school advantages! It shows that the farmer is at last coming to his own.

Often regret for the good old school of thirty or forty years ago is heard—from fifty to a hundred pupils to the teacher. Three or four real bright ones in the lot—ten per cent of the whole getting what the whole are now getting. People wish today to compare the work of this little three or four with the entire school population today. Well they may do so for the whole now compare most favorably with that little three or four. If there is any dispute about it, the matter can easily be proven by a comparison with the finished product of the "old school."

But this is not what we wish. Schools today are good. They do, however, educate the boy and girl away from the farm. The gospel of paint, plants and pictures must be preached.

CHAPTER VIII.

Deforestation and Reforestation—Denudation in Western Montgomery County—Arbor Day—Adirondack and National Forest Preserves—The Forests and the Water Supply.

In no part of the Mohawk watershed has the denudation of the original foresct been more complete than in Montgomery county. There is left none of the virgin forest as the last piece of the ancient woods was destroyed within the past decade. Only a few scattered patches of woods remain and even they are being made way with. In view of the pitiful remains of the once great wood of the Mohawk valley, it seems incredible that this region was once entirely covered by a magnificent forest and that its trees furnished giant masts for the greatest sailing vessels and massive timbers for construction and building purposes.

For the sake of the land, the rainfall and the welfare of the inhabitants scientific reforestation must be praetised. It is hoped that nature study, which is being largely taught American children today, will aid in the future, in an intelligent understanding of the subject of forests. Our forefathers, whom we praise so highly, seem to have been utterly deficient in foresight. Much of the land they cleared so recklessly is useful only for wood growing and its intelligent reforestation would have ensured many a farmer a sure, continuous and growing income today with the increasing price of all useful woods.

The case of the trees is so plain that it hardly seems worth arguing. Foreign lands from which the forests have been removed have often become worthless. Trees enrich the earth with their leaves, their roots, forming a network in the ground, hold the water, prevent floods and consequent soil erosion. Forest regions are blessed with rain just as desert wastes repel the water clouds. The constant temperature of trees (54 degrees) tends toward an equable temperature, winter and summer. The continual circulation of water from roots to leaves and from leaves into the air tends to make the earth healthful and properly drained and fills the air with the moisture necessary to produce rain. Without a proper water supply man cannot exist and it has been truly said that the population of a given area depends more upon the rainfall of that section than any other item. This rainfall is essential, in this neighborhood, for power purposes as the increasing cost of fuel will force the utilization of every stream available. It is also needed to give a sufficient depth of water in the Barge canal. The rainfall of Central New York has been steadily decreasing for a century, doubtless due to continued deforestation. Trees purify the air and their healthful properties are recognized by the sick who seek to return to normal conditions by living in the woods.

All waste places should be planted to forests. Some trees, such as the valuable cedar, will grow where nothing else will. All country roads should be tree planted on both sides, also side hills and all availabè places. Waste and unused land in villages and towns should be forested, including spaces about schools. We have seen how attractive a spot can be made by the planting of trees and shrubs in the example of the New York Central station at Fort Plain. Every home should be made (with native trees, shrubs and flowers) at least as attractive as a railroad station. As a Mohawk valley writer has truly said: "Learn about our grand native trees and teach your children about the land, its trees and their uses, and your posterity will long live to enjoy the naturally beautiful land you have adopted." The New York Botanical Gardens, Bronx Borough, New York city, publishes a work (price 25 cents) on "Native Trees of the Hudson Valley." The Mohawk valley forms a section of the Hudson valley and the greater part of these are found in our watershed. This is one of the most instructive and cheapest works on our native trees and is quite fully illustrated with examples of the chief varieties. "Trees Every Child Should Know" (50 cents) is part of a nature library published by Doubleday, Page & Co. and is an interesting book for old and young.

A list of the principal native trees of the Mohawk valley has been compiled, from "Native Trees of the Hudson Valley" and from the tree exhibits at the New York Museum of Natural History, as follows:

Pine, spruce, hemlock, fir, cedar, arbor vitae, poplar, willow, basswood (or linden), oak, elm, plane (also called sycamore, buttonwood, buttonball), maple, ash, birch, beech, hickory, butternut, crabapple, plum, wild cherry, choke cherry, hornbeam (ironwood), hackberry (or sugarberry), serviceberry, witchhazel, sassafras, sour gum, sweet viburnum, thorn, sumac. Many of these trees have a number of varieties. Some trees which are quite common, such as the horsechestnut, are not native, but imported.

In sections distant from the Mohawk considerable land is reverting to wilderness, due to the abandonment of farmlands. This abandoned land, however, generally runs to scrub growth instead of to forest, as it would if properly tree planted. In a few waste places, in western Montgomery county, young native trees have replanted themselves and are reoccupying the land. They are pleasant sights.

Not only have we seen the disappearance of the virgin forest of the Mohawk but we have also been witnesses of the passing away of much of the beautiful verdure which made the Mohawk river such a picturesque stream a quarter of a century and more ago. The Barge canal is completing this destruction and it is up to the state to replant where they have destroyed, not only for the sake of beauty but to protect the canalized-river banks from the current. With the introduction of electric lights in the villages of western Montgomery county, much of the foliage of the trees in the streets has been mutilated to allow the electric lights to illuminate the surrounding grounds. Our village trees have suffered more from unintelligent trimming in the past twenty years than in their whole life previous. Some of our village trees have grown to magnificent proportions (particularly our elms) and it is hoped that they will be spared both trimming and destruction. Shade trees actually need no trimming whatever. The most beautiful specimens . are those which have been untouched, as witness the Prospect hill (Fort Plain) giant elm, oak, maple, beech or pine which has grown to stately and pleasing proportions, untouched by the hand of man.

In regard to the subject, the following, from the bulletin of the Tree Planting association, will be found of interest:

How few realize as they pass a tree on the street that, although silent and fixed in its position, it is more intimately related to our lives than any living object. It is only by grace of that tree that we "live and move and have our being" on this earth. Destroy it and its kind and human life would be impossible on this planet.

Science teaches that the food of the tree is the poisonous carbon dioxide which we exhale at every breath, and that the vitalizing element of the air we inhale is the life-giving oxygen which the tree through its leaves supplies abundantly.

As we enter the shade of a tree in full leafage, on a hot summer day, we feel a thrill of energy which quickens our footsteps, expands our chests, brightens our thoughts, and gives a new impulse to all our vital processes. What has happened? We have thrown out of our lungs the depressing dioxide and replaced it with the exhilarating oxygen from the nearby tree.

If we cross one of our avenues on a hot day when the temperature is 130 degrees F. and pass into the shade of a tree we are refreshed by the cool air. What makes the change? Not the shade alone, but chiefly because we are in the presence of a body that has a fixed temperature of 54 degree F., or 76 degrees F. cooler than the street. If on a cold winter's day we pass from a temperature of the street, at zero, into a group of trees, we are surprised at the warmth. This is not only due to the shelter they afford, but more largely to the warmth of the tree, which at 54 degrees E. is 54 degrees F. warmer than the street.

These facts suggest that if our streets were well supplied with vigorous trees we should have much cooler summers and warmer winters, as the temperature of the tree never varies from 54 degrees F. in summer's heat or winter's cold.

The tree has the power of absorbing and thus removing from the air the malarial emanations from the street, and from putrifying waste matter, so abundant in cities. In this respect they are the scavangers of the air and protect people from a large number of what are known by sanitarians as "filth diseases." The older physicians record the fact that as the forests were removed new and fatal fevers, hitherto unknown, appeared.

Transpiration is another function of a tree which contributes greatly to man's comfort and health. This act consists in absorbing large quantities of water from the earth and emitting it as by spraying, into the surrounding air, by its leaves. This is a very cooling process and tends powerfully to reduce excessive temperature in the vicinity of the tree. The amount of water thus thrown into the air by a single tree varies with the weather, increasing as the temperature rises and diminishing as it falls.

The value of a single tree in thus modifying temperature was strikingly shown by the late Prof. Pierce of Harvard college, who made a mathematical study of the foliage of the famous "Washington Elm." The tree was then very old and decayed, but he found that it bore a crop of 7,000,000 leaves, exposing a surface of 200,000 square feet, or about five acres of foliage. Now, as one acre of grass emits into the air 6,400 quarts of water in 24 hours, it follows that this old tree sprayed into the surrounding air 32,-000 quarts, or 8,000 gallons, or upward of 260 barrels of water every day.

Concrete examples are necessary in order to impress upon people certain truths. The general public's familiarity with Bible lands may help to show forcibly, by the reading of the following extract, the value of forests to all lands—to the Mohawk valley as well as to Palestine. The following is from the Christian Herald:

One of the most remarkable illustrations in all history of the ill effects of the disappearance of forests may be observed in Palestine. In the days when Joshua conquered the promised land Palestine was a wonderfully fertile country, a land flowing with milk and honey. The Lebanon mountains were heavily wooded, and a large population was supported in comfort.

The general devastation of the forests brought about, however, a gradual deterioration of the country. The hills of Galilee, which had long served as pasture lands for large herds of cattle and sheep, are now sterile. The Jordan has become an insignificant stream, and several smaller rivers are now completely dried up throughout the greater part of the year. Some few valleys in which fertile earth washed down from the hills has been deposited have retained their old fertility. The land today supports only one-sixth the population of the time of Solomon.

New York state has taken the most advanced position as to forestry of any of the United States. Its Adirondack state park, established by the act of 1892, will contain 2,800,000 acres when completed and embraces the northern part of Herkimer county, all of Hamilton and parts of St. Lawrence, Franklin, Essex and Warren counties, an area equal to that of Connecticut. This contains the highest peaks of the Adirondacks, including the highest peak, Mt. Marcy. The region is filled with 1,200 lakes and is drained by twenty large rivers. It is well stocked with fish and game.

A considerable part of the northern Mohawk valley watershed lies in the Adirondack Park, as the headwaters of the West Canada and East Canada creeks are in this public domain. East Canada creek, as we all know, forms the western border of the town of St. Johnsville in western Montgomery county. Both those streams furnish abundant water power and it is reassuring to know that their water flow is largely protected by their sources being within the Adirondack Park. They also furnish a great volume of water to the Barge canal and hence their water supply is of the greatest importance to New York state.

New York also has the Interstate Park, as the west bank of the lower Hudson, and other forest lands.

Arbor Day was originally advocated by the Nebraska State Board of Agriculture in 1874, the second Wednesday in April being suggested as a school holiday, trees to be planted on that day and appropriate school exercises to be held. This school observance of this day has been adopted by about forty states, New York among them. In 1912, the school children of western Montgomery county planted 103 trees on their school grounds. Arbor Day was established by New York state about twenty-five years ago and if the proportion of three planting has been kept up during that time then over 2,000 trees have been set out by our school children, a record of which they may be proud.

Our social and patriotic societies might well aid the cause of forestry. Our women's organizations could do much toward the care, protection and planting of village and countryside trees. Also our fishing and sporting clubs should foster the woods on which their sports and pleasure depend and they should aim to protect the woods as well as the game and to plant new woods wherever possible. The business men should, by acts and public sentiment, aid the protection of our watercourses and the forests of their basins. On the woodlands of streams used for power purposes depends the constant supply of that power by the conservation of the water. On this conservation depends the electric light, heat and power furnished by these power developments, which will form such a feature of communities in the future, when coal and oil have become exhausted in supply. This is true of the West Canada and Caroga creeks which have been electrically developed and should also apply to the valleys of all the larger streams of western Montgomery which will be utilized electrically in time.

There is at least one instance of the practical application of scientific forestry in the Mohawk valley. The local officials of Dolgeville are interesting themselves in a project to apply principles of scientific forestry to the classification and cultivation of trees in Schuyler Ingham Park, the beautiful 100-acre tract of wooded hillside that was given to the village by Mr. Ingham. The proposition is to form a park improvement society and ascertain the best methods of tree culture, so that a practical demonstration may be had of what can be done along this line.

CHAPTER IX.

1894-1914—Western Montgomery County Hydro-Electric Development on East and Caroga Creeks.

Few sections of New York of such comparatively small area (about 125,-000 acres) have seen such important hydro-electric development within or on its borders as western Montgomery county. In the twenty years, from 1894 to 1914, has been witnessed the erection of dams and power plants on East creek and Caroga creek. With the increasing cost of fuel other streams may be electrically developed and it is not improbable that the Otsquago, Canajoharie, Flat Creek, Yatesville, Zimmerman, Timmerman, Crum creek and even other western Montgomery county streams may be utilized for electrical power purposes. Just as it is now (1914) prophesied that the old time sailing vessels will soon again be carrying the slow freight of the seas, so is the manufacturer again turning to our first motive power—water; and both for the same reason—the increasing cost of coal and oil with no prospect of relief. For the same reason waterways, such as the Barge canal, will be the heavy and slow freight carriers of the future.

For hydro-electric development purposes and to protect our waterways, we must conserve our forests and woods about the headwaters of the streams utilized. This shows how the subject of forestry has become important at it interlocks with so much of our industrial and commercial life.

At Ephratah 5,400 H. P. is developed, at East Creek, 2,000 H. P., at Ingham's Mills, 8,000 H. P. and at Dolgeville 2,500 H. P., in all 17,900 H. P. generated by East and Caroga creeks, with possibilities of still further increase.

This electric power is claimed to be as cheap as any furnished in the eastern states and eventually is bound to make the villages of western Montgomery county industrial centers of importance. The towns in western Montgomery county, which are particularly interested in this electrical generation are St. Johnsville, Fort Plain-Nelliston and Canajoharie-Palatine Bridge, while the villages or hamlets in western Fulton county interested in the development or use of this power are Dolgeville (7 miles from the Mohawk); Ingham's Mills, in the town of Manheim and Oppenheim (4 miles from the Mohawk); Caroga, in the town of Ephratah (9½ miles from the Mohawk); Ephratah, in the town of Ephratah (6 miles from the Mohawk). The foregoing are all airline distances.

The first conservation of water power on a considerable scale in Montgomery or Fulton counties seems to have been accomplished by Amsterdam manufacturers. In 1848 a dam was built across the Chuctanunda above the Forest paper mill. In 1855 the Galway reservoir covering 450 acres (at Galway, Saratoga county, northeast of Amsterdam), was built. This was enlarged in 1865 and 1875 to an area of stored water of 1,000 acres. This water system has been largely responsible for the industrial importance of Amsterdam.

The following was written during the summer of 1913 by William Irving Walter of St. Johnsville with regard to hydro-electric development of East creek:

"A gradual development of the electrical energy from the powers supplied by the falls at East Creek and its progress in eliminating steam as a motive power in St. Johnsville, vicinity and, in fact, throughout the Mohawk valley is just beginning to attract a small portion of the attention that such a feature in the never-ceasing industrial revolution deserves. The announcement that the Lion Manufacturing Co., the pioneer in the knitting industry in St. Johnsville, has just completed the installation of electricity instead of steam in all its departments excepting for heating purposes, and that the same work is now going forward in the piano action factory of F. Engelhardt & Sons is an epoch in the local industrial development.

"This leaves steam as a motive power only in the Union Mills (Royal Gem knitting mills) and the Clark Machine Co.'s works with the possibility that these exceptions may at no distant day be eliminated. This attracts public attention to the great development of the forces which for years ran to waste unheeded at our doors, from the days when the Mohawk, sole lord of the valley passed the cataract with indifferent eyes. 'As the brown bear blind and dull to the grand and beautiful.' It was in 1894, during one of the most severe depressions the country has ever known, that Guy R. Beardsley began the revival of East Creek as a factor in business conditions of the Mohawk valley. We say revival, for at the beginning of the nineteenth century East Creek bid fair to become one of the leading centers of the state. John Beardslee (born in Sharon, Conn., November, 1759, died at East Creek October 3, 1825), who came to the Mohawk valley in 1787, as a builder and a millwright, left his impress upon this part of central New York. The construction by the authorities of Montgomery county of the old covered bridge at East Creek, brought him to East Creek where he purchased a large tract of land and erected saw and grist mills and a carding mill half a mile north of the turnpike. These were operated in 1794. These were followed by stores, hotels, a distillery, nail factory, brewery, etc., until about 1800 'Beardslee's city' as it was colloquially termed had few if any superiors west of Schenectady. The opening of the turnpike road giving access to western New York and turning immigration that way, and the fact that only the ruder sorts of manufacturing establishments were called for in the social and industrial conditions then existing, operated against the permanence of the East Creek settlement, and the construction and completion of the Erie canal (1817-25) completed its ruin. The settlement dwindled until finally the Jerome hotel, the last survivor of the old East Creek went out of existence about the time Mr. Beardslee began the revival of East Creek as an industrial factor. Causes not to be discussed here postponed the conversion of the valley into a great manufacturing hive until the years succeeding the Civil war and almost simultaneously with the revival of business which succeeded the depression of 1893-7, the East Creek Electric works passed from hope to reality, March, 1898. Within a decade and a half the electricity developed by the East Creek Electric Light and Power Co. has become a prime factor in the industrial, economic and social life of St. Johnsville, Fort Plain, Canajoharie and Sharon Springs. It operates the Fonda, Johnsown and Gloversville railroad and also, in conjunction with the Utica electric works, from Amsterdam to Rome with the connecting point at that marvelous fabric of engineering and electrical skill at Inghams Mills.

"The Union Knitting Co. (Wesley Aliter & Son) was the first establishment in St. Johnsville to discard steam for electricity and with the present system of separate motors doing away with so much shafting and belting and the consequent waste of power. In the piano works the amount of power required is such that a separate sub-station for those extensive works is now in course of construction.

"The Royal (now Royal Gem) knitting mill founded in 1898 by J. H. Reaney and O. W. Fox in the building now occupied by the extensive music roll business of F. Engelhardt & Sons, was equipped from the beginning with electrical motive power, but when in December, 1901, the business was removed to the present Royal Gem Mill on New street, it had so outgrown the electrical development of East creek falls that steam power was installed. Since that time the Union Mills management has begun the installation of electric energy in some departments with the probability of increasing its use. Mr. Beardslee found it necessary for the utilization of the falls to increase his riparian holdings and finally his successors, the East Creek Electric Light and Power Co. controlled both banks of the East Canada creek until the immediate vicinity of

Dolgeville is reached, the height of the Inghams Mills dam having been regulated by the tail race of the Dolgeville plant of the Utica Gas and Electric Co., thus placing the whole power derived from this stream under the control of managements which work in unison for the development of the forces which for uncounted ages ran to waste.

"The East Creek falls are about three-quarters of a mile in length, descending in that distance one hundred and eighty feet, the descent beginning at the Snell farm. Six of the descents deserve the name of cataract. The scenery has not been marred but rather improved by the erection of the electrical works, for "Dance of waters, and mill of grinding, both have beauty and both are useful." The fall of water utilized by the dam here is 120 feet, which drives two turbines each of 1,000 horse power, both connected with generators, one of 450 and the other of 500 K. W. power with turbine governors and exciters duplicated with the exception of step-up transformer. The surplus of the power generated here is transferred when needed to the lines of the Utica Gas and Electric Co. at a point between Dolgeville and Little Falls.

"The East Creek Electric Light and Power Co. came into being in 1902. In 1893 when Mr. Beardslee decided upon this undertaking which has grown far beyond his anticipation, he applied to the authorities of Little Falls for a franchise for the purpose of supplying the city with electric light and power. Although the people of Little Falls were very insistent at that time in their demands for a city charter they were too conservative to seize this opportunity and Mr. Beardslee turned his attention to the lower valley. In 1895 the firm of Roth & Engelhardt (whose successful establishment of the piano action industry at St. Johnsville during a period of phenomenal business depression was attracting considerable attention and placing themselves and the village of their location among the influences to be considered in the business world) added a lighting plant to

their St. Johnsville piano works. This Mr. Beardslee purchased of Roth & Engelhardt in 1898.

"The dam at Dolgeville was constructed by Alfred Dolge in 1897, and an electric plant installed, which ultimately passed into the hands of the Utica Gas and Electric Co. This plant generates about 2,500 H. P.

"Mr. Beardslee, who initiated the East Creek improvement, has for some years taken little or no part in its management but has devoted himself to his private interests and especially to his dairy, composed of thoroughbred blooded stock. He suffered severe losses in the winter of 1907 by the burning of his barn and destruction of his dairy, but he was not disheartened and set himself to work repairing his losses with the indefatigable energy which deserved and achieved success. His father, Augustus Beardslee, son of John Beardslee, was a well known character in his day. He was born at East Creek August 13, 1801, died there March 15, 1873. An alumnus of Fairfield seminary and Union college he was admitted to the bar and filled the positions of judge of the court of common pleas and member of assembly. Outside of these his studies and his private business occupied his time, and, thoroughly conservative, he felt no inclination to become a pioneer in the work of industrial development which may be said to have only begun in his declining years. In politics he was a Democrat of the old school and attended a national convention at Charleston, S. C., in April, 1860, as a member of the Mozart hall delegation. The failure of this movement left him out of touch with political conditions and he took no pains to adapt himself to the new situation and issues evolved by the Civil war, but passed his latter years as one of the surviving Democrats of the Jacksonian school.

"The present chapter in the history of the East Creek electrical development opened with the construction of the Inghams Mills dam and power plant. Of the thousands that pass every day up and down the Mohawk valley, few realize what a work of art, science and utility exists a few miles up the wild-appearing gorge which they pass with hardly a glance as the Twentieth Century or the Empire State trains fly by. In fact, the approach to the twin plants of the East Creek Electric Light and Power Co. is more in keeping with our ideas of the scenes of Scott's novels and poems of the Scottish Highlands than of Central New York. Inghams Mills, like many of the country hamlets, had its rise and decadence. The grist mill now disused was constructed in 1802 by Col. William Feeter and in the last years of its operation was the oldest grist mill in Herkimer county. The village became a busy place for years but as steam became the accredited agent of propulsion it slowly lost its position until 1909, when the electric plant was begun, to be completed in 1912. The dam, one of the show places of the valley, is 123 feet in height, 87 feet thick at the bottom, 12 feet at the top and 605 feet in length, setting back the water three miles, to the village of Dolgeville. The brick building containing the power plant, is one of the most complete of its kind. Two turbines each connected with a generator of 4,000 H. P., 8,000 in all, generate the mysterious element of which we know so little, but fear and dread so much. The plant at Inghams Mills is duplicated throughout more completely than that at East Creek. A breakage or other accident to one turbine or generator would cause no inconvenience to patrons of the system, the parts of the machinery being interchangeable. The use of induction motors is another great improvement over the former system but is one of those things, which while the results are appreciated by the general public, involves technicalities which are not easily understood by those who have not been initiated into the mysteries of electrical science. One plant being known as a 25 cycle plant with 3,000 alternations per minute, the other a 60 cycle plant with 7,200 alternations per minute, it became necessary to have some point where what is termed a change of frequency can take place.

This is provided at the sub-station in Manheim, where connection is made with the line of the Utica company.

"We will close by calling attention to the work at present being done to insure a larger and more regular supply of water. The Durey Lumber Co. is now engaged under a contract with the East Creek Electric Light and Power Co. in constructing storage dams at the outlet of Irving pond, Pine lake and Nine Corners lake in the near Adirondacks for the purpose of securing a uniform supply of water power. The subject of erecting an additional storage dam between East Creek and Inghams Mills has also been mooted. The work is being done under the supervision of Viele, Blackwell & Buck, engineers and builders of New York city, who also constructed the Inghams Mills dam, a piece of workmanship which owing to its secluded situation is visited by comparatively few people, but which is worthy of much more attention from the public than it has received."

E. W. Tuttle. formerly of Fort Plain, furnished the following concerning the electric development of the water power of Peck Pond and East and West Caroga lakes and Caroga creek by the Mohawk Hydro-Electric company, whose two main lines run to Fort Plain and to Gloversville-Johnstown. The Fort Plain line was opened in 1912.

Recent developments in electrical transmission of power have exerted a marked influence on the manufacturing activities of the Mohawk valley. An example in point is found in Fort Plain, N. Y., where, with the completion of the direct transmission line of the Mohawk Hydro-Electric company, in February, 1912, a new phase of industrial possibilities was entered upon.

A feature of special interest in connection with this hydro-electric development is its storage system, which utilizes natural sources of supply in such a manner as to be practically independent of rainfall variation. This enables the company to deliver a reliable, uninterrupted primary power throughout the year at the lowest rate known in the Eastern states.

The reservoir system of the development consists of three considerable natural lakes and an artificial reservoir. The lakes are: Peck's, with an area of 1,500 acres, which is owned by the company; and East and West Caroga, with a combined area of 700 acres, from which the company has the right to draw 4½ feet of water. The level of Peck's lake has been raised 24 feet by a dam 900 feet long and 36 feet high, of arch and buttress construction. The water from both of these bodies is conveyed to the main reservoir, a distance of 12 miles, through the natural channel of Caroga creek. This main reservoir, located at Garoga village, about two miles from the power station, has an area of 50 acres. It is formed by a concrete arch and buttress forebay dam 720 feet long, 58 feet high and having a spillway 260 feet in length.

A surface pipe line or tunnel conducts the water from the forebay pond to the power station, a distance of 11,430 feet. This tunnel is of varied construction, to meet the pressure requirements of its several sections. From the dam the first 400 feet is a concrete conduit; the next section, 8,700 feet in length, is a 72-inch wood stave pipe, enlarging into a 1,460-foot section of 96-inch pipe of the same construction; and the terminal section, 1,010 feet long, is a 96-inch steel pipe. Excessive surges or water-hammer in the pipe have been guarded against by a surge tower of reinforced concrete, 55 feet high and 25 feet in diameter, situated on the brow of the hill from which the pipe finally descends to the turbines. The effectual head developed is 285 feet, with a loss of approximately 10 feet in pipe line, with 3 units full load.

The power station is of concrete foundation and rubble masonry walls, designed for four generating units, of which three have been installed. The hydraulic equipment consists of three 1,800 H. P. Smith-Francis turbines of the horizontal single runner type, operating at 720 revolutions per minute. The electrical equipment of each unit is a 3 phase, 60 cycle, 2,300 volt generator of 1,250 K. V. A. capacity. The current from the generators is delivered to two banks of three transformers (and one spare), of 500 K. V. A. each, which step it up from 2,300 to 23,000 volts. The out-going lines are equipped with electrolytic lightning arresters.

There are two transmission lines known as the Gloversville-Johnstown and the Fort Plain lines. The former is a 10-mile, 23,000 volt line, transmitting power to the Fulton County Gas & Electric company, which corporation, purchasing in bulk, serves the cities of Gloversville and Johnstown and adjacent communities. The latter is a 7-mile, 23,000 volt line, direct to the sub-station at Fort Plain. The transmission towers are of two types—4-legged and "A" frames. They are designed for two 3-phase circuits on the first named line and one circuit on the Fort Plain line—the latter consisting of three No. 1 hard drawn solid copper wires.

The sub-station at Fort Plain is of hollow tile and brick construction and has complete equipment for stepping down from 23,000 to 2,300 volts, together with approved protective devices and measuring instruments.

During the first eighteen months of its operation the plant has carried the entire load of the cities of Johnstown and Gloversville, serving a population of over 36,000 people continuously 24 hours a day, with but one interruption of six minutes. This operating period includes the summer months of 1911 and 1912, which were seasons of unusual dryness. In spite of these severe conditions the storage at Peck's lake has had a draught of only three feet made on it at the end of the present summer season, leaving a reserve of over a billion cubic feet of stored water. The electric regulation on the company's power circuit has been remarkably good, the management of the Fulton county company's system stating that both as to reliability and regulation the service is far superior to that which they had been able to obtain from their own steam plant.

The complete plant was designed by Barclay, Parsons & Klapp,' New York city. Work was started in May, 1910. The Gloversville-Johnstown load was taken on in February, 1911, and the Fort Plain service inaugurated in February, 1912.

CHAPTER X.

1825-1913—Western Montgomery County and the Five Townships of Minden, Canajoharie, Root, Palatine and St. Johnsville.

This is the second chapter relating to western Montgomery county and its five towns of Minden, Canajoharie, Root, Palatine and St. Johnsville. The first treated of the period in this territory from 1689, the date of settlement of Palatine by Hendrick Frey, to 1825—the year of the completion of the Erie canal, and covered details local to these towns not contained in the more general historical chapters. This chapter deals with the later period during the years from 1825 to 1913.

Among the wonderfully varied country of land, water and mountains contained within New York state that of the Mohawk valley holds a justly famed position. From the days of the earliest settlers our river and its watershed were celebrated throughout the thirteen colonies and in Canada. The Canadian Indians with Champlain sang to him praises of this then primeval region. The old Canajoharie and Palatine districts and its river sections contained in western Montgomery county, hold much that is beautiful and typical of the Mohawk valley. This territory formed a large part of the old Indian country of Canajoharie and later of the civil divisions of the Canajoharie and Palatine districts of Tryon county. Together with the added towns of Danube and Manheim of Herkimer county it comprised the entire river section of those districts.

Western Montgomery county is a country of high, rolling hills and fertile flats. Much of its farm lands are rich, some are today (1913) much "run out." It is a noted farming section and famous dairying region, growing hay, oats, corn, fruit and poultry. On the south side hops were once raised generally, now only slightly. From its surface the forest, which originally overspread this river region, as well as the greater part of the eastern United States, has been almost completely denuded. It should be the work of the valley men of today and the future to bring back to that land, which is poorly suited for agriculture but adapted to forest growth, those great woods and trees of old, which enrich the land, store up pure water and induce rains, and which give life and health to the people. These same valley men should bring, from the small remnants of these woods, the trees, shrubs and flowers which are typical of this old region of the earth, and surround their homes with these native growths, making places of beauty where now are frequently barren, naked grounds.

The Mohawk, in western Montgomery county, runs a course from northwest to southeast, from Palatine Church to below Canajoharie—a distance of seven miles out of the seventeen miles of river which wind through the five western towns. This course, which varies from the general eastern direction of the Mohawk, was noted by the Dutch travelers and explorers whose journey here in 1634 is mentioned in Chapter I of this work. The Mohawk of fifty years ago was a river of much beauty, with tree-lined banks, faintly suggesting that wonderful stream of the seventeenth century running between forest covered hills. Until the Barge canal operations it retained much of this attractiveness in parts. Most of the beautiful views obtainable, in the region we are considering, are to be seen from the highlands directly bordering the river. Such a low elevation (of 100 feet above the river) as Prospect Hill in Fort Plain, gives charming vistas while the outlook westward from the west side of the Big Nose, at an elevation of 600 feet, gives a view of the valley which is magnificent.

Several of the Mohawk's most important tributaries enter the river in western Montgomery county. Two of these, the East and Caroga creeks run down through their hill-bordered valleys from the lakeland of Fulton county and enter their parent stream at East Creek and Palatine Church, respectively. Both produce abundant water power. On the south shore, the Otsquago, entering the Mohawk at Fort Plain, the Canajoharie at Canajoharie, Flat creek at Sprakers, and Yatesville or Wasontha, at Randall, are tributaries of the river of the second class. Much of the most beautiful scenery in this section is contained along the valleys of these streams. The small falls and rapids above East Creek station on East creek are of considerable beauty.

On Flat creek, a mile or more south of Sprakers, is a considerable fall of water, but most attractive of all the landscape features of western Montgomery county is the Canajoharie Falls at the upper end of the famed Canajoharie gorge which begins at the Canajoharie of yore and the Canajoharie of today—the old stone "pot" in the creek's bed which lies on the southern limits of the village itself.

Situated in the middle of this fertile river farming country are three centers of population which, today are modern, progressive, well-kept American villages of the best type and of which their citizens may well be proud. These are St. Johnsville, Fort Plain (including Nelliston) and Canajoharie (including Palatine Bridge). All these three places are market towns for the surrounding country and much manufacturing is done in them all, many of the products being famous the country over. All are excellent places of residence, not as yet (1913) being overrun with a foreign population, alien in every way to the thoroughly American population of western Montgomery county. It is to be hoped that this condition will continue in spite of that urban growth which is sure to come. The villages mentioned are typical of other small towns and even of the cities of the Mohawk valley. As the town giving its title to this work, Fort Plain has been selected as the village whose story is detailed from 1825 to 1913, but the same social, agricultural, labor and manufacturing details noticed are largely true of St. Johnsville and Canajoharie and of the countryside also, so that in reading the story of Fort Plain and the town of Minden, we scan that of western Montgomery county and its villages as well. Although imaginary lines of geographical demarcation are of but little real value, it may interest the reader to know that western Montgomery contains about 125,000 acres (about half the area of the county) and is about the size of Schenectady county. Its combined population is about 16,000.

In western Montgomery county are located three of the historic churches and several of the pre-Revolutionary houses of the Mohawk valley.

The population of western Montgomery county in 1840 was 16,378 and in 1850, 15,939 divided as follows: Minden, 4,623; Canajoharie, 4,097; Root, 2,736; Palatine, 2,856; St. Johnsville, 1,627. The populations of Min-

den and St. Johnsville only have increased from 1850 to 1910 and this has been due entirely to the growth of the villages of St. Johnsville and Fort Plain. The incorporated places of Fort Plain and Canajoharie (then the only ones in western Montgomery) did not have their population given separately in the census of 1850.

The census of 1880 was the first in which the population of all the villages of the west end of Montgomery county were returned. The census figures of 1880 by towns follow: Minden, 5,100; Canajoharie, 4,294; Root, 2,275; Palatine, 2,786; St. Johnsville, 2,002. Total population of the five western towns of Montgomery county (1880), 16,457. Population of the villages: Fort Plain, 2,443; Canajoharie, 2,013; St. Johnsville, 1,072; Nelliston, 558; Palatine Bridge, 332.

The 1910 population of the five western towns of Montgomery county— Minden, Canajoharie, Root, Palatine, St. Johnsville—was 15,932, divided among the townships as follows: Minden, 4,645; Canajoharie, 3,888; Root, 1,512; Palatine, 2,517; St. Johnsville, 3,369. The population of the five villages was as follows: Fort Plain, 2,762; St. Johnsville, 2,536; Canajoharie, 2,273; Nelliston, 737, Palatine Bridge, 392.

While there are five incorporated villages in western Montgomery there are but three centers of urban population, viz: Fort Plain-Nelliston, combined population 1910. 3,499; Canajoharie-Palatine Bridge, 2,665; St. Johnsville, 2,536. The growth of St. Johnsville has been very considerable in the past decade and if continued it will become the largest population center in western Montgomery county before the passage of many years.

Although a union of the villages of Fort Plain and Nelliston and of Canajoharie and Palatine Bridge is not now contemplated, nor even desired by the inhabitants of the smaller places, it probably will eventually come to pass.

The total population of the five west end villages in 1910 was 8,700. Outside of these incorporated places are probably 1,000 people whose living is not derived from the land. This would give a farming population of 6,200 and a non-farming population of 9,700. Over half the agricultural population of Montgomery county is located in the western half, as the people engaged in the cultivation of the soil, in Montgomery county, probably do not exceed 11,000 in number. The producing farm population of the five western towns of Minden, Canajoharie, Root, Palatine and St. Johnsville, is about half what it was in 1850, while the non-food-producing public has more than doubled. This condition, which is common to the entire country, is responsible for the high and increasing cost of food stuffs, and this condition will not be bettered except by a great increase in the number of food producers.

The foregoing chapters of this work have detailed the history of western Montgomery and the Mohawk valley from the time of the earliest Dutch explorers and its Mohawk Iroquois inhabitants. We have seen the events of settlement by Dutch, British and Germans and how the location of Hendrick Frey in 1689 in Palatine was the first in the limits of old Tryon county and the first in the valley west of the Schenectady county line. In western Montgomery county was the forest home of Sir George Clarke, one of the British colonial governors. The stirring Revolutionary events of this section have been detailed and the great part its inhabitants played in the defense of this frontier. Later we have had the Mohawk river commerce described and that of the turnpikes and the building of the canal, railroad and Barge canal. The part the men of the middle Mohawk valley played in the wars of 1812 and 1861-5 has been told with much particularity. The following will describe this section of recent years and at the present time (1913).

CHAPTER XI.

1825-1913—Western Montgomery County—The Town of St. Johnsville and St. Johnsville Village.

The town of St. Johnsville is the most westerly, with the town of Minden, in Montgomery and is bounded on the north by Fulton county (town of Oppenheim and a small part of the town of Ephratah), on the east by Palatine, on the south by the Mohawk river and the town of Minden, and on the west by Herkimer county. Its surface consists of broad flats along the Mohawk, with broken uplands rising to the north to a height of over 1,000 feet sea elevation and over 700 feet above the river. The principal streams, all of which flow in a southerly direction and empty into the Mohawk, are East Canada, Crum, Fox, Zimmerman, Timmerman and Mother creek. Mason's History (1892) says: East Canada creek is noted for a succession of falls and rapids, descending 75 feet in a distance of 80 rods, this being a mile from its mouth. The soil of the town is a fine quality of gravelly loam, and that portion lying near the river is adapted to grain and hay, while farther north the land is well suited to grazing. Discovery has been made of three distinct mineral veins, on or near East Canada creek, which are distinguished as the lower, middle and upper mines. The first mentioned consists largely of lead, with a trace of gold, the second is a mixture of copper, lead and zinc, and the last mentioned is mostly copper. [None of these have ever been really worked.]

St. Johnsville was formed from the town of Oppenheim [now in Fulton county] at the time Montgomery county was divided [into Montgomery and Fulton counties], April 18, 1838. In area it is the smallest town in the county. A large portion of it was formerly comprised in the Harrison patent of 12,000 acres, dated March 18, 1722. The town is divided into four school districts.

The town is supposed to have been settled at about 1725 or before. It was part of the Palatine district and its history is largely that of Palatine which was settled about 1712, by Palatine Germans. These with a few Dutch comprised the settlers prior to the Revolution. Mention has been made in the former chapter on western Montgomery county [1689-1825] of the settlements, industries and schools here prior to 1825. St. Johnsville formed part of the town of Palatine from 1772 to 1808, when the town of Oppenheim, then in Montgomery county, was set off. In 1838 the town of St. Johnsville, Montgomery county, was formed as previously stated. The first town meeting of the new town was held May 1, 1838, at the house of Cristopher Klock, one mile east of the later village of St. Johnsville. The number of votes polled was 271. During the civil war St. Johnsville furnished a large number of federal soldiers, considering its small area.

The village of St. Johnsville is situated on Zimmermans creek about in the center of the town and dates its first settlement from 1775 when David and Conrad Zimmerman located there and built a grist mill on the stream. George Klock built a grist mill in 1801 and David Quackenbush another in 1804. In 1825 James Averill built here a stone grist mill and distillery. These buildings were twice destroyed by fire and as often rebuilt and eventually became a paper-mill, making straw board. St. Johnsville village was long known as "Timmerman's," a name derived from its first settlers, the names Timmerman and Zimmerman being equivalent.

The name of the village and town was taken from St. John's Reformed church, as mentioned in a foregoing chapter on the five Revolutionary churches of western Montgomery county, of which St. John's was one. This church was formed prior to 1756 and a church erected in 1770 below the village. In 1804 this was removed to its present location. In 1881 the present St. John's Reformed church of brick was erected.

It has been stated that the name of the town and village was adopted in honor of Alexander St. John, who was

a pioneer of what is now Northampton, Fulton county, and who was a well-known engineer and surveyor of his time. On April 4, 1811, the New York legislature passed an act authorizing John McIntyre of Broadalbin, Alexander St. John of Northampton, and Wm. Newton of Mayfield, to lay out a new turnpike road "from the house of Henry Gross in Johnstown to the house of John C. Nellis, in the town of Oppenheim," terminating in the Mohawk turnpike near the present village of St. Johnsville. St. John did the surveying and largely superintended the construction of the turnpike. He was at "Timmerman's" a great part of the time and when a postoffice was established there it is said to have been named in his honor, St. Johnsville. It may be that the historic old Reformed church and the capable and popular surveyor both contributed to the adoption of the name, but the subject will probably continue to be a matter of dispute.

The construction of the Erie canal in 1825 and the Utica and Schenectady railroad in 1836, boomed the little village and in 1857 the population had grown to 720. On Aug. 1, 1857, the place was incorporated.

Besides St. John's Reformed church the following religious societies have been organized in the village: Grace Christian church, organized in 1874; Union church, erected in 1849 by Lutherans and Methodists and a few other denominations no longer in existence; Methodist Episcopal church, built in 1879; St. Patrick's Roman Catholic church, built 1889; Episcopal.

The following newspapers have been published in St. Johnsville, with the dates of their establishment: Interior New Yorker, 1875; Weekly Portrait, St. Johnsville Times, St. Johnsville Herald, St. Johnsville Herald-Times; St. Johnsvile Leader, 1886; St. Johnsville News, 1891; St. Johnsville Enterprise, 1897.

The First National bank of St. Johnsville was organized in 1864 with a capital of $50,000. The Board of Trade of St. Johnsville was organized 1892. Exceptionally good educational facilities are afforded by the St. Johnsville High and Grammar school.

St. Johnsville has a fine public library housed in its own building. Like Fort Plain and Canajoharie, its sister villages, it has many social, fraternal, religious and patriotic societies. St. Johnsville Lodge, No. 611, F. and A. M., was organized in 1866.

The manufactures of the village are (1913) player pianos and piano actions (manufacture began 1889), agricultural implements, condensed milk, carriage hardware, knit goods, carriages, wagons, sleighs, paper, straw board, sash and blinds, cigars, iron castings. The manufacture of knit goods began in 1892.

The following is from the Industrial Directory of 1912, issued by the New York State Department of Labor:

St. Johnsville (Montgomery county), incorporated as a village in 1857; estimated population in 1913, 2,735. St. Johnsville is situated in the valley of the Mohawk river on the New York Central railroad [the station of South St. Johnsville is on the south side of the Mohawk on the West Shore railroad and the Erie canal]. The principal manufactures are knit goods and pianos [player pianos and piano actions]. The village is the trading and shipping center for a rich dairy farming section. There is building sand in St. Johnsville. The village has sewers, electric lighting service and municipal water works.

With 990 operatives in an estimated (1913) population of 2,735, St. Johnsville is an unusual valley industrial center, on account of the large proportion of manufacturing employes to the total population—over one-third. It is the leading industrial town of western Montgomery county. Its factories (1914) generally employ electric power derived from the power stations at East Creek and Inghams Mills. See the chapter on Western Montgomery county hydro-electric development, in which its relation to the manufactories of St. Johnsville is detailed by William Irving Walter, the well-known writer on historical and general subjects, of St. Johnsville.

The growth of St. Johnsville, due to its flourishing industries, has been very rapid since 1890 and the village has all improvements such as sewers,

electric lights and water supply. It boasts the first modern opera house built in western Montgomery county. The Mohawk turnpike is excellently paved through the village with brick and a variety of experimental road building materials further west. The only hamlet in the town is that of Upper St. Johnsville, about one and a half miles west of the village proper, of which it will doubtless eventually form a part.

The population of St. Johnsville township was in 1850, 1,627; 1880, 2,002; 1910, 3,369.

The population of St. Johnsville village was 720 in 1857, 1,376 in 1870, 1,072 in 1880, 1,263 in 1890, 1,873 in 1900 and 2,536 in 1910.

CHAPTER XII.

1825-1913—Western Montgomery County—The Town of Palatine.

Says Mason's History (1892): The present town of Palatine lies north of the Mohawk, and directly east of St. Johnsville. It is bounded on the north by Fulton county [town of Ephratah] and on the east by the town of Mohawk [and on the south by the Mohawk river and the towns of Minden, Canajoharie and part of Root]. The surface of the town is mostly an upland [200 to 700 feet above the valley], broken by deep, narrow ravines and descending irregularly toward the river. Garoga [or Caroga] creek, a beautiful mill stream, which rises in the Garoga lake [and Peck's Pond] flows in a southwesterly direction through the western part of the town and empties into the Mohawk at Palatine Church. Mill creek, a tributary of the Garoga; Smith creek, at the Smith farm; Nelliston creek, at Nelliston; Flat creek, on the Gros farm; Saltsman creek, below Palatine Bridge; the Kanagara, emptying into the Mohawk a short distance below Sprakers [at the County Home], are the principal water courses of the town. The soil consists in a great measure of dark, clayey loam, containing more or less gravel, and is highly fertile when properly cultivated. It is especially adapted to grazing and, in the manufacture of cheese, Palatine is one of the leading dairy townships.

The story of the town of Palatine has been brought in previous chapters down to 1825. It is exclusively an agricultural town, its two villages of Nelliston and Palatine Bridge, being in reality residence sections respectively of Fort Plain and Canajoharie, without industries of any size. The Palatine district, on the formation of Tryon county in 1772, was called the "Stone Arabia district." On March 8, 1773, the name was changed to "Palatine district." Salisbury, Herkimer county, was the first town set off from Palatine in 1797. Stratford (Fulton county) was formed from it in 1805; Oppenheim (embracing also the present town of St. Johnsville) in 1808; Ephratah in 1827, but a portion of the latter was re-annexed upon the division of the county in 1838.

"The territory of Palatine," says Mason's History, "originally comprised three historic land grants, the first being the Van Slyck patent of 6,000 acres, granted 1716. It lay along the north bank of the Mohawk, extending west from the Nose and a mile or more above Palatine Bridge, also including the 'Frey place.' Next was the Harrison patent, containing 12,000 acres, and including nearly all of what is now St. Johnsville. This was bought from the Indians in 1722 by Francis Harrison and others. The third was the Stone Arabia patent of 1723, comprising 12,700 acres, and granted mostly to 27 Palatines and Herrdrick Frey, who were already settled on the land." The oldest structure in Palatine is Fort Frey, a stone house built in 1739, and located in the present village of Palatine Bridge.

Mention has been made of the three Revolutionary churches of Palatine, the Reformed church of Stone Arabia and the Lutheran churches of Stone Arabia and Palatine Church. Aside from these is Salem Church of the Evangelical Association of America, later called "the German church," first organized in 1835 and incorporated in 1877, the present edifice being erected

in 1871, and the Methodist church of Nelliston, built about 1890.

Palatine is divided into eleven school districts. It comprises, besides the incorporated villages of Nelliston and Palatine Bridge, the hamlets of Palatine Church, Wagners Hollow, Stone Arabia and McKinley (formerly Oswegatchie). The villages of Nelliston and Palatine Bridge are advantageously located. They have residential, educational and social advantages which should ensure a future considerable growth. Both have factory and home sites in abundance. Palatine Bridge is (1914) putting in a village sewage system.

The population of Palatine was 2,856 in 1850, 2,786 in 1880, 2,517 in 1910.

The population of Palatine Bridge was 493 in 1870, 332 in 1880, 392 in 1910.

The population of Nelliston was 558 in 1880, 737 in 1910.

CHAPTER XIII.

1825-1913—Western Montgomery County—The Town of Root.

Mason's History (1892) says: "Root is the central town of the county on the south of the Mohawk. It is bounded on the east by Glen and Charleston; on the south by Schoharie county and on the west by Canajoharie. The surface of this town presents a variety of natural features surpassing in extent and grandeur any other portion of the county, in fact it is doubtful if any other equal area in the Mohawk valley contains so many interesting works of nature. The geologist and naturalist here find subjects for thought and discussion, while the admirer of beautiful scenery is charmed with the prospect from the heights in the northern and central portions of the town. The majestic hills, that rise abruptly from the Mohawk to a height of 630 feet, form the northern crest of an undulating upland, the soil of which varies from a dark colored loam and clay bottom, near the eastern border, to a gravelly loam in the center, and more or less clay and light soil in the western portion of the town. A fine quality of building stone crops out on some of these summits, but, owing to the steep hills and heavy grades, these quarries have seldom been worked. An abundance of black slate is found near the center of the town. Agriculture is the principal interest and, although hay is the chief crop, oats, barley, corn and buckwheat are raised in abundance. In the vicinity of Currytown, hops are grown with much success. The adaptability of the soil to grazing was recognized by the farmers at an early day, and thus we find extensive dairies and cheese factories scattered throughout the town."

The two principal streams in Root are Yatesville and Flat creeks. The former [Yatesville] enters the town on its eastern border from Charleston and flows in a northerly direction, emptying into the Mohawk at Randall, formerly Yatesville. This stream was called by the Indians Wasontha. A beautiful cascade is to be seen about one mile north of Rural Grove, where this stream falls twenty or twenty-five feet, affording a scene of picturesque attraction. Flat Creek, which takes its name from the shallowness of a portion of its stream, enters the extreme southern part of the town and flows in an irregular northerly direction, making a circuitous detour into Canajoharie and emptying into the Mohawk at Sprakers. A large portion of the course of this stream is composed of natural features differing from those to which it owes its name. For a number of miles it flows through an inclining stratum of gravel and slate, its banks forming steep and rugged ravines, and at a point a mile above Sprakers there is a fall of sixty-five feet. At several points along its course, prospecting parties have successfully brought to the surface mineral ore containing fifty per cent of lead and fifteen per cent of silver, as shown by the assay of the state geologist, and this led to the formation of the Canajoharie Mining Co. [but the veins have never been worked]. Besides these there are two other small streams in the town of Root—Big Nose creek, just east of the Big Nose, and Allston creek in the eastern part of the

town, emptying into the Mohawk in the town of Glen.

Facing the river, on the northern border of Root, about two miles east of Sprakers, is a bold promontory, which is mentioned in connection with a similar spur on the opposite or north side of the Mohawk as "the Noses." These lower uplifts of the Mohawk have been noted at length in connection with the history and geography of the Mohawk valley and of the geology of the middle Mohawk valley. The scenery and landscape on and about the Noses and their aspect from the river and the broad flatlands above and below them, constitutes one of the most picturesque features of the Mohawk valley. The editor of this work would suggest "the Noses" and their adjoining country and the Canajoharie falls as the two most attractive landscape items in western Montgomery county. The southern nose is known as "the Big Nose." On it is located Mitchell's cave, a seeming fault in the rock, enlarged by water action and which has been descended to its bottom for several hundred feet. It drops at a sharp angle toward the Mohawk river. Its exploration is attended with considerable danger and should only be undertaken by a party of men with ropes, lanterns, etc. There is a similar hole north of Little Falls known as Hinman's Hole. The Big Nose has also been called "Anthony's Nose."

Root is the largest town of Montgomery county. The eastern half was formerly in the Mohawk district of Tryon county while the half west of the Big Nose was in the Canajoharie district. It was formed from Canajoharie and Charleston in 1823 and named in honor of Erastus Root of Delaware county, a political leader of that time. Its territory embraces parts of nine different land grants as follows: Burnet patent, 1726, 775 acres, in Randall village; Provost patent, 1726, 8,000 acres, lying west of Randall; Roseboom patent, 1726, 1,500 acres, including the hill known as "Anthony's Nose" and extending southeast within a mile of Currytown; Kennedy patent, 775 acres, granted 1727, and including

Stone Ridge; Bagley and Williams. patent, 4,000 acres, granted 1837, in the south part of Root, extending into southeastern Canajoharie; Corry's patent, 25,400 acres, granted 1737, embracing parts of Charleston, Glen and Root; Winne's patent, 4,000 acres, including Flat Creek village, granted 1741; Gros patent (title secured by John Daniel Gros, pastor of the Canajoharie Reformed Dutch church at Fort Plain) embracing parts of Root and Canajoharie, title granted 1786.

The first permanent white settler known who located in Root was Jacob Dievendorf, who settled at Currytown. The first town meeting and election of officers was held shortly after the organization of the town in January, 1823. In 1825 the population of the town was 2,806. In 1910 it was 1,512. The first schools in Root were German schools but the first school of which we have any record was an English school taught by one Glaycher near the Noses in 1784. There are now fourteen school districts in Root.

Rural Grove is the largest and most important center in Root, and is located on Yatesville creek, about five miles south of the Mohawk. It is said to date its settlement from 1828, when Abram H. Vanderveer and Henry Stowitts erected a dwelling and large tannery on the site of the residence of the late John Bowdish. The cluster of houses which grew up around the tannery was named Unionville by Stowitts and later was called Leatherville. The present name of Rural Grove was suggested by a beautiful grove of elms on the west border of the little village and residents began using this name in 1850 and it was adopted by the postoffice department in 1872. The Currytown postoffice was removed to Rural Grove in 1832. The place has about 250 population, stores and a grist mill and cheese factory. The Rural Grove Methodist church was built in 1845, but a Methodist society had existed long before that date. The Christian church was organized in 1854 and a church built which was enlarged in 1874.

Sprakers is an attractive hamlet on the Mohawk at the mouth of Flat creek and on the south side of the Erie canal. It is a station on the West Shore road and connected by ferry with the Central railroad station of Sprakers opposite on the north shore. It was named for Jost Spraker, a pioneer of the well known valley family of that name. George Spraker, son of Jost Spraker, built a tavern here which was kept for years, until it burned down. Daniel Spraker built the first store in 1822 and until the canal was completed was engaged in the business of transferring freight between the unfinished sections. Another store was started by Joseph Spencer, who sold out to John L. Bevins, who built the fine stone store still standing and occupied as a place of business, on the south bank of the canal, by S. W. and Oscar Cohen (1913). Sprakers was for a long time a supply place for the canal trade. A postoffice was established here early in the nineteenth century. The Reformed church of Sprakers was erected in 1858 on the site of a much older church building. Sprakers has a hotel, creamery and several stores and a population of about 200.

Currytown is the oldest settlement in the town of Root, and here a store was established about 1800 by John McKernan, who subsequently built a bridge across the Mohawk at Randall which was carried away by high water in 1820 or shortly after. At Curry town was established the first postoffice in the town of Root, the mail being brought by a post-rider. This was removed to Rural Grove in 1832 but one was again established in the latter part of the nineteenth century. Currytown is today a strictly residential hamlet of prosperous farmers. The Reformed church of Currytown is the oldest religious organization in Root, having been organized in 1790 and a church built in 1809. It was remodeled in 1849 and was rebuilt in 1883.

Randall is a postoffice and village in the northeastern part of the town, on the Erie canal, West Shore railroad and Mohawk river and at the mouth of Yatesville creek. It was originally called Yatesville, which name was some of these summits, but, owing to the steep hills and heavy grades, these quarries have seldom been worked. An abundance of black slate is found near the center of the town. Agriculture is the principal interest and, although hay is the chief crop, oats, barley, corn and buckwheat are raised in abundance. In the vicinity of Currytown hops are grown with much success The adaptability of the soil to grazing was recognized by the farmers at an early day, and thus we find extensive dairies and cheese factories scattered throughout the town."

The two principal streams in Root are Yatesville and Flat creeks. The former [Yatesville] enters the town on its eastern border from Charleston and flows in a northerly direction emptying into the Mohawk at Randall formerly Yatesville. This stream wa called by the Indians Wasontha. beautiful cascade is to be seen abou one mile north of Rural Grove, wher this stream falls twenty or twenty-fiv feet, affording a scene of picturesqu attraction. Flat Creek, which take its name from the shallowness of portion of its stream, enters the ex treme southern part of the town an flows in an irregular northerly direc tion, making a circuitous detour int Canajoharie and emptying into th Mohawk at Sprakers. A large portio of the course of this stream is com posed of natural features differin from those to which it owes its name For a number of miles it flows through an inclining stratum of gravel an slate, its banks forming steep an rugged ravines, and at a point a mil above Sprakers there is a fall of sixty five feet. At several points along it course, prospecting parties have suc cessfully brought to the surface min eral ore containing fifty per cent o lead and fifteen per cent of silver, a shown by the assay of the state geol ogist, and this led to the formation o the Canajoharie Mining Co. [but th veins have never been worked]. Be sides these there are two other smal streams in the town of Root—Big Nos creek, just east of the Big Nose, an Allston creek in the eastern part of th

town, emptying into the Mohawk in the town of Glen.

Facing the river, on the northern border of Root, about two miles east of Sprakers, is a bold promontory, which is mentioned in connection with a similar spur on the opposite or north side of the Mohawk as "the Noses." These lower uplifts of the Mohawk have been noted at length in connec tion with the history and geography o the Mohawk valley and of the geolog of the middle Mohawk valley. Th scenery and landscape on and abo the Noses and their aspect from tl river and the broad flatlands above a below them, constitutes one of t most picturesque features of the M hawk valley. The editor of this w would suggest "the Noses" and t adjoining country and the Canajoh falls as the two most attractive l scape items in western Montgor county. The southern nose is kn as "the Big Nose." On it is lo Mitchell's cave, a seeming fault in rock, enlarged by water action which has been descended to its tom for several hundred feet. It d at a sharp angle toward the Moha river. Its exploration is attended wi considerable danger and should only undertaken by a party of men wi ropes, lanterns, etc. There is a simi lar hole north of Little Falls known a Hinman's Hole. The Big Nose has also been called "Anthony's Nose."

Root is the largest town of Mont gomery county. The eastern half was formerly in the Mohawk district of Tryon county while the half west of the Big Nose was in the Canajoharie district. It was formed from Canajo harie and Charleston in 1823 and named in honor of Erastus Root of Delaware county, a political leader of that time. Its territory embraces parts of nine different land grants as fol lows: Burnet patent, 1726, 775 acres, in Randall village; Provost patent, 1726, 8,000 acres, lying west of Randall; Roseboom patent, 1726, 1,500 acres, in cluding the hill known as "Anthony's Nose" and extending southeast within a mile of Currytown; Kennedy patent, 775 acres, granted 1727, and including

Stone Ridge; Bagley and William patent, 4,000 acres, granted 1837, in the south part of Root, extending into southeastern Canajoharie; Corry's patent, 25,400 acres, granted 1737, embracing parts of Charleston, Glen and Root; Winne's patent, 4.000 acres, including Flat Creek village, granted 1741; Gros patent (title secured by John Daniel Gros, pastor of the Canajoharie Reformed Dutch church at Fort Plain) embracing parts of Root and Canajoharie, title granted 1786.

The first permanent white settler known who located in Root was Jacob Dievendorf, who settled at Currytown. The first town meeting and election of officers was held shortly after the organization of the town in January, 1823. In 1825 the population of the town was 2,806. In 1910 it was 1,512. The first schools in Root were German schools but the first school of which we have any record was an English school taught by one Glaycher near the Noses in 1784. There are now fourteen school districts in Root.

Rural Grove is the largest and most important center in Root, and is located on Yatesville creek, about five miles south of the Mohawk. It is said to date its settlement from 1828, when Abram H. Vanderveer and Henry Stowitts erected a dwelling and large tannery on the site of the residence of the late John Bowdish. The cluster of houses which grew up around the tannery was named Unionville by Stowitts and later was called Leatherville. The present name of Rural Grove was suggested by a beautiful grove of elms on the west border of the little village and residents began using this name in 1850 and it was adopted by the postoffice department in 1872. The Currytown postoffice was removed to Rural Grove in 1832. The place has about 250 population, stores and a grist mill and cheese factory. The Rural Grove Methodist church was built in 1845, but a Methodist society had existed long before that date. The Christian church was organized in 1854 and a church built which was enlarged in 1874.

Sprakers is an attractive hamlet on

basin
eek,

[text obscured] of the west [text obscured] name. George Sprakes, [text obscured] kept for years. Daniel Spraker built [text obscured] 1822 and [text obscured] was engaged in [text obscured] erring freight [text obscured] sections. [text obscured] y Joseph Spraker [text obscured] ohn L. Bevins [text obscured] tone store still [text obscured] s a place of business [text obscured] ank of the canal [text obscured] Cohen (1913). Sprakers [text obscured] ime a supply place [text obscured] rade. A postoffice [text obscured] ere early in the [text obscured] The Reformed church [text obscured] rected in 1858 on the site [text obscured] lder church building [text obscured] otel, creamery and [text obscured] nd a population of about [text obscured]

Currytown is the oldest [text obscured] n the town of Root, and has [text obscured] as established about 1800 by [text obscured] cKernan, who subsequently [text obscured] ridge across the Mohawk [text obscured] hich was carried away by high water [text obscured] n 1820 or shortly after. At this [text obscured] own was established the first postoffice [text obscured] ce in the town of Root, the mail being brought by a post-rider. This was [text obscured] emoved to Rural Grove in 1832 but one was again established in the latter part of the nineteenth century. Currytown is today a strictly residential hamlet of prosperous farmers. The Reformed church of Currytown is the oldest religious organization in Root having been organized in 1790 and a church built in 1809. It was remodeled in 1849 and was rebuilt in 1883.

Randall is a postoffice and village in he northeastern part of the town, on he Erie canal, West Shore railroad nd Mohawk river and at the mouth of Yatesville creek. It was originally alled Yatesville, which name was changed to Randall when the postoffice was established in 1863. A Christian church was formed about 1850 at Randall and a church was built in 1885. The bridge connecting Randall and Yosts on the north shore was swept away, as mentioned previously, in 1820, shortly after its erection. Population about 150.

Flat Creek is located on the stream of that name four miles south of the Mohawk. Considerable business was transacted here at one time and then the place had two hotels or taverns. A postoffice was established here in the latter part of the nineteenth century. A cheese factory and saw and feed mill are here located. A Baptist church was built in 1860, but later the society disbanded. The True Dutch Reformed church of Flat Creek was built in 1885.

Bundy's Corners, Lyker's Corners and Brown's Hollow are the names of hamlets of Root consisting each of a few houses. At Brown's Hollow, Henry Lyker erected a grist mill at an early day, which later was bought by John Brown, who increased the water power by tunneling 1,000 feet through the hill. The mill was burned but subsequently rebuilt. A distillery, linseed oil mill, carding machine and fulling mill were at one time in operation at Brown's Hollow but have discontinued operation.

Population Root township: 1850, 2,736; 1880, 2,275; 1910, 1,512.

CHAPTER XIV.

1825-1913—Western Montgomery County—The Town of Canajoharie and Canajoharie Village.

The town of Canajoharie lies on the south side of the Mohawk. It is bounded on the north by the river and the town of Palatine; on the east by the town of Root; on the south by Schoharie county and on the west by Minden. Its surface consists of undulating uplands rising from the Mohawk to heights of almost 1,000 feet in the southern part of the town. Its territory lies almost entirely in the watershed of Canajoharie creek, which enters the southwestern part of the town and flows almost directly east to the little hamlet of Waterville, when it turns north and flows in a zig-zag course to its outlet into the Mohawk at Canajoharie village. About one and a half miles from its mouth occur the picturesque Canajoharie falls, with a perpendicular drop of about forty feet to the deep pool at its base. Here begins the Canajoharie gorge of slate and stone walls, over a hundred feet in height in places, hemming in the stream on both sides and forming a miniature canyon of great beauty about three-quarters of a mile or more in length. It ends at the southwestern outskirts of Canajoharie village, about three-quarters of a mile from the junction of the creek with the Mohawk river. At the end of the gorge is located the original "Canajoharie" or "pot which washes itself." This is a hole in the solid rock of the creek bed about twenty feet wide and ten feet or more in depth although the depth is probably much greater in the rock. This is a gigantic pot hole, probably worn by the action of small stones at some time when the course of the stream facilitated their grinding action. Happy Hollow Brook, about one mile north of Canajoharie village, is the only other stream outside of a few rivulets, in the township.

The soil of the town is a gravelly loam, derived from the disintegration of the underlying slate, in some places intermixed with clay. It is easily and profitably cultivated and Canajoharie has been noted, from its earliest settlement, for its rich and valuable farms. When the first German and Dutch settlers of the town of Canajoharie came here about 1720 they found the Mohawks cultivating the flatlands, particular the island located in the river just below Fort Plain and the island a mile and a half below the creek. Here corn, beans, squashes and tobacco were growing.

Canajoharie is the remaining portion of the old Tryon county district of that name, designated at the time of the setting off of Tryon county March 24, 1772. Cherry Valley town was formed from it in 1791; Minden in 1798; a part of Root in 1823; and a part (the Freysbush district) was taken from it and added to Minden in 1849.

The prinicpal land grants in the present town of Canajoharie were the Canajoharie tract of 12,450 acres dated 1723; the Bradt patent of 3,200 acres granted in 1733; Bagley's patent of 4,000 acres in 1737; two Colden patents and the Cosby, Dick, Lyne and Morris patents of 2,000 acres each.

The following relates to the centers of population in Canajoharie township:

The history of Canajoharie village from about 1777 to 1825 is contained in the first chapter dealing with western Montgomery county. The village was incorporated April 30, 1829, and since that time it has had a slow but sure growth and has never gone back in population. It suffered extensive losses by severe fires in 1840, 1849 and 1877, in each instance a large part of the business section being burned. The construction of the West Shore railroad in 1883 somewhat injured the lower and business part of the town. The Canajoharie Local train runs west to Syracuse and return over the West Shore railroad.

The old stone school, known as district No. 8, was built in 1850. In 1893 the present fine stone school house was built, housing grammar, high school and training school departments. It is one of the finest examples of school architecture in the county and a leading feature of those substantial stone structures which make Canajoharie such a well-built, solid and substantial looking town.

The Canajoharie Water Works Co. was organized in 1852 and the village supplied by water taken from springs by gravity, to which were later added rams for fire purposes. In 1876 this system was extended and the supply was added to from larger springs. In 1881 the Cold Spring Water Co., a competing corporation, put in new works. In 1888 the older company sold out and in 1889 the Canajoharie Consolidated Water Co. was organized, receiving the property and franchises

of both companies. The catch basin was located on Canajoharie creek, three-fourths of a mile from the village center, the pond one-half mile and the reservoir one-quarter mile. The present village water supply system was inaugurated in 1912.

A union church was erected in 1818 and the Erie canal was built so close to it as to seriously interfere with services here. The Reformed church of Canajoharie (village) was organized in 1827 and a stone church was erected in 1842, which later was occupied by the Methodist society when the present handsome stone church was built in the latter part of the nineteenth century. St. Mark's Lutheran church was formed in 1839 and soon purchased the old Union church near the canal. The present attractive vine-covered church was built in 1870. St. John's German Evangelical Lutheran church was organized in 1835. The present stone church dates from 1871. In 1852 the Church of the Good Shepherd, Protestant Episcopal, was formed. Its present handsome stone church was erected in 1873. The Methodist Episcopal church socety had its birth on the opposite side of the river in Palatine where it built a church in 1828. It occupied the first Reformed church in 1841. In 1863 it was rebuilt and enlarged. St. Peter and St. Paul's Roman Catholic church was built in 1862.

The village has the beautifully situated Canajoharie Falls cemetery and a public library.

Hamilton lodge, No. 79, F. and A. M., received its charter in 1806, being at that time number ten in the list of state lodges. The first master was Dr. Joshua Webster. A number of other fraternal and social organizations are located in town. Among these is the Fort Rensselaer club, located in the old stone Van Alstine house (built 1750). At the public square is the monument commemorating Gen. Clinton's army's presence at Canajoharie in 1779, placed there by the local D. A. R.

Canajoharie's first newspaper was the Telegraph, started in 1825. Other papers have been: Canajoharie Sentinel, 1827; Canajoharie Republican, 1827; Montgomery Argus, 1831; Canajoharie Investigator, 1833; Canajoharie Radii, 1837; Mohawk Valley Gazette, 1847; Montgomery Union, 1850; Canajoharie Courier, 1879; Hay Trade Journal, 1892. The Radii, Courier and Hay Trade Journal are prosperous papers today.

The National Spraker bank was established as the Spraker bank in 1853. It was reorganized and incorporated under the national banking act of 1865. Its capital is $100,000. The Canajoharie National bank was first organized as a state bank in 1855 and became a national bank in 1865, with a capital of $100,000, which has been increased to $125,000.

The manufacture of and printing of paper and cotton sacks and bags was started in 1859 and the firm (Arkell & Smiths) is today one of Canajoharie's leading industries. The output is many·millions of sacks annually and 126 hands were employed in 1912.

The manufacture of food-stuffs by the Beech-Nut Packing Co. began, about 1890. The firm was then known as the Imperial Packing Co. and started business curing "Beech-Nut" hams and bacon. This has developed into one of the model pure food factories of the world, with an enormous and constantly increasing output. The employes are generally natives of Canajoharie and the industry is one in which Canajoharie justly takes the greatest pride. Its perfect factories are in sight from the Central railroad and Canajoharie has justly been termed "Beech-Nut Town." The output of this concern averages $3,000,000 yearly and 380 hands were employed in 1912.

Aside from these two leading industries there were 7 small factories in 1912 employing 23 hands. The total number of operatives in Canajoharie's manufactories in 1912 was 529. Palatine Bridge has one factory with 9 employes, so that there are 538 people employed in manufacturing in Canajoharie-Palatine Bridge.

Canajoharie village consists of a lower portion on the flats from which streets rise to hills of a considerable height, affording fine valley views. On the Seeber Lane road, a mile northwest from the town, is a U. S. Government geodetic survey station, at a sea elevation of 800 feet, or 500 feet above the Mohawk. From here may be obtained a fine panoramic valley view to the southeast, as well as one of the Cherry Valley hills to the west.

Canajoharie is a center of a steady trade with the farming country around about it including much of Montgomery and Schoharie county to the south and southwest of it. Together with Palatine Bridge, its sister village directly across on the north bank of the Mohawk, it forms an ideal residence community with all the features of trade, social, educational, industrial and agricultural life which go to make up a progressive twentieth century American village. It may justly be said that all these qualities are shared by the three sister villages of western Montgomery county — Canajoharie, Fort Plain and St. Johnsville, all of similar character, size and population. They all should experience a growth of population, industries, wealth and business and an educational and social development. Their situation and the sterling character of their inhabitants ensures these things for the future.

The 1912 Industrial Directory of the New York State Department of Labor contains the following regarding Canajoharie:

Canajoharie (Montgomery county), incorporated a village in 1829; estimated population in 1913, 2,325. Canajoharie is situated in the valley of the Mohawk river on the Erie canal and the West Shore railroad. The village of Palatine Bridge, on the New York Central railroad, is industrially and commercially an integral part of Canajoharie, a bridge over the Barge canal, which here follows the course of the Mohawk river, connects the villages. The principal industries are the manufacture of paper and cotton bags and the packing of food products. Canajoharie is surrounded by a rich farming section devoted to general agriculture [dairying and hay raising in particular].

Population of Canajoharie village, 1870, 1,822; 1890, 2,089; 1910, 2,273. 1910, Canajoharie - Palatine Bridge, 2,665.

Population Canajoharie township: 1850, 4,097; 1880, 4,294; 1910, 3,889.

The village life of these three western Montgomery county centers, during the past century, is described in the chapter devoted to Minden township and Fort· Plain, the central one of the three villages.

Buel is a hamlet in the southern part of the town of Canajoharie, the first settlement here having been made by John Bowman about 1760. He purchased a large tract of land near the headwaters of Canajoharie creek and, for over half a century thereafter (and during the Revolution), the stream, the settlement of Buel and a large part of the southern part of Canajoharie township were all known as "Bowman's Creek." In 1830 a postoffice was established at Buel. In 1823 the Central Asylum for the instruction of the deaf and dumb was established at Buel. In 1836 it was united with a similar institution in New York city. Buel took its name from Jesse Buel, at one time prominent in state agricultural circles.

Sprout Brook is a small hamlet and postoffice on the Canajoharie creek in the extreme southwestern part of the town. The history of its settlement is largely that of Buel and the Bowman's Creek section.

Ames, in the Canajoharie valley, two miles east of Buel, was named in honor of Fisher Ames. It is said that the first settler near here was named Taylor. In 1796, the Free Will Baptist church of Ames was located here, it having been organized, in 1794, a few miles to the west. Most of the early settlers of Ames were New Englanders, instead of being Germans as in most of the neighboring settlements, particularly in the immediate vicinity of the Mohawk river. Its population is estimated at about 200·

The early history of Mapletown has been mentioned in a previous chapter. It takes its name from the numerous sugar maples left standing by the pioneers. It is on the old Indian trail from Canajoharie to New Dorlach and about four miles from Canajoharie. Early in the nineteenth century a small

Dutch Reformed church was built here.

The little hamlet of Marshville is on the Canajoharie creek near the center of the town. Here in early days was a large saw mill owned by one of the Seeber family. How the place received the nickname of "Muttonville" is told in the first chapter on western Montgomery county. Population of Marshville, about 100.

Van Deusenville lies near Sprout Brook and Waterville, another little hamlet. between Ames and Mapletown.

The first school within present Canajoharie town was in Seebers Lane, on the north line of the Goertner farm, a mile and a half southwest of Canajoharie village. When the common school system was adopted this became district No. 1 of Canajoharie. The town is divided (1913) into fourteen school districts.

CHAPTER XV.

1825-1913—Western Montgomery County—Fort Plain Village and Minden Township.

The history of the town of Minden, from the time of the construction of the Erie canal to the date of the compiling of these articles, is largely its development in relation to agriculture and the part its men played in the great war of the rebellion.

The story of the village of Fort Plain, for a similar period, is typical of the development of Mohawk valley towns during the nineteenth century. It has also been the growth of the canal and market town of 1830 into the manufacturing village and farming community center of the twentieth century. At the completion of the great Barge canal work, it will undoubtedly regain its place as an "inland port," which it held before the decline of traffic on the Erie canal, due to railroad competition. Fort Plain was incorporated as a village in 1832. Like Canajoharie, Fort Plain is a "canal town"—that is, its early growth was largely the result of the great impetus to trade and commerce in the valley due to the construction of the Erie canal. The founding and development of industries, except on a small scale, came later. Through all the changes of the nineteenth century, it has remained a trading center for an important agricultural and dairying section. Situated at the mouth of the Otsquago valley and practically (by road) at the outlet of the Caroga valley, it has formed a center of trade for those two extensive natural thoroughfares and their adjacent country. With the present rapid improvement of the highways, its advantageous location will continue to be of marked aid to the trade centering about the town, and its projected Barge canal terminal will give it a position of prominence in the traffic of that great waterway. The Caroga valley road, a mile and a half north of Nelliston, leads north up the Caroga valley into the lakeland of northern Fulton county. The Otsquago valley roads, south into the Susquehanna valley, lead to Richfield Springs, Springfield Centre, Cooperstown, Cherry Valley and other points.

Fort Plain originally was a hamlet of a few houses, a hotel, store and mill, which grew up at the foot of Prospect Hill and along the south shore turnpike (now Willett street) and the Otsquago creek, which then ran along the flats to the foot of Fort Hill (or the eminence on which the fortification of Fort Plain stood), a half mile north of the business center of present Fort Plain. As we have seen, during the building of the Erie, the business concerns at Sand Hill, on the northern end of the present village, moved to the present business site. Fort Plain, as a hamlet, dates from about the building of the Canajoharie Reformed Dutch church on Sand Hill in 1750, when the nucleus of a little settlement was established here at the river ferry and the beginning of the Dutchtown road. Both Sand Hill and the Prospect Hill hamlets formed parts of the present Fort Plain village limits—about a square mile of territory.

Fort Plain and Nelliston form what is virtually one town as before stated. They are separated by the Mohawk river, Nelliston being on the north shore and Fort Plain on the south. Nelliston dates its growth from about 1850. The original river bridge connecting the present villages was built in 1829. The first Mohawk river bridge at Fort Plain was built across the Island in 1806. Nelliston is a beautiful residential section and is more adapted to the site of future residential growth of the two villages than Fort Plain itself. For articles relative to Fort Plain in connection with the building of bridges, highways, canals and railroads, turn to the separate chapters on these subjects.

Fort Plain lies partly on the flats and partly on the high ground rising to Prospect Hill on the east and to Institute and Cemetery Hill and Fort Hill on the west and north. It also extends up the Otsquago valley nearly a mile. Nelliston lies on a tableland on a small hill rising directly from the river.

Trade and business houses rapidly sprang up in Fort Plain, both before and immediately after the Erie was completed in 1825, and for a number of years it shared in the commerce of what was then a great water route of passenger and freight traffic. For years the Fort Plain canal docks were lively and busy places and continued as such up to about 1880, when the competition of the railroads began to be seriously felt. Since about that time the canal traffic has been rapidly falling off until now it is but a small fraction of its former volume and the same docks are practically deserted by canal men. Reference should be made to the chapter on the Erie canal for an idea of this phase of life in Fort Plain in the first half of the nineteenth century.

At this period and until the time railroads entered the country to the south of us, Fort Plain as a market and canal town and later a railroad town as well, drew a great amount of trade to itself from what is now Otsego county. Teams loaded with merchandise arrived from and departed for towns and settlements as far south as Oneonta and even beyond. Its position at the outlet. of this country, by way of the Otsquago valley, gave it a lively trade and these facts and its place as a station on the canal and railroad contributed to build up a solid business section much larger and more important than in most towns of its size. Indeed, in the days when the village only had half its present (1913) population, the business section was practically of its present area and importance. A man who lived in Minden in the 40s, made Fort Plain a visit in 1911 and to a query, by the writer, as to how the town looked to him, in comparison with the Fort Plain of his boyhood, he replied: "Oh, about the same." This is true of the business section but the manufacturing and residential portions have enlarged and changed to a marked extent from the town of the quoted man's youthful days. The size of stocks, completeness and enterprise of the stores of Fort Plain have been a matter of valley knowledge and local pride for almost a century.

Some of Fort Plain's merchants of the early and middle nineteenth century did an enormous business, considering the size of the village. Stocks were then carried which made Fort Plain the best shopping center between Schenectady and Utica. It was in those days that Fort Plain's business center was developed, a business section which presents a more metropolitan and citylike appearance than any town between Schenectady and Utica, not excepting Little Falls and Amsterdam, which are many times the size of Fort Plain. We talk of modern business methods but they are nowise superior to those of the early nineteenth century merchants.

From the beginning Fort Plain was an important market town. Manufacturing on any scale did not appear until the establishment of the Fort Plain Spring and Axle Works in 1870. These are said to have been the largest works of their kind in the country and are mentioned later. With the decline of agriculture hereabouts its importance as a market center diminished and its country trade was split up somewhat with other towns. The building of railroads in the Susquehanna valley attracted to southern railroad centers the trade which largely came north through the Otsquago valley to Fort Plain, as its natural outlet, prior to 1870.

The Utica and Schenectady railroad was completed in 1836 and the growing town of Fort Plain became a lively place on the new road. The original small station was later used as a hay barn and stood just to the south of the river bridge, on the Nelliston side, until about 1890. August 1, 1836, the day of the opening of the road, was a great event for Fort Plain as well as the rest of the Mohawk valley towns and crowds gathered to watch the first train pass. The new Central station and grounds is one of the model ones along the line and was built of stone in 1902.

The first newspaper in Fort Plain was the Fort Plain Watch Tower, established in 1827 or 1828. After many changes this became the Mohawk Valley Register in 1854. The Fort Plain Standard was established in 1876 and the Fort Plain Free Press in 1883. Other publications have been issued from time to time, the village at one time having a little-needed daily paper. The Clionian Argus, later the Clionian, was a monthly publication issued for over fifteen years (1883 1890) by one of the literary societies of Clinton Liberal Institute. The Register is (1913) Montgomery county's old est newspaper.

As has been stated, from the canal completion in 1825 until the Civil war period is the Fort Plain era of the development of business and transportation. This time was one of building and general village growth. Many large and imposing brick dwellings were erected, which today, with their generally attractive grounds, give an air of solidity and permanence to the village as a whole. This period was also one of broader social life in many ways, compared with today, and the homes were more generally the attractive scenes of social gatherings, often of considerable size. Later house construction, as a rule, has been of smaller dwellings of frame and these have been built in very closely toward the center of the town.

A public school was already located in the village when incorporated in 1832. The old wooden building, a veritable firetrap, was replaced in 1879 by the present brick structure, which has since been enlarged. In 1893 this was made into the Fort Plain High school, with a primary and grammar school department. A school conducted in the "Lockville" section was united with the main one at that time. A new site and building for the Fort Plain High school is now (1914) under consideration.

The Fort Plain Bank was organized Dec. 25, 1838. The National Fort Plain Bank was the name after a reorganization in 1864. The Farmers and Mechanics Bank, a state institution, was inaugurated 1887.

The Fort Plain Seminary and Collegiate Institute was erected in 1853, by a stock company with a capital of $32,000 and chartered by the regents of the university, Oct. 20 of that year. The first scholastic year of the institution began Nov. 7, 1853, with 513 students. Iu 1879 this large brick structure was remodeled into a still larger building of five stories and occupied by Clinton Liberal Institute, which removed here from Clinton. This was a school under the patronage of the Universalist denomination and continued to fill an important educational mission until it was unfortunately destroyed by fire in 1900. Instruction was given in academical, college preparatory and commercial courses and there was an important and largely attended fine arts department which schooled in music, elocution, and drawing and painting. In its latter years a military department was added and plans were on foot to make it exclusively a boys' military school when it was destroyed. It occupied a beautiful site of about ten acres on high ground and had, beside the main building, a gymnasium, a large armory and athletic field. Crowds came to witness the field sports and

the baseball and football matches in which this preparatory school frequently competed successfully with college teams. "C. L. I." was a center of culture for all the people of the middle Mohawk valley and its destruction was a great educational loss to not only Fort Plain, but a great area of country about it. Its park-like site was known first as "Seminary Hill" and later as "Institute Hill." An effort was made to have it converted into a public park and site for the High school, but this unfortunately failed of a majority in a village election held in 1909. Over 200 students were in attendance at C. L. I. during some years.

The town of Minden, including Fort Plain, bore its full share of the terrible cost, in lives and treasure, of the War of the Rebellion. Minden as a whole furnished 518 men at an expense, beside the county bounty, of $154,143. This is according to Beer's 1878 History. The Grand Army of the Republic is (1913) represented in Fort Plain by Klock Post, G. A. R., named after Capt. Klock of St. Johnsville. See the chapter on Montgomery county in the Civil war.

The construction of the West Shore railroad in 1883 made Fort Plain a station on the new line, which has lately been denominated South Fort Plain to differentiate it from the New York Central station and to avoid confusion among shippers. The completion of the West Shore railroad in 1883 was marked by a disastrous wreck on that road at Diefendorf Hill to the north of Fort Plain. Two passenger trains, scheduled to pass each other at the Fort Plain station at noon, collided through some misunderstanding of orders. Several lives were lost and the wreck was most spectacular, one of the engines being shoved upright into an almost perpendicular position. What was to have been a day of celebration was changed into one of gloom at Fort Plain. The wreck was viewed by large crowds of people.

Shortly before the completion of the West Shore, occurred a riot of Italian laborers and several of them were wounded by townspeople who broke up the gathering in front of the Zoller house, which they besieged, as in it was hidden the contractor who owed them their wages. The day was one of great excitement for Fort Plain.

About 1870 the Fort Plain Spring and Axle Works was established in Fort Plain, the business having been originally located in Springfield Centre. This was a large industry, employing a considerable force of men, many of them mechanics of the highest class earning high wages. This plant was the first important village manufacturing concern and its removal to Chicago Heights in 1894 was a distinct loss to the village for several years. Two important silk mills were located in Fort Plain in a period between about 1880 and 1884. The largest, located on Willett street, was burned in 1884 and this was an event temporarily disastrous to the town.

One of the largest Canal street firms doing business had its grain elevator and mill burned in a spectacular fire in 1883. After this date the canal business fell off rapidly. At present in the village of Fort Plain are industries devoted to the manufacture of furniture, knit goods, silk, toy wagons, paper boxes, broombands, lithographed tin, corn huskers, hose bands, can openers, pickles, cabinet and bookcase work, condensed milk and many minor industries.

The 1912 Industrial Directory of the State of New York issued by the Department of Labor gives the following manufacturing statistics relative to Fort Plain:

'Fort Plain (Montgomery county), incorporated as a village in 1832; estimated population in 1913, 2,857. Fort Plain is situated on the Mohawk river, the Erie [Barge] canal, and the West Shore railroad. The village of Nelliston, on the opposite [north] side of the river on the New York Central rail road, is a part of Fort Plain industrially. The principal manufactures are knit goods and furniture. The village is an important trading center for the surrounding country, which is devoted to dairy farming and general agriculture. Building stone is found in the vicinity of the village; there is considerable undeveloped water power within ten miles. [There is also the electric power derived from the power station of the Mohawk Hydro-Electric Co. by direct transmission line from Ephratah, six miles distant.] Fort Plain has a sewer system, municipal water works and electric lighting [and power] service.

Twenty-two manufactories with 737 employes. Those employing over 10 hands are, Bailey Knitting Mills, knit goods, 441; A. & C. A. Hix, furniture, 86; Duffy Silk Co., silk throwing, 52; Fort Plain Knitting Co., knit goods, 46; Empire State Metal Wheel Co., children's wagons, 21; Century Cabinet Co., bookcases, 16; Borden Condensed Milk Co., condensed milk (in Nelliston), 15; J. M. Yordon, paper boxes, 11. 14 small factories, 49. The principal industries are knit goods with 487 employes and furniture with 102 employes.

Fort Plain has gas and electric light. It also has electric power furnished by the Mohawk Hydro-Electric Co. The concern has rights to the use of the water in the Caroga lakes and is one of the few water power companies that has a dependable water supply, particularly during the summer months. The introduction of this power into Fort Plain in 1912 undoubtedly means much to the future industrial growth of this town, as it is claimed that power can be developed here as cheaply as anywhere in the east. The Mohawk Hydro-Electric company gave the free use of electricity to the merchants of Fort Plain during the street fair of 1912, which resulted in a brilliant electric display in the village streets, quite unique among the towns of the valley. See the chapter on western Montgomery county hydro-electric power development.

In 1884 a Woman's Literary society was organized in Fort Plain with a membership of about forty. Shortly after this organization was effected it was decided that the efforts of its members should be directed toward the establishment of a public library. With this idea in view a "book reception" has held at the home of one of its members, and a number of books and some contributions of money were received. It was resolved to work under the name of the Women's Library Association of Fort Plain and the constantly growing collection of books was housed at a number of places, until 1909 when the children of the late James H. Williams, in conjunction with Miss Sadie J. Williams, all of Brooklyn, gave the use of the house at the corner of River and Willett streets to the Fort Plain Public Library, which had been incorporated under that name. This was presented as a memorial to one of Fort Plain's first merchants, Harvey E. Williams, and his son, James H. Williams, who was born here. The library was also willed $1,000 by the late John Winning and $2,000 by the late Homer N. Lockwood. Aside from these library gifts, the Catherine Nellis Memorial chapel and a drinking fountain presented by the late Charles Tanner, are the only public benefactions to the people of Fort Plain within the writer's knowledge.

Fort Plain has many fraternal, social and church organizations. The Old Fort Plain band has been a high-class musical organization for a half century, and at one time the town had two bands. The volunteer fire department has generally maintained a high degree of efficiency. The Fort Plain club was originally organized as an athletic and social club of young men in 1891. It took in business men as members the same year and became a business men's social organization. The merchants and manufacturers of the town are organized under the title of the Associated Business Interests of Fort Plain. Fort Plain Lodge, No. 433, F. and A. M., was organized June 17, 1858.

A railroad, from Fort Plain to Richfield Springs and Cooperstown, has been agitated ever since an initial meeting of townspeople, to further that object, in 1828. In 1894 work was actually begun, a right of way having been obtained. Much of the road bed was constructed but the contractors failed and the project fell through.

In the fall of 1898 a number of Main street merchants got up, on the spur of the moment, a display of farm fruits and produce on the sidewalks in front of their stores, and this was the nucleus of the Fort Plain street fair, famed throughout Central New York. Great crowds come by horse and automobile conveyances and by trains from up and down the valley to this September carnival. Excellent displays of fruit, farm produce, field crops and poultry are held under canvas covered booths on the brick pavement of Canal and Main streets. As many as 50,000 visitors are estimated to have attended the fair, during the week in which it is held, and 15,000 are said to have been present on a single day. The management is vested with the Fort Plain Street Fair association and the necessary funds are raised by private subscriptions. Free attractions are annually offered and the crowds, while full of the fair and carnival spirit and addicted to much noise, are invariably orderly and arrests and petty crimes are almost unknown.

In the years from 1880 to 1910, Fort Plain established water, electric light and sewage systems. The water system was originally owned by a private company, with reservoir in Freysbush. The village instituted its own plant in 1895, with reservoir in Palatine, a mile northeast of the town. Its water is taken from North creek, a branch of the Caroga. In 1903 parts of Canal and Main streets were paved with brick and since that time the main thoroughfares have been so paved. About 1885 occurred the development of Prospect Hill as a residential section.

In 1911, Atwood, the aviator, made his epoch-making trip by aeroplane from St. Louis to New York. He landed in a field on the E. I. Nellis farm in Nelliston. This was his only overnight stop in the Mohawk valley which he used as his route from Syracuse to Castleton on the Hudson. He landed near Glen village, Montgomery county, on the day following his stop in Nelliston. The history of Nelliston it might be here remarked, is practically coincident with that of Fort Plain, since about 1850 when Nelliston began to grow into the pleasant and attractive town it now is. The date of Atwood's landing at Nelliston was Aug.

22, 1911. Atwood slept that night in
Fort Plain, where he was accorded, as
he said, the best reception of his whole
journey.

In 1911 the Fritcher opera house
was burned and the Fort Plain theatre
was erected in the same year. A U. S.
Government building, housing the
postoffice and costing, with site, $65,-
000, is provided for and will soon be
erected.

The following gives the known figures of the population of Fort Plain:
1825, 200; 1832, 400; 1860, 1,592; 1870,
1,797; 1880, 2,443; 1890, 2 864; 1900,
2,444; 1910, 2,762. Fort Plain and Nelliston, combined, population figures:
1880, 3,001; 1890, 3,585; 1900, 3,078;
1910, 3,499. Fort Plain and Nelliston
are virtually one community, on opposite sides of the Mohawk.

The following are the population figures for the town of Minden: 1850,
4,623; 1860, 4,412; 1870, 4,600; 1880,
5,100; 1890, 5,198; 1900, 4,541; 1910,
4,645

The Reformed society moved from
Sand Hill to Fort Plain and built a
church in 1834 on its present site.
This burned and in 1835 a structure,
long known as "the brick church," was
built which was repaired in 1872.
While these were building, the congregation used the church at Sand Hill,
but upon the completion of the brick
one the old structure to the west of
the village, was demolished. The ec-
clesiastical relations of this church are
with the classis of Montgomery and
through it with the General Synod of
the Reformed Church in America. In
1887 a new and architecturally important brick church was built by the
Reformed society and an adjoining
frame dwelling was purchased and became the parsonage.

The first Methodist class in Fort
Plain was formed, June 24, 1832. In
early times the Methodist services
were occasionally held in the Sand
Hill church, but more frequently in
the second story of a building that
stood near the Clark place on Upper
Canal street. When this building was
moved to a spot near the present Shin-

aman drug store, the Methodists continued its use as a meeting place.
Then for several years before 1842
services were held in what was at
that time the district school house,
which occupied the site of the present
one. The first Methodist church was
dedicated Feb. 20, 1845. In 1854 it
was enlarged and re-dedicated. In
1879, a large new brick structure was
erected on the old site. A Methodist
church (of frame construction) was
built in Nelliston in 1895.

The first Universalist society of
Minden was organized April 6, 1833,
and the first church was dedicated
Dec. 25, 1833. It was remodeled in
1855 and 1874. In 1896 the old frame
structure was torn down and a large,
brick church was erected on the site.

The (German) Lutheran church society held its first meetings in 1842 in
private houses. The first church
building was built in 1853. The present brick structure was completed in
1874. A Baptist society was formed
in 1891 and a brick church was built
in 1892. A Catholic frame church was
erected in 1887. An Episcopal church
was erected on Prospect Hill in 1887
and in 1899 was removed to the corner
of Lydius and Washington streets.

Fordsbush or Minden, in the southwest corner of the town of Minden,
has two churches, Lutheran and Universalist. The Universalist was organized in 1838 and the church was
enlarged and rebuilt in 1874.

The Freysbush Lutheran church was
organized in 1834. In 1841 a house of
worship was built, and a large team
shed adjoining in 1845. A parsonage
and barn were erected in 1868. Methodist services have been held in Freysbush since 1812, but the place did not
become an independent pastoral charge
until 1847. The church building of the
society is the second occupied by
them, its predecessor having been the
first Methodist church built in the
town of Minden.

The association managing the cemetery of Fort Plain was organized
March 4, 1864. It occupies, on the
heights in the northwest corner of the
village territory, a large and beautiful

location. The view of the valley obtained from it is very fine and this park-like burial place is one of the most important in Central New York. The stone Catherine Nellis Memorial chapel, of much beauty and architectural merit, is the gift of Mrs. H. H. Benedict of New York, in memory of her mother, and was erected in 1907.

Minden today is a prosperous dairying and farming section and it is famed for the beauty of its rolling hills and wooded valleys. Fort Plain has many advantages, and some disadvantages of location. In Prospect hill, it has a sightly viewpoint, the equal of which is not possessed by any valley town excepting Little Falls. The vistas opened up to a spectator on this hill are wide and exceedingly pleasing in their variety of river, canal, fertile fields and distant wooded hills. It is a valley section and a village with a situation and a setting, which offers unusual opportunities for the factory, for the dwellers in the town or on the fertile farms round about it.

Prospect Hill is a valley eminence and a little hill of the world—a place of today and of yesterday; though but of comparatively low elevation it has the breath of the far uplands and the clear upper summits of the Mohawk valley. Along its margins yet remain a few vestiges of the ancient forest, which covered this viewpoint and stretched away in every direction to the summits of the distant high hills in the days of the Mohawks. Here are oaks, elms, a few pines, and other of our noble native trees. To the southward Prospect Hill rises to a noble height of two hundred feet above the river. This portion of this upland was the Tarahjohrees, or "the hill of health" of the Mohawks, and its summit would be easily accessible, from the wooded little valley and brook (which lies just south of the southern limits of the village of Fort Plain and enters the Mohawk at the upper end of Nellis island) were it not for many barbed-wire fences intervening. From Prospect Hill one can easily imagine the valley as it was—perhaps as it will be—and view it as it is. Its aloofness suggests pictures of the past while its close proximity to village, railroads and canal, gives an intimate insight into the valley and village life of today. Its triangular bluff point, abutting on Otsquago creek should become a village park, to prevent its use for other purposes.

Mason's 1892 History of Montgomery County published the following on the town of Minden: "This is the southwest corner town of the county and lies on the south bank of the Mohawk. Its boundaries are formed by the Mohawk on the north, Canajoharie on the east, Otsego county on the south and Herkimer county on the west. The surface of Minden consists chiefly of an undulating upland with steep declivities bordering on the streams. Otsquago creek [which rises almost twenty miles away in Otsego county] flows in a northeasterly direction, receiving the waters of the Otsquene creek (its principal tributary) about the center of the town, and emptying into the Mohawk at Fort Plain. Otsquago is derived from the Mohawk word 'Oxsquago,' signifying 'under the bridge.' The other streams of the town are of minor importance. The branches of the Otsquago radiate largely through the greater part of the town." There are besides, eight small brooks running into the Mohawk to the north of Fort Plain. The largest of these is the picturesque one which flows through Oak Hill and alongside the Dutchtown road for a distance of four miles. One of the most interesting little brooks of Minden is the Little Woods creek, which flows through a pretty little valley along the northern side of the plateau on which stood old Fort Plain. This rivulet forms the northern limit of the village limits of Fort Plain. Just to the south of the village limits lies another little brook running from Prospect Hill into the Mohawk, and the 2½ square miles of Fort Plain's territory lie, generally speaking, between these two little streams. The greatest length of Minden from, northeast to southwest, is ten miles, and its greatest breadth, along the river is eight miles.

"The soil throughout the greater part of the town is a fine quality of gravelly and clayey loam, and is well adapted to grazing. In dairy products, Minden has always been in advance of the neighboring towns, and the cultivation of hops has also been an important feature in agricultural pursuit [but has now ceased to be.]" ˑ

Minden is said to be the largest producer of dairy products of the five towns of the famous dairying section of western Montgomery county. Like the balance of western Montgomery county, hay, oats and corn are the principal crops. The Fort Plain Milk Co. controls (1914) a number of dairies and the milk from 3,000 cows.

"Much interest is added to the history of Minden by the fact that it contains the remains of one of those ancient fortifications, which are not uncommon in central and western New York, but are rare in the eastern part of the state. They indicate that the country was inhabited long prior to the advent of the [Iroquois] Indians, and, with the exception of similar remains recently discovered in Ephratah, are the farthest east thus far discovered even by the geologist. They are situated four miles south of Fort Plain on a promontory ["Indian Hill" on the Otsquene, a half mile from its junction with the Otsquago], 100 feet above the stream, the declivities being almost precipitous. Across the promontory, at its narrowest part, is a curved line of breastworks, 240 feet in length, enclosing an area of about seven acres. A gigantic pine, six feet in diameter, stands upon the embankment, giving added proof that the work must have been of great antiquity." The facts here given concerning this prehistoric Indian site are credited to "Smithsonian Contributors," Vol. 2, article 6.

Indian Hill is a most interesting place, well worthy a visit, and evidencing markedly the picturesque beauty of the Otsquago valley. Many Indian remains (pottery, arrowheads, etc.) have been here uncovered.

Minden has the following hamlets within its borders: Mindenville, Minden, Hallsville, Brookmans Corners, Salt Springville (part in Minden and part in Otsego county), and Freysbush. Its elevation above the sea ranges from about 300 feet, at the Mohawk at Fort Plain, to 986 feet at Salt Springville. Between the sites of Fort Windecker and Fort Willett the land is 894 feet elevation. Oak Hill has an elevation above the Mohawk of 500 feet and Prospect Hill of over 100 feet. A furlong or more below the village limits curious spurs or small, sharp "noses" abut on the flatlands. One of these is over 200 feet above the river and the Erie canal is almost at its feet. A magnificent view up and down the valley for a distance of twelve miles or more is here obtained and this is probably the highest ground so close to the river between Fall Hill and the Noses. A point on the Seebers Lane road, a mile south of the village on the Canajoharie-Minden line, has an elevation of 500 feet or more above the Mohawk and a sea level elevation of over 800 feet. This is probably the highest land near the village. From all these sightly points magnificent views may be obtained. They are the principal elevations of the eastern end of the town lying along the river, from which they may be readily seen.

However, the beauty of Minden scenery is not alone in these lofty lookouts but also along the Otsquago, in the woodlands, and on the upland meadows where graze the peculiarly marked and belted Holstein-Frisian cattle, making curious spots of black and white on a background of attractive landscape. The numerous farms, with their buildings, may generally be objects of pride to the people of Minden.

───

Miss Margaret B. Stewart is the author of the following paper on "The Founding of Fort Plain:"

"Long before Fort Plain [the present village] was even thought of and before the Erie canal was dreamt of, there were but few residents who owned the soil on which Fort Plain now stands. The mercantile, postoffice and other business was transacted at Sand Hill. 'Pingster Day' was a great holiday for the slaves. They had a peculiar dance they called 'To-to' dance, which always met at Wagner's tavern, and as [this part of] Fort Plain had no name, it was commonly known as 'To-to-ville' and next as Wagnersville [probably from the tavern]. Just as soon as the project of the canal became a fact, the ground for a village was surveyed and staked out, a map drawn, and, before the canal was finished, the sale of lots began and immediately buildings were erected, ready for business on the canal. At this period there were no churches, no halls, and all the ground from Mohawk and Canal streets up to the Crouse bluff was vacant, up as far as Abeel's along the canal [with the exception of a few buildings as noted in previous chapters].

"Religion and politics ran high for those were stormy days. As I said before, there were no churches then, and the Methodists, Dutch Reformed and Universalists held their meetings in the schoolhouse, which stood on its present site. First one would occupy it, then the other, and the other. The doctrine of the Universalists was new to Fort Plain, and the orthodox opened fire on them and threw hot shell into their camp, and the Universalists fired back. Each tried to hold the fort and a fierce discussion in the schoolhouse, in the streets, stores and shops was kept up, which entirely divided the community—a kind of cat and dog religion. The Methodists brought out their heaviest gun—Elder Knapp, one of the most popular and redhot revivalists in the state. He hurled the Universalists into hell, without giving them time to pull off their boots. The Dutch Reformed brought on their big gun, Ketcham of Stone Arabia, who helped kindle hell's fire and get it boiling. Then the Universalists got Dr. Skinner, of Utica, with a cartload of ice and put out the fire. So it went and the people took sides and the schoolhouse was too small. The result was that the Universalists built their church and the Dutch Reformed built

their church — a frame building — on the site where the brick building now stands. The churches were built and finished at the same time and were to be dedicated the same day.

"The night before dedication, the Dutch Reformed church burned down, but money was raised and a brick church was erected on the same spot. Next came up the subject of incorporating the village, and in 1831 there was no opposition, except in the name. Some wanted the village named Fort Plank and others Fort Plain. Finally Fort Plain was agreed upon and on the 25th of April, 1832, the village was incorporated."

———

Fort Plain was the home of George W. Elliott and Jeptha R. Simms, both known through their literary labors.

Jeptha R. Simms was born in Canterbury, Conn., Dec. 31, 1807. His father, Capt. Joseph Simms, removed to Plainfield, N. Y., in 1824. Beginning 1826, J. R. Simms was a clerk in Canajoharie, for three years, going from there to New York city. In the fall of 1832 he returned to Canajoharie and went into business with Herman I. Ehle, a former employer. After a clerkship for a time in Schoharie, Mr. Simms set about collecting the scattered materials for his "History of Schoharie County and Borders Wars of New York," published in 1845. In 1846 he published a Revolutionary tale entitled the "American Spy" and, in 1850, the "Trappers of New York." In 1882 was issued his "Frontiersmen of New York," in two volumes, dealing with Mohawk valley history, principally of the Revolution, and particularly with that of the neighborhood immediately adjacent to Fort Plain. It is largely owing to his labors that so much of local record has been preserved. Mr. Simms died in Fort Plain in 1883, aged 76 years.

Simms lived in Fultonville for a number of years and while there published his "Border Wars" in 1845; and also erected a very handsome residence built of cobblestones, every one of which he gathered in the vicinity and for the outside course he sized them through a hole in a board to have them uniform. This dwelling, still in fine condition, is in possession of Starin Industrial and Benevolent association and called Cobblestone Hall.

. George W. Elliott was a resident of Fort Plain in the sixties ahd married Mary Bowen, daughter of Solomon Bowen, who for years conducted Montgomery Hall (later the Lipe House), which was remodeled into the present building of the Farmers and Mechanics Bank. Elliott was editor of the (Fort Plain) "Mohawk Valley Register" for a time and wrote much pleasing poetry. His best known production is "Bonny Eloise, the Belle of the Mohawk Vale," which has become the song of the valley. It is said he composed the words to this popular melody while on a railroad journey from New York to Fort Plain, addressing his song to his sweetheart, Mary Bowen (with a change of name). The work bears copyright date of 1858 and J. R. Thomas was the composer of the plaintively sweet melody to which Mr. Elliott's words are sung. The lyric follows:

Bonny Eloise.

Oh, sweet is the vale where the Mo-
    hawk gently glides
On its clear winding way to the sea,
And dearer than all storied streams on
    earth besides
Is this bright rolling river to me.

(Chorus)

But sweeter, dearer, yes dearer far
    than these,
Who charms where others all fail,
Is blue-eyed, bonny, bonny Eloise,
The belle of the Mohawk vale.

Oh, sweet are the scenes of my boy-
    hood's sunny years,
That bespangle the gay valley o'er,
And dear are the friends seen through
    memory's fond tears
That have lived in the blest days of
    yore.

(Chorus)

Oh, sweet are the moments when
    dreaming I roam
Thro' my loved haunts now mossy
    and grey,
And dearer than all is my childhood's
    hallowed home,
That is crumbling now slowly away.

(Chorus)

Lossing wrote, in 1848, concerning Fort Plain and its surrounding country, as follows, in his "Pictorial Field Book of the American Revolution:"

"Fort Plain (at the junction of the Otsquago creek and the Mohawk) one of the numerous comely children brought forth and fostered by the prolific commerce of the Erie canal, is near the site of the fortification of that name erected in the Revolution.
* * * * * *

"At Fort Plain I was joined by my traveling companions, * * * and made it my headquarters for three days, while visiting places of interest in the vicinity. It being a central point in the hostile movements - in Tryon county, from the time of the flight of St. Leger from before Fort Stanwix until the close of the war, we will plant our telescope of observation here for a time, and view the most important occurrences within this particular sweep of its speculum. * * *

"Who that has passed along the Valley of the Mohawk, near the close of a day in summer, has not been deeply impressed with the singular beauty of the scene? Or who, that has traversed the uplands, that skirt this fruitful garden, and stretch away to other valleys, and mingle with the loftier hills or fertile intervals within the borders of ancient Tryon county, is not filled with wonder while contemplating the changes that have been wrought there within a life-span? When the terrible drama, which we have been considering, was performed almost the whole country was covered with a primeval forest. Clearings were frequent along the Mohawk river and cultivation was assiduous in producing the blessings of abundance and general prosperity; but the southern portions of Herkimer and Montgomery, * * * [much of] Schoharie and all of Otsego, down to the remote settlements of Unadilla, were a wilderness except where a few thriving settlements were growing upon the water courses. The traveler as he views the 'field joined to field' in the Mohawk valley, all covered with waving grain, green pastures, or bending fruit trees, inclosing, in their arms of plenty, elegant mansions; or watches the vast stream of inland commerce that rolls by upon the Erie Canal; or the villages of people that almost hourly sweep along its margin after the vapor steed; or rides over the adjacent hill country, north and south, enlivened by villages and rich in cultivation, can hardly realize the fact that here, seventy years ago, the wild Indian was joint possessor of the soil with the hardy settlers, and that the light of civilization was as scattered and feeble, and for a while as evanescent and fleeting, in these broad solitudes, as is the sparkle of a firefly on a summer evening.. Yet such is the wonderful truth; and as I passed down the canal, at the close of the day, from Fort Plain to Fultonville, surrounded with the activity, opulence and beauty of the Mohawk valley, I could not, while contrasting this peacefulness and progress with the discord and social inertia of other lands, repress the feelings of the Pharisee."

On the streets of Fort Plain, those who look aloft see, silhouetted against the sky, a giant elm on the crest of Prospect Hill—a presiding spirit of the hill and of the village—a landmark known to all who dwell or have dwelt within its range. Under its great branches one may view for miles the quiet valley and the Mohawk winding northward. Truly it is a spirit of the hill, the town and the valley for it has been a silent witness of all the many changes of animal and plant life along the Mohawk from the day when the dusky Iroquois sped in his bark canoe upon the rippling waters till that eventful evening when a bird man came flying high over the glooming hills from the far westward. For this noble tree must have graced this spot from the day when the very first white settler made his forest home within sight of "Tahraghjorees, 'the hill of health,'" well beloved of the Mohawks. Here came the first Dutch traders, of whom we have a record, to the Iroquois village of Osquago and

here they were well received by its chieftain, Ognoho, "the wolf."

The big tree of Tahraghjorees has been a witness of the coming of the Dutch, German and British; it has seen the destruction of that immense forest, of which it was once a unit, and with it the passing of the Mohawks who dwelt upon its hill.

Now from this great elm have been visible many sights of interest to all our people. Let these visions arise once more in fleeting succession:

Here come the first white men toiling with poles to push their laden flatboats up stream to their future woodland homes; some driving their cattle and carts along the river trails.

Many of these same pioneers, with their women and children, later flee eastward, for the French and Indians have burned the village at German Flatts and murdered its people.

Long lines of soldiers stream up and down the turnpike at the foot of the hill, going to and returning from battles with the Canadian French and Indians. Here come ten thousand soldiers—militia and regulars—marching slowly up the valley; drums beat, trumpets sound, arms and red coats glitter in the sunlight; on the river the batteaux slowly creep westward bearing army supplies and munitions. It is General Amherst's great army on its way to capture Montreal and Canada from the French.

On a hill to the west sturdy Germans are building the blockhouses and stockade of old Fort Plain.

Up the valley march the patriot farmers on their way to the gory field of Oriskany; back come the straggling survivors, carrying their wounded comrades in litters and on river boats.

The green summer landscape is spotted with the fire and smoke of burning buildings, while Brant and his merciless savages are raiding over the Minden hills; distant tiny figures are fleeing toward the fort; bands of naked, yelling brutes are in chase, striking down bloodily those they catch.

Here comes a great column of American soldiers; Van Rensselaer is riding at their head; they beg him to lead on to Stone Arabia where smoke is rising from the fires set by Johnson's raiders; the listless general, unheeding, rides on to the fort to fill his stomach to the full; his men cursing cross the river at the island and chase the foe up the river; the red and white savages escape in the night.

A rider gallops furiously along the turnpike, plunges through the creek and up to the fort; drums beat and a battalion of fighting men come swarming like bees from out a hive; there they go rapidly tramping by to the field of Johnstown; at their head rides the big, powerful figure of Marinus Willett.

Washington and Clinton, with their escort of Continental officers, ride out from old Fort Plain over the trail to Otsego lake.

Now come the settlers' caravans, the "prairie schooners," rolling to the distant west over the valley highways; great flat-wheeled freight wagons crawl slowly eastward and westward. The first mail stagecoach comes rattling cheerily up the southern turnpike. Its arrival is a lively event to the valley folk. People go to the tavern to see if the stage has brought them letters or newspapers.

Men are tearing down the fort on the distant hillside; farmers are drawing away its timbers and palisades.

Up the river, at the Island, the sturdy valley men are making the first bridge in sight across the Mohawk.

River boats, heavily laden with arms and supplies, move laboriously up the Mohawk. Columns of the men of 1812 march to the westward to defend the New York frontier from British invasion; many sons of the valley are in the ranks.

Myriads of tiny figures are digging a great ditch parallel with the river, in which to float greater freight and passenger boats; they are changing the channel of the Otsquago at the foot of the hill; streets are being laid out, dwellings and stores are going up on the flatlands, where before were but a few scattered houses; the noise of building is heard all the day long.

A railroad has been built on the east or "north" bank of the Mohawk; crowds of people gather at the Fort Plain station to watch the first trains go by, crowded with cheering travelers; all make this a great holiday.

Men are stringing wires on poles along the railroad; to the incredulous watchers they say men will signal and talk through the tiny metal wire.

Drums are beating in the valley below; crowds are watching the "boys in blue" marching to entrain for southern battlefields where northern brother will clash with southern brother; ere long the black hearse wends its way up the hillside to the white, monument-dotted cemetery, bearing one killed in this dread war; sorrowing women, children and men follow to the soldier's grave, where on Decoration day waves a tiny flag of red, white and blue.

Brick factories arise on the river flats.

Another railroad is being made along the south or "west" bank of the river; here and there are clusters of shanties, housing the brawny, swarthy men who do the necessary vigorous labor.

The first automobile whirls through the village streets; it becomes one of the many nine-day wonders the valley people have seen.

Men raise a great dam and lock of cement across the Mohawk, filling the stream to its bank tops; where, in the old days the Indian canoe danced on the dark waters and the laden batteaux slowly floated, great barges will glide from lakes to ocean and from ocean to lakes.

Out of the summer evening sky to the north a great bird shape comes sailing and drops on a Palatine meadow. People run madly to greet its man pilot.

From the northern hills comes a line of great wires, strung on iron pillars, running across the fields and through the opposite village to Fort Plain, bringing the electric power generated by the waters of the Caroga—power which, in the future, will supplant coal, which will heat and light and furnish the energy to turn the humming factory wheels of the town.

On the hills is in evidence much of the agricultural detail of these broad rolling farmlands, stretching miles away to the far horizon—the roads, fields, crops, woods, farmhouses, barns and herds—the living moving dots of people and animals seeming no larger than the tiny ants scurrying about in the grass at our feet. The loaded haywagon moves slowly toward the big barn on the distant hilltop; the milk wagon rattles along the road with its load bound for the village creamery or condensed milk factory; countless automobiles glide swiftly along the turnpikes; the farm boy and his dog drive homeward the black and white cattle at nightfall; the evening sun casts it orange radiance on the eastern hills—here and there a farmhouse window glows like a point of living fire.

Down in the valley are all the signs of busy village life; the dawn breaks over the Palatine hills through the gray river mist; a few people walk about in the streets; smoke rises from the chimneys in the houses where breakfast is cooking; factory whistles blow; workers are going to their tasks; a storekeeper unlocks his store door and waits upon the farmer who has just driven into town; the schoolbell rings; children troop to their daily lessons, singly and in little groups; tiny dark figures, motor cars, dot the brick pavements; farm wagons cross the river bridge and come rapidly down the Otsquago road; trains whistle, they rush by, east and west, some stopping at the stations; school is out and the happy youngsters skip to play or dawdle homewards; a solitary canal boat floats into sight on the Erie; a tug is unloading goods on the once busy docks; workers come from their toil; lights are lit and crowds are astir along the bright thoroughfares; a black mass of people gathers at the street corner and the sound of a band playing comes softly to the hilltop—it is "Bonnie Eloise" the musicians are playing; black night comes on; the moon rises and illumines the twin pale strips of river and canal; lights blot out in the house and the town, the people, the countryside go to sleep; the night wind softly stirs the branches of the great tree.

It is Sunday; the village church bells ring clangingly, ponderously; a knell for the past, brave notes for the now and the days to come; couples of young people climb the hill, clad in their best; the father, the mother and the children slowly walk to the summit; they refresh themselves with a view of the broad stretches of the valley and the winding river.

Many human animals have seen this changing panorama in the years gone by; most have lived, some happily and some unhappily, and have gone to their long rest on the distant hilltop.

The big elm, too, saw all that makes up the human story of old Fort Plain and of the winding valley; its great branches still stand against the sky; its message—"I have seen it all; I shall see much that is to come."

APPENDIX

MOHAWK VALLEY CHRONOLOGY

The following list of dates forms a chronology of the Mohawk valley and its six counties of Oneida, Herkimer, Montgomery, Fulton, Schoharie and Schenectady. The editor of this work has found it impossible to secure dates of secondary importance, which will explain their absence to those who think they should have been included. All the dates of the main events of importance in the history of the Mohawk valley are here included:

1524—John de Verezzano, Italian navigator, enters harbor of New York; possibly first discoverer of territory of New York.

1540—French fur traders build trading post on Castle Island, in Hudson, near Albany; destroyed by freshet same year and abandoned.

1604—Canada's first permanent white settlement made at Port Royal, Nova Scotia, by the French.

1608—Champlain settles Quebec.

1609—Champlain and Canadian Indians defeat Mohawks on west shore of Lake Champlain, near Ticonderoga, making Mohawks lasting enemies of the French.

1609—Sailors from the Dutch ship, Half Moon, pass the mouth of the Mohawk.

1614—Dutch trading post established at Castle Island, near Albany.

1614—Probable first visit of white men (two Dutch traders) who came up the Mohawk and went south to Otsego, probably by way of the Otsquago.

1615—Champlain's expedition against the Iroquois defeated in the Onondaga country.

1616—First French-Canadian priests enter Mohawk valley on missionary work.

1621—Dutch West India Company formed, taking possession of New Netherlands.

1624—First permanent settlement of Albany; Fort Orange built; New Amsterdam (New York) settled permanently same year.

1626—New Netherlands (embracing New York and New Jersey) made a province or county of Holland.

1634—Three Dutch traders from Fort Orange journey on the south side of Mohawk river through western Montgomery county. They visited eight Mohawk villages from the Big Nose to opposite Caroga creek, seven on the south and one on the north side of the Mohawk river.

1646—Jogues, French Jesuit priest, put to death by Mohawks. Shrine at Auriesville, Montgomery county, marks this event.

1658—Four settlers said to have been located at Schenectady—Van Slyck, Lindsay, Glen and Teller. Place said to have been occupied by white men at and before 1642.

1659—Council at Caughnawaga between Dutch and Mohawks; first held in the valley.

1661—Schenectady settled by Dutch; historically regarded as the first white settlement in Mohawk valley, although Schenectady was settled by white men before this date.

1664—New Netherlands captured by the English. Name changed to New York. New Amsterdam renamed New York and Fort Orange renamed Albany.

1666—French and Indians destroy Mohawk villages; Mohawks escape.

1669, August 18—Mohawks defeat Mohicans in battle at Towereune, near Hoffmans, Schenectady county, ensuring Mohawk control of valley.

1670 (about)—Jan Mabie stone house built at Rotterdam, Schenectady county; oldest existing structure in Mohawk valley.

1673—Dutch retake New York state from the English.

1674—Dutch turn over New York again to the English.

1682 — Reformed Dutch church of Schenectady built; later demolished.

1689—Mohawks and Iroquois raid Canada and Montreal.

1689—Hendrick Frey and family settle at Palatine Bridge.

1689-1697—First French-British war in America, known as King William's war.

1690—Schenectady burned and people massacred by French and Indians; neighborhood repopulated soon after.

1692—French-Indian war party attacked and burned Oneida castle. The Onondagas, fearing attack, burned their villages and retreated to the wilderness.

1693—French-Indian-Canadian expedition, under Count Frontenac, attacks, captures and burns the three Mohawk castles; hard fight at upper castle; 300 Mohawks made prisoners; Albany militia, under Col. Peter Schuyler, pursued and retook 50 captives.

1698—White population of Mohawk valley estimated at 300, mostly in Schenectady county.

1700—Vrooman house (brick) Schenectady city, built.

1700—Schenectady fort rebuilt. It was originally destroyed in the massacre of 1690. It was later rebuilt and strengthened in 1735 and in 1780.

1701-1713 — Second French-British war in America, known as Queen Anne's war.

1709—Four Mohawk chiefs, of whom King Hendrick was one, accompany Col. Peter Schuyler of Albany to England; received by Queen Anne; object of trip to ally Iroquois closely to England.

1710 — Three Mohawk chiefs and Schuyler return from England to Albany; one chief dies on trip; council at Albany at which Iroquois renew allegiance to England.

1711—Fort Hunter built.

1712—Queen Anne's (Episcopal) chapel built at Fort Hunter for religious instruction of Indians; stone parsonage built and still standing; chapel destroyed in building Erie canal, 1817-1825.

1713—Glen Sanders house, Scotia, Schenectady county, built; oldest large house standing in the valley.

1713 (about)—First settlement by Palatine Germans at Stone Arabia and on Schoharie creek.

1713 (about)—First church of logs, built at Stone Arabia—Stone Arabia Reformed Dutch church.

1714—Tuscaroras, driven by whites out of Carolinas, settle among Iroquois, who become Six Nations after this date.

1723, Oct. 19—Stone Arabia patent of 12,700 acres granted to 27 heads of families, nearly all Palatine Germans.

1725—Burnetsfield patent granting land to Palatine German settlers, from Little Falls to Frankfort; this year found the Mohawk valley settled along the river by Germans from the Noses westward to Frankfort; also the Schoharie valley settled by Germans and Dutch; eastern end of Mohawk valley settled by Holland Dutch.

1730—Major Glen house, Scotia, Schenectady county, built.

1735—Governor Yates brick house, Schenectady city, built.

1738—William Johnson settles in Florida, Montgomery county, and builds Fort Johnson (first house of three).

1738-42—Sir George Clarke, governor of province of New York, builds a stone house on site of Fort Plain and lives there parts of four years.

1739—Fort Frey (stone) built at Palatine Bridge; oldest house in Palatine.

1742—Fort Johnson (stone house) built, town of Amsterdam, Montgomery county. This was first named Mount Johnson and later called Fort Johnson, when fortified; this has made considerable confusion between Johnson's first two houses.

1743—Butler frame house, Mohawk town, Montgomery county, built.

1743-1748—Third French-British war

in America, known as King George's war.

1745—William Johnson appointed justice of peace of Albany county and colonel of Albany county militia; sets about organizing Mohawk valley militia; appointed commissioner of Indian affairs for New York province.

1746, August 4—Party sent by Col. William Johnson against French and Indians, ambushed at Chambly.

1748—Battle of Beukendaal, Schenectady county, between valley militia and Canadian Indians; militia ambuscaded, defeated; 30 killed, 13 captured.

1750—Van Alstine stone house built on Canajoharie creek (probably oldest in town of Canajoharie).

1750—Colonel William Johnson made one of governor's council.

1754—Commissioners from the colonies attend a Colonial conference at Albany, to discuss colonial defense against French; said to be the first step in the formation of the United States; Col. Wm. Johnson and King Hendrick and delegation of Iroquois attend; King Hendrick makes famous speech.

1754-1763 — Fourth French-British war in America, known as the Seven Years war. Officially it lasted from 1756-1763—but in America it began in 1754 and ended in 1760.

1755—Fort Canajoharie built at present Indian Castle (Herkimer county) to protect Mohawks at Canajoharie castle.

1755—Major-General William Johnson in command of British-American army defeats French in Battle of Lake George; 250 Mohawk warriors in force; King Hendrick, Mohawk chief killed. Johnson made a baronet and reappointed Indian superintendent.

1756—Fort Klock (stone house) built in town of St. Johnsville, Montgomery county.

1756—Fort Herkimer erected. Fort Herkimer (Herkimer county) stone Reformed Dutch church completed; oldest church standing in Mohawk valley and probably second oldest in state (Sleepy Hollow church antedating it).

1756—Gen. Webb with British regiment and supplies passes up Mohawk valley to reinforce Fort Oswego; French capture fort; Webb returns; Johnson with militia and Indians returns.

1756, August—Gen. Johnson leads militia and Indian party to join Gen. Webb's relief expedition for Fort William Henry, on Lake George; expedition fails; Fort William Henry is captured by French.

1756, Nov. 12—French and Indians destroy Palatine village at present Herkimer, and massacre inhabitants.

1758—French and Indian attack at Fort Herkimer (Herkimer county) repulsed.

1758—April—Col. William Johnson calls together the Mohawk valley militia at Canajoharie (Fort Plain) to repel invasion of French and Indians at Fort Herkimer. Enemy fled. The valley militia were with their commander (later Sir William Johnson) in many of his military expeditions in the French-Indian war, 1754-1763.

1758, July 8—Sir William Johnson and 400 Iroquois warriors join Gen. Abercrombre's English army at Ticonderoga where the army of 7,000 British and 9,000 provincial troops were totally defeated.

1758—Fort Stanwix (Rome) built.

1759, Jan. 18—Conference of Mohawk and Seneca chiefs with Sir William Johnson at Canajoharie Castle. In April, at same place, Iroquois pledge their assistance to Johnson's expedition against Fort Niagara; 700 warriors later follow Johnson to victory at this place.

1759—British-American army under Sir William Johnson captures French Fort Niagara; 700 Iroquois warriors and body of militia with Johnson.

1759—St. George's Episcopal church, Schenectady, built.

1759—Johnstown founded by Sir William Johnson.

1760, June 12—Gen. Amherst's British American army of 10,000 (6,000 provincials, 4,000 regulars) leaves Schenectady and passes up valley en route to Montreal, which it captures, ending French power in America;

army's supplies and munitions go
north on Mohawk river. Sir William
Johnson later joins expedition with
1,300 Iroquois warriors in his force.
Amherst's army largest ever in Mohawk valley.

1760—First white settlement in Oneida county by Johannes Roof. Settlement abandoned in 1777. Johannes
Roof jr., first white child born in Oneida county, born this year.

1763—Caughnawaga (Fonda), Montgomery county, Reformed Dutch
parsonage built. Church erected 1763;
pulled down in 1868.

1763—Johnson Hall, Johnstown, Fulton county, built; Sir William Johnson
removes from Fort Johnson (first called Mount Johnson), to Johnson Hall,
now owned by New York state.

1764—Herkimer (brick) house built
by (General) Nicholas Herkimer at
Danube, Herkimer county; now owned
by state.

1765—Campbell house, Schenectady
city, built.

1766—Guy Park, stone house, Am-
sterdam, Montgomery county, built by
Sir William Johnson for his nephew,
Guy Johnson.

1768—Council between Sir William
Johnson, British colonial authorities
and Iroquois at Fort Stanwix in which
Six Nations relinquish large part of
their lands to British Crown.

1769—Indian Castle, Herkimer county, frame church built, largely for Mohawk Indians' instruction.

1770—Palatine Evangelical Lutheran
(present stone) church built.

1772 — Schoharie Reformed Dutch
church built at Schoharie Court
House; used as Revolutionary American post—known as the Lower Fort.

1772—Formation of Tryon county
and the districts of Mohawk, Canajoharie, Palatine, German Flats and
Kingsland. Canajoharie, on south
side, and Palatine, on north side, extended from the Noses to Little Falls.
Johnstown made county seat; jail and
court house built. Population of whole
Mohawk valley estimated at about
15,000; Tryon county, over 10,000.

1774—First patriotic meeting in
Tryon county, held in Palatine.

1774—Sir William Johnson dies at
Johnstown; was major-general of New
York militia and Indian superintendent
for all British American colonies; son,
Sir John Johnson succeeds to his es-
tate of 173,000 acres.

1775-1783 — American Revolution of
the thirteen British-American colonies; independence declared.

1775—Formation of Palatine Committee of Safety at home of Adam
Loucks in Palatine (first committee of
safety in Tryon county).

1775, May 24 — First meeting of
Tryon County Committee of Safety
held at William Seeber's in Canajoharie district at later Fort Plain.

1775, June 11—Tryon County Committee of Safety at Gose Van Alstine's house, in Canajoharie, appoints
Christopher P. Yates and John Marlatt
as delegates to New York Provincial
Congress.

1775—Col. Guy Johnson and large
body of Mohawk Indians and Tories
leave the valley for Canada.

* 1775—Liberty pole erected by Fort
Herkimer patriots; later cut down by
Tory Sheriff White.

1776, Jan. 18—Gen. Schuyler and
force meets Col. Herkimer and the
Tryon County militia at Caughnawaga;
review held there on the ice on Mohawk river.

1776, Jan. 19—Gen. Schuyler's and
Col. Herkimer's American forces disarm Johnson and 400 Tories at Johnstown.

1776—Fort Plain and Fort Plank
(town of Minden) built; Fort Dayton
built; Fort Herkimer, Fort Stanwix
(renamed Fort Schuyler), Fort Hunter
repaired and rebuilt; Johnstown jail
made Fort Johnstown.

1776—Sir John Johnson and Tory
followers escape from Johnstown to
Canada, as Col. Dayton's American
party enters town to capture them.

1776, August 22—Tryon county brigade of American militia organized.
Nicholas Herkimer made chief colonel.

1777—Fort Paris, in Palatine, Fort
Clyde (in Freysbush district of Minden), Fort Windecker in Minden, built;
three Schoharie valley forts—upper,
middle and lower—constructed; Upper

Fort near Brakabeen; Middle Fort near Middleburg; Lower Fort at Schoharie.

1777, May—Gen. Nicholas Herkimer and the Tryon County Militia go from Fort Plain to Cherry Valley to Otsego lake to hold conference with Joseph Brant and his Indian army at Unadilla, with the idea of winning the Indians to the American cause or making them neutral. The conference is ineffectual and battle is narrowly avoided.

1777, August 2—Fort Schuyler (garrisoned by 750 Americans under Col. Peter Gansevoort) invested by British-Tory-Indian army under General St. Leger (1,600 men).

1777, August 4—Tryon county militia, commanded by Brig.-Gen. Nicholas Herkimer, starts march from Fort Dayton to relieve Fort Schuyler.

1777, August 6—American national flag—the stars and stripes—first flown in battle over Fort Schuyler.

1777, August 6—Battle of Oriskany between Tryon county American militia and St. Leger's British army; Willett's sortie; drawn battle; 200 British-Tories-Indians killed or wounded; 200 Americans killed or wounded; General Herkimer mortally wounded; Tryon county militia retreats to Fort Herkimer; bloodiest and hardest fought Revolutionary battle.

1777, August 8—Col. Willett and Lieut. Stockwell start from Fort Schuyler for Gen. Schuyler's headquarters at Stillwater, on the Hudson, to secure relief force for Fort Schuyler.

1777, August 12—Col. John Harper rides from Schoharie to Albany to secure aid to repel McDonald's Tory and Indian invasion of Schoharie valley.

1777, August 13—Col. John Harper, with 28 regular American cavalrymen and body of Schoharie militia repulse and drive off Capt. McDonald's 150 Indians and Tories at Vroomans; known as "Flockey Battle."

1777, August 16—General Herkimer dies at his home, Danube, Herkimer county, of wounds received at Oriskany.

1777, August 22—St. Leger's British force flees from Fort Schuyler on approach of Gen. Arnold's American army.

1778, February — Council between New York state commissioners and Iroquois Indians at Johnstown. Oneidas and Tuscaroras renew allegiance; other four tribes, represented by a few Mohawks and Onondagas, remain hostile.

1778—Brant and enemy destroy Andruston, south of German Flatts, Herkimer county.

1778, March—Invasion of Fairfield, Herkimer county, by party of Tories and Indians.

1778 April—Indian and Tory raid of Manheim, Herkimer county.

1778, May 1—Company of American soldiers from Fort Paris, Stone Arabia, go in pursuit of party of 20 Indians and Tories who raided Ephratah, the day before, April 30, 1778. Raiders escape.

1778, May 30—Battle of Cobleskill; 300 Indians and Tories under Brant ambuscade 50 American regulars and militia, defeat and almost annihilate them.

1778, May—Springfield, Otsego county, raided by Brant's invaders.

1778, May—Lieut. Matthew Wormuth shot by Brant and Indians in Takaharawa Glen, near Cherry Valley. Col. Klock and the Palatine battalion go to Cherry Valley but Brant's party flees.

1778, Sept. 1—Brant and enemy raid German Flats. Helmer, American scout's heroic run, saves settlers; settlements destroyed.

1778, Nov. 10—Massacre at Cherry Valley by party of enemy under Walter Butler and Brant. Col. Klock and the Palatine batallion of the Tryon county militia march to the relief of Cherry Valley, but the enemy escapes.

1779, April 18—American expedition, under Col. Van Schaick, sent from Fort Schuyler against Onondaga villages; Onondagas fled and Americans burned their villages.

1779—Gen. Clinton's American army of 1,500 men, enroute to join Gen. Sullivan's army invading the Iroquois country, reach Canajoharie from Schenectady, the supplies, etc., coming by river batteaux. June 17 Clinton began moving his troops and supplies and batteaux (by wagon) to Otsego lake, which he reached June 30. At Canajoharie two Tory spies were hanged. Clinton used the regular roads from Canajoharie to Otsego, building only short stretches of new road. Sullivan and Clinton's American army defeated enemy at Elmira, Aug. 29, and afterward ravaged the Iroquois country.

1780—Fort Plain blockhouse built.

1780, May 21—Sir John Johnson, commanding 500 Indians and Tories, raids from Johnstown to the Mohawk and up the valley to western Montgomery county. Buildings burned and patriots murdered.

1780, Aug. 2—Minden raid by Indians and Tories under Joseph Brant. Col. Wemple and militia march to Fort Plain but enemy escapes.

1780, Sept. 1 (about)—Fort Plain made headquarters of Mohawk valley forts.

1780, Oct. 16—Johnson and raiders enter Schoharie valley and commence great raid of Schoharie and Mohawk valleys. Feeble attacks made on Middle and Lower Schoharie forts.

1780, Oct. 19—Col. John Brown and American force of 135 defeated at Stone Arabia by Sir John Johnson's raiders. Brown killed. Palatine raided and buildings burned.

1780, Oct. 19—Skirmish at Klock's Field, St. Johnsville town, fought by Gen. Van Rensselaer's American army and Johnson's invaders. Johnson's force retreats and escapes.

1781—Fort Willett, in Dutchtown section of Minden, built.

1781, June—Col. Marinus Willett appointed commander of Mohawk valley military with headquarters at Fort Plain.

1781, July 2—Capt. Solomon Woodworth's company of rangers ambuscaded at Fairfield, Herkimer county, by Indians and but few escape; 50 Americans, 80 Indians in Fairfield battle; Woodworth and 37 of his men killed; bloodiest Revolutionary encounter in Mohawk valley.

1781, July 9—Raid at Currytown by 500 Tories and Indians under Capt. Dockstader, a valley Tory.

1781, July 10 — Battle of Sharon Springs. Col. Willett and 260 men start from Fort Plain, pursue the enemy and defeat them at Sharon Springs.

1781, Oct. 24—Raid by enemy under Ross and Butler, through town of Root to Mohawk river, south to Amsterdam and northwest to Johnstown. Col. Willett starts from Fort Plain in pursuit with 400 men.

1781, Oct. 25—Battle of Johnstown; American victory.

1781, Oct. 29—Battle of West Canada creek; American victory; Butler killed.

1781—Christian Schell, his wife and six sons make heroic defense of his blockhouse home (five miles north of Fort Dayton), repulsing 60 Tories and Indians; killing 11, wounding 15, including enemy's captain, McDonald, mortally wounded and captured.

1782—Washington visited Schenectady.

1782, July—Fort Herkimer neighborhood raided by enemy; repulsed from fort; last large raid of the war; settlements destroyed.

1783, Feb. 9—Col. Willett's attempt to capture Fort Oswego fails.

1783, April 17—News of cessation of hostilities reaches Fort Plain from Washington's headquarters at Newburgh. April 18, Capt. Thompson and four companions start on journey with the peace news to British post of Fort Oswego.

1783—Population of Tryon county, about 4,000.

1783, July 30—Gen. Washington and staff reach Fort Plain on return from valley trip westward to site of Fort Schuyler. Washington stops over night at house of Peter Wormuth in Palatine. July 31, Washington and staff dine at Fort Plain and journey to Cherry Valley. Aug. 1, Washington's party visits Otsego lake and returns to Canajoharie, dining with Col. Clyde in Van Alstine house and remaining here over night. Aug. 2, Washington's party continues east on their return down the Mohawk valley to the Hudson and thence to American army headquarters at Newburgh.

1783—Fort Herkimer made military depot for far western American posts.

1784—James Duane of New York and Duanesburgh, Schenectady county, first mayor of New York city after the British evacuation.

1784—First permanent white settlement of Oneida county; Whitestown, Oneida county, settled; era of immigration into valley, especially western end, largely from New England.

1784 — Council at Fort Schuyler (Rome), Oneida county, between New York authorities and Six Nations; treaty made; great foot race concludes council.

1785—Oneidas and Tuscaroras, in council at Fort Herkimer, cede all territory between Chenango and Unadilla rivers to New York state.

1786—Three houses on site of Utica; owned by Demuth, Christian and Cunningham.

1786—Population Tryon county about 15,000; of the entire Mohawk valley, approximately, 20,000.

1787—Stone Arabia Reformed (present stone) church built.

1787—Dutch Reformed church of Middleburgh, Schoharie county, built. Former church burned in raid of 1780.

1788—Council between New York state authorities and Iroquois Indians at Fort Schuyler (Rome), Oneida county. Indian title to New York state lands extinguished and territory opened for settlement.

1790 (about)—Bridge built at Little Falls, probably first bridge built over the Mohawk.

1790—Mail stages begin running from Albany to Schenectady to Johnstown to Canajoharie.

1791—Herkimer county formed.

1792—Stone Arabia Lutheran (present frame) church built at Stone Arabia, Montgomery county.

1792—Inland Lock & Navigation Co. formed.

1793—Bridges over East and West Canada creeks built and north side turnpike opened to Utica.

1795—First newspaper in the Mohawk valley established at Whites-

town. The Utica Herald-Dispatch is a descendant of this paper.

1795 — Union college, Schenectady, founded.

1795—Schoharie county formed.

1796—"The Mohawk Mercury," first newspaper established in Schenectady.

1796—Mohawk river navigation improved by Inland Lock Navigation Co. with locks and canals at Little Falls, Wolf's Rift, Rome, Wood Creek.

1797—Mohawk and Hudson turnpike, from Albany to Schenectady, begun.

1798—Schenectady made a city.

1798—Oneida county formed.

1798 — Fort Hunter, Montgomery county, bridge built over Schoharie creek; Great Western turnpike built.

1800 (about)—Manufacture of cheese for outside markets begun in Mohawk valley. Dairying became a large valley industry about 1825. Cheese making for market purposes was introduced into the Mohawk valley by New England immigrants into Herkimer county.

1800 — Improvement of Mohawk (north shore) turnpike begun.

1800—Population of present six Mohawk valley counties, 72,522, including 1,352 slaves.

1803—First Canajoharie bridge over Mohawk river built.

1803—Fairfield academy founded at Fairfield, Herkimer county. Medical school later added; academy discontinued in 1903.

1806—First Fort Plain bridge over Mohawk river built, at "the Island."

1807—Woolen factory established at Frankfort.

1809—James Burr and Tallmadge Edwards start business of dressing leather and making leather mittens in Kingsboro (now Gloversville), Fulton county; this was the beginning of the leather and glove industry of Fulton county. Credit for inception of this industry has been given to others also.

1809 — Schenectady county formed from Albany county.

1812—Hamilton college founded at Clinton, Oneida county; successsor to Indian school founded by Kirkland.

1812-14—Mohawk valley militia take part in second war with England.

1812-1814—Great numbers of American troops pass west (to defend New York-Canadian frontier) and return over Mohawk turnpike. Large amount of American army stores and arms pass west over Mohawk turnpike and on Mohawk river.

1816—Gloversville known as "Stump City."

1817—Herkimer county line moved east from Little Falls to a line running north and south from East Creek. Town of Danube, Herkimer county, cut off from Minden; town of Manheim cut off from Oppenheim town, including present St. Johnsville town.

1819—Business part of Schenectady burned.

1820—Manufacture of plows begun at Utica.

1823—Erie canal (begun 1817) completed eastward to Sprakers.

1823-5—Joseph C. Yates of Schenectady elected governor of New York.

1825, Oct. 26—Erie canal officially completed and Gov. Clinton starts east from Buffalo on the packet Seneca Chief, on his triumphal canal tour to New York.

1825 — Era of manufacturing and town building begins in Mohawk valley following completion of Erie canal.

1830—Harry Burrell of Salisbury, Herkimer county, makes first shipment of cheese to England (10,000 pounds).

1831—Eliphalet Remington jr. opens forge for manufacture of gun barrels and firearms at Ilion, Herkimer county; he had previously made same from 1816 on his father's farm at Steele's Creek, Herkimer county.

1831 — Egbert Egberts invents a frame for knit goods manufacture, operated by power, at Albany, N. Y. Timothy Bailey aids in invention. Removed to Cohoes in 1832.

1831—Mohawk and Hudson (Albany to Schenectady) railroad opened; first steam passenger train trip in America.

1832—Utica made a city.

1832—Manufacture of knit goods begun at Cohoes by Egberts & Bailey; probably the inception of the knit goods business of the country; the Mohawk valley now (1914) being the center of American knit goods manufacture.

1833 — Incorporation of Herkimer Manufacturing and Hydraulic Co. (capital $100,000) to erect a dam across West Canada creek to produce water power.

1835—Enlargement of Erie canal begun.

1836 — Chenango canal, Utica to Binghamton, built; later abandoned.

1836—Manufacture of axes and other edge tools begun in Cohoes.

1836 — Manufacture of ready-made clothing begun at Utica.

1836—Manufacture of cotton cloth (white goods) introduced at Cohoes by Peter Harmony, a Spaniard, who founded the Harmony Mills Co. In building the foundation of additional Mill No. 3, of this industry, in 1866, skeleton of a mastodon was unearthed at the bottom of a great "pot hole," 60 feet deep. This mastodon is now mounted and on exhibition in Geological Hall, Albany, N. Y.

1836, August 1—Opening of Schenectady and Utica (later part of N. Y. C. & H. R.) railroad.

1836 — Montgomery county court house removed from Johnstown to Fonda.

1836, Oct. 19—Dedication of a monument to Col. John Brown at Stone Arabia Reformed Dutch church burial ground; largely attended, some veterans of the Stone Arabia battle, in which Brown was killed, being present.

1838—Separation of Montgomery and Fulton counties and town of St. Johnsville set off from town of Oppenheim, now in Fulton county.

1840—Baseball invented by (later General) Abner C. Doubleday at Cooperstown, Otsego county; not in Mohawk valley, but near it. Fort Plain, Montgomery county, was Cooperstown's trade and road outlet to the Mohawk valley, in 1840.

1840—Manufacture of ingrain carpets begun at Hagaman's Mills by Wait, Green & Co.; later J. Sanford & Son of Amsterdam.

1842—Manufacture of woolen goods begun at Little Falls.

1843—Stages discontinued on the Mohawk turnpike.

1843-1845—William C. Bouck (Democrat) of Schoharie county, governor of New York.

1844—Match making business established at Frankfort.

1845—First through line of steam canal boats started from Buffalo to New York.

1845—First college course in civil engineering instituted at Union college, Schenectady.

1845 (about)—Manufacture of yarn begun at Little Falls.

1845—Manufacture of railroad steam locomotives begun at Schenectady.

1846 — First kid glove factory of Johnstown established.

1846-1848—War with Mexico.

1847—Manufacture of worsteds begun at Utica.

1848—Manufacture of linseed oil begun at Amsterdam.

1848—Manufacture of cotton cloth (white goods) begun at Utica; now (1914) largest center of this industry in New York state.

1848—Power dam across North Chuctanunda creek built at Amsterdam. This water power subsequently greatly developed in 1855, 1865 and 1875.

1849—Black River canal built connecting at Rome, Oneida county, with Erie.

1850—Population of Mohawk valley, 193,575 (mostly agricultural).

1853—Fort Plain Seminary founded.

1853—New York Central railroad formed.

1853-1855—Horatio Seymour (Democrat) of Utica, Oneida county, governor of New York.

1854—Utica and Black River railroad opened to Boonville; extended to Carthage in 1870; now branch of New York Central and Hudson River railroad.

1855 (about)—First telegraph line constructed through Mohawk valley, from Albany to Utica, by New York Central railroad.

1857—Manufacture of knit goods begun at Amsterdam.

1858—Webster Wagner of Palatine Bridge completes the sleeping car.

1858, Sept. 1—Sleeping cars, invented by Webster Wagner of Palatine Bridge, Montgomery county, begin running on the New York Central railroad.

1859—Manufacture of paper and cotton bags begun at Canajoharie.

1859—Elevated passenger car roof, with side ventilators, invented by Webster Wagner of Palatine Bridge, Montgomery county.

1861-5—Civil war, in which many men from the Mohawk valley took part. (See Mohawk valley military statistics.)

1861-5 — Great numbers of Union troops and stores moved over New York Central railroad. Great quantity of Union army stores moved east on Erie canal.

1861-5—Remington arms works at Ilion (with branch at Utica) produces great quantity of arms for Union armies; as does the Watervliet arsenal, at the mouth of the Mohawk.

1863—Manufacture of knit goods begun at Utica.

1863—Manufacture of knit goods machinery on a large scale begun in Cohoes.

1863-1865—Horatio Seymour (Democrat) of Utica, Oneida county, governor of New York; one of the strongest Union "war governors."

1865—Remington breech-loading rifle perfected at Ilion prior to this date.

1865—Albany to Binghamton railroad, through Schoharie valley, built. Branches to Cherry Valley and Sharon Springs built, 1870. This road was leased to the Delaware and Hudson in 1871.

1866 — "Athens branch" railroad, Schenectady to Athens, built.

1867—Schoharie valley railroad built.

1867—Wagner palace car invented by Webster Wagner of Palatine Bridge, Montgomery county; Wagner Palace Car Co. and Pullman Palace Car Co. consolidated about 1890.

1867—Utica, Clinton and Binghamton railroad opened from Utica to Hamilton.

1868—Blood's broom factory established at Amsterdam; first large broom factory of that city.

1868 — Middleburg and Schoharie railroad built.

1868—Horatio Seymour, of Utica, Oneida county, Democrat, defeated for presidency by Gen. U. S. Grant, Republican; Grant 214 electoral votes; Seymour 80 electoral votes.

1869—New York Central and Hudson River Railroad incorporated, embracing railroad lines from New York to Buffalo.

1869—Cohoes made a city.

1870—Rome made a city.

1870—Completion of Fonda, Johnstown and Gloversville railroad; extension of same to Northville in 1875; branch runs to Broadalbin, Fulton county. All of this railroad is in Fulton county, except the two miles from Fonda to Sammonsville, close to the Fulton-Montgomery line.

1870—Utica, Chenango and Susquehanna railroad, from Utica to Waterville and Richfield, completed.

1872—Manufacture of knit goods begun at Herkimer.

1872—Manufacture of knit goods begun at Little Falls.

1875—Alfred Dolge locates at Dolgeville and begins manufacture of felt goods, etc.

1873—Manufacture of present Remington typewriter begun at Ilion by Remington Arms Co., in connection with James Densmore, the inventor.

1873—"Schenectady and Duanesburg railroad" completed.

1877—Centennial celebration of the battle of Oriskany at Oriskany, Oneida county; battle monument erected here later.

1878—Manufacture of brass begun at Rome, Oneida county.

1880 (about)—First (high) bicycles used in Mohawk valley.

1880 (about)—Electric lights, telephones and phonographs first introduced into Mohawk valley.

1881—Manufacture of dairy preparations begun at Little Falls.

1883—West Shore railroad completed west to Syracuse.

1883—West Shore railroad shops established at Frankfort; later removed to Depew, with exception of the foundry.

1885—Mohawk and Malone railroad opened from Herkimer north to Malone; now branch of the N. Y. C. and H. R. R.

1885—Amsterdam made a city.

1885 (about)—Safety bicycles first used in Mohawk valley.

1885 (about)—Period of electric trolley car line construction began in Mohawk valley. Until 1914 lines were built running up the river from Schenectady to Amsterdam, Johnstown, Gloversville and Fonda and from Little Falls to Rome. Trolley lines connect (1914) Utica with Clinton and with Syracuse and Buffalo. A trolley line runs south from Herkimer to Richfield Springs and Oneonta with branch to Cooperstown. Also east and north from Schenectady to Albany and Troy and Saratoga Springs.

1886 — Manufacture of desks and typewriter cabinets begun at Herkimer.

1887—Manufacture of knit goods begun at Fort Plain.

1887—Manufacture of copper begun at Rome, Oneida county.

1888—General Electric Co. moves to Schenectady.

1888 (about) — Building of Little Falls and Dolgeville railroad.

1890—Gloversville made a city.

1890 (about)—Manufacture of food stuffs begun at Canajoharie.

1892 — Report of Martin Schenck, state engineer and surveyor, advocating a Barge canal. Hon. Martin Schenck was a native of Palatine, Montgomery county.

1892—Manufacture of knit goods begun at St. Johnsville.

1895—Johnstown made a city.

1895—Little Falls made a city.

1895 (about)—Automobiles first used in Mohawk valley.

1895—First college course in electrical engineering instituted at Union college, Schenectady.

1896—Monument erected over grave of General Nicholas Herkimer at Danube, Herkimer county.

1898—Electrical development of East Creek water power at East Creek (2,000 H. P. generated). Later development at Dolgeville (1897) and Inghams Mills (1912).

1898—Spanish-American war; some

valley men enlisted in American army.

1905—Work begun on Erie division of the Barge canal.

1907—Unveiling of statue of General Herkimer at Herkimer; Burr Miller, sculptor; Warner Miller, donor; occasion, Herkimer village's centennial.

1908—William H. Taft of Cincinnati, Ohio, elected president and James S. Sherman of Utica (Oneida county), New York, elected vice president of the United States on the Republican national ticket.

1909—18,457 farms in six Mohawk valley counties, producing $30,000,000 annually, exclusive of lumber.

1910—Population of six Mohawk valley counties 424,704. That of New York state, 9,113,614. That of the United States, 91,972,266.

1911—Centennial celebration of Little Falls as a village.

1911—Mohawk Hydro-Electric company completes dams and plants at Pecks Pond, Caroga and Ephratah; line run to Johnstown-Gloversville; line run to Fort Plain in 1912.

1911—Harry N. Atwood alights at Nelliston, after flight of 95 miles from near Syracuse, en route by aeroplane from St. Louis to New York.

1912—Wm. H. Taft of Cincinnati, Ohio, and James S. Sherman of Utica (Oneida county), New York, renominated for president and vice president on the Republican national ticket. James S. Sherman died in October, 1912, before the election. Wilson, Dem., elected; Taft, Rep., and Roosevelt, Prog., defeated.

1912—1,321 factories with 88,271 operatives in six Mohawk valley counties, producing goods valued at about $200,000,000 annually. Chief manufactures: Knit goods, electrical apparatus, leather gloves, white goods, rugs and carpets.

1912—Route of Gen. Herkimer, from Danube to Oriskany, marked by bronze tablets, under the auspices of the Daughters of the American Revolution.

1912—Dam and plant for hydroelectric power development, built at Inghams Mills on East creek, in town of Manheim, Herkimer county.

1914—General Herkimer house in Danube, Herkimer county, purchased by state and placed under the care of the Daughters of the American Revolution and the German-American Alliance.

1914—Second war with Mexico. Vera Cruz occupied but no official declaration of war as yet (April 28, 1914) and none of the valley militia as yet called out for service.

WESTERN MONTGOMERY COUNTY DATES.

The following dates have an especial reference to Western Montgomery county:

1750 — Reformed Dutch church (frame) of Canajoharie built at Sand Hill, later Fort Plain.

1756—Reformed Dutch church built in town of St. Johnsville.

1790—Dutch Reformed church organized at Currytown, being the first church body in the town of Root.

1794—Free Will Baptist church organized, west of Ames, being the first known church organization in Canajoharie town.

1795, March 31—Union academy of Palatine (at Stone Arabia) incorporated by the State Regents. Building built in 1799, burned in 1807 and never rebuilt.

1798—Town of Minden formed from Canajoharie.

1799—Funeral services in honor of General Washington held at the Reformed Dutch church at Sand Hill (Fort Plain).

1804—St. John's Reformed Dutch church moves from its original location, east of St. Johnsville, to that village.

1808—Town of Oppenheim (including present St. Johnsville town) set off from Palatine.

1810—Cornplanter, with Indian suite, visits relatives at Fort Plain, where Cornplanter raided with Brant's party in 1780.

1818—Union church built at Canajoharie village, the first there erected.

1823—Town of Root formed.

1825, Oct. 26—Celebration of completion of Erie canal. Dinner and ball in celebration at Fort Plain. Oct. 31, Governor Clinton and party on packet, Seneca Chief, pass east on their triumphal tour of Erie.

1825—First newspaper in western Montgomery county, the "Telegraph," established at Canajoharie.

1827—First existing newspaper in western Montgomery county, the Fort Plain Watch Tower, established—now known as the Mohawk Valley Register (oldest paper in Montgomery county in 1914).

1829—Canajoharie village incorporated.

1829—First Fort Plain bridge at present site built over Mohawk river.

1832—Fort Plain village · incorporated.

1834—Reformed Dutch church at Sand Hill removed to Fort Plain, ending Sand Hill as a hamlet.

1849—Freysbush district taken from town of Canajoharie and added to Minden, making last change in territory of five western Montgomery towns.

1852 — First St. Johnsville bridge across Mohawk river built.

1857—St. Johnsville village incorporated.

1865—Furniture manufacturing begun at Fort Plain.

1867—Palatine Bridge village incorporated.

1870—Manufacture of springs and axles begun at Fort Plain. Factory removed to Chicago Heights, Ill., in 1894. Factory came from Springfield to Fort Plain.

1878—Nelliston village incorporated.

1879—Clinton Liberal Institute removed to Fort Plain, supplanting the Fort Plain Seminary on Seminary Hill; C. L. I. burned 1900.

1880 (about)—Manufacture of silk begun at Fort Plain.

1889—Manufacture of player pianos and piano actions begun at St. Johnsville.

1898—First Fort Plain street fair held.

1900—Clinton Liberal Institute destroyed by fire; armory and gymnasium uninjured. Institute not rebuilt.

MOHAWK VALLEY MILITARY STATISTICS.

The following Mohawk valley military statistics include not only military operations along the Mohawk, but those in which valley men were engaged elsewhere:

Early French-Indian Hostilities— 1609-1689.

1609—Champlain and Canadian Indians defeat Mohawks on west shore of Lake Champlain, near Ticonderoga; two Mohawk chiefs killed; action makes Iroquois enemies of French and friends of Dutch and English.

1666—The Mohawk villages burned by French-Indian Canadian expedition; Mohawks escape into the woods.

Indian Wars.

1669, August 9—Battle of Towereune, near Hoffmans, Schenectady county, in which Mohawks defeat Mohicans and gain mastery of valley.

King William's War—1689-1697.

1689—Mohawks raid Montreal.

1690—Schenectady burned by French and Indians; population massacred or captured.

1692—French-Indian war party burns Oneida castle; Onondagos burn their villages and escape to woods.

1693—French-Indian-Canadian expedition, under Count Frontenac, attacks, captures and burns the three Mohawk castles; hard fight at upper castle; 300 Mohawks made prisoners; Albany militia, under Col. Peter Schuyler, pursued and retook 50 captives.

King George's War—1743-1748.

1746, August 4—Party sent by Col. William Johnson against French and Indians ambushed at Chambly.

1748—Battle of Beukendaal, Glenville town, Schenectady county, in which valley American militia were ambuscaded by Canadian Indians and American force almost destroyed. Beukendaal means, in Dutch, Beechdale.

Seven Years War—1754-1760.

During the Seven Years War (which is also called the French and Indian War), large bodies of British-American troops passed up and down the valley, the Mohawk river being largely used for the transportation of their supplies and munitions.

1755—British-American army under Major-Gen. William Johnson defeats French at Lake George—Mohawks and militia with Johnson.

1756—Attack by French and Indians at German Flats (Herkimer), settlement destroyed and inhabitants captured or massacred.

1756—Gen. Webb with British regiment and supplies passes up Mohawk valley to reinforce Fort Oswego; French capture fort; Webb returns; Johnson with ·militia and Indians returns.

1756, August—Gen. Johnson leads party of Indians and militia to join Gen. Webb's expedition for relief of Fort William Henry, at the head of Lake George; expedition fails through Webb's incapacity and Fort William Henry is captured by French.

1758, April—Gen. William Johnson calls together the Mohawk valley militia at Fort Canajoharie (present Indian Castle)˙ to repel invasion of French and Indians at Fort Herkimer. Enemy repulsed from Fort Herkimer by garrison and flees back to Canada.

1758, July 9—Johnson and 400 Iroquois warriors at disastrous defeat by French of Gen. Abercombie's British-American army before Fort Ticonderoga.

1758—Repulse of French and Indians from Fort Herkimer.

1758—British-American army under Sir William Johnson captures French Fort Niagara; 1,000 Iroquois warriors and body of militia with Johnson.

1760—Gen. Amherst's British-American army of 10,000 passes up Mohawk to conquest of Montreal. Johnson with 1,300 Iroquois join army later.

Revolution—1775-1783.

Only the main military events and movements of the Revolution are here given:

1777, August 6—Battle of Oriskany at Oriskany, Oneida county, between Tryon County Militia, commanded by General Herkimer, and British-Tory-Indian army commanded by General

St. Leger; drawn battle, both armies retire from field; aim of Americans to relieve Fort Schuyler unsuccessful.

1777, August 6—Sortie by Willett's command from Fort Schuyler (now Rome, Oneida county) against St. Leger's camp; American success; stars and stripes first flown here in battle.

1777, August 13—Battle of Flockey, Vroomans, Schoharie county, where American regulars and Schoharie militia under Col. Harper drive off invading force of enemy under Capt. McDonald; American success.

1778, May 30—Battle of Cobleskill, Schoharie county; ambuscade of 50 Americans by Brant and 300 Indians; American defeat.

1778, Nov. 10—Cherry Valley massacre. Place attacked by enemy under Butler and Brant.

1778, Sept. 1—German Flatts raided by enemy under Brant.

1779, June 19—Gen. Clinton and American army of 1,500 start overland march from Canajoharie to Otsego lake to join Gen. Sullivan's army at Tioga, August 22; defeat enemy at present Elmira, August 29; Indian country later devastated.

1780, May 21—Johnson and enemy raid Johnstown and Caughnawaga neighborhoods. American force pursues; Johnson escapes.

1780, August 2—Brant and enemy raid in Minden about Fort Plain; militia gathers; enemy escapes.

1780, Oct. 16—Johnson and enemy pass Upper Fort on the Schoharie and begin raid of Schoharie and Mohawk valleys, ending with action at Klock's Field, Oct. 19.

1780, Oct. 19—Battle of Stone Arabia, Palatine town, Montgomery county; defeat of American force of 140 men under Col. Brown by Johnson's raiders, numbering about 800.

1780, Oct. 19—Battle of Klock's Field or Battle of St. Johnsville (Montgomery county). Virtually a skirmish between Van Rensselaer's American militia (numbering 1,500) and Johnson's raiders (numbering 800); American success; enemy flees and escapes.

1781, July 2 — Battle of Fairfield,

Herkimer county. Capt. Woodworth's company of 50 American rangers, ambuscaded by 80 Indians and patriot force nearly destroyed—killed or captured; American defeat—38 killed out of 50; bloodiest valley Revolutionary action.

1781, July 9—Currytown, Montgomery county, raided by enemy under Dockstader.

1781, July 10 — Battle of Sharon Springs, Schoharie county, between 250 American militia under Col. Willett and 500 of enemy under Capt. Dockstader; American success; enemy driven off.

1781, Oct. 24—Enemy under Ross and Butler begin raid of Montgomery and Fulton counties, ending with battle of Butler's Ford, West Canada creek, Oct. 29.

1781, Oct. 25—Battle of Johnstown, Fulton county, between 400 Americans under Col. Willett and Maj. Rowley and 700 British-Tory-Indian raiders under Ross and Butler; American success; enemy driven off.

1781, Oct. 29 — Battle of Butler's Ford, West Canada creek, Herkimer county, between 400 American pursuing force under Col. Willett and 700 of enemy under Ross and Butler, retreating from Johnstown; American victory; enemy driven off and Butler killed.

1782, July—Enemy raids Fort Herkimer district; repulsed from fort.

1783, Feb. 9—American force under Col. Willett, fails on expedition to surprise British Fort Oswego; guides lost; expedition discovered; Americans return to Mohawk river.

War of 1812-1814.

Following is a record of the passing and arrival of American troops at Utica during the second war with England, known as the War of 1812. It will serve to show how the Mohawk valley was used as a military road just as the Mohawk river was used as a military waterway for the transportation of arms, munitions and supplies for the American armies on the New York frontier:

1812, August, Flying Artillery (130

men) from Lancaster, Pa.; September, 800 drafted men under Gen. Dodge of Johnstown; Sept. 20, Fifth U. S. regiment; Sept. 22, 2 companies light artillery; Sept. 30, 90 sailors bound for Sackett's Harbor; Oct. 5, 150 sailors, 150 wagons, on their way to Buffalo; Oct. 6, 130 U. S. soldiers, 20 wagons; Oct. 10, 130 U. S. marines; Oct. 13, parties of marines; Oct. 14, "Republican Greens" (190 men); Oct. 23, 23d U. S. regiment (300 men) from Albany; 130 field artillery.

1813, April 6, 150 light horse reach Utica from Sackett's Harbor, which they have been compelled to leave on account of lack of provisions, and on April 13, 150 more light horse reach Utica, probably for the same reason; April 15, 200 light artillery moving west; April 24-25, 500 soldiers, 100 sailors for Sackett's Harbor; 500 horse and foot for Buffalo; May 12, 2d U. S. regiment on way to front; May 15 and 16, 900 Massachusetts soldiers on way to front; May 23, 600, 21st U. S. for west; May 26, 750 U. S. soldiers for west; June 15, 14th U. S. (300 men) and a rifle company for the front; June 16, 49th English regiment, prisoners of war, pass down the valley; June (latter part), numbers of soldiers and sailors en route to defense of Sackett's Harbor; July 10, 3d and 25th U. S. (270 men); Aug. 9, 100 Canadian and British prisoners on their way down the valley under guard; summer and autumn, constant passing east and west of American soldiers, sailors and militia; Oct. 15, 2 companies Walleville's English regiment (captured on lake transports) went east as prisoners under guard; Oct. 31, 800 U. S. regulars from Fort George, going west; Nov. 23, Com. Oliver Hazard Perry (hero of Lake Erie naval battle) given great public dinner at Utica, and passes down Mohawk in a batteaux, everywhere given a great reception.

The 10th, 11th and 13th (Mohawk valley militia) regiments of the Fourth Brigade of New York were engaged in this war on the St. Lawrence and Niagara frontiers. See Chapter IX., Series II., on the War of 1812.

Mexican War—1846-1848.

No valley military organizations took part in this conflict. Two regiments from New York are reported to have been engaged; they were regular army regiments.

Civil War—1861-1865.

1861-1865—The following is a record of the Civil war military organizations in which the Union soldiers of the six valley counties were enrolled. It is compiled from county histories. During the Civil war, thousands of troops went to the front over the New York Central railroad and great quantities of supplies went forward to the Union armies over the Erie canal and on the railroad.

Oneida county: The principal Civil war organizations recruited from this county were: 14th infantry; 26th infantry; 81st infantry (350 men); 97th (from Oneida, Lewis, Herkimer and Fulton); 117th infantry; 146th infantry. Oneida county had representation also in 50th (engineers), 53d, 57th, 61st, 68th, 71st, 75th, 76th, 78th, 81st, 93d, 101st infantry regiments, 3d, 8th, 11th, 13th, 15th, 20th, 22d, 24th cavalry; the Oneida cavalry, 1st mounted rifles, 1st, 2d, 3d, 13th, 14th, 16th artillery.

Herkimer county: The principal Civil war organizations largely recruited from this county were 34th infantry, known as "the Herkimer county regiment," five companies coming from this county. 97th infantry. Cos. C, D, E, F and I were largely of Herkimer county men. 121st infantry, from Herkimer and Otsego counties. 152d regiment from Otsego and Herkimer counties (360 men from Herkimer). 16th artillery (over 100 men). Other organizations in which Herkimer men were represented were 14th infantry, 26th infantry, 1st light artillery (Battery A), 2d light artillery (Battery K), 2d rifles, 18th N. Y. cavalry.

Montgomery county: The principal Civil war organizations in which Montgomery county was represented are the following: 115th infantry, 421 men; 153d infantry, 329 men; 32d infantry (Cos. B and D), 130 men; 43d infantry (Co. E), 69 men; 1st artillery (Co. K), 65 men; 16th artillery, 36 men; 13th artillery, 33 men.

Fulton county: The principal Civil war organizations in which Fulton county was represented are the following: 153d infantry, 269 men; 115th infantry, 162 men; 77th infantry, 101 men; 10th cavalry (Co. I), 92 men; 13th artillery, 71 men; 97th infantry, 53 men; 93d infantry (Co. D), 51 men; 2d cavalry, 31 men.

Schoharie county: The principal Civil war organizations from Schoharie county were 134th regiment, N. Y. S. V., recruited from Schoharie and Schenectady counties. This might fittingly be called "the Schoharie county regiment," as it contained about 800 men from Schoharie. Co. I, 76th N. Y. S. V., had about 80 Schoharie county men and several hundred other Schoharie men were enlisted in many other organizations.

Schenectady county: The principal Civil war organizations in which Schenectady county was represented are: 30th infantry, 44 men; 77th infantry, 50 men; 43d infantry, 31 men; 2d cavalry, 110 men; 69th infantry, 55 men; 18th infantry, 141 men; 134th infantry, about 380 men; 91st infantry, 156 men; 13th cavalry, 58 men; 25th cavalry, 1st rifles, 13th artillery, 177th infantry, 192d infantry.

Spanish-American War—1898.

Several military organizations and a number of Mohawk valley men were enlisted in the American army.

Second War With Mexico.

1914—Second war with Mexico. Vera Cruz occupied but no official declaration of war as yet (April 28, 1914) and none of the valley militia as yet called out for service.

FIFTEEN DATES FOR SCHOOL USE

Following are fifteen Mohawk valley principal dates, suggested for school use. They form a brief and easily understood history of the Mohawk valley. They cover the six Mohawk valley counties of Oneida, Herkimer, Montgomery, Fulton, Schoharie and Schenectady and are suitable for use in any of the schools of these counties. It is here suggested that students learn first the main date, and later the subsidiary matter.

1661—Schenectady settled by Dutch; burned by French and Indian war party in 1690 and its people killed or captured; rebuilt shortly after.

1713—Mohawk and Schoharie valleys settled by Palatine Germans.

1753-1760—Seven Years War. Mohawk Indians and valley militia take part in victories of British-American armies (under Sir William Johnson) at Lake George and Niagara; also in other military movements. Burnetsfield (present Herkimer) burned and its people generally massacred or captured in 1756. French and Indian attack on Fort Herkimer repulsed in 1758. Large bodies of British and American troops passed up and down the valley; munitions and supplies going on the river. In 1760, Gen. Amherst's British-American army of 10,000 men went north, by way of the Mohawk valley, and captured Montreal from the French, which ended the war. Quebec was taken from the French by the English under Wolfe in 1759. The people of the Mohawk valley were in almost constant danger of massacre, from 1661 to 1760, by French and Indian scalping parties.

1775-1783—Revolutionary War. Chief battles in the Mohawk valley were Oriskany, 1777 (drawn battle); Stone Arabia, 1780 (American defeat); Klock's Field or St. Johnsville, 1781 (American victory); Sharon Springs, 1781 (American victory); Johnstown, 1781 (American victory); West Canada Creek or Butlers Ford, 1781 (American victory). There were many skir-

mishes, raids and massacres in the Mohawk valley during these years. The valley American troops made a generallly successful defense of the valley but the country and its people suffered from invasion more than in any other part of the thirteen colonies; Mohawks left valley, with the Johnsons, and went to Canada in 1775, where they enlisted and fought barbarously, under the British flag, against their old American valley neighbors, as did also most of the valley Tories.

1777, August 6—Battle of Oriskany between the Tryon County American militia (800 men) and St. Leger's British - Tory - Indian army (1,600 men); drawn battle and the hardest fought action of the Revolution; successful American sortie from Fort Schuyler, over which stars and stripes were first flown in battle on this day.

1783—Washington makes a tour of the Mohawk valley; he visited Schenectady in 1782.

1784—Oneida county permanently settled at Whitestown; a large immigration began in this year into and through the Mohawk valley from New England and other American colonies. Utica and Rome were permanently settled about 1785.

1796 — Mohawk river navigation improved by locks and canals at Little Falls, Wolf's Rift, Rome and Wood Creek; this work was done by the Inland Lock and Navigation Co.; formed in 1792.

1800—Mohawk (north shore) turnpike begun from Schenectady to Utica; period of the stage coach and great freight wagons. A turnpike then ran from Albany to Buffalo, now used largely as an automobile road.

1812-1814—Second War with England; 10th, 11th and 13th (Mohawk valley) militia regiments engage in defense of New York frontier. Large bodies of troops pass up and down Mohawk turnpikes; army supplies and munitions go west on river boats and on turnpike wagons.

1817-1825—Construction of Erie canal from Buffalo to Albany; length of canal, 387 miles; 72 locks; 7 feet deep; 70 feet surface width; length of Erie canal through Mohawk valley (Cohoes to Rome) about 110 miles. An era of town building, manufacturing and dairy production for outside markets began in the valley, following the construction of the Erie canal. From 1862 until abandonment of Erie for Barge canal boats 98x17½x6 and of 240 tons were in use.

1831 — Mohawk and Hudson railroad (17 miles long), from Albany to Schenectady completed. This was the first steam passenger railroad in America. The Utica to Schenectady railroad was completed August 1, 1836, and both roads became parts of the New York Central and Hudson River railroad in 1869. West Shore railroad was completed 1883, and is now part of N. Y. C. & H. R. R.R.

1861-5—Civil War or War of the Rebellion, during which thousands of Mohawk valley men enlisted in the Union armies; many thousands of Union troops passed over the New York Central railroad and enormous quantities of army supplies and munitions passed east over the railroad and the Erie canal. Remington Arms factories at Ilion and Utica produced great amount of arms for the Union army, as also did the Watervliet arsenal.

1905—Construction of Erie branch of the New York State Barge canal begun. Erie branch is 323 miles long with 35 locks, and utilizes the channel of the Mohawk river from Rome to Waterford, about 110 miles. Great reservoirs for Barge canal water storage purposes have been constructed at Delta, Oneida county, and at Hinckley, the latter being in Oneida and Herkimer counties, and also being the largest body of water (nine miles long) in the Mohawk valley. Barge canal types of boats are not (1914) definitely decided upon. They may be of from 3,000 tons downward, the idea being for one motor engine or power boat to draw about 3,000 tons through the locks without breaking up the boats.

Boats of 1,500 tons to run tandem or of about 800 tons to run in quadruplets (one to be a power boat) are probable types.

1911 — Aeroplane flight of Atwood through the Mohawk valley, en route from St. Louis to New York, 1,266 miles. Atwood flew from near Syracuse to Nelliston, Montgomery county, 95 miles, August 22, 1911, spending the night at Fort Plain, across the Mohawk; he flew from Nelliston to Castleton, on the Hudson, 65 miles, August 23, with a short stop for repairs, in the morning, near Glen, Montgomery county.

———

Statistical Summary (for school use; also see map; the figures are from the 1910 U. S. census).

The six Mohawk valley counties:

Oneida; county seat, Utica.

Herkimer; county seat, Herkimer.

Montgomery; county seat, Fonda.

Fulton; county seat, Johnstown.

Schoharie; county seat, Schoharie.

Schenectady; county seat, Schenectady.

Area six Mohawk valley counties (in round numbers), 2,860,000 acres, divided as follows: Oneida, 800,000; Herkimer, 934,000; Montgomery, 355,-000; Fulton, 330,000; Schoharie, 410,-000; Schenectady, 132,000.

Population, six Mohawk valley counties, census of 1910 (in round numbers), 425,000, divided as follows: Oneida, 154,000; Herkimer, 56,000; Montgomery, 58,000; Fulton, 45,000; Schoharie, 24,000; Schenectady, 88,000.

Largest cities, census of 1910 (in round numbers), Utica, 74,000; Schenectady, 73,000. Other cities in order, Amsterdam, Gloversville, Rome, Little Falls, Johnstown. Cohoes, near the mouth of the Mohawk, is a city of the valley, but is not in one of the six Mohawk valley counties, being located in Albany county.

Number of farms in six Mohawk valley counties (in round numbers), 18,000, raising $30,000,000 worth of products yearly.

Number of factories in six Mohawk valley counties (in round numbers), 1,300, with 88,000 employes, producing about $200,000,000 worth of goods yearly. Principal manufactures: Knit goods, electrical apparatus, leather gloves, white goods, rugs and carpets.

CHRONOLOGY OF MOHAWK VALLEY PRE-REVOLUTIONARY HOUSES AND CHURCHES.

Following is a list of the principal pre-Revolutionary houses and churches of the Mohawk valley, with approximate date of erection. Many of the best houses along the Mohawk were destroyed by the Indian and Tory raids from 1777-1782. Where a house is called a fort it means it was strongly built to resist attack or was palisaded. None of these "forts," or fortified houses, were actual army posts.

This does not include all the pre-Revolutionary houses standing in the Mohawk valley; there are a number of others; but the following are generally recognized as the most important and typical of their time.

Schenectady county, with Albany and Saratoga counties, embraces about 30 miles of the lower Mohawk valley. During the Revolution this section did not suffer from Tory and Indian raids, as did the other five Mohawk valley counties, and consequently more ancient structures there remain. For some of these pre-Revolutionary houses no dates are known or available to the editor of this work and consequently none are given. All however, were constructed prior to the close of the Revolutionary war. The editor of this work desires to express his indebtedness to Miss Marion Abbott of Fonda, author of a most interesting and entertaining essay on "The Remaining Revolutionary Residences of the Mohawk Valley." This essay was awarded the prize offered to students of the Fonda High school by Caughnawaga chapter, D. A. R., of that village, and was published in the Fonda Democrat.

The following gives a list of 33 pre-Revolutionary Mohawk valley houses. As before stated there are others, some of which, however, are difficult to authenticate. There are two or three small structures at Sand Hill, Fort Plain, which possibly antedate the Revolution. One is a small frame building now used as a barn, standing near the beginning of the Dutchtown road, and which is said to have been the parsonage of the old "Canajoharie (now Fort Plain) Reformed Dutch church." Probably research could increase the number of pre-Revolutionary Mohawk valley residences to 50 or more. The following 33 are the best known of these interesting seventeenth and eighteenth century valley residences:

1670—Jan Mabie stone house, Rotterdam, Schenectady county. This is the oldest existing building in the Mohawk valley. 1686 is also given as the date of its erection.

1680 (about)—Vrooman brick house, Schenectady city.

1700 (or before) — Van Guysling house, Rotterdam, Schenectady county; also said to have been built in 1664.

1711—Johannes Peek house, Schenectady county.

1712 — Fort Hunter, Montgomery county, Queen Anne (Episcopal) parsonage of stone; chapel was destroyed in building Erie canal 1817-1825.

1713—Glen Sanders house, Scotia, Schenectady county. This is the oldest large house standing in the valley; still (1914) in Sanders family.

1720 (about)—Toll (brick) house, Glenville town, Schenectady county.

1730—Abraham Glen house, Scotia, Schenectady county.

1735—Governor Yates brick house, Schenectady city.

1736—Arent Bradt house, Rotterdam, Schenectady county.

1739—Fort Frey (stone house), Palatine Bridge, Montgomery county (still in Frey family).

1742—Fort Johnson (stone), Montgomery county; built by Sir William Johnson and originally called Mount Johnson; Johnson's second house; home of Montgomery County Historical society. Johnson lived here from 1742 until 1763 when he removed to Johnson Hall.

1743—Butler (frame) house, Mohawk town, Montgomery county.

1750—Wagner stone house, Palatine town, Montgomery county; forms part of house now standing.

1750 (about)—Van Alstine stone house, Canajoharie, Montgomery county. Washington was probably here in 1783. This house is sometimes erroneously called Fort Rensselaer.

1752—Ehle (stone) house, Nelliston, Montgomery county; house now (1914) in ruins.

1756—Fort Klock (stone house), St. Johnsville town, Montgomery county; also called Fort House, from its builder.

1762—Van Schaick (brick) house, Van Schaick Island, Cohoes city, Albany county. This house was American Revolutionary headquarters for a time during the Saratoga campaign of 1777, when the American Army of the North had fallen back to the mouth of the Mohawk.

1763—Drumm house, Johnstown city.

1763—Johnson Hall (frame), Johnstown, Fulton county; built by Sir Wm. Johnson; his third house. Owned by New York state. Johnson lived here from 1763 until his death, in 1774.

1764—Herkimer (brick) house, Danube, Herkimer county; built by (later General) Nicholas Herkimer; owned by New York state.

1765—Campbell house, Schenectady city.

1766—Guy Park (stone), Amsterdam, Montgomery county; built by Sir Wm. Johnson for his nephew, Guy Johnson; owned by city of Amsterdam.

1767 (before)—Lansing house, Cohoes city; altered from original form.

1767 (before) — Derek Hemstreet house, Cohoes city; altered from original form.

Schermerhorn house, Schenectady county; still in Schermerhorn family (1914).

Voorhees house, Amsterdam, Montgomery county; built by Garret Roseboom and used as a tavern during old Mohawk turnpike days.

Bergen house, Sand Flats, Mohawk township, Montgomery county; altered from original form.

DeGraff (frame) house, Glenville town, Schenectady county; now (1914) in ruins.

Cochran house, Palatine town, Montgomery county; home of Dr. John Cochran, surgeon general of the American Revolutionary army.

General William North house, Duanesburgh town, Schenectady county; Gen. North was an aide of Baron Steuben in the Continental American army and a son-in-law of Judge Duane.

Judge James Duane house, Duanesburgh town, Schenectady county; also called Featherstonhough house. Judge Duane was a great Revolutionary American jurist and, in 1784, first mayor of New York city after the British evacuation.

There are but five existing pre-Revolutionary churches in the Mohawk valley and four of these are of stone construction, which speaks well for the early valley men. Many houses of worship were destroyed by the enemy during the war for independence, 1777-1782. The churches built before the Revolution and now standing are:

1756 — Fort Herkimer Reformed (Dutch) stone church, Fort Herkimer, Herkimer county.

1759—St. George's (Episcopal) stone church, Schenectady city.

1769—Indian Castle (frame) Union church; at Indian Castle, Danube town, Herkimer county.

1770 — Palatine Lutheran stone church, Palatine town, Montgomery county.

1772—Schoharie Reformed (Dutch) stone church, Schoharie, Schoharie county.

The Fort Herkimer church is not only the oldest in the valley but is probably the second oldest in the state, being antedated only by the Sleepy Hollow stone church, near Tarrytown, on the Hudson, made famous by Irving's "Legend of Sleepy Hollow." Fort Herkimer church was included in the stockade of Fort Herkimer.

The Indian Castle church was erected by order of Sir William Johnson, colonial superintendent of Indian affairs, to furnish religious instruction to the Mohawks there resident at the

upper or Canajoharie Castle. Johnson's faith was the Episcopalian but
he gave support and financial aid to
every church erected in the Mohawk
valley during his time. The Indian
Castle church was built by Col. Samuel
Clyde of Cherry Valley, under Johnson's orders.

The Schoharie church formed part of
the Lower Fort, on the Schoharie
creek, during the Revolution.

It is greatly to be regretted that the
most interesting church structure ever
raised in the Mohawk valley—Queen
Anne's chapel at Fort Hunter, Montgomery county, should have been destroyed during the building of the Erie
canal. Architects and builders would
do well to study these old pre-Revolutionary buildings, as well as those
erected in the half century following
the close of the Revolution, with a view
to the modern adoption of their best
features for valley structures of today.
All the good Mohawk valley traditions,
whether of building or of other phases
of human life, are worthy of preservation.

1715-1774—CHRONOLOGY OF WIL-LIAM JOHNSON.

The following is a chronology of the
principal events in the life of Sir William Johnson relative to the Mohawk
valley and its inhabitants.

1715 — William Johnson born in
County Down, Ireland.

1738—William Johnson settled in
Florida town, Montgomery county, and
built his first house (of three) which
he named Fort Johnson. Johnson came
to the Mohawk valley to manage the
landed estate of his uncle, Admiral
Warren.

1742—William Johnson builds stone
house, mill and store at present Fort
Johnson, Amsterdam town, Montgomery county. This house was named
first Mount Johnson. After it was fortified some ten years later it became
known at Fort Johnson, which name it
now bears. The similarity of name in
Johnson's first two houses has been the
cause of considerable confusion. Ref-

erences in this work to Fort Johnson
mean the present Fort Johnson, town
of Amsterdam.

1745—Johnson appointed justice of
the peace of Albany county and colonel
of Albany county militia; organized
Mohawk valley militia.

1746—Johnson appointed commissioner of Indian affairs for New York
province.

1746—Johnson made a chief of the
Mohawk tribe under the name of War
raghegagey.

1750—Johnson resigns position of superintendent of New York province Indian affairs.

1750 — Col. Wm. Johnson made a
member of the governor's council of
the province of New York.

1754—Col. Johnson and party of Iroquois, including King Hendrick, attend
colonial conference at Albany, held to
discuss means of common defense, by
the American-British colonies, against
France.

1755 — Fort Canajoharie, at Indian
Castle, Herkimer county, built for protection of Mohawks, under supervision
of Col. Johnson.

1755—Johnson tendered an ovation
and public reception in New York city,
for his victory at Lake George.

1755 — Major-General Johnson, in
command of British-American army,
defeats French in Battle of Lake
George; 250 Mohawks in Johnson's
army; King Hendrick, Mohawk sachem, killed; Johnson was made a baronet and made colonial Indian superintendent and voted £5,000 by the English parliament, for this victory.
Johnson was wounded in the thigh in
this battle.

1758—Gen. Johnson with militia and
Indians starts for support of Gen.
Webb's British-American expedition to
reinforce Fort Oswego. Webb turns
back, Fort Oswego falls and Johnson's
party returns.

1756, August—Gen. Johnson leads In
dians and militia to assist Gen. Webb's
party for relief of Fort William Henry,
at the head of Lake George; expedition fails through Webb's incapacity
and Fort William Henry is captured by
French.

1758, April—Fort Herkimer attacked; Johnson calls out valley militia, but enemy escapes.

1758, July 8—Johnson and 400 Iroquois warriors join Gen. Abercrombie's British-American army at Ticonderoga, where it is disastrously defeated by French.

1759—Gen. Johnson succeeds to command of British-American army before Fort Niagara, after Gen. Prideaux is killed, and takes that French fort; 700 Iroquois in Johnson's force.

1759 — Johnson founds Johnstown, Fulton county.

1760—Gen. Johnson joins Gen. Amherst's British-American army which captures Montreal; 1,300 Iroquois warriors in Johnson's expedition.

1760—British Crown grants to Johnson the "Royal Grant" of 69,000 acres in Herkimer county, north of the Mohawk; previously deeded to him by the Mohawks.

1760 (about)—Johnson builds a summer residence, called Castle Cumberland, in Broadalbin town, Fulton county; also a fishing lodge on the Sacandaga in the town of Northampton, Fulton county.

1763 — Johnson completes Johnson Hall at Johnstown, Fulton county, and removes thence from Fort Johnson.

1764—Johnson holds a grand Indian council at Fort Niagara. From 1763-5 Johnson was continually occupied with affairs relative to the Pontiac Indian insurrection in the west. In 1763, Johnson Hall was fortified.

1766—Johnson supervises erection of St. George's Episcopal church at Schenectady. The same year he fitted up a Masonic lodge room, for the use of the fraternity at Johnson Hall.

1768—Council between Sir William Johnson, Indian colonial superintendent, together with British colonial authorities, and Iroquois at Fort Stanwix (now Rome), in which Six Nations relinquish large part of their lands to British Crown.

1771 — Johnson builds St. John's (Episcopal) church at Johnstown; school established here by Johnson about this time.

1772—Tryon county formed, through the influence of Johnson, and Johnstown made county seat.

1772—Gov. Tryon reviews three regiments of Mohawk valley militia (numbering 1,400 men), under command of Gen. Johnson at Johnstown, Burnets field (present Herkimer) and German Flats.

1774, July 11—Sir William Johnson dies at Johnstown, during Indian council. Funeral attended by 2,000 people, including many colonial officials and Indian chiefs. Sir John Johnson succeeds to his estate, including 173,000 acres of land.

1634-1911—MOHAWK VALLEY TRAVELERS' CHRONOLOGY.

This work contains accounts of twelve journeys through the Mohawk valley or over the Mohawk river, and this is a more complete list of these historic accounts than is contained in any work on the Mohawk valley, so far as the editor of this work knows. These interesting accounts throw a personal and vivid light on the history of this locality and they are as follows:

1634 (Series I., Chapter I)—Account of Dutch explorers, particularly of the valley from the Noses to a point opposite Caroga creek.

1757 (Series I., Chapter VI.)—French account of the Mohawk valley, north and south shore roads, from Fort Canajoharie (Indian Castle) to Schenectady.

1760 (appendix)—Account of Mrs. Grant of Laggan (author of the Memoirs of an American Lady) of Mohawk river voyage from Schenectady to Wood creek, and thence to Oswego, with stop at Fort Canajoharie (Indian Castle).

1783 (Series I., Chapter XVIII.)—Capt. Thompson's journey from Fort Plain to Fort Oswego, bearing news of cessation of Revolutionary war hostilities.

1788 (appendix)—First Mohawk valley trip of Elkanah Watson, Schenectady to Fort Schuyler (Rome).

1791 (appendix)—Second Mohawk valley trip of Elkanah Watson and companions, Albany to Oneida lake,

Oswego river, Onondaga lake, Cayuga and Seneca lakes, resulting in the formation of the Inland Lock and Navigation Co. and improvement of Mohawk river in 1796.

1792 (Series I., Chapter I.)—Account of traveler's trip through the Mohawk valley in 1792, from Schenectady to Oneida Castle.

1802 (Series II., Chapter I.)—Account of Rev. John Taylor's valley trip from Tribes Hill to Little Falls. See also account of Little Falls in Series II., Chapter VI., by Rev. Mr. Taylor.

1807 (Series II., Chapter VI.)—Christian Schultz's trip by packet batteau up the Mohawk river to Wood creek.

1825 (Series II., Chapter VII.)—Thurlow Weed's stagecoach journey over the Mohawk turnpike.

1848 (Series III., Chapter II.)—Trip of Lossing, the historian, from Currytown to Sharon Springs to Cherry Valley to Fort Plain; also reference to Erie canal packet boat trip from Fort Plain to Fultonville in Series III., Chapter XV.

1911 (Series III., Chapter V.)—Aeroplane flight of Atwood from Syracuse to Nelliston and from Nelliston to Castleton, on his St. Louis to New York air journey. The Mohawk river portion of the trip is described in a sketch by Atwood entitled "Following the Mohawk."

MOHAWK VALLEY MANUFACTURING CHRONOLOGY — SKETCHES OF PRINCIPAL INDUSTRIES AND OF CHEESE DAIRYING.

Following is a chronology of Mohawk valley manufacturing, inclusive of the manufacture of dairy products. This does not cover all the industries of the six Mohawk valley counties but it does include the principal industries, in which the great majority of the wage-earners of the valley are engaged. This chronology gives at a glance the beginnings and development of the leading manufactures.

1800 (about)—Manufacture of cheese for outside markets begun in Mohawk valley. Dairying became a large valley industry about 1825. Cheese making for market purposes was introduced into the Mohawk valley by New England immigrants into the Mohawk valley, principally in Herkimer county.

1807—Manufacture of woolen cloth began at Frankfort.

1809—James Burr and Tallmadge Edwards start business of dressing leather and making leather mittens in Kingsboro (now Gloversville), Fulton county; this was the beginning of the leather and glove industry of Fulton county.

1820—Manufacture of plows begun at Utica.

1830—Harry Burrell of Salisbury, Herkimer county, makes first shipment of cheese to England (10,000 pounds).

1831—Eliphalet Remington jr. opens forge for manufacture of gun barrels and firearms at Ilion, Herkimer county. He had previously made same from 1816 on his father's farm at Steele's Creek, Herkimer county.

1831 — Egbert Egberts invents a frame for knit goods manufacture, operated by power, at Albany, N. Y. Timothy Bailey aids in invention. Removed to Cohoes in 1832.

1832—Manufacture of knit goods begun at Cohoes by Egberts & Bailey; probably the inception of the knit goods business of the country; the Mohawk valley now (1914) being the center of American knit goods manufacture.

1836—Manufacture of axes and other edge tools begun in Cohoes.

1836 — Manufacture of ready-made clothing begun at Utica.

1836—Manufacture of cotton cloth (white goods) introduced at Cohoes by Peter Harmony, a Spaniard, who founded the Harmony Mills Co.

1840—Manufacture of ingrain carpets begun at Hagaman's Mills by Wait, Green & Co.; later J. Sanford & Son of Amsterdam.

1842—Manufacture of woolen goods begun at Little Falls.

1845 (about)—Manufacture of yarn begun at Little Falls.

1845—Manufacture of railroad steam locomotives begun at Schenectady.

1846 — First kid glove factory of Johnstown established.

1847—Manufacture of worsteds begun at Utica.

1848—Manufacture of linseed oil begun at Amsterdam.

1848—Manufacture of cotton cloth (white goods) begun at Utica; now (1914) largest center of this industry in New York state.

1857—Manufacture of knit goods begun at Amsterdam.

1859 — Manufacture of cotton and paper bags begun at Canajoharie.

1863—Manufacture of knit goods begun at Utica.

1863—Manufacture of knit goods machinery on a large scale begun in Cohoes.

1865—Manufacture of furniture begun at Fort Plain.

1868—Blood's broom factory established at Amsterdam; first large broom factory of that city.

1872—Manufacture of knit goods begun at Herkimer.

1872—Manufacture of knit goods begun at Little Falls.

1875—Alfred Dolge locates at Dolgeville and begins manufacture of felt goods, etc.

1878—Manufacture of brass begun at Rome, Oneida county

1886 — Manufacture of desks and typewriter cabinets begun at Herkimer.

1887—Manufacture of copper begun at Rome, Oneida county.

1887—Manufacture of knit goods begun at Fort Plain.

1888—General Electric Co. moves to Schenectady.

1889—Manufacture of player pianos and piano actions begun at St. Johnsville.

1890 (about) — Manufacture and packing of foodstuffs begun at Canajoharie.

1892—Manufacture of knit goods begun at St. Johnsville.

We have seen, in this review of events, the development of agriculture and manufactories in the valley. From a line of general crops raised on the farm we have witnessed a gradual change to dairying and haying with corn, oats, hops and barley as subsidiary crops. Also there has been a gradual increase in poultry, fruit-raising and market gardening. The raising of broom corn and hops, once important crops, have practically ceased except in Schoharie county, where hops are yet raised.

In 1909, in the six Mohawk valley counties, there were 18,457 farms, with about 1,350,000 acres of improved farm land, raising over $30,000,000 of products, exclusive of lumber.

Manufacturing in the Mohawk valley was generally introduced by New England men, who settled in the valley, after the close of the Revolution. Men of "Mohawk Dutch" descent also soon joined in this industrial movement, after it was brought well under way by the valley "Yankees."

Following the completion of the Erie canal came a boom in town building and the gradual growth of manufactures, which, however, had their greatest development in the valley after the Civil war. Today we see Utica a great knit goods and white goods manufacturing center, Rome a large producer of brass and copper goods, Frankfort of tools, Ilion the state's largest manufacturing center of typewriters and firearms, at Herkimer a great desk and furniture industry, Little Falls, St. Johnsville, Fort Plain, Amsterdam and Cohoes, centers for knit goods manufacturing, Dolgeville, New York's leading felt producing town, at Gloversville and Johnstown 80 per cent of the country's leather glove industry, Amsterdam the second carpet and rug manufacturing center in New York and the first broom-making city, and Schenectady the largest producer of electrical apparatus in the world, and the first New York city in the manufacture of locomotives. Those cited are only the leading industries of each town and there are other important and interesting industries, such as the making of player pianos at St. Johnsville, the manufacture of bags and the packing of food stuffs at Canajoharie, and a hundred other kinds of important industries located within the confines of the six Mohawk valley counties—aside from Schoharie, which is almost entirely an agricultural section, possessing but few manufacturing establishments.

It was about the middle of the nineteenth century and particularly at the close of the Civil war that the Mohawk valley changed from an agricultural to a manufacturing district—now one of the most important in the United States.

In the Mohawk valley, at Palatine Bridge, was developed the sleeping and palace car and the elevated car roof; at Newport, the Yale lock and, at Ilion, the modern typewriter, while Cohoes was the birthplace of the knit goods industry. Herkimer county was also the birthplace of American cheese making for market. Today at Schenectady the laboratories of the General Electric Company are continually producing new electrical devices.

A study of local manufacturing and agricultural interests is advised for public school pupils, in connection with the study of valley history. They should be considered in connection with their birth, growth and present importance.

In 1912 in the six Mohawk valley counties there were 1,321 factories, employing 88,271 operatives, producing goods of an estimated value of $200,-000,000 annually.

For detailed New York state manufacturing information consult the New York State Department of Labor Industrial Directory.

The following sketches of the principal manufacturing industries of the Mohawk valley, properly belong in the section of this work devoted to "Additions." However, as the manufacturing chronology belongs under the Mohawk Valley Chronology it has been thought best to publish both the manufacturing chronology and the historical and descriptive sketches of Mohawk valley manufactures in this place. The industries of the valley are varied, unique and important, and, besides those mentioned, there are here represented many of the manufactures of the United States. The leading industries are agriculture, knit goods, electrical machinery, leather gloves and leather, white goods, rugs and carpets and wood working.

Industries of the six Mohawk valley counties which employ over 1,000 hands are here described. Two others —broom making and felt manufacturing—which employ nearly 1,000 hands and which soon will probably exceed that number, are also included. The leading industries are here described in their chronological order, beginning with cheese dairying, which was the first to develop and which the editor of this work considers as much manufacturing as any other industry.

———

1785-1914—Cheese dairying and general dairying in Herkimer county and the Mohawk valley.

The following account comprises a history (from 1785 to 1914) and description of cheese-making and dairying in Herkimer county and the Mohawk valley. It may be remembered that the same conditions, etc., apply to the valley adjacent to Herkimer, except in the earliest years of cheese-making, particularly to Montgomery and Oneida counties, as well as Herkimer. It is a fine line which divides some agricultural from industrial work or manufacturing. It is difficult to understand why cheese-making or butter making is not as much a manufacturing enterprise as the making of locomotives, a rug or an undershirt. Also why cheese-making should be considered an agricultural pursuit and the manufacture of condensed milk a manufacturing enterprise is a question.

From Hardin's History of Herkimer County (1893), Chapter VII., on "History of Cheese Dairying in Herkimer County," taken from a chapter written (in 1878) by X. A. Willard. The following contains almost the entire paper:

The rock, which underlies a large share of the lands in the towns north of the Mohawk, is the Utica slate. It is of a dark color, of a soft or flaky nature, is found cropping out in numerous places, and, when exposed to the atmosphere and frosts, readily falls to pieces and is mingled with the soil. The rock contains considerable organic matter (according to Emmons, more than ten parts in one hundred), is charged with sulphur and contains lime, and, when near the surface, forms a soil rich in fertilizing elements and not easily exhaustible. Instances can be pointed out where fields of this black slate have been plowed and cultivated for more than twenty years in succession without the application of manures and yielding good returns each year; and there are pastures and meadows that have lain in grass for thirty or forty years and which are still yielding abundant crops.

In the towns south of the Mohawk river, the Utica slate is found only to a limited extent, the Frankfort slate, limestone and Marcellus shales being the characteristic underlying rocks.

It is the modifying influence which these rocks are supposed to exert on the grasses and the comparatively large surface over which they extend, together with the abundant supply of never-failing streams and springs of pure water, that render Herkimer county peculiarly adapted to grazing, giving a richness and flavor to her cheese product not easily obtained in less favored localities.

The fall of rain and snow during the year is considerably more here than in many other parts of the state, and this is supposed to act favorably on the grasses and in the preservation of meadows. The grasses usually grown and considered most productive are timothy, June or Kentucky blue grass, red top and orchard grass, with the clovers, red and white. These grow on the sward and are well adapted to the soil and climate. White clover and June grass are indigenous and are deemed of great value for pasturage.

* * * At first and for many years after dairying had become established, farmers raised their own stock by seleeting calves from their best cows, and in this way the milking stock was greatly improved. The early settlers along the Mohawk came mostly from Germany and Holland and they brought with them what was known as the "Dutch cow." She was medium in size, black and white, often red and white, very hardy, a good feeder and of deep milking habit. The early dairymen got their best cows from this breed. * * * As the price of cheese advanced, the praetise of filling up the herds, with stock driven from other counties, often from remote localities, obtained; and, although this means of keeping good the herd was more or less deprecated by farmers as unsatisfactory, still the practise grew and became pretty general. [In the thirty-six years—from 1878 to 1914—since the writing of this article there has been an almost complete reversion to the Dutch cow of the first settlers—the Holstein-Frisian breed, which is in general use by the progressive dairymen of the Mohawk valley. Short-Horn Durhams, Devons, Ayrshires and Jerseys were introduced between 1830 and 1900, but they have been generally discarded now (1914) for the "Dutch cow."]

Herkimer county may justly claim the honor of giving birth to cheese dairying as a specialty in America. It was from Herkimer county that the business began to spread to the adjoining counties, and from thence to the different states and to Canada. In many instances, Herkimer county dairymen, removing to distant localities, were the first to plant the business in their new homes; while in many instances, cheese-dairying was commenced by drawing upon Herkimer for cheese makers to manage the dairies. Often too, parties were sent into the county to obtain a knowledge of cheese making, and, returning home, carried the art into new districts. Thus for many years Herkimer was the great center from which the new districts drew the necessary information and skill for prosecuting the business of cheese dairying with profit and success.

Cheese was made in small quantities in the county as early as 1800. In 1785 a number of persons, emigrating from New England, settled in the town of Fairfield [Herkimer county]; among them may be named Cornelius Chatfield, Benjamin Bowen, Nathan Arnold, John Bucklin, Daniel Fenner, Nathan Smith, the Eatons, Neelys, Peter and William Brown and others. Some of these families, coming from Cheshire, Mass., brought with them a practical knowledge of the method by which cheese was made in a small way in Cheshire. But notable among these families were Nathan Arnold, Daniel Fenner and the Browns, who settled in the southern part of the town of Fairfield and near each other. Arnold's wife was a cheese maker, and he is the first, it is believed, who began cheese dairying in the county.

Except along the Mohawk nearly the whole county was then a dense forest. Brant, the famous Mohawk chief, and his bloody warriors, had been gone several years but traces of their pillage and murders were fresh among the early settlers in the valley and along the river. * * *

From 1800 to 1826 cheese-dairying had become pretty general in Herkimer county but the herds were mostly small. As early as 1812-1816 the largest herds, numbering about forty each, were those belonging to William Ferris, Samuel Carpenter, Nathan Salisbury and Isaac Smith in the northern part of the county, and they were regarded as extraordinary for their size.

About 1826 the business began to be established in adjoining counties, in single dairies here and there, and generally by persons emigrating from Herkimer county. The implements and appurtenances of the dairy were then very rude. The milking was done in open yards and milking barns were unknown. The milk was curded in wooden tubs, the curd cut with a long wooden knife and broken with the hands. The cheeses were pressed in log presses standing exposed to the weather. The cheeses were generally thin and small. They were held through the season and, in the fall, when ready for market, were packed in rough casks made for the purpose and shipped to different localities for home consumption. Prices in those days were low, ranging from 4 cents to 6 cents per pound. * * *

In 1826, Harry Burrell of Salisbury, Herkimer county, then a young man full of enterprise and courage, having learned something of the sly methods of Ferris and Nesbith [of Massachusetts, then the leading valley buyers of cheese] resolved to enter the field as their competitor. He pushed his operations with great vigor and bought a large share of the cheese at a price above that figured by the Massachusetts firm. He afterwards became the chief dealer in dairy goods in Central New York, often purchasing the entire product of cheese made in the United States.

Mr. Burrell was the first to open a cheese trade with England, commencing shipping as a venture in 1830 or 1832, at the suggestion of Erastus Corning of Albany. The first shipment was about 10,000 pounds. He was the first also to send cheese to Philadelphia [first shipping there in 1828. Mr. Burrell's business, on his death, was carried on by his sons, D. H. Burrell and E. S. Burrell of Little Falls, which place was the home of Harry Burrell during the last twenty years of his life].

From 1836 to 1860 several Herkimer county merchants had entered the field as cheese buyers, the most notable of whom were Samuel Perry of Newport, V. S. Kenyon of Middleville, A. H. Buel of Fairfield, Perry & Sweezy of Newport, Benjamin Silliman of Salisbury, Lorenzo Carryl of Salisbury, Frederick Ives, James H. Ives, Roger Bamber of Stark, Simeon Osburne of Herkimer and several others. Cheese during this time was usually bought on long credits, the dealers going through the country and purchasing the entire lot of cheese made or to be made during the season, advancing a small part of the money and agreeing to pay the balance on the first of Jan-

uary following. Failures would occur from time to time and the farmers selling to these unfortunate speculators not unfrequently lost the bulk of their labor for the season.

Up to 1840 the dairymen of Herkimer had made but little improvement in farm buildings or in appliances for the dairy. Lands were comparatively cheap and it was no unusual thing for men with little or no means to buy farms and pay for them by dairying. About this time or a little earlier the smaller farms of the county began to be absorbed by well-to-do dairymen and the plan of renting farms on what is known as the "two-fifths" system began to be adopted. * * *

In 1840 farmers had become so prosperous from dairying that they began to pay more attention to the care and management of stock. They not only looked more closely to the comfort of the herds, but "milking barns" for their own convenience and comfort began to be pretty generally substituted for the open yard in milking.

About this time also the first dairy steamer for making cheese was brought out by G. Farmer of Herkimer. It consisted of a boiler for the generation of steam, attached to a stove or furnace, with a pipe for conveying steam from the boiler to the milk vat, on the same principle as the milk vats now in use.

A branch of the steam pipe was connected with a tub for heating water for washing utensils used in the dairy. This apparatus of course was a crude affair compared with the modern, highly-improved cheese vat and steam boiler, but it was the first invention of the kind and led to grand results in labor-saving appliances in the dairy. In about ten years after Farmer's invention, which was extensively introduced into Herkimer and other counties, William G. Young of Cedarville brought out the steel curd-knife, which was a great improvement over the wire and tin cutters that Truman Cole of Fairfield had invented and had got into general use. The log presses were also fast going out of use—their place being supplied by the Kendall press. The Taylor and Oysten presses, both invented by Herkimer county men, were further improvements brought out between 1850 and 1860.

From 1850 to 1860 dairying began to assume formidable proportions. Prices had gradually risen from 5 to 7 cents, from 7 cents to 9 cents, and the business was considered more prosperous than any other farm industry. During this period the farmers of Herkimer county had generally acquired wealth or a substantial competence, and this was shown in the improved buildings and premises.

In 1857 Jesse Williams of Rome,

Oneida county (a dairyman who had learned cheese-making in Herkimer) conceived the idea of the factory system, but it did not begin to attract much attention until 1860, when plans were inaugurated for testing the system in Herkimer. The first factories were erected by Avery & Ives of Salisbury and by Mr. Shell of Russia. The system did not spread so rapidly at first in Herkimer, as it has in some new sections, because cheese-making was better understood by the mass of the farmers here than elsewhere; and the cheese of Herkimer having a high reputation in many of the large dairies, the dairymen were at first a little doubtful as to the success of the factories. They, however, soon wheeled into line, and now the last state census gives the number of factories in Herkimer county, in 1874, at 88, aggregating a capital of $235,070, and paying out annually in wages the sum of $48,-181. The number of cows in the county, whose milk was sent to the factories that year, was 32,372 and in 1875, 34,070; the number of patrons was 1,303.

[In 1861] * * * Dairymen and dealers began to meet at Little Falls on certain days of the week, for the purpose of making transactions in cheese. There was a large number of home dealers, some of them acting as agents for New York, Philadelphia and Baltimore houses, while others were seeking transactions on their own account. The fact that so many dairymen had lost money the previous year and the desire, on their part to sell for cash or short credits helped to start "Sales day" or a public market at Little Falls. Dairymen commenced in the Spring to bring small parcels of cheese into town on Mondays, offering it for sale to resident dealers and transactions were readily made, * * * and "market days," for the sale of dairy products at Little Falls, were inaugurated. At first two days in the week, Mondays and Wednesdays, were agreed upon, and the plan worked well and was satisfactory to all concerned. Soon dealers from New York and other cities began to visit the market, making such selections as they desired, while the dairymen, selling for cash and meeting with buyers who were ready to compete for their goods, were so pleased with the arrangement that they did not care to dispose of their cheese in any other way. * * *

In 1864 the first weekly reports of the Little Falls market, then and now [1878] the largest interior dairy market in the world, began to be made by the writer in the Utica Morning Herald. Previous to 1864, farmers relied on city quotations which were believed to be in the merchants' favor. Indeed so sharp was the competition at Little Falls that the prices paid at this market every week were not infrequently above New York quotations, and dairymen from other sections sought eagerly for these reports before selling. The factories also were sending their salesmen on the market; not only from Herkimer but from the adjoining counties, the "sales day" now being on Monday only of each week. From 1864 to 1870, the Little Falls cheese market had acquired so high a reputation that it was considered the center of the trade in America, and its weekly transactions had a controlling influence in establishing prices on the seaboard. Reports of the market at its close, were telegraphed, not only to parties engaged in the trade in our leading cities, but to the great cheese centers of Liverpool and London. During this time, besides a great number of farm-dairymen attending the market weekly, salesmen from 300 factories have sometimes been present while the regular list of factories doing business in the market numbered about 200. The quantity of cheese annually sold on the market has been estimated at 25,000,-000 to 30,000,000 pounds, but the actual shipment of dairy produce from the county was considerably less, as the factories after selling their goods by sample, shipped them at the railroad depots nearest the factory.

The "export" quantity (other than sold for local use) of cheese sent out from Herkimer county in 1864 was 16,-767,999 pounds, and, of butter, 492,673 pounds. In 1869 it was 15,570,487 pounds of cheese and 204,634 pounds of butter.

Up to 1871 the butter market at Little Falls had been held in the open street, but, early in January of that year, steps were taken to organize a Dairy Board of Trade for the State, with headquarters at Little Falls, that being the chief and only dairy market in the interior of the country.

In February, 1871, the New York State Dairymen's Association and Board of Trade was organized at Little Falls, at a public meeting there, this being the first dairymen's board of trade organized on the continent. Similar associations shortly followed at Utica, N. Y., and Elgin, Ill., and in other sections. Shortly after the organization of the Little Falls Dairymen's Association and Board of Trade, the citizens of Little Falls fitted up a board of trade room. In 1878 nearly all the factory made cheese of Herkimer county went to England.

Butter making has never been extensively practised as a specialty in Herkimer county, although considerable quantities of butter are made in the spring and fall in connection with cheese manufacture. The usual plan, in these seasons, when milk is delivered at the factories, is to allow farmers to skim one day's milk or the night mess of milk and then deliver the skimmed milk. In farm dairies the milk is set for a longer or a shorter period, and the skimmed milk made into cheese. - But this practise obtains for the most part only in spring and fall, while some of the factories will not allow any skimming, believing that a high reputation can only be maintained by manufacturing at all times nothing but "full-milk cheese." A few creameries have from time to time been operated in the county.

Commenting on the above [1878] article Hardin's [1892] History of Herkimer County, says:

Since the foregoing paper was written but few changes have taken place in cheese-dairying in Herkimer coun ty. The annual production of dairy products shows slight fluctuations from year to year, but has neither materially increased or decreased. The changes which have occurred have been mostly along the line of advanced methods of manufacture. The introduction of improved machinery into cheese and butter factories and of better blood into dairy herds. The machine recently [1892] invented by Dr. Babcock of the Wisconsin Experiment Station, Madison, Wis., for testing milk to determine the quantity of butter fats, is now in use in some creameries and factories, while the separator is quite extensively employed in the manufacture of butter.

Dairymen are giving more attention to means for increasing the capacity of their herds both with regard to production and quality of milk. The introduction of full-blooded males of the Holstein-Frisian [Dutch cow], Jersey and Guernsey breeds, for the accomplishment of this end, is consequently receiving considerable attention, which, with the better care and management, is gradually improving the average of the dairy cows of the county. The silo too, is beginning to command attention from the most progressive dairy farmers, a dozen or more being in successful operation in different localities in the county. A movement is also being made in the direction of winter dairying, which bids fair to add new impetus to this already important and prosperous industry.

In 1892 Herkimer county sold for "export" (other than home use), 206,-058 boxes of cheese, at an average of 60 lbs. per box, or a total for the year of 12,363,483 lbs., at an average price of .0915 cents per lb. The total value of this was $1,131,258, which, with the addition of $87,404 worth of dairy cheese, made a grand total for Herkimer county, in 1892, of $1,218,662. Prices from 1890 to 1892 ranged from 6¾c to 11c per pound.

There have been considerable general changes in the conditions of Mohawk valley dairying from the year when the foregoing was written (in 1878 and 1893) until the present (1914). In the last twenty years there seems to have been a tendency away from cheese-making—toward the production and shipping of milk and cream to cities and toward the manufacture of milk into products such as butter and condensed milk. There seems also to be a tendency among farmers toward combination in dairy production, a natural sign of the present times (1914).

Since 1893 the Dutch or Holstein-Frisian cow has resumed its old-time supremacy along the Mohawk, it being the animal favored by local dairymen. Also since 1893 Utica has vied with Little Falls as an interior first-hand market for cheese, and for a number of years the volume of cheese business transacted in Utica exceeded that of Little Falls. In 1913, however, Little Falls did a larger business than Utica, regaining once more its paramount position as the leading eastern cheese market.

The Fort Plain market, Feb. 22, 1914, quoted 16½ cents as the price paid producers of cheese for their product, while 22 cents was quoted as the retail price. In cities and points remote from dairy sections, the retail price of "American cheese" is greater (1914). Pasteurized milk sold in New York in 1914 for 10 cents per quart bottle, while the prediction was made, by those in a position to know, that it would not be many years before the metropolitan retail price per quart bottle would be 15 cents. Notwithstanding this increase in price paid to farmers, creameries and cheese factories for milk and milk products, it is said that the dairy herds of New York state are decreasing in size and that farmers are going into other lines of agricultural production. It was stated that in 1913 the dairy herds of the state decreased 30,000 cows. This condition is certainly peculiar. The requirements of the State Board of Agriculture may have affected the situation. All dairy farms and premises nowadays must be perfectly sanitary, or, rather, they are supposed to be. Rigid cattle inspection is practised and frequently farmers lose a considerable part of their herds because their cattle become infected by tuberculosis and are killed by state orders. It may be that in the future a general applica tion of the laws of sanitation to farms will make sickly cows a rarity and the farmer, adapting himself to new conditions, will make a fair profit at the business of dairying, for its products are bound to increase in value. Many farmers find profit in the business in this year—1914.

In 1912, in the six Mohawk valley counties, there were condensed milk factories located at Deansboro and Holland Patent, Oneida county; Newport, Herkimer county; St. Johnsville, Nelliston and Fultonville, Montgomery county. The Mohawk valley furnishes a large part of the New York city milk supply, as well as a large part of its cheese and butter.

There are (1914) manufactures of dairy machinery (165 employes) and of butter color and dairy preparations (21 employes) at Little Falls. A tendency toward organization among valley dairymen has become marked in recent years and there are many town and county dairymen's associations in existence. Very recently (April, 1914) a movement has been started toward a comprehensive association of the dairy producers of the three principal valley dairy counties of Oneida, Herkimer and Montgomery, as the following clipping will show:

Herkimer Citizen, April 7, 1914: Tuesday, in Herkimer, there was a meeting held of those interested in the formation of a Dairymen's League for this vicinity. The meeting was informal and was for the purpose of talking over the matter. It is proposed to have the organization take in the milk producers from Fort Plain to Holland Patent. A committee of sellers can act for the entire district. The following milk stations were represented at

the meeting: Fort Plain, Little Falls, Middleville, Newport, Holland Patent, Prospect, Remsen, Trenton, Gravesville, Indian Castle, Poland, Cedarville and Inghams Mills.

That great good is expected as a result of the organization is shown by a comparison of the prices in this [Herkimer] section with those that prevail ed at Holland Patent, where a Dairy men's League has been formed and is in operation. The average for the Bor den prices in this section is $1.20 for the six months. At Trenton it is $1.47½, at Holland Patent $1.55½ and at Gravesville $1.54 1-6.

1805-1809—Fulton county's glove and leather industry first started.

Beers's "History of Montgomery and Fulton Counties" (1878) on page 175, gives a history of the origin of the glove and leather dressing business in Fulton county. It is in part as follows:

The business started first, as such, in Kingsboro (now on the northern limits of Gloversville) in 1809. That village and the surrounding country was orig inally settled by people from New Eng land, many of whom were skilled in the manufacture of tin. They were of gen uine Yankee stock, cute and indus trious and unlike their Dutch neigh bors along the Mohawk, took more naturally to manufacture and to trade than to farming. Hence they were ac customed to manufacture tin, load a horse with it and, leading the beast up the Mohawk and "Chenango country," as it was then called, would exchange the tinware for wheat, also for any other products which they needed or could readily sell.

The deer skins, one of which they generally bought for a medium sized tin basin, were sometimes rather a burden, for they were not used for much else than jackets and breeches, being prized more particularly for the latter purpose, because of their lasting qualities—no small consideration in those days of comparative poverty, economy and hard work.

The inhabitants had learned to tan the skins for clothing, according to the Indian process, using the brain of the deer itself, when convenient, but at this time often substituting the brains of hogs for that purpose. It is said that the brains of a deer will tan the hide, containing as it does the same elements as the "soda ash" fat liquor in use at the present day. * * * * *

About 1809 Tallmadge Edwards, formerly a leather-dresser in England, * * * moved from Massachusetts to Johnstown. In that year James Burr * * * * hired Edwards to come to

Kingsboro and teach them his art of dressing leather. Mr. Burr, in 1809, made up a few pairs of mittens which he took up the Mohawk and bartered off. In the following year he made a considerable number and sold at least part of them by the dozen, the first transaction of the kind. He subsequently made material improvements in the process of dressing skins, the most noticeable of which was the invention of the "bucktail," for which he received a patent. The apparatus is still in use, but the invention, like many others, proved rather a loss than otherwise to the inventor.

At this time, and much later, no gloves were manufactured, but only rough heavy mittens, which were needed to protect the hands of farmers and woodmen in cold and heavy labor. Even the leather which was produced up to a quite recent date [prior to 1878] was unfit for the manufacture of gloves, being too stiff and heavy. As lately as about * * * [1850], it is said, gloves were seldom cut, except an occasional pair, taken from the thinnest and most pliable parts of the skins. Gloves were originally cut, it is said, by laying a pasteboard pattern on the leather and following it with the shears. But very indifferent progress could be made in that way with the elastic leather now in use, and this fact shows the difference in quality quite distinctly. E. P. Newten started, in 1859, the first general machine works in Fulton county for the manufacture of glove and mitten cutting machines. The goods made in earlier days, however uncouth, furnished a good means of disposing of surplus deer skins, which, instead of being a drug on the market, were eagerly sought for, and when made up, were returned, with the next parcel of tinware, to be rebartered to parties from whom the skins had been obtained, besides being put upon the market for sale to any who wished to purchase. Elisha Judson, it is said, carried east, about 1825, the first load of gloves ever driven into Boston. The trip took six weeks.

In justice to others it may be said that the inception of Fulton county's glove business has been ascribed to others than those above mentioned. William C. Mills, in 1805, and Ezekiel Case (a former Cincinnati citizen) in 1806, are said to have started leather dressing and glove making operations. However it is certain that some time, during the years from 1805 to 1809, the leather dressing and glove making business of Fulton county began the start of its remarkable later growth.

In 1912 over 7,000 persons were employed in the glove industry and leather dressing business of Fulton county, and Johnstown and Gloversville did 80 per cent of the glove making of the United States. Johnstown and Gloversville are today (1914) the first towns in New York state in the manufacture of leather gloves and the dressing and preparation of leather. The latest invention in this industry is that of washable leather.

1831—Eliphalet Remington establishes an arms factory at Ilion. 1873— Typewriter construction begun in Remington works at Ilion.

In 1831, Eliphalet Remington jr. started a forge, at Ilion, Herkimer county, for the manufacture of gun barrels and firearms. He had previously had a small forge on his father's farm at Steele's Creek, Herkimer county. The business developed rapidly and during the years, 1861-5, furnished a large amount of arms to the Union armies, from the Remington factory at Ilion and a branch factory in Utica. About this time the Remington breech-loading gun was completed. In 1873, James Densmore, the inventor of the typewriter, came to Ilion and interested the Remingtons in his invention and shortly after the manufacture of typewriters began here, an industry which has developed into one of the largest in the valley.

In 1912, in the Remington typewriter works, 2,851 hands were employed and in the Remington arms works, 1,127 people were employed. Over 300 hands are employed in a fire arm factory in Utica, making about 1,500 people engaged in the manufacture of arms in the Mohawk valley

----

1832—Cohoes knitting industry established.

The father of the knitting business in this country was Egbert Egberts. While living in Albany in 1831, he became interested in the making of knit goods. Here he made his primary experiments in the construction of a knitting frame to be operated by power. Timothy Bailey, a practical mechanic, became associated with Egberts in this work of experimentation. Bailey built a wooden frame, which, when turned by hand, accomplished, in a small way, what Egberts desired. A knitting machine had already been invented. One was bought in Philadelphia by Bailey and brought to Albany, and his contrivance was applied, so as to produce knit goods by turning a crank. In 1832 Egberts and Bailey removed to Cohoes. The new machine was arranged to run by water power. Soon eight of these machines were constructed by Timothy Bailey and set in motion. The next step was to commence carding and spinning, thus preparing their own yarn. In this way the foundation was laid for the extensive knit goods business, which is an industry of the greatest importance in the Mohawk valley, and in the United States as well.

For some time the new invention was kept a secret. The doors were fastened by spring locks. Even Gen. George S. Bradford, who ran the mill by contract, was compelled to make an agreement that he would not enter the knitting room. Timothy Bailey, and a foreman who worked with him, were the only ones who understood the machines.

In 1853 there were three knitting mills in Cohoes, employing 750 hands and producing 45,000 dozen goods annually. In 1883 there were 25 knitting mills in Cohoes, with 177 sets of cards, 595 knitting cylinders and 4,140 operators. $1,600,000 was estimated to have been paid out annually, about this period, to employes in the Cohoes knit goods business. In 1863 the manufacture of knitting machinery was begun on a considerable scale at Cohoes, the birthplace of the knitting industry, which is now (1914) one of the two mammoth industries of the valley—knit goods and the making of electrical machinery. In 1912, 17,000 persons were employed in the knit goods industry in the Mohawk valley. There were factories in nineteen valley towns, with Utica, Amsterdam, Cohoes and Little Falls, the principal points of production in the order named.

1836—Cohoes, Harmony Mills (for the manufacture of white goods) established.

Peter Harmony, a Spaniard, was the founder of these mills and from him they have taken their name. Associated with him were many local public-spirited men and capitalists (largely of Dutch ancestry).

The company bought a tract of land about a quarter of a mile south of the Cohoes falls, and in 1837 erected a brick building, 165 feet long, 50 feet wide and four stories high, which complete with water-wheels, flumes, etc., cost $72,000. Three brick blocks were built at the same time, just west of the mill and divided into tenements for the use of the operatives. The mill was equipped with the best cotton machinery then in use, and the manufacture of cotton cloth [or white goods] began under the most favorable circumstances.

Bad management or some other cause handicapped the project from the start and, in the thirteen years, from 1837 to 1850, the only year which showed a profit was the single year of 1838. In 1850, under compulsory sale, the property was purchased by Garner & Co. of New York, and Alfred Wild of Kinderhook. The annual product of the mill at that time was 1,500,000 yards of print cloth; 700 bales of cotton were consumed, and 250 hands employed, a large number for that period in the valley.

Under new management, the Harmony mills prospered wonderfully and in 1883 they were the largest and most complete cotton manufacturing establishment in the United States. New mills of the company, or acquired by it were built in 1844, 1846, 1849, 1853, 1857, 1867, 1872. The north wing of the "Mastodon" or No. 3 mill, was built in 1866-7. In excavating for the foundation at the north end, a large pot hole was found in the bed of what had once been a stream of water. The pot hole was very deep, filled with peat, and at its bottom, 60 feet below the surface of the street, was found the almost perfect skeleton of a mastadon mammoth of a former age. The bones were carefully removed and presented to the state. They are now mounted and on exhibition in Geological Hall in Albany.

In 1912, 5,650 employes were at work in the white goods factories of the Mohawk valley, distributed as follows: Utica, 2,750; New York Mills, 1,800; Cohoes, 600; Capron, 250; New Hartford, 150; Little Falls, 100. Utica is the center of this industry for New York state.

1840—Amsterdam Carpet industry.

In 1840, Wait, Greene & Co. of Hagamans began the manufacture of carpets.

In 1842 William K. Greene withdrew from the firm of Wait, Greene & Co. of Hagamans Mills and came to Amsterdam where he started a carpet factory in a small factory where now stands the Greene Knitting Co. works. A few years later John Sanford acquired an interest in the business, which then removed to the old Harris mill further up the stream. Later Mr. Greene retired from the business and the firm thereafter became known as J. Sanford & Son. In 1853 the senior member retired and Stephen Sanford became sole proprietor. Later on the firm became S. Sanford & Sons and the Sanfords soon built up one of the largest carpet manufactories in the country. Several other carpet making establishments followed.

In 1912, in Amsterdam, 4,100 persons were employed in the manufacture of carpets and rugs.

1845—The Schenectady Locomotive Works.

About 1845 Schenectady became interested in the manufacture of locomotives. Some enterprising citizens, among them Hon. Daniel D. Campbell, Simon C. Groot and others, conceived the idea of here erecting locomotive works. Associated with the incorporators was John Ellis, "one of the shrewdest, ablest, hardheaded, Scotch men and skilful mechanics the state has ever known." The Norris brothers of Philadelphia, about as eminent locomotive builders as lived in the land, came to take control of the little plant. The Norrises started well, but for some reason, made a bad failure in the end. The stockholders took charge in 1850.

A disagreement occurred, in fact grew chronic among the shareholders. Ellis (the original practical man of the company) had the strength of his convictions and, when disputes arose, would not give way. He was the only real mechanic of the outfit and believed he understood his business. The stockholders endeavored to get rid of him but with true Scottish tenacity he stuck to the works. Walter McQueen was associated with Ellis, and McQueen was a grand mechanic, understanding every phase of the business. The McQueen engine soon became known all over the United States. One of them, purchased by the government, rolled into Fairfax Court House, one fine afternoon in the fall of 1862, when the 134th was lying there drilling for the awful experience they were to undergo. The Schenectady men recognized an old friend, and, swarming about it, patted it like a horse and would have hugged it if they could. The genius of McQueen and the business ability of Ellis were building up an immense plant, soon to rival the Baldwins of Philadelphia and the Rogers of Paterson.

Yates's Schenectady County (1902) says: "Today the plant is one of the largest in the world, its workmanship unsurpassed and, in recent trials, outstripping every locomotive on earth. '999' of the Empire State Express, was the admiration of every sightseer at the Columbian Exposition in Chicago [in 1893]. Yet '999' is an everyday engine now besides the monster of the type of 2207 [and of still later types]."

In 1912 in Schenectady, 3,300 employes were engaged in the manufacture of locomotives; in Rome 250 were employed in this industry, a total for the valley of 3,550 employes in locomotive manufacturing.

1874—Dolgeville felt manufacturing established.

In 1874, Alfred Dolge, a young German who was engaged in the importing of piano material in New York, and who also had started the domestic manufacture of piano felt in Brooklyn, came up to Dolgeville, prospecting for spruce wood, which is used in the manufacture of piano sounding boards. He purchased the tannery property and, in April, 1875, began his manufacturing operations, which later developed into the largest of their kind in the United States and included (1893) felt mills, felt shoe factories, factories for piano cases, piano sounding boards, piano hammers and lumber yards. In 1875 Dolgeville's population numbered 325. Alfred Dolge subsequently failed and removed to California, where he founded another Dolgeville. His industries in Dolgeville (Herkimer and Fulton counties) have been continued in other hands and the felt industry is now the largest of its kind in New York state.

In 1912, in Dolgeville, 713 persons were engaged in the manufacture of felt, and in Oriskany, 120, making a total for the felt industry of the valley of 833 employes.

1878—Rome brass industry. 1887—Rome copper industry.

In 1878 the manufacture of brass began at Rome and in 1887 the manufacture of copper began there. These are among the largest of the valley industries. In 1912, in the Rome brass works, 1,800 employes were engaged; in Rome copper works, there were 600 hands employed.

1888—The General Electric Company comes to Schenectady.

In 1888 there came a corporation to Schenectady which was destined to make it one of the chief manufacturing and electrical centers of the world. The Jones Car Works of Green Island had come to Schenectady (in 1872) and had established a plant on the present site of the General Electric Company. It failed (in 1884) and went into the hands of a receiver. Under the dircetion of the court, its real estate was offered for sale. Hon. John A. De-Remer, the receiver, obtained an order from the court for the sale of the property for $45,000. The attention of the Edison Machine Works of Georck street, New York city, was attracted

to it and negotiations were entered into. The company, then by no means a large corporation, examined the situation and were struck by its advantages. Its directors discovered that they could not get in New York what they needed. Here then were railroad and canal connections, with all points of the compass at the door of their shops, and opportunities for experimental work along the bank of the canal were unequalled anywhere. But they would give but $37,000 for the whole outfit. The citizens took hold of the matter and private and personal subscription soon made up the $45,000. The original industry grew, daily increasing its output enormously and bringing work and workmen to the town. A connection was formed with Thompson and Houston, with immense plants in Lynn, Mass., and Orange, N. J. The works doubled in size and business. Like in all factory towns a great number of cheap saloons sprang up on Kruesi avenue, leading to the General Electric Works. The General Electric Company established its own restaurant in its works and desired to close up this street of saloons, besides which the company needed the land for the enlargement of its own works.

In 1899 the citizens of Schenectady raised $30,000 by subscription, the street was purchased and given to the General Electric Company, the gift guarded only by the promise that if the plant removed from Schenectady, the property was to revert to the subscribers to the fund. The corporation soon showed its appreciation of this generosity of the people by a subscrip tion of $15,000 to the local public li brary and by many later public bene factions.

In 1897, the General Electric Com pany did a business of $11,170,319; in 1901, of $27,969,541. 60 per cent of this business was done at Schenectady. In 1901, the employes of the company at Schenectady numbered 7,651, with a pay roll of $100,000 per week.

In 1912, in the General Electric Co.'s works at Schenectady, 17,000 persons were employed. The works are constantly enlarging and form one of the world's great industries. They have made Schenectady from a quiet village of 1880 into a great city in 1914.

The woodworking establishments of Herkimer, including desks, house and office furniture, and wood trim, employed 1,202 hands in 1912.

The wood manufactures of the Mohawk valley, including the above and other branches, constitute one of the largest industries of the six valley counties. About 2,500 persons were engaged in the wood manufactures in these counties (1912), principally in Herkimer, Oneida and Montgomery, in the order named. Herkimer was the center of this industry and Herkimer county employed nearly four-fifths of the operatives in valley wood manufactures, principally at Herkimer, Little Falls and Ilion.

Metal manufactures and iron founding employed several thousand people in the Mohawk valley in 1912, in many widely varying industries, including the making of metal beds and heating apparatus, at Utica and Rome.

Clothing, millinery, etc., manufactures, in 1912, employed over 1,700 persons in the six Mohawk valley counties, 1,600 of whom were operatives in Utica industries of this character.

Silk manufactures and silk throwing and winding employed, in 1912, over 1,500 persons in the six Mohawk valley counties.

The packing of food products, including canned goods, employed over 1,500 operatives, in the six Mohawk valley counties in 1912. Over 1,100 of these were hands employed in factories in Oneida county, over 300 in Canajoharle, Montgomery county, and the balance in several small factories elsewhere.

Broom factories, in 1912, in the six Mohawk valley counties, employed over 900 operatives. Broom corn growing was at one time an important feature of valley agriculture, but has been entirely discontinued for about twenty years. Broom making machinery and broom appliances are also made in the valley. Amsterdam was the center of Mohawk valley broom making, over 800 hands being there employed in 1912.

APPENDIX

ADDITIONS, NOTES, CORRECTIONS

The editor of this work regrets that the greater part of the matter in this Appendix could not be contained in the main body of this book; a number of causes prevented its insertion there. This Appendix contains some of the most interesting matter concerning the history of our valley. In any future edition of this work the following pages will be put in their proper place in the main body of this book. The following series and chapter headings relate to similar ones in the major portion of the work. That is the Appendix chapter numbers indicate the chapter to which its matter properly belongs in the main body of the book. The editor of this work suggests the main chapters be read first and that the reader then turn to the Appendix and read the added matter relative to each chapter herein contained.

SERIES I.

CHAPTER I.

The Mohawks and Six Nations—The Iroquoian Tribes of North America— The Iroquois Legend of Hiawatha.

With the continued publication of this work, in weekly newspaper form, it has grown from a study dealing with a section of the middle Mohawk valley into a general historical review of life along the Mohawk river. It is therefore deemed best by the editor to add the following general sketch of the Mohawk Indians and of the Five Nations or later Six Nations (also called the Iroquois confederacy), of which the Mohawks were a part. The Five Nations formed themselves only a part (although the most powerful) of a great family of Indian tribes which is

called the Iroquoian. The life, customs, wars and legends of the Five Nations were common to all the five tribes, including of course the Mohawks. Therefore the life and story of the Mohawk tribe forms most interesting reading to the valley people of the present. However, it is a most voluminous subject, and the reader is referred to works dealing especially with the Iroquois. In these pages the story of the Mohawks is interwoven with that of the white peoples of the valley. The following general sketch and the great legend of the Iroquois, Hiawatha, is given in the following pages and will be found of interest.

The Delawares have a legend that their remote ancestors and those of the Iroquois originally formed one tribe long ages ago, which, through the centuries, gradually worked their way from westward of the Rocky mountains to east of the Alleghanies, the two peoples eventually separating into two nations.

The Mohawk valley and the six Mohawk valley counties formed the home of two of the tribes of the Iroquois league—the Mohawks in the eastern half and the Oneidas mostly in Oneida county.

The Mohawks (also formerly written Mohocs) are commonly regarded by historians as among the most powerful and intelligent of our savage aborigines; of good stature and athletic frames, naturally warlike and brave, they possessed in large measure all the qualities making up the savage's highest type of man. Simms says the word Mohawk comes from an Indian word meaning "muskrat" and the river was so called because of the numerous muskrats which lived in its banks. In the eighteenth century the country of the Mohawks extended from the mouth of their river westward to about the present location of Frankfort. West of that was the country of the Oneidas extending westward to the Onondaga country. The Oneidas were mostly located in the county of that name, their chief castle being on Oneida creek, the western boundary of Oneida county, about six miles from where it empties into Oneida lake.

From a historical address delivered by Percy M. Van Epps of Glenville, Schenectady county, in 1913, at a reunion of the Rockefeller family in Amsterdam:

Here in our valley we have with us the handiwork and traces of several different peoples. Not to speak at all of certain forms of stone implements, that by some have been called paleolithic and assigned a great antiquity, we come to a class of objects about which we can speak with more certainty.

In the closing days or centuries of the glacial period, when, due to some unknown climatic change, the great shect of ice was melting and its southern border was slowly creeping northward, there came a time when the ancient valley of the St. Lawrence, yet blocked by the retreating glacier front, held back its waters, causing for a time the existence of a mammoth interior lake, occupying not only the present sites of Lake Erie and Lake Ontario but of much additional territory. This ancient glacial lake is known to scientists as Lake Iroquois.

For a time the Mohawk valley served as an outlet for this lake or rather interior sea [of fresh water]. It now appears certain that a race or tribe of people followed closely the retreating glacier front and lived for a time in our valley, while yet it served as an outlet for Lake Iroquois. It is very likely that they were a people closely resembling the Eskimos, perhaps their ancestors. The river at this period flowed at a far higher level than at present and the traces of this people have all been found at high levels along the sides of the valley, or on the bluffs and hills above.

After the glacier and the fur clad people had disappeared far to the north, a new race came into the valley, probably from the west. They were probably predecessors of the Indians of colonial times, but the class of relics left by this race differs greatly from the Indian relics of later date. Little is known about this people. * * Next in order, as we interpret the rec-

ords, came the Mohicans or Eastern Indians. They evidently occupied the eastern end of our valley for a long time and perhaps three-fourths of all the surface relics found were left by them.

The Mohawks came to this valley for a permanent home, not until after Jacques Cartier had made his memorable voyage up the St. Lawrence [in 1534]. Cartier found Mohawks living at Hochlega, above the present site of Montreal.

Some time after this date the Mohawks had a bloody battle with an Algonquin nation and were whipped and well nigh exterminated. The remnant fled southward through the wilderness and sought shelter in three secluded glens bordering our river. Here in their fortified villages they lived until they again became a strong nation, when, abandoning their forest homes they built their long houses on the very banks of the Mohawk. This happened just prior to the arrival of the Dutch in our valley in 1623-30. [Indian Hill, near Fort Plain, Montgomery county, is supposed to be the site of one of these three castles referred to.]

The Mohicans disputed the Mohawks' claims to the valley and in 1669, despite the strong protest of the English, sent an expedition against them from Massachusetts. A battle was fought below Amsterdam, and, in the second day's fight (which occurred at the foot of a steep hill at Hoffmans called Towereune), the Mohicans were utterly routed with many of their number killed, among whom was their chief, Chic-a-tau-bet.

Beers's History says:

It is difficult to locate the sites of the Mohawk villages, designated castles, a term which implied places furnished with palisades or some other protection that distinguished them from more migratory and less defensible villages. At an early day these Indians built their huts near together, the better to resist the invading foe. Great danger from an enemy, however, sometimes compelled a migration of the camp, or convenience of hunting and fishing dictated it. The Mohawks once had a strong castle nearly four miles south of Fort Plain, in a well-chosen position on an elevated tongue of land between two streams, called Indian Hill [See Chap. XV., Series III., P. 301 of this work]. This plateau presents, on the west toward the Otsquene, an impracticable bluff. The northern declivity of the hill is more gentle, and thirty or forty rods below its termination the stream mentioned [the Otsquene] empties into the Otsquago. Upon the hillside the entrance of the castle may still be traced, as the ground has never been cultivated. The relics found here, including fragments of pottery, bones, bone implements, fresh water clam shells, etc., indicate that the place was probably early and long one of the chief strongholds of the tribe. It is believed that the occupancy of this site should be dated more than 250 years ago. The Mohawks also had a castle within the present limits of Fort Plain, at the termination of the high ground on the east side of the Otsquago, now called Prospect Hill. The site was occupied much later than the other, as shown by the discovery of rings, wampum shells, etc., introduced by the Jesuits or others of the first white men who ventured into the valley. The position of this village was also well chosen for defence and observation. It is said to have been called by the Indian Ta-ragh-jo-rees— "Healthy Place." [This village is called Osquage in the Dutch account of 1634. This may have been the name of the village while Taraghjorees was the name of the hill on which it stood. Taraghjorees has been translated "hill of health."]

For a description of some of the Indian villages along the Mohawk in 1634, see the account of Dutch travelers of that date in Chap. I., Series I. of this work. This book does not pretend to place the sites of Mohawk villages in the valley. It is a much discussed question. In this work authorities are quoted, which seem to the editor reasonable and logical.

It has been previously noted that, practically throughout the eighteenth century, the Mohawks had but two principal towns or castles along our river—one at Dyiondarogon (or Tiononderoga) at Fort Hunter, Montgomery county, and the other at Canajoharie or Fort Canajoharie (after the erection of a fortification there in 1755), at present Indian Castle in the town of Danube, Herkimer county. Canajoharie was called the upper and Dyiondarogon the lower Mohawk castle.

Dyiondarogon or Tionderoga is also written Icanderoga and Teondeloga. It is said the meaning of one (or all) of these words is "two streams coming together," referring to the junction of the Schoharie with the Mohawk at present Fort Hunter, near which this Mohawk palisaded village or lower "castle" was located. Canajoharie, the name of the upper "castle" has been (as before mentioned) translated by Brant as meaning "the pot that washes itself," referring to that natural curiosity, the great pothole at the end of the gorge of Canajoharie creek in Canajoharie village. The Mohawks gave the name Canajoharie to the whole river country between the Noses and Little Falls, as before stated, and the Canajoharie village and fort, at present Indian Castle, took its name from this Indian district.

Because it was the most warlike tribe of the Six Nations or the Iroquois confederacy, the war chief of the league was selected from the Mohawk nation. The council fire was kept by the central tribe, the Onondagas. The Five Nations numbered about 13,000 at the advent of the Dutch in 1609, with over 2,000 warriors.

The following relative to the Iroquoian Indians (of which the Six Nations were a part), is largely taken or condensed from an article on the subject by J. N. B. Hewitt in Appleton's Encyclopedia:

The Indians of the Six Nations or the Iroquois confederacy were a branch of the Iroquoian family of red men, perhaps the most important of the Indian families of tribes in North America. As before stated the Iroquois confederacy or Six Nations of the eighteenth century was composed of the Mohawks, Oneidas, Tuscaroras, Onondagas, Cayugas and Senecas, in the order named, from east to west. The Mohawks occupied the valley of the river to which they gave their name. The word Iroquois is said to mean in Algonquin "real, natural snakes"—an application which seemed natural to the Algonquin tribes who were deadly enemies of the Iroquois.

The Iroquois of the Six Nations called themselves the Aguinoshioni or Konoshioni, signifying cabin makers or people of the Long House. This "Long House" became figurative of their political organization, extending from the shores of Lake Erie to the banks of the Hudson. The Mohawks kept the "eastern door" the Senecas the "western door."

The chief tribes of the Iroquoian Indians were the Hurons, Wyandots, Tionontates (or Tobacco nation), the Attiewendaronk (or Neuter nation), the Eries or Cat (Raccoon) nation, the Canastogas (or Susquehannocks), the Tceroki (Cherokee) nation, the Nottoways and the Six Nations or the Iroquois confederacy—Mohawks (or Caniengas), Oneidas, Tuscaroras, Onondagas, Cayugas and Senecas. These latter are generally termed the Iroquois. [All these Iroquoian Indians were probably descendants of one original tribe, which later became many times subdivided. The Six Nations probably formed one tribe at one time, which later became divided into the six tribes or nations.]

The Iroquoian Indians, before the coming of the white man, occupied New York, Pennsylvania, the region about Lake Erie, north of Lake Ontario and the St. Lawrence valley. Others of the kindred tribes of the Iroquoian family lived in two areas in the present southern states—one in the eastern Carolinas, and the other partly in the western Carolinas, and parts of the states of Georgia, Alabama, Tennessee, Kentucky and the Virginias. (See map of the "Linguistic Stocks of American Indians North of Mexico," Vol. VI., Appleton's Enclopedia.)

The Huron or Wyandot tribe lived about Lake Simcoe and the St. Lawrence; the Tionontates (or Tobacco nation), west of Lake Ontario and south of the Hurons and in New York; the Eries or Cat (Raccoon) nation, south of Lake Erie; the Wenrohronan, southeast of the Eries in Pennsylvania; the Canastogas (or Susquehannocks), and their allies, along the Susquehanna; and the Iroquois or Five Nations in Central New York.

The western southern Iroquoian area was occupied by the Tceroki (Cherokees) and the eastern southern Iroquoian area was the home of the Tuscaroras, the Nottoways and other kindred but unimportant tribes. Many of the tribes mentioned, although of kindred blood, were deadly enemies and waged a constant war against each other.

Says Hewitt regarding Iroquoian characteristics:

The marriage tie was not a bond of strength, being broken for the good or the convenience of the persons or families concerned. * * *. The line of descent was in the female, and the children were virtually the property of the clan rather than of the family, which was only a subdivision of the clan.

In the Iroquoian pantheon the gods of the sky, the sun, the moon and earth, the stars, thunder and lightning, storm and wind, fire and of dreams (the mouthpiece of the sky god) were the chief and most influential. The treatment of disease and wounds was in the hands of the shamans [medicine men] mainly.

Long-houses of bark and saplings for dwellings, and caches of riven pieces of timber for the storage of their [maize], vegetables, roots, squashes and gourds, were built by these people. They constructed palisades around their chief towns or villages. The tillage of the land was carried on mainly by the women and girls, but labor was not considered degrading. They raised tobacco and many kinds of vegetables, including a kind of potato. They also manufactured sugar and syrup from the sap of the maple tree, and it was from them that the white people learned the process of this manufacture.

Their government was in the hands of chiefs divided into two classes, one of each class belonging to every clan. These chiefs were nominated by the suffrages of the women of the clan to which they belonged by birth or adoption, but such nomination had to be passed upon by the tribal, and among the Iroquois (Five Nations) by the federal council as well. The chiefs held office for life unless deposed for cause. In statecraft the Iroquois were politic and crafty but, magnanimous to captives [provided they were spared from torture]. Their cunning and caution were proverbial among their Indian neighbors. The adoption of captives into full citizenship with the free Iroquois, to replace those who had been lost in battle or by capture, was a marked policy of the Iroquois league; and it was by means of these adopted aliens under the discipline of Iroquoian institutions and under the guidance of Iroquoian commanders, that the confederacy was able to complete its war-parties, depleted by almost incessant warfare, and to hold high its name and power for so long a period. During the long period of their intercourse with the Dutch and English colonists before the Revolution, these Indians were remarkably noted for their good faith, when once their word was given.

Woman's position was high among the Iroquois. Property was vested in them and they could command cessation of war. They were the suffrage sex, as previously mentioned. The general council of the Five Nations consisted of two delegates from the Senecas, the most numerous tribe, and one each from the Mohawks, Oneidas, Onondagas, and Cayugas.

In the foregoing the word "Iroquoian" refers to the entire North American Indian family, of many tribes as stated but of similar blood. The word Iroquois has been applied to that particular New York state confederation of these people known first as the Five Nations and after 1722, as the Six Nations. It is to this people, of which the Mohawks formed a part, that reference is made when the Iroquois are mentioned in the following lines:

Notwithstanding all their wars, which were chiefly undertaken to maintain national independence, there is to be found, among the nobler traits of the Iroquois, a strong love for peace, a great regard for law and custom, a reverent homage paid to ancestral greatness, a lively sentiment of the brotherhood of man, and strong social and domestic affections.

The league was originally designed to be a permanent central government, rather than a temporary union of peoples and common interests.

Local matters concerning individual tribes were to be determined, as formerly, by the local council, but after that the council was to be guided by the principles of the federal constitution. The federal government was lodged in the hands of fifty chiefs of the highest order, divided unequally among the tribes, who were also members of the tribal council of the tribe to which they belonged. The tenure of office of these chiefs was for life, unless deposed for cause, and their official acts in all things was acknowledged throughout the entire confederacy. One of the distinctive features of this league was the avowed purpose of its founders to abolish war and murder by the peaceful expansion of the confederacy so as to induce all the tribes of men to adopt its principles and to agree to live under its institutions; notwithstanding this, the history of the league is one of almost incessant warfare.

The first known act of the league from the valley of the St. Lawrence, the direct result of which was to embroil the [Iroquois] confederates with the Huron tribes living about Lake Simcoe, to whom the fugitives from the St. Lawrence had fled for protection.

In 1534 Cartier met a tribe of Iroquoian stock, living on the Bay of Gaspe, and his is the first historic mention of this most interesting Indian people. Before the year 1600, the Five Nations had waged war with all the Algonquian tribes whose lands were coterminous with those from which the Hurons had been expelled. In 1622 this struggle was at its height. In the year 1609, Champlain, espousing this quarrel of the Hurons and Algonquians, marched with them and several Frenchmen against the Iroquois and succeeded in defeating a party of these [probably Mohawks] on the banks of Lake Champlain. The confederacy never forgave the French, and the Iroquois opposition thus aroused eventually cost France her North American possessions. In 1615, Champlain, who had invaded the Iroquois country, was defeated in the Onondaga section, and, wounded himself, was driven back to Canada.

The wars of the Iroquois to maintain independence continued with a few short intervals, until 1649, when the Iroquois drove from their Simcoe country the remnants of the Huron tribes whom they had not killed or taken into captivity. The victorious Iroquois then began a war with the Neuter nation, which culminated in 1651 in the utter dispersion of this people by death or capture. In the meantime the Tobacco nation had been compelled to flee to the region about Lake Superior to seek an asylum among Algonquin tribes. The Eries or Cat (Raccoon) nation also were almost annihilated and the survivors were forced to abandon their country in 1655. In 1657 a long and bloody war broke out between the Iroquois and the Canestogas and, with short cessation, lasted until the year 1676, when the Iroquois succeeded in dispersing the remnants of this brave and warlike people. In the south the Iroquois were at times engaged in war with the Tceroki [Cherokees], their hereditary enemies, and a people of their own lineage [as were also many of the foes of the Iroquois with whom they waged warfare]. The Iroquois again were almost constantly at war with their Algonquian and other neighbors, east, west, north and south of them. The Abenakis, Mohegans, Ojibwas, Etchemins, Montagnais, Delawares, Illinois, Miamis, Nanticokes, Shawnees, Tuteloes, Saponys, Catabas and various other tribes, at one time and another, felt the displeasure of the Iroquois. [The struggle between the Mohicans and Mohawks, ending with the victory of the Mohawks, in a great two day battle in 1669 at Towereune, near Hoffmans, Schenectady county, has been previously mentioned.] In these same wars the Iroquois carried out their policy of adopting their captives by tribes, clans and by individuals; but it is also true that they burned at the stake many of their prisoners to intimidate their enemies, but mainly as a sacrifice to the god of war. Notwithstanding that the successful career of the Iroquois places them, intellectually and physically, among the highest developed people on the continent, it is equally true that other causes contributed materially to give them the vast power and influence they acquired over their neighbors during the century and a half ending with their defeat in 1779 by Gen. Sullivan [and Gen. Clinton and their American forces at Elmira]. The chief of these is the fact that the Dutch, finding that the Iroquois preferred guns and powder to other merchandise, began selling firearms and ammunition to the Iroquois.

The Tuscaroras, in attempting to resist the encroachments of the white settlers of the Carolinas, became engaged in a war with those pioneers. The red men were defeated and came and found homes among the Iroquois in 1714. The Five Nations allowed the Tuscaroras to settle on lands lying on the affluents of the Susquehanna and a few probably joined themselves at this time to particular tribes of the Five Nations. After 1722 the Five Nations became called the Six Nations, the Tuscaroras being the sixth tribe of the confederacy.

There were white settlers at Schenectady in the Mohawk country as early as 1642 and probably before. In 1661 Schenectady was officially settled by Dutch colonists on land bought from the Mohawks. By 1700 the valley of the Mohawk was occupied by white pioneers from the mouth of its river to Hoffmans, a distance of nearly thirty miles. The Mohawks were generally kind to these Dutch settlers and several marriages between the two races occurred. Some of the most prominent early men of the valley had Mohawk blood in their veins. In 1689 Hendrick Frey settled at Palatine Bridge on lands he purchased from the Mohawks. In 1713 Palatine Germans located along the Schoharie and on the Mohawk on lands bought or given them by the valley Indians. It is said these Schoharie settlers would have perished had not the Indians provided them with food and shelter. About this time the Mohawks began to lose their lands, through fraudulent purchases and grants by the Crown to provincial favorites and schemers. Many of the grants were proper and just but even more were doubtless crooked and unjustly deprived the valley Indians of their lands. The tribe had become weakened by alcohol and the diseases brought in by the white settlers. The leading men of the Mohawks fought the traffic in liquor and the Dutch-Mohawk council at Caughnawaga, held in 1659, had the suppression of the sale of spirits among the red men as one of its objects. In one winter of the seventeenth century it is said 1,000 Mohawks died of smallpox which originated among the Dutch at Fort Orange. With these diseases and excesses came a degeneracy of the Mohawk character and physique.

Among the more important events affecting the Mohawks, which transpired in the valley from the beginning of the eighteenth century to the commencement of the French and Indian war, were the following: In 1709 four Mohawk chiefs, representing the Iroquois league, accompanied Col. Peter Schuyler to England, with the object of cementing the Iroquois-English alliance. King Hendrick, of the upper or Canajoharie Castle, was one of these. In 1738 William Johnson settled near present Amsterdam. He was the greatest white friend the Mohawks ever had, from 1738 until his death in 1774, and always fought the liquor traffic among them. About 1745 he was made a chief of the Mohawks by that tribe. (See Chronology of Sir William Johnson's life in Mohawk Valley Chronology.)

In 1754 (then Col.) Johnson attended that momentous council of representatives from some of the colonies, which met at Albany to discuss plans for colonial defense against the French, and which is said to have been the initial step in the formation of the United States. Johnson in full Indian regalia was present with a party of Mohawks and other Iroquois. King Hendrick here made a celebrated speech (quotations from which are made in Chap. II., Series I.) and which shows him a great orator as well as a great Iroquois character. Hendrick was killed while leading a party of Mohawks in the battle of Lake George, which the English, under Gen. Johnso's leadership, won from the French.

The part the Iroquois played in the wars between France and England in America, their general resistance to France (particularly in the case of the Mohawks) and their course and part in the Revolution are told in the body of this book and in the Mohawk Valley Chronology and in the Mohawk Valley Military Statistics in the appendix of this work. It was almost entirely the powerful influence of Sir William

Johnson, the colonial Indian superintendent for the British crown, that kept the Iroquois sided with the English cause against the French in the dread Seven Years War which made all North America an English-speaking empire, as it is today in the two political divisions of the United States and Canada.

In 1768 at a council held at Fort Stanwix the Iroquois deeded a considerable part of their lands to the British Crown. In 1776 the greater part of the Mohawks left the valley for Canada, with Col. Guy Johnson, superintendent of Indian affairs. They fought under the British colors during the Revolution and their savage record of unspeakable barbarity is written in these pages. In their cruel and vile methods of guerilla warfare they were equalled by the Tories who frequently painted themselves as red men and were called blue-eyed Indians. The Mohawks, Onondagas, Cayugas and Senecas sided with England in the Revolution, while the Oneidas and part of the Tuscaroras fought on the side of the colonists. The Oneidas lived during the war at Fort Hunter and Schenectady and formed a scouting force of great service in American valley military operations. Most accounts say it was an Oneida who shot, killed and scalped the infamous Walter Butler at the battle of Butler's Ford on West Canada creek in 1781. Simms, however, says it was a friendly Mohawk. In 1784 and 1788 councils between the Iroquois and New York state authorities were held at Fort Stanwix. On account of their fight against the colonists the Iroquois's title to their lands was extinguished and their country was thrown open for settlement. Reservations for the Six Nations were made in different parts of the state. The Iroquois threatened war but wiser counsel prevailed and the red men accepted the inevitable. The Mohawks and many of the other tribes settled in Canada on lands granted them by the Crown.

The Mohawk tribe of the eighteenth century produced two great Indian chiefs—King Hendrick and Joseph Brant. The eminent historian, John Fiske, calls Joseph Brant the most remarkable Indian in our history. His clever sister, Molly Brant, who was the second wife of Sir William Johnson, exemplified the possibilities of the feminine Indian character. All three of these interesting Mohawks were residents, a large part of their lives, of Canajoharie or Fort Canajoharie (also called Fort Hendrick) at present Indian Castle in the town of Danube, Herkimer county.

As before stated, it is said that the successful example of the Iroquois republic had a great influence with the founders of the United States of America in the formation of our own greater republic

A few friendly Mohawks and other Indians remained in the valley after the war but by 1850 probably the last of these remnants of a once powerful race in the valley had died out or moved away with the exception of what Oneidas may have been then remaining in Oneida county.

Says Appleton's Encyclopedia:

The tribes and portions of tribes that sided with Great Britain [in the Revolution] are now situated on the Grand river, Canada, on lands granted them by the crown. These consist of Mohawks, Cayugas, Oneidas, Onondagas, Senecas and Tuscaroras, who maintain nearly unchanged their ancient form of government under the protection of the British government. They hold their lands by patents, individually. Their farms are well cultivated, and their industry is markedly in contrast with that of some of their brethren in New York state. They have a flourishing agricultural society which holds semi-annual sessions, and their exhibits of produce and stock fully equal, and in some instances surpass, those of the towns surrounding them. The fostering care of the Canadian government is directed wisely for their advancement.

Other reservation residences of the Six Nations are as follows: Oneidas, south of Oneida, New York, and at Green Bay, Wisconsin; these are said to be the most prosperous of the Six Nations living in the United States today (1914); Onondagas, south of Syracuse, New York; Senecas in New York at Cattaraugus, Allegany, Tonawanda; Tuscaroras in Niagara county, New York, who are said to be "as a whole, more enlightened and better educated than any other tribe in the state, and are self supporting. Their farms are fairly well tilled and they have many fine orchards."

The total number of Iroquoian Indian tribes or all peoples of Iroquoian blood in the United States and Canada in 1910 may be estimated at close to 60,000, making them the most numerous Indian family of North America. This includes the Cherokees, who live in the eastern part of Oklahoma, in what was formerly the Indian territory, to which they emigrated early in the nineteenth century. Appleton's says "they are the most highly developed and enlightened North American Indians." They numbered 42,000 in 1910. The Cherokees are said to be the richest tribe of people in the world. In 1910 New York had 6,029 Indians, almost entirely Iroquois, on its different reservations.

The 1890 population of the Six Nations, in both the United States and Canada, was as follows: Mohawks, 6,656; Oneidas, 3,129; Senecas, 3,055; Cayugas, 1,301; Onondagas, 890; Tuscaroras, 733. Total, 15,764.

With the Iroquois, and their tribes of Mohawks, Oneidas, Tuscaroras, Onondagas, Cayugas and Senecas, is associated the greatest legend of the North American continent, one of the greatest also of world myths—the story of Hiawatha.

The legend of Hiawatha belongs as much to the Mohawks as to the Onondagas, although the scene of Hiawatha's life is at Lake Teonto, or Cross lake, and at Onondaga lake. Cross lake lies a mile or two north of the Seneca river into which it flows, about fifteen miles west of Syracuse. It lies in the watershed of the Oswego river and forms part of the border line between Onondaga and Cayuga counties and is about four or five miles long by about a mile in width. It should bear the name Teonto instead of Cross lake. Onondaga lake, which marks the final scene of Hiawatha's life, is at Syracuse.

The Hiawatha poem of Longfel-

low, derived from the Iroquois legend, is a beautiful heroic epic, embodying not only the essence of ideal Indian life but of human life as well. While it varies markedly from the Iroquois legend it contains the same basic elements. The story of a divine redeemer of humanity living among his chosen people (as did Hiawatha) is common to all the higher races of mankind, the world over, as is also the idea of sacrifice, for humanity's benefit, which is part of the Iroquois legend as it is of so many others. Here we have also the return to his divine home by the redeemer as the final scene of his earthly life. Doubtless there are, in the legend of Hiawatha, many fundamental truths concerning the history of the Iroquois.

The Iroquois of the Six Nations believed they sprang from the earth itself—a common tradition among the primitive peoples. Their legends say:

In the remote ages the Iroquois had been confined under a mountain near the falls of the Osh-wa-kee or Oswego river, whence they were released by Tharonhyjagon, the Holder of the Heavens. Bidding them go forth to the east, he guided them to the valley of the Mohawk and, following its stream, they reached the Hudson which some of them descended to the sea. Retracing their steps toward the west they originated in their order and position the Mohawks, Oneidas, Onondagas, Cayugas, Senecas and Tuscaroras—six nations—but the Tuscaroras wandered away to the south and settled on the Cantano or Neuse river in North Carolina, thus reducing the number to five nations. Each of the tribes thus originated was independent of the others and they warred with each other as well as with the surrounding tribes. Tharonhyjagon still remained with the tribes; gave them seeds of various kinds, with the proper knowledge for planting them; taught them how to kill and roast game; made the forests free to all the tribes to hunt, and removed obstructions from the streams. After this he laid aside his divine character and resolved to live with the Onondagas that he might exemplify the maxims he taught. For this purpose he selected a handsome spot of ground on the southern banks of the lake called Teonto, being the sheet of water now known as Cross lake. Here he built a cabin and took a wife of the Onondagas, by whom he had an only daughter, whom he tenderly loved and most kindly and carefully treated and instructed. The excellence of his character and his great sagacity and good counsels led the people to view him with veneration and they gave him the name of Hi-a-wat-ha, signifying a very wise man. From all quarters people came to him for advice and, in this manner, all power came naturally in his hands, and he was regarded as the first chief in all the land. Under his teachings the Onondagas became the first among all the original clans. They were the wisest counselors, the best hunters, and the bravest warriors. Hence the Onondagas were early noted among all the tribes for their pre-eminence.

The balance of the story of Hiawatha is from an account by Abraham Le Fort, an Onondaga chief and a graduate of Geneva college. He calls Lake Teonto, or Cross lake, Lake Tioto. Many Indian names have several variations of pronunciation and spelling.

On the banks of Tioto, or Cross lake, resided an eminent man who bore the name of Hiawatha, or the Wise Man. This name was given him, as its meaning indicates, on account of his great wisdom in council and power in war. Hiawatha was of high and mysterious origin. He had a canoe which would move without paddles, obedient to his will, and which he kept with great care and never used except when he attended the general council of the tribes. It was from Hiawatha the people learned to raise corn and beans; through his instructions they were enabled to remove obstructions from the water courses and clear their fishing grounds; and by him they were helped to get the mastery over the great monsters which overran the country. The people listened to him with ever increasing delight; and he gave them wise laws and maxims from the Great Spirit, for he had been second to him only in power previous to his taking up his dwelling with mankind.

Having selected the Onondagas for his tribe, years passed away in prosperity; the Onondagas assumed an elevated rank for their wisdom and learning, among the other tribes, and there was not one of these which did not yield its assent to their superior privilege of lighting the council-fire.

But in the midst of the high tide of their prosperity, suddenly there arose a great alarm at the invasion of a ferocious band of warriors from the North of the Great Lakes; and as these bands advanced, an indiscriminate slaughter was made of men, women and children. Destruction fell upon all alike.

The public alarm was great; and Hiawatha advised them not to waste their efforts in a desultory manner, but to call a council of all the tribes that could be gathered together, from the East to the West; and, at the same time, he appointed a meeting to take place on an eminence on the banks of the Onondaga lake. There, accordingly, the chief men assembled, while the occasion brought together a vast multitude of men, women and children, who were in expectation of some marvellous deliverance.

Three days elapsed and Hiawatha did not appear. The multitude began to fear that he was not coming, and messengers were despatched for him to Tioto, who found him depressed with a presentment that evil would follow his attendance. These fears were overruled by the eager persuasions of the messengers; and Hiawatha, taking his daughter with him, put his wonderful canoe in its element and set out for the council. The grand assemblage that was to avert the threatened danger appeared quickly in sight, as he moved rapidly along in his magic canoe; and when the people saw him, they sent up loud shouts of welcome until the venerated man landed. A steep ascent led up the banks of the lake to the place occupied by the council; and, as he walked up, a loud whirring sound was heard above, as if caused by some rushing current of air. Instantly, the eyes of all were directed upward to the sky, where was seen a dark spot, something like a small cloud, descending rapidly, and as it approached, enlarging in its size and increasing in velocity. Terror and alarm filled the minds of the multitude and they scattered in confusion. But as soon as he had gained the eminence, Hiawatha stood still, causing his daughter to do the same— deeming it cowardly to fly, and impossible, if it was attempted, to divert the designs of the Great Spirit. The descending object now assumed a more definite aspect; and, as it came nearer, revealed the shape of a gigantic white bird, with wide-extended and pointed wings. This bird came down with ever increasing velocity, until, with a mighty swoop, it dropped upon the girl, crushing her at once to the earth.

The fixed face of Hiawatha alone indicated his consciousness of his daughter's death; while in silence he signalled to the warriors, who had stood watching the event in speechless consternation. One after the other stepped up to the prostrate bird, which was killed by its violent fall, and selecting a feather from its snow-white plumage, decorated himself therewith.

But now a new affliction fell upon Hiawatha; for, on removing the carcass of the bird, not a trace could be discovered of his daughter. Her body had vanished from the earth. Shades of anguish contracted the dark face of Hiawatha. He stood apart in voiceless grief. No word was spoken. His people waited in silence, until at length arousing himself, he turned to them and walked in calm dignity to the head of the council.

The first day he listened with attentive gravity to the plans of the different speakers; on the next day he arose and said: "My friends and brothers; you are members of many tribes, and have come from a great distance. We have come to promote the common interest, and our mutual safety. How shall it be accomplished? To oppose these Northern hordes in tribes singly, while we are at variance often with each other, is impossible. By uniting in a common band of brotherhood we may hope to succeed. Let this be done, and we shall drive the enemy from our land. Listen to me by tribes. You, the Mohawks, who are sitting under the shadow of the great tree, whose branches spread wide around, and whose roots sink deep into the earth, shall be the first nation, because you are warlike and mighty. You, the Oneidas, who recline your bodies against the everlasting stone that cannot be moved, shall be the second nation, because you always give wise counsel. You, the Onondagas, who have your habitation at the foot of the great hills, and are overshadowed by their crags, shall be the third nation, because you are greatly gifted in speech. You, the Senecas, whose dwelling is in the dark forest, and whose home is all over the land, shall be the fourth nation, because of your superior cunning in hunting. And you, the Cayugas, the people who live in the open country and possess much wisdom, shall be the fifth nation, because you understand better the art of raising corn and beans, and making lodges. Unite, ye five nations, and have one common interest, and no foe shall disturb and subdue you. You, the people who are the feeble bushes, and you who are a fishing people, may place yourself under our protection, and we will defend you. And you of the South and West may do the same, and we will protect you. We earnestly desire the alliance and friendship of you all. Brothers, if we unite in this great bond, the Great Spirit will smile upon us, and we shall be free, prosperous and happy; but if we remain as we are, we shall be subject to his frown. We shall be enslaved, ruined, perhaps annihilated. We may perish under the war-storm, and our names be no longer remembered by good men, nor be repeated in the dance and song. Brothers, those are the words of Hiawatha. I have spoken. I am done."

The next day his plan of unison was considered and adopted by the council, after which Hiawatha again addressed the people with wise words of counsel, and at the close of this speech bade them farewell; for he conceived that his mission to the Iroquois was accomplished, and he might announce his withdrawal to the skies. He then went down to the shore, and assumed his seat in his mystical canoe. Sweet music was heard in the air as he seated himself; and while the wondering multitude stood gazing at their beloved chief, he was silently wafted from sight, and they saw him no more. He passed to the Isle of the Blessed, inhabited by Owayneo [the Great Spirit] and his manitos.

And they said, "Farewell forever!"
Said, "Farewell, O Hiawatha!"
And the forests, dark and lonely,
Moved through all their depths of
    darkness.
Sighed, "Farewell, O Hiawatha!"
And the waves upon the margin,
Rising, rippling on the pebbles,
Sobbed, "Farewell, O Hiawatha!"
And the heron, the shuh-shu-gah,
From her haunts among the fen-lands,
Screamed, "Farewell, O Hiawatha!"
    Thus departed Hiawatha,
Hiawatha the Beloved,
In the glory of the sunset,
In the purple mists of evening,
To the regions of the home-wind,
Of the northwest wind, Keewaydin,
To the Islands of the Blessed,
To the kingdom of Ponemah,
To the land of the Hereafter.
["The Song of Hiawatha," By H. W. Longfellow.]

<hr/>

CHAPTER II.

The Six Mohawk Valley Counties and the Mohawk Valley Considered as a Historical and Geographical Unit— Dutch Settlement and Influence in the Hudson and Mohawk Valleys— Importance of the Hudson Valley, Geographical, Commercial, Industrial, Agricultural, Social.

It is more than probable that the historian of the future will no longer seat himself on Boston Common, for contemplation and meditation on the history of the United States, but will perch himself on some eminence overlooking the Hudson or the Mohawk, through which the march of empire has taken its course westward. The Hudson and Mohawk valleys form a national road of commerce and a great highway of American history; they form a main artery of American life, industry and transportation—perhaps the main artery. So the first Europeans who settled along these streams take on an additional importance— and this people was the Holland Dutch.

The Mohawk valley may be separated for convenience into four general divisions—first, the upper valley, embracing Oneida county; second, the middle valley, including Herkimer, Montgomery and Fulton counties; third, the Schoharie valley; fourth, the lower valley embracing Schenectady and the parts of Saratoga and Albany counties, abutting on the Mohawk.

The six Mohawk valley counties are for statistical convenience taken to represent the Mohawk valley, but they do not include about fifteen miles of its lower course. Also parts of the six Mohawk valley counties are not in the Mohawk valley as previously shown. Also some ten other counties contain portions of the Mohawk watershed, those areas of the six counties not in the valley and those areas of the watershed located in other counties about balancing each other. At times both the six Mohawk valley counties and the lower Mohawk valley (including the city of Cohoes and parts of Saratoga and Albany counties) are included in statistical totals in this work under the title of the six Mohawk valley counties and the Mohawk valley. By far the greater part of the population of the six Mohawk valley counties and the Mohawk valley, is located close to the Mohawk river itself, 80 per cent probably living within 5 miles of the river; so it is a very defined area of population we are considering in Mohawk valley subjects and history.

The following relates to the six Mohawk valley counties and their consideration as a historical whole, to the first settlement of the Mohawk valley by the Dutch at Schenectady and to the Dutch and their influence, in the Hudson valley, including the Mohawk, and the United States at large.

The editor of this work believes the history of counties will eventually be considered according to their natural geographical divisions rather than by states. The growth of the United States as a country can be viewed as that of the Atlantic seaboard and its valleys (including the Hudson and the Mohawk), that of the Great Lakes region, that of the Mississippi valley, that of the plains region, the southwest and the Pacific slope. Just so we must study the development of the Mohawk valley as a whole. The histories of the six Mohawk valley counties can form supplementary readings to this general study.

The history and present day consideration of the Mohawk valley must embrace that of the six Mohawk valley counties of Oneida, Herkimer, Montgomery, Fulton, Schoharie and Schenectady. This is because the Mohawk valley is a real geographical division and the counties are purely imaginary demarcations of its area. Schenectady should have as much, if not more, attention paid its history as the other counties. Because it was not included in the old Tryon county it is frequently left out of Mohawk valley historical studies, and as a result errors and a disjointed idea of valley history ensue. As a consequence we have seen a historical paper which claimed the Palatines as the first settlers of the Mohawk valley. The Dutch at Schenectady were the first settlers along the Mohawk and they had been here present for fifty years or more before the Palatine Germans arrived. One hundred years before Stone Arabia (in 1713) was settled by Palatines two Dutch traders had passed the Palatine hills on their way to the Otsego coun try (in 1614).

The Holland Dutch settlers have not been "written up" like the New Eng land or Virginia settlers. They probably numbered over half or two-thirds of the 300,000 people in New York and New Jersey in 1775 and their influence in colonial and national life was considerable and permanent. Holland in the seventeenth century was the then "United States" of Europe. Its people are closely akin to the English in blood and language and their civilization and commerce were superior to that of European nations, including Britain. Civil and religious liberty and intellectual tolerance prevailed in Holland

and attracted the persecuted from many lands—including Palatines and Pilgrims. New York, in its early years, similarly received those fleeing from the fanatical religious persecutions of New England. Holland of the sixteenth and seventeenth centuries possessed great political and military leaders, statesmen, teachers, philosophers, artists and writers. It was practically the birthplace of modern art and, although it is little known, north European art here developed, years before that of Italy. Holland of those days was the home of large industries, a great merchant marine, a wonderful world commerce and great merchants.

The Dutch settlers of New York and New Jersey strongly influenced the life of our nation, because they were largely located in the Hudson valley (of which the Mohawk forms a part) and came in touch with the moving population of the colonies and the later United States. Our American Christmas observance and our American political, religious and intellectual tolerance are descended from those descendants of the Batavii whom Caesar could scarce conquer. People who are uninformed on the subject, must remember that this hardy race was called "Low Dutch," simply because of the geographical position of Holland. Caesar found their ancestors dwelling in the marshes of the lowlands bordering the North Sea. Little Holland's fight against mighty Spain was one of the most heroic struggles in history and dwarfs our own Revolutionary war. Dutch success ensured political and religious liberty and modern European and American civilization.

At the time of the Revolution the Dutch element was preponderant in the Hudson valley and in the eastern Mohawk valley about Schenectady and it extended to all parts of the settled Mohawk valley. Among men of this race we find Gansevoort, Van Schaick, Van Benschoten, Visscher, Schuyler and other Revolutionary first-rate fighters, Van Buren, the president, Lossing, the great historian of New York state, Vanderlyn, the painter, and many other political and intellectual leaders of early New York. Even the best pre-Revolutionary pugilist, in the Mohawk valley, was Van Loan, the mighty Schoharie Dutchman.

Later came into the Hudson valley other races which finally made the Dutch and Palatine elements a minority. Today they form a thoroughly American element so amalgamated as to no longer be a definite racial item. Just as the Indians influenced our first settlers, so our first settlers have affected the later comers. In the Revolution it fell largely to the New York Dutch militiaman to guard the Hudson valley (key to the colonies) from the British. This he helped to do successfully. While not exaggerating its great importance, let us give due credit to the Dutch and their influence on America and American history. For it is as great, in its way, as that of any other and as said before, it has not been "written up."

The reader is referred to Mrs. Grant's "Memoirs of An American Lady" for the best picture of Dutch colonial life (about Albany) extant.

The Dutch immigration was continuous into New York state from the earliest permanent settlements, about 1624, up until the Revolutionary war. It did not cease with the conquest of New Netherland by the English in 1664.

The original territory occupied by the Dutch in New York and New Jersey is shown geographically by the names they gave their towns, the streams and other natural features. Where they did not use the Indian names, the streams became kills (Dutch for creek or river). These Dutch names are scattered all through the Hudson and Mohawk valleys and northern New Jersey—the territory of Dutch colonization.

A very considerable element of United States population today (1914) is of Dutch or partial Dutch extraction. It may be safely estimated that five million Americans possess some Dutch blood in their veins. In 1914 there were in the United States about 370,000 people (N. Y. World Almanac figures) of Dutch-Flemish-Frisian birth or parentage and speaking these allied languages.

The first settlements by the Dutch of the Hudson valley, New York harbor and Manhattan island take on great importance, because the Hudson valley, in its relation to man, is one of the great river valleys of the world; because New York harbor is the world's greatest sea and inland (on the Hudson) water port and New York city by 1920 will, doubtless, be the world's greatest city. New York, in 1915, is estimated by the U. S. Census Bureau to be but little smaller than London and in another half decade the American metropolis will surpass the British world center in population.

The Hudson valley is the most important section, commercially and socially, of the leading state of the United States. The Hudson valley is the vital spot in American history, in it has been thoroughly exemplified the development of our country in manufactures, agriculture, political, industrial, commercial, transportation, social, urban and rural life. In it have been developed many of our great modern inventions. On its shores were built the first successful steamboat and the locomotive which drew America's first passenger train, within its borders (from Albany to Schenectady). Its early water route, from the Hudson to the Great Lakes by way of the Mohawk valley, was utilized in the Erie canal and the later greater Barge canal, joining the world's oceans to the thousands of miles of America's great and wonderful inland water system of lakes and river. Similarly the early Indian trails and later turnpikes became still later great continental railroad systems. Over the waters of the Hudson took place the first American long distance air flight, from Albany to New York, by Curtiss in 1910, but seven years after the Wright brothers made their first glide with a heavier than air machine at Kitty Hawk, N. C., in 1903.

In the Civil war the Hudson valley furnished thousands of men to the Union armies, while over the Hudson-Mohawk railroads, rivers and canals vast quantities of army supplies went to the front. On its river and railroads hundreds of thousands of Union soldiers were transported and within its limits were made great amounts of arms for the federal armies.

The Hudson valley is today America's greatest land and water traffic and transportation route. A waterway like the Panama canal is of secondary importance compared with it. It is virtually a sea inlet for one hundred seventy miles, from New York to Troy, as well as the channel of a great fresh water river. As a landscape feature the Hudson valley and its hills, mountains, fields, rivers, lakes and forests, is without a peer.

Politically the Hudson valley has played a great part and it has given two presidents to the United States—Van Buren and Roosevelt, both descendants of its first Dutch settlers. In literature, art and music, the Hudson valley has long been regarded as the center for the western hemisphere. Its great city is a wonderful study in itself much as we may disapprove of it as a human abiding place. It is easy to understand, from the foregoing how vital the history of the Hudson valley is to the eight million people (1915) gathered about that estuary of the Hudson river—New York bay; and this history includes, of course, that of that part of the Hudson valley known as the Mohawk valley—its whole and all its parts.

A great amount of legendary and patriotic interest attaches to the Hudson valley (of which the Mohawk forms a part). With it is concerned the stories of Sleepy Hollow and Rip Van Winkle, which while purely fictitious and products of Irving's genius reflect early Dutch eighteenth century Hudson river life. Song and story embody the spirit of the Hudson and the Mohawk. At Rensselaer (old Greenbush), opposite Albany, Yankee Doodle was born to the accompaniment of American fifes and drums and the lusty voices of the farmer soldiers. At Fort Stanwix, on August 6, 1777, the stars and stripes were first flown in battle and at Saratoga in 1777, the Americans won the decisive action of the Revolution. At Poughkeepsie in 1786, the New York state assembly ratified the United States constitution, making the ninth state to take such action and thereby putting it in force.

In 1754 at Albany was held a convention of colonial delegates, previously mentioned in this work, which is said to have been the initial step in the formation of the United States. The Mohawk river section of the Hudson valley was the home of two tribes of the Iroquois republic—the Mohawks and the Oneidas. It is said the example of the successful Iroquois league of the Six Nations had a powerful influence in the formation of our own greater present-day American republic.

In the realm of sport, the Hudson valley boasts the birthplace of the inventor of baseball—Ballston Springs, where Gen. Doubleday was born, who invented the great national pastime at Cooperstown.

These mentioned are but a few of the items of interest to all the nation, which have had their origin in the Hudson valley. Much of the foregoing life, trade and traffic had its birth in the Hudson valley in the early days when the Dutch influence was predominant. It must be remembered that other races were also mingled together in New York province, but the Dutch were predominant in numbers and influence prior to the Revolution. In regard to this subject see Lossing's "Empire State," also Series I., Chapter VII. of this work. Before (in the early nineteenth century) the railroads and Hudson river steamboats made urban intercommunication rapid and cheap Albany held the position, for two centuries, of the metropolis of the upper Hudson and the Mohawk valleys. Schenectady was a subsidiary center for the Mohawk valley—market town, turnpike and river traffic terminal. Both were typical Dutch towns up to the beginning of the nineteenth century.

It is the peculiar geographical position of the Hudson and its tributary, the Mohawk, which contributed to make New York the great city it is

today (1914), offering as it does a "water level route" to the west—being the only low break through the Appalachian range of mountains. The completion of the Erie canal in 1825 made New York city the foremost metropolis of the continent and this was greatly added to by the later railroads traversing the state from east to west. The great importance and population of the Hudson valley is bound to increase tremendously with the coming years.

Of the great traffic and travel route and waterway, which stretches 425 miles across our state from New York to Buffalo, 250 miles (from New York to Rome) lies in the Hudson valley. This is one-twelfth of the distance across the continent.

Its manufactures, trade, traffic, land and water commerce and the ten millions (1915) which are located on its shores and that of its estuary—New York bay—make the Hudson valley the most important river valley in the world. Therefore its first settlement by the Dutch and their predominance therein for over a century and a half thereafter, become subjects of much importance. It must be thoroughly borne in mind that the Mohawk valley is part of the greater Hudson valley, in considering the history of the Hudson valley and its first settlement by the Holland Dutch.

The estimated population of New York city in 1914 was 5,500,000. In addition to this there were estimated to be over 1,500,000 people on the shores of the lower Hudson adjoining New York and on the borders of New York bay and its adjoining waters, all within a twenty-mile radius of New York city hall. The principal of these places were Newark, Jersey City, Yonkers, Elizabeth and Hoboken. This gives a combined population of 7,000,000 located at the mouth of the Hudson. The twenty-two Hudson valley counties of Essex, Warren, Hamilton, Washington, Saratoga, Oneida, Herkimer, Montgomery, Fulton, Schoharie, Schenectady, Albany, Rensselaer, Greene, Columbia, Ulster, Dutchess, Orange, Putnam, Rockland, Westchester, Bronx had a combined population in 1910 of 1,633,000 in round numbers. Adding to this the 1910 population of New York city, 4,767,000 and the four New Jersey counties of Bergen, Hudson, Eessex and Union and parts of Middlesex and Monmouth (all of which abut on New York bay) with a 1910 population of about 1,400,000 gives a 1910 population of the Hudson valley and the cities at its mouth of 7,800,000, compared with a 1910 population for the United States of 92,000,-000. By 1915 this population will be probably 9,000,000, as compared with an estimated U. S. population of over 100,000,000. By 1920 the Hudson valley population will probably be 11,000,000 out of a U. S. population of 110,000,000. By 1950 the Hudson valley population may be 20,000,000 and that of the United States 175,000,000. The population of the twenty-two Hudson valley counties and New York city in 1910 was 6,400,-000 as compared with 9,113,000 for New York state. The twenty-two Hudson valley counties (above New York city) and the five New York city counties (Bronx, New York, Richmond, Kings and Queens) comprised twenty-seven of the sixty-two counties of New York state. From the foregoing it can readily be seen what an important section of the United States and of North America the Hudson valley forms, containing as it does about one-eleventh of the population of our country and about one-twelfth of that of North America (excluding Mexico), north of the Rio Grande. Not all of the territory of the twenty-two Hudson valley counties lie in the Hudson river watershed but the greater part of their territory does and all but a small fraction of their population is gathered along the Hudson and its tributaries and within its watershed.

An interesting center of population in the Hudson valley is that which lies at the junction of the Hudson and its principal tributary, the Mohawk. The Albany-Troy section had a population in 1910 of 230,000 in round numbers. Including Schenectady and its suburb Scotia this group of Hudson-Mohawk

cities in 1910 had a population of 306,-000. This has since increased and probably will increase rapidy in the future, as this family of cities lies at the end of Hudson tide water navigation and at the beginning of Mohawk river-Barge canal navigation and is also a great railroad, industrial and agricultural center. The reader's attention is directed to a study of the map of New York state river valleys and to the remarkable way in which the Hudson and Oswego river valleys carry water navigation three-quarters of the way over the great New York to Buffalo trade route. A people located along this great trade route are fortunate in being daily in touch with its industrial, commercial, agricultural, political, social and historical features.

1661—Dutch Settlement of Schenectady

"Schenectady, Ancient and Modern;" Joel Henry Monroe, 1914:

Regarding the settlement of Schenectady in 1661, the above work says:

Arent Van Curler, a native of Holland, superintended for many years this great [Rensselaer] estate. He was a man of unusual force and ability, an influential figure in the affairs of the colony, and also among both the Indians and the French. Van Curler was something of a diplomatist too, honest in public matters, was fearless and withal progressive. He was highly esteemed by the Iroqouis and often acted as ambassador in disputes and in humane matters arising between them and the French. The latter also regarded him in the highest favor.

.Van Curler was familiar with the surrounding country. He had had occasion to make many trips up and down the valley during the twenty years past and had taken special note of the charming country lying west of Beverwyck [Albany]. * * * * * *

The contour of the land and the geographical location combined to render the site chosen a most eligible one, and, by reason of its situation on the Mohawk river, it was destined to be at the foot of navigation. The broad river, skirting the proposed town on the west, formed a spacious bay or Binne Kill, which would afford an ample harbor. The land, to be sure, was still in possession of the Mohawks; it had been their hunting ground and corn ground for many centuries. In fact the site of Schenectady, according to tradition, was the seat of an Indian capitol at some remote period. * * *

The names of the petitioners, asking to settle at Schenectady, in 1661, were Van Curler, Brouwer, Glen, Van Velsen, Veeder, Van Woggleum, Bancker, Teller, DeWinter, Borsboom, Van Olinda, Wemp, Van Slyck.

The town of Schenectady is referred to, in the original Indian deed to the Dutch settlers as Schonowa. The name of the Indian village there was Connochariguharie, which pronounced rapidly, sounds suspiciously like Canajoharie. Possibly the whole region of the Mohawk valely north may have been so-called by the Mohawks, as so many of their localities and towns had a similarly sounding name.

The name Schenectady is supposed to be (by some) Dutch and not Mohawk in its derivation. Yates's (1902) "Schenectady County" says: "The name the county now bears is said to have a beautiful origin:—Schoon (beautiful) Acten (valuable) Deel (portion of land)." Is this right or is it a "guess?" Can "Schenectady" be a final settling down of the various attempts of various nationalities to pronounce Canajoharie, which may have been the name the Mohawks gave their whole country? In lieu of a better translation, however, it is well to accept that of Yates.

The Mohawks a Bar to Early White Settlement Along the Mohawk.

The average reader of history, in scanning the accounts of the settlement of the British colonies, generally wonders why the rich agricultural section of the Mohawk valley was not settled earlier in the history of our country. That it was not was entirely due to the fact that the early authorities, both Dutch and English, secured the alliance of the powerful Iroquois nation and wished them to continue as a defence against the encroaching French power on the St. Lawrence. To have settled in their country would have broken up this alliance and made the Iroquois the enemies of the white men then resident in the Hudson valley. The Mohawks and Iroquois greatly admired Van Curler and therefore allowed him to settle at

Schenectady in 1661. Doubtless they also figured that this white chief would help them in their never-ending battle with the French and the Canadian Indians if he were located among them. So great was their admiration for Van Curler that, for years after his death, they gave the New York governor the title of "Corlaer." The settlement of Schenectady was the entering wedge and soon other white settlements were made farther up the Mohawk valley among the Mohawks, then enfeebled and depleted by alcohol and the vices introduced among them by the white men. Fort Stanwix (or Schuyler) remained the western boundary of the New York settlements until after the Revolution, as the tribes of the other Six Nations, aside from the Mohawks, remained an insurmountable barrier to any further encroachment. After the council of 1788 at Fort Schuyler, the Indian title to lands west of that point was extinguished and immigration in great volume at once set in.

1709—Trip of Four Mohawk Chiefs to England.

In 1709 four chiefs of the Mohawk nation accompanied Col. Peter Schuyler of Albany to England. The expenses of the trip were paid by the British nation and the journey was made with the idea of allying the Iroquois more closely with the English cause, particularly as the French were continually making overtures of friendship to the Five Nations. The Mohawk chiefs represented the Iroquois confederacy and they would only go on the condition that their friend Schuyler, accompany them. For, they trusted him implicitly, saying "he never told a lie and always thought before he spoke." King Hendrick was one who made the journey and in England he had his portrait painted in a court suit presented him by Queen Anne, who received these savage chieftains several times. To Schuyler she offered knighthood, but he, true democrat that he was, courteously declined the honor. The trip was undertaken with the idea of showing the Iroquois people the real military and commercial greatness of England, and, under Schuyler's skilful direction, it proved a great success. On the return of the Mohawk chieftains to Albany in 1710, a council was there held at which the Iroquois made a strong league of friendship with the English New York provincial authorities, a course due to the forceful representations of the returned travelers. One of the Mohawks died on the voyage. Col. Peter Schuyler was one of the leading men of his time in the upper Hudson and Mohawk valleys, of which Albany was the center.

1760—Mrs. Grant's Mohawk River Trip

Mrs. Anne Grant's "Memoirs of An American Lady (Margaret Schuyler)" is mentioned several times in this work. Mrs. Grant was Anne McVicar, the daughter of a Scotch officer in the English army, and lived her childhood in Albany and vicinity. In 1758 she with her mother came from Scotland and located at Claverack-on-the-Hudson, where Capt. McVicar was stationed. In 1760 she accompanied her parents to Ft. Oswego and on her return from there located in Albany until 1768, when they all returned to Scotland. Mrs. Grant describes Albany and vicinity, of that time, in a most graphic manner. She is most enthusiastic in her praise of the descendants of the Hollanders who made Albany a Dutch city until the nineteenth century. She also speaks very highly of the Palatine German element of the population tributary to Albany, and of the Mohawk nation as well, for whose savage virtues she had a great appreciation. Her trip from Claverack to Oswego, by boat on the Mohawk to Wood creek, Oneida lake and the Oswego river, is described most entertainingly. She, with her parents, visited Sir William Johnson at his first two Mohawk river homes (Johnson Hall at Johnstown not being then built); also King Hendrick at Fort Canajoharie or Fort Hendrick (now Indian Castle). This was the son of the famous King Hendrick, who fell in battle under Sir William Johnson, at

Lake George in 1755. Of her Mohawk river trip in 1760 she says, in part:

"The first day we came to Schenectady, a little town, situated in a rich and beautiful spot, and partly supported by the Indian trade. The next day we embarked, proceeded up the river with six batteaux, and came, early in the evening, to one of the most charming scenes imaginable, where Fort Hendrick was built; so called in compliment to the principal sachem or King of the Mohawks. He resided, at the time, in a house which the public workmen, who had lately built this fort, had been ordered to erect for him in the vicinity. We did not fail to wait upon his majesty; who, not choosing to depart too much from the customs of his ancestors, had not permitted divisions of apartments or modern furniture to profane his new dwelling. It had the appearance of a good barn and was divided across by a mat hung in the middle. King Hendrick, who had indeed a very princely figure and a countenance that would not have dishonored royalty, was sitting on the floor beside a large heap of wheat, surrounded by baskets of dried berries of different kinds. Beside him his son, a very pretty boy, somewhat older than myself, was caressing a foal, which was unceremoniously introduced into the royal residence. A laced hat, a fine saddle and pistols, gifts of his good brother, the Great King, were hung round on the cross beams. He was splendidly arrayed in a coat of pale blue, trimmed with silver; all the rest of his dress was of the fashion of his own nation, and highly embellished with beads and other ornaments. * * * Add to all this, that the monarch smiled, clapped my head and ordered me a little basket, very pretty, and filled, by the officious kindness of his son, with dried berries. Never did princely gifts, or the smile of royalty produce more ardent admiration and profound gratitude." Mrs. Grant speaks of "sitting from morning to night, musing in the boat * * * having my imagination continually amused with the variety of noble, wild scenes, which the beautiful banks of the Mohawk afforded."

The party making the trip consisted of a number of British soldiers, under Captain McVicar, with some of their wives. They all camped for the night several times on this journey to Fort Oswego and the howling of the wolves was so terrific that it made several of the women hysterical. A considerable portion of the work is given to Fort Oswego, which was then a frontier post, completely isolated in the great forest; its only connection with civilization being by the waterway to Albany mentioned. Fort Oswego, as shown in this work, played a great part in Mohawk valley Revolutionary history.

Mrs. Grant mentions the knowledge of nature possessed by the early colonists of New York province. This nature lore was early acquired and even children early learned its rudiments. Mrs. Grant speaks of the young Albanian of the middle eighteenth century, in this regard as follows:

"It is inconceivable how well these young travelers, taught by their Indian friends and the experimental knowledge of their fathers, understood every soil and its productions. A boy of twelve would astonish you with his accurate knowledge of plants, their properties, and their relation to the soil and to each other. Said he: 'Here is a wood of red oak; when it is grubbed up this will be loam and sand, and make good Indian corn ground. This chestnut wood abounds with strawberries, and is the very best soil for wheat. The poplar wood yonder is not worth clearing; the soil is always wet and cold. There is a hickory wood, where the soil is always rich and deep, but does not run out; such and such plants that dye blue or orange, grow under it.'"

In the conflicting racial prejudices of Mrs. Grant's day, it is amusing to note her hostility to the New England people who were then beginning to come into New York state. This is particularly edifying considering the widely differing views of Elkanah Watson, a New Englander himself, who made the same trip by batteaux about thirty years later.

1760—Gen. Amherst's Expedition.

In 1760 Gen. Amherst's British and Provincial American army passed up the Mohawk valley on its way to the investment of Montreal. Amherst's army caused the fall of Montreal and the final extinction of French power in Canada. The invading force left Schenectady, June 12, 1760, and marched up the valley, the supplies and munitions going up the river by batteaux. The army numbered 10,000 men—6,000 provincial troops and 4,000 regulars. With this expedition were Gen. Amherst, Gen. Thomas Gage (later English commandant of Boston), Col. Haldemand (afterward governor-general of Canada during the Revolution), Sir William Johnson (superintendent of Indian affairs), Gen. John Bradstreet and Lieut.-Col. Israel Putnam, the famous American Revolutionary leader. Later Johnson joined the expedition with 1,300 Iroquois warriors in his force. This was the largest Indian body ever attached to a British general's command. Amherst's army, when it invested Montreal, numbered 17,000 men. That part of it which went up the Mohawk, in June, 1760, numbering ten thousand, was the largest army which ever entered this valley. Thus, from the Mohawk, went forth the American and British fighting force which ended French empire along the St. Lawrence. The foregoing is briefly mentioned in Series I., Chapter II.

Regarding this we quote as follows from Wager's "History of Oneida County—Our County and Its People (1896)":

In 1760 a final campaign was ordered by the British government to drive the French forces, which had converged around Montreal, from Canada. One English army was to proceed from Quebec, another from Lake Champlain, and a third from Albany up the Mohawk, via the Oneida carrying place, to Oswego, thence over Lake Ontario and down the St. Lawrence. General Amherst commanded the last, consisting of 4,000 English regulars, 6,000 Provincials and 600 Indians under Sir William Johnson. * * * * In September of that year (1760) the English forces converged at Montreal, where the French army had been driven, and all Canada passed into the hands of the English.

This great movement of British forces through the Mohawk valley, which resulted in the American-British conquest of North America from the French, is hardly even mentioned in the various histories and stories of the Mohawk valley. Its tale is worth a volume in itself.

CHAPTER III.
Sir William Johnson, an Appreciation.

It is regrettable that the great achievements of Sir William Johnson should be befogged, in the eyes of the casual reader of history, by the revamping of ancient stories as to his marriage relations. Johnson was an empire builder like several other strong Americans of early days. Beloved by his red and white neighbors, his fine manly figure looms large and clear in the light of history. William Johnson founded schools, churches, forts and a town, he built roads, aided his neighbors to improve their condition and their farming methods. He introduced seeds, plants, animals, trees, etc., into the Mohawk valley. His battles for his country found a record in a bullet in his thigh.

Sir William Johnson thoroughly organized the Mohawk valley militia, and this discipline was useful to them during the Revolution. Although other tribes of the Six Nations wavered, Johnson always kept their mightiest warriors, the Mohawks, in the English ranks. His power over the Iroquois, his well-trained militia and his military talents, together with his defense of the Mohawk and his victories at Lake George and Niagara largely contributed to the final British conquest of Canada. To Johnson, as much as to any man of his time (not excepting Washington) are we responsible for the English-speaking American race which dominates the great continent of North America from the Rio Grande to the North Pole.

From his appointment, in 1750, to be one of the Governor's Council of the Province of New York, until his death at Johnstown in 1774—a period of a quarter century—Johnson was probably the most important and influential figure in the state. His influence was particularly telling as it was exerted during one of the most important formative periods in the state's history.

A "world man," modern in the most modern sense, for he was without prejudice or intolerance and a guiding, governing brother to Mohawk, Hollander, German or British resident of the valley in his time. With the power of a prince, he was simple, strong and manly, though he well knew how to entertain and impress the spectator with a show of military power or the signs of wealth. There is no stronger figure in our Colonial history than that of Johnson, and the rehashing of his alleged immoralities, etc.—veritable historical back-fence tattle—should be discountenanced. The praise of a contemporary is praise indeed and we find a glowing tribute to the Mohawk valley baronet in the "Memoirs of An American Lady" by Mrs. Anne Grant, who traveled through the Mohawk valley in the middle eighteenth century and who visited Johnson at his first and second houses on the Mohawk. Sir William's memory has suffered from the Toryism and vandalisms of his son Sir John Johnson and the "Johnson party," but it is a perversion of "Mohawk Dutch" whiggery to vent this resentment on William Johnson. Johnson's achievements would remain just as great even had he been possessed of as many concubines as an ancient biblical patriarch. However there is every reason to believe Sir William was married to both Catherine Wisenberg and Molly Brant. Their children inherited under the law as legal and legitimate heirs. Johnson was married to his first wife at Queen Anne's chapel, Fort Hunter, by Mr. Barkley, the Episcopal minister, and, by at least the Indian form of marriage, he was tied up as fast to his second wife, Molly Brant, as any Mohawk valley daddy of today is spliced to his lady boss, by dominie, priest or squire.

See chronology of Johnson's life in chronology of William Johnson, under the Mohawk valley chronologies.

When in 1742, Sir William Johnson built his stone house, at present known as Fort Johnson, he called it Mount Johnson. About ten years later, at the beginning of the French and Indian war, it was fortified and, then or later, became known as Fort Johnson. This has been the cause of considerable confusion as Johnson called his first house, in present Florida township, by the name of Fort Johnson.

CHAPTER V.

In the "1772—Tryon County and the Canajoharie and Palatine Districts" chapter V. the statement is made that "It was almost entirely the influence of Sir William Johnson which made Tryon county a region unfavorable to the cause of independence." The idea really meant is not that Sir William would have been a Tory had he lived, but rather that a strong Tory party had grown up around him. Many writers incline to the belief that John son would have cast his lot with the colonies, or would have at least remained neutral.

CHAPTER VIII.
1764—The General Herkimer House—A 1913 Description.

The following is an excellent description of the General Herkimer house, in Danube, Herkimer county, at the time of its being turned over to the care of the Daughters of the American Revolution and the German-American Alliance, after its purchase by the state of New York in 1913.

As before stated the Herkimer house was built by Nicholas Herkimer in 1764, on his removal from his former home at German Flatts to Danube and his location on the Herkimer patent at Fall Hill, granted to his father, Johan Jost Herkimer. It was later occupied by his brother, George Herkimer, and George's son, John Herkimer, up to 1817. It was not "built of bricks brought from Holland" and probably but very few houses were, the popular tradition to the contrary notwithstanding. The bricks were doubtless made

in the Mohawk valley somewhere and brought here on the river. The burial plot has always been the property of the descendants of Capt. George Herkimer, as the editor of this work understands it.

For reference to the Herkimer house (as it has been generally called in the family) see Chapter XIII, Series I. The following account is from the Albany Knickerbocker Press, Oct. 1, 1913:

The house is a two-story brick structure with basement and attic. The foundation is of limestone. The bricks are shorter than those made nowadays and about six inches wide. The fire places are immense affairs, and are found in the basement as well as on the first and second floors. The hallway running through the center of the house is a very wide one, and has in it a partition shutting off the stairway. This partition may not have been in the original house. The walls are thick and the windows are panel backed and have window seats. The stair risers are from one inch to two inches higher than those now built. The boards in such of the original floors as remain are from twenty inches to two feet wide and it is evident that they were never run through a planer. The laths used are split by the use of a hatchet, and the roof timbers are hewn out of red pine and very substantial. In one part of the cellar are port holes, indicating that it was built to withstand a siege, and in the other to the right of the fireplace are the remains of what appears to have once been a tunnel leading out to the powder magazine.

All the rooms on the first and second floors are generous in size, and adjoining the main rooms are what may have been recesses or sleeping rooms, connected by an arch and treated like an alcove. On the first floor are few decorative features. On the second floor is a guest chamber, said to be the room in which General Herkimer died. The panels in the doors and under the windows are in gothic designs, and also have a Greek pattern. The moulding around the mantel and archway is ornamented by rosettes, some of which have been abstracted by vandals. This room easily might be restored with good effect. In the attic, the roof is supported by trusses and these are skilfully and substantially built.

While the outside of the walls might be improved by pointing up, it is noticeable that the mortar is solid and holds the bricks firmly. Although these walls were built 150 years ago, the mortar is more solid than that in the stone walls surrounding the cemetery laid in 1896. The roof is hipped, having a double slant. The powder magazine is situated under the large barn in the rear of the house and about forty yards distant. This is an underground masonry structure about 18x24 feet and ten feet high. It has an arched ceiling of heavy masonry. At the front are two port holes.

In the dooryard is a granite marker with bronze tablet, placed ,there by the German-American Alliance of the state, June 14, 1912. It is surrounded by an iron fence. Nearby is what appears to have been a neighborhood graveyard containing perhaps a hundred marked graves of members of his family. This graveyard is surrounded by a massive stone wall laid random. It is covered with a creeping vine, which just now is scarlet, and the bright blue of the Michaelmas daisies make a strong contrast in colors.

The granite shaft erected by the state of New York in 1896, rises to a height of about seventy-five feet and is a stately monument worthy of the man. It can be seen for miles.

1777—Account of the Herkimer-Brant Conference at Unadilla by Joseph Wagner, a Palatine Militiaman.

The Fonda Democrat under date of May 22, 1913, printed (from the papers in the possession of the Sammons family of Fonda) a statement made by Joseph Wagner (probably of Palatine) regarding the famous conference in the spring of 1777 between Herkimer with a party of Tryon county militia and Brant and his warriors, at Unadilla. Wagner was with Capt. Fox's company in Col. Klock's regiment of Palatine militia. Col. Cox and Major Eisenlord are mentioned as also being in the force of 300 men under the command of Gen. Herkimer. The party went to Cherry Valley, evidently by way of Fort Plain, where they stayed one week, "thence to Lake Otsego, now Cooperstown, where we remained one day and a night." From here Herkimer sent "an express" to Brant at Ockwago asking him to come to Unadilla for a conference. The Americans then marched to Unadilla where they waited a week for the Indians to appear. Brant arrived with 500 warriors, "accompanied by Capt. A. Bull, William Johnson, son of Sir William Johnson by an Indian woman, and also an Indian chief." Wagner's statement continues: "Brant, having encamped, took 40 of his Indians and, together with Bull, Johnson and the chief, proceeded to where Herkimer had encamped. A circle was now formed by Herkimer, in which Brant with the chief and the other officers entered. A conversation having been entered into, Brant, for some reason or other, became irritated and sent his 40 Indians to their encampment, when, they all at once fired off their rifles as a signal for battle. Before Brant left he agreed to meet Herkimer at 9 o'clock next morning in the same place. In the morning Gen. Herkimer called on me and informed me that he was about communicating something in confidence, which I must keep a perfect secret. He then told me. that he had selected myself and three others to be present in the circle when Brant and those with him should arrive, that each was to choose and know his man, and, on a given signal, to fire on Brant and the three with him. Brant arrived, accompanied the same as the day before, when he addressed Gen. Herkimer, as follows: 'Hundred warriors with me, well-armed and ready for battle, you are in my power but, as we have been friends and neighbors, I will not take advantage. I will go back again and for the present you may rest assured that no hostilities will be committed. by the Indians.' Herkimer made Brant a present of the dozen head of cattle he had brought along and Brant's warriors immediately. killed them with spears and tomahawks." The statement continues: "It is very probable that Herkimer's object was to get Brant to take part in the war against Great Britain or, at least, during said war to remain neutral. But Brant informed him that it was now too late and the Indians would not remain neutral. Brant went west, joined St. Leger at Oswego and went with him to the siege of Fort Stanwix." Brant's irritation at the first day's conference arose from a dispute with and abuse by Col. Cox.

Herkimer has been severely criticised by some historians for the foregoing order, but it was a dictate of common sense, made necessary by the dangers of border warfare with a barbarous race and was thoroughly justified.

Christopher P. Yates.

Christopher P. Yates is frequently mentioned in the Revolutionary accounts of Tryon county. He was a member of the well known Mohawk valley Yates family and was born in 1750, died 1815. Yates was a man of education and force in support of the American cause, was a lawyer and practised in the Tryon and old Montgomery county courts. In 1774 he held a captain's commission and was a commissary of then Colonel Nicholas Herkimer's brigade. He went with Montgomery to Canada as a volunteer and it has been suggested that his admiration for his ill-fated commander made him instrumental in changing the name of Tryon to Montgomery county. Yates raised a company of rangers during the war and in 1776 was made a major in the First New York line regiment. He was early identified with the Tryon county committee of Safety. Christopher P. Yates was a delegate, from Tryon county, to the first and third provincial congresses, a member of assembly, 1774-85-88, 1800-1-2, and the first county clerk of Montgomery county, being in office from 1777 to 1800, and also surrogate 1778-87. He was a member of the New York state convention which ratified the federal constitution, thereby putting it in force, and a member of the first board of regents of New York. He married Maria Frey, daughter of Hendrick Frey, in 1774 and the Fonda Democrat (from which the foregoing facts are taken) under date of July 3, 1913, says that "he is buried on his old farm, and his grave lies uncared for and neglected on what is now known as the Devoe farm, near Freysbush, in the town of Minden." A portrait of Yates painted in 1803, was unearthed in 1913, restored and hung in the county clerk's office in Fonda. Christopher P. Yates was one of the first patriots of Tryon

county during the Revolutionary struggle and a leader in the life and events of the constructive period in the valley, following the war for independence.

CHAPTER IX.

In Simms's "Frontiersmen of New York" a picture is printed representing a view of the blockhouse and, in the distance, the Reformed Dutch church of Canajoharie district standing on Sand Hill. Such a view would have been actually impossible, as the church was burned by Brant's raiders in August, 1780, and the construction of the blockhouse was not begun until a few months later.

CHAPTER XI.

1777—The Battle of Oriskany Described by Miller and Seeber, Soldier Participants.

This work contains something unique in Mohawk valley Revolutionary history and in American Revolutionary history in its accounts of valley Revolutionary battles told by soldier participants in the actions and campaigns which they describe. Chief of these (to be found in the appendix) is the account of Johnson's great valley raid of 1780 and the resultant actions at the Middle and Lower Schoharie forts and at Stone Arabia and Klock's Field or the Battle of St. Johnsville. This wonderfully clear and vivid description is by Hon. Thomas Sammons, a private with Capt. McKean's American volunteers, who was in the battle of Klock's Field and who knew of the other actions by hearsay from their soldier participants. The second account in importance, is to be found in the appendix, and is that of Lieut. Wallace, who guided the detachment under Major Rowley to the rear of the enemy under Ross at the Johnson Hall battle, which resulted in the victory of Rowley's battalion over a much superior force. A companion description to this is that of Philip Graff, a private with Willett's expedition up West Canada creek in pursuit of Ross's retreating little army. Graff describes the battle of Butler's ford and the killing of Butler. This is contained at the end of Chapter XX., Series I.

In addititon there are two accounts in the appendix of the Oriskany battle by two soldiers engaged in that bloody struggle. These foregoing descriptions of valley actions by Revolutionary soldier participants are from the Sammons papers, and, so far as the editor of this work knows, have never before been contained in any valley historical work. They were all published in the Fonda Democrat, during the year 1913. In this book are also published the Oriskany soldiers' anecdotes (from Simms), published in Chapter XIII., Series I., and the well-known statement concerning the American sortie from Fort Schuyler, written by the commander of that movement, Col. Willett and originally published and contained in Chapter XI., Series I.

Thus, in "The Story of Old Fort Plain and the Middle Mohawk Valley," are Revolutionary soldiers' accounts of Oriskany, the sortie from Fort Schuyler, the actions at the Middle and Lower Schoharie forts, Stone Arabia, Klock's Field (or St. Johnsville battle), Johnstown, West Canada creek (or Butler's Ford)—eight Mohawk valley Revolutionary battles and skirmishes—including all the more important valley actions of the war for independence excepting that of Sharon Springs, of which there is a chapter based on that in Simms, which was written by him from the accounts of American soldier participants. No other book than this contains all these most important Revolutionary documents.

The first of these soldiers' statements, chronologically, are those concerning the battle of Oriskany by Adam Miller, who then lived in the present town of Glen, Montgomery county, and of Henry Seeber of Canajoharie township, Montgomery county. They follow:

Adam Miller, a soldier of the Revolutionary army [from the present town of Glen, Montgomery county], states that he was, in the year 1777, enrolled in Capt. John Davis's company of mi-

litia in Col. Frederick Visscher's [Mohawk district of Tryon county] regiment and said company, being ordered out for militia service [he was], engaged in a battle with the [British] enemy at Oriskany, about four miles above [present] Utica. Col. Cox [of the Canajoharie district regiment] and Gen. Herkimer [commanding the Tryon county brigade of militia] held a consultation previous to the day [of the battle, August 6, 1777] upon the propriety of an attack, supposing the enemy to be greater in number [as they proved to be]. Gen. Herkimer expressed a desire to send for a reinforcement to which Col. Cox replied, "It will not do." Gen. Herkimer then replied "March on." They all proceeded without delay to march towards the enemy with advanced and flank guards. After marching a short distance the guards were shot off and the main body of the army instantly surrounded by the enemy. A bloody battle then ensued. Col. Cox, Capt. Davis and Capt. Van Slyck were killed at the commencement of the battle. Miller was taken prisoner by Capt. John Hare soon after Capt. Davis was killed. Col. Bellinger [of the German Flatts regiment] fired upon the party having him prisoner, which set him at liberty, and he again joined in battle against the enemy. Soon after this the enemy advanced with fixed bayonets, in which a close attack ensued without the firing of guns from either side. Capt. Gardinier, on the side of the American, and Lieut. MacDonald, of the enemy, were actually clinched together, in which Capt. Gardinier was thrown to the ground and there fastened down with two bayonets which were driven through his thighs, from which he was liberated by Miller. The enemy appeared to be the strongest party and succeeded in taking a number of arms from the American army. Capt. Gardinier instantly followed Lieut. MacDonald and thrust a spear into his side. Many others were actually clinched together with bayonets and spears were clashing together from both parties. Col. Willett having commenced firing from the Fort [Schuyler] and the brave officers and soldiers unwavering [and continuing] the battle with great energy, they succeeded in driving the enemy from the field, leaving, among the slain, Capt. Hare and Lieut. MacDonald on the field of battle, Lieuts. Watts and Singleton wounded. They then proceeded to make biers [litters] for the purpose of removing the wounded, in which they succeeded in removing them from the field of battle unmolested.

Henry Seeber, of the Canajoharie district, in the Sammons papers, gives the following statement regarding part of the battle of Oriskany:

He was ordered out in Col. Cox's regiment and marched to the German Flatts. On the fifth of August marched with Gen. Herkimer, who commanded a regiment of the Tryon county militia, to Thompson's farm, five or six miles west of the flats and the last on the south side of the river. Here Herkimer wished to wait for a reinforcement or until Gansevoort could make a sally from the fort in his favor. Herkimer sent an express to the fort and, if the express could pass the enemy's camp and reach the fort, requested Gansevoort to give notice to it by firing three cannons. Herkimer was very desirous, on the morning of the battle, to remain where he was until he should receive the signal from the fort, but was urged and even accused of cowardice by some of his officers and some of the principal men of Tryon county. He therefore attempted to pass the enemy; when, after marching some distance, his advanced guard came upon some of the enemy. A few minutes told him he was completely within the ambush of the enemy. We were engaged most warmly on our south side as on the north to the river was very swampy ground. One Jacob Peeler commenced forming [men in] a circle, without having orders from any officers, about an hour after the battle had commenced, and all soon followed his example.

Jacob Peeler's name does not appear on any Oriskany roster. Many names could be added, probably, with further effort. The tactics of forming the Americans into circles during the Oriskany battle has been credited to others than Peeler.

Miller's description would indicate that Col. Willett's sortie from Fort Schuyler, against the British camp, drew off such a large portion of the British force, engaged in attacking the valley militia, that they were thereafter able to withdraw unmolested from the Oriskany battlefield. Without this help from Col. Gansevoort's garrison, the Tryon county farmers might have been utterly destroyed and defeated. Also it is more than probable that a well-arranged and concerted attack on St. Leger's army by the Tryon county militia and Gansevoort's garrison [their combined American forces equalling the British party] would probably have defeated and have effectually repulsed the British invaders. It was such an attack that Gen. Herkimer planned and the execution of which was prevented by the insubordination of his officers and soldiers.

The Indian word from which Óriskany was derived was Ole-hisk, meaning "the nettles"—a most appropriate title considering the conflict there.

1777—Capt. McDonald's Tory and Indian Invasion of Schoharie—Flockey Battle.

Capt. McDonald with 150 Indians and Tories invaded the Schoharie valley at Brakabeen on August 10, 1777, four days after the battle of Oriskany. The valley was then in a defenseless condition and Col. John Harper, the famous Schoharie patriot, rode to Albany for aid in repelling this irruption of the enemy. He was followed by two hostile Indians, whom he compelled to fly at the points of his pistols. Harper reached Albany, August 12; 28 cavalrymen were dispatched back to the Schoharie country with Col. Harper. After a ride from Albany of 45 miles the cavalrymen, joined by the Schoharie militia under Col. Harper, met the enemy at the house of

Adam Crysler, near the upper end of Vroomanland, near a place called "The Flockey," August 13, 1777. A few shots and a charge by the cavalry made the invaders fly in disorder. David Wirt, lieutenant of the cavalry, was killed and he was the first patriot to fall in the Schoharie country. Two privates were wounded—one, named Rose, mortally. Some 20 Schoharie Tories joined the enemy on their retreat to Niagara. This is known as the "Battle at the Flockey," the name meaning "the swamp" or swampy ground, and was the first Revolutionary action in the Schoharie valley.

CHAPTER XIII.

The New York legislature of 1913 passed an act authorizing the purchase by the state of the Gen. Herkimer homestead in Danube, which bill has been signed by Gov. Sulzer. The house is to be under the joint care of the German-American Alliance and the Daughters of the American Revolution. A movement is on foot (1913) looking toward the purchase of the Oriskany battlefield.

CHAPTER XIV.
1778—Battle of Cobleskill.

1778, May 30, occurred what is known as the battle of Cobleskill. Brant and 300 of the enemy ambuscaded 50 American regulars and militia under Capts. Patrick and Brown. Twenty-five Americans were killed or wounded and the rest, together with the settlers of Cobleskill, escaped to Schoharie.

Additional Facts Concerning Helmer's Heroic Run of 1778.

Herman Green of Seattle, Wash., writes (1913) as follows concerning the great feat of John Adam Helmer in his long run to warn the Fort Herkimer-German Flats section of the approach of Indian raiders in 1778: "When Helmer got back as far as the old Warren road, about one-half mile south of the river road, just west of the village of Mohawk at the top of the first long hill, he met an Indian and each of them dodged behind a large hemlock tree. Neither of them dared step out. Helmer put his hat on his ramrod and held it out so that the Indian could see it. The Indian shot and the hat fell. He came to scalp his supposed victim and Helmer shot him. The Indians were camped just east of the road in a valley. The trees were pointed out to me seventy years ago, and I always looked for those trees when passing that way. My brother Walter and I went there in September and located the places where the trees stood. I would like to see the place marked."

CHAPTER XV.
1779—Gen. Clinton's Route From Canajoharie to Otsego Lake.

The route of General Clinton from the Mohawk valley to Otsego lake, in 1779, has been the subject of endless controversy. The Canajoharie, Happy Hollow and Fort Plain (Otsquago valley) roads have all been stated to be the way by which this American army and its supplies and flatboats journeyed to join Gen. Sullivan's force. It is probable that some of the troops, at least, went by the Fort Plain road. The route from Canajoharie is the generally accepted one on which the main body and the wagons carrying the batteaux, baggage and supplies went. S. L. Frey says that the Clinton expedition used the roads then in existence to Otsego lake, although the American troops may have cut a road from Springfield to the head of the lake near Hyde Hall, where the boats were probably launched. It would have been practically impossible for Clinton's men to make a new road from present Canajoharie village to Otsego lake in the few weeks the American army was in this vicinity and roads (probably very bad ones) were already in use. Mr. Frey gives the following as Clinton's probable route from Canajoharie village to the lake: "It * * * * led from the mills on the creek to Lindsey's Bush, as Cherry Valley was first called. Some parts of it are still in use. It is 'the old Cherry Valley road.' From the mills it climbed the hill, past the Diedrick Sloan place; then straight on westward north of the French place; past the reservoir; then on past the Amos Klinkhart place and the Bullock and Goertner farms, and so on to Marshville; past the Kougher farm, and then on to Buel and Sprout Brook, where it separated, one branch going to the left to Cherry Valley, the other branch going straight on to Springfield." From here the American soldiers may have cut a road to Hyde Bay through a few miles of wilderness. This last short stretch is known as "the Continental road." The Canajoharie, Happy Hollow and Fort Plain roads to Cherry Valley, Springfield and Otsego lake were all in existence in 1779 and probably followed prior Indian trails. It is possible all three may have been used and Fort Plain probably figured in some of Clinton's preparations, as it was the nearest army post to his point of departure from the Mohawk. A monument, erected by the D. A. R. in Canajoharie village, marks Clinton's point of departure from that place for Otsego lake.

CHAPTER XVII.

The Sammons papers give an account of a militiaman, who was with Col. Wemple's Albany and Schenectady militia which went to the relief of Fort Plain when Brant made his Minden raid of August 1, 1780. Wemple's force exceeded Brant's and the Americans marched up to Fort Plain and formed for battle there, on the flats, with cannon. Wemple evidently expected Brant to attack him but the Indian commander seems to have leisurely withdrawn up the Otsquago valley, without being hindered by Wemple, who seems to have been very derelict. A party of Tryon militia, largely on their own initiative, pursued a small party of Indians and recaptured one of their white prisoners.

CHAPTER XVIII.

1780—Johnson's Raid and Battles of Stone Arabia and Johnstown Described by Thomas Sammons, an American Volunteer.

The following account of Johnson's great raid of 1780 through the Scho harie and Mohawk valleys and the actions of Stone Arabia and Klock's Field was written by Thomas Sammons, who was a militiaman with Capt. McKean's volunteers, and who joined Van Rensselaer's American army at Caughnawaga. Accounts of Revolutionary battles and marches by soldier participants are rare. This is the third account of a Mohawk valley Revolutionary action by a soldier-participant and by far the most important. In all there are five such descriptions in this work, as before mentioned. For these unique documents we are indebted to the Sammons papers and their publications in the Fonda Democrat by its editor, William B. Wemple, an authority on valley history, whose frequent printings of valuable historical papers have been of the greatest assistance in the preparation of this work.

So far as the editor of this work knows, this is the only book which contains these five Revolutionary militiamen's accounts of Mohawk valley battles in which they were engaged and the only publication which embodies a similar number of such Revolutionary accounts by soldier participants published anywhere. The soldiers' experiences at Oriskany, published in Simms, are anecdotes of the fight and not accounts of battles, like the five Revolutionary valley militiamen's descriptions published in "The Story of Old Fort Plain and the Middle Mohawk Valley."

Thomas Sammons gathered a great deal of Mohawk valley Revolutionary history at first hand and he well deserves the title of our first valley historian. He was a congressman from old Montgomery county, a member of the well-known Sammons family (his father was the pioneer, Sampson Sammons) of the town of Mohawk, Montgomery county. Col. Simeon Sammons, of 'the 115th New York Volunteer Regiment, was the son of Thomas Sammons.

Sammons's account of Johnson's great raid and the battles of Stone Arabia and Klock's Field (St. Johnsville) follow:

"In the fall of the year 1780 Sir John Johnson made an incursion upon our frontiers, in which he unfortunately too well succeeded. He started from Lachine in Canada, his forces consisting of three companies of his own regiment and one company of German Yagers, and came to Oswego, where he was joined by one company of regulars of the 8th Regt., Butler's rangers and about 200 Indians under the command of Joseph Brant, his whole number consisting of about 800 or 1,000 persons, including Indians. Sir John Johnson had with him one three pounder and two brass mortars which were dragged through the woods by horses having poles or shafts attached to their breasts. Each man was supplied with eighty musket cartridges and every two alternately carried a cartridge for their cannon.

"From Oswego he proceeded in boats as far as Onondaga lake, where he concealed his boats in a creek and proceeded on his march for Schoharie, going by way of Service's place on the Charlotte river and arrived at Schoharie on the morning of the 16th of October, passed by the upper fort and, coming near the middle fort, some of his party set fire to a building, which was seen by the sentinel. This middle fort was under the command of Major Wolsey, having 150 state troops and 50 militia. Lieut. Spencer was ordered to take 60 volunteers and examine into the cause of the fire. On calling for volunteers all wished to go and forty were counted from the right. Lieut. Spencer advanced in the direction of the fire and soon fell in with the advanced part of Sir John's party and after firing three rounds upon them retreated into the fort without having lost a man. The alarm gun being fired, Major Wolsey prepared for

defending the fort and again sent out Lieut. Spencer with his volunteers to protect a barn and some stacks of grain that were near the fort; in doing so lost one man named L. Yons. The enemy passed from the south to the northeast of the fort keeping up a continual fire with small arms. They stopped within a short distance to the northeast and placed their three pounder on the brow of a hill from whence they commenced firing upon the fort. Some five or six cannon balls were fired into different buildings belonging to the fort and three into the mud walls. Some bombs were also thrown by the enemy which caused no other mischief than falling in one of the buildings fired a lud which was soon extinguished.

"The fort, having no port holes in the direction from which the fire of the enemy was received, a platform was raised and a cannon being placed upon it, the first fire of which silenced them. A white flag was seen to approach the fort to demand a surrender and orders were given by Major Wolsey that firing should discontinue in the fort. Murphy, a soldier, stationed himself at a port hole opposite to where the flag was advancing. He was one of those whose noble daring on many occasions, had cost the enemy much loss and knew that for himself, if taken, there would be no mercy and said he would not be taken alive. He was ordered not to fire and one of the officers threatened to dispatch him with his sword but, being supported by the militia, he fired upon the flag and it retreated. Again it advanced and again he fired. A third time it advanced from another quarter and a third time he fired. Then Sir John immediately commenced his march towards the lower fort, burning, plundering and destroying cattle, etc.; having passed to the west side of Schoharie creek where he encamped until the following morning; when, passing down along said creek, late in the afternoon of that day he arrived at Fort Hunter on the Mohawk river. Somewhere between the lower fort and Fort Hunter on a low, marshy piece of ground the two brass mortars were sunk and yet remain there. When Sir John Johnson arrived at Fort Hunter he sent Capt. Duncan to the north side of the Mohawk with some Indians and three companies of his Greens; the rest of his men he retained with himself on the south side of the river. Sir John, on the south, and Captain Duncan, on the north, commenced their march west along the Mohawk, burning and destroying everything possible in their course, until near daybreak when they came at a place called the Nose Hill where they encamped opposite each other. [Oct. 19, 1780.]

"General Robert Van Rensselaer was in pursuit of Sir John on the south side of the river with a strong force of militia and encamped at Charles Van Epps's, a short distance below and opposite Caughnawaga the same time Sir John encamped at the Nose Hill. The next morning, as Van Rensselaer was marching up the south side of the Mohawk, he was joined by Capt. McKean, with some eighty volunteers who joined with the Oneida Indians. He now numbered about fifteen hundred [in his army].

"Sir John decamped before Van Rensselaer came up with him, and going a short distance farther up the river crossed to the north side by fording, leaving on the north bank of the river 40 men to prevent Van Rensselaer crossing. Capt. Duncan, who was on the north side, turned from the river at the Nose Hill and went in the direction of Oswegotchie. Sir John continued marching west along the river until he came to Sprakers, where he sent off north a detachment. These, as well as those with Capt. Duncan, were plundering and destroying all they could to meet Sir John on the old Stone Arabia; he himself, after continuing along the river for about two miles further, turned off for Stone Arabia and was met by the detachment he had first sent off.

"Col. Brown was in Fort Paris and the night before had received orders from Gen. Van Rensselaer that if Sir John should approach Stone Arabia, that he, Brown, with those in the fort,

should engage Sir John in front while Van Rensselaer would at the same time engage him in the rear.

"Consequently Col. Brown sallied from the fort having 135 soldiers, and after marching three miles met [Oct. 19, 1780] to engage Sir John about one mile from the river on a farm owned by Shaver; but, being unsupported, was soon killed with forty of his men and the rest escaping as best they could to the fort. Capt. Duncan had not joined Sir John. He now dispersed his men in small companies for a distance of five or six miles round the country. Later in the afternoon Sir John reunited his forces and, leaving Stone Arabia one complete waste, marched to the river road east of Caroga creek and, passing around Fox's Fort, continued his march west.

"In the meantime Gen. Van Rensselaer was on the south side of the river, in the morning when he came opposite the forty men Johnson had left to guard the fording place; halted but made no attempt to cross the river. Van Rensselaer had with him a number of field pieces. William Harper rode to the banks of the river, was fired at by one of the enemy to whom he took off his hat, and returned on a walk. Van Rensselaer still remaining on the south side marched west when opposite to where Col. Brown had engaged Sir John the firing was distinctly heard as also the warwhoops of the Canada Indians. Van Rensselaer, about 11 o'clock a. m., halted opposite to Peter Ehle's [in present Nelliston village], three miles below where the Caroga creek enters into the Mohawk river. A few of Brown's men at this place came running to the river and, jumping in, forded to the south side. As they came to the bank Van Rensselaer enquired of them where they came from. One, Samuel Van Alter, a militia officer, answered:

"'Escaped out of Brown's battle.'

"'How has it gone?'

"'Col. Brown is killed with many of his men. Are you not agoing there?'

"'I am not acquainted with the fording place,' was Van Rensselaer's reply.

"He was answered that it was not difficult. Van Rensselaer then asked Van Alter if he could go before, who, though tired, said he could.

"Col. Lewis Dubois at this moment rode up to Gen. Van Rensselaer who instantly mounted his horse and, as was understood, went to Fort Plain to take dinner with Col. Dubois. Col. Lewe and Capt. McKean marched the Indians and volunteers through the river to the north side, expecting Gen. Van Rensselaer would do the same. Van Rensselaer's baggage wagons were now driven into the river into a line and stopped, reaching most of the way across the river; his men then commenced crossing in a single line by getting on the back part of the first wagon, crossing over it, walking on the tongue between the horses, and thus to the next wagon and so on until they came to the end of the wagons; they then got into the river and forded to the north bank. In this manner they continued crossing until four o'clock in the afternoon when Gen. Van Rensselaer returned just as the last man was over. When Gen. Van Rensselaer came to the south bank Col. Louis shook his sword at him and called him a Tory and when he came to the north bank he was addressed by William Harper who thought by this unnecessary delay too great a sacrifice of property and lives had been made. Col. Lewis Dubois marched his regiment of state troops into the river and crossed in a few minutes; the cannons were all left on the south side of the river.

"Gen. Van Rensselaer now appeared in much haste and, being assisted by Major Van Benschoten and Col. Dubois, the men were formed into three divisions, except the Oneida Indians and the volunteers under McKean, who continued by themselves without any regular order.

"Gen Van Rensselaer marched two of his divisions on the flat ground and the third under command of Col. Dubois some distance above the road in the woods. The volunteers of McKean and the Oneida Indians, under command of Col. Louis [the friendly Oneida chieftain] were directly opposed to the

Canadian Indians and Yagers. Sir John stood fast and Gen. Van Renselaer advanced firing at a distance. The Canada Indians gave the war whoop and were answered by the Oneidas; they rushed simultaneously forward until near together. Col. Dubois had no one to oppose him. Some of his men came to the assistance of the Oneidas and volunteers. They then advanced upon the Canada Indians and Yagers who fled with greatest precipitancy crossing the road and running in the rear of Sir John's men on the flats to cover themselves. This was all the fighting that was done, for, as Johnson saw his Indians and Yagers running, he fled with them, leaving his men, crossed the river and escaped as fast as they could.

"It was now near evening. Major Van Benschoten of Col. Dubois's division was hastening to Gen. Van Rensselaer to request orders to fall upon the rear of the enemy. At this moment when Sir John had fled from his own men and they were thrown into perfect confusion, Gen. Van Rensselaer marched his three divisions to the road and, turning east, traveled back three miles to Foxe's Fort [at Palatine Church], where he encamped for the night. Col. Louis and Capt. McKean did not obey orders but remained that night in buildings that were near. After dark some of the Tryon county militia who had volunteered, as also some of the Indians, took some prisoners, a number of knapsacks, guns and the field piece.

"Johnson's Greens, finding their commander had deserted them, broke their ranks and hid in a cornfield and the regulars for some time remained in their ranks without doing anything and finally went in pursuit of their officer.

"The following morning Col. Louis and McKean crossed the river to pursue the enemy. Between 8 and 9 o'clock Gen. Van Rensselaer came back upon the battleground. While McKean was waiting for Gen. Van Rensselaer to cross the river one of his volunteers [Thomas Sammons], hearing there were some prisoners in a small picket fort nearby, called Ft. Windecker, went to it where an Indian was shot the evening before trying to look into it. On going in he found nine prisoners and one of them he knew and had been a near Tory neighbor. On asking him how he got there he said he was ashamed to tell him. The volunteer's statement was as follows:

" 'I went into Windecker's to see the prisoners, and spoke to the prisoners, one of them having been a near neighbor of my father [by name] Peter Cass. He also informed me they had concealed themselves in a corn field till after dark before they crossed the river. I am satisfied if McKean and Louis had us, the volunteers and Indians, immediately out in pursuit of the enemy after Van Rensselaer's retreat they would have taken two or three hundred prisoners without much difficulty. How strange it is that such men as DuBois and Van Benschoten obeyed orders. [Said Cass]: Last night after the battle we crossed the river; it was dark; we heard the word 'Lay down your arms.' Some of us did so; we were taken and nine of us marched into this little fort. Seven militia took nine of us prisoners out the rear of about 300 of Johnson's Greens, who were running promiscuously through one another. I thought Van Rensselaer's whole army was in our rear. Why did you not take us prisoners yesterday after Sir John ran off with his Indians and left us? We wanted to surrender.' "

"Sir John with the Indians and Yagers, thinking the rest of his forces had been taken prisoners, under cover of the woods, directed his course for the Onondaga lake, where his boats had been concealed. Those he left behind after crossing the river, continued on the main road west until Herkimer, where, avoiding the fort, took to the woods and overtook Sir John before he reached Oneida.

"Gen. Van Rensselaer, having crossed to the south side, pursued in the direction of the enemy until he reached [Fort] Herkimer, where he was met by Gov. Clinton. He accompanied Van Rensselaer but did not assume the command. Col. Louis and Cap. McKean, being in the advance, received positive orders from Gen. Van Rensselaer to advance with all possible despatch, overtake and engage Johnson's

men and that he would close in the rear and support him. Col. Louis and McKean advanced and the next morning, coming where the trails of Sir John's Indians and his men that followed him met, they halted, knowing that they were some distance in advance of Gen. Van Rensselaer, until he should come nearer. A few were sent forward to reconnoitre. Col. Dubois came to bring orders from Gen. Van Rensselaer ordering McKean and Col. Louis to hasten forward, engage the enemy and assuring them of support. McKean and Louis hastened forward and soon came where the enemy had just decamped leaving their fires burning. The volunteers were anxious to engage, but the Oneidas for the first time hesitated. Col. Louis shook his head and, pointing in the direction of Gen. Van Rensselaer, refused to advance until he should come near. There was a halt for some time when a Doctor Allen came up stating that Gen. Van Rensselaer was returning and was at least four miles distant and if he had not overtaken them there would not have gone farther for he [Allen] was just on the point of going back.

"The night previous Gen. Van Rensselaer sent an express to Fort Stanwix ordering Capt. Vrooman to precede Johnson with 100 men and burn the boats which had been left at Onondaga Lake. Captain Vrooman immediately set out as directed. When he came to Oneida one of his men pretended to be sick and was left there. His object in staying was to inform Sir John of Capt. Vrooman's intention which he did. Sir John soon came up with this wicked informer and, knowing the deplorable situation in which he would be left should his boats be burned, immediately sent forward his Indians and Butler's rangers with all possible despatch. At Caughnawaga [not the Montgomery county Caughnawaga, or Fonda, but a place of the same name in the Oneida country] they overtook Capt. Vrooman and came upon him when eating dinner, taking him and all his men prisoners without firing a gun. Sir John then proceeded unmolested on his return, which after much fatigue, he with difficulty effected, having lost about 100 of his men killed and taken prisoners.

"The news that Dr. Allen brought Capt. McKean and Col. Louis, who then had about 160 militia and Indians, caused them to retreat as fast as they could; overtook Gen. Van Rensselaer at Herkimer and encamped that night in the woods. The Tryon county militia were dismissed and the Oneida Indians returned to Schenectady, where they removed some time previous, and remained there until peace was declared. [They] were always ready in rendering many profitable services in repelling the frequent and destructive incursions of the enemy.

"Gen. Van Rensselaer returned and dismissed his men at Schenectady, Albany and Claverack where they had been enrolled. It is here proper to add that when Sir John marched up the south side of the Mohawk river Gen. Van Rensselaer was very near to him, Sir John passing Van Epps' just before dark and Van Rensselaer encamping there, just after Sir John occupied the greater part of the night in going six miles, the river separating him from a large portion of his men; burning a great many buildings, destroying property and plundering and laying waste the country in the very face of Gen. Van Rensselaer. Sir John's men were tired with their long marches and laboring under knapsacks heavily laden with provisions and plunder, whereas Gen. Van Rensselaer's were fresh troops and unburdened. The delay of Gen. Van Rensselaer, his orders to Col. Brown, those to Capt. McKean and Col. Louis as also those to Capt. Vrooman, could not have been given in any way in which they would have more assisted Sir John, either in effecting his retreat or doing injury to the country. * * * *

"When my father's buildings were burned and my brothers taken prisoners the pain that I received was not as great as this conduct on the part of Gen. Robert Van Rensselaer.

"With regard to the battle on Klock's farm and the facts stated in the annexed papers, I would say that I joined with Capt. McKean as a volunteer and met Gen. Van Rensselaer on the south side of the river, opposite Caughnawaga, early in the morning [of Oct. 19, 1780, the day of the battle of Stone Arabia, in the morning, and of Klock's Field, in the evening]; of my own knowledge know most of the facts to be as they are stated; stayed with the volunteers after the battle, and had the conversation with one of the prisoners in Windecker fort as is stated; was with Capt. McKean when he had orders to advance and overtake Sir John, and a short time after saw Dr. Allen who came to inquire as to why Van Rensselaer was returning. With regard to the route of Sir John Johnson, that [is] from those of his own party who are now living and men of undoubted veracity.

"THOMAS SAMMONS."
—From Fonda Democrat, June, 1913.

Thomas Sammons was engaged in a number of valley Revolutionary military movements. He was with the militia under Col. Wemple when it marched to the relief of Fort Plain at the time of Brant's raid about that post in 1780. Sammons was also in the Johnstown battle in 1781, where he captured a British prisoner at the end of the action and brought him in to the Johnstown jail, where he, Sammons, counted 37 British prisoners taken on that day.

CHAPTER XIX.
Monuments to and Portraits of Colonel Willett.

Although the editor of these chapters knows of no monument erected to the memory of Colonel Marinus Willett, in the Mohawk valley, there are two memorials to him, erected at Albany and at New York. The one in Washington park, Albany, is a bronze tablet, affixed to a massive boulder and was erected by the Sons of the Revolution. It commemorates particularly Willett's services in the defense of the New York state frontier.

The inscription on the tablet to Col. Willett, at the corner of Broad and

Beaver streets, New York City, is as follows:

"Marinus Willett: Oriskany, Monmouth, Ticonderoga, Fort Stanwix, Peekskill.

"To commemorate the gallant and patriotic act of Marinus Willett, in here seizing, June 6, 1775, from British forces, the muskets with which he armed his troops, this tablet is erected by the Sons of the Revolution, Nov., 1892."

There are portraits of Col. Willett in the New York City hall and in Independence Hall, Philadelphia.

CHAPTER XX.

1781 — Lieut. Wallace's Story of the Battle of Johnstown.

The papers, collected by Hon. Thomas Sammons, the Revolutionary patriot, and known as "the Sammons papers" contain an account of the battle of Johnstown by Lieutenant William Wallace. He was the guide who evidently piloted the Tryon county militia detachment, under the command of Major Rowley, to take up their position in the rear of and attack Ross's force from behind while Col. Willett made the frontal attack. Willett's men were defeated but Rowley's soldiers made such a stubborn attack against three times their number that the enemy fled when Willett returned to the attack. It would seem from Wallace's narrative that the victory was almost entirely due to the regulars and local militia under Major Rowley, who was severely wounded. The date of the Johnstown battle was October 25, 1781.

Col. Willett's force numbered only 416 men and Ross had over 700. Hence Willett resorted to the strategy of an attack in front and rear at the same time. His forces were evidently about evenly divided, giving about 200 men under Willett and 200 under Rowley. The latter had 60 Massachusetts regulars and about 150 Tryon county militia. Willett attacked Ross in front, evidently before Rowley got up. Greatly outnumbered, Willett's men were driven back to Johnstown shortly

after which Rowley attacked Ross in the rear with great success and when Willett returned to the fight the enemy fled to the woods and the American victory of Johnstown was complete. After Willett was reinforced in Johnstown village by a party of Tryon militia, it is evident that over half his force, which then numbered 500, were Mohawk valley militiamen.

Lieut. Wallace's account is a most interesting document relative to this important valley campaign and it is seemingly the best description of the Johnstown battle that has come under the notice of the editor of this work. It was originally published in the Mohawk Valley Democrat of Fonda, and is here reprinted in full, as follows:

"Col. Willett, having sent Rowley on with the militia to come in the rear of Ross, continued his march with the state troops on the main road through the village of Johnstown to the Hall farm, where Ross had arrived a little before. When Willett advanced, Ross fell back a short distance in the woods [and] formed an ambush. Willett's advance guard advanced in the woods while Willett formed his men on the field, with his field piece, for battle. His advance was repulsed with some loss. Ross ordered his men to leave their knapsacks where the ambush was formed and formed his men for battle. [He] advanced up to Willett on the field with his whole force [and] attacked him very furious. In a few minutes, Willett's men retreated and run in confusion to the village of Johnstown [and] left their field piece with the enemy. [The enemy] pursued Willett's men until near the village of Johnstown, about one mile. Ross * * * * [did not know] the militia was in his rear [and] expected he had defeated all the forces Willett had collected, so Major Rowley came on them unexpectedly, while some were as much as a mile apart looking for plunder. Willett and Ross had commenced their engagement about one o'clock. Rowley attacked Ross about two o'clock.

"Lieut. William Wallace, who brought on the Tryon county militia, [had been] appointed by Col. Willett as a pilot under the command of Major Rowley of Massachusetts. This detachment was sent from Col. Willett [over] the road leading to the river on the hill south of the village [of Johnstown] and crossed the creek near where Nicholas Yost's mill is and went onward till some distance above the Hall, then came downward to the east on the north side of the Hall creek, when, coming near or by the clear lands they discovered the enemy in different places on the Hall farm.

"The enemy soon formed some of their men. Rowley's men advanced, fired on the enemy, [and] the enemy immediately advanced with some of their men to the right of Rowley along or near the Hall creek. Rowley ordered Wallace to meet them. Some of the men volunteered [and] they run to meet them. Wallace told the men not to fire till he told them, but one of his men fired and killed the officer [who] marched forward. When they fired from both parties, the enemy's detachment run. Rowley found the enemy collected [in] considerable force and stood. * * * [He] then received a ball through the ankle. He was carried back and the enemy then retreated back of a fence from where they were soon routed to another place where they made a stand. The enemy, having left some men with a field piece they had taken from Willett, they were also attacked by some militiamen. They abandoned it, the ammunition was blown up [and] the field piece was no more used that day. The militiamen left the cannon and fell on the enemy [and] generally routed the enemy; but in some part of the scrimmaging [the enemy] drove the militia back. None of the militia left the field, they continued to prevent Ross from uniting his men together and, about sunset, Ross's men had all left the field and the militia had gained a complete victory. About this time Willett returned from the village of Johnstown. The militiamen brought [in] about 40 prisoners, picked forth from scattered men of Ross's men— probably not above two or three taken together.

"Willett, when he fell back to the village, received about 100 of the Tryon county militia. Why this delay of Willett was is difficult to know—from two to six o'clock. [He had] a much superior force in the village to Rowley, after he was joined with 100 militiamen. After Major Rowley was wounded, it is difficult to know, who was commander. Some privates, where small parties met, assumed command. The officers, wherever they were, did their duty—no confusion or none left the field until the enemy was completely drove from the field.

"Thus, for a second time, the militia of Tryon county, defeated the enemy with a very inferior number. At Oriskany, the enemy were two to one in a battle of about five hours [and] were completely drove back [and] left Herkimer unmolested to make biers [litters] and carry their wounded off. With Ross left, then 250 [American soldiers] drove Ross from the field with seven or 800 men—like bulldogs, 'hold fast or die with the holt.' "

CHAPTER XXI.

The "Sammons papers" give an account by Jacob Timmerman of his capture, in the Palatine district, "by Indians who came over from Oswegatchie, about 25 in number." This was in 1782, while Timmerman was out with a scouting party of six. The Indians fired on them, killing two. Two escaped and Timmerman, who was wounded, and Peter Hillicos were captured. The party took a week to return to Oswegatchie, from whence they were taken to Montreal, where Timmerman was put in a hospital to be cured of his wound. He and Hillicos were afterward closely confined until the end of hostilities.

CHAPTER XXV.

The Part Played by the Women, Children and Youth in Mohawk Valley History.

An effort has been made, in "The Story of Old Fort Plain and the Middle Mohawk Valley," to give due prominence to the life and events, with which the women and children of the valley have been connected, as well as those in which men have borne a part. The editor of this work regrets that more detailed records are not available concerning the women and their children.

However, if the reader will look through the foregoing chapters, he will find much of interest and considerable detail regarding these matters, particularly of the first two centuries after the entrance of the white man upon the shores of the Mohawk. The farm life, church scenes, sport, travel, household work and details respecting the women and children of the valley have been given great attention.

The American women of the Revolution played fully as heroic or even a more heroic part, in that great struggle, as the American men. The women frequently did the hard work of the farms, as well as the household, after fathers, husbands and sons had left the homes to join the patriot armies. This was particularly true of the Mohawk valley and here, throughout seven years of the most horrible and savage border warfare, these women frequently remained on their homesteads with their husbands and families. When the men were called out to do militia duty the women were more exposed to the dangers of this barbaric conflict than the men, for they were left behind alone and liable at any moment to be murdered by lurking Tories and Indians. It is remarkable that any of the Mohawk valley families remained on farms distant from forts but there seem to have been many such instances. Frequently the women planted, tended and harvested the crops—a mighty task in the days when all farm labor was done by hand. When Daniel Olendorf and his wife were captured in the Minden raid of 1780, they were taken in his barn, where they were "mowing away" a load of hay. This is one incident of many showing that women did the hardest kind of farm work.

Nothing could be more worthy than the erection of a suitable monument raised in some fitting place in the valley to the memory of the American Revolutionary frontiersmen of the Mohawk valley—men, women and children. It is time that the trials and heroism of the women of our locality of that day be fittingly recognized, as well as the suffering, tragic endings, and frequent heroism of the little ones of the period—the Revolutionary boys and girls of the Mohawk valley. At the time of this writing (1914) an article is announced for publication in the Herkimer Citizen dealing with Revolutionary women, their lives and heroism. This is a good move in the right direction in the portrayal of a side of eighteenth century life that has been somewhat slighted by historical writers until recently. History should consider the population as a whole, without regard to sex or age.

The word pictures of feminine life along the Mohawk, contained herein, are most absorbing, down through the years, from the December day in 1634, described by a Dutch explorer, when "three Indian women came from the Senecas peddling fish" to the Mohawk village of Canagere (near present Canajoharie). These Seneca ladies prove most interesting as showing (in these days of feminism) the early business activities of the fair sex along the Mohawk, and as suggesting that our river and neighboring waters always afforded poor fishing. Coming to a later evidence of woman's industrial activity along the Mohawk, it is probable that the first professional cheese-maker in the valley was Mrs. Nathan Arnold, who settled in Fairfield, Herkimer county, in 1785.

Among the women of whom particular mention has been made are the following: Mrs. Guy Johnson, Mrs. Daniel Claus, both daughters of Sir William Johnson; Molly Brant, Johnson's second wife; Mrs. Gardinier, wife of Capt. Gardinier of Oriskany fame; Mrs. Samuel Campbell, wife of Col. Samuel Campbell of Cherry Valley and colonel of the Canajoharie battalion of the Tryon County militia; Mrs. Samuel Clyde, wife of Col. Clyde, acting colonel of the Canajoharie battalion in the later years of the war; Mrs. Gros, wife of Rev. Johan Daniel Gros, dominie of the Fort Plain (Sand Hill) Reformed Dutch church; many women of Minden who suffered during Brant's raid of 1780, and several tragic and other incidents regarding the women of the valley, elsewhere.

Among the Minden women who endured the horrors of Brant's raid were: Mrs. Miller of Freysbush, who was captured with a nursing infant, and who, by main force, many times prevented her weak and crying child from being tomahawked, during the long journey of the Minden captives to Canada; Mrs. Pletts, another young captive Freysbush mother, who was "treated with marked kindness" by the Indians on their arrival in Canada because she was "a tidy woman" and kept her captors' household spick and span; Mrs. George Lintner, who saved her baby by hiding all night with it under a hollow tree in "the bush." When Mrs. Lintner and her infant were safely rejoined by the rest of her children and her husband next day she gazed upon the ruins of her burned homestead and said in German, "Now, although we have lost everything but the clothes we have on, I feel richer than I ever did before in all my life."

Among the terrific tragic pictures, in which women figured in this region during the Revolution, were the diabolical scenes at Cherry Valley; Mrs. Knouts, found lying dead in her Freysbush dooryard after the Minden raid with her three murdered children in her arms, all killed by Tory and Indian fiends; Mrs. Dorenberger speared to death and scalped by her own Tory brother, while berrying along the banks of the West Canada creek. Such were the barbarous methods of warfare countenanced by British and Tory military authorities.

The red and white savages, enlisted under the British Revolutionary colors, murdered women and children as well as the male and soldier population. The women and children showed as great (and sometimes even greater) courage as the men.

During the entire Revolutionary war the Schoharie valley and the Mohawk from Amsterdam to Frankfort were exposed to the danger of massacre by Tories and Indians. It is very remarkable that about 4,000 settlers were still in this region at the end of hostilities in the valley in the spring of 1783.

In chapter III, series III., reference is made to the need of a satisfactory history of the Mohawk valley in the Civil war, and it is there suggested that our women of that time have their part in that struggle recorded—both as nurses and as homeworkers for the soldiers at the front. The editor of this work is not one who believes that valley history means merely Revolutionary affairs. The happenings of yesterday and of today are as much history as those of a century ago, so that our valley life during the Rebellion or in recent years should have its proper place in our valley records. Some stray thought in your neighbor's mind, some trifling occurrence in your community may be the tiny germ of some large event. Great things, like the telegraph and the steam engine doubtless originated in some wayward speculation in the mind of some seemingly obscure individual in some obscure locality. Let us not forget that "all the world's a stage."

The schoolboys of today and members of the Boy Scouts will find in these pages, many instances of the heroism and exciting adventures of the boys of long ago. The boy of today will read with interest how Francis Putman, a fifteen-year-old lad, captured Lieut. Hare, a most bloodthirsty Tory, who was subsequently hung by General Clinton on Academy Hill in Canajoharie; how Jacob Dievendorf, a lad of ten, was captured at Currytown, scalped after the battle of Sharon, recovered and lived almost eighty years afterward; how John Gremps, a fifteen-year-old soldier of Palatine, fought with his elders at Oriskany (probably like a number of others but little older) and came unhurt from the battlefield; how the boys of Minden were killed, captured and escaped from the savages during Brant's 'Minden raid of 1780; and lastly, to lend a humorous touch to these bloody records, we have the good story of the Nelliston boy who was the first to greet Atwood, the aviator, when he alighted there on his St. Louis to New York trip in 1911. When asked by Atwood where he had landed, the lad replied: "In the Nellis pasture," an answer that should go down into history as a bit of geographical information to an airman who had slidden down out of the clouds after a hundred-mile flight.

Probably among the incidents of Washington's valley trip in 1783, which pleased him was that of the company of Fort Plain schoolboys who, lined up along the road by the good wife of Dominie Gros, gave the General a rousing cheer as he rode up the hill to the fort; also at Cherry Valley where he saw and talked with the boys of the heroic Mrs. Campbell, all of whom had been captives of the Indians in Canada or at Niagara.

Concerning the little girls of the Revolution we also know considerable. Simms has preserved for us many interesting details of them during the Minden raid of 1780, those details which give us such an insight, not only into the horrors but into the life of the Revolution. We also have the dramatic incident of the captive ten-year-old Magadelena Martin, who rode on a horse behind the fiendish Walter Butler, on a cold October night of 1780 (when Johnson made his great raid up the valley), and who warmed her cold little hands in Butler's fur-lined pockets.

One of the most pathetic incidents of the Revolution in the valley was the return of Capt. Veeder and his company from the battlefield of Sharon, tenderly bearing on litters back to Fort Plain, two poor little children—a boy and a girl—scalped by the fiends whom Willett's men drove from the field. Fate deals queer cards, for Jacob Dievendorf, the boy, lived for seventy-nine years after that dreadful day, while the little girl, Mary Miller, passed away in the arms of a soldier who was giving her a drink from his canteen as the party neared Fort Plain.

When we consider the rage that must have filled the valley's fighting men at these many diabolical deeds done by the enemy, we are filled with wonder that they never made a single reprisal in revenge on the wives and children of Tories who lingered in the valley throughout the war. Truly our American fighting men of the Revolution were as high types of civilization as the world has seen before or since.

To offset these tragic stories we have more amusing and entertaining details such as the old-fashioned picture of little seven-year-old Anne McVicar (who later wrote the famous "Memoirs of An American Lady") sitting all day in a Mohawk river batteaux, propelled slowly upstream by the red-coated British soldiers of her father's company; also her visit to King Hendrick's son at Indian Castle, when "the monarch smiled, clapped my head and ordered me a little basket, very pretty and filled by his son with dried berries."

Campfire Girls take notice of the following:

Among the many dramatic incidents of Brant's raid about Fort Plain in 1780, are those concerning the young Bettinger, Strobeck and Sitts girls, who were captured and taken to Canada, where they liked life among the Indians so well that they refused to return and remained north and married red husbands (such instances were not uncommon in our early history); the five-year-old Sophia Sitts (who was taken in Brant's Minden raid but released by her squaw captor because the little girl was too much of a burden to carry pickaback) who became one of the best harvest hands of her section (in a day when women worked with men on the farm) and who lived to the great age of 108; and lastly, the little five-year-old girl, Evan Myers, who was made a prisoner the same day and thought her life was spared, because, unlike her little brothers (who were killed), when she was captured, as she subsequently told it, "I did not cry."

Appleton's Encyclopedia says that, of the 231,000 Continental or regular American troops engaged in the Revolution, New York state furnished 17,-800. New York in the Revolution gives the number of New York state Revolutionary militia 51,972, the latter being the correct figure.

SERIES II.

CHAPTER I.

1784—First Permanent Settlement of Oneida County—New England Immigration.

In 1784 the first permanent white settlement was made in Oneida county. Johannes Roof settled at Fort Stanwix about 1760, a few years after the construction of that advanced outpost. On St. Leger's approach in 1777, Roof was forced to abandon his farm and moved down the valley to the General Herkimer place. Later he settled at Canajoharie where he kept tavern when General Clinton was there in 1779 and during General Washington's visit in 1783. In 1784 the first considerable settlement was made in Oneida county at Whitestown. Utica and Rome were permanently settled a few years later. When Elkanah Watson made his first Mohawk river journey in 1788 the river section of Oneida county was practically a "howling" wilderness with the exception of a few settlements and clearings. The "howling" was actual as the wolves made sleep almost impossible with their night howling. Utica took on its first importance as being located at a river ford and when a bridge was built here and a road opened westward to "the Indian country" its future was assured. Then as now it became the hub of a series of roads (and later railroads) running north, east, south and west. Rome grew up on the site of Fort Schuyler (first called Fort Stanwix) and was important as being located at the carry from the Mohawk into Wood creek. Oneida county is about the size of the state of Rhode Island and its first settlers, after the Revolution, were largely from New England. These "Yan-

kees" also settled largely in Herkimer and Fulton counties at points more or less distant from the Mohawk, as these river lands were already occupied. Montgomery, Schoharie and Schenectady received less of this immigration. Utica, Rome and Oneida county grew rapidly in population, trade, agriculture and industry, after 1800, and Oneida soon became the most populous of the six Mohawk valley counties. Today (1914) over a third of the population of the Mohawk valley is located in Oneida county, and the latter forms a very important link in the industrial chain extending from Cohoes to Rome, along the banks of the Mohawk. Oneida is also the most important agriculturally of the six Mohawk valley counties.

CHAPTER VI.

Elkanah Watson's Mohawk River Trips of 1788 and 1791—His Views on and Efforts for Improved Mohawk River Navigation.

Elkanah Watson was a wide traveler and "gentleman of leisure" of Providence, R. I. Watson was greatly interested in canals, a subject which was generally discussed in the latter eighteenth century, and he had observed many of the old world artificial waterways. About 1788, while traveling in the Mohawk valley he took note of the commercial possibilities of that stream, as many public-spirited men had before him, and soon he began to propose, through the press, its improvement. In September, 1791, a party, piloted by Mr. Watson, covered the line of the improved waterway he had advocated. It consisted of Jeremiah Van Rensselaer, Gen. P. Van Cortland, Stephen N. Bayard and Watson. They left Albany and went to Schenectady, where they hired two batteaux, engaged six men and laid in a stock of provisions to last six weeks. The flatboats went up the river to Fort Herkimer where they were joined by the four principals who went thence by land. The whole party went to Fort Stanwix by river, where the two mile carry was made into Wood creek. The bargemen took the two batteaux through this waterway to Oneida lake, a very difficult and obstructed piece of navigation, used however by the Mohawk river boats of the time. The investigating party proceeded through Oneida lake into Oswego river and investigated Seneca river, Onondaga, Seneca and Cayuga lakes. They, satisfied themselves of the feasibility of the improvements proposed by Watson. They secured the influential assistance of Gen. Philip Schuyler and in 1792 the Inland Lock Navigation Co. was organized with Gen. Schuyler as president. In the face of great difficulties the improvement of the Mohawk river was carried through and completed from Oneida lake to Schenectady, in 1796. This included a canal and five locks at Little Falls with a 44½ ft. lift. The canal was 4,752 feet long and 2,550 feet of this was through solid rock. At Wolf's Rift, below Ft. Herkimer, was a canal 1¼ miles long with three locks. At Rome a canal 1¾ miles long connected the Mohawk with Wood creek on which there were four locks. See Chapter VI., Series II.

The labors of Elkanah Watson make him as much the "father" of New York state inland navigation as anyone, his being the first practical efforts for state waterway improvement. Watson was born in Massachusetts in 1758 and died at Port Kent, Lake Champlain, 1842, aged 84 years.

Watson kept a diary of his journeys through the Mohawk valley in 1788 and in 1791. In 1856 Mr. W. C. Watson published a memoir of his father, Elkanah Watson, under the title "Men and Times of the Revolution, or Memoirs of Elkanah Watson." This contained summaries or verbatim extracts from journals of the elder Watson's interesting travels. In 1788, Elkanah Watson visited Hudson, Albany, Schenectady and Johnstown, and at the latter place learned of the great Indian council shortly to occur at Fort Schuyler, or Stanwix as it was still generally called. He resolved to attend it and proceeded from Johnstown, northward.

His memoirs contain the following concerning this, his first valley trip of 1788:

"The country between Schenectady and Johnstown was well settled by a Dutch population, generally in a prosperous condition." The Watson memoirs further say:

From Johnson Hall, he proceeded up the Mohawk, through a rich region, under high cultivation and adorned by luxuriant clover pastures. This lovely valley was almost on a level with the river and was bounded on the north by a lofty range of hills, whose cliffs at times seemed impending over him. The fields were only separated by gates, with no fences on the roadsides. The beauty of the country, the majestic appearance of the adjacent mountains, the state of advanced agriculture, exhibited in a long succession of excellent farms, and the rich fragrancy of the air, redolent with the perfume of the clover, all combined to present a scene he was not prepared to witness on the banks of the Mohawk.

The territory, known as the German Flats, had been long inhabited and was densely occupied by a German population. This people had suffered severely during the War of Independence, from the ravages of the Tories and Indians and had been nearly extirpated. Their safety was only secured by the erection of numerous block houses, which were constructed in commanding positions, and often mounted with cannon. Many of these structures were yet standing, and were seen in every direction.

On this trip, Watson suffered from hunger, on account of the scarcity of taverns, in the upper valley. He stopped at Whitesboro, then a considerable settlement of log houses. At Oriskany he passed several hundred Indians and visited the battlefield, piloted by two German settlers, and saw the ground strewn with human bones. Beyond Oriskany he rode alone through a band of drunken, half-naked Indians, who danced, whooping and yelling, about him. He finally reached Fort Stanwix and found "the whole plain around the fort covered with Indians of various tribes, male and female. Many of the latter were fantastically dressed in their best attire— in the richest silks, fine scarlet clothes bordered with gold fringe, a profusion of brooches, rings in their noses, their ears slit, and their heads decorated with feathers. Among them I noticed some very handsome countenances and fine figures."

Watson secured quarters in the garret of the dwelling where Gov. Clinton and the eight New York Commissioners were housed, and attended all the doings at this celebrated Indian council, in which the red men were forced to give up their title to' their lands in New York state and farther west— about 4,000,000 acres. While here Watson examined the carry into Wood Creek, and started on a western waterway voyage but was turned back by a heavy rain.

Of his return trip down the Mohawk, Watson says in part: "My curiosity satisfied, I sent my horse towards Albany and embarked on board a returning bateau, and proceeded down the Mohawk to Little Falls, anxious to examine that place with an eye to canals. We abandoned ourselves to the current of the river, which, with the aid of our oars, impelled us at a rapid rate. We met numerous bateaux coming up the river, freighted with whole families, emigrating to the 'land of promise.' I was surprised to observe the dexterity with which they manage their boats, and the progress they make in poling up the river, against a current of at least three miles an hour. The first night we encamped at a log hut on the banks of the river and the next morning I disembarked at German Flats." From here he returned to Albany.

Watson's journal, of the Mohawk river investigating committee of 1791, is intensely interesting to Mohawk valley people as it describes pioneer conditions along the Mohawk. His remarks in regard to the "Mohawk Dutch" (for this term included both the High and Low Dutch) must be considered in the light of the fact that he was a cultured New Englander, that he was considering a different race whose very rude strength had aided in their partial conquest of the wilderness, and also that his enthusiasm for the "rudiments of literature" was not shared by a people who were schooled only in the rudiments of frontier life and had no time for anything else. While a majority of the valley people of 1791 were crude, rough and unlettered they also possessed many sterling qualities. There were also among them men of education, keen perceptions, and strong, solid intellectual powers. Watson came through western Montgomery county by way of Johnstown, through Stone Arabia to Caroga creek and thence up the valley. He was an observer of wide experience and his picture of frontier life on the Mohawk river in 1791 is perhaps the most valuable in existence, as it showed conditions as they generally existed here throughout the eighteenth century. It is to be regretted that his journal of his travels up and down the valley cannot be given verbatim. His entries are largely summarized by his son. Wherever his journal has reference to the Mohawk valley it is here reprinted (from the Memoirs of 1856) in full. The first verbatim entry, of the 1791 journey, was evidently written at Palatine Church, Sept. 4, 1791. The following are verbatim extracts:

1791, Sept. 4—We proceeded on our journey with a miserably covered wagon, and in a constant rain, until night, which brought us to Major Schuyler's mills in Palatine [on Caroga creek at Palatine Church], settled by the descendants of German emigrants, intermingling on all sides with the enterprising Sons of the East [New Englanders] between whom mutual prejudices ran high. These feelings will gradually be overcome by intermarriages and other modes of intercourse. Thus far the German and Dutch farmers have been, in a manner, totally remiss in cultivating the first rudiments of literature, while the descendants of the English in New England have cherished it as a primary duty. Hence the characteristics of each people are distinctly variant. * * * * I have noticed with pleasure that the German farmers begin to use oxen in agriculture instead of horses. For this salutary improvement they are indebted to the New England men.

I am induced to believe, should the Western canals ever be made, and the Mohawk River become, in one sense, a continuation of the Hudson River by means of canals and locks, that it will most clearly obviate the necessity of sending produce to market in winter by sleighs [then the general custom, the farmers going to Albany in winter with the surplus products they had for sale]. On the contrary, it would be stored on the margin of the Mohawk in winter, and be sent, in the summer months, by batteaux, to be unloaded aboard vessels in the Hudson.

The bottoms or lowlands along the Mohawk are laid off into rich inclosures, highly cultivated, principally by industrious Germans. Narrow roads and contracted bridges still exist.

On the south side of the river the country is thicker settled and many pleasant situations, old farms, and wealthy farmers appear, but these evidently are far behind those of Germany or England in the profitable science of agriculture. We crossed a new wooden bridge [over the Caroga creek] near Schuyler's Mills, 75 feet long, with a single arch supported by framed work above. I was glad to notice this an enterprising wedge to more extended improvements.

[1791] Sept. 7.—This morning we ascended Fall Hill, over a craggy road of one mile. From its summit we commanded an extensive and picturesque view of the surrounding country in the north, partly settled, but generally in nature's original brown livery, spotted here and there by an opening. We left Little Falls on our right and descended into the rich settlement of German Flats. At Eldridges tavern, near Fort Herkimer, we overtook our batteau, all well and embarked the same evening, stemming fourteen miles against a strong current, with an awning spread over our heads. Each boat was manned by three men, two in the bow and one in the stern to steer. They occasionally rowed in still water, setting with short poles at the rapids, with surprising dexterity. In this mode their average progress is three miles an hour, equal to truck-shute travelling in Holland; but it is exceedingly laborious and fatiguing to the men. At night we encamped in a log hut on the margin of the river.

[1791] Sept. 8.—A pleasant sail of ten miles this fine morning brought us to Old Fort Schuyler. Here we were joined by Gen. Van Cortland and Mr. Bayard, who were waiting for us, which completes our number to thirteen.

From Little Falls, thus far, the river is nearly competent to inland navigation, with the exception of a serious rapid and a great bend at the German Flats, called Wolf-riff, which must be subdued, either by a cut across the neck of land, upward of one mile, or by removing the obstructions.

An Indian road being opened from this place [later Utica] to the Genesee country, it is probable that the position of Fort Stanwix and this spot will become rivals as the site of a town, in connection with the interior, when it shall have become a settled country. If, however, the canals should be constructed, I think Fort Stanwix will take the lead at a future day. Such was my impression when here in 1788. Since then only a few houses and stores have been erected here, also a tolerable tavern to administer comfort to the weary traveler, which I experienced the want of three years past.

In the afternoon we progressed thirteen miles, meeting many obstructions in consequence of the cruel conduct of the new settlers, who are wonderfully increased since I was here [three years before], filling the river with fallen trees cut on its margin, narrowing it in many places, producing shoals where the deepest waters had been accustomed to flow, and impeding the progress of our boats. We pitched our Camp on the right hand bank of the river in the midst of woods. We soon had a roaring fire and our tents pitched —open on one side to the fire and closed at each end with canvas. We found an excellent substitute for feathers, laying our buffaloes on hemlock twigs; although the ground was moist we were effectually protected from any inconvenience. We enjoyed a pleasant night, with ten times more comfort than we could in the miserable log huts along the banks of the river.

[1791] Sept. 9.—At noon we reached Fort Stanwix, to which place, with some aid of art, the river continues adapted to inland navigation for boats of five tons burthen. Emigrants are swarming into these fertile regions in shoals, like the ancient Israelites seeking the land of promise.

We transported our boats and baggage across the carrying place, a distance of two miles, over a dead flat and launched into Wood Creek, running west. It is a mere brook at this place, which a man can easily jump across.

In contemplating this important creek as the only water communication with the immense regions in the west, which are destined to bless millions of freemen in the approaching century, I am deeply impressed with a belief, considering the great resources of this State, that the improvement of our internal navigation cannot much longer escape the attention of our law-makers, and more especially as it is obviously practicable. When effected, it will open an uninterrupted water communication from the immense fertile regions in the West to the Atlantic.

Sept. 10, 1791, Watson and party began to descend Wood creek, to Oneida lake, a most tortuous stream and difficult piece of navigation, so narrow that the bow and stern of a batteau scraped opposite banks in making the turns, obstructed by logs in the stream and crossed by boughs and limbs so closely overhead that in some places it obliged "all hands to lie flat."

On Sept. 12 they reached the Royal block-house at the east end of Oneida lake. Sept. 13 they "wrote home by a boat coming from the west loaded with hemp, raised at the south end of Cayuga lake." Sept. 14 they came to Fort Brewerton at the entrance to the present Oneida river, after sailing down Oneida lake, which evoked the warmest admiration from Mr. Watson, although he found it "extremely turbulent and dangerous."

Watson's journal is replete with surmises and prophecies on the future of United States internal waterway navigation, much of which has come to pass. The influence of what one in telligent, energetic man, with imagination and a working control of his specialty, can achieve is seen in the improved Mohawk river which Watson's efforts brought about, and which, in itself led up to the Erie and the Barge canal. All honor to Elkanah Watson!

CHAPTER VII.
1800 (About)—The Mohawk and Albany Pikes—Toll Gates.

Rufus A. Grider's paper on "The Mohawk Turnpike," says that the Great Western turnpike started from Albany and ran by way of Carlisle, Cherry Valley, Otsego, Chenango, Owego, Dannsville, Aurora, to Buffalo. In 1790 the first mail stage west of Schenectady ran from Albany to Schenectady, Johnstown and Canajoharie each week. The fare was three cents per mile. In 1792 the route was extended to Fort Plain, Old Fort Schuyler (now Utica), and Whitestown, every two weeks. In 1794 the line was further extended to Geneva and Canandaigua. Stage fares of this period, generally averaged about four cents a mile.

The Mohawk and Hudson turnpike (chartered in 1797) from Albany to Schenectady was a fine macadamized road lined with poplars. The Mohawk turnpike (chartered 1800) was of broken stone, sixty feet wide, with a center raised eighteen inches above the sides. There were twelve toll gates on this pike, four of them being located in western Montgomery county. Mr. Grider gives their location as follows:

1. Schenectady.
2. Cranesville.
3. Caughnawaga (now Fonda).
4. Schenck's Hollow (near the north side Nose, now the Montgomery county home).
5. Junction of Wagner's Hollow road in Palatine (a short distance east).
6. Caroga creek (short distance east).
7. St. Johnsville (lower end).
8. East Creek bridge (west end).
9. Fink's Ferry (at Fall Hill).
10. West Canada Creek (Herkimer).
11. Sterling (six miles east of Utica).
12. Utica (formerly Old Fort Schuyler).

In 1811 a fast line ran, day and night, from Albany to Buffalo, in three days. The horses were trotted almost continuously and were changed every nine to twelve miles. Four coaches were sent east and four coaches west by this line daily.

Over 200 automobiles were counted in one hour passing westward through the village of Nelliston on a summer Sunday afternoon in 1914 over the Mohawk turnpike.

"Everyman's Literary and Historical Atlas of North and South America" gives an interesting map of the early highways of the United States from east to west. The principal ones noted are the Iroquois trail and Genesee road (the Mohawk turnpike and Genesee road from Albany to Buffalo with an extension to Boston); the Philadelphia to Pittsburg turnpike; the Washington to Cumberland to Wheeling road (later extended to Indianapolis and St. Louis); the Richmond to Cumberland Gap to Louisville road. Of these, the "Iroquois trail" was the principal one and the only one (as it is today) which afforded practically continuous water communication (as well as land communication) with the Great Lakes region. The Iroquois trail also extended eastward from the junction of the Hoosac river with the Hudson to Massachusetts bay. This was also called the Mohawk trail.

CHAPTER XI.

1914 — Mohawk Valley Railroads — Railroad Development.

There are coal pockets on the New York Central's Mohawk division at St. Johnsville and coal pockets were established on the West Shore at Indian Castle in 1913. The West Shore division of the New York Central has a foundry located at Frankfort. Schenectady, Fonda, Herkimer, Utica and Rome are important railroad centers in the Mohawk valley.

In 1914 the invention was announced of an electrically propelled railroad system capable of a speed of 300 miles an hour.

The following is of interest as marking a stage in the development of railroad freight transportation in the Mohawk valley:

The longest freight train that ever ran over the New York Central railroad passed through the Mohawk valley, Monday morning, May 18, 1914. The train was composed of 125 cars some of which were loaded, while others were empty. One engine hauled them.

The train was known as a "test train." For some time past, the N. Y. C. has been trying to determine how many cars an engine would haul, and it was believed that the limit was 125. The trial May 18 appeared to be successful as the big load rode easily.

The 125 cars made a train about one mile in length. Each car will average 40 feet in length or a total of 5,000 feet. Neither caboose nor engine were included in the 125 cars and these are about one hundred feet in length, or making an estimated total length of the train as over 5,100 feet. If loaded to capacity, the train carried about

3,750 tons or a little more than two tandem canal barges are expected to haul.

In 1914 an Erie railroad freight locomotive drew 250 loaded freight cars.

It may fittingly here be remarked that the American railroads are in a critical condition at the time of the issuance of this work, 1914. Increased operating expenses and frequently past financial irregularities have made it barely possible for the roads to earn expenses. Increased rates and better financial methods will doubtless bring future improvement.

SERIES III.

CHAPTER I.

Mohawk Valley Governors, Yates 1823-5; Bouck, 1843-5; Seymour, 1853-5, 1863-5—Vice President Sherman, 1908-12.

The Hudson valley, of which the Mohawk forms a part, has given two presidents to the United States—Van Buren and Roosevelt. The Mohawk valley has furnished three governors to New York state—Yates of Schenectady, Bouck of Schoharie and Seymour of Oneida—and one presidential candidate, Seymour, who ran as a Democrat against Grant, Republican, in 1868, and one vice president, Sherman of Oneida.

Governor Joseph C. Yates was born in Schenectady in 1768. He was a founder of Union college, the first mayor of Schenectady after it was made a city in 1798 and governor of New York, 1823-25. He died in 1837. Yates county was named for him.

William C. Bouck was the second governor of New York state from the Mohawk valley. He was born at Fulton, Schoharie county, in 1786. He was a lawyer, member of assembly, 1814-15 17, and a state senator in 1819. He was colonel of the 18th N. Y. infantry, a member of the state canal board and a superintendent of a section of the Erie canal under construction, 1817-25. He was canal commissioner for 19 years. In 1840 he was the unsuccessful Democratic candidate for governor and in 1842 he was elected. He was a member of the constitutional convention of 1846 and treasurer of New York customs, 1846-9, after which he resumed the occupation of a farmer. He died in 1859, aged 73 years. Bouck's Falls, in Schoharie county, was named for his family by the historian Simms.

Horatio Seymour was born at Pompey, Onondaga county, in 1810. In childhood his family removed to Utica, Oneida county, where Mr. Seymour made his home for the rest of his life. He became a lawyer in 1832, although he did not actively practise as he was engaged principally in the management of a large estate inherited from his father. Seymour was elected as a Democrat to the New York state assembly in 1841 and for three succeeding terms, being speaker in 1845. He was mayor of Utica in 1842 and an unsuccessful Democratic candidate for governor in 1850. He was elected governor in 1853, serving till 1855. In 1862 he was again elected and became one of the famous "war governors," heartily supporting the union. He was defeated for re-election in 1864. In 1868, against his wishes, Seymour was nominated for the presidency by the Democratic party and was defeated by U. S. Grant, who received 214 electoral votes to Seymour's 80. He died at Utica in 1886, aged 75 years. Governor Seymour was a learned and entertaining writer on Mohawk valley history and an eloquent orator. He frequently spoke at valley patriotic gatherings and his addresses at such times are local historical classics. Seymour inspired Frederic to the writing of "In the Valley."

The Mohawk valley has furnished one vice president to the United States —James S. Sherman of Utica, Oneida county. Mr. Sherman was born in Utica in 1855 and died there in 1912, aged 57 years. He served as congressman from the Oneida district for a number of years and was nominated on the Republican presidential ticket of 1908 and elected with William H. Taft, the nominee for president. He was renominated with Taft on the Re-publican ticket of 1912, but died before the election.

The Hudson valley, of which the Mohawk forms a part, furnished the following vice presidents to the United States: George Clinton, qualified 1805; Martin Van Buren, qualified 1833; Schuyler Colfax, qualified 1869; Theodore Roosevelt, qualified 1901; James S. Sherman, qualified 1909. Of these five, Van Buren and Roosevelt subsequently became presidents. Eight of the twenty-eight vice presidents came from New York state and four presidents, of the twenty-seven who have served from Washington in 1789 to Wilson in 1914.

CHAPTER IV.
Prospective Barge Canal Commerce.

The 1910 tonnage of two of the great canals of the world is given in this chapter as follows: Sault Ste. Marie (connecting Lakes Huron and Superior), 36,395,687; Suez, 23,054,901. Their 1912 tonnage, according to the N. Y. World almanac, was Sault Ste. Marie, 72,472,676; Suez, 20,125,120. The 1913 tonnage of vessels engaged in traffic on the Great Lakes was 2,949,924, almost double that of 1900. The commerce of our inland seas is growing at such a rate that even the foregoing figures will doubtless be surpassed in a few years. This "Soo" canal carries only part of this traffic as that of Lake Michigan does not pass through it. Its commerce is almost four times that of Suez. It is reasonable to suppose that a very large part of the Great Lakes traffic will find an outlet through the Barge canal, and that its tonnage will exceed that of Suez and of Panama. It is human nature to be fascinated by fireworks rather than solid achievement and so we see the Panama canal, with its picturesque and romantic features, receive the widest publicity in the American press while the Barge canal, fully as great and interesting a work, is practically ignored. We all remember the proverb of a prophet being honored save in his own country and, if a canal very similar to the Panama canal was being constructed in our populous eastern states, it would probably get as little public attention as the Barge canal receives. The latter work also suffers from the fact that the more spectacular Panama canal is being built at the same time as our big state waterway.

The Barge canal in the Mohawk valley is practically the Mohawk river. So, indeed, was the Erie canal which was virtually a side stream of the Mohawk, as the latter furnished most of the water for that artificial river.

A ship canal has been several times proposed from Waterford on the Hudson to Oswego on Lake Ontario, by way of the Mohawk, Oneida lake, Oneida river and Oswego river. Its length would be about 170 miles, 110 of which would be through the Mohawk valley, from Waterford to Rome.

The Barge Canal Bulletin, Series VI., 1913 (December, 1913), published a very interesting map with regard to the Barge canal. This showed that, within two miles of the Barge canal and its natural extensions, the Hudson river and Lake Champlain, there lived 73½ per cent of the population of the state, within five miles of these waterways lived 77 per cent of New York's population, and within twenty miles, 87 per cent of the state's people. This twenty-mile strip constituted 46 per cent of New York state's territory.

♦Fully 80 per cent, or about 400,000 of the probable 1915 population of 500,000 in the Mohawk valley and the six Mohawk valley counties, is located within 5 miles of the Barge canal.

Barge canal types of boats are not (1914) definitely decided upon, according to the Barge Canal Bulletin. They may be of from 3,000 tons downward, the idea being for one motor engine or power boat to draw about 3,000 tons through the locks without breaking up the boats. Barges of 1,500 tons, to run tandem, or of about 800 tons each, to run in quadruplets (one to be a power boat) are probable types. The lockage capacity of the Barge canal will be about six times that of the old Erie. This is sufficient for present needs; time alone will show whether it will

take care of the east-west waterway commerce of the future.

The year of the publication of this work (1914) marks an era of the practical finishing of three great American canal projects. In July, 1914, the Cape Cod canal, giving inside water route communication between New York and Boston was opened. The Panama canal, early in 1914, passed boats on trial trips and the New York State Barge canal was largely completed and the expectations were that it would be open for traffic in 1915.

Forty of the sixty-two counties of New York state directly abut upon or are crossed by the Barge canal of New York state. These forty counties had a population combined of 7,911,000 (in 1910) as compared with the 1910 New York state population of 9,113,000 and a U. S. population of 92,-000,000. Seven counties of New Jersey border the Hudson river section of the Barge canal or are located on its immediate terminal waters, thus making forty-seven counties of the two states which are directly served by this great waterway. It is well to observe how largely this important world canal serves the great majority of the New York state territory and its population, a matter which is frequently overlooked by many in considering canal questions.

The forty New York state Barge canal counties as before stated, have a population of 7,911,000, while the seven New Jersey Barge canal counties have a population of 1,753,000, making a combined New York-New Jersey population served by the Barge canal of 9,644,000 (in 1910).

To the New York state territory open to the commerce of the canal can very properly be added the counties of Chautauqua, Jefferson, St. Lawrence, Nassau and Suffolk, which reach the Barge canal through navigable adjacent waters on Lake Erie, Lake Ontario, St. Lawrence river and Long Island Sound. Including these counties would give forty-five New York state Barge canal counties out of a total of sixty-two, or about 80 per cent of the state's territory accessible to the canal. These forty-five New York state Barge canal counties have a combined population of 8,413,000 out of a New York state population of 9,113,000. Including the seven New Jersey Barge canal counties, the fifty-two New York-New Jersey Barge canal counties had a total population of 10,166,000 in 1910.

The entire New York state population of the forty-five Barge canal counties can safely be estimated in 1915 as about 9,400,000. Estimating the 1915 population of the five New Jersey Barge canal counties at 2,000,-000, would give a combined population of the fifty-two New York-New Jersey Barge canal counties of 11,400,000 for the year of the canal's opening (1915). The most important sections, commercially and industrially, of New York and New Jersey are served by the new waterway. Extensions of the canal are projected which would add three more counties to the canal territory—Chemung, Tioga, Broome. Steuben and Lewis could be added to this list by possible extensions, making forty-eight New York state counties which would be within the Barge canal territory. Of course a much greater territory of the United States and Canada is covered by this New York state waterway and over half of the United States and a population of 75,000,000 or more will directly or indirectly be accessible to the transportation advantages of this great water freight route. Persons interested in the ramifications of this canal should send to the office of the State Engineer and Surveyor, Albany, New York, for the small canal map of the state of New York. Of course the entire Atlantic sea coast and its navigable rivers are open to the commerce of the Barge canal barges.

Twenty miles of the left bank of the lower Hudson lies in New Jersey, also the western and southern shore lines of upper and lower New York bay. It is the desire of this work to show the natural geographical, industrial, commercial and social American divisions rather than the artificial ones and in

this case the subdivision of these important waters by the purely imaginary boundaries of states is misleading and somewhat ridiculous.

The seven New Jersey Barge canal counties comprise one-fifth of the territory of that state and two-thirds of its population. The portions of these counties on navigable waters connecting with New York bay, New York city and the lower part of Westchester county, are all generally spoken of as the "Metropolitan District." By the census of 1910 this area had a population of 6,400,000 in round numbers. In 1915, the year of the expected opening of the Barge canal, its population will be, as estimated, about 7,500,000. It is estimated that New York city alone grew over eight hundred thousand between 1910 and 1915. Its 1915 population is estimated at over 5,600,000. All of the meropolitan district lies within twenty-five miles of the New York city hall.

For an idea of the possibilities of a still greater waterway see Chapter V., Series II. of "The Story of Old Fort Plain." Attention is also called to the map of the rivers of New York state (published at the front of the book) which shows very clearly how a remarkable series of rivers carry the Barge canal along and across the state and northward to Lake Ontario and Lake Champlain. Of the 475 miles of Barge canal waterway from New York to Buffalo, the Hudson, and its tributary, the Mohawk, and the closely connected valley of the Oswego carry the canal 350 miles or more of the route. The Hudson-Mohawk section comprises over 250 miles of the cross-state waterway and rail way route.

In closing this subject it may be here said that the forty New York counties directly abutting on the canal or its terminals are Erie, Niagara, Orleans, Monroe, Wayne, Ontario, Yates, Tompkins, Schuyler, Seneca, Cayuga, Oswego, Onondaga, Madison, Oneida, Herkimer, Montgomery, Fulton, Schenectady, Albany, Saratoga, Washington, Warren, Essex, Clinton, Rensselaer, Greene, Columbia, Ulster,

Dutchess, Orange, Putnam, Rockland, Westchester, Bronx, New York, Richmond, Kings, Queens.

The seven New Jersey Barge canal counties are Bergen, Passaic, Hudson, Essex, Union, Middlesex and Monmouth.

The five additional New York state counties now practically open to Barge canal navigation are Chautauqua on Lake Erie; Jefferson, and St. Lawrence on Lake Ontario and the St. Lawrence river and Nassau and Suffolk on Long Island Sound. The New Jersey counties are all located on New York bay and its adjacent navigable waters.

Fulton county is included in the foregoing because its twin cities of Johnstown and Gloversville are but three and six miles distant from the canal and within easy trucking distance. Moreover geographically Fulton and Montgomery counties are virtually one.

Additions to the Barge canal are being surveyed and were treated of in State Engineer Bensel's 1914 report. They are from the foot of Seneca lake to Chemung river, following the route of the old Chemung canal. This would open up communication between the 540 miles of the New York state Barge canal and the Susquehanna river and thence with the coal country of Pennsylvania. The other additions considered were the Glens Falls feeder, and two canals on the Greater New York section of Long Island, one from Newton creek to Flushing Bay and the other across the island from Flushing Bay to Jamaica Bay. Barge canal improvement of the Black river, from Lake Ontario to Carthage, has also been projected. A 27-foot ship channel from Hudson to Albany, is projected in 1914. It must be remembered that the Hudson river and New York bay are parts of the Barge canal.

By way of the Chicago Drainage canal, connecting Lake Michigan with the Mississippi, the Barge canal has communication with the Mississippi valley, the Gulf of Mexico and with three-quarters of the navigable inland waterways of the United States. From

Lake Superior through Rainy lake and Lake of the Woods to Lake Winnipeg, the building of a canal would connect the Great Lakes and the Barge canal with the great Canadian northwest and would open up water communication with over half of the navigable inland waterways of North America. This great area is now (1914) probably the seat of population of 90,000,000 people and eventually may hold a population of four or five hundred millions.

In all this remarkable connecting system of rivers, lakes and canals, it is interesting to note that it is the Mohawk valley which makes possible this easy and direct communication between the tidal waters of the Hudson and Atlantic and America's great system of inland fresh waterways. Fortunate is the individual and the community situated along this water route system.

See maps on these subjects.

Twenty million dollars have been appropriated by New York state for the construction of terminal docks or small harbors and practically every town of importance along the main route of the Barge canal (and on its branches as well) will have such a terminal for the reception and dispatching of freight, which will doubtless be hauled by slow freight and fast freight boats and lines of boats, after the completion of the canal. Five million dollars has been appropriated by the national government for the improvement of the upper Hudson river, $1,300,000 of which is to be spent at and near Troy. Great concrete docks are also being built at the latter place and Albany (1914).

Predictions are made by residents of the Albany-Troy group of cities that a great metropolis will grow up at that point—the head of the tidewater navigation and the beginning of the Erie and Champlain branches of the Barge canal and in the center of a network of railroads and automobile roads and a great industrial, commercial and agricultural center as well. Some of these (1914) predictions sound extravagant to the limit. Congress-

man Ten Eyck of Albany claims a fu
ture population for this greater Albany-Troy of five millions. It is not
improbable, however, that a great
center of a million people will eventually be located on the Hudson and Mohawk near the mouth of the latter
stream.

By 1925 the New York metropolitan
district will number 9,500,000 people
and by 1950 probably more than 15,-
000,000, with a New York state population of about 25,000,000. By the year
2000 it may have 20,000,000 people and
by 2200 35,000,000 after which time its
population will probably stand still or
even considerably decrease as the
United States population reaches its
maximum of 400,000,000. These figures
are all provided present conditions continue. A marked decrease in the rainfall in the next century would make
the estimated population at the mouth
of the Hudson an impossibility. There
is nothing particularly noteworthy
about such enormous population centers; in fact they are deplorable as
regards the great majority of their
population, so that a decrease in their
population means progress in reality.
It may be that the course of industrial
and commercial life in the next century (1914-2014) may diffuse these
great populations over many sub-cen-
ters of human activity. But whatever
the future populations they seem now
(1914) bound to be very great and the
New York State Barge canal will be a
necessity for bringing foodstuffs and
supplies (in conjunction with the railroads) from the American northwest
and from foreign countries to the
great cities in the industrial belt lying
along the New York State Barge canal.
By 1925 the metropolitan district of
New York, with 9,500,000 people, will
be the greatest population center of
the world, excelling London which it
now (1914) nearly equals.

It is expected that the Barge canal
structures and its deepening of the
Mohawk river channel will in the future prevent the spring freshets which
have often been so disastrous and always inconvenient to the valley towns.

At the time of the publication of
this book (1914) a $3,500,000 company
was in process of incorporation, which
had for its object the navigation of the
Barge canal and the institution of a
fast freight line from New York to
Albany to Buffalo, serving principally
the Erie section from Albany to Buf
falo. Thirty electrically driven boats
are projected, the type of which was
not in 1914 definitely decided upon.

CHAPTER V.
1914—Aeroplanes.

The year 1914 was marked by the
construction of the aeroplane "America," destined for a trans-Atlantic trip.
Several routes were in contemplation
in 1914, one from Newfoundland to
the Azores to Spain and the other by
way of Greenland-Iceland and Great
Britain. Aeroplanes were used for the
first time in war in the Italian-Turkish
war in Tripoli in 1911-1912, in the Bal-
kan wars (Turkey vs. Greece-Servia-
Montenegro-Bulgaria and Bulgaria vs.
Servia-Greece, 1912-13), in the Mexi-
can revolution of 1913-1914. A great
European war involving all of the
great European powers is beginning
at the time of this writing (August
1, 1914) and aeroplanes will doubtless
play a large part in this conflict,
should it unfortunately long continue.
Dirigible balloons form part of the
military equipment of many European
nations. A continuous succession of
fatalities has marked the use of airships of both kinds.

August 4, 1914, the first great battle
of this war was being fought at Liege,
Belgium, between an invading force of
Germans and its Belgian defenders.
Russia, France, England, Belgium and
Servia are arrayed against Germany
and Austria, with other powers liable
to be involved.

In 1914, the year of going to press of
this book, a speed of 124 miles per hour
by aeroplanes flying over a measured
course has been recorded. It was only
in 1903 that the first flight occurred of
a man-directed heavier-than-air aeroplane at Kitty Hawk, N. C., managed
by the Wright brothers, virtual inven-

tors of the aeroplane. In 1913 the tenth anniversary of this event was celebrated by New York city aeronauts and a thrilling race, or Metropolitan Aeroplane Derby, was held around Manhattan Island. The winner made 60 miles in 52 minutes.

Across-the-Atlantic and around-the-world flights are being considered and projected (1914).

The aeroplane stabilizer, a Wright invention, was brought out in 1914. Up to 1914 the greatest distance flown over a circuit without stop by an aeroplane was 627 miles. Accidents and deaths of aeronauts are (1914) of almost daily occurrence. The aeroplane corps of the United States army have aeroplanes in service at Vera Cruz in Mexico (1914) and all nations are utilizing aeroplanes and dirigible airships for war purposes. The Hudson and Mohawk valleys were the scenes of the notable Albany-New York flight by Curtiss in 1910, and in part the route of Atwood from St. Louis to New York in 1911. Both of these events were epoch-making in American aeronautics.

Incorrect Historical Illustrations.

Simms's "Frontiersmen of New York" contains many illustrations which are apt to give the uninitiated a false impression of the people and costumes of the Revolution. Revolutionary men are depicted therein in silk hats and spike-tail coats, which is ridiculous and misleading. For good pictures of our valley ancestors and their costumes see "In the Valley" by Harold Frederic, illustrated by Howard Pyle.

A similar instance is the engraved supposed portrait of General Herkimer printed in the publications of the Oneida Historical society. This is taken from an interesting old painting representing a middle-aged man, in his shirt sleeves, smoking a pipe. Its authenticity has never been established but it has been used as a basis for later representations of Herkimer—notably the fine statue of him by Burr Miller at Herkimer. But the picture used by the Oneida Historical society shows General Herkimer in a "Prince Albert" coat, and modern turn-down collar and necktie—an attire absolutely unknown in Revolutionary times and not worn at all until about the time of the Civil war. This portrait of Herkimer is absolutely unworthy of such a distinguished body as the Oneida Historical society—one which has done a great work in the preservation of valley records and the marking of sites—and this plate should be suppressed.

Such pictures, like careless historical references, give the general public a disjointed and foggy view of valley history.

The Marking of the Site of Old Fort Plain — Valley Historical Societies and Their Accomplishments — Boy Scouts and Campfire Girls.

Among the several patriotic projects of recent years, one of the most laudable is that of the Fort Plain Chapter, Daughters of the American Revolution, having in view the marking of the site of old Fort Plain with a suitable memorial. Consideration of the reproduction of the blockhouse on its original site, has been made. No more suitable memorial could be constructed. Fort Plainers would benefit by the moderate walk to the site and the view of the valley, which is here particularly interesting. It probably would be much visited if made accessible. Fort Plain is a central point in the Mohawk valley and a very suitable place for a collection of historical objects and exhibits of present day interest, particularly so as such large crowds gather here from up and down the valley during street fair week. It would also have a tendency to continually attract a considerable number of people to Fort Plain which would be to the constant advantage of the town. It would also be, an object of educational interest to students. The D. A. R. have done splendid work in the marking of historic sites and the arousing of public interest in valley history, and the permanent marking of old Fort Plain on Fort Hill and the preservation of a suitable plot of ground about it, with accessible walks, would be one of the best achievements of these public-spirited women. It may be mentioned here that too much credit cannot be given the patriotic and historical societies of the valley for their notable achievements in marking sites, preserving historic buildings and erecting monuments.

Among the accomplishments by these societies and also by public-spirited individuals in recent years have been the erection of monuments on the battlefields of Oriskany, Johnstown and Stone Arabia, over the grave of General Herkimer, the preservation of the Herkimer house, Fort Johnson, the Van Alstine house, Johnson Hall, several of our Revolutionary churches, the erection of a fine statue to Herkimer at Herkimer, and the marking, with tablets, of the line of march of the Tryon County Militia to Oriskany, from the Herkimer house to the battleground, and the monument marking the start of Clinton's overland march from Canajoharie in 1779; as well as lesser monuments, markings and preservations. Many of these are referred to elsewhere in this work.

We have in America today two organizations which, while not of an ostensibly patriotic or historical character, will have a future great influence on our country. They are the Boy Scouts and the Campfire Girls—the former one of the greatest organizations ever instituted and the latter with great possibilities. Both bring the young in touch with nature, the land, outdoor life and the history of rivers and localities and are bound to influence for good coming American men of the future. It is almost impossible to get a Mohawk valley man of today (1914) to walk out and get acquainted with his home valley. The Boy Scouts and Campfire Girls encourage enjoyable, vigorous, out-door exercise and consequent strong, hardy bodies — matters in which the average town-dwelling American of today (and he constitutes the majority of our American element) is sadly lacking, and in which our outdoor ancestors excelled as a matter of course. All honor to Baden-Powell,

who instituted the Boy Scout movement, which has spread from Britain to the United States, Canada, Australia, South Africa and all other English speaking communities the world over.

___

Yankee Doodle and the Yankee Doodle Boys.

The following is from the recently published diary of Baron Closen, a young French officer who was with Count de Rochambeau in the Yorktown Campaign of 1781. It may be remarked here that the young French officer was much fascinated by the Revolutionary American girls. The paragraphs quoted describe the surrender of Yorktown and have nothing whatever to do with the Revolutionary history of the Mohawk valley. It gives such a good picture of the American soldier and the hatred that existed between them and the (shall we say, snobbish) British that it is worth publication—all the more because it brings to mind a sketchy outline of what our Mohawk valley Revolutionary fighting men may have been like. Of the surrender of Cornwallis at Yorktown, Va., Closen wrote in his diary of Oct. 19, 1781:

At 2 o'clock the garrison of York marched out before the allied army, which was formed in two lines, the French standing opposite to the Americans and wearing their gala uniforms. While passing between the two lines the English showed the greatest contempt for the Americans who, to say the truth, did not cut much of a figure compared with our army in appearance and equipment, for the greater part of these unfortunates were dressed in little white cloth jackets, dirty and ragged, and many of them were almost barefooted. The English had given them the nickname "Janckey Dudle."

But what of that, the sensible man will ask—these people are all the more praiseworthy and brave for fighting as they do, when they are so badly provided with everything.

"Janckey Dudle," as Closen wrote it, is a French rendering of "Yankee Doodle." It was at old Greenbush, now Rensselaer, on the Hudson, opposite Albany, that the song "Yankee Doodle" was first vamped together and sung and played by the American Provincial soldiers. So it was in the Hudson valley (at Rensselaer) that our national song "Yankee Doodle," was born and in the Hudson valley (on the Mohawk at Fort Schuyler) that the stars and stripes were first flown in battle. Evidently the British called our American soldiers "Yankee Doodles."

"Landmarks of Rensselaer County," by George Baker Anderson (published under the auspices of the Troy Press, 1897), has the following account of the birth of "Yankee Doodle" at Greenbush (Rensselaer) during the French-Indian war (1754-1760):

During the last of the French and Indian wars, Major-Gen. James Abercrombie, with more than 10,000 British-American troops, in 1758, encamped in the lower part of what is now Greenbush [Dutch, "Greenbosch"— Green bush or green woods]. Soon after sixteen colonial regiments arrived and a little later four more regiments from Connecticut. It was while these troops were in camp at this point that the song known as "Yankee Doodle," originally intended as a satire on the Connecticut regiments, was composed by Dr. Shackburg, a [Dutch?] surgeon in the British army. The general appearance of these troops greatly amused the well-drilled and well-informed British soldiers and they were laughed at and derided until they became a byword, not only in the camp but in Albany. They were called "Yankee Doodles," and the song which Dr. Shackburg composed was dedicated to and named after them. The music was adopted from an old song written in England many years [centuries?] before, and for a long time preserved in rhymes of the nursery:

"Lucy Locket lost her pocket,
Kitty Fisher found it;
Nothing in it, nothing in it,
But the binding round it."

Just what Dr. Shackburg's composition was it is impossible, at this day to tell, for parody after parody has been written since that time. The tune, however, is practically the same today as it was when the original Yankee Doodle was written, except for the interpolation of a few notes to fit the increased number of syllables in the stanzas. The purpose of the composition was fulfilled and the Connecticut soldiers, who took the joke good-naturedly, called it "Nation-Fine." Less than a score of years afterward,

upon the surrender of General Burgoyne, October 17th, 1777, the captured enemy marched between the lines of the victorious Yankees to the tune which a British soldier had composed, and which, by that time, had become the only national air which the Americans had.

_____

"Value of the Study of Local History."

On July 1, 1914, Dr. Sherman Williams, Chief of School Libraries of the University of the State of New York, made an address before the Montgomery County Historical Society at the home of the society, Fort Johnson. His paper which is entitled "The Value of the Study of Local History," is the best exposition of the matter the editor of this work has seen and portions of it are here reprinted. In this connection it may be here remarked that the editor of "The Story of Old Fort Plain and the Middle Mohawk Valley," has prepared a short "School History of the Mohawk Valley, and the Six Mohawk Valley Counties," which is a condensation of this work, and a gazeteer of Mohawk valley as well. Portions of Dr. Williams's address, which are always pertinent to our valley and its history, follow:

It is to be regretted that while the courses of study in the public schools of the state provide for seven years' work in history, no time whatever is given to the study of the history of New York except incidentally, and very incidentally, in connection with the study of the history of the United States. This seems to be a violation of all the old pedagogical principles such as that we should go from the known to the related unknown, the simple to the complex, etc. Just why this condition of affairs has come about is a little difficult to see. It may be because there is too common a belief that knowledge and education are synonymous terms which, of course, is very far from being true. Whatever the cause may be, no change is likely to take place unless a demand for such change comes from the people of the state pretty generally.

It seems to me that this is a matter that local historical societies and patriotic organizations might very properly take into consideration. It is not that the knowledge of the history of our state is of more value than the knowledge of other history, but that the effect of such knowledge is helpful, stimulating and uplifting. A person who believes in his family and is proud of it is a better member of his family because of that fact. So, a person who believes in and is proud of the history of his locality or his state, and the people who constitute the community and state, is likely to be a better citizen. A recent writer has said: "Europeans regard a general knowledge of the history of their country, province and city as an essential factor in even an elementary education. Inquiry by the American visitor will lead to the discovery that almost every intelligent peasant boy is at least fairly informed about the annals of the locality; its heroes are his own, its glory is reflected in the enthusiasm with which he recites their deeds to the passing stranger. But when the immigrant, emerging from such a background, arrives in America he is apt to find that those among whom his social lot is cast know little of our national history and virtually nothing of the career of the state or city; his children are not even taught local history in the public schools. Small wonder if he concludes that America has no history worth the telling, no state or city heroes worthy the name; that America 'just grew up' and is merely a land of opportunity in which to make dollars.

"Can American patriots be made out of these foreigners in the face of such neglect? Can a man be taught to love his country or his state or city unless he is taught that great deeds have been done, that her high ideals are cherished; that his locality has been and is a factor in civilizing the New World? Are even our American born boys and girls being made into the same sort of patriots that they rear abroad? Is it not time that as teachers we pay some regard to our state and local history; that we begin to cultivate a taste in this study in the minds of youth, and therein lay the foundation for that love of locality, which is the essence of civic patriotism?"

* * * * * * * * *

The Battle of Bunker Hill was not followed by any momentous consequences. It did not change history. If the battle had not been fought, or if it had and the patriots had run like frightened sheep at the first charge of the British, the general result would have been the same. The city of Boston would still have been surrounded by thousands of patriots, the British would still have been driven out. It is not claimed that the Battle of Bunker Hill was of no consequence. Far from it. It showed that the patriots could withstand a charge by British regulars and it greatly cheered and en-

couraged the Americans. But the battle was not followed by any momentous consequences.

The following year a battle was fought in New York. That was not without important consequences. It was the bloodiest battle of the Revolution, that is, the largest proportion of those engaged were killed or wounded. This battle was followed by important consequences. It was the turning point of the Revolution. I refer to the Battle of Oriskany. That is not known to every schoolboy so that he can actually see it. Many of them have never even heard of it. Many of our school histories do not even mention it. But it was at Oriskany that the Battle of Saratoga was really won. It was this that led to the support of the French.

I might spend the afternoon in calling attention to the important events in the history of our state that are not mentioned in our schools or school books and then fail to exhaust the subject.

How is it with your own valley? No portion of our state is richer in historical associations. It was fore-ordained that New York should be great whether you consider it from the military or the civic standpoint—great in commerce, great in manufactures, great in wealth, great in population, great in all that tends to make a state. The Hudson river flows through the only low-lying, wide-open gap in the whole Appalachian system. There is none other from the St. Lawrence on the north to the Gulf of Mexico on the south. From New York to Troy is practically a dead level, the tide rising and falling at the latter place. From here through the valley of the Mohawk and across the western part of the state to the Great Lakes was the easiest route to the west. The physical make-up of the state made it certain that any people who occupied this state would be great. This has always been the case. It always must be. It was true when the Mohawks and the other members of the Five Nations controlled Central New York from Albany to Lake Erie. Not only is the history of your section worthy of study because of its general importance but it is no less so because of the events that occurred in it and the men who took part in those events. We are meeting in the first real home of the man who perhaps was second to no other in that part of our colonial history that precedes the Revolution. I refer, of course, to Sir William Johnson. His brief stay in a little hut at Warren's Bush is not forgotten but that hut was hardly a home. Here he was the dominating character, not only of the valley but of the whole frontier. No other person began to exercise the influence over the Indians that he did. It is perhaps not too much to say that but for him this state, New England and the regions of the Great Lakes would have fallen under the control of the French and it might have resulted in making the greater part of what now constitutes the United States a great "New France." You probably know well the history of Sir William Johnson. Your children also ought to possess that knowledge and they ought to be able to get it in the schools. His story, however, should be told by some one who has not the New England prejudice against everything in New York—a prejudice that leads even so able a writer as Parkman to sneer at Johnson and to speak of his wife as an ignorant German wench.

* * * * * * * *

Your society does well in trying to perpetuate the memory of these things but you will do better if you make the story of this valley known, through the schools, to every boy and girl who attend them. I most earnestly entreat you to do what you may to see that the history of your valley is taught in the schools round about you.

* * * * * * * *

Whether or not New York shall come to her own, when the story of the history of our country is told, will depend largely upon the attitude of societies such as yours.

2200 Population of Hudson Valley— Ultimate Mohawk Valley Populations

The editor of this work estimates the Hudson valley population of the year 2200 at 40,000,000. Of this over 35,000,000 should lie in the vast city at its mouth which should then include the greater part of northeastern New Jersey about New York bay, Staten Island, Manhattan Island, Western Long Island, both shores of the Hudson river along the whole Tappan Zee north of Peekskill, and the most of Westchester county. Its center would probably then have shifted northward from its present location—34th to 42d streets—to north of Yonkers in Westchester county and its face will be an entire new one, with (let us hope) much of civic unity, comfort and beauty. By that future date the population of the Hudson valley will have reached its zenith.

In the year 2200 (only three centuries hence) the population of the United States may be 350,000,000 and that of Canada 150,000,000 giving a combined North American population of 500,000,000, which Noah Webster (of dictionary fame) estimated as our ultimate North American population. Estimating the English speaking population of outside of North America at 200,-

000,000 would give a total world English-speaking population of 700,000,000, vastly greater than that of any other single-language-speaking population. The English-speaking population of the world in 1914 was estimated at about 160,000,000 (the largest in the world), of which 110,000,000 was in North America. In the year 2200, North America (with the United States and Canada then in close alliance) may with Russia and Japan-China control the destinies of the world. After that period doubtless South America and Africa will rise in importance. In those days let us hope, a union of civilized nations will make peace and justice reign and see that no man lacks work and no mother or child food, clothing and shelter.

For the year 2200 the editor of this work predicts some ultimate populations for the present towns in the Mohawk valley and the six Mohawk valley counties. This is merely a personal guess and if the reader's local pride is injured he can make one probably equally as accurate which will please him better. Location and accessibility to trade routes and water power have been considered in this estimate. Only valley towns with populations of 1,000, according to the census of 1910, are considered. On or before 2200 the Mohawk valley should have a population of about 1,500,000.

This is in no sense a boost for large populations. Frequently a town of half a thousand population is a better abiding place for the average citizen than any of the world's greatest capitals. Many causes may conduce to make this estimated population impossible such as food, fuel and water shortage. This estimate is based on present increases.

Some towns may reach these figures and then decrease before 2200. The estimate for that year follows, beginning with Oneida county and following the Mohawk and its tributaries southward:

Boonville, 5,000.
Camden, 5,000.
Rome, 50,000.
Oriskany, 8,000.
Waterville, 5,000.
Clinton, 5,000.
Whitesboro-New Hartford-New York Mills-Utica, or Greater Utica, 250,000.
Frankfort - Ilion - Mohawk - Herkimer, 75,000.
Little Falls, 50,000.
Dolgeville, 12,000.
St. Johnsville, 12,000.
Fort Plain, 12,000.
Canajoharie, 12,000.
Fonda-Fultonville, 8,000.
Johnstown-Gloversville, 75,000.
Northville, 8,000.
Schoharie, 3,000.
Cobleskill, 8,000.

Middleburg, 3,000.
Amsterdam, 75,000.
Schenectady-Scotia, 400,000.
Cohoes, 75,000.
Schenectady - Scotia - Cohoes - Water-
ford - Watervliet - Troy - Greenbush -
Albany, or Greater Albany-Troy-Sche
nectady, 1,000,000.

Scenic Features of the Mohawk Valley.

It is impossible to enumerate in this
volume all the scenic beauties and
items of topographic interest in the
Mohawk valley.

Of the hills along the Mohawk, noble
old Yantapuchaberg, towering over a
thousand feet above the Mohawk back
of Rotterdam, is probably the most im
pressive. The Noses and Fall Hill are
fine bluffs and hills.

West Canada creek has, among its
other scenic features, a picturesque
gorge and falls at Trenton Falls. There
are attractive rapids at East Creek
falls, on East Canada creek, about a
mile above the East Creek station.
Canajoharie gorge and falls are famous
in the valley. Bouck's falls in Scho-
barie county and the falls of the Plat-
terkill, in the hills back of Rotterdam,
the falls of Tequetsera near Hoffmans,
the Adriutha, near Amsterdam, Butter-
milk falls near Cranesville and Flat
creek falls near Sprakers, are all cascades of considerable beauty.

Aside from the scenic beauty of the
river, its flats, hills, woods, creeks and
brooks, and their falls, glens and valleys, the Mohawk valley possesses several lakes of considerable beauty,
among them, Canada, Caroga, Peck,
Jerseyfield and Honnedaga. The upper part of Fulton county is dotted
with lakes and ponds draining into
East creek, the Caroga or Sacandaga.
The large lakes formed by the Barge
canal reservoirs at Delta and Hinckley
are the largest bodies of water in the
Mohawk watershed, and possess added
interest on account of the great engineering work necessary to their construction.

At Howe's Cave in Schoharie, is a
very considerable cave, which has been
much visited.

The main beauty of the Mohawk
valley seems to be in the pleasing harmony and variety of the lines and
forms of its wood-covered hills, the
winding course of the Mohawk and the
pastoral beauty of its fertile farm
lands. Each lover of the valley landscape, and their name has been legion,
finds some particular personal interest
in its varied scenery.

NOTES.

It is suggested that the reader of
this book follow this order in reading
this work:

First: Read the Fifteen School Dates
in the Mohawk Valley Chronologies in
the appendix.

Second: Read the Mohawk Valley
Chronology (the first and main one),
which starts the appendix.

Third: Read the main body of the
book.

Fourth: At the conclusion of each
chapter turn to the appendix and read
therein the matter relative to the chapter in the main body of the book, which
the reader has just completed. The
appendix additions carry the main
body chapter heads, to which the appendix matter properly belongs.

A reading of the "Short School History of the Mohawk Valley and the
Six Mohawk Valley Counties," by Nelson Greene, the editor of this book,
will give good rudimentary historical
valley knowledge. If off the press by
the time of the publication of this
book, the reader is advised to peruse
it first, unless he or she is well versed
in Mohawk valley history. The author
also has in preparation a "New York
to Buffalo Book," which forms a gazeteer of the towns on and the country
along the N. Y. C. & H. R. R. R. All
three works can be read with mutual
enlightenment.

The word British, used in this work,
of course refers to all the peoples of
the British Isles—English, Scotch,
Irish and Welsh. Of the British pre-
Revolutionary elements of the Mohawk
valley population, the Scotch seems to
have been the greatest numerically.

Hon. Robert Earl, in a paper on Fort Dayton, read before the Herkimer Historical society in 1898, says Walter Butler "was killed, on the banks of the West Canada creek, about ten miles above Trenton Falls," at a place on the creek called "Broadwaters," north-westerly of Ohio City, and east of the hamlet of Northwood (the West Canada here runs east and west).

A census of Schenectady, taken by the city's letter carriers, gave a population of 94,000 in 1914. If this is correct and the rate of increase continues the population of the six Mohawk valley counties in 1915 will be about 470,-000. Adding to this the population of the lower Mohawk valley in Albany and Saratoga counties, would give a 1915 population, of the six Mohawk valley counties and the Mohawk valley combined, of over 500,000.

On the Mohawk and the Hudson, near the mouth of the Mohawk, is located an interesting group of seven cities and villages which virtually form one great city or community, as they all lie within a radius of about ten miles or less. They are Albany, Rensselaer, Watervliet, Green Island, Cohoes, Waterford and Troy. The New York Industrial Directory of 1912 estimates their population at 240,000 in round numbers. With the addition of Schenectady their combined population, according to the same authority, is 325,000 in round numbers. If these communities were organized in one civic government it would be the third city in the state. They form an industrial and commercial center of great importance.

This publication does not pretend to give all the known or recorded episodes, tragedies and adventures of the Revolutionary history of the Mohawk valley, or even all of those which happened within the immediate vicinity of old Fort Plain. Only such as bear upon the major events and the main story of the valley are brought out here —such as are necessary to the picture of the three centuries of life along the Mohawk. Other works will aid the

reader who is interested in the thrilling and tragic features of the Revolutionary war in this locality. The reader is particularly referred to Simms's "Frontiersmen of New York."

Recent years have seen a great growth of public spirit and local and town pride in the Mohawk valley. Practically every village and city along the Mohawk now has its public library which has been frequently given in whole or part to the community by some public-spirited citizen. In March, 1914, David H. Burrell of Little Falls announced a gift of $50,000, to the city of Little Falls, for a City hall, provided a similar amount was raised by other citizens or by the municipality. Mr. Burrell had previously given a public gymnasium and building to his city. On March 12, 1914, the Weller Free Library of Mohawk was opened. This was a gift of the fine brick mansion of the late Mr. and Mrs. Frederick N. Weller of Mohawk. Mr. and Mrs. Weller also left the village a business block and $52,000 in U. S. bonds to provide for the library's support. An era of broad world interest is opening for the people along the Mohawk and the day of narrow provincialism is ending. It is proved by the spirit which actuated the donors of these public edifices and enterprises.

"Everyman's Literary and Historical Atlas of North America and South America" gives the battle of Oriskany as one of the twenty-five principal battles of the War of Independence. The Revolutionary principal actions fought on New York state soil are given in that publication as follows: Fort Ticonderoga, 1775; Long Island, Aug. 27, 1776; White Plains, Oct. 28, 1776; Fort Washington (Manhattan island), Nov. 16, 1776; Fort Ticonderoga (Saratoga campaign), July 5, 1777; Oriskany (Saratoga campaign), Aug. 6, 1777; Saratoga (Saratoga campaign), Sept. 19, 1777; Saratoga (Saratoga campaign), Oct. 17, 1777. Stony Point, 1779, and the battle of Elmira, 1779, should be here included. More Revolutionary principal battles were fought in New York than in any other of the thirteen colonies.

The editor of this work regrets the somewhat local character of this historical study. By the elimination of the chapters relative to western Montgomery county exclusively, this book will be found to be a general review of Mohawk valley history. However it is probable that a more natural picture of Mohawk valley life can be given by a historical study of that portion of the middle Mohawk valley, from Herkimer to Amsterdam (which is the section here particularly treated), than by a historical analysis of life in large valley urban centers such as Schenectady or Utica.

A fertile subject for discussion, debate and essays in the public schools of the Mohawk valley could be the possibilities of future valley life as viewed in the light of the past and as influenced by present day forces.

Fully one-third of this work is given up to the description and discussion of subjects which concern Mohawk valley modern life—its railroads, canals, river, highways, manufacturing, agriculture, commerce and social life—all subjects which promise to be timely to the reader for centuries to come. In no other historical work has there been such a comprehensive treatment of the Mohawk valley and its present (1914) life.

"The Story of Old Fort Plain and the Middle Mohawk Valley" was originally published in the Fort Plain Standard and republished, a week or more, after its initial appearance, in the Mohawk Valley (Fonda) Democrat. There were also some twenty republications of chapters, or the greater portions of chapters, in nine other papers in the Mohawk valley, from Frankfort to Schenectady.

In a letter to the Herkimer Citizen of July 21, 1914, E. J. Klock says that factory cheese was first made on May 10, 1851, by Jessie Williams and his sons, Dewitt and George Williams, at the "first cheese factory in the world," erected on the Williams farm, two miles north of Rome, Oneida county. Refer to the article on Herkimer county and Mohawk valley cheesemaking in this Appendix, pages 331-335.

Simms in his list of the Mohawk's tributaries omits Kuyahoora as the Indian name of West Canada creek. The Geisenberg neighborhood, frequently referred to in this work, relates to the Hallsville section of Minden township. The spelling Caroga is used for the creek of that name in this book, whereas the universal pronunciation (and probably that of the Mohawks) was Garoga. Such a spelling would be used in any future edition. It may be remarked here that Schoharie is translated as meaning "driftwood."

The maps herein contained are from reliable sources or were drawn by the author from maps issued by the office of the New York State Engineer and Surveyor or from standard maps.

In addition to the hydro-electrical plants located on Caroga and East creeks it may be mentioned that there is a similar development at Trenton Falls on West Canada creek, north of Utica. Others will follow doubtless, but these three streams are at present (1914) the Mohawk valley ones which have been developed hydro-electrically.

In the industrial map of the Erie railroad system (published 1913) the Mohawk river section from Rome to Utica is given as one of the regions in which oil or gas is produced. This region is the most easterly on this map. Gas was discovered in a small quantity in Root, Montgomery county, in 1913. It exists in generally small pockets in many Mohawk valley sections.

In 1914 the holding of a September street fair in Fort Plain was abandoned for the first time since its in ception fifteen years before. Its holding had become burdensome to the merchants who yearly organized and conducted it. The suggestion is here made that the fair be held yearly in rotation by the sister villages of western Montgomery county—Canajoharie, Fort Plain, St. Johnsville. In this way this typical Mohawk valley affair could be continued.

The editor of this work desires to acknowledge the assistance of the following persons in aiding in the collection of material and the use of their writings in this work: James A. Holden, New York State historian, Albany, N. Y.; Noble E. Whitford, State Engineer's office, Albany, N. Y.; Dr. Sherman Williams, University of the State of New York, Albany, N. Y.; James A. Wendell, Albany, N. Y.; P. M. Van Epps, Glenville, N. Y.; John Fea, Amsterdam, N. Y.; Rev. Washington Frothingham, William B. Wemple, Miss Marion Abbott, Fonda, N. Y.; S. L. Frey, Palatine Bridge, N. Y.; Abram Devendorf, Mrs. Horace L. Greene, Fort Plain, N. Y.; N. Berton Alter, Nelliston, N. Y.; William Irving Walter, St. Johnsville, N. Y.; Col. John W. Vrooman, A. T. Smith, Herkimer, N. Y.; Margaret B. Stewart; E. W. Tuttle; Harry N. Atwood (Saturday Evening Post); the United States Census Bureau, Washington, D. C.; office of State Engineer and Surveyor, Albany, N. Y.; Albany Knickerbocker Press, and others.

Particularly does the editor wish to acknowledge the great assistance he has had from Messrs. George O'Connor and W. W. O'Connor, publishers of the Fort Plain Standard, who have given the utmost care to the proper assembling and printing of these chapters and in the preparation of this review of Mohawk valley history. Also acknowledgment is due to William D. Ludwig, linotype operator for the Standard, whose careful and skilled typography and knowledge of valley names has made errors at a minimum, in the newspaper and book publication of this work—a work where opportunities for erroneous typography were innumerable. Also credit is due Fred H. Kelsey, pressman of the Standard, for his careful printing of this book. Standard printing exemplifies at its highest the care and high degree of excellence that has characterized the best of Fort Plain's printing art for the last half century (prior to 1914). It is a great pleasure for the editor of this work, who has the utmost respect and admiration for the great art of printing, to make this acknowledgent.

As the last forms of this work are going to press the city of Utica is holding a week of celebration (August 3 to 8, 1914), including a pageant representing the battle of Oriskany and the dedication of a statute of Baron Steuben, the "drillmaster" of the Revolutionary American army, who died and is buried in the town of Steuben, Oneida county, to the north of Utica.

CORRECTIONS

SERIES I.

CHAPTER II.

In chapter II. it is stated that LaCarnon, a French Canadian priest, was the first white man to explore the upper reaches of the Mohawk, in 1616. Later researches show that even he was probably preceded by the Dutch who doubtless had gone into the lower Mohawk valley considerably before that date. Mr. Frey says: "It is certain, also, that three Dutchmen, before 1614, had passed up the Mohawk, crossed over to Otsego lake, and gone down the Susquehanna as far as Wyoming, whence, crossing the mountains to the Delaware, they were ransomed; the Mohawks having taken them prisoners, mistaking them for Frenchmen." They probably came to the Otsquago and went up its valley to Otsego lake.

CHAPTER II.

Schenectady was settled by Van Curler and his companions in 1661. It was officially plotted by the Fort Orange (Albany) authorities in 1663. White settlers were resident there years before 1661, however—perhaps before 1640.

CHAPTER II.

Isaac Jogues was a prisoner in 1642 and was killed in 1646 at Osseruenon, on the south side of the river, not at Caughnewago, on the north side. The site where Jogues was killed is marked by the Shrine at Auriesville. All the Mohawk villages of that date were on the south side. The Jesuits only converted a part of the Mohawks. These were transferred to villages on the St. Lawrence and were known as the "Praying Indians." St. Catherine, "the Lily of the Mohawk," was one of them. The above correction is by S. L. Frey.

This chapter says that Jogues, "through the influence of the Dutch, was released and returned to France."

The actual facts are that he escaped at night from his barbarous captors while they stopped with him at Albany and, with the aid of the Dutch commandant of Fort Orange, hid himself on a Dutch boat, which later sailed for Holland. The Mohawks were greatly incensed at his escape, but the Dutch commandant professed ignorance.

CHAPTER III.

Joseph Brant used the "Wolf" totem, showing that his mother was of that clan. So, of course, his father could not have been a "Wolf," as members of the same clan could not marry Correction by S. L. Frey.

CHAPTER VIII.

A paragraph says "Nicholas Herkimer and Ebenezer Cox were residents (in 1775) of the present town of Danube." Beers makes this statement which is an error. Herkimer lived in Danube but Col. Ebenezer Cox resided on the south side of the Mohawk, in the present town of Minden, about a mile from the present village of St. Johnsville. Simms said in 1882 that the Cox farm was then owned by Samuel F. Smith, whose wife was a granddaughter of Col. Cox, and that the Cox farm had always been in the possession of the Cox family. Three of the eight members of the Tryon County Committee of Safety of the Canajoharie district were (in 1775) from the present town of Minden— William Seeber, John Pickard, Ebenezer Cox.

CHAPTER IX.

This chapter has the following: "At the close of the French war there were, in the valley army fortifications at Fort Stanwix (now Rome, erected 1758), at Fort Herkimer (1756) and at Fort Hunter (1711)." There was also, in addition to the above, the fort called Fort Canajoharie at Indian Castle, which was erected in 1755 by Sir William Johnson to protect the Mohawks there residing.

CHAPTER X.

In the "Adjacent Settlers (to Fort Plain)—1776" chapter X. it was said that "Willett did not command here (at Fort Plain) after 1782." This is an error. Willett commanded here, although not constantly at this post, at least in 1781, 1782, 1783 and possibly later.

SERIES II.

CHAPTER I.

This chapter says that the council of 1784, between the Iroquois and Gov. Clinton and commissioners, at Fort Schuyler or Stanwix (now Rome), was the last Indian council in the valley. This is an error. The council of 1788 at Fort Schuyler, in which the Iroquois finally extinguished the title to their 4,000,000 acres of land, was the last Indian council in the valley. Note the table of dates at the end of the regular chapters.

CHAPTER II.

Gen. Doubleday, the inventor of baseball, is spoken of as a schoolboy of the old Canajoharie district. Strictly speaking this is probably erroneous as Otsego lake lies in what was the old German Flats district. The matter is apropos, however, as Cooperstown and Fort Plain interests have always been closely identified. As Doubleday was about 21 in 1840 he may have been a teacher or assistant in Green's Cooperstown school or a visitor there rather than a schoolboy.

CHAPTER V.

A sentence in this chapter, says that "two small lakes or ponds, one at the headwaters of Oriskany creek and the other at the source of the South Chuctanunda, are the only ponds of a size worthy of mention on the south side of the Mohawk watershed." This is a mistake of a map consulted, which connected the lake at Hamilton with the Oriskany instead of the Chenango. A small pond lies at the head of Fox creek (a tributary of the Schoharie) in

Albany county. Including the ponds at Mariaville in Schenectady county, which is the source of the South Chuctanunda, and the Fox creek headwater pond, there are three small lakes or ponds on the south side Mohawk watershed.

CHAPTER X.

In this chapter, Judge Forman's residence is given as both Onondaga and Ontario county. Joshua Forman, who introduced the first legislative canal act in 1808, was from Onondaga county.

In the opening paragraph of the Mohawk Valley Chronology on page 307, it says: "The editor of this work has found it impossible to secure dates of secondary importance." It should read: "The editor of this work has found it impossible to secure some dates of secondary importance." Practically all dates of first and secondary importance in the history of the Mohawk valley are contained in the chronology, which the editor of this work considers one of its most important features.

In the Mohawk Valley Chronology in the appendix, under the date 1758, April, it says: "Col. William Johnson calls together the valley militia at Canajoharie (Fort Plain) to repel invasion of French and Indians at Fort Herkimer." There are two errors here: Johnson should have been called General Johnson, as he had that title in 1758, and the militia were called together probably at Fort Canajoharie (present Indian Castle).

In the Statistical Summary for School Use on Page 323, the area of Montgomery county is given as 355,000 acres. It should read 255,000 acres. With the exception of a few months during the early newspaper publication of this book (when he was in Fort •Plain) the editor of this work has been in New York during its publication in Fort Plain. Owing to his inability to read press proofs certain errors have crept in which are corrected herewith.

A FINAL WORD

This book will have served its purpose to some extent if it shows the intimate relation of the individual and his community to the surrounding areas and to the world at large. The hamlet is as much the hub of the world as the great city. Yonder railroad turning westward goes far beyond your horizon, on and on to the plains, the high western mountains and the wide Pacific. The waterway, with its loaded boats, at the foot of this hill does not end around that turn of the valley, but flows along to the boundless salt sea. That stream running through the flats to the Mohawk comes from the far silent glades of the big North Woods. Those eastern hills rise on and on to the mile high peaks of the Adirondacks.

Willy nilly, you daily touch hands with the whole world, just as the life and history of the Mohawk valley touches everywhere that of the great world of which it is relatively a tiny part.

On a still day you stand at the edge of the pond and toss in a stone—the ripples widen to its farthest bank.

The scientist tells us that our lives, whether sordid or great, whether happy or miserable, have their effect chemically on the atoms of the universe—on this small globe whirling through space and on those bright worlds which, across the great black midnight heavens, make a bridge of light, which seems to lead the human soul up and up to a dim vision of the infinite.

CPSIA information can be obtained
at www.ICGtesting.com
Printed in the USA
BVOW04s1347031116

466853BV00010B/64/P